目　录

扫码观看琦叔教你如何使用 3K 系列书籍

List 1

Unit 1

■ ABANDON	■ ABASE	■ ABASH	■ ABATE	■ ABBREVIATE
■ ABDICATE	■ ABERRANT	■ ABET	■ ABEYANCE	■ ABHOR

abandon [əˈbændən]
【考法 1】 *v./n.* 放纵：carefree, freedom from **constraint**
例 abandon oneself to emotion 感情用事
近 unconstraint, uninhibitedness, unrestraint
【考法 2】 *v.* 放弃：to **withdraw** from often in the face of danger or encroachment
例 abandon the home 离家
反 salvage 救援

abase [əˈbeɪs]
【考法】 *v.* 降低(地位、职位、威望或尊严)：to **lower** in rank, office, prestige, or esteem
例 He was unwilling to abase himself by pleading guilty to a crime that he did not commit. 他不愿意屈就自己去承认一个莫须有的罪名。
近 debauch, degrade, profane, vitiate, discredit, foul, smirch, take down
反 elevate, ennoble, uplift, aggrandize, canonize, deify, exalt 使高贵，使有声望

abash [əˈbæʃ]
【考法】 *vt.* 使尴尬，使羞愧：to destroy the self-possession or **self-confidence** of, disconcert, **embarrass**
例 feel abashed in public 当众感到羞愧
近 discomfit, disconcert, discountenance, faze, fluster, nonplus, mortify
反 embolden 使大胆

abate [əˈbeɪt]
【考法 1】 *v.* 减轻(程度或者强度)：to **reduce** in **degree** or **intensity**
例 abate his rage/pain 平息他的愤怒／减轻他的痛苦
近 moderate, recede, subside, remit, wane, die (away or down or out), let up, phase down, taper off
反 intensify 加强，加剧
【考法 2】 *v.* 减少(数量)，降低(价值)：to **reduce** in **amount or value**
例 abate a tax 降低税收
近 de-escalate, deplete, downscale, dwindle, ratchet (down)
反 augment, promote 增加

abbreviate [əˈbriːvieɪt]
【考法】 *v.* 缩写，缩短：to make **briefer**
例 abbreviate the word "building" as "bldg." 将"building"缩写作"bldg"。
近 abridge, curtail, cut back, syncopate, truncate
反 extend, protract, elongate, lengthen, prolong 延长

abdicate [ˈæbdɪkeɪt]
【考法】 *v.* 正式放弃(权力、责任)，不干了：to renounce a **throne**, to relinquish (power or responsibility) formally
例 abdicate the throne/crown 退位
近 cede, relinquish, renounce, resign, step down (from)
反 constitute, assume, usurp 任命；承担；篡位

aberrant [æˈberənt]
【考法】 *adj.* 异常的，非常规的：**deviating** from the usual or natural type
例 aberrant behavior 异常行为
近 abnormal, anomalous, peculiar, singular, unwonted, uncustomary
反 normal, natural, regular, standard, typical 正常的，标准的，典型的

abet [əˈbet]

【考法】 v. 鼓励: to actively **encourage** (as an activity or plan)

例 abet someone's opinion 支持某人的观点

近 aid, assist, back, support, prop (up)

反 stymie, frustrate, obstruct, thwart, impede, forestall, hinder 阻挠

abeyance [əˈbeɪəns]

【考法】 n. 中止，搁置: temporary **inactivity**

例 hold the plan in abeyance 使计划暂停

近 doldrums, quiescence, moratorium, latency, dormancy, suspension, cold storage, deep freeze

反 continuance, fulfillment 继续；履行

abhor [əbˈhɔːr]

【考法】 vt. 深恶痛绝，极度厌恶: to regard with **extreme repugnance**

例 abhor violence 厌恶暴力

近 abominate, despise, detest, execrate, loathe

反 greatly admire 非常崇拜

Unit 2

■ ABIDING	■ ABJECT	■ ABJURE	■ ABNEGATE	■ ABOMINATE
■ ABOVEBOARD	■ ABRADE	■ ABRIDGE	■ ABROGATE	■ ABSCOND

abiding [əˈbaɪdɪŋ]

【考法】 adj. 持久的: lasting for a long time; **enduring**

例 an abiding love of Espanol 对西班牙语持久的热爱

近 ageless, enduring, eternal, everlasting, perennial, perpetual, timeless

反 evanescent, ephemeral 短暂的

abject [ˈæbdʒekt]

【考法 1】 adj. (地位、身份)悲惨、凄凉的: sunk to or existing in a **low state** or condition

例 abject poverty 让人绝望的贫穷

【考法 2】 adj. 卑微的，讨好的: expressing or offered in a **humble** and often ingratiating spirit

例 abject flattery 卑躬屈膝般的恭维 ‖ an abject apology 讨好般的道歉

近 base, humble, menial, servile, slavish

abjure [əbˈdʒʊr]

【考法 1】 v. 发誓放弃: a firm and final **rejecting** or **abandoning** often made under oath

例 abjure one's belief 发誓放弃信仰

近 recant, renege, renounce, abnegate, forswear, repudiate

反 affirm, espouse, embrace 接受，拥护

【考法 2】 v. 抵制，避免: to **resist** the temptation of

例 abjure extravagance 抵制铺张浪费

近 keep (from), refrain (from), withhold (from)

反 bow to, give in to, submit to, succumb to, surrender to, yield to 屈从于

abnegate [ˈæbnɪgeɪt]

【考法】 v. 否认: **deny**, **renounce**

例 abnegate the idea of freedom 放弃自由的观念

近 recant, renege, repudiate, unsay, forswear, take back

反 reaffirm 再肯定，重申

abominate [əˈbɑːmɪneɪt]

【考法】 v. 痛恨，厌恶: to hate or loathe intensely, **abhor**

例 abominate slavery 痛恨奴隶制

近 despise, detest, execrate, loathe

反 esteem, love, adore 尊敬，爱

aboveboard [əˈbʌvbɔːrd]

【考法】 adj. 无欺诈的，光明正大的: **free from** all traces of **deceit or duplicity**

例 aboveboard transactions 光明正大的交易

反 surreptitious, underhanded 偷偷摸摸的

abrade [əˈbreɪd]

【考法】 v. 磨损，精神上折磨: to rub or **wear away** especially **by friction**; wear down spiritually

例 Their | gossips abrade her | into restlessness. 他们的流言蜚语使她心烦意乱。

近 chafe, excoriate, rasp, graze, scuff

反 augment 增加

abridge [əˈbrɪdʒ]

【考法】 *v.* 缩短，缩小：to **shorten** in duration or extent

例 The modern transportation | abridges distance | . 现代运输方式缩短了路途。

近 curtail, truncate, cut back

反 extend in length, protract, amplify 延长，放大

abrogate [ˈæbrəɡeɪt]

【考法1】 *v.* 官方的正式废除：to abolish by authoritative action, **annul**

例 | abrogate the law | /treaty 废除法律、条约

近 disannul, invalidate, nullify, quash, rescind, roll back, strike down

反 embrace, uphold, institute 采纳；支持；建立

【考法2】 *v.* 无视（某事）存在：to treat as **nonexistent**

例 | abrogate their responsibilities | 抛开、不顾他们的责任

abscond [əbˈskɑːnd]

【考法】 *v.* 偷偷离开：to **depart secretly** and hide oneself

例 | abscond from the prison | 越狱

近 flee, lam, run off, break out (of), clear out

Unit 3

| ■ ABSOLUTE | ■ ABSOLVE | ■ ABSTAIN | ■ ABSTEMIOUS | ■ ABSTRACT |
| ■ ABSTRUSE | ■ ABSURD | ■ ABUNDANT | ■ ABUSE | ■ ACQUAINTED |

absolute [ˈæbsəluːt]

【考法1】 *adj.* 专制的：**unconstrained** by constitutional or other provisions

例 | absolute ruler | 专制的统治者

近 arbitrary, autocratic, despotic, dictatorial, monocratic, tyrannical

【考法2】 *adj.* 无限的：**unqualified** in extent or degree; total

例 | absolute silence | 鸦雀无声

近 complete, utter, deadly, downright, out-and-out

反 qualified 有限的，有保留的

【考法3】 *adj.* 完美的，纯净不掺杂的：**free from imperfection**; free or relatively free from **mixture**

例 | absolute alcohol | 无水酒精（纯酒精）

近 plain, refined, unadulterated, unalloyed, undiluted, unmixed

反 adulterated, alloyed, diluted, impure, mixed 掺杂的，不纯的

【考法4】 *adj.* 不容置疑的，确凿的：positive, **unquestionable**

例 | absolute proof | 确凿的证据

近 clear, deciding, decisive, definitive

反 inconclusive, indecisive, unclear 不明确的

absolve [əbˈzɑːlv]

【考法】 *v.* 使无罪，解除责任：to set **free from** an obligation or the consequences of **guilt**, **exculpate**

例 | absolve somebody from blame | 使某人免受责备

近 acquit, exonerate, vindicate

反 blame, criminate, incriminate 定罪

abstain [əbˈsteɪn]

【考法】 *v.* 自我克制，主动戒绝：to **refrain** from something **by one's own choice**

例 | abstain from smoking | /voting 戒烟；弃权

近 forgo, keep from, refrain from, withhold (from)

反 bow to, give in to, submit to, succumb to, surrender to, yield to 屈服于

abstemious [əbˈstiːmiəs]

【考法】 *adj.* （吃喝等）有节制的，节俭的：marked by **restraint** especially in the consumption of **food or alcohol**, **sparing**

例 an | abstemious diet | 有节制的饮食 ‖ | abstemious meals | 节俭的饭餐

近 continent, temperate, self-abnegating, self-denying

反 indulgent 放纵的

abstract [æbˈstrækt]

【考法1】 *vt.* 做总结，概括：to make an **abstract** of, **summarize**
例 abstract an essay 概括一篇文章
近 digest, recapitulate, synopsize, sum up, boil down
反 elaborate 详细描述

【考法2】 *vt.* 使分心：to draw **away** the **attention** of
例 abstract my attention from work 转移我对工作的注意力
近 detract, divert, call off, throw off
派 abstraction *n.* 心不在焉
反 attention 关注

abstruse [əbˈstruːs]

【考法】 *adj.* 难以理解的：difficult to comprehend: **recondite**
例 the abstruse calculations 复杂深奥的计算
近 arcane, esoteric, hermetic (*also* hermetical), recondite
反 accessible, patent, shallow, superficial 可了解的，肤浅的

absurd [əbˈsɜːrd]

【考法】 *adj.* 不合理的：ridiculously **unreasonable**, unsound, or incongruous
例 an absurd argument 无稽之谈
近 wild, bizarre, ludicrous, insane, nonsensical, preposterous, half-baked
反 rational, sensible, realistic, reasonable 理性的，合理的

abundant [əˈbʌndənt]

【考法】 *adj.* 大量的：marked by **great plenty** (as of resources)
例 an abundant land 一片富饶的土地
近 ample, cornucopian, teeming, replete, abounding
反 infrequent, rare, uncommon, inadequate, scanty, scarce 稀少的，罕见的

abuse [əˈbjuːz]

【考法1】 *v.* 辱骂，抨击：to **condemn or vilify** usually unjustly, intemperately, and angrily
例 He alleged that he was verbally abused by his colleagues. 他声称受到了同事的言语攻击。
近 assail, bash, castigate, excoriate, lambaste
派 abusive *adj.* 辱骂的

【考法2】 *v.* 不正当或不合理使用：to put to a **wrong or improper use**；过分过量使用：to **use excessively**
例 abuse a privilege 滥用特权 ‖ abuse alcohol 酗酒
近 misemploy, misuse

acquainted [əˈkweɪntɪd]

【考法】 *adj.* 熟悉的：**having information** especially as a result of study or experience
例 He was well acquainted with the literature of France, Germany and Holland. 他对于法国、德国和荷兰的文学了如指掌。
近 familiar, conversant, knowledgeable, informed, versed, well-informed
反 ignorant, unacquainted, unfamiliar, uninformed, unknowledgeable 不了解

Unit 4

■ ABYSMAL	■ ACCEDE	■ AD HOC	■ ACCESSIBLE	■ ACCESSORY
■ ACCIDENTAL	■ ACCLIMATE	■ ACCOLADE	■ ACCOMMODATE	■ ACCENTUATE

abysmal [əˈbɪzməl]

【考法】 *adj.* (程度)很深的；极端的：**immeasurably great**
例 abysmal ignorance 极端的无知
近 profound
反 shallow, shoal, skin-deep, superficial 浅的；肤浅的

accede [əkˈsiːd]

【考法】 *v.* 赞成：to express **approval** or give **consent**
例 accede to public demand 顺应民意
近 acquiesce, assent, consent, subscribe, come round
反 demur, dissent 反对

ad hoc	[ˌæd ˈhɑːk]
【考法】	_adj._ 专门的：concerned with a **particular end** or purpose
例	an _ad hoc_ investigating committee 一个专门的调查委员会
近	specific, specified

accessible	[əkˈsesəbl]
【考法1】	_adj._ 可以到达的：situated **within easy reach**
例	the town accessible by rail 有铁路通达的城镇
近	handy, reachable
反	inconvenient, unhandy, unreachable, untouchable 无法到达的，不方便的
【考法2】	_adj._ 可理解的：capable of being **understood** or appreciated
例	accessible to general audience 对于普通读者浅显易懂
近	apprehensible, fathomable, legible, scrutable
反	abstruse, incoherent, incomprehensible, inscrutable, insensible 深奥的；难以理解的

accessory	[əkˈsesəri]
【考法】	_adj._ 辅助的，附属的：having a **secondary**, **supplementary**, or **subordinate** function
例	accessory features such as call-waiting 类似呼叫等待的附属功能
近	peripheral, supplementary
反	of primarily importance, chief, main, principal 主要的

accidental	[ˌæksɪˈdentl]
【考法】	_adj._ 意外发生的，偶然的：occurring **unexpectedly** or by chance
例	accidental death 意外死亡
近	incidental, fortuitous, unintended, unintentional, unpremeditated, unwitting
反	calculated, deliberate, intended, planned, premeditated 预先计划好的

acclimate	[ˈækləmeɪt]
【考法】	_vt._ 使适应：to change (something) **so as to make it suitable** for a new use or situation
例	acclimate oneself to a nine-to-five office job 适应朝九晚五的坐班生活
近	adjust, accommodate, shape, suit, tailor
反	make unfamiliar with 使不熟悉

accolade	[ˈækəleɪd]
【考法1】	_n._ 同意，赞赏：an expression of **approval**
例	The director won virtually every accolade that the film world offered. 这位导演赢得了电影界几乎一致的赞赏。
近	applause, credit, distinction
反	disapprobation 不赞成
【考法2】	_v._ 赞扬：to **praise** or honor
反	excoriate, criticise, reprobate, castigate, derogate, reproof, denigrate, denunciate 批评，谴责

accommodate	[əˈkɑːmədeɪt]
【考法1】	_v._ 改变以适应新情况、新场景：to change (something) so as to **make** it **suitable** for a new use or situation
例	accommodate to the life overseas 适应海外的生活
近	acclimate, adjust, condition, conform, doctor, edit, shape, suit, tailor
【考法2】	_vt._ 使和谐：to bring to a state **free of conflicts**, inconsistencies, or differences
例	The idea that the United States could harmoniously accommodate all was a fiction. 认为美国能够和谐一切的想法只是幻想。
近	attune, conciliate, conform, coordinate, reconcile
反	disharmonize 使不和谐

accentuate	[əˈksentʃueɪt]
【考法】	_v._ 强调：to make (something) more **noticeable**
例	accentuate the importance of communication skill 强调沟通技巧的重要性
近	accent, emphasize, foreground, highlight
反	de-emphasize, play down, downplay 轻描淡写

Unit 5

accrete ［æ'kriːt］
【考法】 *v.* 逐渐增长：to **grow** or increase **gradually**, as by addition
例 accrete the public interest 增加公众利益
近 accumulate, build up, pile（up）, stack（up）
反 wear away 衰退
派 accretion *n.* 慢慢增加

accumulate ［ə'kjuːmjəleɪt］
【考法】 *vi.* 逐渐增长：to **increase gradually** in quantity or number
例 accumulate a fortune 积攒了一笔财富
近 mount, swell, garner, snowball, build up, bulk（up）
反 dissipate, diminish, dwindle, recede, wane 消散，减少

acerbic ［ə'sɜːrbɪk］
【考法】 *adj.*（心情、心境或者语调）尖酸的：marked by the use of **wit** that is intended to **cause hurt feelings**
例 acerbic commentary 尖酸的评论
近 pungent, sardonic, satiric, scalding, scathing
反 sweet, saccharine 甜的
派 acerbity *n.* 尖酸，刻薄

acme ［'ækmi］
【考法】 *n.* 顶点，极点：the **highest** point or stage, as of achievement or development
例 the acme of his career 他事业的巅峰
近 culmination, pinnacle, tip-top, high-water mark
反 bottom, nadir, rock bottom 最低点

acquiesce ［ˌækwi'es］
【考法】 *v.* 勉强同意；默许：to **accept**, comply, or submit **tacitly or passively**
例 acquiesce to my own fleecing 默许我的敲竹杠行为
近 assent, consent, subscribe, come round
反 resist, defy, dissent 抵制，不同意
派 acquiesence *n.* 听话，顺从

acrid ［'ækrɪd］
【考法】 *adj.* 刻薄的：marked by the use of **wit** that is intended to **cause hurt feelings**
例 acrid temper 刻薄的性情
反 gentle 温和的

acrimonious ［ˌækrɪ'moʊniəs］
【考法】 *adj.* 刻薄的，充满仇恨的：having or showing **deep-seated resentment**
例 the acrimonious debate between the two candidates 两位候选人之间言辞激烈的辩论
近 embittered, hard, rancorous, resentful, sore

acumen ［'ækjəmən］
【考法】 *n.* 不同寻常的洞察力和鉴别力：**exceptional discernment and judgment** especially in practical matters
例 the business acumen 商业方面的洞察力
近 keenness, shrewdness, canniness, clear-sightedness, hardheadedness
反 unable to discern 不能辨别的

acute ［ə'kjuːt］
【考法 1】 *adj.* 敏锐的：marked by **keen discernment** or intellectual perception especially of subtle distinctions, penetrating
例 an acute thinker 思维敏锐的思想者
近 delicate, fine, keen, perceptive, sensitive
【考法 2】 *adj.*（程度、影响）极强的：**extreme** in degree, or effect
例 She was experiencing acute distress over the misunderstanding with her best friend. 她因与死党之间发生误会而陷入了深深的痛苦中。
近 dreadful, excruciating, profound
反 light, moderate, soft 温和的

adamant	[ˈædəmənt]

【考法】 *adj.* 固执的，不可动摇的：**unshakable** or insistent especially in maintaining a position or opinion, **unyielding**; **inflexible**

例 adamant about staying here 执意留下来

近 hardheaded, headstrong, intransigent, pertinacious, obdurate, uncompromising

反 vacillatory, incline to yield, amenable, compliant, relenting, yielding 动摇的，易屈从的

Unit 6

■ ADAPT	■ ADDICT	■ ADHERE	■ ADJOURN	■ ADJUNCT
■ AD-LIB	■ ADMONISH	■ ADORE	■ ADULATE	■ ADULTERATE

adapt	[əˈdæpt]

【考法】 *v.* 修改，使(适应)：to **modify** according with the changing circumstances

例 adapt to the change 适应变化 ‖ adapt the novel for the screen 改编小说为影视作品

近 adjust, conform, edit, accommodate, shape, suit, tailor

addict	

【考法】 [əˈdɪkt] *v.* 沉溺，上瘾：to devote or **surrender** (oneself) to something habitually or **obsessively**
[ˈædɪkt] *n.* 对某事上瘾的人：a person with a strong and **habitual liking** for something

例 be addicted to drug/alcohol 沉溺于毒品、酒 ‖ science-fiction addicts who eagerly await each new installment in the series 科幻小说爱好者，等待着系列的每一次更新

近 devotee, enthusiast, fanatic, maniac

反 nonfan 非粉丝

adhere	[ədˈhɪr]

【考法】 *v.* 服从，遵守：to act **according to the commands** of

例 adhere to the rules 遵守规定

近 cling to, hew to, stand by, stick to, comply with

反 defy, disobey, rebel against 不服从，反抗

adjourn	[əˈdʒɜːrn]

【考法】 *vi.* 延期，休会：to **suspend** a session indefinitely or to another time or place

例 The meeting adjourned for a week. 会议延期一周。

近 prorogate, prorogue, recess, suspend

反 convoke 召集，召开会议

adjunct	[ˈædʒʌŋkt]

【考法】 *n.* 附属物，非必须部分：something joined or added to another thing but **not essentially a part** of it

例 an important adjunct to drug treatment 药物治疗的重要辅助

近 appendage, appliance, attachment, add-on

反 essential element 重要部分

ad-lib	[ˌædˈlɪb]

【考法】 *adj.* 即兴的：made or done **without previous thought or preparation**

例 not bad for an ad-lib comedy routine 对即兴喜剧表演来说已经不错了

近 extemporary, impromptu, improvisational, offhanded

反 considered, planned, premeditated, rehearsed 预先计划的

admonish	[ədˈmɑːnɪʃ]

【考法 1】 *v.* 建议：to **give advice** to

例 admonish the patient to eat more healthy foods 建议患者多吃健康食品

近 counsel

【考法 2】 *v.* 责备：to **reprove gently** but earnestly

例 admonish her for littering 责备她乱扔垃圾

近 chide, reprimand, reproach, reprove, tick off

派 admonishment *n.* 责备

adore	[əˈdɔːr]

【考法 1】 *vt.* 喜爱，因…感到愉悦：to take **pleasure** in

例 I adore those earrings. 我相中那对耳环了。

近 fancy, relish, savor, delight in, rejoice in

【考法 2】 *vt.* 宠爱：to feel passion, devotion, or **tenderness** for

例 adore his wife 宠爱他的妻子

近 cherish

反 abhor, abominate, despise, detest, execrate, loathe 讨厌，嫌弃

adulate [ˈædʒəleɪt]

【考法】 *v.* 极度谄媚，拍马屁: to **praise too much**

例 adulate his/her boss 拍老板马屁

近 overpraise, belaud, soft-soap, butter up

反 scorn, disdain, vituperate, disparage 鄙视

• adulterate [əˈdʌltəreɪt]

【考法】 *vt.* 掺杂，加入低等成分: to corrupt, debase, or make **impure** by the **addition** of a foreign or inferior substance or element

例 adulterate its products with cheap additives 在产品中掺杂廉价的添加剂

近 alloy, contaminate, pollute, taint, water down

反 enrich, fortify, strengthen 加入(养分)使增强

Unit 7

■ ADUMBRATE	■ ADVENTITIOUS	■ ADVERSARY	■ ADVERT	■ ADVOCATE
■ AFFABLE	■ AFFINITY	■ AFFLUENT	■ AGGRANDIZE	■ AGGRAVATE

• adumbrate [ˈædəmbreɪt]

【考法】 *vt.* 预示: to **give a slight indication** of beforehand

例 The strife in Bloody Kansas adumbrated the civil war that would follow. 发生在堪萨斯州的流血冲突预示了之后的南北内战的爆发。

近 forerun, harbinger, herald, prefigure

• adventitious [ˌædvenˈtɪʃəs]

【考法】 *adj.* 外来的，后天的，非内在的: coming from another source and **not inherent or innate**

例 adventitious viruses 外来病毒

近 alien, extraneous, external, foreign, supervenient

反 constitutional, essential, intrinsic, inborn, inbred, innate, inherent 天生的，内在的

adversary [ˈædvərseri]

【考法】 *n.* 敌手，对手: one that contends with, opposes, or **resists**: **enemy**

例 political adversary 政敌

近 antagonist, foe, opponent

反 ally, amigo, friend 联盟；朋友

advert [ədˈvɜːrt]

【考法】 *vi.* 引起注意；提到: to call attention; **refer**

例 He adverted to the problem in the opening paragraph. 他开门见山地提出了问题。

派 advertent *adj.* 留意的

反 inattentive, remiss, heedless, negligent 疏忽的

advocate [ˈædvəkeɪt]

【考法】 *vt.* 支持，提倡: to speak, plead, or argue in favor of; **support**

例 advocate traditional teaching methods 提倡传统教学方法

近 back, champion, endorse, patronize

反 impugn 提出异议

affable [ˈæfəbl]

【考法】 *adj.* 和蔼的，温和的: characterized by **ease** and **friendliness**

例 an affable manner 随和的举止

近 cordial, genial, hospitable, sociable, good-natured, good-tempered, well-disposed

反 irascible, testy, ill-tempered, unamiable, ungenial 易怒的，不随和的

affinity [əˈfɪnəti]

【考法 1】 *n.* 喜欢，倾向: a habitual **attraction** to some activity or thing

例 She always had an affinity for nurturing living things. 她总是喜欢养一些活物。

近 bent, penchant, predilection, predisposition, proclivity, propensity

反 aversion, repugnance, antipathy 厌恶

【考法 2】 *n.* 相似: the fact or state of having something **in common**

例 share obvious affinities 有明显的相似性

近 association, kinship

affluent [ˈæfluənt]
【考法】 *adj.* 富裕的: having a generously **sufficient** and typically increasing supply of material possessions
例 affluent society 富裕的社会
近 opulent, loaded, deep-pocketed, silk-stocking, well-endowed, well-off, well-to-do
反 needy, impecunious, impoverished, indigent, penurious 贫困的

aggrandize [əˈɡrændaɪz]
abase abase 贬义
【考法】 *vt.* 增加、提高(力量、财富、地位、声誉)等: to **enhance** the power, wealth, position, or reputation of
例 exploit the situation to aggrandize himself 借势而上使得自己地位提升、财富增长
近 augment, boost, expand, magnify, add (to), pump up
反 relegate, disparage, efface, abase, demean 降级; 贬低

aggravate [ˈæɡrəveɪt]
【考法】 *vt.* 加重, 恶化: to make **worse**, more **serious**, or more **severe**
例 Stress and lack of sleep could aggravate the situation. 压力和睡眠不足使情况恶化。
近 complicate, worsen
反 alleviate, succor, console, assuage, mitigate, relieve 减轻, 抚慰

Unit 8

■ AGGREGATE	■ AGGRESSIVE	■ AGGRIEVE	■ AGITATE	■ AGOG
■ AGONIZE	■ AIRTIGHT	■ ALACRITY	■ ALIBI	■ ALIENATE

aggregate
【考法】 [ˈæɡrɪɡət] *n.* 集合体: a mass or body of **units or parts** somewhat loosely **associated** with one another [ˈæɡrɪɡeɪt] *v.* 集合, 聚集: to **collect or gather** into a mass or whole
例 An empire is the aggregate of many states under one common head. 帝国是由一个共同领袖领导的若干国家的集合体。‖ aggregate content from many other sites 搜罗集合许多其他网站的内容
近 sum, summation, totality; coalesce, join together
反 isolated units 隔离的单位; disperse 分散
派 disaggregate *v.* 分解

aggressive [əˈɡresɪv]
【考法1】 *adj.* 好斗的: having a quality of anger and determination that makes it ready to **attack** others
例 aggressive behavior 具有攻击性的行为
近 fierce, assaultive, combative, militant, confrontational, go-getting, self-assertive, truculent, pugnacious
反 even-tempered, nonbelligerent, pacific, uncombative, uncontentious 心平气和的, 不好斗的
【考法2】 *adj.* 强有力的, 强烈的: marked by or uttered with **forcefulness**
例 an aggressive campaign to win the African-American vote 一次能够获得非裔美国人选票的强有力的竞选
近 dynamic, energetic, full-blooded, vigorous

aggrieve [əˈɡriːv]
【考法】 *vt.* 使苦恼, 使悲痛: to give **pain** or **trouble** to, **distress**
例 be aggrieved at insult 因为被侮辱而悲痛
反 gratify 使高兴, 满足
派 aggrieved *adj.* 苦恼的, 怨念的
例 a line of aggrieved ticket-holders, demanding a refund for the cancelled play 一队心怀怨念的购票者为取消的话剧要求退款
近 discontent, disgruntled, displeased, dissatisfied, malcontent

agitate [ˈædʒɪteɪt]
【考法1】 *v.* 煽动, 激起: to attempt to **arouse** public feeling
例 agitate for better conditions 为得到更好的条件而煽动
近 debate, dispute, bat (around or back and forth), hash (over or out), talk over
【考法2】 *vt.* 使不安: to excite and often **trouble the mind** or feelings of: **disturb**
例 There's no need to agitate the patient about little things. 没必要因为鸡毛蒜皮的事让患者烦躁。
近 bother, discomfort, discompose, perturb
反 calm, compose, soothe, tranquilize 平息, 抚慰

agog [əˈɡɑːɡ]
【考法】 *adj.* 极度感兴趣的: showing **urgent desire or interest**
例 Children were agog over new toys. 孩子们见到了新玩具极其兴奋。
近 avid, ardent, enthusiastic, solicitous, voracious
反 apathetic, indifferent, uneager, unenthusiastic 漠不关心的, 冷淡的

agonize [ˈæɡənaɪz]

【考法】 *v.* (使)非常痛苦: to (cause to) feel **deep sadness** or mental pain

例 agonizes over every decision 做每一个决定都非常痛苦

近 anguish, suffer

airtight [ˈertaɪt]

【考法】 *adj.* 无瑕疵的: having **no** noticeable weakness, **flaw**, or loophole

例 an airtight argument 滴水不漏、无懈可击的论断

alacrity [əˈlækrəti]

【考法】 *n.* 反应迅速, 乐意, 欣然: promptness in response: cheerful readiness

例 accept the invitation with alacrity 欣然接受邀请

近 amenability, gameness, obligingness, willingness

反 dilatoriness, hesitance and reluctance 拖延、犹豫和不情愿

alibi [ˈæləbaɪ]

【考法】 *n.* 不在场的证明; 托辞, 借口: an **excuse** usually intended to avert blame or punishment (as for failure or negligence)

例 He always has a very creative alibi for undone homework . 他对于不完成作业总是有各种新奇的借口。

近 defense, justification, plea, reason

alienate [ˈeɪliəneɪt]

【考法】 *v.* 疏远, 离间: to **make unfriendly**, or indifferent especially where attachment formerly existed

例 He has alienated most of his colleagues with his bad temper. 因为他的坏脾气, 很多同事都和他疏远了。

近 disaffect, disgruntle, sour

反 unite, reunite, reconcile 联合, 重新联合, 和好

Unit 9

■ ALIGN	■ ALLAY	■ ALLEGIANCE	■ ALLEVIATE	■ ALLUDE
■ ALLURE	■ ALLY	■ ALOFT	■ ALOOF	■ ALTRUISM

align [əˈlaɪn]

【考法】 *vt.* 调准, 校准: to **adjust** to produce a proper relationship or orientation

例 align the wheels of the truck 调整卡车的轮子

派 aligned *adj.* 对准的, 均衡的

反 improperly adjusted, irregular 调整不当的, 不规则的

allay [əˈleɪ]

【考法】 *vt.* 减轻: to **subdue** or **reduce** in **intensity or severity**, alleviate

例 allay one's fears or doubts 减轻某人的恐惧或怀疑

近 assuage, ease, mitigate, mollify, palliate, relieve, soothe, alleviate

反 excite, aggravate, foment, increase the intensity of, exacerbate 激起, 使加重

allegiance [əˈliːdʒəns]

【考法】 *n.* 忠诚: **devotion or loyalty** to a person, group, or cause

例 They swore their allegiance to the USA. 他们宣誓效忠美国。

近 commitment, dedication, piety, faithfulness, steadfastness

反 inconstancy, infidelity, perfidiousness, treachery 不忠实, 背叛

alleviate [əˈliːvieɪt]

【考法】 *v.* 缓和, 减轻: **relieve, lessen**

例 alleviate pain /suffering 减轻痛苦

近 ease, assuage, mitigate, mollify, palliate, soothe, allay, relieve

反 excite, aggravate, foment, increase the intensity of, exacerbate 激起, 使加重

allude [əˈluːd] *imply*

【考法】 *vi.* 间接提到: to **convey** an idea **indirectly**

例 He also alluded to his rival's past marital troubles . 他还间接提到了对手过去的婚姻问题。

近 imply, indicate, infer, insinuate, intimate, suggest

allure [əˈlʊr]

【考法】 *vt.* 吸引: to **attract or delight** as if by magic

近 entice, seduce, solicit, tempt, captivate, enchant, lead on

派 alluring *adj.* 诱惑的, 有吸引力的

例 an alluring smile 迷人的微笑

反 unattractive 无吸引力的

ally

【考法】 [ˈælaɪ] *n.* 盟友，支持者: one in helpful **association** with another

[əˈlaɪ] *v.* 加入联盟: to **enter** into an alliance

例 enter the war as an ally of America 以美国的同盟者身份加入战争 ‖ several tribes allied to fend off the invaders 几个部落联合起来抵抗侵略者

近 supporter, confederate, sympathizer

反 adversary, rival 对手；disband 解散

aloft

[əˈlɔːft]

【考法】 *adv.* 在空中: in the air especially: **in flight** (as in an airplane)

例 The balloon stayed aloft for days . 气球在空中停留了很多天。

近 overhead

反 grounded 着陆地

aloof

[əˈluːf]

【考法】 *adj.* 高冷的: removed or **distant** either physically or emotionally

例 an aloof composer who never worry about public opinion 不关心民意的高冷作曲家

近 detached, offish, unsociable, withdrawn, standoffish

反 sociable 好社交的

altruism

[ˈæltruɪzəm]

【考法】 *n.* 利他主义，无私: **unselfish** regard for or devotion to the welfare of others

例 ambition that is masked as altruism 利他主义掩盖下的野心

反 egoism 利己主义

派 altruistic *adj.* 利他的

反 egotistic, self-centered, self-concerned, selfish 自私的

Unit 10

■ AMALGAMATE	■ AMBIGUOUS	■ AMBLE	■ AMBROSIAL	■ AMELIORATE
■ AMENABLE	■ AMENITY	■ AMIABLE	■ AMICABLE	■ AMITY

amalgamate

[əˈmælɡəmeɪt]

【考法】 *v.* 合并，混合: to **combine** into a **unified** or integrated whole; **unite**

例 amalgamate with an American company 与一家美国公司合并

近 mix, fuse, intermix, compound, meld, mingle, integrate, intermingle

反 separate, isolate 分开，隔离

ambiguous

[æmˈbɪɡjuəs]

【考法】 *adj.* 不确定的: open to **more than one** interpretation; **doubtful** or **uncertain**

例 Students have ambiguous feelings about their role in the world. 学生们为他们在世界中的角色感到迷茫。

frustrated by ambiguous instructions 因为不明确的指示而受挫

近 doubtful, equivocal, unclear, uncertain

反 distinct, pellucid, patent, blatant, explicit, lucid, perspicuous 清楚的，明显的

amble

[ˈæmbl]

【考法】 *vi./n.* 漫步，闲逛: to **walk slowly** or **leisurely**; **stroll**

例 Every evening, they ambled along the bank . 他们每晚沿河边散步。

近 ramble, saunter, stroll, wander, dally, dawdle

反 step quickly 快走

ambrosial

[æmˈbroʊziəl]

【考法】 *adj.* (食物)特别美味的；香的: something **extremely pleasing** to taste or smell

例 The ambrosial aroma of the roast stimulated our appetites. 烤肉的香气刺激了我们的食欲。

近 savory, aromatic, perfumed, redolent, odorous

反 fetid, noisome, stenchy, malodorous, rancid 恶臭的

ameliorate

[əˈmiːliəreɪt]

【考法】 *vt.* 改善，改进: to make or **become better**; **improve**

例 ameliorate the suffering of people who have lost their jobs 缓解失业人员的痛苦

近 improve, recuperate

反 aggravate, worsen, deteriorate (使)恶化

派 ameliorator *n.* 改良物

反 damper 抑制因素

amenable [əˈmiːnəbl]

【考法】 *adj.* 顺从的，服从的：readily brought to **yield**, **submit**, or cooperate

例 The high-spirited and rebellious girl is not at all amenable to persuasion . 这个泼辣而反叛的女孩根本不听从劝告。

近 compliant, docile, submissive, tractable, obedient

反 intransigent, contumacious 不妥协的；intractable, recalcitrant, refractory 倔强的；uncontrollable, ungovernable, unruly 难管束的

amenity [əˈmenəti]

【考法1】 *n.* (环境、设备等的)舒适，人性化：something that conduces to **comfort**, convenience, or enjoyment

例 the amenity of the new surroundings 新环境的舒适宜人

近 comfort, convenience, affability

【考法2】 *n.* 融洽，和谐：the quality of being **pleasant** or **agreeable**

例 a discussion conducted in perfect amenity 在和谐融洽的气氛中进行的讨论

近 agreeability, harmony, accord, concord, consonance

反 discordance, inharmony 不和谐

amiable [ˈeɪmiəbl]

【考法】 *adj.* 好脾气的，友好易相处的：being **friendly**, sociable, and congenial

例 an amiable teacher not easily annoyed 一个不易惹恼、易相处的老师

近 friendly, affable, amicable, genial, easy to get along with

反 disagreeable, ill-natured, ill-tempered, unamiable, ungenial, ungracious, unpleasant 坏脾气的，令人不愉快的

amicable [ˈæmɪkəbl]

【考法】 *adj.* 友善的：characterized by **friendly** goodwill; **amiable**

例 maintain amicable relations 保持友好关系 ‖ an amicable divorce 和平离婚

近 friendly, affable, amiable, genial, easy to get along with

反 antagonistic, hostile, unfriendly 有敌意的

amity [ˈæməti]

【考法】 *n.* 友好关系，亲善和睦：**friendship**; especially: **friendly** relations between nations

例 live in amity with his neighbors 与邻居和睦相处 ‖ They parted in amity . 他们友好地分别了。

近 friendship

反 enmity, hostility 敌意

Man errs so long as he strives.

人只要奋斗就会犯错误。

——德国诗人、剧作家 歌德

(Johann Wolfgang Goethe, German poet and dramatist)

List 2

"壮丽的诗篇要以信念作为舞台，融着几多苦乐的拼搏历程是我想要延续的抚慰和寄托。"

（金宇航，Verbal 720，Quantitative 800，
录取院校：哈佛大学工程与应用科学）

Unit 1

■ AMORPHOUS　　■ ANODYNE　　■ ANARCHIST　　■ ANATHEMA　　■ ANCILLARY
■ ANECDOTE　　■ ANEMIC　　■ ANESTHETIC　　■ ANIMATE　　■ ANIMUS

amorphous ［əˈmɔːrfəs］ *7h→form*
- 【考法】 *adj.* 无固定形状的：having no **definite** form: **shapeless**
- 例 an amorphous cloud mass 一团无定形的云
- 近 shapeless, unformed, unshaped

anodyne ［ˈænədaɪn］
- 【考法】 *adj.* 无害的：**not causing** or being capable of causing injury or **hurt**
- 例 The otherwise anodyne comments sound quite inflammatory when taken out of context. 当脱离语境的时候，本来没有冒犯意味的评论听起来惹人生气。
- 近 harmless, benign, innocuous, inoffensive
- 反 adverse, baleful, baneful, deleterious, detrimental, nocuous, pernicious 有害的

anarchist ［ˈænərkɪst］
- 【考法】 *n.* 反抗权威的人：a person who **rebels against any authority**, established order, or ruling power
- 例 a large anarchist community 庞大的无政府主义群体
- 同 rebel, insurgent
- 派 anarchy *n.* 混乱：a state of lawlessness or political disorder due to the absence of governmental authority
- 近 chaos, disarray, topsy-turviness, commotion, turmoil
- 反 order 有序

anathema ［əˈnæθəmə］
- 【考法】 *n.* 令人讨厌的人或事：something or someone that is **hated**
- 例 Violence was anathema to them. 他们对暴力深恶痛绝。
- 近 abhorrence, abomination, antipathy, aversion, detestation, execration
- 反 love 爱

ancillary ［ˈænsəleri］
- 【考法1】 *adj.* 次要的：of **secondary importance**
- 例 The company hopes to boost its sales through ancillary products. 公司想通过辅助产品来增加销量。
- 近 subordinate, subsidiary
- 反 main, paramount 主要的
- 【考法2】 *adj.* 辅助的，补充的：**auxiliary, supplementary**
- 例 the need for ancillary evidence 对补充证据的需要 ‖ Some practice in the deft use of words may well be ancillary to the study of natural science. 某些熟练使用文字的练习对于自然科学的研究也是有辅助作用的。
- 近 auxiliary, supplementary

anecdote ［ˈænɪkdoʊt］
- 【考法】 *n.* 短小有趣的故事，段子：a usually **short narrative** of an **interesting, amusing**, or biographical incident
- 例 He told us all sorts of humorous anecdotes about his childhood. 他告诉了我们所有关于他童年的奇闻趣事。
He is a master raconteur with endless anecdotes. 他是讲故事的超级高手，总有讲不完的奇闻趣事。

anemic ［əˈniːmɪk］ *animate*
- 【考法】 *adj.* 缺乏力量、活力、精神的：**lacking force**, vitality, or spirit
- 例 an anemic economic recovery 毫无活力的经济复苏 ‖ Investors are worried about the stock's anemic performance. 投资者担心股市低迷的表现。
- 近 sapless, infirm, feeble, decrepit, wan, pale, pallid, effete, lethargic
- 反 vigorous, spirited 精力充沛的；forceful 有力量的

13

anesthetic	[ˌænəsˈθetɪk]
【考法】	*adj.* 无感觉的，麻木的：**lacking awareness or sensitivity**
例	be anesthetic to their feelings 对他们的感受麻木不仁
反	sensate 有感觉的

animate	
【考法 1】	*adj.* 有活力的：having much **high-spirited energy** and movement
例	Animate dance will get the blood pumping. 有活力的舞蹈会让人热血沸腾。
近	bouncing, brisk, energetic, sprightly, vivacious
反	inactive, lackadaisical, languid, listless, leaden 没有活力的，无精打采的
【考法 2】	[ˈænɪmeɪt] *vt.* 使有活力，支持：to give **spirit** and **support** to
例	The writer's humor animates the novel. 作者的幽默使小说富有生命力。
近	brace, energize, enliven, invigorate, ginger (up), pep up, vitalize 使有活力
反	damp, dampen, deaden 使没活力，使沮丧
派	animation *n.* 生命力，活力：the quality or condition of being alive, active, spirited, or vigorous
反	lassitude, lethargy 疲倦，疲乏

animus	[ˈænɪməs]
【考法】	*n.* 敌意：a usually prejudiced and often **spiteful** or **malevolent** ill will, **enmity**
例	She felt no animus toward those who had wronged her. 她对那些冤枉了她的人没有敌意。
近	animosity, antagonism, antipathy, hostility, rancor
反	friendliness, amity, amenity 友好

Unit 2

■ ANNOY	■ ANNUL	■ ANOMALOUS	■ ANONYMOUS	■ ANTAGONIZE
■ ANTEDILUVIAN	■ ANTERIOR	■ ANTIC	■ APATHY	■ APHORISM

annoy	[əˈnɔɪ]
【考法】	*vt.* 不断烦扰：to **disturb** or irritate especially by **repeated** acts
例	Mosquitoes annoy us in the summer. 夏天蚊子总是不断烦扰我们。
近	aggravate, bother, chafe, gall, grate, irk, nettle, peeve, pique, rile, ruffle, spite, vex
反	soothe, defuse, allay, conciliate, propitiate, mitigate, assuage, appease, pacify, placate, calm, settle, subdue, solace, mollify 平息，抚慰

annul	[əˈnʌl]
【考法】	*vt.* 宣告无效，取消：to declare or make **legally invalid** or void
例	annul the contract 废除合同
近	disannul, cancel, invalidate, abrogate, nullify, repeal, rescind
反	make legal 使合法；enact 制定

anomalous	[əˈnɑːmələs] *normal → abnormal*
【考法】	*adj.* 不普通的，不平常的：being **out** of the **ordinary**
例	He is in an anomalous position as the only part-time teacher in Weichen. 他和别人不一样的是，他是微臣唯一的兼职老师。
近	aberrant, abnormal, atypical, phenomenal, singular, uncustomary, unwonted
反	unexceptional, unextraordinary 普通的，平常的
派	anomaly *n.* 反常：deviation or departure from the normal or common order, form, or rule

anonymous	[əˈnɑːnɪməs]
【考法】	*adj.* 匿名的：**not named** or **identified**
例	He made an anonymous phone call to the police. 他给警察打了一个匿名电话。 ‖ anonymous donor 匿名捐赠者
近	incognito, innominate, unnamed, unidentified, untitled
反	dubbed, named, termed 有名字的

antagonize	[ænˈtægənaɪz]
【考法 1】	*vt.* 与…敌对，反对：to act in **opposition** to：**counteract**
例	antagonize a bill 反对一项议案
近	counteract, disagree
反	agree, concede, grant，win over (使)同意

【考法2】 vt. 激怒：to **incur** or **provoke** the **hostility** of
例 His remark antagonized his friends. 他的评述激怒了他的朋友。
近 aggravate, exasperate, gall, inflame, nettle, provoke, peeve, pique, irritate, rile, roil, chafe, grate, ruffle, vex
反 soothe, defuse, allay, conciliate, propitiate, mitigate, assuage, appease, pacify, placate, calm, settle, subdue, solace, mollify 平息，抚慰

antediluvian [ˌæntidɪˈluːvɪən]
ante→before (lu→水 (上帝淡水，方舟)
洪水之前
【考法】 *adj.* 非常古老的；过时的：**extremely old** and **antiquated**
例 He has antediluvian notions about the role of women in the workplace. 他对职场女性抱有老掉牙的看法。
an antediluvian automobile 古董级的汽车
近 aged, age-old, prehistoric, antique, immemorial
反 modern, new, recent 新的

anterior [ænˈtɪrɪər]
【考法】 *adj.* 前面的：coming **before** in time or development
例 finish the work anterior to the schedule 提早完成任务 ‖ tests anterior to the college entrance examination 高考前的考试
近 antecedent, foregoing, former, forward, precedent, preceding, prior
反 after, ensuing, following, posterior, subsequent, succeeding 后面的，后来的

antic [ˈæntɪk]
【考法】 *adj.* 滑稽可笑的：characterized by **clownish** extravagance or absurdity
例 The clown came on with many antic gestures. 那个小丑上场表演了许多滑稽动作。
近 chucklesome, comedic, comic, droll, farcical, laughable, ludicrous, hilarious
反 humorless, unamusing, uncomic, unfunny, unhumorous 不好笑的；grave, serious, solemn, somber 严肃的，庄重的

apathy [ˈæpəθi]
没感觉   *sympath 同情*
【考法】 *n.* 缺乏兴趣，不关心：**lack** of **interest** or **concern**
例 She heard the story with apathy. 她毫无兴趣地听完了这个故事。 ‖ Her poor grades are proof enough of her apathy concerning all matters academic. 她可怜的分数足以证明她对所有的学术问题都没兴趣。
近 disinterestedness, disregard, incuriosity, insouciance, nonchalance, unconcern
反 concern, interest, regard 关心，有兴趣，在意

aphorism [ˈæfərɪzəm]
【考法】 *n.* 格言，警句：a **short witty** sentence which expresses a general truth or comment
例 When decorating, remember the familiar aphorism, "less is more." 装修时需要记住一句格言"少即是多"。
近 adage, epigram, maxim, proverb

Unit 3

■ APOCALYPTIC ■ APOCRYPHAL ■ APOPLECTIC ■ APOSTASY ■ APPALL
■ APPEAL ■ APPEALING ■ APPLAUSE ■ APPOSITE ■ APPRECIABLE

apocalyptic [əˌpɑːkəˈlɪptɪk]
【考法1】 *adj.* 预言的，启示的：of a revelatory or **prophetic** nature
例 No one listened to her apocalyptic predictions. 没有人听她的预言。
近 prophetic, predictive, prognostic, farsighted
【考法2】 *adj.* 重要的，转折点的：of, relating to, or being a **major turning** point
例 The apocalyptic Battle of Stalingrad led to the ultimate defeat of Nazi Germany. 具有转折点意义的斯大林格勒战役导致了最后纳粹德国的战败。
反 trivial, petty, minor, immaterial, inconsequential, insignificant 不重要的

apocryphal [əˈpɑːkrɪfl]
【考法】 *adj.* 假的：of **doubtful authenticity**: **spurious**
例 an apocryphal story about the president's childhood 一个关于总统童年的假的故事
近 spurious, unauthentic, ungenuine
反 factual, true, truthful, authentic 真的

apoplectic [ˌæpəˈplektɪk]

【考法】 *adj.* 极度愤怒的: **extremely angry**; **furious**

例 He became apoplectic about wasteful government spending . 他对政府的浪费开销感到怒不可遏。

近 choleric, enraged, furious, incensed, indignant, infuriated, irate, ireful, outraged

反 angerless, delighted, pleased 不生气的，高兴的

apostasy [əˈpɑːstəsi]

【考法】 *n.* 背叛: **abandonment** of a **previous loyalty**: defection

例 He was looked down upon for apostasy . 他因为背叛而受到鄙视。

近 defection, perfidy, treacherousness, recreancy

反 fidelity, allegiance, loyalty, piety 忠诚，虔诚

appall [əˈpɔːl] *pall→脸色白 ap→皮*

【考法】 *vt.* 使惊恐: to overcome with **consternation**, shock, or dismay

例 He felt appalled by the whole idea of marriage so we broke up. 结婚使他恐惧，因此我们分手了。

近 dismay, terrify, intimidate, frighten, horrify, daunt, deter

反 embolden, encourage, nerve 使大胆，鼓起勇气

appeal [əˈpiːl]

【考法 1】 *n.* 申请: an **application** (as to a recognized authority) for corroboration, vindication, or decision

例 a piteous appeal for help 哀怜地请求帮助 ‖ make an appeal to the public to donate needed blood 向公众提出献血请求

近 adjuration, conjuration, entreaty, petition, pleading, supplication

【考法 2】 *n.* 起诉: to **charge** with a **crime**: **accuse**

例 My lawyer said the court's decision wasn't correct and that we should file for an appeal . 我的律师说，法庭的判决不对，我们应该起诉。

近 charge, accuse, incriminate, inculpate, indict

反 absolve 赦免；exonerate, exculpate 开脱罪责；vindicate 辩护

appealing [əˈpiːlɪŋ]

【考法】 *adj.* 吸引人的: **attractive**, **inviting**

例 an appealing offer 一个诱人的 offer

近 alluring, captivating, charismatic, charming, enchanting, engaging, entrancing, luring, seductive

反 repellent, repelling, repugnant, repulsive, unalluring 令人厌恶的，不吸引人的

applause [əˈplɔːz]

【考法】 *n.* 鼓掌；认可: **approval** publicly expressed (as by clapping the hands)

例 Her appearance was greeted with applause . 她的出现被报以热烈的掌声。

近 acclamation, cheer, cheering, ovation, plaudit, rave

反 hissing, booing 发出嘘声

apposite [ˈæpəzɪt] *pos→放 position 放一起 =(重要的)*

【考法】 *adj.* 相关的，合适的: highly **pertinent** or **appropriate**: apt

例 enrich his essay with some very apposite quotations from famous people 用名人名言来丰富他的文章

近 applicable, apropos, germane, pointed, relative, relevant

反 extraneous, irrelevant, impertinent, irrelative, pointless 无关的

appreciable [əˈpriːʃəbl]

【考法】 *adj.* 可感知的，明显的: capable of being perceived or measured; **perceptible**

例 the appreciable changes in temperature 气温明显的变化 ‖ There doesn't seem to be any appreciable difference between this piece and that one. 这个和那个看上去没什么明显的差别。

近 apprehensible, perceptible, detectable, discernible, palpable, distinguishable, sensible

反 impalpable, imperceptible, inappreciable, indistinguishable, insensible, undetectable 不能感知的

Unit 4

| ■ APPREHENSION | ■ APPRISE | ■ APPROBATION | ■ APPROPRIATE | ■ APROPOS |
| ■ APT | ■ ARCHAIC | ■ ARCHETYPE | ■ ARDOR | ■ ARDUOUS |

apprehension [ˌæprɪˈhenʃn]

【考法 1】 *n.* 忧虑，恐惧: **suspicion** or **fear** especially of future evil

例 She had a strong apprehension about her sister's health . 她非常担心她姐姐的健康。

近 dread, foreboding, misgiving, anxiousness, unease, uneasiness, worry

反 composure, equanimity 镇定；unconcern 冷漠

【考法 2】 *n.* 理解 : the knowledge gained from the process of coming to know or **understand** something
例 sudden apprehension of something strange 突然间领悟了陌生事物
近 understanding, comprehension
反 incomprehension

apprise [əˈpraɪz] *inform*
【考法】 *v.* 通知，告知 : to give notice to; **inform**
例 apprise him of the danger that may be involved 告知他可能涉及的危险
近 inform, acquaint, make known to
反 withhold information 隐瞒信息

approbation [ˌæprəˈbeɪʃn] *approve*
【考法】 *n.* 同意 : an expression of warm **approval**
例 The proposal met his approbation. 这项建议得到了他的同意。
近 approval, favor
反 disapproval, disapprobation, disfavor 不同意

appropriate
【考法 1】 [əˈprouprieɪt] *v.* 私自挪用 : to **take possession** of or make use of exclusively for oneself, often **without permission**
例 appropriate private property 盗用私人财产 ‖ The economy has been weakened by corrupt officials who have appropriated the country's resources for their own use. 经济因为腐败的官员们私自挪用国家资源而被削弱了。
近 purloin, pirate, embezzle, peculate, usurp
【考法 2】 [əˈproupriət] *adj.* 适当的 : especially **suitable** or compatible: **fitting**
例 Red wine is a more appropriate choice with the meal. 红酒更适合这顿饭。
近 apt, becoming, felicitous, fitting, proper, meet, suitable, apposite, apropos
反 improper, inapposite, inappropriate, inapt, unmeet, unseemly, unsuitable 不合适的

apropos [ˌæprəˈpou]
【考法 1】 *adj.* 相关的 : being both **relevant** and opportune
例 The actor announced to reporters that he would only answer to apropos questions about the movie. 演员向记者表示，他只回答和电影有关的问题。
近 applicable, apposite, germane, pointed, relative, relevant
反 extraneous, irrelevant, impertinent, irrelative, pointless 无关的
【考法 2】 *prep.* 关于，有关 : **having to do with**
例 make a number of telling observations apropos the current political situation 做了很多关于当前政治形势有力的观察
近 apropos, apropos of, as far as, as for, as regards (*also* as respects), as to, concerning, regarding, respecting, touching, toward (*or* towards)

apt [æpt]
【考法 1】 *adj.* 恰当的，合适的 : exactly **suitable**; **appropriate** △
例 apt remark/choice/description 恰当的评述/选择/描述
近 apropos, germane, relative, relevant, appropriate
反 extraneous, irrelevant, impertinent, irrelative 无关的; inappropriate, improper, unseemly 不恰当的，不合时宜的
【考法 2】 *adj.* 聪明的 : keenly **intelligent** and **responsive**
例 an apt pupil 一个聪明的小学生 ‖ He is apt at mathematics. 他擅长数学。
近 brilliant, clever, quick-witted, ready-witted, smart
反 foolish, dull, dumb, stupid, unintelligent 傻的，愚蠢的

archaic [ɑːrˈkeɪɪk] *archaeology* 考古学
【考法】 *adj.* 过时的，久远的 : **no** longer **current** or applicable; **antiquated**
例 archaic laws 过时的法律
近 antiquated, outdated, outmoded, prehistoric, superannuated
反 fashionable 流行的; up-to-date, fresh, modern, new, novel 新的
派 archaism *n.* 古语 : the use of archaic diction or style
反 modern diction 新语

archetype [ˈɑːkitaɪp]

【考法】 *n.* 典范，榜样：an **ideal** example of a type

例 an archetype of the successful entrepreneur 成功企业家的典范

近 ideal, a perfect example, quintessence

ardor [ˈɑːrdər]

【考法】 *n.* 狂热：**strong enthusiasm** or **devotion**; **zeal**

例 His ardor was damped. 他的热情被泼了冷水。

近 avidity, zeal, fervor, fervency, fervidness, passion, passionateness, vehemence

反 apathy, torpor, impassivity, insensitivity 冷漠，麻木

arduous [ˈɑːrdʒuəs]

【考法】 *adj.* 难以做到的，费劲的：hard to accomplish or achieve: **difficult**

例 a long and arduous undertaking 一项长期艰苦的任务 ‖ an arduous journey across miles of desert 艰苦的沙漠之旅

近 grueling, laborious, taxing, onerous, burdensome

反 easy, simple, unchallenging, undemanding, facile, effortless 不费劲的

Unit 5

■ ANTHROPOGENIC ■ ARREST ■ ARRESTING ■ ARRHYTHMIC ■ ARROGANCE
■ ARTICULATE ■ ASCENDANT ■ ASCETIC ■ ASEPTIC ■ ASKEW

anthropogenic [ˌænθrəpəˈdʒenɪk]

【考法】 *adj.* 人为的：resulting from the **influence of human beings** on nature

例 anthropogenic degradation of the environment 人类造成的环境恶化

近 caused by human

arrest [əˈrest]

【考法1】 *n./v.* 停止：the **stopping** of a process or activity; to bring to a **standstill**

例 Science cannot yet arrest the process of aging. 科学不能阻止衰老。

近 cease, cessation, closure, conclusion, discontinuance, discontinuation, ending, halt, stop, termination; check, stop, cease, close, conclude, discontinue, end, halt, terminate

反 continuance, continuation 继续

【考法2】 *v.* 逮捕：to take or **keep** under one's control by authority of law

例 She was charged with resisting arrest. 她因为拒捕受到起诉。

近 apprehend

反 discharge 释放

【考法3】 *v.* 吸引（某人）注意力：to **hold** the **attention** of as if by a spell

例 The behavior of the daredevil arrested pedestrians. 冒失鬼的行为吸引了行人们的注意力。

近 enchant, fascinate, bedazzle, grip, hypnotize, mesmerize

arresting [əˈrestɪŋ]

【考法】 *adj.* 吸引人的：**attracting** and holding the attention; **striking**

例 an arresting spectacle 吸引人的奇观

近 absorbing, engaging, engrossing, enthralling, fascinating, gripping, immersing, intriguing, riveting

反 boring, drab, tedious, monotonous, uninteresting 乏味的，单调的

arrhythmic [əˈrɪðmɪk]

【考法】 *adj.* 不规律的：**lacking** rhythm or **regularity**

例 arrhythmic pulse 不规律的脉搏

近 irregular, disorderly

反 regular, orderly 规律的

arrogance [ˈærəgəns]

【考法】 *n.* 傲慢，自大：**overbearing pride**

例 Her arrogance has earned her a lot of enemies. 她的傲慢给她带来了很多敌人。

近 assumption, bumptiousness, haughtiness, hauteur, imperiousness, loftiness, peremptoriness, pomposity, pompousness, presumptuousness, superciliousness

反 humility, modesty, humbleness, unassumingness 谦虚，谦逊

articulate

【考法 1】 [ɑːrˈtɪkjuleɪt] *v.* 清晰地表达: to utter **clearly** and **distinctly**

例 He cannot articulate his thoughts . 他不能清楚地表达他的想法。

近 enunciate

反 murmur, mumble, mutter, slur 含糊地说

【考法 2】 [ɑːrˈtɪkjələt] *adj.* 表达清晰的: **able** to **express** oneself **clearly** and well

例 The television crew covering the science fair were looking for photogenic and articulate students to explain their projects on the air. 负责报道科学展览的电视工作人员正在寻找上镜的、表达清晰的学生，请他们在节目中解释其(科学)项目。

近 eloquent, fluent, silver-tongued, well-spoken

反 inarticulate, ineloquent, unvocal 表达不清楚的

ascendant [əˈsendənt]

【考法】 *adj.* 有影响力的，主宰的: **dominant** in position or **influence**; **superior**

例 This idea was in the ascendant . 这种思想处于主导地位。

近 superior, dominant, sovereign

反 having no influence/power 没有影响力的

ascetic [əˈsetɪk]   *abstemious 节俭的.*

【考法】 *n./adj.* 自制的（人）: practicing strict **self-denial** as a measure of personal and especially spiritual discipline

例 This is an ascetic diet of rice and beans. 这是一顿苦行餐，只有米饭和豌豆。

近 abstemious, abstinent, self-denying

反 sumptuous, luxurious 奢侈的; licentious, sybaritic, voluptuous 放荡的，沉溺于酒色的

· aseptic [ˌeɪˈseptɪk]   *aseptic monk 苦行僧*

【考法】 *adj.* 消毒的，无菌的: **preventing infection**

例 Surgery must be in aseptic environments . 手术必须在无菌环境下进行。

近 sterile, germfree

反 germy, unsterile 有细菌的; contaminated, tainted 被污染的

askew [əˈskjuː]

【考法】 *adj./adv.* 不成直线的(地)，歪的(地): out of line, **awry**

例 The picture hung askew . 画挂歪了。

近 crooked, cockeyed, oblique, lopsided, skewed, aslant, slanted, slanting, listing, tilted, awry

反 aligned 列成一行的; straight, erect 直的

Unit 6

■ ASPECT	■ ASPERITY	■ ASPERSION	■ ASPIRANT	■ ASSENT
■ ASSERT	■ ASSERTIVE	■ ASSESS	■ ASSIDUOUS	■ ASSUAGE

aspect [ˈæspekt]

【考法】 *n.* 外表，容貌: **appearance** to the eye or mind

例 His face had a frightening aspect . 他的脸很吓人。

近 appearance, look, figure, presence, mien

· asperity [æˈsperəti]

【考法 1】 *n.* (举止、性情)粗暴: **roughness** of manner or of temper

例 She responded with such asperity that we knew she was offended by the question. 她如此粗鲁地回答问题，我们知道这个问题冒犯了她。

近 roughness, crudity, rudeness, poignancy, harshness

反 softness, mildness 脾气好

【考法 2】 *n.* (环境)艰苦: **rigor**, **severity**

例 He has encountered more than his share of asperities on the road to success . 在成功的道路上，他已经遇到过比他应该承受的更多的艰辛。

近 severity, hardness, hardship, rigor

aspersion [əˈspɜːrʒn]

【考法】 *n.* 诽谤，中伤: a false or misleading charge meant to **harm** someone's **reputation**

例 cast aspersions on my loyalty 诽谤我的忠诚

近 defamation, besmirchment, calumny, calumniation, maligning, obloquy, vilification

反 glowing tribute, eulogy, extolling, laudation, praise, commendation, compliment 热情赞赏，表扬; flattery, adulation 拍马屁

aspirant [əˈspaɪərənt]

【考法】 *n.* 有抱负者，有野心者：one who **aspires**, as to advancement, honors, or a high position

例 an aspirant to social honor 追求名声的人

近 seeker

反 noncandidate 非候选人

assent [əˈsent]

【考法】 *vi.* 同意：to **agree** to something especially after thoughtful consideration

例 assent to the request of customer 同意了消费者的需求

近 accede, agree, consent, subscribe, come round

反 dissent, disagree 不同意

assert [əˈsɜːrt] *assertive 傲慢武断*

【考法】 *vt.* 断言，肯定地说出：to state or **declare** positively and often **forcefully** or **aggressively**

例 assert one's innocence 坚称自己无罪

近 aver, allege, avow, avouch, insist

反 deny, gainsay 否认

assertive [əˈsɜːrtɪv]

【考法】 *adj.* 自信的：inclined to **bold** or confident **assertion**; aggressively **self-assured**

例 assertive foreign policy 自信的外交政策

近 assertory, self-assured, self-assertive, peremptory

反 diffident 不自信的

assess [əˈses]

【考法1】 *v.* 评估（重要性、尺寸、价值等）：to **determine** the importance, size, or **value** of

例 assess the performance 评估表现

近 evaluate, appraise, guesstimate

【考法2】 *v.* 征收费用（如罚款）：to establish or apply as a **charge** or **penalty**

例 The utility company will assess a fee if your payment is late. 如果你付款晚了，公共事业公司会罚款。

近 assess, charge, exact, fine, lay, levy, put

反 remit 免除（债务）

assiduous [əˈsɪdʒuəs] *sid→坐在桌前*

【考法】 *adj.* 勤勉的，专心仔细的：marked by **careful** unremitting attention or persistent application; busy

例 He always tended his garden with assiduous attention. 他总是专心仔细地照看他的花园。 ‖ The project required some assiduous planning. 该项目需要细心的规划。

近 diligent, industrious, sedulous

反 idle, inactive, unbusy, unemployed, unoccupied 空闲的

派 assiduity *n.* 勤勉：persistent application or diligence; unflagging effort

assuage [əˈsweɪdʒ]

【考法】 *vt.* 缓和，减轻：to **lessen** the **intensity** of

例 He couldn't assuage his guilt over the divorce. 他无法减轻自己在离婚中的内疚。

反 aggravate, exacerbate 加强，使恶化

Unit 7

■ ASTOUNDING	■ ASTUTE	■ ASUNDER	■ ASYLUM	■ ASYMMETRICAL
■ ATONE	■ ATROCIOUS	■ ATTENUATE	■ AUDACIOUS	■ AUGUR

astounding [əˈstaʊndɪŋ] *tound→thunder*

【考法】 *adj.* 令人吃惊的，出乎意料的：causing **astonishment** or **amazement**

例 astounding undersea environment 令人震惊的海底环境

近 amazing, astonishing, blindsiding, dumbfounding, shocking, startling, stunning, stupefying

反 unsurprising 平常的

astute [əˈstuːt] *acute*

【考法】 *adj.* 机敏的，有洞察力的：having or showing **shrewdness** and **perspicacity**

例 Astute salesmen know how to invest emotionally. 精明的推销员知道如何进行感情投资。

近 canny, smart, shrewd, perspicacious, clear-eyed, clear-sighted, savvy, hardheaded

反 unknowing 无知的

asunder [əˈsʌndər]

【考法】 *adv.* 分离地: apart from each other in position

例 A quiet conscience sleeps in thunder, but rest and guilt live far asunder . 平静的良心能在雷声中入睡，而安宁和负罪则无法毗邻。 ‖ Our opinions are wide as the poles asunder. 我们的意见完全相反。

近 apart

反 together 在一起

asylum [əˈsaɪləm]

【考法】 *n.* 收容所，保护所: an inviolable place of **refuge** and protection giving shelter to criminals and debtors/something (as a building) that offers cover from the weather or **protection** from danger

例 an insane asylum 疯人院 ‖ The embassy serves as an asylum for that country's nationals in need of help. 大使馆作为那国需要帮助的公民的保护所。

近 harbor, haven, refuge, sanctuary, sanctum

asymmetrical [ˌeɪsɪˈmetrɪkl]

【考法】 *adj.* 不平衡的，不对称的: having **no balance** or **symmetry**

例 the asymmetrical construction 非对称的建筑

近 asymmetric, nonsymmetrical, unsymmetrical, unbalanced

反 symmetrical 对称的；balanced 平衡的

atone [əˈtoʊn]

【考法】 *v.* 赎罪，弥补: to make **amends**, as for a sin or fault

例 Blood must atone for blood . 以命抵命。 ‖ Even death cannot atone for the offence. 罪不容诛。

近 redeem

atrocious [əˈtroʊʃəs]

【考法】 *adj.* 极坏的，极其残忍的: **extremely wicked**, brutal, or cruel

例 Murder is an atrocious crime . 谋杀是一种极其恶劣的犯罪活动。

近 heinous

反 benign, kind, kindhearted, benignant, good-hearted, humane, sympathetic, tenderhearted 善良的，好的

attenuate [əˈtenjueɪt]

【考法】 *v.* 降低(数量、力量、价值): to **lessen** the amount, force, magnitude, or value of

例 an investment attenuated by inflation 一项因通货膨胀而贬值的投资

近 cheapen, devalue, downgrade, reduce, write down

反 appreciate, enhance, upgrade, mark up 升值，提升

派 attenuation *n.* 减弱，贬值

audacious [ɔːˈdeɪʃəs]

【考法 1】 *adj.* 大胆的，(但往往)愚勇的: **fearlessly**, often **recklessly** daring; bold

例 an audacious plan 一个冒进的计划

近 bold, adventurous, brash, brassy, brazen, rash, reckless

反 cautious, circumspect, guarded, wary 小心谨慎的

【考法 2】 *adj.* 令人吃惊的: very bold and **surprising** or shocking

例 His audacious writing style is designed to surprise or to startle. 他令人吃惊的写作风格旨在惊吓读者。

近 striking, surprising, startling, shocking amazing, astonishing, stunning

augur [ˈɔːɡər]

【考法】 *n.* 预言家 *vt.* 预言: to **tell** of or describe **beforehand**

例 The fortune-teller augured nothing but a series of calamities for me. 占卜人预言在我身上将会有一系列大灾难发生。

近 forecast, predict, presage, prognosticate, prophesy, forebode

Unit 8

- ■ AUTHENTIC
- ■ AUTHORITY
- ■ AUTOCRACY
- ■ AUTONOMY
- ■ AVARICE
- ■ AVER
- ■ AVERSE
- ■ AVID
- ■ AWASH
- ■ AWE

authentic [ɔːˈθentɪk]

【考法】 *adj.* 真实的，非仿造的: being **exactly** as appears or as claimed   *genuine*

例 authentic self 真实的自我

近 bona fide, certified, genuine

反 bogus, counterfeit, fake, mock, phony, spurious 伪造的

派 authenticity *n.* 真实，真实性

authority [ə'θɔːrəti]

【考法 1】 *n.* (某领域的)权威人士：a person with **a high level of knowledge** or skill in a field
- 例 a leading authority on neural anatomy 一名神经解剖学领域的权威人士
- 近 expert, connoisseur, maestro, master, virtuoso
- 反 amateur 业余爱好者；inexpert 非专家

【考法 2】 *n.* 管辖权，控制：**lawful control** over the affairs of a political unit (as a nation)
- 例 The sheriff had authority over the whole county. 郡守对于整个郡都有管辖权。
- 近 administration, governance, regime, regimen

autocracy [ɔː'tɑːkrəsi]

【考法】 *n.* 独裁政府：**government** in which a person possesses **unlimited power**
- 例 It signified the British rejection of autocracy by constituting the first formal restraining of the power of the monarch. 英国对于独裁体制的反抗表现在它对君王权力进行的正式约束。
- 近 absolutism, dictatorship, totalitarianism, tyranny
- 反 democracy 民主，民主制度
- 派 autocratic *adj.* 独裁的

autonomy [ɔː'tɑːnəmi] = *independent*

【考法 1】 *n.* 政治上的独立：the quality or state of being **self-governing**
- 例 The province has been granted autonomy. 这个省份被授予了自治权。
- 近 self-governance, sovereignty
- 反 dependence, subjection 附属，依赖

【考法 2】 *n.* 自我主导的自由，(尤其是)精神独立：self-directing freedom and especially moral **independence**
- 例 a teacher who encourages individual autonomy 一个鼓励精神独立的老师
- 近 independence, liberty, free will
- 反 constraint, duress 限制
- 派 autonomous *adj.* 自治的

avarice ['ævərɪs]

【考法】 *n.* 贪财，贪婪：excessive or **insatiable** desire for wealth or gain
- 例 can not satisfy his avarice 无法满足他的贪婪
- 近 acquisitiveness, avidity, covetousness, cupidity, greediness, rapacity
- 反 generosity, magnanimity 慷慨
- 派 avaricious *adj.* 贪婪的

aver [ə'vɜːr]

【考法】 *v.* 声称为真：to **state** as a fact usually **forcefully**
- 例 was tearfully averring his innocence 涕泪俱下地声明他的清白
- 近 allege, assert, avouch, avow, declare, purport, warrant
- 反 deny, gainsay 否认

averse [ə'vɜːrs] *verse versatile* 转(多面手) *adversary* 敌手 *adversity* 逆境

【考法】 *adj.* 反对的：having a natural **dislike** for something
- 例 I'm not averse to broccoli if it's cooked right. 如果烹饪得当，我不反对花椰菜。
- 近 antipathetic, antagonistic, hostile, opposed, resistant, repulsed, revolted

avid ['ævɪd]

【考法】 *adj.* 急切渴望的：marked by keen interest and **enthusiasm**
- 例 avid movie fans 急切的影迷
- 近 agog, ardent, eager, keen, impatient, thirsty
- 反 apathetic, indifferent 不在乎的

awash [ə'wɔːʃ]

【考法】 *adj.* (如洪水般)泛滥的：**filled**, **covered**, or completely **overrun** as if by a flood
- 例 The program is currently awash in submissions and will not be accepting any more until next term. 该项目的申请人数过多，因此下一轮之前不会再接受任何申请。
- 近 abounding, abundant, flush, fraught, replete, swarming, teeming, thronging
- 反 dearth, insufficient, scant 匮乏的

awe [ɔː]

【考法】 *n./v.* 敬畏：an emotion variously combining **dread**, **veneration**, and **wonder** that is inspired by authority or by the sacred or sublime
- 例 She gazed in awe at the great stone. 她敬畏地凝视着那块巨石。
- 近 admiration, reverence, respect, veneration; admire, revere, respect, venerate
- 反 irreverence, insolence, scorn, superciliousness 蔑视，不敬
- 派 awesome *adj.* 令人敬畏的

Unit 9

■ AWKWARD　　　　■ AVANT–GARDE　　　　■ AWRY　　　　■ AXIOMATIC　　　　■ BABBLE
■ BACKHANDED　　　■ BADGER　　　　■ BADINAGE　　　　■ BAIT　　　　■ BALE

awkward ［ˈɔːkwərd］
【考法 1】 *adj.* 缺乏灵活性和技巧的：**lacking dexterity** or skill
例 awkward dance step 笨拙的舞步
近 handless, maladroit
反 adroit, deft, dexterous, proficient, skilled 灵巧的
【考法 2】 *adj.* （处理问题）缺乏手段和智谋的：showing or marked by **a lack of skill and tact** (as in dealing with a situation)
例 Her awkward handling of the seating arrangements resulted in many hurt feelings. 她那缺乏智谋的座次安排伤害了许多人的感情。
近 botched, bungling, fumbled, inept, inexpert, maladroit

avant-garde ［ˌævɑːˈɡɑːrd］ *avant → advanced*
【考法】 *n.* （尤指艺术上的）先锋派：an intelligentsia that **develops new or experimental concepts** especially in the arts
例 To this theater world's avant-garde , silent films seemed like a very old-fashioned play whose time had come and gone. 对于这个影视先锋派而言，无声电影似乎已是辉煌不再的过时表演方式。
近 forerunner, harbinger, pioneer, precursor, vanguard
反 conservative, diehard 保守者，顽固分子

awry ［əˈraɪ］
【考法】 *adj./adv.* 出差错的(地)：**off** the correct or expected **course**
例 Operation Redwing was initially launched by US special-operation troops in hopes of capturing or killing a Taliban leader but went awry. 由美军特种部队发起、代号为"红翼"的军事行动的最初目的是捕获或击杀一名塔利班头目，然而行动在执行过程中出现了差错。
近 amiss, aside, astray, erroneous
反 right, well 无差错的

axiomatic ［ˌæksiəˈmætɪk］
【考法】 *adj.* 不言自明的：taken for granted, **self-evident**
例 an axiomatic truth 一个不言而明的真理
近 self-evident, prima facie
反 controversial 有争议的

babble ［ˈbæbl］
【考法】 *v.* 发出含糊无意义的嘟囔声，胡乱说：to **utter** a **meaningless** confusion of words or sounds
例 Babies babble before they can talk. 婴儿在会说话以前含糊不清地发音。
近 drivel, gabble, gibber, jabber, prattle
反 articulate 清晰地说出

backhanded ［ˌbækˈhændɪd］
【考法】 *adj.* 间接的：**indirect**, devious, especially sarcastic
例 a backhanded compliment 虚情假意的恭维话
近 feigned, roundabout, sarcastic, hypocritical, two-faced, double-faced, left-handed
反 forthright 直截了当的；artless, candid, genuine, honest, sincere真挚的，真诚的

badger ［ˈbædʒər］
【考法】 *vt.* 不断纠缠或骚扰：to **harass** or annoy **persistently**
例 badger him into purchasing 不断地骚扰劝说他购买
近 bait, plague

badinage ［ˌbædənˈɑːʒ］
【考法】 *n.* 打趣，善意的玩笑：playful repartee, **banter**
例 the sophisticated badinage of the characters in plays by Oscar Wilde 奥斯卡·王尔德作品中意味深长的玩笑话
近 banter, persiflage, repartee

bait	[beɪt]
【考法】	*vt.* 引诱：to **lead away** from a usual or proper course by offering some pleasure or advantage
	n. 诱饵：**something** (as food) used in **luring** especially to a hook or trap
例	The investment scheme baits the greedy and the unscrupulous. 这份投资计划吸引贪婪者和轻信者上钩。
近	allure, decoy, entice, seduce；allurement, snare, trap, temptation

bale	[beɪl]
【考法】	*n.* 痛苦，悲哀：woe, **sorrow**
例	relieve spirit from the bale 从悲痛中解脱
近	misery, suffering, anguish, grief
反	joy 快乐

Unit 10

■ BALEFUL	■ BALK	■ BALKY	■ BALDERDASH	■ BALLOON
■ BALM	■ BANAL	■ BANE	■ BANISH	■ BANTER

baleful	[ˈbeɪlfl] bale 灾祸
【考法】	*adj.* 有害的：**harmful** or malignant in intent or effect
例	a policy with baleful effects 一个带来不良后果的政策
近	harmful, pernicious, detrimental
反	beneficent 有益的

balk	[bɔːk]
【考法 1】	*vt.* 阻碍：to **check** or stop by or as if by an **obstacle**
近	circumvent, frustrate, foil, thwart
反	advance, forward, foster, nurture, promote 推进
【考法 2】	*v.* 不愿接受，拒绝：to show **unwillingness** to accept, do, engage in, or agree to
例	She balked at the very idea of compromise. 她固执地拒绝了妥协的想法。
近	decline, refuse, spurn, repudiate, turn down
反	accept, approve 同意
派	balky *adj.* 倔强的

balky	[ˈbɔːlki]
【考法】	*adj.* 不服管束的，倔强的：**refusing** or likely to refuse to proceed, act, or function as directed or expected
例	a balky mule 犟骡子
近	contumacious, defiant, perverse, intractable, obstreperous, refractory, unruly, wayward, willful
反	compliant, docile, subdued, submissive, tractable 顺从的

balderdash	[ˈbɔːldərdæʃ]
【考法】	*n.* 胡言乱语，废话，无意义的话：words or language **having no meaning** or conveying no intelligible ideas; **nonsense**
例	What a load of balderdash! 简直是一派胡言！
近	babble, blabber, drivel, nonsense, prattle, mumbo jumbo

balloon	[bəˈluːn]
【考法】	*v.* 迅速增加：to **increase** rapidly
例	The use of computers has ballooned in recent year. 近年来，电脑的使用量迅速增长。
近	inflate, escalate, expand, burgeon, mushroom, snowball
反	decrease, taper, dwindle, diminish, recede, wane 减少

balm	[bɑːm]
【考法】	*n.* 香油，止痛膏；安慰物：a **sweet-smelling oil** that heals wounds or reduce pain; things that **soothe** the mind
例	Friendship is the finest balm in need. 危难关头，友情是最好的安慰。
反	irritant 刺激物
派	balmy *adj.* 止痛的

banal	[bəˈnɑːl]

【考法】 *adj.* 非原创的，陈腐的：lacking originality, freshness, or novelty; **trite**
例 banal slogan 陈旧的口号
近 cliché, hackneyed, stereotyped, threadbare, trite, timeworn, shopworn, stale, moth-eaten
反 novel, innovative, arresting 新颖的
派 banality *n.* 陈腐

bane	[beɪn]

【考法】 *n.* 有害的物质：a substance that by chemical action can **kill or injure a living thing**
例 a plant that is believed to be the bane of the wolf 一种被认为对狼有毒害作用的植物
近 toxic, toxin, venom
派 baneful *adj.* 有害的

banish	[ˈbænɪʃ]

【考法】 *vt.* 驱逐出境：to require by authority to **leave** a **country**
例 banish the diplomats from the country 将外交官驱逐出国
近 deport, exile, expatriate, expel
反 repatriate 遣返

banter	[ˈbæntər]

【考法】 *n./v.* 幽默、打趣的(地)谈话：good-**humored**, playful conversation
例 banter with someone 和某人调侃
近 badinage, persiflage, repartee

Today is the first day of the rest of my life, I wake as a child to see the world begin. On monarch wings and birthday wonderings, want to put on faces, walk in the wet and cold. And look forward to my growing old, to grow is to change, to change is to be new, to be new is to be young again, I barely remember when.

——美国乡村歌手约翰·丹佛（John Denver）

List 3

"没有风雨怎么见彩虹，无悔的拼搏为我带来加州的阳光和硅谷的清风。"

（朱晨光，2007 年 6 月，Verbal 720, Quantitative 800, AW 5.0，
录取院校：斯坦福大学计算机系）

Unit 1

■ BARB	■ BARBAROUS	■ BAREFACED	■ BARGAIN	■ BAROQUE
■ BARRAGE	■ BARREN	■ BARRICADE	■ BARTER	■ BEGUILE

barb [bɑːrb]
【考法】 *n.* 尖锐而严厉的批评: a biting or pointedly **critical** remark or comment
例 The teacher's barb stung his students . 这个老师的批评刺伤了他的学生。
近 affront, criticism, offense, outrage, sarcasm
反 praise, applause, compliment 称赞

barbarous [ˈbɑːrbərəs]
【考法】 *adj.* 野蛮的，凶残的: **mercilessly** harsh or cruel
例 insulted by barbarous language 被粗暴的言语侵犯
近 brutal, atrocious, fiendish, heartless, savage, truculent, vicious
反 merciful, benevolent , humane, sympathetic 仁慈的

barefaced [ˈberfeɪst]
【考法】 *adj.* 公然的，厚颜无耻的: undisguisedly bold; **brazen**
例 a barefaced lie 一个公然的谎言
近 apparent, plain, bald, evident, manifest, obvious, perspicuous
反 secret, furtive, clandestine, surreptitious 秘密的

bargain [ˈbɑːrgən]
【考法 1】 *n.* 协议: an **agreement** between parties settling what each gives or receives in a transaction
例 They made a bargain that one would help the other next week. 他们达成了一项协议：下周其中一人将帮助另外一人。
近 accord, compact, contract, covenant, deal, pact, settlement
【考法 2】 *vi.* 讨价还价: to **negotiate** over the terms of a purchase
例 bargain over the price 讨价还价
近 haggle, negotiate

baroque [bəˈroʊk]
【考法】 *adj.* 装饰华丽的，过分雕琢的，复杂的: characterized by **extravagance**, **complexity**, or **flamboyance**
例 a baroque prose 一篇辞藻华丽的散文
近 byzantine, complicated, convoluted, elaborate, fancy, intricate, knotty, labyrinthine, lavish, tangled
反 austere, plain, simple 朴实无华的

barrage [bəˈrɑːʒ]
【考法】 *n.* 有压倒之势的、集中的倾泻(如言语): an **overwhelming**, concentrated **outpouring**, as of words
例 The announcement was met with a barrage of criticism and protests. 此公告一出，批评和抗议的声音四起。
近 salvo, hail, cannonade, shower, storm, volley

barren [ˈbærən]
【考法 1】 *adj.* 不产生结果的，无效的: producing **no results**; unproductive
例 That line of investigation proved barren, so the police tried other avenues. 那个方向的调查已经被证明是没有结果的了，所以警察开始尝试其他的途径。
近 bootless, ineffective, inefficacious, unavailing, vain
反 effective, successful, productive, virtuous 有效的，成功的

【考法 2】 *adj.* 贫瘠的: **deficient** in production of vegetation and especially crops
- 例 barren deserts and wastelands 贫瘠的沙漠和荒野
- 近 desolate, impoverished, waste
- 反 arable, fruitful, luxuriant, verdant 富饶的，繁茂的

barricade [ˌbæriˈkeɪd]
【考法 1】 *n.* 障碍物: an **obstruction** or **rampart** thrown up across a way or passage
- 例 The police put up barricades to block off the parade route. 警察设立了路障来阻挡游行的队伍。
- 近 fence, hedge, wall, barrier, obstacle, blockade, obstruction
【考法 2】 *vt.* 用障碍物阻止通过: to **prevent access** to by means of a barricade
- 例 Streets have been barricaded by authorities. 街道被当局封锁了。
- 近 bar, check, hinder, impede, obstruct, wall off
- 反 permit 允许

barter [ˈbɑːrtər]
【考法】 *v.* 以物换物: to **trade** (goods or services) **without** the exchange of **money**
- 例 barter wheat for cotton 以小麦换棉花
- 近 swap, trade

beguile [bɪˈɡaɪl]
【考法】 *v.* 欺骗: to cause to **believe what is untrue**
- 例 He used his newspapers to beguile the readers into buying shares in his company. 他利用他的报纸诱骗读者买他公司的股票。
- 近 deceive, bluff, con, cozen, delude, dupe, gull, hoodwink, snooker, trick
- 反 undeceive 使…不受欺骗

Unit 2

| ■ BATHETIC | ■ BEFUDDLE | ■ BEDECK | ■ BELABOR | ■ BELEAGUER |
| ■ BELIE | ■ BELLWETHER | ■ BENEFICENT | ■ BENIGN | ■ BERATE |

bathetic [bəˈθetɪk]
【考法】 *adj.* 平凡的，陈腐的: characterized by exceptional **commonplaceness**
- 例 a bathetic funeral scene 平凡的葬礼场面
- 近 trite, cliché, commonplace, hackneyed, stale, stereotyped
- 反 offbeat 离奇的；exceptional 不平常的，非凡的
- 派 bathos *n.* 平凡的事物

befuddle [bɪˈfʌdl]
【考法】 *v.* 使困惑: to throw into a state of **mental uncertainty**
- 例 most of the applicants were befuddled by the wording of one of the questions on the driving test 大多数的申请者被驾校考试中一个问题的措辞弄得晕头转向
- 近 confuse, baffle, bewilder, confound, disorient, flummox, muddle, perplex, puzzle
- 反 assure, reassure, satisfy 打消疑虑；enlighten, inform 使知道

bedeck [bɪˈdek]
【考法】 *vt.* 装饰，点缀: to **make more attractive** by adding something that is beautiful or becoming
- 例 bedeck with jewels 用珠宝装饰
- 近 adorn, beautify, decorate, dress, embellish, emblaze
- 反 strip 剥去；blemish, deface, mar, spoil 损害，破坏

belabor [bɪˈleɪbər]
【考法 1】 *vt.* (当众)严厉批评: to **criticize** harshly and usually publicly
- 例 It's not wise to belabor other people's flaws when you're hardly perfect yourself. 如果你自己还做不到完美，去指责他人是不明智的。
- 近 beat, baste, batter, excoriate, lambaste, abuse, assail, vituperate, scathe
- 反 applaud, extol, eulogize, endorse, acclaim 赞扬
【考法 2】 *vt.* 就…作过度的说明，喋喋不休: to **explain** or insist on **excessively**
- 例 belabor the obvious 就显而易见的问题喋喋不休
- 近 dwell on, harp on
- 反 disregard, omit, ignore, neglect, slight, slur over 忽略

beleaguer [bɪˈliːgər]

【考法】 *vt.* 使困扰，使烦恼，使消沉：**trouble**, harass, beset

例 We are still beleaguered by the very problem. 我们仍然为这一个问题感到困扰。

近 annoy, harass, pester, plague, tease

反 delight 使愉悦

派 beleaguering *adj.* 扰人的

belie [bɪˈlaɪ]

【考法 1】 *vt.* 掩饰：to keep secret or **shut off from view**

例 Security Council issued false assurances that belied the true gravity of the situation. 安理会发布了不真实的承诺，掩盖了局势的严重性。

近 conceal, curtain, disguise, mask

反 disclose, expose 揭露

【考法 2】 *vt.* 与…相对立；与…相矛盾：to be **counter** to; contradict

例 a theory belied by facts 一个和事实矛盾的理论

近 contradict, contravene

反 agree 与…相一致

bellwether [ˈbelweðə]

【考法】 *n.* 领导者，带头人：one that takes the **lead** or initiative

例 Paris is a bellwether of the fashion industry. 巴黎是一座引领时尚潮流的领头羊。

近 leader, pacemaker, pilot, trendsetter

反 follower, disciple, imitator 跟随者，弟子，模仿者

beneficent [bɪˈnefɪsnt]

【考法 1】 *adj.* 仁慈的，好慈善的：characterized by or performing acts of kindness or **charity**

例 a beneficent couple who are regular volunteers at an orphan 一对常在孤儿院做义工的慈善的夫妇

近 kind, altruistic, benevolent, philanthropic, benign, compassionate, sympathetic

反 atrocious, barbarous, truculent, vicious 残忍的

派 beneficently *adv.* 仁慈地

【考法 2】 *adj.* (对个人或社会)有益的：promoting or **contributing** to personal or social well-being

例 the beneficent effect of sunshine 日光浴的益处

近 helpful, advantageous, favorable, kindly, profitable, salutary

反 detrimental, harmful, noxious, toxic 有害的

benign [bɪˈnaɪn]

【考法】 *adj.* 无害的：**not causing** or being capable of causing injury or **hurt**

例 a benign tumor 良性肿瘤

近 harmless, innocent, innocuous, inoffensive

反 baleful, deleterious, detrimental, harmful, injurious, pernicious 有害的

berate [bɪˈreɪt]

【考法】 *vt.* (长时间)严厉指责：to **scold** or condemn **vehemently** and **at length**

例 He berated them in public. 他公开谴责他们。

近 castigate, flay, lambaste, scold, rail, upbraid, reproach, reprimand

反 commend, compliment, praise 表扬，赞颂

Unit 3

■ BESEECH	■ BESMIRCH	■ BIFURCATE	■ BIGOT	■ BLAND
■ BLANDISHMENT	■ BLASÉ	■ BLAST	■ BLATANT	■ BLAZON

beseech [bɪˈsiːtʃ]

【考法】 *vt.* (急切地)恳求：to **beg** for urgently or anxiously

例 They besought the military to act immediately. 他们恳求军方立即采取行动。

近 appeal, conjure, entreat, implore, petition, plead, supplicate

反 demand (依据权力等)要求

besmirch [bɪˈsmɜːtʃ]

【考法】 *vt.* 诽谤，玷污：to **detract from the honor** or luster of

例 besmirch your reputation by fabricating scandals 通过捏造丑闻来玷污你的名声

近 defile, smear, soil, stain, smirch

反 honor 授予荣誉

bifurcate	['baɪfərkeɪt]	
【考法】	*v.* (使)分成两支：(to cause) to divide into **two branches** or parts	
例	Their visions of the company's future slowly began to bifurcate. 我们关于公司未来的构想慢慢出现分歧。	
近	divide, diverge, fork	
反	coalesce 联合；converge 汇合	

bigot	['bɪgət]	
【考法】	*n.* 固执己见者，有偏见的人：a person **obstinately devoted** to his own opinions and prejudices	
例	a religious bigot 宗教偏执者	
近	dogmatist, partisan	
反	depreciator, disparager 贬低他人的人	
派	bigoted *adj.* 固执己见的	

bland	[blænd]	
【考法】	*adj.* 无趣的：**dull**, insipid	
例	a bland story with naïve plot 一个情节幼稚的无聊故事	
近	banal, sapless, insipid	
反	riveting, enchanting 诱人的	

blandishment	['blændɪʃmənt]	
【考法】	*n.* 甜言蜜语，讨好某人的话：something that tends to **coax** or **cajole**	
例	Our blandishment left her unmoved. 纵使甜言蜜语她也无动于衷。	
近	flattery, adulation	

blasé	[blɑː'zeɪ]	
【考法】	*adj.* (过度放纵之后)厌倦享乐的，腻烦的：**apathetic** to pleasure or excitement as a result of excessive indulgence or enjoyment	
例	Years of extravagance has made him totally blasé. 长期的奢华生活已使他彻底麻木。	
近	indifferent, jaded, unconcerned, world-weary	
反	zealous, fanatic 狂热的；curious 好奇的	

blast	[blæst]	
【考法1】	*n.* 爆炸：an **explosion** or violent detonation *vt.* 炸裂，爆破：to **cause to break open** or into pieces by or as if by an explosive	
例	blast wave of a nuclear bomb 原子弹的冲击波	
近	burst, detonation, eruption, outburst；demolish, explode, smash, blow up	
反	implosion 向内爆裂	
【考法2】	*vt.* 斥责，抨击：to **criticize harshly** and usually publicly	
例	blast the new governor for every little misstep 就每一个小的失误抨击新的执政官	
近	abuse, assail, belabor, castigate, lambaste, scathe, vituperate	

blatant	['bleɪtnt]	
【考法】	*adj.* (让人生厌地)惹人注目的：very **noticeable** especially for being incorrect or bad	
例	a blatant lie 明目张胆的谎言 ‖ a blatant error in simple addition 简单加法运算中的一个明显错误	
近	conspicuous, flagrant, glaring, patent, striking, pronounced	
反	subtle, unimpressive 细微的	

blazon	['bleɪzn]	
【考法1】	*vt.* 使知名：to **make known openly** or publicly	
例	Their very public canoodling has pretty much blazoned the fact that they are having an affair. 他们彼此间公开的亲昵举动让他们之间的恋情大白于天下。	
近	annunciate, broadcast, declare, publicize, proclaim	
反	withhold 保留，不透露	
【考法2】	*v.* 修饰，装扮：to **make more attractive** by adding something that is beautiful or becoming	
例	The university's dormitory has been blazoned with banners celebrating graduation. 大学宿舍被那些庆祝毕业的横幅装饰一新。	
近	adorn, bedeck, embellish, garnish	
反	blemish, deface, mar, spoil 损害，破坏	

Unit 4

blemish ['blemɪʃ]

【考法 1】 *n.* 缺点，污点：a noticeable **imperfection**
例 The first LCD had several blemishes on its surface, so we took it back to the store. 第一块液晶显示屏有许多坏点，所以我们拿回商场去退货了。
近 blotch, defect, fault, flaw, mar, spot, scar

【考法 2】 *vt.* 损害，玷污：to **reduce** the soundness, effectiveness, or perfection of
例 A scratch blemished the finish on the car. 一道刮痕破坏了车子表面的涂层。
近 break, disfigure, harm, hurt, impair, injure, spoil, vitiate
反 fix, renovate, repair, revamp 翻新，维修
派 unblemished *adj.* 纯洁的，无瑕疵的

blight [blaɪt]

【考法 1】 *v.* (使)枯萎：to **affect** (as a plant) with blight
近 wither, shrivel
反 flourish 生长繁茂

【考法 2】 *v.* 损害：to **impair** the quality or effect of
例 Illness blighted his career. 伤病毁了他的职业生涯。
近 damage, deteriorate, harm, impair, mar, ruin
派 blighted *adj.* 枯萎的；毁坏的

bliss [blɪs]

【考法】 *n.* 极度快乐：extreme happiness; **ecstasy**
例 Ignorance is bliss——The Matrix. 无知者，幸也。(电影《黑客帝国》)
近 beatitude, joy, ecstasy, elation
反 grief, misery 悲痛

blithe [blaɪð]

【考法 1】 *adj.* 愉快高兴的：of a **happy lighthearted** character or disposition
例 Everyone loved her for her blithe spirit. 所有人都喜欢她开朗的性格。
近 bright, buoyant, gay, jocular, jocund, jovial
反 dour, gloomy, morose, saturnine, sulky, sullen 忧郁的

【考法 2】 *adj.* 无忧无虑的；漫不经心的：having or showing **freedom from worries** or troubles
例 He has a blithe attitude about ever having to earn a living because he knows there's a trust fund in his future. 他对生活无忧无虑，因为他知道他的未来有信托基金可以倚靠。
近 debonair, insouciant, lighthearted
反 careworn 焦虑的

blueprint ['bluːprint]

【考法】 *vt.* 事先计划：to **work out** the details of (something) **in advance**
例 blueprint the schedule of events for the festival right down to the last detail 把节日活动的每一个细节都事先安排好
近 arrange, budget, calculate, organize, frame, lay out

blunder ['blʌndər]

【考法】 *n.* 过失 *v.* 犯错误：a gross **error** or **mistake** resulting usually from stupidity, ignorance, or carelessness
例 a series of political blunder 一连串政治错误
近 mistake, gaffe, lapse, error

blunt [blʌnt]

【考法 1】 *vt.* 使变钝：to make **less sharp** or definite
近 dull, deaden, hebetate, benumb, enfeeble
反 whet, sharpen 磨尖

【考法 2】 *adj.* 直率的：being or characterized by **direct**, **brief**, and potentially rude speech or manner
例 He values honesty and is quite blunt about telling people what he doesn't like about them. 他重视诚实，经常直率地告诉别人他们何处使他不满。
近 abrupt, bluff, brusque, curt, gruff
反 circuitous, mealy-mouthed 拐弯抹角的

blur	[blɜːr]

【考法 1】 *v.* (使)变得朦胧，(使)变得不清楚：to (cause sth. to) become **vague** or indistinct

例 Sorrowful tears blurred her eyes. 悲伤的眼泪模糊了她的双眼。

近 shroud, becloud, befog, obscure

反 clear 使清晰

派 blurring *adj.* 朦胧的

【考法 2】 *vt.* 使不易理解：to make (something) **unclear to the understanding**

例 An article for the layman that blurs the distinction between the two kinds of cholesterol. 一篇针对普通读者的文章对两种胆固醇的区别表述得含糊不清。

近 obfuscate

反 clarify, illuminate 阐明，说清楚

blurt	[blɜːt]

【考法】 *vt.* 突然说出，冲动地说：to utter **abruptly** and impulsively

例 blurt out the secret 脱口说出了秘密

近 burst, bolt, ejaculate, cry out

反 muffle, mute 使缄默

bluster	['blʌstər]

【考法 1】 *v.* 狂妄自大地大声说：to speak in a **loudly arrogant** or bullying manner

例 He was blustering alone in the meeting, which triggered wide dissatisfaction. 他一人在会议上夸夸其谈，引得众人不满。

近 roar, clamor, rattle

反 whisper 小声嘀咕

【考法 2】 *n.* 喧闹的状态：a state of **noisy**, confused activity

例 a mayor who got things done without a lot of bluster 一个能把事情低调解决的市长

近 disturbance, pandemonium, tumult, turmoil

派 blustering *adj.* 大吵大闹的

Unit 5

■ BOGGLE	■ BOISTEROUS	■ BOLSTER	■ BOMBAST	■ BONHOMIE
■ BOO	■ BOON	■ BOORISH	■ BOOTLESS	■ BOUND

boggle	['baːgl]

【考法】 *v.* (因为怀疑、恐惧)犹豫：to **hesitate** because of doubt, fear, or scruples

例 boggle at the dilemma 身处困境而犹豫不决

近 hesitate, falter, waver

boisterous	['bɔɪstərəs]

【考法】 *adj.* 喧嚷的，吵闹的：**noisily** turbulent

例 a boisterous queue in front of the pavilion 场馆前喧闹的队伍 ‖ boisterous mirth 喧闹的欢笑

近 rowdy, vociferous, blatant, clamorous, raucous, rambunctious

反 quiet, sedate 安静的

派 boisterousness *n.* 喧闹

bolster	['boulstər]

【考法 1】 *n./v.* 支撑(物)：a structural part designed to eliminate friction or **provide support** or bearing

例 pillars that bolster the building 支撑房屋的柱子

近 brace, buttress, bear, sustain, undergird, underpin, uphold, prop up

【考法 2】 *vt.* 鼓励，使有精力：to give a **boost** to

例 news that bolsters the morale of the troops 鼓舞军队士气的消息

近 buoy, reinforce

反 dampen 泼冷水

bombast	['baːmbæst]

【考法】 *n.* 夸大的言辞：grandiloquent, **pompous** speech or writing

例 "Their eloquence is all bombast", said Charles Kingsley. "他们的雄辩是虚张声势"，查尔斯·金斯利如此说道。

近 braggadocio, grandiloquence, exaggeration

反 understatement 保守的观点

派 bombastic *adj.* 夸大的

| bonhomie | [ˌbɑːnəˈmiː] |

【考法】 *n.* 温和，和蔼：a pleasant and affable disposition; **geniality**

近 affability, amiability, geniality

派 bonhomous *adj.* 和蔼的

| boo | [ˈbuː] |

【考法】 *n./v.* 嘘（以表示不满或嘲笑）：a sound uttered to show **contempt**, **scorn**, or **disapproval**

例 boo the actor off the stage 把演员嘘下舞台

近 jeer, scorn

反 applaud 鼓掌

| boon | [buːn] |

【考法】 *n.* 恩惠，福利：**benefit**, favor

例 The new solar battery booster is a boon for photographers. 这个光伏充电器是摄影师们的福音。

近 gift, benevolence, present, windfall

反 misfortune, scourge 灾祸

| boorish | [ˈbʊrɪʃ] |

【考法】 *adj.* 粗鲁无礼的：having or showing crudely insensitive or **impolite** manners

例 Yelling for service in restaurants is a kind of boorish behavior. 在餐厅里大喊大叫是一种粗鲁无礼的行为。

近 churlish, classless, loutish, uncouth

反 couth, cultivated, polished, refined, well-bred, courteous, polite 有教养的，优雅的

派 boor *n.* 粗鲁的人

| bootless | [ˈbuːtləs] |

【考法】 *adj.* 无用的：**useless**, unprofitable, futile

例 The meeting turns out to be a bootless attempt. 这个会议被证明是一次徒劳的尝试。

近 barren, ineffective, futile, abortive, fruitless, vain

反 worthy 有价值的

| bound | [baʊnd] |

【考法1】 *n.* 界限：a real or imaginary point **beyond which a person or thing cannot go**

例 The language in the novel really is beyond the bounds of decency. 这本小说的语言实在太不得体了。

近 environs, limit, confines, perimeter

反 unrestrainedness 无边无际

【考法2】 *adj.* 投入的，坚定的：**fully committed** to achieving a goal

例 I am bound and determined to write a novel before I turn 30. 我下定决心在 30 岁之前要写本小说。

近 resolute, determined, single-minded, bent on

反 faltering, hesitant, vacillating, wavering, weak-kneed 动摇的

派 boundless *adj.* 无边无际的，无约束的

Unit 6

■ BOYCOTT	■ BRACING	■ BRAKE	■ BRASH	■ BRASSY
■ BRAVADO	■ BRAVURA	■ BRAZEN	■ BREACH	■ BREVITY

| boycott | [ˈbɔɪkɑːt] |

【考法】 *vt.* 联合抵制，拒绝参与：to engage in a **concerted refusal** to have dealings with（as a person, store, or organization）usually to express disapproval or to force acceptance of certain conditions

例 This brand is being boycotted for damaging environment. 因为破坏环境，这个品牌正在被抵制。

近 refuse

反 patronize 经常光顾

| bracing | [ˈbreɪsɪŋ] |

【考法】 *adj.* 令人振奋的，给人带来活力的：**giving strength**, vigor, or freshness

例 a bracing news from the frontline 来自前线的振奋人心的消息

近 invigorating, rejuvenating, reviving, stimulating

反 vapid 乏味的

派 brace *v.* 支持，使充满活力

	brake	[breɪk]
	【考法】	v. 刹车: to cause to move or proceed at a **less rapid** pace
	例	A seagull swooped down in front of her car, causing her to slam on the brakes . 一只海鸥忽然俯冲到车窗前，她猛踩刹车。
	近	decelerate, retard, slacken
	反	accelerate, hasten, rush, speed up 加速

	brash	[bræʃ]
	【考法】	adj. 愚勇的，鲁莽的: **foolishly adventurous** or bold
	例	a brash decision 一个鲁莽的决定
	近	audacious, brassy, daredevil, madcap, reckless, temerarious
	反	circumspect, guarded, heedful, prudent, wary 谨慎的

	brassy	[ˈbræsɪ]
	【考法】	adj. 厚脸皮的，不知羞耻的: displaying or marked by **rude boldness**
	例	brassy reporters 厚颜无耻的记者
	近	audacious, bold-faced, brazen, impertinent, impudent, insolent
	反	diffident, unassertive, retiring, timid 羞怯的，谦逊的

	bravado	[brəˈvɑːdəʊ]
	【考法1】	n. 假装勇敢: a **pretense** of bravery
	例	I remembered his youthful bravado . 我还记得他的年少鲁莽。
	【考法2】	n. 虚张声势: blustering **swaggering** conduct
	例	out of sheer bravado 完全源于虚张声势

	bravura	[brəˈvʊərə]
	【考法】	adj./n. 优秀演技(的): **brilliant** technique or style in performance
	例	a truly bravura performance of the ballet 一场极其精彩的芭蕾舞演出
	近	adroit, artful, dexterous, masterful
	反	amateur, artless, unprofessional, unskillful 业余的，拙劣的

	brazen	[ˈbreɪzn]
	【考法1】	adj. 蛮横大胆的，厚颜无耻的: marked by **contemptuous boldness**
	例	a brazen disregard for the rules 蛮横大胆地漠视规则
	近	bold-faced, impertinent, impudent, insolent
	反	modest, self-effacing, diffident, retiring, timid 谦虚的，胆小的
	【考法2】	v. 大胆自信地去面对或从事: to face or undergo with **bold self-assurance**
	例	brazen out the crisis 沉着面对危机
	近	confront, outface, defy
	反	dodge, duck, shirk, sidestep 躲开，避谈

	breach	[briːtʃ]
	【考法】	v. 违背: to **fail to keep**
	例	a builder being sued by a homeowner for breaching a contract 建筑商因违约被房主起诉
	近	contravene, fracture, infringe, transgress
	反	obey, observe, comply with, conform to 遵守

	brevity	[ˈbrevəti]
	【考法】	n. 简短，简洁: **shortness** of duration
	例	Brevity is the soul of wit. 〈谚〉言贵简洁。
	近	briefness, conciseness, shortness
	反	lengthiness 冗长

Unit 7

■ BRIBE	■ BRIDLE	■ BRISK	■ BRISTLE	■ BRITTLE
■ BROACH	■ BROMIDE	■ BROOK	■ BROWBEAT	■ BRUIT

	bribe	[braɪb]
	【考法】	v. 贿赂，收买: to **give** something, such as **money** or a favor, to a person in a position of trust to influence that person's views or conduct
	例	They bribed him to keep quiet about the incident. 他们收买他，希望其保持缄默。
	近	corrupt, pay off, square

bridle	[ˈbraɪdl]
【考法】	*v.* 限制: to **keep from exceeding** a desirable degree or level (as of expression)
例	Try to bridle your criticism next time so that it is helpful and not hurtful. 下回尽量控制好批评的语气，让其既顺耳又有益。
近	check, contain, curb, constrain, inhibit, regulate, restrain, tame, rein in

brisk	[brɪsk]
【考法】	*adj.* 充满生机的，有活力的: marked by much life, movement, or **activity**
例	brisk and concise response 轻快而简洁的回答
近	animated, bouncing, bustling, frisky, kinetic, sprightly, vibrant
反	lackadaisical, languid, leaden, dead, inactive, lifeless 没有生机的

bristle	[ˈbrɪsl]
【考法】	*v.* 怒不可遏，咆哮: to express one's **anger** usually violently
例	bristle at the suggestion of gay marriage 对基情怒不可遏
近	bluster, fulminate, rampage, fume, storm
反	cower 畏缩

brittle	[ˈbrɪtl]
【考法 1】	*adj.* 易碎的，脆弱的，易坏的: easily **broken**, cracked, or snapped
例	as brittle as glass 像玻璃一样脆弱
近	crispy, crumbly, flaky, friable
【考法 2】	*adj.* 不热心的，不真心的: **lacking in friendliness** or warmth of feeling
例	a brittle apology that was anything but heartfelt 一个毫不真诚的道歉
近	chilly, frigid, frosty, glacial, unfriendly, unsympathetic
反	cordial, genial, warmhearted 热心的

broach	[broʊtʃ]
【考法】	*vt.* 提出讨论: to **present** or bring forward for discussion
例	broach the topic of plans for next year's parade 将明年的游行活动计划提上讨论日程
近	moot, place, raise, bring up

bromide	[ˈbroʊmaɪd]
【考法】	*n.* 陈词滥调: a commonplace or **hackneyed** statement or notion
例	A newspaper editorial offered the timeworn bromide that people should settle their differences peacefully. 报纸编辑又拿出那一套呼吁和平解决纷争的陈词滥调。
近	banality, cliché, platitude, homily, truism, chestnut, shibboleth

brook	[brʊk]
【考法】	*vt.* 忍受，容许: to stand for, **tolerate**
例	brook no interference with his plans 不能容忍别人对他的计划进行干涉
近	abide, countenance, endure, stomach

browbeat	[ˈbraʊbiːt]
【考法】	*vt.* 恐吓: to **intimidate** by a stern manner or arrogant speech: bully
例	They would often browbeat the younger child . 他们总是欺负小朋友。
近	blackjack, bulldoze, bully, cow, hector, intimidate

bruit	[ˈbruːt]
【考法】	*vt.* (未经证实地)散播(消息): to **make** (as a piece of information) **the subject of common talk** without any authority or confirmation of accuracy
例	It's been bruited that... 到处传播…
近	circulate, whisper, noise about
反	keep secret 保持秘密

Unit 8

■ BUCK	■ BUDGE	■ BULGE	■ BULLY	■ BUMPTIOUS
■ BUNGLE	■ BUOY	■ BUOYANT	■ BURGEON	■ BURLESQUE

buck	[bʌk]
【考法】	*v.* 阻止，反对: to **refuse assent**, to refuse to give in to
例	buck the system 不遵守制度
近	defy, fight, oppose, repel, withstand
反	assent to, bow to, submit to, succumb to, surrender to, yield to 赞成，服从

budge	[bʌdʒ]

【考法】 *v.* 停止抵抗，屈服：to **cease resistance** (as to another's arguments, demands, or control)
例 Despite hours of intense pressure, she refused to budge from her position . 尽管被连续施压几小时，她仍旧不肯让步。
近 concede, relent, submit, succumb, surrender
反 resist 拒绝，抵抗

bulge	[bʌldʒ]

【考法】 *n.* 凸起：a **protuberant** or swollen part or place
例 a bulge in his jacket 他衣服上鼓起来的一块
近 convexity, projection, protrusion, protuberance, swell
反 depressed region, cavity, dent, indent, recess, pit 凹陷，坑
派 bulging *adj.* 凸起的
例 bulging eyes 暴鱼眼

bully	[ˈbʊli]

【考法】 *n.* 欺凌弱小者，恶霸：a person who habitually treats others in an overbearing or **intimidating manner**
例 They had to deal with the local bullies . 他们要对付当地恶霸。
近 bullyboy, hector, intimidator
反 underdog 被欺负的人

bumptious	[ˈbʌmpʃəs]

【考法】 *adj.* 专横傲慢的，自以为是的：having a feeling of **superiority** that shows itself in an overbearing attitude
例 be bumptious over one's inferiors 对下级态度傲慢
近 assumptive, supercilious, imperious, overweening, peremptory, pompous, presuming, presumptuous, self-assertive, haughty
反 humble, modest, unarrogant, unpretentious 谦虚的，低调的

bungle	[ˈbʌŋgl]

【考法】 *vt.* 办糟，失败：to act or **work clumsily** and awkwardly
例 bungle a job 搞砸了一项工作
近 boggle, bumble, fumble, mess up, screw up
反 bring off 成功

buoy	[bɔɪ]

【考法】 *vt.* 使充满勇气和力量，使振作：to fill with **courage or strength** of purpose
例 The sudden improvement in his health buoyed him up . 身体的突然好转让他很振奋。
近 embolden, hearten, inspire, bear up, buck up
反 daunt, discourage, dishearten, dispirit 使沮丧，泼冷水

buoyant	[ˈbuːjənt]

【考法】 *adj.* 心情好的：having or showing a **good mood or disposition**
例 in a buoyant mood 轻松快乐的心情
近 blithe, chipper, eupeptic, lightsome, upbeat, winsome, effervescent
反 dour, gloomy, morose, saturnine, sullen 沮丧的

burgeon	[ˈbɜːrdʒən]

【考法】 *vi.* 迅速成长扩大，蓬勃发展：to **grow** and expand **rapidly**; **flourish**
例 My confidence began to burgeon . 我的信心开始迅速增强。
近 accelerate, accumulate, balloon, boom, build up, escalate, mount, multiply, mushroom, proliferate, roll up, snowball, wax, flourish, prosper
反 wane, wither, waste away, subside, subdue 衰退

burlesque	[bɜːrˈlesk]

【考法】 *n./v.* 夸张滑稽地模仿以嘲弄他人的文学艺术作品，恶搞：to copy or exaggerate (someone or something) in order to **make fun of**
例 Burlesquing the teacher's nervous tic isn't very nice. 恶搞老师紧张的痉挛不是好的行为。
近 caricature, imitate, mock, parody, spoof, travesty

Unit 9

| ■ BURNISH | ■ BUTTRESS | ■ BYZANTINE | ■ CACHE | ■ CACHET |
| ■ CACOPHONY | ■ CAVALIER | ■ CAJOLE | ■ CALCIFY | ■ CALIBRATE |

burnish ［ˈbɜːrnɪʃ］
【考法】 *v.* 擦亮，磨光：to **make smooth or glossy** usually by repeatedly applying surface pressure
例 burnish the knife 磨光刀
近 buff, polish, furbish, grind, smoothen

buttress ［ˈbʌtrɪs］
【考法】 *vt.* 为…提供支撑的证据或者信息：to **provide evidence or information for** (as a claim or idea)
例 A mass of circumstantial evidence buttresses the prosecutor's case. 大量证据都支持起诉人的案件。
近 back, bolster, corroborate, reinforce, substantiate, shore up
反 contravene, challenge 反对，质疑

byzantine ［ˈbɪzəntiːn］
【考法】 *adj.* 错综复杂的：**complicated** or **secretive**, having many parts or aspects that are usually **interrelated**
例 a bill to simplify the byzantine tax structure 一项试图简化繁琐税收制度的提案
近 convoluted, intricate, involved, labyrinthine, sophisticated, tangled
反 straightforward, plain, simple, uncomplicated 直截了当的，不复杂的

cache ［kæʃ］
【考法】 *n.* 囤货，藏货：a **supply** stored up and often hidden away
例 maintain a cache of food in case of emergencies 保存食物，以防万一
近 stash, stockpile, store, deposit, hoard, reserve

cachet ［kæˈʃeɪ］
【考法 1】 *n.* 同意：an indication of **approval** carrying great prestige
近 approval, authorization, concurrence, endorsement, license, permission, sanction, warrant
反 interdiction, prohibition, proscription 禁止
【考法 2】 *n.* 威望，声望：**prestige**; a **mark or quality**, as of distinction, individuality, or authenticity
例 Federal courts have a certain cachet which state courts lack. 联邦法院拥有州立法院所不具备的威信。
being rich...doesn't have the cachet it used to 富甲一方，再也不像过去拥有那么高的声望了
近 credit, distinction, esteem, homage, kudos, prestige
反 infamy, notoriety 不好的名声

cacophony ［kəˈkɑːfəni］
【考法】 *n.* 刺耳的声音：loud, confused, and usually **inharmonious sound**
例 the cacophony of a pet store full of animals 宠物商店里各种动物叽叽呱呱的声音
近 blare, bluster, clamor, din, discordance, racket
反 quiet, silence, still, stillness 安静

cavalier ［ˌkævəˈlɪr］
【考法 1】 *n.* 有骑士精神的人，彬彬有礼的绅士：one having the spirit or bearing of a knight; **a courtly gentleman**
例 Though grew up in a slum, he possessed an amazing spirit of cavalier. 他虽然生长于贫民窟，但有着令人难以置信的骑士精神。
近 chevalier
反 culprit, devil, felon, fiend, miscreant, rapscallion, rascal, reprobate, villain 流氓，恶棍
【考法 2】 *adj.* 傲慢的：having a **feeling of superiority** that shows itself in an overbearing attitude
例 I cannot tolerate such an arrogant and cavalier attitude toward others. 这种对待他人的高傲态度让我无法忍受。
近 arrogant, assumptive, bumptious, haughty, imperious, lofty, overweening, peremptory, pompous, presumptuous, supercilious
反 humble, modest 谦卑的

cajole ［kəˈdʒoʊl］
【考法】 *v.* 哄骗：to urge with gentle and repeated appeals, teasing, or flattery; **wheedle**
例 He cajoled her into doing his laundry for him. 他哄骗她帮他洗衣服。
近 blandish, blarney, palaver, wheedle, soft-soap, sweet-talk

calcify	[ˈkælsɪfaɪ]
【考法】	*vt.* 使僵化: to make **inflexible** or **unchangeable**
例	a calcified theory 一个僵化的理论
近	harden, ossify
反	make malleable, make pliant, make more flexible 使灵活

calibrate	[ˈkælɪbreɪt]
【考法】	*vt.* 调整，使标准化: to **standardize** （as a measuring instrument）by determining the deviation from a standard so as to ascertain the proper correction factors
例	calibrate the polling procedures to ensure objectivity 为保证客观性而使投票过程标准化
反	unstandardize 使不标准

Unit 10

■ CALLIGRAPHY	■ CALLOUS	■ CALLOW	■ CALUMNIATE	■ CAMARADERIE
■ CATHARSIS	■ CAMOUFLAGE	■ CANARD	■ CANDOR	■ CANON

calligraphy	[kəˈlɪɡrəfi]
【考法】	*n.* (优美的)书法: artistic, stylized, or **elegant handwriting** or lettering
例	She specializes in scrollwork with beautiful calligraphy . 她很擅长花体字。
近	longhand, manuscript, penmanship, script

callous	[ˈkæləs]
【考法】	*adj.* 无同情心的, 冷漠的: emotionally hardened; **unfeeling**
例	a callous indifference to the suffering of others 对他人痛苦的漠不关心
近	affectless, uncharitable, unsparing, remorseless, indurate, ruthless
反	sympathetic, compassionate, merciful, tender, warmhearted 有同情心的

callow	[ˈkæloʊ]
【考法】	*adj.* 不老练的, 不成熟的: **lacking** in adult **experience** or maturity
例	callow young man 未经世事的年轻人
近	green, immature, inexperienced, juvenile, unfledged, unripened, puerile
反	adult, experienced, grown-up, mature, ripe 成熟的

calumniate	[kəˈlʌmnieɪt]
【考法】	*v.* 诽谤，造谣，中伤: to utter maliciously **false statements**, charges, or imputations about
近	asperse, blacken, defame, libel, malign, smear, traduce, vilify
反	vindicate 辩护
派	calumnious *adj.* 造谣的
反	flattering 谄媚的
派	calumny *n.* 诽谤，中伤: a false statement maliciously made to injure another's reputation
反	approbation 嘉许

camaraderie	[ˌkɑːməˈrɑːdəri]
【考法】	*n.* 友情: a spirit of **friendly** good-fellowship
例	There is great camaraderie among the teammates . 组员之间有着深厚的情谊。
近	brotherhood, comradeship, fellowship
反	enmity 敌意

catharsis	[kəˈθɑːrsiːs]
【考法】	*n.* 情绪的宣泄、释放: **elimination of a complex** by bringing it to consciousness and affording it expression
例	The author calls reading a perfect practice of catharsis , one that cleanses him of feelings of fury and frustration. 作者声称阅读是一种宣泄情绪的极佳方式: 所有的愤怒与失望都随之消失。
近	cleansing, expurgation, lustration, purgation, purification
派	cathartic *adj.* 宣泄情绪的

camouflage	[ˈkæməflɑːʒ]
【考法】	*v./n.* 伪装; 伪装手段: behavior or artifice designed to **deceive** or **hide**
例	The soldiers must wear protective jungle camouflage while on patrol. 士兵们在巡逻的时候必须穿上迷彩服来保护自身安全。
近	costume, guise, cloak, dress up
反	unmask 揭露

canard	[kəˈnɑːrd]

【考法】 *n.* 谣传，误传：an unfounded or false, deliberately **misleading** story.

例 It's a popular canard that the actress died under scandalous circumstances. 有一种广泛的说法声称，女演员死于绯闻的压力。

近 story, whisper

candor	[ˈkændər]

【考法】 *n.* 坦白，直率，诚挚：unreserved, **honest**, or **sincere** expression

例 The members of the rock band speak with candor about their recent squabbling. 摇滚乐队成员对于他们最近的内讧直言不讳。

近 bluntness, forthrightness, frankness, unreservedness, straightforwardness

反 artifice, mendacity, dissembling, dissimulation, indirection 谎言，不直接

canon	[ˈkænən]

【考法1】 *n.* 准则，标准：a basis for judgment; a **standard** or **criterion**

例 the canons of polite society 文明社会的法规

近 dogma

【考法2】 *n.* 真经，正典：the **authentic** works of a writer

反 apocrypha 伪经

派 canonical *adj.* 正统的，标准的：conforming to a general rule or acceptable procedure : orthodox

反 heterodox, nontraditional 非正统的

派 canonize *v.* 作为神圣的来对待，使神圣化：to treat as sacred; glorify

近 adore, adulate, idolize, deify, worship

反 abase, degrade, demean, humiliate 贬低

Ordinary people merely think how they shall spend their time; a man of talent tries to use it. 普通人只想到如何度过时间，有才能的人设法利用时间。

——德国哲学家 叔本华（Arthur Schopenhauer, German philosopher）

List 4

Unit 1

■ CANVASS　　　　■ CAPITULATE　　　　■ CAPRICE　　　　■ CAPTIVATE　　　　■ CAREWORN
■ CARDINAL　　　　■ CARICATURE　　　　■ CARNAL　　　　■ CAROUSE　　　　■ CARP

canvass ['kænvəs]
【考法 1】 *v.* 仔细检查，详尽讨论：to **examine carefully or discuss thoroughly**; scrutinize
例 The evidence had been repeatedly canvassed in American courts. 该项证据已在美国的法庭中反复被审查过。
【考法 2】 *v.* 游说，去（一个地区）的各处或找到（个人）来拉选票或订单：to go through（a region）or go to（persons）to **solicit votes or orders**
例 canvass voters 拉选票
近 interview, poll, solicit, survey

capitulate [kə'pɪtʃuleɪt]
【考法】 *v.* 投降，默许：to **give up all resistance**; acquiesce; yield
例 One side finally capitulated when it became clear that they couldn't win the argument. 意识到他们不能拿下这场辩论后，该方投降了。
近 budge, concede, relent, submit, succumb, surrender, knuckle under
反 resist, oppose 抵抗

caprice [kə'priːs]
【考法】 *n.* 反复无常，善变：an inclination to **change** one's mind **impulsively**
例 His decision is pure caprice. 他的决定完全是心血来潮。
近 freakishness, impulsiveness, whimsicalness
反 confirmation 确认
派 capricious *adj.* 反复无常的，善变的
反 steadfast, resolute, constant, pertinacious 坚定不变的

captivate ['kæptɪveɪt]
【考法】 *vt.* 吸引：to **attract** and hold by charm, beauty, or excellence
例 I was captivated by her brilliant mind. 我被她的才华横溢所吸引。
近 allure, beguile, bewitch, enchant, fascinate, magnetize
反 repulse 使反感

careworn ['kerwɔːrn]
【考法】 *adj.* 忧心忡忡的，焦虑的：showing the effect of **grief** or **anxiety**
例 a careworn face 忧心忡忡的脸
反 lighthearted 心情愉快的

cardinal ['kɑːrdɪnl]
【考法】 *adj.* 主要的，非常重要的：of **foremost importance**; **paramount**
例 the cardinal rule of medicine: do no harm 药物的首要标准就是无害
近 dominant, overbearing, overriding, paramount, preeminent, primal, supreme
反 minor 次要的

caricature ['kærɪkətʃər]
【考法 1】 *n.* 用讽刺歪曲等手法的夸张，漫画，讽刺画：**exaggeration** by means of often ludicrous distortion of parts or characteristics
派 caricaturist *n.* 漫画家

【考法 2】 *v.* 嘲笑性模仿或夸张：to **copy** or **exaggerate**（someone or something）in order to make fun of
例 caricature the supervisor's distinctive walk 模仿督导员独特的走路方式
近 burlesque, imitate, mock, parody, spoof, travesty

carnal [ˈkɑːrnl]
【考法 1】 *adj.* 肉体的，物质的：relating to the **physical**
例 seen with carnal eyes 用肉眼看 ‖ carnal remains 遗体
近 corporal, corporeal, fleshly, material, somatic
反 spiritual 精神的
【考法 2】 *adj.* 世俗的：**worldly**
例 a carnal mind 凡心
近 earthborn, mundane, temporal, terrestrial, worldly

carouse [kəˈraʊz]
【考法】 *vi.* 畅饮，狂饮作乐：to **drink** liquor **freely** or excessively
例 stay at home instead of going out and carousing with friends 呆在家里而不是出去和朋友们狂饮作乐
近 binge, revel, roister, wassail

carp [kɑːrp]
【考法】 *vi.* 对小事吹毛求疵，挑剔，表现不满：to make often **peevish criticisms** or **objections** about matters that are minor, unimportant, or irrelevant; to **express dissatisfaction**, pain, or resentment usually **tiresomely**
例 carp about the order of names on the wedding invitations 对于婚礼请柬上的名单顺序吹毛求疵
近 cavil, fuss, niggle, nitpick, gripe, grizzle, grouch, grouse, grumble, wail

Unit 2

■ CLIQUISH	■ CAST	■ CASTIGATE	■ CATALYZE	■ CATASTROPHE
■ CATEGORICAL	■ CATHOLIC	■ CAUSTIC	■ CAVEAT	■ CAVIL

cliquish [ˈkliːkɪʃ]
【考法】 *adj.* 小集团的：bound together by feelings of **very close association**
例 MI6 is a separate, self-perpetuating department of government of somewhat cliquish upper-crust origins .
军情六处是小集团的上层起源的政府的独立、能自我永存的部门。
近 clannish, cliquey, close-knit

cast [kæst]
【考法 1】 *vt.* 提出：to put forth, **give off**, to place as if by throwing
例 cast doubt on their reliability 对它们的可靠性提出质疑
近 discharge, emanate, irradiate, issue, shoot, throw out, give out
【考法 2】 *v.* 抛弃：to **get rid of** as useless or unwanted
例 Once she became rich and didn't need them anymore, she cast off all her old friends like so much junk.
当她有钱了不再需要朋友了，她把老友像糟粕一样抛弃了。
近 ditch, dump, jettison, toss

castigate [ˈkæstɪgeɪt]
【考法】 *vt.* 强烈（公开）指责：to **criticize** harshly and usually publicly
例 The author castigated the prime minister as an ineffective leader. 该作者谴责首相行政无作为。
近 berate, chastise, lambaste, reprimand, reproach, rebuke, vituperate, excoriate, rail（at or against）
反 approbate, accolade, extol 认可，赞美

catalyze [ˈkætəlaɪz]
【考法】 *vt.* 成为…的导火索，导致：to **be the cause of**（a situation, action, or state of mind）
例 A reinstitution of the draft would catalyze protests around the country. 草案的提出会激发全国范围的抗议。
近 breed, beget, effectuate, engender, generate, prompt, spawn, yield, result in , bring（about）
反 retard, prevent, inhibit 阻挠，抑制
派 catalyst *n.* 催化剂：an agent that provokes or speeds significant change or action
例 a catalyst for change of lifestyle 生活方式变化的催化剂
反 inhibitor 抑制剂

catastrophe [kəˈtæstrəfi]
【考法 1】 *n.* 大灾难：the final event of the dramatic action especially of a **tragedy**
近 apocalypse, calamity, cataclysm, debacle, tragedy

【考法 2】 *n.* 彻底的失败：**utter failure**: fiasco
例 The party was a catastrophe . 该派对就是一个杯具。
近 bummer, debacle, disaster, fiasco, fizzle, washout
反 blockbuster, hit, smash, success, winner 大胜

categorical ［ˌkætəˈɡɔːrɪkl］
【考法】 *adj.* 没有例外的；绝对的：being **without** exception or **qualification**; **absolute**
例 a categorical denial 完全的否认
近 definite, downright, fair, utter, thorough, unalloyed, unconditional, unqualified
反 conditional, qualified 有条件的

catholic ［ˈkæθlɪk］
【考法】 *adj.* 普遍的，包容的：**not limited or specialized** in application or purpose
例 a catholic taste in music 对于音乐的兼容并包的品味
近 unlimited, unqualified, unrestricted, unspecialized, all-around（also all-round）
反 narrow, limited, restricted, specialized 狭隘的

caustic ［ˈkɔːstɪk］
【考法】 *adj.* 挖苦讽刺的，刻薄的：marked by **incisive sarcasm**
例 caustic movie reviews 尖酸刻薄的影评
近 acerbic, acrid, barbed, mordant, pungent, sardonic, satiric, scathing, sharp
反 genial, smooth, kind, innocuous 和蔼的，（言论行为等）无害的

caveat ［ˈkæviæt］
【考法】 *n.* 警告，告诫：a **warning of a specific limitation** of something such as information or an agreement
例 a final caveat 最终的告诫
近 warning, admonish

cavil ［ˈkævl］
【考法】 *v.* 挑剔，吹毛求疵：to find fault unnecessarily; raise trivial objections: **quibble**
例 cavil about the price of a cup of coffee 对一杯咖啡的价钱挑剔
近 carp, fuss, niggle, nitpick, quibble

Unit 3

■ CATACLYSMAL　　■ CEDE　　　■ CEMENT　　　■ CENSOR　　　■ CONCOMITANT
■ CENSURE　　　　■ CHIC　　　　■ CESSATION　　■ CHAFF　　　 ■ CHAGRIN

cataclysmal ［kætəˈklɪzəməl］
【考法】 *adj.* 灾难性的：bringing about **ruin** or misfortune
例 a cataclysmal decision to plunge the nation into war 一个让国家陷入战争的灾难性的决策
近 calamitous, catastrophic, destructive, disastrous, ruinous, unfortunate

cede ［siːd］
【考法】 *vt.*（根据条约）放弃，割让：to **surrender possession of**, especially by treaty
例 cede the island to America 把岛屿割让给了美国
近 relinquish, render, yield, renounce, resign, turn in, turn over, step aside (from), give up, hand over, lay down
反 possess 拥有

cement ［sɪˈment］
【考法】 *n./v.* 粘合，粘合剂：a **uniting** or **binding** force or influence
例 the cement of society 社会的凝聚力
近 cord, knot, link, tie

censor ［ˈsensər］
【考法】 *vt.* 审查并删除不良的东西：to **examine** in order to suppress or **delete** anything considered objectionable
例 censor the news 审查新闻
近 bowdlerize, expurgate, red-pencil, clean up
派 censorship *n.* 审查制度
派 censorious *adj.* 挑剔指责的: highly critical
例 censorious comment 尖刻的评论
反 eulogistic 赞美的

concomitant [kənˈkɑːmɪtənt]

【考法】 *adj.* 伴随的，同时发生的：present at the **same time** and place

例 An improvement in the facilities led to a concomitant improvement in morale . 设施的改进导致伴随而来的士气提升。

近 accompanying, coexistent, coincidental, concurrent

censure [ˈsenʃər]

【考法】 *v.* 公开表示反对，谴责：to express **public** or **formal disapproval** of

例 He was censured by the committee for his failure to report the problem. 他因为未上报事故受到了委员会的指责。

近 condemn, denounce, objurgate, rebuke, reprimand, reproach, reprehend, pan

反 commend, extol, laud, endorse 支持，赞同

chic [ʃiːk]

【考法】 *adj.* 时髦的，潮的：being in the latest or **current fashion**

例 a chic new hairstyle that makes her look very sophisticated 一个时髦的发型使得她看起来非常精致

近 stylish, fashionable, modish, trendy, voguish

反 outmoded, unchic, unfashionable, unmodish, unstylish 不时尚的

cessation [seˈseɪʃn]

【考法】 *n.* 终止，暂停：the **stopping of a process** or activity

例 a cessation of hostilities 停止敌对行动

近 check, cutoff, closure, discontinuance, expiration, halt, shutdown, termination

反 commencement, start, continuation 开始，继续

chaff [tʃæf]

【考法】 *v.* 开玩笑：to **make jokes**

例 A coworker likes to chaff at others' expense , and this often results in hurt feelings. 同事喜欢开别人玩笑，往往会伤害他人感情。

近 banter, jape, jest, quip

chagrin [ʃəˈɡrɪn]

【考法】 *n.* （因为失败、出糗而导致的）不安，焦虑：disquietude or **distress of mind** caused by humiliation, disappointment, or failure

例 Edgar's chagrin at having bungled the simple assignment was clear from his trembling lips and averted eyes. 从埃德加颤抖的嘴唇和躲闪的目光中可以看出他搞砸简单任务之后的不安。

近 anxiety, concern, disquiet, inquietude, restiveness, solicitude, unease, unrest, worry

反 aplomb, composure, countenance, equanimity, sangfroid 镇定自若，淡定

Unit 4

■ CHAMELEON	■ CHAMPION	■ COMPULSIVE	■ CHIMERA	■ CHARLATAN
■ CHARY	■ CHASE	■ CHASM	■ CHAUVINISTIC	■ CHECK

chameleon [kəˈmiːliən]

【考法】 *n.* 变色龙，善变的人：a person who dexterously and expediently **changes or adopts opinions**

例 At the summer resort he acquired a reputation as a social chameleon —someone who could be whatever his hosts wanted him to be. 在度假胜地，他被称为"社交多面手"——可以变成主人想要的任何角色。

近 chancer, opportunist, temporizer, timeserver, trimmer, weathercock

champion [ˈtʃæmpiən]

【考法】 *vt.* 支持：to fight for, defend, or **support** as a champion

例 champion the cause of civil rights 支持民权事业

近 advocate, back, endorse, patronize, plump for

反 disparage, impugn, oppose 贬低，反对

compulsive [kəmˈpʌlsɪv]

【考法】 *adj.* 不能自拔的：caused by or suggestive of an **irresistible urge**

例 a frightening, compulsive novel 一本令人欲罢不能的惊悚小说

近 besetting, driven, obsessive

chimera	[kaɪˈmɪrə]

【考法】 *n.* 虚构的事物，幻觉：an **illusion or fabrication** of the mind，especially an unrealizable dream

例 EU is just a chimera that can't prevent old nations from playing their dices. 欧盟只不过是一个虚构的存在，它根本不可能阻止那些老国家按照自己的一套规则办事。

近 conceit, daydream, delusion, fantasy, figment, hallucination, illusion, phantasm, vision

反 actuality, fact, reality, truth 事实，现实

charlatan	[ˈʃɑːrlətən]

【考法】 *n.* 骗子，装懂的人：a person who makes elaborate, **fraudulent**, and often voluble claims to skill or knowledge; a quack or fraud

例 a charlatan in music 冒充音乐家的人

近 fake, fraud, hoaxer, mountebank, phony, pretender, quack, imposter

chary	[ˈtʃeri]

【考法】 *adj.* 非常谨慎的：very **cautious**

例 chary investors who weren't burned by the dot-com bust 那些没有受到互联网萧条影响的谨慎投资者们

近 alert, cautious, circumspect, conservative, gingerly, guarded, heedful, wary

反 rash, bold 鲁莽的

chase	[tʃeɪs]

【考法】 *v.* 驱赶：to drive or **force out**

例 chase the enemy 驱赶敌人

近 banish, dismiss, expel, extrude, kick out, cast out

chasm	[ˈkæzəm]

【考法】 *n.* 分歧，(意见、利益或忠诚上的)明显差异：a **pronounced difference** of opinion, interests, or loyalty

近 contradiction, dissent, disjunction, discord, conflict, rift, rivalry, dichotomy

chauvinistic	[ˌʃoʊvɪˈnɪstɪk]

【考法】 *adj.* 盲目爱国的：having or showing **excessive favoritism** towards one's own country

例 chauvinistic behavior 盲目爱国的行为

近 jingoist, jingoistic, nationalistic, superpatriot

check	[tʃek]

【考法1】 *vt.* 使突然停止，阻止：to **arrest** the motion **abruptly**

例 A tree finally checked the skidding car. 一辆滑行的车终于被大树停住了。

近 arrest, stall, bridle, contain, curb, tame, bring up, draw up, hold up, pull up

反 propagate, goad, hasten 扩增，驱使，促进

【考法2】 *v.* 同意，一致：to be **in agreement** on every point

例 Their story of what happened checks with the report of the eyewitness. 他们的说法和目击者的供词一致。

近 accord, cohere, conform, correspond, dovetail, fit, harmonize, jibe, tally

反 differ, disagree with 反对

Unit 5

■ CHERUBIC	■ CHICANERY	■ CHIDE	■ CHOLERIC	■ CHORD
■ CHROMATIC	■ CHRONIC	■ CHURLISH	■ CIPHER	■ CIRCUITOUS

cherubic	[tʃəˈruːbik]

【考法】 *adj.* 天使般可爱的：innocent-looking usually chubby and **rosy**

例 A representation of Cupid as a naked, cherubic boy usually is used as a symbol of love. 丘比特作为小天使般的少年裸体画像被用作爱的象征。

反 fiendish, devilish 恶魔般的

chicanery	[ʃɪˈkeɪnəri]

【考法】 *n.* 诡计多端，欺骗：**deception** by artful subterfuge or sophistry

例 Well-doer never does chicanery and person who is good at chicanery does not belong well-doer. 善者不辩，辩者不善。

近 deception, artifice, legerdemain, wile, subterfuge

反 aboveboard action 光明正大的行为；honest dealing 诚实的行为；forthrightness 坦白

chide	[tʃaɪd]

【考法】 *v.* 责备: to **scold mildly** so as to correct or improve
例 chide sb. for sth. 因为某事责备某人。
近 reprove, reprimand, reproach, tick off
反 praise, commend 称赞

choleric	[ˈkɑːlərɪk]

【考法】 *adj.* 易怒的,暴躁的: easily **angered**; bad-tempered
例 choleric disposition 易怒的性情
近 crabby, cranky, irascible, peevish, petulant, bad-tempered, hot-tempered, short-tempered, testy
反 difficult to provoke, pacific, placid, calm, serene, tranquil, composed, nonchalant 难以被激怒的,平静的
派 choler *n.* 易怒: ready disposition to irritation: irascibility also: anger

chord	[kɔːrd]

【考法】 *vi.* 与…和谐一致;符合: to be in **accord**; **agree**
例 The revised system chords perfectly with the original goals. 新版的系统非常符合最初的目标。
近 accord, agree, conform, consist, correspond, dovetail, fit, harmonize, jibe, rhyme, square, tally
反 differ from, disagree with 与……不同,有分歧

chromatic	[krəˈmætɪk]

【考法】 *adj.* 彩色的: relating to **colors** or color
例 the chromatic paintings of Matisse and the other Fauvists 马蒂斯和其他野兽派画家的彩色画
近 colored, colorful, motley, multicolored, multihued, varicolored, variegated, kaleidoscopic
反 colorless, pallid, blanched 无色的; monochromatic, monochromic, monotone, self-colored 单色的

chronic	[ˈkrɑːnɪk]

【考法】 *adj.* 经常发生的,复发的: marked by long duration or **frequent recurrence**
例 chronic disease 慢性病
近 frequent, usual, routine
反 sporadic 偶然发生的; infrequent 不经常的

churlish	[ˈtʃɜːrlɪʃ]

【考法】 *adj.* 粗鲁无礼的: having or showing crudely insensitive or **impolite manners**
例 as valiant as the lion, churlish as the bear "像狮子般勇猛,像狗熊般粗鲁"
近 boorish, classless, loutish, uncouth
反 couth, cultivated, polished, refined, well-bred, courteous, polite 有教养的,优雅的
派 churl *n.* 粗鲁的人

cipher	[ˈsaɪfər]

【考法】 *n.* 密码: a method of transforming a text in order to **conceal** its meaning
例 convert their messages into cipher 把他们的信息转换成密码
近 code, secret message

circuitous	[sərˈkjuːɪtəs]

【考法】 *adj.* 迂回的,不直接的: **not** being **forthright** or **direct** in language or action
例 We took a circuitous route to the airport so as to avoid the massive traffic jam. 我们走了一条迂回的路线去机场来躲避堵车。
近 indirect, circular, roundabout
反 direct, straight, straightforward 直接的
派 circuity *n.* 不直接: lack of straightforwardness
反 straightforwardness, direction 直接

Unit 6

■ CIRCUMLOCUTION	■ CIRCUMSCRIBE	■ CIRCUMSPECT	■ CIRCUMVENT	■ CIVILITY
■ CHOKEHOLD	■ CLANDESTINE	■ CLARION	■ CLARITY	■ CLASP

circumlocution	[ˌsɜːrkəmləˈkjuːʃn]

【考法】 *n.* 冗长: the use of **too many** words to express an idea
例 Your papers have to be five pages long, but that's five pages of substance, not circumlocution. 你的论文要求是5页,但是那5页都是实质内容,不是废话。
近 diffuseness, diffusion, long-windedness, prolixity, redundancy, verbalism, verboseness, verbosity, windiness, wordage, wordiness
反 conciseness, concision, pithiness, succinctness, terseness 简洁

circumscribe [ˈsɜːrkəmskraɪb]

【考法】 *vt.* 限制：to **limit** narrowly; restrict

例 Teammates circumscribed his enthusiasm so as not to make the losing side feel worse. 队员们抑制了他们的热情，为了不让失败者更难过。

近 cap, limit, confine, delimit, restrict

反 exceed 超过，超越

circumspect [ˈsɜːrkəmspekt]

【考法】 *adj.* 谨慎的，小心的：**careful** to consider all circumstances and possible consequences: prudent

例 The banks should have been more circumspect in their dealings. 银行本应该在它们的交易当中更加谨慎。

近 alert, careful, gingerly, guarded, heedful, prudent, cautious, chary, wary

反 careless, incautious, unmindful, unwary 不小心的，不谨慎的；audacious, reckless 大胆的，鲁莽的

circumvent [ˌsɜːrkəmˈvent]

【考法】 *vt.* 躲避，不遵从：to **avoid** having to **comply** with (something) especially through cleverness

例 circumvent all the red tape 绕过所有官方程序繁文缛节 ‖ He found a way to circumvent the law. 他发现了一个逃避法律的方法。

近 avoid, bypass, dodge, sidestep, skirt, get around

反 comply with, follow, obey, observe 遵从；confront, directly encounter 直接面对

civility [səˈvɪləti]

【考法】 *n.* 彬彬有礼：**courteous** behavior; **politeness**

例 They greeted us with civility. 他们有礼貌地招呼我们。

近 politeness, courtesy, politeness, genteelness, gentility, graciousness

反 discourteousness, discourtesy, impoliteness, incivility, rudeness, surliness, ungraciousness 无礼，粗鲁

chokehold [ˈtʃoʊkhoʊld]

【考法】 *n.* 压制 a force or influence that **stops** something from **growing or developing**

例 have a chokehold on the city's finances 压制城市的财政

clandestine [klænˈdestɪn]

【考法】 *adj.* 隐藏的，秘密的：kept or done in **secret**, often in order to conceal an **illicit** or **improper** purpose

例 their clandestine love affair 他们的秘密恋情

近 secret, covert, furtive, surreptitious, sneaky, stealthy, undercover, underground, underhand, underhanded

反 open, overt, public 公开的；aboveboard 光明正大的

clarion [ˈklæriən]

【考法】 *adj.* 清楚响亮的：**loud** and **clear**

例 clarion call for democracy 对民主的高声呼吁

反 soft and indistinct 柔和而模糊的

clarity [ˈklærəti]

【考法】 *n.* 清晰，清楚：the quality or state of being **clear**: **lucidity**

例 Clarity of diction is vital for a XDF teacher. 发音清楚对新东方老师来说是至关重要的。

近 clarity, explicitness, lucidity, lucidness, perspicuity, perspicuousness

反 obscureness, obscurity, unclarity 模糊，不清晰

派 clarify *v.* 澄清，使清晰：to free of confusion

例 clarify his mind 理清思路；clarify a subject 澄清某一问题

近 purify, clear, elucidate, explain, illuminate, illustrate

反 obfuscate, obscure 使模糊

clasp [klæsp]

【考法】 *n./v.* 紧握：the act or manner of **holding**

例 He clasps her hands. 他紧攥着她的手。

近 clench, grapple, grasp, grip, handgrip, handhold

Unit 7

■ CLEMENT	■ CLICHÉ	■ CLOG	■ CLOT	■ CORDIAL
■ CLOUT	■ CLOYING	■ CLUMSY	■ COAGULATE	■ COALESCE

clement [ˈklemənt]

【考法 1】 *adj.* 宽容的，善良的：**tolerant** and **kind** in the judgment of and expectations for others

例 Clement judge reduced the sentence. 仁慈的法官减轻了刑罚。

近 charitable, lenient, merciful

反 harsh, severe, stern, strict 严厉的，严格的
派 clemency *n.* 仁慈
【考法2】 *adj.* 气候温和的：marked by temperatures that are **neither** too **high** nor too **low**
例 Hawaii is known for its delightfully clement climate . 夏威夷以它宜人的温和气候著称。
近 mild, genial, gentle, balmy, equable
反 harsh, inclement, severe 严酷的

cliché [kliːˈʃeɪ]
【考法】 *n./adj.* 陈词滥调（的）：a **hackneyed** theme, characterization, or situation
例 Cliché is a feature of bad news. 拙劣新闻的特征是使用陈词滥调。
近 banality, bromide, platitude; trite, bathetic, hackneyed, stereotypical
反 fresh, new, original, creative 新的，创造性的

clog [klɑːɡ]
【考法】 *n.* 阻碍物：**something** that makes **movement** or **progress difficult**
v. 阻碍：to create **difficulty** for the work or activity of
例 impede with a clog 用障碍物阻止 ‖ They always clog the courts . 他们一直阻挠法庭工作。
近 balk, bar, block, deterrent, drag, fetter, holdback, hurdle, impediment, inhibition, interference, obstacle, obstruction, shackles, stop, stumbling block, trammel; encumber, fetter, hinder, hold back, hold up, impede, inhibit, interfere with, obstruct, shackle, stymie, tie up, trammel
反 aid, assist, help 帮助；facilitate 促进

clot [klɑːt]
【考法1】 *n.* 密集的一群：a **number of things** considered as **a unit**
例 A clot of daisies occupied one corner of the flower bed. 一簇雏菊占据了花床的一角。
近 array, assemblage, band, block, bunch, cluster, clutch, collection, constellation, grouping, huddle, knot, lot, muster, package
【考法2】 *v.* 凝结：to turn from a liquid into a substance resembling **jelly**
例 clotted blood 凝结的血块
近 congeal, jell, jelly

cordial [ˈkɔːrdʒəl]
【考法1】 *adj.* 热情的，友好的：showing a natural **kindness and courtesy** especially in social situations
例 We received a cordial greeting from our host at the party. 我们受到了聚会主人的热情欢迎。
近 affable, genial, hospitable, sociable, warmhearted
反 aloof, apathetic, brittle, detached, distant, offish, remote, unbending 冷淡的，无感情的
【考法2】 *adj.* 令人振奋的，令人焕然一新的：having a **renewing effect** on the state of the body or mind
例 He insisted that nothing but a cordial nip of vodka would be the right choice for someone suffering from cold. 他坚信受到风寒困扰的人们只需一小口伏特加便能精神百倍。
近 bracing, invigorating, refreshing, rejuvenating, restorative, reviving, stimulating, vital, vitalizing
反 debilitating, draining, enervating, enfeebling, exhausting, sapping 令人疲倦的

clout [klaʊt]
【考法】 *n.* 权力，影响力：**influence**; pull
例 The queen may have privilege but she has no real political clout . 女王有特权，但无真正的政治影响力。
近 power, influence, capacity, heft, leverage
反 impuissance, impotence 无力

cloying [ˈklɔɪɪŋ]
【考法】 *adj.* 甜得发腻的；感情用事的：excessively **sweet**; **sentimental**
例 the cloying sentiments of so many Mother's Day cards 这么多母亲节贺卡(所蕴含)的甜蜜感情
近 lovey-dovey, maudlin, mawkish, saccharine, sentimental
反 unsentimental 不动感情的

clumsy [ˈklʌmzi]
【考法】 *adj.* 笨拙的：**lacking** or showing a lack of **nimbleness** in using one's hands; a **lack** of **skill** and tact
例 turn out to be a clumsy sleight of hand 弄巧成拙
近 awkward, ham-handed, heavy-handed, maladroit, unhandy, bungling, inept
反 adroit, deft, dexterous, handy 熟练的，灵巧的

coagulate [koʊˈæɡjuleɪt]
【考法】 *v.* (使)凝结，(使)变稠：to (cause to) become viscous or thickened into a **coherent** mass: curdle, **clot**
例 The blood coagulates to stop wounds bleeding. 血液会凝结以防止伤口流血。

近	clot, congeal, jelly
反	melt, liquefy, fluidify, dissolve 融化，溶解；thin 使变稀薄
派	coagulant *n.* 凝结剂：an agent that causes a liquid to coagulate

coalesce ［ˌkoʊəˈles］
【考法】	*v.* 合并，融合：to unite into a **whole**：fuse
例	Different units coalesced into one army . 不同的党派融合成了一支部队。
近	associate, combine, conjoin, connect, couple, fuse, interfuse, join, link (up), unify, unite
反	break up, dissever, section, separate, sever, split, sunder, unlink, disband 分开，解散

Unit 8

■ COAX	■ CODA	■ COERCE	■ COEVAL	■ COGENT
■ COGNIZANT	■ COLLAPSE	■ COLLUDE	■ COLOSSAL	■ COLTISH

coax ［koʊks］
【考法】	*v.* 哄骗：to persuade or try to persuade by **pleading** or **flattery**；**cajole**
例	coax a child to take his medicine 哄小孩吃药
近	blandish, cajole, wheedle, palaver

coda ［ˈkoʊdə］
【考法】	*n.* 终曲：the **concluding passage** of a movement or composition
例	A song includes prelude, loud song and coda . 一首歌包括前奏、高潮和尾声。
近	finale, epilogue
反	overture, prelude 前奏

coerce ［koʊˈɜːrs］
【考法】	*vt.* (以武力)强制：to achieve by **force** or **threat**
例	be coerced into agreeing 被迫同意
近	force, threaten, compel
派	coercion *n.* 强力压迫：the act of persuading someone forcefully to do something that they do not want to do
反	voluntary behavior 自愿的行为

coeval ［koʊˈiːvl］
【考法】	*adj.* 同时代的，同龄的：of the same or **equal age**, antiquity, or duration
例	Two stars thought to be coeval because they have nearly the same mass and brightness. 两个星星被认为是同龄，因为他们的质量和亮度几乎相同。
近	coetaneous, coexisting, concurrent, contemporaneous, simultaneous, synchronic, synchronous
反	asynchronous, noncontemporary, nonsimultaneous 不同时的

cogent ［ˈkoʊdʒənt］
【考法1】	*adj.* 令人信服的：appealing forcibly to the mind or reason：**convincing**
例	Six Sigma is one of the most cogent methods for modern enterprises to control quality and optimizing process. "六西格玛"方法是现代企业进行质量控制和工艺优化最令人信服的方法之一。
近	convincing, compelling, conclusive, telling, persuasive, satisfying
反	unconvincing, unpersuasive 不令人信服的
【考法2】	*adj.* 相关的：**pertinent**, relevant
例	a cogent analysis 一项相关的研究
近	apropos, germane, relative, relevant
反	extraneous, irrelevant, impertinent, irrelative 无关的

cognizant ［ˈkɑːgnɪzənt］
【考法】	*adj.* 知道的，意识到的：fully informed; conscious; **aware**
例	We are cognizant of the problem . 我们已经意识到了这个问题。
近	aware, conscious, witting, apprehensive, sensible
反	oblivious, unconscious, unaware, unmindful 没意识到的
派	incognizance *n.* 不认识；没知觉

collapse ［kəˈlæps］
【考法】	*v./n.* 失败：to be **unsuccessful**; a falling short of one's goals
例	The legal case collapsed in the face of the opposition's evidence. 面对反方的证据，这个法律案件败诉了。

近 defeat, nonachievement, nonsuccess
反 accomplishment, achievement, success 成功，成就

collude [kəˈluːd]
【考法】 v. 串通，共谋（做坏事）: to act **together secretly** to achieve a **fraudulent**, illegal, or **deceitful** purpose; **conspire**
例 collude with competitors to control the price 与竞争者合谋以控制价格
近 connive, conspire, contrive, intrigue, machinate, put up
反 act independently 单独行动

colossal [kəˈlɑːsl]
【考法】 adj. 巨大的: of a **size**, **extent**, or **degree** that elicits awe or taxes belief; **immense**
例 a colossal waste of public money 对公共财产的巨大浪费
近 huge, giant, titanic, gargantuan, mammoth, tremendous, elephantine, prodigious
反 tiny, micro, minute, miniature, minuscule, wee, infinitesimal 微小的

coltish [ˈkoʊltɪʃ]
【考法】 adj. 爱开玩笑的: given to good-natured **joking** or **teasing**
例 Off camera the actor is high-spiritedly coltish, but turns serious once the camera starts rolling. 镜头下这个演员很喜欢开玩笑，但是当镜头开启，他就马上变得严肃起来。
近 antic, frisky, frolicsome, larky, sportful
反 earnest, serious-minded, sober 严肃的

Unit 9

■ COMA　　　　　■ COMBUSTIBLE　　　　■ CLUSTER　　　　■ COMITY　　　　■ COMMENCEMENT
■ COMMEND　　　■ COMMENSURATE　　　■ COMMINGLE　　■ COMMITMENT　　■ COMMITTED

coma [ˈkoʊmə]
【考法】 n. 昏迷，深度无知觉: a state of **profound unconsciousness** caused by disease, injury, or poison
例 The girl lay in a coma for three days after the accident. 那个女孩在事故之后昏迷了三天。
近 insensibility, blackout, knockout
反 consciousness, awareness 有知觉

combustible [kəmˈbʌstəbl]
【考法1】 adj. 可燃的: capable of **igniting** and burning
例 release a combustible gas 释放出可燃性气体
近 burnable, combustive, flammable, ignitable, inflammable
反 incombustible, nonburnable, noncombustible, nonflammable, noninflammable, unburnable 不可燃的；fireproof 防火的
【考法2】 adj. 容易激动的: **easily excited**
例 a high-strung combustible temper 一碰就火的性格
近 excitable, agitable, touchy

cluster [ˈklʌstər]
【考法】 n. 一群人: a usually **small number of persons** considered as a unit
例 A small cluster of reporters waited by the courthouse door. 一小群记者等候在法院门口。
近 array, batch, bunch, group, clutch, constellation, crop, grouping

comity [ˈkɑːmɪti]
【考法】 n. 友好，社会和谐: **friendly** social atmosphere: social **harmony**
例 group activities promoting comity 促进和谐氛围的团队活动 ‖ comity of nations 国际礼节
近 compatibility, concord, peace
反 conflict, discord, dissension 冲突，不和

commencement [kəˈmensmənt]
【考法1】 n. 开始: a **beginning**; a start
例 There was a large turnout at the commencement of the conference, but the numbers dwindled as it progressed. 在会议开始的时候，有很多人出席。但是随着会议的进行，人慢慢变少了。
近 birth, onset, outset, start, genesis, inception, nascence, threshold
反 close, conclusion, end, ending 结束
【考法2】 n. 毕业典礼: the ceremonies or the day for **conferring** degrees or diplomas
例 The purpose of a commencement speaker is to dispense wisdom. 毕业典礼上演讲者的目的是传播智慧。
反 matriculation 录取入学

commend [kəˈmend]

【考法】 *vt.* 赞扬：to mention with **approbation**: **praise**

例 Jason commended his students' studious attitude . Jason 表扬了他的学生用功的态度。

近 approbate, praise, acclaim, applaud, compliment, eulogize, extol

反 blame, criticize, reprehend, reprobate, chide, rebuke, reprimand, reproach, reprove, censure, admonish berate, deplore, execrate 责备，批评，谴责，憎恶，痛骂

commensurate [kəˈmenʃərət]

【考法 1】 *adj.* 同样大小的：**equal** in measure or extent

例 Five yards is commensurate with fifteen feet. 5 码等于 15 英尺。

近 equal, tantamount

反 unequal, disparate, preponderant 不相同的，（重量，重要性，数量上）超过的

【考法 2】 *adj.* 相称的，相当的：corresponding in size or degree; **proportionate**

例 a job commensurate with her abilities 一份与她能力相称的工作

近 commensurable, proportionate

反 disproportionate 不相称的

commingle [kəˈmɪŋgl]

【考法】 *v.* 充分混合：to **blend** thoroughly into a harmonious whole

例 Fact and fic-tion commingle in the story . 事实和虚构混合成了故事。

近 amalgamate, fuse, mix, immix, commix, compound, mingle, immingle, intermingle, intermix, merge

反 break down, break up, separate, unmix 分开

commitment [kəˈmɪtmənt]

【考法 1】 *n.* 致力，投入：the state or an instance of being **obligated** or emotionally **impelled**

例 a commitment to a cause 投身于某项事业

近 dedication, devotedness, fealty, piety, steadfastness

【考法 2】 *n.* 承诺，表态：the act of **revealing one's view** of

例 He made a commitment to pay the rent on time . 他承诺按时交房租。

反 ambivalence, equivocation 矛盾，含糊其辞

committed [kəˈmɪtɪd]

【考法】 *adj.* 忠诚的，忠实的：**loyal** to a belief, organization, or group, and willing to work hard for it

例 remain committed to one's youthful ideal 坚持不懈地追求自己年轻时的理想

近 loyal, faithful, allegiant

反 disloyal 不忠诚的

派 noncommittal *adj.* 不明确的：giving no clear indication of attitude or feeling

例 a noncommittal reply 一个不明确的回答

反 confirmable 确定的

Unit 10

| ■ COMMODIOUS | ■ COMMONSENSICAL | ■ COMMOTION | ■ COMPENDIUM | ■ COMPLACENCY |
| ■ COMPLAISANCE | ■ COMPLIANT | ■ COMPLIMENT | ■ CLOWNISH | ■ COMPOSE |

commodious [kəˈmoʊdiəs]

【考法】 *adj.* 宽敞舒适的：comfortably or conveniently **spacious**: roomy

例 a commodious closet 宽敞的衣橱

近 spacious, roomy

反 constricted, cramped, snug, constringed 狭窄的

commonsensical [ˌkɑːmənˈsensɪkl]

【考法】 *adj.* 符合常识的，有依据的：displaying **common sense**, based on **sound** reasoning or information

例 The only commonsensical solution would be to divide the children into groups according to age. 唯一合理的解决办法就是按照年龄把孩子分成组。

近 justified, logical, rational, reasonable, reasoned, valid, well-founded, levelheaded

反 groundless, illogical, invalid, irrational, nonrational, nonsensical, nonvalid, unfounded, uninformed, unjustified, unreasonable, unreasoned, unsound 无逻辑的，不合理的；preposterous 荒谬的

commotion [kəˈmoʊʃn]

【考法】 *n.* 骚乱：an agitated **disturbance**

例 The commotion was created when the nation's top rock band arrived in town. 当全国顶级摇滚乐队来到小镇时，人们骚乱了。

近 tumult, turmoil, pandemonium, hurry-scurry
反 tranquility, calmness, quiet, serenity 安静；order 有序

compendium [kəmˈpendiəm]
【考法】 *n.* 摘要：a brief **summary** of a larger work or of a field of knowledge: **abstract**
例 a compendium of information 资料概要
近 abstract, brief, overview
派 compendious *adj.* 简洁而全面的：concise and comprehensive
例 his compendious knowledge of this subject 他关于这一学科的全面知识
近 concise, brief, laconic, compendiary, succinct

complacency [kəmˈpleɪsnsi]
【考法】 *n.* 自满，无忧患意识：a feeling of **self-satisfaction**, coupled with an **unawareness of trouble**
例 Complacency is the enemy of study. 自满乃学习之敌。
近 conceit, pomposity, pompousness, pride, self-admiration, self-assumption, smugness, vanity
反 anxiety 忧虑；humbleness, humility, modesty 谦虚

complaisance [kəmˈpleɪzəns]
【考法】 *n.* 愿意顺从，讨好，彬彬有礼：disposition to please or **comply**: **affability**
例 She speaks with complaisance. 她说话彬彬有礼。
近 affability, amenability, amiability, good-naturedness
反 obstinacy 固执；churlishness 粗野

compliant [kəmˈplaɪənt]
【考法】 *adj.* 顺从的：ready or disposed to comply: **submissive**
例 a corrupt regime aided by a compliant television station 一个在顺从的电视台帮助下的腐败政府
近 amenable, conformable, docile, submissive, tractable
反 balky, contumacious, disobedient, incompliant, insubordinate, intractable, noncompliant, obstreperous, rebel, rebellious, recalcitrant, refractory, unamenable, ungovernable, unruly, willful, wayward 顽固的，难驾驭的

compliment *n.* [ˈkɑːmplɪmənt] *v.* [ˈkɑːmplɪment]
【考法1】 *n./vt.* 称赞，恭维：an expression of **praise**, admiration, or congratulation
例 a man meriting the compliments and homage of his fellows 一个值得他的伙伴们尊敬和称赞的人
近 praise, commend, eulogize, extol, laud
反 vituperate 责骂
派 complimentary *adj.* 称赞的：expressing or containing a compliment
反 vituperative 责骂的
【考法2】 *n.* 敬意，免费赠送的礼物：formal and **respectful** recognition: honor
例 How about a delicious dessert then, with our compliment? 给您上点甜点怎么样，算是我们小小的敬意。

clownish [ˈklaʊnɪʃ]
【考法】 *adj.* 滑稽可笑的：acting in a silly or **funny way**
例 Clownish though he is, Mr Bossi has acute political antennae. 尽管贝卢斯科尼滑稽可笑，但是他有着敏锐的政治直觉。
近 boorish, churlish, classless, cloddish, loutish, uncouth

compose [kəmˈpoʊz]
【考法1】 *vt.* 使镇定：to free from agitation: **calm**
例 She took a deep breath and composed herself. 她做了一个深呼吸，使自己安定下来。
近 contain, settle
反 agitate, discompose, disquiet, disturb, perturb, upset, vex 使激动，使不安
派 composed *adj.* 镇静的，安定的：free from agitation: calm
反 distraught, restless 发狂的，不平静的
派 composure *n.* 镇定：a calmness or repose especially of mind, bearing, or appearance
【考法2】 *v.* 组成，构成：to **form** the substance of: **constitute**
例 composed of many ingredients 由很多配料组成
近 constitute, comprise, make up

List 5

Unit 1

■ COMPOUND	■ COMPRESS	■ COMPROMISE	■ COMPUNCTION	■ CONCATENATE
■ CONCOCT	■ CONCEAL	■ CONCEDE	■ CONCENTRATE	■ CONCERTED

compound

【考法 1】［ˈkɑːmpaʊnd］ *n.* 混合物：**something composed** of or resulting from union of separate elements, ingredients, or parts

［ˈkɑːmpaʊnd］ *adj.* 混合的：**consisting** of two or more substances, ingredients, elements, or parts

［kəmˈpaʊnd］ *vt.* 混合：to put or bring **together** so as to form a new and longer whole

例 mixed the chemicals together to form a new compound 将化学试剂混合形成新的化合物 ‖ a compound word 复合词 ‖ "Steamboat" is a compound noun . "汽船"是一个复合名词。‖ the German language's propensity for compounding words 德语喜欢复合单词

近 admixture, alloy, amalgam, amalgamation, cocktail, combination, composite, fusion, intermixture, meld, mix, conflation, synthesis; amalgamated; chain, conjugate, couple, hook, interconnect, interlink, join, link, yoke

反 noncompound 非混合的；disconnect, disjoin, disjoint, dissever, disunite, separate, unchain, uncouple, unhitch, unyoke 分开

【考法 2】 *vt.* 使恶化，加重：to **make worse**, more serious, or more severe

例 Additional bloodshed and loss of life will only compound the tragedy in this nation. 额外的流血和牺牲只会加重这个国家的悲剧。

近 aggravate, complicate, exacerbate, intensify, worsen

反 allay, alleviate, assuage, mitigate, mollify, palliate, relieve, soothe 缓和，减轻

compress ［kəmˈpres］

【考法】 *vt.* 压缩（体积）：to **reduce** in **size** or **volume** as if by squeezing

例 compress a computer file 压缩电脑文档 ‖ The science textbook compresses a lot of information into a few short chapters. 科学教科书将人类的繁育知识压缩成了几个短章节。

近 capsule, collapse, compact, condense, constrict, constringe, contract, shrink, telescope

反 increase in volume, decompress, expand, balloon 体积增大；outspread, outstretch 伸展，扩张

compromise ［ˈkɑːmprəmaɪz］

【考法 1】 *v.* 妥协：to adjust or settle by mutual **concessions**

例 Eventually we reached a compromise on the number of hours per week that would be devoted to piano practice. 最后我们在每周练琴的时间上妥协了。

近 accommodation, negotiation

【考法 2】 *vt.* 使危险：to place in **danger**

例 Officials were concerned that his statements would compromise national security . 官员们认为他的言论会危害国家安全。

近 hazard, imperil, jeopardize, menace, peril, venture

compunction ［kəmˈpʌŋkʃn］

【考法】 *n.* 焦虑，内疚，良心不安：**anxiety** arising from awareness of **guilt**

例 compunction of conscience 良心不安 ‖ a brutal murderer who killed without compunction 一个野蛮没有良心的杀人犯

近 anxiety, misgiving, scruple

反 absence of misgiving 不担忧

concatenate ［kənˈkætɪneɪt］

【考法】 *v.* 连结，混合：to put or **bring together** so as to form a new and longer whole

例 The movie actually concatenates several episodes from various books into one narrative . 这部电影把很多书中的片段混合成了一个故事。

近 catenate, chain, couple, hook, interconnect, interlink, join, link, yoke

反 disconnect, disjoin, disjoint, dissever, disunite, separate, unchain, uncouple, unhitch, unyoke 分开

concoct ［kənˈkɑːkt］

【考法】 *v.* 捏造，编造：to **invent** or develop especially in order to **deceive someone**

例 The prisoner concocted the story to get a lighter sentence. 囚犯为了获轻罚编造了这个故事。

近 invent, construct, devise, fabricate, make up, manufacture

conceal ［kənˈsiːl］

【考法】 *v.* 隐藏，隐瞒：to **prevent disclosure** or recognition of

例 Robert could not conceal his relief . Robert 无法掩饰他如释重负的心情。

近 cache, secrete, disguise, mask, occult, ensconce

反 display, exhibit 展示；bare, disclose, expose, reveal, uncover, unmask 揭露

concede ［kənˈsiːd］

【考法】 *vt.* 承认：to **grant** as a right or privilege

例 She grudgingly conceded his point . 她不情愿地承认了他的观点。

近 acknowledge, grant, confess

反 refuse to grant, deny 拒绝承认，否认

派 concession *n.* 让步：the act of yielding

反 aggression 侵犯

concentrate ［ˈkɑːnsntreɪt］

【考法 1】 *vt.* 浓缩：to make **less dilute**

例 Prolonged boiling is required to concentrate the sap when making maple syrup. 制作枫糖浆时，要进行长时间的煮，使汁液充分浓缩。

近 condense

反 dilute, water down 稀释

【考法 2】 *v.* 聚集：to come **together** in one body or place

例 Recent immigrants tend to concentrate in port cities . 近来的移民倾向于聚集在海港城市。

近 accumulate, amass, assemble, collect, congregate, garner

反 dispel, disperse, dissipate, scatter, break up, disband 驱散，解散

concerted ［kənˈsɜːrtɪd］

【考法】 *adj.* 共同完成的：planned or **accomplished together**

例 The ITER project, commendable though it is, should be merely a component of a concerted effort . "国际热核聚变实验堆"计划虽然是值得称赞的，但是它仅仅是(人类)齐心协力的一部分。II A victory results from the concerted effort of the entire team . 一项成功来自整个团队的齐心协力。

近 collaborative, combined, cooperative, united

反 separate 分开的；individual, single, sole, solitary 单独的

Unit 2

■ CONCILIATE	■ COMMONPLACE	■ CONCORD	■ CONCUR	■ CONDESCENDING
■ CONDIGN	■ CONDOLE	■ CONDONE	■ CONDUCIVE	■ CANTANKEROUS

conciliate ［kənˈsɪlieɪt］

【考法】 *v.* 平息，抚慰：to **lessen the anger** or agitation of

例 A principal tried to conciliate the parents who did not receive their tickets to the graduation ceremonies. 校长试着平息没有收到他们学校毕业晚会门票的家长的气愤情绪。

近 appease, pacify, assuage, mollify, placate, propitiate, calm (down), ease, soothe, palliate, disarm

反 annoy, enrage, vex, nettle, rile, incense, inflame, exasperate, infuriate, discompose, disturb, perturb, upset 烦扰，激怒，打扰

commonplace	[ˈkɑːmənpleɪs]
【考法】	*adj/n.* 司空见惯的(事物),陈旧的(事物): used or heard **so often** as to be **dull**
例	a thriller that uses the commonplace plot twist of the evil twin 一部使用了恶魔兄弟的老套剧情的恐怖片
近	banal, cliché, stale, hackneyed, moth-eaten, musty, shopworn, stereotyped, threadbare, timeworn, trite
反	fresh, new, novel, original, unhackneyed 新的

concord	[ˈkɑːŋkɔːrd]
【考法】	*n.* 一致,和睦: **harmony** or **agreement** of interests or feelings; accord
例	No discord, no concord. 不打不成交。
近	comity, compatibility, peace
反	conflict, discord, dissension, variance 冲突,不和

concur	[kənˈkɜːr]
【考法1】	*vi.* 同意: to express **agreement**
例	concur with an excellent opinion 同意一个好的想法
近	agree, coincide
反	differ, disagree 不同意
【考法2】	*vi.* 同一时间发生、存在: to occur or exist at the **same time**
例	The race to the moon, the Vietnam War, and the civil rights movement all concurred in the 1960s. 登月、越战和人权运动都发生在二十世纪六十年代。
近	coexist, synchronize, co-occur
【考法3】	*vi.* 团结合作: to participate or assist in a **joint** effort to accomplish an end
例	All people concurred to pass the reform legislation. 所有人都联合起来使改革法案通过。
近	band together, collaborate, concert, conjoin, league, team up, unite

condescending	[ˌkɑːndɪˈsendɪŋ]
【考法】	*adj.* 摆出高人一等的姿态的: displaying a **patronizingly superior** attitude
例	treat sb in a condescending manner 以屈尊俯就的态度对待某人
近	patronizing
派	condescension *n.* 屈尊俯就: patronizing attitude or behavior

condign	[kənˈdaɪn]
【考法】	*adj.* 应得的,恰当的: **deserved**, appropriate
例	condign punishment 应得的惩罚 ‖ A suspension without pay is condign punishment for breaking the company's code of business ethics. 停职是违反公司商业道德准则应得的惩罚。
近	due, deserved, merited, justified, warranted
反	undeserved, undue, unmerited 不应得的

condole	[kənˈdoʊl]
【考法】	*vi.* 表达同情: to express **sympathetic** sorrow
例	We condole with him on the death of his father. 我们对他父亲的死深表同情。
近	compassionate, sympathize with, yearn over
派	condolence *n.* 同情: sympathy with another in sorrow

condone	[kənˈdoʊn]
【考法】	*vt.* 宽恕;忽视: to overlook, **forgive**, or disregard (an offense) without protest or censure
例	By his silence, he seemed to condone their behavior. 他的沉默流露出了他对他们行为的宽恕。
近	disregard, ignore, overlook, remit, shrug off, gloss over
反	denounce 谴责; exact 强求

conducive	[kənˈduːsɪv]
【考法】	*adj.* 有益的,有促进作用的: tending to **promote** or assist
例	be conducive to education 于教育有利的 ‖ The state's long-standing low tax is conducive to entrepreneurship. 政府长期的低税率有利于创业者。
近	facilitative, useful
反	unhelpful, useless 无用的

cantankerous	[kænˈtæŋkərəs]
【考法】	*adj.* 脾气不好的: having or showing a habitually **bad temper**
例	They are cantankerous egotists, the kind of men who are unwelcome in the modern corporation. 他们是脾气不好的自我主义者,是现代企业中不受欢迎的一群。
近	acid, ill-tempered, dyspeptic, ill-natured, surly
反	amiable, affable, good-humored, good-natured, good-tempered 脾气好的

Unit 3

confine [kənˈfaɪn]

【考法】 *vt.* 限制：to keep within **limits**

例 Please confine yourself to the subject . 请只限于讨论这个话题。

近 limit, circumscribe, restrict

反 exceed 超越，超过

confluence [ˈkɑːnfluəns]

【考法】 *n.* 汇合，混合：the coming **together** of two or more things to the **same** point

例 a happy confluence of beautiful weather and spectacular scenery during our vacation 旅途中美好的天气和壮丽的景色——令人欣喜的汇合

近 conjunction

反 divergence 分叉

confront [kənˈfrʌnt]

【考法】 *vt.* 直接对抗，直面：to come **face to face** with, especially with defiance or hostility

例 You must confront your fear in order to conquer it. 敢于面对恐惧才能克服恐惧。

近 affront, brazen, encounter, face, meet

反 dodge, duck, parry, shirk, sidestep 躲避

派 confrontation *n.* 对抗，冲突

confound [kənˈfaʊnd]

【考法1】 *vt.* 使困惑：to throw into a state of mental **uncertainty**

例 We are all confounded by his self-contradictory claims . 我们都对他自相矛盾的言论感到困惑。

近 baffle, bewilder, confuse, muddle, perplex, puzzle

反 clarify 使清醒

【考法2】 *vt.* 证明为假，证伪：to prove to be **false**

例 new discoveries that confounded much of what archaeologists thought they have known about the ancient Mayan civilization 一些新的发现颠覆了考古学家们长期以来对于古代玛雅文明的认识

近 belie, debunk, falsify, disprove, rebut, refute

反 confirm, validate, verify 证实，证明为真

派 confounding *adj.* 使人困惑的

congeal [kənˈdʒiːl]

【考法】 *v.* 凝固，固化：to change from a fluid to a **solid state** by or as if by cold

例 congealed blood 凝结的血液

近 coagulate, solidify, indurate, clot

反 melt, liquefy 熔化，液化

派 congealment *n.* 凝固

congenial [kənˈdʒiːniəl]

【考法】 *adj.* 和善的，友好的：having or marked by **agreement** in feeling or action

例 a congenial host who invited us for a feast 一位邀请我们美餐一顿的友好主人

近 agreeable, amicable, compatible, unanimous

反 discordant, incompatible 不和睦的，不和谐的

派 congeniality *n.* 友善

congruent [ˈkɑːŋgruənt]

【考法1】 *adj.* 和谐一致的：being **in agreement**, harmony, or correspondence; congruous

例 a theory congruent with the known facts 一个与已知事实相一致的理论

近 consonant, compatible, consistent, harmonious, accordant

反 disagreeable 不一致的；conflicting, incompatible 冲突的，不可协调的

派 congruity *n.* 和谐一致

【考法2】 *adj.* 全等的：**coinciding** exactly when superimposed

例 congruent triangles 全等三角形

近 identical, exact

反 disparate 迥异的

conjecture [kən'dʒektʃər]

【考法 1】 *n.* 推测，猜测：a **conclusion** deduced **by surmise** or guesswork
例 based on conjecture 基于推测
近 speculation, supposition, surmise, theory
反 fact 事实；axiom 公理

【考法 2】 *v.* (没有依据地)认为：to **form an opinion** from little or no evidence
例 conjecture the cause, of disease 揣测疾病的原因
近 assume, imagine, presume, speculate, suppose

connive [kə'naɪv]

【考法】 *vi.* 暗中合作，共谋：to **cooperate secretly** or have a secret understanding; collude
例 They connived to take over the throne . 他们密谋篡位。
近 conspire, intrigue, plot, collude, machinate, put up
派 conniver *n.* 共谋者

connoisseur [ˌkɑːnə'sɜːr]

【考法 1】 *n.* 鉴赏家(尤指艺术领域)：a person who enjoys **with discrimination** and **appreciation** of subtleties and details especially in matters of culture or art
例 a connoisseur of wine and cigarette 烟酒鉴赏的行家
近 aesthete, cognoscente

【考法 2】 *n.* 专家：a person with a **high level of knowledge** or skill in a field
例 works that are highly prized by connoisseurs of art glass 被玻璃艺术制品专家高度赞誉的作品
近 adept, artist, authority, maestro, master, maven, proficient, virtuoso
反 amateur, inexpert, nonexpert 业余者，非专业者；tyro, neophyte 新手

Unit 4

■ CONSCIENTIOUS	■ CONSENSUS	■ CONSEQUENCE	■ CONSERVATIVE	■ CONSERVATORY
■ CONSILIENCE	■ CONSIDERABLE	■ CONSOLE	■ CONSOLIDATE	■ CONSONANT

conscientious [ˌkɑːnʃi'enʃəs]

【考法 1】 *adj.* 仔细的，一丝不苟的：taking, showing, or **involving great care** and effort
例 a conscientious researcher 一丝不苟的研究者
近 careful, exact, heedful, meticulous, painstaking, scrupulous
反 careless, remiss 粗心大意的

【考法 2】 *adj.* 有良心的，正直的：**governed by** or conforming to the dictates of **conscience**
例 a conscientious police officer 一名有良心的警察
近 conscionable, ethical, honest, moral, upright, principled, scrupulous
反 unscrupulous 不正直的
派 conscience *n.* 良心

consensus [kən'sensəs]

【考法】 *n.* 一致同意：**general agreement**; unanimity
例 The board has finally reached a consensus . 董事会最终达成了一致。
近 accord, assent, agreement, harmony, unanimity, unison
反 disagreement 不同意见

consequence ['kɑːnsəkwens]

【考法 1】 *n.* 结果：something **produced by** a **cause** or necessarily following from a set of conditions
例 negative consequences of the war 战争带来的负面后果
近 aftermath, effect, outcome, result
反 source, origin, cause, antecedent 根源，原因

【考法 2】 *n.* 重要性，价值：significance; **importance**
例 a mistake of no consequence 不重要的错误
近 moment, magnitude, weight
反 triviality 琐碎的事
派 consequential *adj.* 重要的

conservative [kən'sɜːrvətɪv]

【考法 1】 *adj.* 守旧的，不愿改变的：favoring traditional views and values; tending to **oppose change**
例 a conservative political stance 一个守旧的政治立场
近 hidebound, reactionary, die-hard
反 radical, aggressive 激进的

【考法2】 *adj.* 不招摇的，低调的：**not** excessively **showy**
例 dressing in conservative outfits so as to make a good impression at job interviews 身着低调得体的套装以期待在面试时留下一个好印象
近 muted, repressed, low-key, understated, unpretentious
反 flamboyant, ostentatious, splashy 浮夸的，张扬的

conservatory [kən'sɜːrvətɔːri]
【考法1】 *n.* 温室：a **greenhouse** for growing or displaying plants
例 The college's conservatory is entirely devoted to cultivating and displaying orchids. 学校的温室几乎全部用于兰花的种植和观赏了。
近 greenhouse, hothouse
【考法2】 *n.* 艺术学院：a **school** specializing in one of the fine **arts**
例 an opera conservatory 歌剧学院

consilience [kən'sɪliəns]
【考法】 *n.* 融合：the **linking together** of principles from different disciplines especially when forming a comprehensive theory
例 The philosopher of science Whewell called this process of independent lines of inquiry converging together to a conclusion a "consilience of inductions". 科学哲学家修艾尔，就把这种经由不同研究途径得到万流归一的结论过程，称作"归纳的融通"。

considerable [kən'sɪdərəbl]
【考法1】 *adj.* (数量上)可观(而值得注意)的：sufficiently **large** in size, amount, or number to merit attention
例 a considerable amount of fortune 一笔可观的财富
近 extensive, substantial, large-scale
【考法2】 *adj.* 值得考虑的，重要的：worth consideration; **significant**
例 a considerable artist 一位举足轻重的艺术家
近 important, significant, consequential, momentous, weighty
反 trivial 不值一提的; insubstantial, negligible, nominal, trifling 不重要的，可忽视的

console [kən'soʊl]
【考法】 *vt.* 安慰，慰藉：to **alleviate** the grief, sense of loss, or trouble of; **comfort**
例 Only her children could console her when her husband died. 当她丈夫去世时，只有她的孩子们才能抚慰她的悲痛。
近 comfort, solace, soothe, calm
反 distress, torment, torture 使痛苦
派 consolation *n.* 安慰

consolidate [kən'sɑːlɪdeɪt]
【考法】 *vt.* 加固，使安全：to **make firm** or secure; strengthen
例 consolidate the defense line 加固防线
近 enhance, strengthen, fortify, reinforce
反 abate, attenuate, undermine, weaken 削弱
派 consolidation *n.* 合并; 加固

consonant ['kɑːnsənənt]
【考法】 *adj.* 和谐一致的：being **in agreement** or harmony; free from elements making for discord
例 His performance was consonant with his reputation. 他的表现与名气大不相符。
近 harmonious, compatible, congenial, consistent, congruous, correspondent
反 conflicting, dissonant, discrepant, inconsistent 不和谐的，不一致的
派 consonance *n.* 和谐，一致

Unit 5

■ CONSPICUOUS	■ CONSPIRE	■ CONSTITUTE	■ CONSTRAIN	■ CONSTRINGE
■ CONSTRUCT	■ CONSUMMATE	■ CONTAGIOUS	■ CONTAMINATE	■ CONTENT

conspicuous [kən'spɪkjuəs]
【考法】 *adj.* 显而易见的; 吸引人的：**obvious** to the eye or mind; attracting attention
例 a conspicuous change in her appearance 她外貌的明显改变
近 apparent, clear, distinct, evident, manifest, plain, patent, noticeable
反 hidden, concealed 隐藏的
派 conspicuousness *n.* 显然，明显性

conspire [kənˈspaɪər]

【考法】 v. 合谋，密谋：to **plan** together **secretly** to commit an illegal or wrongful act or accomplish a legal purpose through illegal action

例 A group of POWs conspired to abscond. 一批战俘密谋潜逃。

近 plot, contrive, connive, cogitate, intrigue, put up

派 conspiracy n. 密谋

constitute [ˈkɑːnstətuːt]

【考法 1】 vt. 指派，任命：to **appoint** to an office, function, or dignity

例 He was constituted manager. 他被任命为经理。

近 nominate, designate, authorize

反 discharge, dismiss 撤除职务；abdicate, resign 退位，辞职

【考法 2】 vt. 构成：**make up**, form, compose

例 Water constitutes the greater part of the human body. 水分构成人体的很大部分。

近 compose, comprise, form

派 constitution n. 构成；宪法；体格

constrain [kənˈstreɪn]

【考法】 vt. 限制：to force by imposed stricture, **restriction**, or limitation

例 Low temperature constrains the chemical reactivity. 低温降低了化学反应活性。

近 bridle, check, confine, imprison, restrain, trammel

反 release 释放

派 constrained adj. 受限的

constringe [kənˈstrɪndʒ]

【考法】 vt. 使紧缩：to make narrow or **draw together**

例 A styptic pencil stopped the bleeding by constringing the small blood vessels at the site of cut. 止血笔通过挤压伤口处的血管阻止了出血。

近 capsule, constrict, narrow, compress, squeeze, telescope

反 broaden, expand, outstretch 扩展，扩宽

construct [kənˈstrʌkt]

【考法 1】 vt. 建造，建立：to **form** by assembling or combining parts

例 construct a new library 建一座新图书馆

近 assemble, build, fabricate, make, produce, rear, set up

反 demolish, destroy, raze 摧毁

派 construction n. 建设，建造

【考法 2】 vt. 创造，想出：to **create** or think of by clever use of the **imagination**

例 He managed to construct a theory that fits all the facts. 他成功提出了一个与所有事实相吻合的理论。

近 contrive, devise, excogitate, fabricate, vamp up

consummate [ˈkɑːnsəmət]

【考法 1】 adj. 专业的，有造诣的：**extremely skilled** and accomplished

例 a consummate liar 一个老练的骗子

近 accomplished, finished, virtuosic, versed, veteran

反 amateur 业余的

【考法 2】 adj. 无纰漏的，完美的：complete in every detail; **perfect**

例 The difficult aria displayed her consummate skill. 高难度的咏叹调展示了她完美的技巧。

近 flawless, impeccable, perfect

反 defective 有漏洞的

contagious [kənˈteɪdʒəs]

【考法 1】 adj. 传染的：**communicable** by contact; catching

例 contagious diseases 传染病

近 infectious, pestilent, transmissible, epidemic

反 incommunicable 不传染的

派 contagiousness n. 可传染性

【考法 2】 adj. (情绪等)唤起共鸣的：**exciting a similar feeling** or reaction in others

例 The enthusiasm of the new club members was contagious. 新成员的热情具有很强的感染力。

近 catching, spreading

contaminate [kənˈtæmɪneɪt]

【考法】 *vt.* 污染，感染：to soil, **stain**, corrupt, or infect by contact or association

例 Bacteria contaminated the wound 细菌感染了伤口。

近 pollute, defile, taint, infect

反 purify, sanitize 净化

派 contamination *n.* 污染；contaminant *n.* 污染物

content

【考法1】 [kənˈtent] *vt.* 使满足：to **appease** the desires of

例 One glass of beer every day could content him. 每天一杯啤酒就能满足他。

近 satisfy, gratify, rejoice

反 discontent 不满足

派 contented *adj.* 满足的

【考法2】 *n.* 内容，内涵：the **idea that is conveyed** or intended to be conveyed to the mind by language, symbol, or action

例 The speech was filled with fancy words but devoid of any real content. 这篇演讲辞藻华丽，但是没什么实质性内容。

近 intention, purport, sense, significance

Unit 6

| ■ CONTENTIOUS | ■ CONTIGUOUS | ■ CONTORT | ■ CONTRACT | ■ CONTRAVENE |
| ■ CONTRITE | ■ CONTUMACIOUS | ■ CONUNDRUM | ■ CONVALESCE | ■ CLOAK |

contentious [kənˈtenʃəs]

【考法1】 *adj.* 引起争论的：likely to cause contention; **argumentative**

例 contentious contents in a movie 电影中引发争论的内容

近 controversial, disputatious, polemical

【考法2】 *adj.* 好争论的，好战的：exhibiting an perverse and wearisome **tendency** to **quarrels** and disputes

例 The Tartars were a contentious people who terrorized much of Asia and eastern Europe during the Middle Ages. 鞑靼是一个好斗的民族，他们在中世纪时期统治了亚洲和东欧的大片土地。

近 belligerent, bellicose, combative, truculent, litigious, pugnacious, scrappy

反 dovish, peace-loving 爱好和平的

contiguous [kənˈtɪɡjuəs]

【考法】 *adj.* 接壤的，相邻的：**sharing an edge** or boundary; touching

例 contiguous nations at war 交战中的邻国

近 adjacent, abutting, neighboring, juxtaposed, verging

反 apart, separate 分开的

派 contiguity *n.* 接壤

contort [kənˈtɔːrt]

【考法】 *vt.* 扭曲：to **twist**, wrench, or bend severely out of shape

例 pain that contorted their faces 痛苦使他们面部扭曲

近 deform, distort, warp, misshape

派 contortion *n.* 扭曲

contract

【考法1】 [ˈkɑːntrækt] *n.* 契约，合同：a **binding agreement** between two or more persons or parties, especially one that is written and enforceable by law

例 a billion-dollar contract from Department of Defense 来自国防部的巨额合同

近 agreement, compact, convention, treaty

【考法2】 [kənˈtrækt] *v.* 收缩：to **reduce** in **size** by drawing together; shrink

例 contract muscle 收缩肌肉

近 compress, condense, concentrate

反 expand 扩展；inflate 膨胀

【考法3】 *v.* 感染疾病：to **become affected** by a disease or disorder

例 He contracted a severe cold that later turned into pneumonia. 他染上了重感冒，最终发展成为肺炎。

近 catch, get, sicken

反 heal 痊愈

contravene [ˌkɑːntrəˈviːn]

【考法】 *vt.* 违反，反对: to **violate**, to **oppose** in argument: contradict

例 contravene the proposal with no reservation 毫无保留地反对这一提案

近 breach, infringe, transgress, fracture, deny, contradict, gainsay, reject

反 uphold, support, buttress 支持; comply, conform, observe 顺从

派 contravention *n.* 反对; 违反，触犯

contrite [kənˈtraɪt]

【考法】 *adj.* （因为有罪孽或过错而感到）后悔悲痛的: feeling or **showing** sorrow and **remorse** for a sin or shortcoming

例 too late to feel contrite 现在后悔为时已晚

近 compunctious, regrettable, remorseful, apologetic, penitent, repentant, rueful

反 impenitent, unrepentant 不知悔改的

contumacious [ˌkɑːntuˈmeɪʃəs]

【考法】 *adj.* 不服从的，倔强的: stubbornly **disobedient**; rebellious

例 Contumacious insurgents refuse to talk. 不愿服从命令的叛军拒绝对话。

近 balky, contumacious, defiant, insubordinate, intractable, obstreperous, rebellious, recalcitrant, refractory, restive, ungovernable, unruly, untoward, wayward, willful

反 obedient, docile, ruly 顺从的

派 contumacy *n.* 不服从，反抗

conundrum [kəˈnʌndrəm]

【考法】 *n.* 无法解决的问题，迷: a paradoxical, **insoluble**, or difficult problem; a **dilemma**

例 a difficult conundrum even for the experts 一道即便是专家也束手无策的难题

近 enigma, mystery, puzzlement, riddle, secret

convalesce [ˌkɑːnvəˈles]

【考法】 *vi.* 渐渐康复，渐愈: to **recover** health and strength **gradually** after sickness or weakness

例 the time needed to convalesce after an operation 手术后需要用来康复的时间

近 heal, recover, recuperate, recoup, snap back

反 aggravate, deteriorate, intensify 恶化，加剧

cloak [kloʊk]

【考法】 *vt.* 遮掩，隐藏: to change the dress or looks of so as to **conceal true identity**

例 cloak his evil purpose under sweet words 用甜言蜜语掩盖邪恶目的

近 belie, camouflage, conceal, cover, curtain, disguise, mask, obscure, occult, screen, sham, shroud, suppress, veil

反 debunk, disclose, display, divulge, expose, reveal, show, uncloak, uncover, unmask, unveil 揭露，揭穿

Unit 7

■ CONVENTION	■ CONVERGE	■ CONVERSANT	■ CONVERT	■ CONSORT
■ CAGEY	■ CONVICTION	■ CONVOKE	■ CONVOLUTED	■ CONVULSION

convention [kənˈvenʃn]

【考法 1】 *n.* 常规，习俗: general **agreement** on or **acceptance** of certain practices or attitudes

例 By convention, north is at the top of most maps. 按照常规，北方在大多数地图的上部。

近 custom, ritual, manner

反 deviation 背离（习俗）

派 conventional *adj.* 传统习俗上的

【考法 2】 *n.* 大会，集会: a **coming together** of a number of persons for a specified purpose

例 attend a convention of mathematicians in California 参加加州的一次数学家集会

近 assembly, congress, council, gathering

converge [kənˈvɜːrdʒ]

【考法】 *v.* 汇集，交汇于一点: tending to **move toward one** point or one another

例 The main streets converge on a central square. 众主干道在中央广场交汇。

近 meet, focus, concentrate

反 diverge, deviate, digress 分离，分岔

派 convergent *adj.* 汇集的; convergence *n.* 汇集

conversant [kənˈvɜːrsnt]

【考法】 *adj.* 熟悉的：having frequent or **familiar** association

例 conversant with the accounting system 熟悉会计系统

近 acquaint, aware, familiar, informed, versed

反 ignorant, unfamiliar 无知的，不熟悉的

派 conversance *n.* 熟知，造诣

convert [kənˈvɜːrt]

【考法】 *vt.* 改变，转化：to **alter** the physical or chemical nature or properties of especially in manufacturing

例 convert water into ice 将水转化成冰

近 alter, change, transform, transfigure

派 converter *n.* 转换器；convertible *adj.* 可转变的 *n.* 敞篷跑车

consort [kənˈsɔːrt]

【考法】 *v.* 结交：to come or **be together as friends**

例 One should consort with those one can learn from. 择其善者而从之。

近 company, consociate, associate, hook up

cagey [ˈkeɪdʒi]

【考法】 *adj.* 不乐意说话的：**not willing to say** everything that you know about something

例 He is cagey about what he was paid for the business. 他遮遮掩掩的，不愿说出在这桩生意中挣了多少。

近 hesitant, disinclined, indisposed, reluctant, reticent

反 disposed, inclined 乐意的

conviction [kənˈvɪkʃn]

【考法 1】 *n.* 深信，确信：the state of **being convinced**

例 a warrior of strong conviction 一名信念坚定的战士

近 assurance, certainty, certitude

反 dubiety, incredulity 怀疑；uncertainty, incertitude 不确定性

【考法 2】 *n.* 证明有罪：state of being found or **proved guilty**

例 evidence that led to the suspect's conviction 证明嫌疑犯有罪的证据

近 sentence

反 acquittal 宣告无罪

派 convict *v.* 宣判有罪

convoke [kənˈvoʊk]

【考法】 *v.* 召集开会：to **bring together** by or as if by summons

例 convoke Parliament 召开国会

近 assemble, convene, summon, muster

反 adjourn 休会

convoluted [ˈkɑːnvəluːtɪd]

【考法】 *adj.* 复杂的，费解的：**complicated**; intricate

例 a convoluted way of describing a simple mechanism 用令人费解的方法解释一个简单的原理

近 complex, knotty, involved, sophisticated, twisted, tangled, labyrinthine

反 straightforward 直截了当的

convulsion [kənˈvʌlʃn]

【考法】 *n.* 骚乱：a violent **disturbance**

例 a regime in convulsion 动荡中的政权

近 commotion, ferment, tumult, upheaval, clamor, tempest, uproar

反 serenity, tranquility 宁静

派 convulse *v.* 剧烈震动；痉挛

Unit 8

■ COOP	■ COPIOUS	■ COQUETTE	■ COUNTERVAIL	■ CORNUCOPIA
■ CORONATION	■ CORPOREAL	■ CORROBORATE	■ CORROSIVE	■ CORRUGATED

coop [kuːp]

【考法】 *vt.* 监禁，困于…之中：to **confine** in a restricted and often crowded area

例 Those restless kids were cooped up in the house on a rainy. 雨天那些好动的孩子们被困在房子里。

近 box, cage, corral, encage, enclose, envelop, fence, hedge, immure, include, pen, wall

反 free, liberate, release 释放

copious [ˈkoʊpiəs]

【考法】 *adj.* 丰富的，大量的：large in quantity; **abundant**

例 a copious harvest 大丰收

近 plentiful, abundant, ample, gushing

反 sparse, dearth, scant 稀少的，缺乏的

---

coquette [koʊˈket]

【考法】 *v.* 调情；不认真对待：to flirt; to deal with something **playfully** rather than seriously

例 He is interested only in coquetting with her, not marrying her. 他只想与她保持暧昧关系，而不结婚。

近 trifle, dally, flirt, mess around

派 coquet *v.* 不认真对待，调情；coquettish *adj.* 调情的

---

countervail [ˈkaʊntərveɪl]

【考法】 *vt.* 抗衡，抵消：to **exert force against**; counteract

例 The extent to which these various unknown factors countervail each other remains uncertain. 这些未知因素彼此之间的抗衡程度仍无法确定。

近 compensate, counteract, counterbalance, counterpoise, neutralize, offset

派 countervailing *adj.* 抗衡的，抵消的

---

cornucopia [ˌkɔːrnjuˈkoʊpiə]

【考法】 *n.* 大量：an **overflowing** store; an abundance

例 a cornucopia of employment opportunities 大量的就业机会

近 plentitude, plethora, wealth, profusion, affluence

反 lack, pittance, deficiency 缺乏，少量

---

coronation [ˌkɔːrəˈneɪʃn]

【考法】 *n.* 加冕，加冕礼：the act or ceremony of **crowning** a sovereign or the sovereign's consort

例 Two different musical pieces by Mozart（a piano concerto and a mass）are both titled "Coronation". 莫扎特两部不同的音乐作品(一部钢琴协奏曲和一部弥撒)都被称作"加冕"。

近 enthronement, crowning

反 abdication 退位

派 coronate *v.* 加冕

---

corporeal [kɔːrˈpɔːriəl]

【考法 1】 *adj.* 肉体的：**not spiritual**

例 corporeal suffering 肉体上的折磨

近 bodily, carnal, corporal, somatic, physical, fleshly

反 spiritual 精神上的

【考法 2】 *adj.* 有形的，实体的：**not immaterial** or intangible

近 material, physical, substantial, sensible, tangible

反 intangible, disembodied, immaterial 无形的，无实体的

---

corroborate [kəˈrɑːbəreɪt]

【考法 1】 *vt.* 用证据或权威证实：to **support with evidence** or authority; make more certain

例 new evidence to corroborate the defendant's story 能证实被告的故事的新证据

近 confirm, authenticate, justify, substantiate, validate, verify

反 controvert, contradict, deny 反驳，否认

【考法 2】 *vt.* 为…提供证据，支持：to **provide evidence** or information for（as a claim or idea）

例 My personal experience does not corroborate your faith in the essential goodness of people. 我的经历可不赞同你关于"人性本善"的信念。

近 back, bolster, buttress, reinforce, support

派 corroboration *n.* 证实

---

corrosive [kəˈroʊsɪv]

【考法 1】 *adj.* 腐蚀性的：tending to **destroy slowly** by chemical action

例 Concentrated sulfur acid is highly corrosive. 浓硫酸有极强的腐蚀性。

近 erosive, caustic

反 noncorrosive 无腐蚀性的

派 corrosion *n.* 侵蚀

【考法 2】 *adj.* 讽刺性的：bitingly **sarcastic**

例 corrosive satire 讽刺性的作品

近 sarcastic, barbed, acerbic, satiric, acrid, mordant, tart

corrugated ['kɔːrəgeɪtɪd]

【考法】 *adj.* 褶皱的：shaped into a series of regular **folds** that look like waves
例　corrugated paper 褶皱的纸
近　wrinkled, creased, folded
反　smooth 光滑的
派　corrugation *n.* 褶皱，折痕

Unit 9

■ COSMOPOLITAN	■ COSSET	■ COUNTENANCE	■ COUNTERFEIT	■ COUNTERMAND
■ COURT	■ COVERT	■ COVETOUS	■ COW	■ COWARDICE

cosmopolitan [ˌkɑːzmə'pɑːlɪtən]

【考法】 *adj.* 有世界性眼光的，包容的：having **worldwide** rather than limited or provincial scope or bearing
例　a cosmopolitan traveler 云游四海的旅行者
近　universal, catholic, global, worldwide
反　insular, provincial 狭隘的
派　cosmopolitism *n.* 世界主义，天下主义

cosset ['kɑːsɪt]

【考法】 *vt.* 宠爱：to treat as a pet; **pamper**
近　caress, cuddle, dote, pet, mollycoddle, coddle
反　slight 怠慢；abuse 虐待
派　cosseted *adj.* 被宠坏的

countenance ['kaʊntənəns]

【考法1】 *vt.* 容忍：to **put up with** (something painful or difficult)
例　The college administration will not countenance cheating. 该大学管理部门决不容忍作弊的存在。
近　abide, endure, stand, stomach, wear
【考法2】 *vt.* 赞成，推崇：to have a **favorable opinion** of
例　I don't countenance such behavior in children of any age. 对于任何年龄的孩子，我都不推崇那种行为。
近　accept, favor, subscribe
反　disapprove, frown 反对

counterfeit ['kaʊntərfɪt]

【考法1】 *adj.* 仿制的，假冒的：made in **imitation** of something else with intent to deceive
例　counterfeit money 假币
近　forged, bogus, spurious, pseudo, feigned, artificial, phony
反　authentic, genuine 真实的
【考法2】 *vt.* 仿制：to make a **fraudulent replica** of
例　counterfeit the signature 仿造签名
近　copy, forge, imitate, simulate, mimic

countermand ['kaʊntərmænd]

【考法】 *vt.* 取消，撤销：to **revoke** (a command) by a contrary order
例　countermand an order 撤销命令
近　annul, repeal, rescind, revoke, cancel
反　approve, permit, sanction 批准

court [kɔːrt]

【考法】 *vt./n.* 追求，献殷勤：to **seek** the **affections** of
例　court the young lady by bring her flowers every day 通过每天送花追求那个年轻女孩
近　woo, pursue, invite
反　spurn, snub 摒弃，怠慢
派　courteous *adj.* 殷勤的；彬彬有礼的

covert ['koʊvɜːrt]

【考法】 *adj.* 隐蔽的，秘密的：**not** openly **shown**, engaged in, or avowed
例　covert alliance 秘密联盟
近　cloistered, hidden, secret, sheltered
反　open, overt, aboveboard 公开的

covetous ['kʌvətəs]

【考法】 *adj.* 贪婪的，渴求财富的：marked by **inordinate desire** for wealth or possessions or for another's possessions

例 cast covetous eyes on their neighbors' fields 对他邻居的土地垂涎

近 acquisitive, avaricious, avid, rapacious, grasping

反 easily-satiated 容易满足的；unenvious 不艳羡的

派 covet *v.* 觊觎，贪婪

cow [kaʊ]

【考法】 *vt.* 恐吓，威胁：to **frighten** with threats or a show of force

例 cow sb. into doing sth 威胁某人做某事

近 intimidate, browbeat, bully, hector, awe

反 embolden, encourage, inspirit 鼓励

派 cowed *adj.* 被吓倒的

cowardice ['kaʊərdɪs]

【考法】 *n.* 懦弱，不坚定：**lack** of **courage** or resolution

例 cowardice in the face of danger 面对危险时的懦弱

近 cravenness, dastardliness, gutlessness, poltroonery, pusillanimity, spinelessness

反 courage, guts, pluck, intrepidness, nerve, stoutness, valiance, valor 勇气

派 coward *n.* 懦夫

Unit 10

■ COWER	■ COZEN	■ CRAMPED	■ CRASS	■ CRAVE
■ CRAVEN	■ CONTINGENCY	■ CREDENCE	■ CREDULOUS	■ CATERWAUL

cower ['kaʊər]

【考法】 *vi.* 畏缩：to **cringe** in fear

例 The dog cowered under the table. 狗吓得蜷缩在桌子下面。

近 fawn, flinch, grovel, quail, recoil, wince

cozen ['kʌzn]

【考法】 *v.* 诱骗：to **mislead** by means of a petty trick or fraud; deceive

例 The salesman cozened the old lady into buying his goods. 推销员诱使老太太买下了他的东西。

近 bamboozle, dupe, cheat, deceive, beguile, delude, take in

cramped [kræmpt]

【考法】 *n.* 狭小的，狭窄的：uncomfortably **small** or restricted

例 a cramped cubbyhole in an office 办公室里狭小的隔间

近 confined, limited, restrained

反 commodious, spacious 宽敞的

派 cramp *n.* 狭窄

crass [kræs]

【考法】 *adj.* 粗俗的，愚钝的：so crude and **unrefined** as to be in discrimination and sensibility

例 crass receptionist 粗俗的招待员

近 coarse, crude, rude, incult, uncouth, vulgar

反 civilized, polished, refined, urbane, genteel 有教养的

crave [kreɪv]

【考法】 *vt.* 热望：to have an **intense desire** for

例 crave alcohols and cigarettes 渴望烟酒

近 need, yearn, desire, pine, thirst, itch, long, yen

反 spurn 摒弃

派 craving *n.* 迫切的渴望

craven ['kreɪvn]

【考法】 *adj.* 非常懦弱的，因胆小而遭人鄙视的：**lacking** the least bit of **courage**; contemptibly fainthearted

例 a craven deserter 一个懦弱的逃兵

近 cowardly, gutless, pusillanimous, spineless

反 dauntless, fearless, gallant, gutsy, intrepid, stalwart, stout, stouthearted, valiant, valorous 勇敢的

contingency	[kənˈtɪndʒənsi]
【考法】	*n.* 可能发生的事：something (such as an emergency) that **might happen**
例	We should be prepared for any contingency. 我们应该对任何应急情况有所准备。
近	case, contingent, eventuality, possibility

credence	[ˈkriːdns]
【考法】	*n.* 坚信：**firm belief** in the integrity, ability, effectiveness, or genuineness of someone or something
例	give credence to gossip 相信绯闻
近	belief, credit, faith, trust, reliance
反	doubt, skepticism 怀疑

credulous	[ˈkredʒələs]
【考法】	*adj.* 轻信的，易受骗的：disposed to believe too readily; **gullible**
例	accused of swindling credulous investors 被控欺骗轻信的投资者
近	believing, unwary, gullible, naïve, unsuspecting
反	disbelieving, skeptical 怀疑的
派	credulity *n.* 轻信

caterwaul	[ˈkætərwɔːl]
【考法】	*v.* 嚎叫：to make a very loud and **unpleasant sound**
例	shrieking and caterwauling in mock distress 无助痛苦中的尖嚎
近	yowl, shriek, howl, scream, shrill, yelp

Every day I remind myself that my inner and outer life are based on the labors of other men, living and dead, and that I must exert myself in order to give in the same measure as I have received and am still receiving.

每天我都提醒着自己：我的精神生活和物质生活都是以别人的劳动为基础的，我必须尽力以同样的分量来报偿我所获得的和至今仍在接受着的东西。

———美国科学家 爱因斯坦（Albert Einstein, American scientist）

List 6

"Just do it. — It pays."

（武阳乐，2007 年 10 月，Verbal 700, Quantitative 800, AW 5.0, 录取院校：Princeton 物理系）

Unit 1

■ CREEP	■ CRESCENDO	■ CREST	■ CRESTFALLEN	■ CRONYISM
■ CROOK	■ CROON	■ CULMINATE	■ CRUCIAL	■ CRUMPLE

creep ［kriːp］
【考法】 *vi./n.* 缓慢地行进：to go very **slowly**
例 creep through the crowd 在人潮中缓慢前行
近 drag, loiter, tarry
反 scurry, run 快步走，跑

crescendo ［krəˈʃendoʊ］
【考法】 *n.* (渐强之后到达的)顶峰：the **peak** of a gradual increase
例 Complaints about stifling smog conditions reach a crescendo. 对让人窒息的烟雾的抱怨到达了顶峰。
近 apex, acme, apogee, climax, crest, peak, pinnacle, summit, zenith
反 nadir 最低点

crest ［krest］
【考法】 *n.* 顶部，浪尖，山顶：the **top**, as of a hill or wave
例 at the crest of her career 在她事业顶峰
近 apex, acme, apogee, climax, crescendo, peak, pinnacle, summit, zenith
反 bottom 底部

crestfallen ［ˈkrestfɔːlən］
【考法】 *adj.* 垂头丧气的，沮丧的：dispirited and **depressed**; dejected
例 be crestfallen at the failure 因失败而垂头丧气
近 downcast, dispirited, low, gloomy, melancholic, sorrowful, woeful
反 elated, buoyant, excited, exhilarated, exultant 激动的，欢悦的

cronyism ［ˈkroʊniɪzəm］
【考法】 *n.* 任人唯亲，对好朋友的偏袒：**favoritism** shown to old **friends** without regard for their qualifications
例 officials practicing cronyism 任人唯亲的官员
近 favoritism

crook ［krʊk］
【考法】 *vt.* 使弯曲：to cause to turn **away from a straight line**
例 Crook your finger to pull the trigger. 弯曲你的手指来扣动扳机。
近 arch, bow, curve, hook, swerve
反 straighten, unbend, uncurl 拉直，伸直

croon ［kruːn］
【考法】 *v.* 低声歌唱或说话：to sing or speak in a gentle **murmuring** manner
例 croon mellow tunes 低声唱柔和的调子
近 whisper, grumble, mumble, murmur
反 shout, yell 大声喊叫

culminate ［ˈkʌlmɪneɪt］
【考法】 *v.* 达到高潮：to bring to a **triumphant conclusion**
例 The Christmas party culminated in the distribution of presents. 圣诞晚会在分发礼物时达到最高潮。
近 cap, climax, crown

crucial ［ˈkruːʃl］
【考法】 *adj.* 非常重要的，决定性的：**extremely significant** or important
例 a crucial step in his professional career 他职业生活中具有决定性的一步
近 critical, decisive, key, pivotal, vital
反 inconsequential, insignificant, trivial 不重要的

crumple	[ˈkrʌmpl]
【考法】	*v.* 弄皱：to press, **bend**, or crush out of shape
例	crumple a piece of paper 弄皱一张纸
近	rumple, crimple, crease, fold, wrinkle
反	smooth 使平滑

Unit 2

crutch	[krʌtʃ]
【考法】	*n./v.* 支撑，支柱：something that **supports** or sustains
例	a crutch for local economy 当地的经济支柱
近	brace, buttress, column, stay, support, underpinning, underpropping

crux	[krʌks]
【考法】	*n.* 中心，关键点：the basic, central, or **critical point** or feature
例	the crux of the problem 问题的核心所在
近	core, substance, kernel, gist, pivot
反	trifle, triviality 无价值之物

cryptic	[ˈkrɪptɪk]
【考法 1】	*adj.* 秘密的：**secret** or occult
例	cryptic message 秘密的信息
近	covert, furtive, secret, stealthy
反	public, open 公开的
【考法 2】	*adj.* 难以理解的：being **beyond one's powers to know**, understand, or explain
例	They were puzzled by the cryptic e-mail message left on his computer. 他们被他电脑里让人费解的电子邮件所迷惑。
近	arcane, enigmatic, impenetrable, inscrutable, mystic, occult, uncanny
反	comprehensible, understandable 可以理解的

culpable	[ˈkʌlpəbl]
【考法】	*adj.* 该受谴责的，有罪的：**deserving** of **blame** or censure as being wrong, evil, improper, or injurious
例	culpable behaviors 该受谴责的行为
近	blameworthy, censurable, guilty, reprehensible, sinful, reproachable
反	inculpable, innocent 无罪的
派	culpability *n.* 有罪

cultivate	[ˈkʌltɪveɪt]
【考法 1】	*vt.* 提升，加强：to **improve** by labor, care, or study
例	cultivate the mind 开化心智
近	educate, instruct, illuminate, nurse
反	degrade, deteriorate, impair 损坏，降低品质
【考法 2】	*vt.* 种植，培养：to **promote** the **growth** of（a biological culture）
例	cultivate vegetables 种植蔬菜
近	grow, breed, produce, raise, develop, nurture
反	balk, frustrate, thwart 阻碍
派	cultivation *n.* 栽培

cumbersome	[ˈkʌmbərsəm]
【考法】	*adj.* 笨重的，难处理的：**difficult to handle** because of weight or bulk
例	a cumbersome piece of machinery 一件笨重的机器
近	unhandy, ponderous, heavy, unwieldy, onerous, thorny
反	light, weightless 轻的；handy 容易处理的

cunning	[ˈkʌnɪŋ]
【考法】	*adj.* 狡猾的：marked by or given to **artful** subtlety and **deceptiveness**
例	cunning tactics 狡猾的战术
近	artful, crafty, devious, foxy, sly, tricky, wily
反	artless, naïve, unsophisticated 天真无邪的

curmudgeon [kɜːr'mʌdʒən]
【考法】 *n.* 脾气坏的、爱抱怨的人：an **irritable and complaining** person
例 a terrible old curmudgeon 一个坏脾气老头
近 crosspatch, fusser, griper, grouser, growler, grumbler, whiner
反 agreeable person 令人愉快的人

cursory ['kɜːrsəri]
【考法】 *adj.* 匆忙的，不注意细节的：acting or done with **excessive or careless speed**
例 a cursory glance at the headline 匆匆地瞥了一眼标题
近 headlong, overhasty, pell-mell, precipitate, precipitous, rash
反 fastidious, thorough, deliberate, unhurried, unrushed 极关注细节的，考虑周到的，不匆忙的

curt [kɜːrt]
【考法】 *adj.* 言词简略的，直接（以至显得粗鲁）的：being or characterized by **direct, brief, and potentially rude** speech or manner
例 his curt reply 他简略而略显粗鲁的回答
近 abrupt, bluff, brusque, downright, unceremonious
反 circuitous, mealymouthed 迂回的

Unit 3

■ CURTAIL	■ CYNIC	■ DABBLE	■ DAFT	■ DAZZLING
■ DALLY	■ DAMPER	■ DANDY	■ DANK	■ DAPPER

curtail [kɜːr'teɪl]
【考法】 *vt.* 缩短，削减：to make **less in extent or duration**
例 curtail your holiday 缩短你的假期
近 abbreviate, abridge, syncopate, truncate, cut back
反 elongate, protract, prolong, extend, lengthen 延长

cynic ['sɪnɪk]
【考法】 *n.* 反人类的喷子：a person who believes all people are motivated by **selfishness**
例 A cynic might think that the governor visited the hospital just to gain votes. 一个反人类的喷子认为州长去医院探视仅仅是为了拉票。
近 misanthrope, naysayer, pessimist

dabble ['dæbl]
【考法】 *vi.* 涉猎，对…浅尝辄止：to work or involve oneself **superficially** or intermittently especially in a secondary interest
例 dabble in arts 对艺术稍有涉猎
反 dedicate, specialize 投入，专门研究
派 dabbler *n.* 涉猎者，浅尝辄止者：one not deeply engaged in or concerned with something
例 He's not a dedicated musician, just a dabbler. 他并不是专门的音乐家，只不过是个业余爱好者。
反 specialist 专家

daft [dæft]
【考法】 *adj.* 不明智的：showing or marked by a **lack of good sense or judgment**
例 This is a daft plan, doomed to wretched failure and merciless ridicule. 这是一个不明智的决定，最终难逃悲催的结局和被无情嘲讽的下场。
近 fatuous, featherheaded, nonsensical, preposterous, senseless
反 judicious, prudent, sagacious, sapient, wise 明智的

dazzling ['dæzlɪŋ]
【考法】 *adj.* 炫目的，耀眼的：giving off or **reflecting much light**
例 The dazzling light from the digital device dizzied me. 来自数字化的设备的耀眼的光使我头昏。
近 beaming, candescent, bright, effulgent, glowing, incandescent, luminous, refulgent, shining
反 dim, dull, lackluster, unbright, unbrilliant 黯淡无光的

dally ['dæli]
【考法】 *vi.* 虚度时光：to spend time **doing nothing**
例 I kept dallying at my desk until I couldn't put off doing my work any longer. 我一直浪费时间直到作业不能再拖了。
近 dawdle, loll, lounge, hang around

damper	[ˈdæmpər]
【考法】	*n.* 抑制因素：one that deadens, **restrains**, or **depresses**
例	Rain put a damper on our picnic plans. 下雨打破了我们的野餐计划。
反	ameliorator 促进物

dandy	[ˈdændi]
【考法】	*n.* 纨绔子弟，爱打扮的人：a man who gives exaggerated attention to personal **appearance**
例	a frivolous dandy 一个轻浮的纨绔子弟
近	fop, gallant

dank	[dæŋk]
【考法】	*adj.* 阴湿的：slightly or moderately **wet**
例	Vegetables tended to go bad quickly in the dank cellar. 蔬菜在潮湿的地下室很容易变坏。
近	damp, wettish

dapper	[ˈdæpər]
【考法】	*adj.* 衣冠整洁的：being **strikingly neat and trim** in style or appearance
例	The students all looked very dapper in their uniforms. 学生们穿着校服显得非常整洁。
近	natty, sharp, snappy, spruce
反	frowsy, unkempt, slovenly 不整洁的

Unit 4

■ DAPPLED	■ DAREDEVIL	■ DART	■ DAUNT	■ DAWDLE
■ DEADPAN	■ DEARTH	■ DEBACLE	■ DEBARK	■ DEBASE

dappled	[ˈdæpld]
【考法】	*adj.* 有斑点的，花的：**marked with small spots** or contrasting with the background; **mottled, spotted**
例	a dappled fawn 一只小花鹿
近	blotchy, mottled, specked, piebald, splotched, stippled, spotted
反	unspotted 没有斑点的

daredevil	[ˈderdevl]
【考法】	*adj./n.* 大胆鲁莽的(人)：**foolishly** adventurous or bold
例	a daredevil test pilot 无畏的试飞员
近	audacious, brash, madcap, overbold, reckless, temerarious
反	circumspect, guarded, heedful, prudent, wary 小心谨慎的

dart	[dɑːrt]
【考法 1】	*vi.* 突然移动，猛冲，狂奔：to move **suddenly** and rapidly
例	The dog darted across the street. 狗飞奔过马路。
近	flitter, flutter
【考法 2】	*n.* 公开侮辱：an act or expression showing scorn and usually **intended to hurt another's feelings**
例	The darts flew fast and furiously when the two former lovers bumped into each other at the party. 旧情人在party 上偶遇，立马开始激烈的人身攻击。
近	affront, barb, offense, sarcasm, slight, slur

daunt	[dɔːnt]
【考法】	*vt.* 使胆怯，吓倒：**to lessen the courage** or confidence of
例	She was not at all daunted by the size of the problem. 她根本没有被问题的大小给吓倒。
近	demoralize, dishearten, dismay, dispirit, frustrate, unnerve
反	embolden, make resolute, hearten 使大胆，鼓舞
派	dauntless, undaunted *adj.* 无畏的，大胆的
反	pusillanimous, trepid, craven, easily discouraged, meek, timorous 胆怯的

dawdle	[ˈdɔːdl]
【考法】	*v.* 拖拖拉拉：to move or act **slowly**
例	If you continue to dawdle, we'll be late for sure. 你要是再拖拉，我们铁定要迟到了。
近	crawl, creep, dally, dillydally, lag, linger, loiter, tarry
反	bolt, hasten, course, dash, speed, scurry 匆忙，疾行

deadpan [ˈdedpæn]
【考法】 *n.* 无趣的，无生气的，不活泼的：marked by **impassively** matter-of-fact, as in style, behavior, or expression
例 a deadpan comedy 一个没有笑点的喜剧
近 expressionless, impassive, inexpressive, stolid, vacant
反 demonstrative, expressive 有表现力的

dearth [dɜːrθ]
【考法】 *n.* 供应不足：an **inadequate** supply
例 a dearth of evidence 证据不足
近 want, deficit, insufficiency, paucity, pinch, scantiness, scarcity, undersupply
反 plethora, spate, copiousness, abundance, adequacy, amplitude, opulence 过剩，丰富

debacle [deɪˈbɑːkl]
【考法】 *n.* 溃败：a **complete failure**; fiasco
例 the debacle of the war 战争的彻底失败
近 bummer, calamity, catastrophe, cataclysm, fiasco, fizzle, flop, washout
反 complete success, éclat, blockbuster 大成功

debark [diˈbɑːrk]
【考法】 *v.* (使)下船(飞机、车等)；卸(客、货)：to **unload**, as **from a ship or an airplane**; disembark
例 The seasick passengers debarked as soon as the ship dropped anchor. 晕船的乘客等到轮船一靠岸抛锚就立即下船。
近 land
反 embark 上船，装货

debase [dɪˈbeɪs]
【考法】 *v.* 贬低，贬损：to reduce to a **lower standing** in one's own eyes or in others' eyes
例 Our failure to win a single game completely debased our image. 我们一场未胜的战绩彻底让我们的形象一落千丈。
近 abase, debauch, degrade, demean, demoralize, deprave, deteriorate, profane, subvert, vitiate
反 aggrandize, canonize, deify, elevate, exalt, ennoble 使神圣

Unit 5

| ■ DEBILITATE | ■ DEBRIS | ■ DEBUNK | ■ DEBUT | DECADENCE |
| ■ DETEST | ■ DECIPHER | ■ DECODE | ■ DECOROUS | DECREPIT |

debilitate [dɪˈbɪliteɪt]
【考法】 *vt.* 使衰弱：to **impair** the **strength** of; enfeeble
例 The virus debilitates the body's immune system. 病毒削弱了免疫系统。
近 devitalize, enervate, enfeeble, prostrate, sap
反 invigorate, fortify, strengthen, beef up 使有活力，加强

debris [dəˈbriː]
【考法】 *n.* 废墟：discarded or useless material
例 the unsightly debris left after mining operations had ceased 采煤工程中止后留下来的难看的废墟
近 dross, dust, litter, offal, refuse, effluvium, junk

debunk [ˌdiːˈbʌŋk]
【考法】 *vt.* 揭穿…的真面目：to reveal the **true nature** of
例 debunk a supposed miracle drug 揭穿所谓的灵丹妙药的真面目
近 uncloak, uncover, undress, unmask, show up
反 camouflage, cloak, disguise, mask 继续伪装，掩盖

debut [deɪˈbjuː]
【考法】 *n.* 初次登台，出道：a **first** public **appearance**
例 made her single debut 完成了她的处女秀
反 farewell performance 告别演出

decadence [ˈdekədəns]
【考法】 *n.* 衰落，颓废：a process, condition, or period of **deterioration** or **decline**; a change to a lower state or level
例 The book condemns the decadence of modern society. 该书批判了现代社会的堕落。
近 degeneracy, degeneration, degradation, deterioration, downfall, eclipse
反 ascent, rise, upswing 提高，提升

detest [dɪˈtest]

【考法】 *v.* 厌恶：to **dislike** (someone or something) very strongly

例 With wisdom and love, the human race as a whole will detest war and embrace peace . 有了智慧和爱，全体人类定当厌恶战争、拥抱和平。

近 abhor, abominate, detest, dislike, hate, loathe

派 detestation *n.* 厌恶

decipher [dɪˈsaɪfər]

【考法1】 *vt.* 破译：to read or **interpret** (ambiguous, obscure, or illegible matter)

例 We deciphered the hidden message to find out when we were supposed to meet. 通过破解暗语，我们得知何时要碰头。

近 break, crack, decrypt, decode

反 cipher, encipher, encode, encrypt 加密

【考法2】 *vt.* 对…有清晰想法，理解，解读：to have a **clear idea** of

例 a convoluted thriller, the plot of which I was never able to actually decipher 一部错综复杂的恐怖电影，情节我一直没有理解

近 apprehend, perceive, recognize, seize, sense, make out

decode [ˌdiːˈkoʊd]

【考法1】 *vt.* 解码：to **change** (as a secret message) from code **into ordinary language**

例 The agents worked into the night to decode the intercepted message from the enemy spy . 情报人员夜以继日地破解从敌方间谍拦截的信息。

近 break, crack, decipher, decrypt

【考法2】 *vt.* 对…有清晰想法，理解，解读：to have a **clear idea** of

例 a complex literary text difficult for many people to decode 一个深奥的文学文本，许多人都无法理解

近 apprehend, perceive, recognize, seize, sense, make out

decorous [ˈdekərəs]

【考法】 *adj.* 得体端正的：following the established traditions of **refined society and good taste**

例 We were asked to be on our most decorous behavior at the formal event. 我们被要求以最端庄得体的行为出席正式活动。

近 decent, proper, respectable, seemly

反 improper, inappropriate, indecent, indecorous, indelicate, unseemly 不得体的

派 decorum *n.* 礼仪，得体

decrepit [dɪˈkrepɪt]

【考法】 *adj.* 虚弱的，衰老的，破旧的：**weakened**, worn out, impaired, or broken down by old age, illness

例 a decrepit old man 一个虚弱的老年人

反 vigorous, sturdy, sound, robust, hale 健壮的

Unit 6

■ DEFAULT	■ DEFER	■ DOCUMENT	■ DEFICIENCY	■ DEVIOUS
■ DEFT	■ DEFUSE	■ DEFY	■ DEHYDRATE	■ DEIFY

default [dɪˈfɔːlt]

【考法】 *n.* 不履行义务，玩忽职守：the **nonperformance** of an assigned or expected action

例 default on a loan 拖欠贷款

近 delinquency, dereliction, misprision, nonfeasance, oversight

defer [dɪˈfɜːr]

【考法1】 *v.* 推迟，延期：to put off; **postpone**; defer

例 We agreed to defer a discussion of the issue . 我们决定推迟问题的讨论。

近 delay, remit, shelve, hold off, hold over, lay over, put off

【考法2】 *vi.* 遵从：to submit to another's wishes, opinion, or governance usually through deference or **respect**

例 defer to her father's wishes 遵从她父亲的意愿

派 deference *n.* 尊崇，顺从：a readiness or willingness to yield to the wishes of others

例 He is shown much deference by his colleagues. 他的同事很尊敬他。

近 acquiescence, compliancy, docility, obedience, submissiveness

反 contempt, defiance, disobedience, intractability, recalcitrance 轻视，不服从

派 deferential *adj.* 表示尊重的，恭敬的：showing or expressing deference

反 imperious, impudent 专横无礼的

document [ˈdɑ:kjument]

【考法】 v. 证实：to **show** the existence or **truth of by evidence**

例 He tried to document a link between ancient civilizations and extraterrestrials. 他企图证明古代文明与外星人之间的联系。

近 demonstrate, prove, establish, substantiate, validate

反 disprove, rebut, refute 反驳

派 documentary *adj.* 基于事实的：based on fact

deficiency [dɪˈfɪʃnsi]

【考法】 n. 缺乏，不足：the quality or state of being deficient: **inadequate**

例 There is a deficiency of fresh food in the diet of many of the working poor. 很多劳工阶层的饮食都缺乏新鲜食物。

近 want, dearth, deficit, famine, paucity, scantiness, scarcity

反 surfeit, abundance, adequacy, amplitude, opulence, sufficiency 过度，充足

devious [ˈdi:viəs]

【考法】 *adj.* 狡猾的：willing to **lie and trick** people in order to get what is wanted

例 a devious politician 一个狡猾的政客

近 beguiling, crafty, cunning, artful, foxy, guileful, tricky, wily

反 artless, guileless, ingenuous, innocent, undesigning 淳朴的

deft [deft]

【考法】 *adj.* 灵巧的，熟练的：characterized by facility and **skill**

例 The pianist has deft fingers. 钢琴家有熟练的手指。

近 cunning, adroit, dexterous, expert, masterful, virtuoso

反 awkward, maladroit, ham-handed, amateur, artless, unprofessional, unskillful 笨拙的，不精通的

defuse [ˌdi:ˈfju:z]

【考法】 *vt.* 抚慰，减轻：to **make less** dangerous, **tense**, or hostile

例 defuse the crisis 平息危机

反 foment 煽动

defy [dɪˈfaɪ]

【考法】 *vt.* 蔑视：to **confront with** assured power of **resistance**

例 defy the court 蔑视法庭

近 mock, rebel, oppose, confront, disregard

反 acquiesce, obey, comply with, conform to 默默接受，遵守；capitulate to, submit to, succumb to, surrender to, yield to 屈服

dehydrate [di:ˈhaɪdreɪt]

【考法 1】 *vt.* 去除水分，使干燥：to **remove water** from; make anhydrous

例 She bought a dehumidifier in order to dehydrate the damp basement. 她买了一个除湿器来给地下室除湿。

近 desiccate, parch, scorch, sear

反 dampen, hydrate, saturate with water, reconstitute 用水浸润

【考法 2】 *v.* 使失去活力：to **deprive of vitality** or savor

例 Years of being trapped in a loveless marriage had dehydrated his spirit. 多年不幸的婚姻消磨了他的活力。

近 deaden, devitalize, enervate, petrify, sap

反 brace, energize, enliven, invigorate, vitalize, vivify 使生机勃勃

deify [ˈdeɪɪfaɪ]

【考法】 *vt.* 尊敬，尊崇：to assign a **high status or value to**

例 Valentino was virtually deified by legions of female fans. 瓦伦蒂诺被大批女粉丝崇拜。

近 aggrandize, canonize, dignify, ennoble, glorify, magnify

反 abase, degrade, demean, humble, humiliate 贬低，羞辱

派 deification *n.* 崇拜

反 debasement 贬低

Unit 7

■ DEJECT   ■ DELETERIOUS   ■ DELIBERATE   ■ DELICACY   ■ DELIRIUM
■ DELUSION   ■ DELUGE   ■ DELVE   ■ DEMAGOGUE   ■ DEMANDING

deject [dɪˈdʒekt]
【考法】 *vt.* 使沮丧：to **lower the spirits** of; **dishearten**
例 Nothing dejects a TV pundit more than the reality check that nobody cares what he thinks. 没有什么比大家都漠不关心更让电视节目专家沮丧了。
近 oppress, sadden, weigh down, bum out
反 brighten, buoy, lighten, rejoice, cheer up 使高兴

deleterious [ˌdeləˈtɪriəs]
【考法】 *adj.* 有害的：**harmful** often in a subtle or unexpected way
例 deleterious to health 对健康有害的
近 adverse, baleful, baneful, detrimental, mischievous, nocuous, noxious, pernicious
反 beneficial, salutary, salubrious, wholesome, benign, harmless, innocuous 有益的，安全无害的

deliberate [dɪˈlɪbərət]
【考法】 *adj.* 深思熟虑的：characterized by or resulting from **careful** and thorough consideration
例 a deliberate decision 一个慎重的决定
近 calculated, considered, reasoned, thoughtful
反 impetuous, casual, unadvised, uncalculated, unconsidered, unstudied 随意的，未经过深思的

delicacy [ˈdelɪkəsi]
【考法】 *n.* (外貌、结构等)精致：**fineness** of appearance, construction, or execution; elegance
例 lace of great delicacy 精致的蕾丝
近 daintiness
反 crudity, coarseness, roughness 粗糙

delirium [dɪˈlɪriəm]
【考法】 *n.* 精神错乱；极度兴奋，发狂：an acute **mental disturbance** characterized by **confused** thinking and disrupted attention usually accompanied by disordered speech and hallucinations; frenzied excitement
例 Shoppers were running around in a delirium the day before Christmas. 购物者在圣诞节前夕疯狂扫货。
近 agitation, distraction, hysteria, rage, rampage, uproar

delusion [dɪˈluːʒn]
【考法】 *n.* 错觉，妄想：a **false** idea
例 This was not optimism, it was delusion. 那不是乐观主义，那是妄想。
近 hallucination, illusion, unreality, falsehood, misconception
反 truth, verity 真实
派 delusive *adj.* 欺骗的：false, deceptive
反 transparent 坦诚的

deluge [ˈdeljuːdʒ]
【考法1】 *n.* 大暴雨：a **drenching rain**
近 cloudburst, downfall, downpour, rainstorm
反 drizzle 毛毛雨
【考法2】 *n.* 大量：a **great flow** of water or of something that overwhelms
例 receive a deluge of offers 收到一大堆 offer
近 cloudburst, downfall, downpour, rainstorm
近 inundation, overflow, spate, torrent

delve [delv]
【考法】 *v.* 探究，钻研：to make a careful or **detailed search for information**
例 The book delves into the latest research. 这本书深入探究了最近的研究。
近 probe, investigate, inquire into, look into, dig into

demagogue ['deməgɑːɡ]

【考法】 *n.* 蛊惑民心的政客：a **leader** who makes use of popular prejudices and **false claims** and promises in order to gain power

例 That politician is just a demagogue who preys upon people's fears and prejudices. 那就是一个蛊惑民心的政客，利用民众的害怕和偏见来欺骗他们。

近 firebrand, fomenter, incendiary, instigator, kindler, provocateur

demanding [dɪ'mændɪŋ]

【考法1】 *adj.* 难取悦的，难满足的：not easily **satisfied** or pleased

例 His mother could be demanding at times. 他母亲有时候很难取悦。

近 exacting, fastidious, finical, finicking, fussy, picky

【考法2】 *adj.* 费时间花心思的：**requiring** much time, effort, or **careful attention**

例 The demanding assignment kept them working all night long. 那项劳神的任务使得他们熬夜。

近 arduous, burdensome, challenging, exacting, grueling, killing, laborious, onerous, persnickety, taxing, toilsome

反 light, unchallenging, undemanding 不费劲的，轻而易举的

Unit 8

■ DEMOLITION	■ DEMONSTRATE	■ DEMORALIZE	■ DEMOTIC	■ DEMUR
■ DENIGRATE	■ DISINGENUOUS	■ DENOUNCE	■ DENT	■ DENUDE

demolition [ˌdeməˈlɪʃn]

【考法】 *n.* 破坏，毁坏：the act or process of wrecking or **destroying**, especially destruction by explosives

例 the demolition of dangerous buildings 危楼的拆毁

近 annihilation, decimation, devastation, havoc, wreckage

反 building, construction, erection, raising 建造

demonstrate ['demənstreɪt]

【考法】 *vt.* （通过证据）证明，表明：to show or **make clear** by **using examples**

例 The paleontologist hopes to demonstrate that dinosaurs once existed in central Peru by unearthing the fos-sil evidence. 通过发掘化石，古生物学家试图证明恐龙曾经在秘鲁中部生活过。

近 exemplify, instance

反 unable to prove 不能证明

demoralize [dɪ'mɔːrəlaɪz]

【考法1】 *vt.* 使士气低落：to undermine the confidence or morale of; **dishearten**

例 demoralize the staff 使员工士气低落

近 daunt, dishearten, dismay, dispirit, unnerve

反 invigorate, cheer 鼓舞

【考法2】 *vt.* 贬低，使堕落：to **lower in character**, dignity, or quality

例 We refused to be demoralized by our humiliating defeat. 我们拒绝由于这场屈辱的战败而被贬低。

近 abase, corrupt, debauch, degrade, demean

反 elevate, ennoble, uplift 使崇高，提升

demotic [dɪ'mɑːtɪk]

【考法】 *adj.* 通俗的，大众化的：popular, **common**

例 demotic entertainments 大众化的娱乐

反 profound 深奥的

demur [dɪ'mɜːr]

【考法】 *n./vi.* 表示异议，反对：to voice **opposition**; **object**

例 demur at the suggestion 反对提议

近 challenge, exception, expostulation, fuss, kick, protest, remonstrance, stink

反 accept, accede 接受

denigrate ['denɪɡreɪt]

【考法】 *vt.* 诋毁，污蔑：to express **scornfully** one's low opinion of

例 denigrate one's opponents 诋毁某人的对手

近 belittle, depreciate, derogate, dismiss, disparage

反 honor, acclaim, applaud, exalt, extol, glorify, magnify 给以…荣誉，赞扬

disingenuous [ˌdɪsɪnˈdʒenjuəs]
【考法】 *adj.* 不真诚的，假惺惺的：**not truly honest** or sincere
例 a disingenuous excuse 一个不真诚的借口
近 insincere, affected, artful, dishonest, guileful
反 artless, guileless, ingenuous, innocent, sincere, honest, undesigning 淳朴的

denounce [dɪˈnaʊns]
【考法】 *vt.* 公开指责：to express **public or formal disapproval** of
例 The governor has denounced the court's decision and vows to press for a constitutional amendment. 州长公开指责法庭判决不公，准备投票进行修宪。
近 condemn, objurgate, rebuke, reprimand, reproach, reprove
反 cite, commend, endorse 支持，称赞
派 denunciation *n.* 谴责：an act of denouncing especially: a public condemnation
反 panegyric, accolade, eulogy 赞颂，颂词

dent [dent]
【考法】 *vt.* (数量、程度上)削弱：to **make smaller** in amount, volume, or extent
例 Hopefully this vacation won't dent our bank account too much. 但愿这次旅行不会让我们银行存款缩水太多。
近 abate, downscale, downsize, dwindle
反 aggrandize, amplify, augment, boost, enlarge, escalate 增大，增强

denude [dɪˈnuːd]
【考法】 *vt.* 脱去，使赤裸：to divest of covering; make **bare**
例 Drought has completely denuded the hills of grass. 干旱"脱去"了山上的草使山变得光秃秃的。
反 cover 遮盖

Unit 9

■ DEPLETE	■ DEPLORE	■ DEPLOY	■ DEPORTATION	■ DEPOSE
■ DEPOSIT	■ DEPRAVITY	■ DEPRECATE	■ DEPRECIATE	■ DEPRESSED

deplete [dɪˈpliːt]
【考法】 *vt.* 耗尽，使衰竭：to decrease the fullness of; to **make complete use** of
例 Miners depleted the vein of copper ore after only a few months. 矿工们在短短几个月内就把一整片铜矿开采完了。
近 consume, devour, drain, exhaust, draw down, play out, use up
反 enrich, renew, replace 使富有，更新

deplore [dɪˈplɔːr]
【考法】 *vt.* 谴责，强烈反对：to **hate or dislike** (something) very much
例 Somehow we had to master events, not simply deplore events. 无论如何，我们必须控制时局，而不能只简单地谴责时局。
近 blame, censure, criticize, denounce, pan, reprehend
反 extol, laud, praise 赞扬

deploy [dɪˈplɔɪ]
【考法】 *v.* (有目的地)展开；调度，部署：to **spread out**, utilize, or arrange for a deliberate purpose
例 deploy a sales force 展开部署销售力量
反 concentrate 集中

deportation [ˌdiːpɔːrˈteɪʃn]
【考法】 *n.* 放逐：the **removal from a country** of an alien whose presence is unlawful or prejudicial
例 the deportation of all illegal immigrants 驱逐所有非法移民
近 banishment, displacement, expatriation, expulsion, relegation

depose [dɪˈpoʊz]
【考法1】 *vi.* 宣誓作证：to **testify** to under oath or by affidavit
例 He was nervous when the time to depose before the jury finally arrived. 他很紧张，在陪审团面前作证的时刻终于到来了。
近 attest, swear
反 perjure 作伪证
【考法2】 *vt.* 废黜，罢免：to **remove from a throne** or other high position
例 a military junta deposed the dictator after he had bankrupted the country 军阀罢黜了使国家陷入赤贫的独裁者
近 defrock, deprive, oust, uncrown
反 crown, enthrone 授予王权

deposit [dɪˈpɑːzɪt]
【考法 1】 *n.* 自然积累，沉积，矿藏：a natural **accumulation** (as of iron ore, coal, or gas)
例 rich deposits of oil and natural gas 丰富的石油和天然气矿藏
近 dregs, precipitate, sediment, settlings, hoard, reserve
反 process of eroding 腐蚀过程
【考法 2】 *vt.* 存钱：to **put in** an **account**
例 We quickly deposited the check in a bank account. 我们火速把支票存入银行账户。
反 withdraw 取款

depravity [dɪˈprævəti]
【考法】 *n.* 道德败坏：**immoral** conduct or practices **harmful or offensive** to society
例 He was sinking into a life of utter depravity. 他自甘堕落。
近 debauchery, iniquitousness, licentiousness, perversion, turpitude, dissoluteness
反 morality, virtue 美德

deprecate [ˈdeprəkeɪt]
【考法 1】 *vt.* 不喜欢：to hold an **unfavorable opinion** of
例 They deprecates TV sitcoms as childish and simpleminded. 他们批评电视情景喜剧既幼稚又脑残。
近 deprecate, discountenance, disesteem, disfavor, frown (on or upon)
反 approve, favor 喜欢
【考法 2】 *vt.* 贬低，轻视：to **express scornfully** one's low opinion of
例 They boys deprecate the comedy as the stupidest movie of the year. 男孩们认为这部喜剧是年度最傻逼电影。
近 belittle, denigrate, dismiss, disparage, cry down
反 acclaim, applaud, exalt, extol, glorify 赞扬

depreciate [dɪˈpriːʃieɪt]
【考法】 *vt.* 贬低…的价值：to **lower** the price or estimated **value** of
例 New cars start to depreciate as soon as they are on the road. 新车一上路便开始贬值。
近 cheapen, depress, devalue, downgrade, mark down
反 appreciate, enhance, upgrade, mark up 提价，升值

depressed [dɪˈprest]
【考法】 *adj.* 不开心的，情绪不高的，消沉的：feeling **unhappiness**
例 I was depressed and didn't feel much like going to the party. 我感到很沮丧，不想去参加聚会。
近 crestfallen, dejected, despondent, gloomy, low-spirited, wretched
反 blissful, buoyant, gleeful, joyous, jubilant 情绪高的

Unit 10

■ DEPRIVATION	■ DERACINATE	■ DERELICT	■ DERIDE	■ DERIVATIVE
■ DESCEND	■ DIVINATION	■ DESECRATE	■ DESICCATE	■ DESIGNATE

deprivation [ˌdeprɪˈveɪʃn]
【考法】 *n.* 匮乏：the condition of being deprived; **privation**
例 serious sleep deprivation caused by long work hours 由长时间工作导致的严重睡眠不足
反 fecundity 丰饶

deracinate [diːˈræsɪneɪt]
【考法】 *vt.* 根除：to **pull out** by the roots; uproot
反 plant 种植

derelict [ˈderəlɪkt]
【考法】 *adj.* 玩忽职守的，不认真的：**lacking** a sense of **duty**; marked by a **carelessly** easy manner
例 The guards were judged derelict in their duty. 守卫们被判玩忽职守罪。
近 disregardful, lax, neglectful, neglecting, remiss, slack
反 extremely careful, attentive, conscientious, nonnegligent 特别仔细的

deride [dɪˈraɪd]
【考法】 *vt.* 嘲弄，嘲笑：to speak of or treat with **contemptuous mirth**
例 My brothers derided our efforts, but were forced to eat their words when we won first place. 我的兄弟嘲笑我们的努力，但是当我们得了第一名以后他们不得不收回那些话。
近 gibe, jeer, mock, scout, shoot down, laugh at

	反	praise 赞美
	派	derision *n.* 嘲弄：contemptuous or jeering laughter; ridicule
	反	veneration 尊敬

derivative [dɪˈrɪvətɪv]

【考法】	*adj.* 非原创的：lacking **originality**: banal
例	their dull, derivative debut album 他们毫无新意的首张专辑
近	secondhand
反	original, innovative, precursory 原创的，先驱的

descend [dɪˈsend]

【考法1】 *v.* 下降：to lead or extend **downward**
例 The pathway descends to the river bank. 通道一直向下延伸到河岸。
近 dip, fall, plunge, sink
反 arise, ascend, climb, mount, upsweep, upturn 上升，登上
【考法2】 *v.* 世代相传：to originate or come from an ancestral stock or source, to **pass by inheritance**
例 The house has descended through four generations. 这座房子已经传了四代。‖ a tradition descending from colonial days 殖民时期传递下来的一项传统
派 descendant *n.* 后代：one deriving directly from a precursor or prototype
例 They are descendants of the original English and Scottish settlers. 他们是最早一批英格兰和苏格兰定居者的后裔。
反 forbears 祖先

divination [ˌdɪvɪˈneɪʃn]

【考法】 *n.* 预言：the art or practice of **foretelling future** events by interpreting omens
例 Divination is an attempt to discern the future that, once again, heads right to the source of power. 占卜是一种试图看清未来的法术，它的终极目标，也是神力的源头。
近 augury, forecast, predictions

desecrate [ˈdesɪkreɪt]

【考法】 *vt.* 亵渎，玷污：to **treat** (a sacred place or object) **shamefully** or with great disrespect
例 desecrate the shrine 亵渎圣地
近 defile, profane, violate
反 sanctify, revere, hallow 尊敬，将…视为神圣

desiccate [ˈdesɪkeɪt]

【考法】 *vt.* 使缺乏活力：to **deprive** of emotional or intellectual **vitality**
例 The students desiccate after tests. 学生们在考试后没有活力。
近 castrate, dampen, deaden, devitalize, enervate
反 brace, energize, enliven, invigorate, stimulate, vitalize 使生机勃勃

designate [ˈdezɪgneɪt]

【考法1】 *vt.* 任命：**to pick** (someone) by one's authority **for a specific position or duty**
例 He has yet to designate his successor as head of the firm. 他还没有给公司选定接班人。
近 assign, commission, constitute, nominate, place
反 discharge, dismiss, expel, fire 解雇，开除
【考法2】 *vt.* 命名：to **give a name to**
例 He was designated Air Jordan by his fans. 他被粉丝们称为"飞人乔丹"。
近 denominate, dub, entitle, label, style, term, title

List 7

"刷词，刷题，刷《再要你命 3000》，为你刷出新世界"

（童心，2007 年 10 月，Verbal 700, Quantitative 800, AW4.0
录取院校：Princeton University 运筹与金融工程）

Unit 1

| ■ DESPICABLE | ■ DESPISE | ■ DESPOTIC | ■ DESULTORY | ■ DETACH |
| ■ DETAIN | ■ DETER | ■ DETERIORATION | ■ DETOUR | ■ DETRACT |

despicable ［dɪˈspɪkəbl］
【考法】 *adj.* 令人鄙视的：arousing or deserving of one's **loathing and disgust**
例 a despicable criminal 一个令人鄙视的罪犯
近 contemptible, detestable, dishonorable
反 admirable, commendable, creditable, meritorious, praiseworthy 值得赞扬的

despise ［dɪˈspaɪz］
【考法】 *vt.* 极其不喜欢：to **dislike strongly**
例 Fools despise wisdom and education. 愚者不喜欢智慧和教育。
近 abhor, abominate, detest, execrate, loathe, disregard, flout
反 love 喜欢

despotic ［dɪˈspɑːtɪk］
【考法】 *adj.* 专制的，暴虐的：arbitrary, autocratic, monocratic, **tyrannical**
例 a despotic tyrant 专制的暴君
近 authoritative, dictatorial, imperious, overbearing, peremptory, tyrannous

desultory ［ˈdesəltɔːri］
【考法】 *adj.* 无计划的，无目的的：**lacking** a definite **plan**, purpose, or pattern
例 a desultory conversation 漫谈
近 digressive, excursive, meandering, rambling, wandering
反 carefully planned, strictly methodical, assiduous 精心计划的，有条理的，专心致志的

detach ［dɪˈtætʃ］
【考法】 *vt.* 使分离：to **separate** or unfasten; disconnect
例 detach the key from the ring 从钥匙圈上取下钥匙
反 tether 束缚

detain ［dɪˈteɪn］
【考法】 *vt.* 拘留，扣留：to **hold** or **keep** in or as if in custody
例 arrest and detain the drug dealers 逮捕并拘留毒贩
反 manumit 释放

deter ［dɪˈtɜːr］
【考法】 *vt.* 吓住，威慑：to **prevent** or **discourage** from acting, as by means of fear or doubt
例 deter criminals from carrying guns 威慑罪犯使其不带枪
近 dissuade, inhibit
反 spur, encourage, persuade 激励
派 deterrent *adj./n.* 威慑的；威慑力量
例 deterrent weapons 威慑性武器 ‖ a deterrent to theft 对偷窃的威慑
反 inducement, incentive 引诱，刺激

deterioration ［dɪˌtɪriəˈreɪʃn］
【考法】 *n.* 恶化；堕落：a gradual **sinking** and wasting away of mind or body
例 a continuing deterioration in relations between the two countries 两国关系的持续恶化
近 decadence, degeneration, deterioration, devolution, downfall, downgrade
反 improvement, recovery, recuperation, rehabilitation, revitalization 改进，改善

detour [ˈdiːtʊr]

【考法】 *n.* 偏离正常标准：a turning **away from** a course or **standard**

例 We'll regard this relapse as just a brief detour on your road to recovery from substance abuse. 我们把这次旧病复发看成你戒瘾道路上的一个小偏离。

近 deflection, departure, deviation, divergency

detract [dɪˈtrækt]

【考法 1】 *vt.* 贬低，降低价值：to **diminish** the importance, value, or effectiveness of something

例 detract from sth. 贬低某事

近 belittle, depreciate, derogate, disparage, dispraise, write off

反 extol, praise, eulogize, laud, panegyrize 赞美

【考法 2】 *vt.* 使分心：to **draw** the **attention** or mind to something else

例 Numerous typos in the text detract the reader's attention from the novel's intricate plot. 许多打印错误让读者分心，不关注复杂的情节了。

近 divert, call off

Unit 2

| ■ DETRITUS | ■ DEVOTED | ■ DEVOUT | ■ DEXTEROUS | ■ DIABOLIC |
| ■ DIAPHANOUS | ■ DIATRIBE | ■ DIDACTIC | ■ DIEHARD | ■ DOVISH |

detritus [dɪˈtraɪtəs]

【考法】 *n.* 废品，碎屑，遗骸：a **product** of **disintegration**, **destruction**, or wearing away: **debris**

例 the detritus of war 战争的残迹

近 debris, residue, wreck

反 valuable product 有用的物品

devoted [dɪˈvoʊtɪd]

【考法】 *adj.* 投入的；忠诚的：characterized by **loyalty** and **devotion**

例 Good teachers are devoted to learning. 好老师会专心学习。

近 constant, loyal, allegiant, dedicated, devout, loyal, pious, staunch, steadfast

反 disloyal, faithless, perfidious, unfaithful 不忠诚的；recreant, traitorous, treacherous 背叛的

devout [dɪˈvaʊt]

【考法】 *adj.* 忠诚的：firm in one's **allegiance** to someone or something

例 devout Maxists 坚定的马克思主义者

近 constant, loyal, allegiant, dedicated, pious, staunch, steadfast

反 disloyal, faithless, perfidious, unfaithful 不忠诚的；recreant, traitorous, treacherous 背叛的

dexterous [ˈdekstrəs]

【考法 1】 *adj.* 动作灵活的：**ready** and **skilled** in physical movements

例 a dexterous surgeon 技术娴熟的外科医生 ‖ The dexterous watchmaker was able to repair the antique watch's delicate gears and parts. 手巧的手表匠能够修理古董手表精密的齿轮和部件。

近 deft, handy

反 ham-fisted, ham-handed, handless, heavy-handed, unhandy 手笨的

【考法 2】 *adj.* 头脑灵活的：**mentally adroit** and **skillful**: clever

近 adroit, clever, cunning

反 dull, foolish, silly, fatuous, unwise 傻的

diabolic [ˌdaɪəˈbɑːlɪk]

【考法】 *adj.* 恶魔一般的：of, relating to, or characteristic of the **devil**

例 The police quickly mobilized to track down the diabolic serial killer. 警察迅速行动起来追查这个恶魔般的连环杀人狂。

近 demoniac, demonian, demonic, devilish, satanic

反 angelic, seraphic 天使般的

diaphanous [daɪˈæfənəs]

【考法 1】 *adj.* 模糊的；非实在的：**vague** or **insubstantial**

例 only a diaphanous hope of success 只有一丝成功的希望

近 vague, obscure, unexplicit, insubstantial, immaterial

反 substantial 实在的；clear, distinct 清晰的

【考法2】 *adj.* (质地精致得)几乎透明的: of such fine texture as to be **transparent** or **translucent**
例 The bride wore a diaphanous veil. 新娘戴着透明的面纱。
近 transparent, translucent, transpicuous, gossamer
反 opaque, impermeable of light 不透明的，不透光的

diatribe [ˈdaɪətraɪb]
【考法】 *n.* 长篇抨击性演讲: a **long** angry speech or **scolding**
例 a diatribe against racism 一个反对种族主义的长篇抨击性演讲
近 tirade, harangue, jeremiad, philippic, rant

didactic [daɪˈdæktɪk]
【考法】 *adj.* 喜欢说教的，思修的: designed or intended to **teach**
例 didactic teaching approach 喜欢说教的教学方法
近 homiletic, preachy, moralistic, sententious
反 undidactic 不喜欢说教的

diehard [ˈdaɪhɑːrd]
【考法】 *adj.* 顽固的，保守的 *n.* 顽固的人，保守的人: strongly or fanatically **determined** or **devoted** / someone who **opposes change** and **refuses** to accept **new ideas**
例 Some diehard smokers belied the doctors' suggestion. 一些顽固的烟民违背了医生们的建议。
近 conservative, hidebound, old-fashioned, reactionary, ultraconservative
反 liberal, nonconservative, open-minded, liberal 自由的，开放的

dovish [ˈdʌvɪʃ]
【考法】 *adj.* 鸽派的，爱好和平的: inclined to **live in peace** and to avoid war
例 The party's dovish faction has regarded the war as a bad idea from the get-go. 党中的鸽派分子认为这场战争从一开始就是一个坏主意。
近 peaceful, pacific, pacifist, peaceable
反 bloodthirsty, hawkish, warlike 好战的

Unit 3

■ DIFFUSE	■ DIGRESS	■ DILAPIDATE	■ DILATE	■ DILATORY
■ DILETTANTE	■ DILIGENT	■ DILUTE	■ DIMINISH	■ DISQUISITION

diffuse
【考法1】 [dɪˈfjuːs] *adj.* 啰嗦的: being at once **verbose** and ill-organized
例 a diffuse report 冗长的报告
近 circuitous, circumlocutory, long-winded, prolix, verbose, windy, rambling
反 concise, pithy, succinct, terse, laconic 简洁的
【考法2】 [dɪˈfjuːz] *v.* 扩展，散开: to **extend**, scatter
例 The photographer uses a screen to diffuse the light. 摄影师用一个屏幕来分散光线。
近 spread, extend, disperse, disseminate, scatter
反 concentrate, center, centralize, focus 集中

digress [daɪˈgres]
【考法】 *v.* 脱离主题: to **turn aside** especially from the **main subject** of attention or course of argument
例 digress from her prepared subject 脱离她准备好的主题
近 excurse, ramble, diverge, get off the subject
派 digressive *adj.* 偏离的
近 discursive
派 digression *n.* 题外话，跑题: the act or an instance of digressing in a discourse
近 aside

dilapidate [dɪˈlæpɪdeɪt]
【考法】 *v.* (使)荒废: to bring into a condition of decay or partial **ruin**
例 The students dilapidated their study. 学生们荒废了学业。
近 ruin, wreck
反 be in use 还在使用；restore 恢复使用；mend, repair 修理；rejuvenate, renew, renovate 翻新

dilate	[daɪˈleɪt]
【考法】	*v.* （使）膨胀，扩大：to **enlarge** or **expand** in bulk or extent; to become **wide**
例	The cat dilated its eyes in the darkness . 猫在黑暗中睁大眼睛。‖ The drug dilates the blood vessels . 药使血管膨胀。
近	expand, amplify, enlarge
反	contract 收缩；narrow 使变窄

dilatory	[ˈdɪlətɔːri]
【考法】	*adj.* 拖延的，磨蹭的：tending or intended to **cause delay**, characterized by **procrastination**
例	dilatory tactics 拖延战术 ‖ The homeowner is claiming that local firefighters were dilatory in responding to the call . 业主声称本地的消防队员对（火警）电话有拖延。
近	delaying, procrastinating, dragging, lagging, tardy
反	rapid, fast, fleet, precipitate, rocketing, swift, hasty, hurrying, scurrying 快速的

dilettante	[ˌdɪləˈtænti]
【考法】	*n./adj.* 业余爱好者（对艺术或知识领域涉猎浅薄者）/缺乏专业技术的：a person having a **superficial interest** in an art / **lacking** or showing a lack of **expert skill**
例	Dilettante watch the scene of bustle , adept guard the entrance. 外行看热闹，内行看门道。
近	dabbler, amateur, nonexpert, cognoscente; nonprofessional, amateur
反	authority, expert, pro, professional, specialist 专家

diligent	[ˈdɪlɪdʒənt]
【考法】	*adj.* 勤勉的，辛勤的：characterized by **steady**, **earnest**, and **energetic** effort: painstaking
例	a diligent and prolific worker 勤奋且出活多的工人
近	assiduous, industrious, sedulous, engaged, hopping, tied-up
反	idle, inactive, unbusy, unemployed, unoccupied 空闲的

dilute	[daɪˈluːt]
【考法】	*vt.* 稀释 / *adj.* 经稀释的：to make thinner or less **concentrated** by adding a liquid such as water/of relatively **low strength** or **concentration**
例	dilute a color 稀释色彩 ‖ a dilute acid that's safe to handle in the classroom 稀释了的可以安全在教室处理的酸
近	thin
反	condense, densify, concentrate, thicken 使浓缩

diminish	[dɪˈmɪnɪʃ]
【考法 1】	*v.* （使）变小，（使）减少：to （cause to） become **smaller** or **less**
例	diminish an army's strength 削弱军队力量 ‖ The sound of the train diminished as our distance from it increased. 当我们距离火车越远时，火车的声音就越小。
近	abate, dwindle, lessen, lower, reduce, decline
反	aggrandize, amplify, augment, boost, enlarge, escalate, expand, increase, raise, balloon 增加，增大
【考法 2】	*v.* 轻视，贬低：to **lessen** the authority, dignity, or reputation of: **belittle**
例	diminish a rival's accomplishments 贬低对手的成就
近	belittle, deprecate, depreciate, disparage
反	acclaim, applaud, exalt, extol, glorify, laud, praise 赞美

disquisition	[ˌdɪskwɪˈzɪʃn]
【考法】	*n.* 专题论文：a **systematic search** for the truth or facts about something
例	Adam Smith's celebrated disquisition on the factors contributing to the wealth of nations 亚当斯密关于导致国家财富的因素的专题论文
近	delving, inquiry, examination, exploration, inquisition, probing

Unit 4

■ DINGY	■ DIOCESAN	■ DIPLOMATIC	■ DIRE	■ DEMOGRAPHY
■ DISABUSE	■ DISAFFECTED	■ DISARM	■ DISARRAY	■ DISAVOW

dingy	[ˈdɪndʒi]
【考法】	*adj.* 昏暗的；肮脏的：**darkened** with smoke and grime; **dirty** or discolored
例	A dingy room is always Dickensian image of the poor. 一个肮脏而昏暗的房间经常作为狄更斯时代的穷人形象。‖ The bed sheets were pretty dingy so we threw them in the laundry pile. 床单太脏了，我们把它扔进了脏衣服堆。

| 近 | darkened, dirty, bedraggled, bemired, besmirched, dusty, mucky, muddy, nasty, smudged, soiled, sordid, stained, sullied |
| 反 | clean, cleanly, immaculate, spotless, stainless, unsoiled, unstained, unsullied 干净的 |

diocesan [daɪ'ɑːsɪsn]

【考法】	adj. 主教管辖区的: of or relating to a **diocese**
例	national or diocesan authority 国家或教区权利
反	ecumenical 世界范围的

diplomatic [ˌdɪplə'mætɪk]

【考法】	adj. 使用策略的, 机智的: employing **tact** and conciliation especially in situations of stress
例	be very diplomatic with awkward clients 总是有办法对付难缠的顾客
近	politic
反	gauche, impolitic, tactless, undiplomatic, untactful 笨拙的, 不机智的

dire ['daɪər]

【考法 1】	adj. 可怕的, 恐怖的: causing **fear**
例	dire consequences 可怕的后果
近	alarming, direful, dread, dreadful, fearsome, forbidding, formidable, frightening, frightful, ghastly, hair-raising, horrendous, horrible, horrifying, intimidating, redoubtable, scary, shocking, terrible, terrifying
【考法 2】	adj. 迫切的: needing **immediate** attention; **urgent**
例	There is a dire need for food and medicine in the famine-stricken country. 在闹饥荒的国家迫切需要食物和药品。
近	immediate, burning, compelling, critical, crying, emergent, exigent, imperative, imperious, importunate, instant, necessitous, pressing, urgent
反	nonurgent, noncritical 不迫切的

demography [dɪ'mɑːgrəfi]

| 【考法】 | n. 人口统计学: the study of **changes** (such as the number of births, deaths, marriages, and illnesses) that occur over a period of time **in human populations** |
| 例 | Even if you look at countries in the same income bracket, there are plenty of factors, from demography to culture, that confuse the picture. 即使观察处在相同收入等级的国家，也有众多的因素如从人口分布到文化差异使情况变得复杂。 |

disabuse [ˌdɪsə'bjuːz]

【考法】	vt. 打消错误念头, 纠正: to **free from error**, **fallacy**, or **misconception**
例	disabuse sb of the notion that... 打消某人的…观点 ‖ I must disabuse you of your feelings of grandeur. 我必须消除你的傲气。
近	disenchant, undeceive
反	lead into error 导致错误; mislead 误导

disaffected [ˌdɪsə'fektɪd]

【考法】	adj. 不满的, 叛逆的: **discontented** and resentful especially against authority; **rebellious**
例	gangs of disaffected teenagers 一群叛逆的年轻人 ‖ The soldiers were disaffected toward the government. 那些士兵对政府不满。
近	discontented, dissatisfied, malcontent, rebellious, insubordinate, contumacious
反	satisfied, contented 满足的
派	disaffect vt. 使不安, 使不满: to fill with discontent and unrest; disaffection n. 不满, 疏远: estrangement
近	dissatisfy, agitate, upset
反	mollify 平息, 抚慰

disarm [dɪs'ɑːrm]

【考法】	vt. 使息怒, 平息, 抚慰: to **lessen** the anger or agitation of
例	disarm her anger 平息她的怒气
近	appease, assuage, conciliate, gentle, mollify, placate, propitiate
反	anger, enrage, incense, inflame, enflame, infuriate, ire, madden, outrage 煽动, 激起

disarray [ˌdɪsə'reɪ]

【考法】	n. 混乱, 无秩序: a **lack** of **order** or sequence vt. 使混乱: to **undo** the proper **order** or **arrangement** of
例	The room was in disarray. 房间一片混乱。
近	confusion, disarrangement, disorder, disorderliness, disorganization, havoc, mess, messiness, misorder, muddle, muss, shambles, jumble, welter; confuse, disarrange, discompose, dishevel, dislocate, disorganize, disrupt, disturb, hash, jumble, muddle, muss, rumple, scramble, upset, mess up, mix up
反	order, orderliness 有序; arrange, array, dispose, order, organize, range, regulate, straighten up 使有序

disavow [ˌdɪsəˈvaʊ]

【考法】 *vt.* 拒绝承认，否认：to **disclaim** knowledge of, responsibility for, or association with; to declare **not** to be **true**

例 disavow the rumor 否认谣言 ‖ She disavowed the testimony that she had given earlier in the trial. 她在审判中否认了自己之前的证词。

近 deny, repudiate, disaffirm, disclaim, disconfirm, gainsay, negate

反 acknowledge, avow, concede 承认

Unit 5

■ DISCERN	■ DISCHARGE	■ DISCIPLE	■ DISCOMBOBULATE	■ DISCOMFIT
■ DISCOMMODE	■ DISCOMPOSE	■ DISCONCERT	■ DISCORD	■ DISCREDIT

discern [dɪˈsɜːrn]

【考法】 *v.* 识别，辨别差异：to **perceive** with the eyes or intellect; **detect**

例 discern the motives 辨识出动机 ‖ too young to discern between right and wrong 太年轻了而辨别不了是非

近 behold, descry, distinguish, espy, perceive, regard, differentiate, discriminate

反 confuse, mix up 混淆

派 discerning *adj.* 有洞察力的，洞悉的：showing insight and understanding

例 a very discerning art critic 眼光敏锐有洞察力的艺术评论家 ‖ She has a discerning palate. 她的味觉很敏锐。

近 insightful, incisive

反 myopic, shortsighted 目光短浅的；undiscerning 无辨别能力的

派 discernible/discernable *adj.* 可辨识的，可辨别的：perceptible

例 a discernible mark 可辨别的痕迹

近 perceptible, detectable, distinguishable

反 indiscernible, imperceptible 不可辨识的

discharge [dɪsˈtʃɑːrdʒ]

【考法 1】 *vt.* 解雇：to **dismiss** from employment

例 discharge a worker/soldier 开除员工/军籍

近 fire, dismiss

反 employ, engage, hire, take on, sign up or on 雇佣

【考法 2】 *vt.* 释放：to set **free** (as from slavery or confinement)

例 discharge the prisoners upon the signing of the peace treaty 根据和平条约释放罪犯

近 disenthrall, emancipate, enfranchise, liberate, loose, manumit, release, spring, unbind, uncage, unchain, unfetter

反 bind, confine, enchain, fetter 监禁，束缚

disciple [dɪˈsaɪpl]

【考法】 *n.* 信徒，追随者：one who accepts and assists in spreading the doctrines of another, **follower**

例 A circle of dedicated disciples who conscientiously wrote down everything the prophet said. 一圈忠实的信徒认真地记下了先知所说的话。

近 acolyte, adherent, convert, epigone, partisan, votary

反 leader, coryphaeus 领导者

discombobulate [ˌdɪskəmˈbɑːbjuleɪt]

【考法】 *vt.* 使不安，使混乱：**upset**, **confuse**

例 invent cool new ways to discombobulate the old order 发明新的好方法打乱了旧秩序

近 upset, addle, baffle, bamboozle, befog, befuddle, confound, fuddle, gravel, muddle, muddy, mystify, perplex, puzzle, vex

反 compose, soothe, calm, pacify 使安定

discomfit [dɪsˈkʌmfɪt]

【考法 1】 *vt.* 使尴尬：to put into a state of perplexity and **embarrassment**

例 He was discomfited by the awkward situation of having his ex-girlfriend meet his current one. 他的前女友看到他现任女友的情况让他很尴尬。

近 embarrass, abash, faze, fluster, mortify, nonplus, rattle

【考法 2】 *vt.* 阻碍: to **prevent** from achieving a goal
例 Constant interruptions discomfited her in her attempt to finish the speech. 经常打断她讲话导致她无法完成演讲。
近 balk, foil, thwart, baffle, checkmate
反 advance, forward, foster, further, promote 推进，促进；encourage 鼓励

discommode [ˌdɪskəˈmoʊd]
【考法】 *vt.* 打扰，使不便: to cause inconvenience to: **trouble**
例 We were discommoded by his late arrival. 他的迟到使我们不便。
近 disturb, trouble, incommode, put out
反 accommodate, assist, oblige, favor 帮忙

discompose [ˌdɪskəmˈpoʊz]
【考法 1】 *vt.* 使不安: to **disturb** the **composure** or calm of; **perturb**
例 GRE does not seem to discompose Jason; on the contrary, he looks rather relaxed. GRE 没有使 Jason 感到慌乱，正相反，他看上去很轻松。
近 agitate, bother, discomfort, disquiet, distemper, disconcert, disturb, perturb, upset, weird out
反 calm, compose, quiet, settle, soothe, tranquilize 平息，抚慰
【考法 2】 *vt.* 使混乱: to **undo** the proper **order** or **arrangement** of
例 The wind discomposed arranged papers. 风吹乱了细心整理的纸张。
近 disarrange, disarray, disorganize
反 arrange, array, order, organize, range 使有序

disconcert [ˌdɪskənˈsɜːrt]
【考法】 *vt.* 使不安: to **disturb** the composure of
例 We were disconcerted by the unexpected changes to the program. 我们对项目未预料到的变化感到不安。
近 abash, discomfit, discountenance, mortify, rattle
反 calm, compose, quiet, settle, soothe, tranquilize 平息，抚慰

discord [ˈdɪskɔːrd]
【考法】 *n.* 意见不一致，不和谐: **lack** of **agreement** or **harmony** (as between persons, things, or ideas)
例 No discord, no concord. 不打不成交。
近 conflict, disaccord, discordance, disharmony, dissension, dissidence, dissonance, disunion, disunity, division, friction, inharmony, schism, strife, row, divergence
反 accord, agreement, concord, concordance, harmony, consensus, unanimity 和谐，一致
派 discordant *adj.* 不和谐的，刺耳的: disagreeable in sound; harsh or dissonant
近 dissonant, cacophonous, disharmonic, disharmonious
反 concordant, harmonious 和谐的

discredit [dɪsˈkredɪt]
【考法 1】 *vt.* 羞辱，使丧失名誉: to **damage** in **reputation**; **disgrace**
例 discredit his opponents 羞辱他的对手
近 abase, debase, degrade, demean, disgrace, dishonor, humiliate, shame, sink, smirch, take down
反 aggrandize 提高名誉；canonize, deify 神化；elevate 提升；exalt 赞扬
【考法 2】 *vt.* 怀疑，不相信: to think **not** to be **true** or **real**
例 discredit the witness 怀疑那个证人
近 negate, doubt, distrust
反 accept, believe, credit 接受，相信；confirm, prove, validate, verify 证实

Unit 6

■ DISCREPANCY　　■ DISCRETE　　■ DISCRETION　　■ DISCRETIONARY　　■ DISCRIMINATE
■ DISCURSIVE　　■ DISDAIN　　■ DISENGAGE　　■ DISGORGE　　■ DISGRUNTLE

discrepancy [dɪsˈkrepənsi]
【考法】 *n.* (在事实和宣称之间的)差异或矛盾: **divergence** or **disagreement**, as between facts or claims
例 a large discrepancy between A and B　A 与 B 之间的巨大差距
近 contrast, disagreement, disparity, dissimilarity, distance, distinction, diversity
反 convergence, concord, consonance 一致，和谐；analogousness, community, resemblance, similarity 相似

discrete [dɪˈskriːt]

【考法】 *adj.* 离散的，不连续的：constituting a **separate** entity

例 a discrete variable 离散变量

近 detached, disconnected, unattached, unconnected, separate

反 continuous 连续的；attached, connected, joined, linked 连接的

discretion [dɪˈskreʃn]

【考法 1】 *n.* 谨慎：the quality of being **discreet**; **circumspection**

例 You must show discretion in choosing your teammates. 你选择队友时必须慎重。

近 discreetness, prudence

反 imprudence, indiscretion 轻率

派 indiscretion *n.* 不谨慎，不符合社会道德规范：an act at variance with the accepted morality of a society

例 resign because of financial indiscretions 因为财政方面的不检点而辞职

【考法 2】 *n.* 自制，节制：the **checking** of one's true feelings and impulses when dealing with others

例 In that job you'll be expected to show discretion and act like a professional at all times. 那项工作要求你时刻保持自制，表现得像一个专业人士。

近 continence, discipline, inhibition, refrainment, restraint, self-control, self-restraint

反 disinhibition, incontinence, unconstraint 不自制，不节制

discretionary [dɪˈskreʃəneri]

【考法】 *adj.* 自主决定的：left to discretion: exercised at **one's own discretion**

例 discretionary income 自主决定的收入

近 elective, voluntary

反 compulsory, mandatory, nonelective, nonvoluntary, obligatory, required 强制性的，非自愿的

discriminate [dɪˈskrɪmɪneɪt]

【考法 1】 *vt.* 区分：to **perceive** the **distinguishing** features of; **recognize** as distinct

例 discriminate different kinds of animals 区分不同的动物

近 differentiate, discern, distinguish

反 confuse, mistake, mix up 混淆

【考法 2】 *vi.* 歧视：to make a **difference** in treatment or favor on a basis other than individual merit

例 The new law discriminated against lower-paid workers. 这条新法律歧视低工资的工人。

派 discriminatory *adj.* 差别对待的：marked by or showing prejudice; biased

近 prejudiced, biased

反 equitable, impartial, unbiased, impersonal, unprejudiced 公平的

discursive [dɪsˈkɜːrsɪv]

【考法】 *adj.* (谈话内容)杂乱的：moving from topic to topic **without order**

例 a long, discursive article 冗长杂乱的文章 ‖ The speaker's discursive style made it difficult to understand his point. 演讲者讲话杂乱，很难让人理解他的观点。

近 desultory, digressional, excursive, meandering, rambling, wandering

反 keen on title, concentrated 关注主题的，集中的

disdain [dɪsˈdeɪn]

【考法】 *vt.* 轻视，鄙视：to look on with **scorn**

例 disdain that man for snobbishness 鄙视那个势利小人

近 contemn, disrespect, slight, sniff, snub, look down

反 honor, respect 尊敬；treat favorably 亲切地对待

disengage [ˌdɪsɪnˈɡeɪdʒ]

【考法】 *vt.* 分开，使脱离：to **set free** from **entanglement** or difficulty

例 seek to disengage myself from the embarrassing situation 试图把我自己从尴尬的气氛中解救出来

近 disengage, disentangle, untangle

反 embroil, entangle 卷入；mesh 啮合

disgorge [dɪsˈɡɔːrdʒ]

【考法】 *v.* 呕吐出：to **discharge** by the throat and mouth; **vomit**

例 He cannot disgorge a fish bone without the doctor's assistant. 没有医生的帮助他吐不出鱼刺来。
The volcano disgorged lava. 火山喷出岩浆。

近 belch, disgorge, eject, eruct, expel, jet, spew, spout

反 swallow, ingest 吞下，咽下

disgruntle [dɪs'grʌntl]
- 【考法】 *vt.* 使发怒，使不满意：to make ill-humored or **discontented**
- 例 be disgruntled with sb 对某人不满
- 近 disaffect, displease, dissatisfy
- 反 content, gratify, please, satisfy 使满意

Unit 7

■ DIGNIFIED	■ DISINCLINATION	■ DISINFECT	■ DISJOINTED	■ DISINTER
■ DISINTERESTED	■ DISJUNCTIVE	■ DISMANTLE	■ DISMAY	■ DISPARAGE

dignified ['dɪgnɪfaɪd]
- 【考法】 *adj.* 高贵庄严的：**serious** and somewhat **formal**
- 例 We want to make sure that every human being has a dignified life. 我们想确保，每个人都过上有尊严的生活。
- 近 august, distinguished, imposing, solemn, stately
- 反 flighty, frivolous, giddy, undignified 轻浮的，不严肃的

disinclination [ˌdɪsˌɪnklɪ'neɪʃn]
- 【考法】 *n.* 不喜欢，厌恶，不情愿：a **lack** of **willingness** or **desire** to do or accept something
- 例 show a marked disinclination 表现出明显的不情愿
- 近 aversion, disfavor, disliking, disrelish, mislike, unwillingness
- 反 appetite, favor, fondness, liking, partiality, preference, relish, inclination 喜欢；willingness 情愿

disinfect [ˌdɪsɪn'fekt]
- 【考法】 *vt.* 消毒，使无菌：to **free from infection** especially by destroying harmful microorganisms
- 例 disinfect with bleaching powder 用漂白粉消毒
- 近 sterilize
- 反 infect, pollute, contaminate, taint 感染，污染

disjointed [dɪs'dʒɔɪntɪd]
- 【考法】 *adj.* 不连贯的：**not** clearly or logically **connected**
- 例 disjointed drunken ramblings 不连贯的酒后胡言乱语
- 近 disconnected, unconnected
- 反 coherent, connected 连贯的

disinter [ˌdɪsɪn'tɜːr]
- 【考法】 *vt.* (从墓地里)掘出：to **take out** of the grave or tomb
- 例 disinter the Egyptia mummy 挖出木乃伊
- 近 unbury, unearth
- 反 bury, inter, tomb, inhume 埋葬

disinterested [dɪs'ɪntrəstɪd]
- 【考法】 *adj.* 公正的，无偏见的：**free from selfish** motive or interest: **unbiased**
- 例 a disinterested decision 公正的决定
- 近 equal, evenhanded, impartial, just, nonpartisan, dispassionate, objective, square, unbiased, unprejudiced
- 反 biased, inequitable, nonobjective, one-sided, partial, partisan, prejudiced, unjust 不公正的，有偏见的

disjunctive [dɪs'dʒʌŋktɪv]
- 【考法】 *adj.* 分离的：marked by **breaks** or **disunity**
- 例 a disjunctive narrative sequence 分散的叙述顺序
- 近 discrete, separate, disconnected, disunited
- 反 combined, connected, jointed, mixed, united 连接的，混合的

dismantle [dɪs'mæntl]
- 【考法】 *vt.* 分解，分拆：to take to **pieces** also: to **destroy** the **integrity** or functioning of
- 例 dismantle a machine 分拆机器
- 近 break down, knock down
- 反 assemble, construct 组装

dismay [dɪs'meɪ]
- 【考法 1】 *vt.* 使失去勇气：to cause to **lose courage** or resolution
- 例 The excessive homework dismayed ourselves. 过量的作业让我们失去了信心。
- 近 chill, daunt, dishearten, dispirit, frustrate, unnerve
- 反 embolden, encourage, hearten, nerve 鼓励，使勇敢

【考法2】 *vt.* 使不安，使焦虑：to **trouble** the mind of; to make **uneasy**
例 dismayed at the cynicism of the youngsters 对年轻人的愤世嫉俗感到焦虑
近 agitate, bother, discomfort, discompose, disquiet, distemper, distress, perturb, unsettle, upset
反 calm, compose, quiet, soothe, tranquilize 平息，抚慰

disparage ［dɪ'spærɪdʒ］
【考法】 *vt.* 贬低；轻蔑地说：to **lower** in rank or reputation; to speak of in a slighting or **disrespectful** way; belittle
例 use the past to disparage the present 借古讽今
近 belittle, denigrate, deprecate, depreciate, derogate, degrade
反 acclaim, applaud, exalt, extol, glorify, laud 赞扬

Unit 8

■ DISPARATE	■ DISPASSIONATE	■ DISPATCH	■ DISPOSE	■ DISREGARD
■ DISSECT	■ DISSEMBLE	■ DISSEMINATE	■ DISSENSION	■ DISSENT

disparate ［'dɪspərət］
【考法】 *adj.* 迥然不同的：fundamentally **distinct** or **different** in kind; entirely **dissimilar**
例 Pull together disparate ideas 把迥然不同的观点汇集起来
近 dissimilar, distinct, distinguishable, diverse, nonidentical, unalike
反 alike, identical, indistinguishable, kindred, like, parallel, same, similar 相似的，相同的

dispassionate ［dɪs'pæʃənət］
【考法】 *adj.* 客观公正的，不易被情绪或偏见影响的：devoid of or **unaffected** by passion, emotion, or **bias**
例 a dispassionate analysis 客观公正的分析
近 disinterested, equal, equitable, evenhanded, impartial, just, nonpartisan, objective, unbiased, unprejudiced
反 biased, inequitable, nonobjective, one-sided, partial, partisan, prejudiced, unjust 有偏见的，不公正的

dispatch ［dɪ'spætʃ］
【考法1】 *n.* 迅速：**promptness** and efficiency in performance or transmission
例 do sth with dispatch 迅速地做某事
近 alacrity, haste, swiftness, expedition, promptitude
反 leisureliness, delay, procrastination 悠然；拖延
【考法2】 *vt.* 发送，派遣：to cause to go or be taken from **one place to another**
例 to dispatch a messenger with urgent news 发送一个紧急消息
近 transfer, transmit, transport, pack off
反 accept, receive 接收

dispose ［dɪ'spoʊz］
【考法1】 *vt.* 使倾向于：to give a **tendency** to: **incline**
例 faulty diet disposes one to sickness 营养不全面导致疾病
派 disposed *adj.* 喜欢的：willing or likely, inclined
例 not feel disposed to argue with her 不喜欢与她争执
近 willing, inclined, predisposed, prone
反 disinclined, indisposed 不喜欢的
【考法2】 *vi.* 处理掉（与 of 连用，dispose of）：to **get rid of**; **throw out**
派 disposal *n.* 处理，不再利用：the act of getting rid of something that is no longer wanted or needed
例 the permanent disposal of radioactive wastes 对放射性废物的永久处理

disregard ［ˌdɪsrɪ'gɑːrd］
【考法1】 *vt.* 漠视，不关注：to pay **no attention** to
例 disregard his feelings 漠视他的感受
近 ignore, overlook, slight
反 heed, mind, regard, attend to 关注
【考法2】 *n.* 缺乏兴趣，缺乏关心：lack of **interest** or **concern**
例 Revelers fired guns in the air with complete disregard for the possible consequences. 饮酒狂欢者朝空中乱开枪，一点也不关心可能产生的后果。
近 apathy, disinterestedness, incuriosity, nonchalance, torpor, unconcern
反 concern, interest, regard 关心，感兴趣

dissect [dɪˈsekt]

【考法】 *vt.* 仔细分析：to **examine**, **analyze**, or criticize in **minute** detail

例 dissect some basic problems in mathematics analysis 仔细研究数学分析中的一些基本问题 ‖ Let's dissect the plot of this thriller to see what makes it thrilling. 让我们来仔细分析一下这个恐怖电影为什么恐怖。

近 analyze

dissemble [dɪˈsembl]

【考法】 *v.* 用假象隐藏真相，掩饰：to put on a **false** appearance

例 dissemble fear with a smile 用微笑来掩饰恐惧 ‖ He dissembled happiness at the news that his ex-girl-friend was getting married to someone else. 他听到前女友结婚的消息后假装高兴。

近 dissimulate, affect, assume, bluff, counterfeit, fake, sham

反 behave honestly 表现诚恳

disseminate [dɪˈsemɪneɪt]

【考法】 *vt.* 散播，传播：to **spread** abroad; **promulgate**

例 disseminate Marxism-Leninism 传播马列主义 ‖ The Internet allows us to disseminate information faster. 互联网让我们更快地传播信息。

近 broadcast, circulate, propagate

反 gather, amass, garner 收集

dissension [dɪˈsenʃn]

【考法】 *n.* 意见不合：**difference** of opinion; **disagreement**

例 a continued dissension on the issue 关于这件事的持续分歧

近 conflict, disaccord, discordance, discordancy, disharmony, dissent, dissidence, dissonance, disunion, disunity, division, friction, inharmony, schism, strife, row, divergence

反 accord, agreement, concord, concordance, harmony, consensus, unanimity 和谐，一致

dissent [dɪˈsent]

【考法1】 *vi.* 持异议，不同意：to **differ** in opinion

例 I dissent from what you said. 我不同意你说的话。

近 differ, disagree, nonconcur

反 agree, assent, concur 同意

【考法2】 *n.* 反对正统：**departure** from a generally **accepted** theory, opinion, or practice

例 a political dissent 一个反对正统政治的人

近 heterodoxy, nonconformity

反 conformity 遵从；orthodoxy 正统

Unit 9

■ DISSIPATE	■ DISSOLUTE	■ DISSOLVE	■ DISSONANCE	■ DISSUADE
■ DISTAIN	■ DISTAL	■ DISTEND	■ DISTILL	■ DISTORT

dissipate [ˈdɪsɪpeɪt]

【考法1】 *vt.* 驱散：to **drive away**; **disperse**

例 The wind finally dissipated the smoke. 风终于吹散了雾气。

近 disband, dispel, disperse, scatter

反 accumulate, gather, amass, cluster, assemble, concentrate, congregate 积聚

【考法2】 *vt.* 浪费：to spend or expend intemperately or **wastefully**: **squander**

例 dissipate too much time and effort 挥霍了太多的时间与精力

近 waste, squander, lavish

反 conserve 节省

dissolute [ˈdɪsəluːt]

【考法】 *adj.* 放荡的，无节制的：lacking moral **restraint**; **indulging** in sensual pleasures or vices

例 lead a dissolute life 过着放荡无节制的生活

近 dissipated, libertine, rakish, reprobate

反 abstinent, abstemious, temperate, ascetic, stoic, spartan, self-denying 自我节制的；pure, uncorrupt, uncorrupted 纯洁的，未堕落的

dissolve [dɪˈzɑːlv]

【考法1】 *v.* 溶解，融化：to cause to pass into **solution**; to reduce (solid matter) to liquid form; **melt**

例 Sugar dissolves in the water. 糖在水中溶解。

近 liquefy, melt

反 coagulate, solidify, freeze 凝结，凝固，结冰

【考法 2】 *v.* 解散：to **break into** component **parts**; **disintegrate**
例 The committee has been dissolved. 委员会被解散了。
近 disintegrate, disband, break up
反 consolidate, unify 使联合

dissonance [ˈdɪsənəns]
【考法】 *n.* (音调)不和谐，刺身；不一致，分歧：a harsh, **disagreeable** combination of sounds; **discord**; lack of agreement, consistency, or harmony; conflict
例 cognitive dissonance 认识上的分歧 ‖ Dissonance among the three partners doomed the project. 三个股东间的不调和注定了那计划的失败。
近 conflict, disaccord, discordance, discordancy, disharmony, dissent, dissidence, disunion, disunity, division, friction, inharmony, schism, strife
反 accord, agreement, concord, concordance, harmony, consensus, unanimity 和谐，一致

dissuade [dɪˈsweɪd]
【考法】 *vt.* 劝阻，反对：to **deter** (a person) from a course of action or a purpose by **persuasion** or **exhortation**
例 dissuade sb from (doing) sth 劝阻/反对某人做某事 ‖ Her parents tried to dissuade her from her intention to drop out of college. 她的父母劝她不要退学。
近 deter, inhibit
反 encourage 鼓励；persuade 说服

distain [dɪsˈteɪn]
【考法】 *vt.* 贬损，伤害(某人的)名誉：to cause to **lose honor**, **respect**, or **reputation**
例 distain the commonplace life 鄙视平庸的生活
近 dishonor, belittle, denigrate, deprecate, depreciate, degrade
反 praise, acclaim, applaud, exalt, extol, glorify, laud 赞扬

distal [ˈdɪstl]
【考法】 *adj.* 远离中心的,(神经)末梢的：**situated away** from the point of attachment or origin or a **central** point
例 the distal end of nerve 神经末梢
反 proximal 接近中心的

distend [dɪˈstend]
【考法】 *v.* (使)膨胀：to (cause to) swell out or **expand** from or as if from internal pressure
例 The stomachs of starving people often distend. 饥民的肚子经常涨起来。
近 expand, dilate, inflate, swell
反 constrict, compress 收缩，压缩

distill [dɪˈstɪl]
【考法】 *vt.* 对…用蒸馏法提高纯度：to **increase** the concentration of, separate, or **purify** by or as if by distillation
例 Distill the water before pouring it in the steam iron. 在把水蒸馏一下
近 purify, filter, refine, fine
派 distillate *n.* 蒸馏物，纯化物，精华：a purified form; an essence

distort [dɪˈstɔːrt]
【考法】 *vt.* 扭曲，歪曲：to **twist** out of the true meaning or proportion
例 A painter may exaggerate or distort shapes and forms. 画家可能会夸张或扭曲形状。
近 deform, misshape, torture, falsify, misinterpret, misrepresent, pervert, twist

Unit 10

■ DISTRACT	■ DISTRAUGHT	■ DIURNAL	■ DIVERGE	■ DIVERSITY
■ DIVERT	■ DIVESTITURE	■ DIVULGE	■ DODDER	■ DODGE

distract [dɪˈstrækt]
【考法】 *vt.* 转移(注意力)，使分心：to **draw** or **direct** (as one's attention) to a **different** object
例 be distracted by a sudden noise 被突然的噪音分心
近 abstract, divert, detract, call off
派 distracted *adj.* 精力分散的
反 rapt 全心投入的

distraught [dɪˈstrɔːt]
【考法】 *adj.* 精神狂乱的，极疯狂的：deeply **agitated**, as from emotional conflict; **insane**
例 a distraught maniac 一个精神狂乱的疯子
近 agitated, delirious, distracted, frenzied, hysterical
反 collected, composed, recollected, self-collected, self-composed, self-possessed 镇静的，平静的

diurnal [daɪˈɜːrnl]
【考法】 *adj.* 白天发生或行动的：occurring or active during the **daytime** rather than at night
例 diurnal animals 昼行性动物
反 nocturnal 夜晚的

diverge [daɪˈvɜːrdʒ]
【考法1】 *vt.* （使）分叉，散开：to (cause to) go or move in **different directions** from a **central** point
例 The river's branches diverged. 河的支流分叉了。
近 branch out, divide, spread
反 converge, join 会合
【考法2】 *vi.* 分歧：to become or be **different** in character or form: **differ** in opinion
近 differ, disagree
反 conform 遵从
派 divergence *n.* 分歧，不同意：disagreement

diversity [daɪˈvɜːrsəti]
【考法】 *n.* 多样性：**variety** or **multiformity**
例 the diversity of species 物种的多样性
近 diverseness, multifariousness, multiplicity, variousness, miscellaneousness

divert [daɪˈvɜːrt]
【考法1】 *vt.* 使转向：to **turn** from one course or use to another: **deflect**
例 divert traffic to a side street 使交通转至辅路
近 deflect, redirect, swing, veer, wheel
反 fix, set, settle 固定
【考法2】 *vt.* 使消遣：to cause（someone）to pass the time **agreeably** occupied
例 A light comedy divert the tired business executive. 一个轻松的喜剧让疲惫的企业主管人员得到了放松。
近 disport, entertain, regale, solace

divestiture [daɪˈvestɪtʃər]
【考法】 *n.* 剥夺：the act of **taking away** from a person
例 Melodramas were popular because they offered the audience a divestiture of neutrality. 情节剧之所以受到欢迎是因为他们给观众一个缺乏中立的(世界)。
近 deprivation, dispossession
反 acquisition 获得；endowment 捐赠

divulge [daɪˈvʌldʒ]
【考法】 *vt.* 泄漏(秘密)：to make **known**（as a **confidence** or **secret**）
例 refuse to divulge details of the negotiations 拒绝透露谈判的细节内容 ‖ We tried to make him divulge the name of the winner, but he wouldn't budge. 我们试图让他透露胜利者的名字，但是他没有那样做。
近 bare, disclose, discover, expose, uncover, unmask, unveil
反 conceal, cover up, hide, mask, shroud, veil 保密，隐藏

dodder [ˈdɑːdər]
【考法】 *vi.* 蹒跚，颤巍巍地行进：to **progress** feebly and **unsteadily**
例 He could only dodder along after the operation. 他手术后只能步履蹒跚地走。
近 careen, lurch, teeter, totter, waddle

dodge [dɑːdʒ]
【考法】 *v.* 躲避：to **avoid**（a blow, for example）by moving or shifting quickly aside
例 dodge a storm of bullets 躲避枪林弹雨 ‖ He dodged the first punch but was hit by the second. 他躲过了第一次打击，但是没有躲过第二次。
近 avoid, escape, shirk, malinger, goldbrick, evade, parry, sidestep, circumvent, fence, hedge, avert, elude, shun, skirt, bilk, eschew, weasel

List 8

"没有野心的人是给自己的懒惰找借口。"

（卢璐，2006 年 10 月，Verbal 750，Quantitative 790，AW 5.5，
就职于 Lazard，中国香港）

Unit 1

■ DOFF	■ DOGGED	■ DOGMATIC	■ DOLDRUMS	■ DOLOROUS
■ DOLT	■ DOMICILE	■ DOMINANT	■ DON	■ DONOR

doff [dɑːf]
【考法】 *vt.* 脱下：to **take off**; **remove**
例 The blazing sun soon had the men doffing their jackets. 炙热的太阳很快就让男人们脱掉了夹克。
近 put off, take off
反 don, put on 穿上

dogged [ˈdɔːɡɪd]
【考法】 *adj.* 固执的，任性的：**sticking to** an opinion, purpose, or course of action in spite of reason, arguments, or persuasion
例 Your dogged adherence to a really lame argument is embarrassing. 你固执地坚持一个站不住脚的观点令人很尴尬。
近 adamant, hardheaded, headstrong, inflexible, intransigent, mulish, obdurate opinionated, ossified, pertinacious, self-opinionated, self-willed, stubborn, unbending, uncompromising, unrelenting, unyielding, willful
反 acquiescent, amenable, compliant, complying, flexible, pliable, pliant, relenting, yielding 顺从的

dogmatic [dɔːɡˈmætɪk]
【考法】 *adj.* 武断的，自以为是的：given to or marked by the forceful expression of **strongly held opinions**
例 a critic's dogmatic insistence that abstract expressionism is the only school of 20th century art worthy of serious study 一个评论家自以为是地坚持认为抽象表现主义是 20 世纪唯一值得严肃研究的艺术学派
近 doctrinaire, opinionated, opinioned
反 latitudinarian, undoctrinaire, undogmatic 不死板的，不拘泥教条的

doldrums [ˈdoʊldrəmz]
【考法】 *n.* 低迷，中断：a state or period of **inactivity**, stagnation, or slump
例 August is a time of doldrums for many enterprises. 对于许多企业来说八月是一个低迷期。‖ The economy is in the doldrums. 经济低迷。
近 abeyance, dormancy, latency, quiescence, moratorium
反 continuation 持续

dolorous [ˈdoʊlərəs]
【考法】 *adj.* 忧伤的：causing, marked by, or expressing **misery** or grief
例 He lifted a pair of sapphire, dolorous eyes. 他抬起了一双忧郁的、蓝宝石般的眼睛。
近 agonized, bemoaning, bewailing, deplorable, grievous, miserable, plaintive, rueful, sorrowful, woeful
反 happy, joyful, jovial, jubilant 高兴的

dolt [doʊlt]
【考法】 *n.* 笨蛋：a **stupid** person
例 What a dolt I have been! 我是多么的愚蠢啊！
近 idiot, fool, moron, simpleton, dullard
反 illuminati, intellectual 智者；genius 天才
派 doltish *adj.* 愚笨的

domicile [ˈdɑːmɪsaɪl]
【考法】 *vt.* 为…提供住处：to establish in or **provide** with a **domicile**
例 The university domiciles students in a variety of buildings in and around its urban campus. 大学在城区校园周围为学生提供了多样化的宿舍。
近 accommodate, bestow, lodge, harbor, put up
反 banish, expel 驱逐

dominant [ˈdɑːmɪnənt]

【考法 1】 *adj.* 处于支配地位的: commanding, **controlling**, or prevailing over all **others**

例 the dominant culture 主流文化

近 ascendant, leading, outweighing, paramount, prevalent, principal, supreme

反 subordinate（等级上）低的

派 dominate *v.* 占主导地位，统治；dominance *n.* 主导，主流

【考法 2】 *adj.* （基因）显性的: of, relating to, or exerting ecological or **genetic dominance**

例 the dominant gene 显性基因

反 recessive 隐性的

派 dominance *n.* （基因的）显性

don [dɑːn]

【考法】 *vt.* 穿上: to put on (an article of clothing)

例 He donned a raincoat for his trip. 他为出行穿上雨衣。

近 assume, wear, put on

反 doff 脱下

donor [ˈdoʊnər]

【考法】 *n.* 捐赠人，给体: one that gives, **donates**, or presents something

例 donors of funds to research foundations 研究基金的捐赠人

近 donator, presenter, contributor, subscriber, patron, sugar daddy

反 acceptor 受体

Unit 2

■ DOODLE	■ DORMANT	■ DOUR	■ DOUSE	■ DOWNPLAY
■ DOOM	■ DOYEN	■ DOZE	■ DRACONIAN	■ DRAWL

doodle [ˈduːdl]

【考法 1】 *vi.* （无目的地）乱涂乱画: to scribble **aimlessly**, especially when preoccupied

例 Google doodle 谷歌涂鸦

近 mess around

【考法 2】 *vi.* 漫无目的地打发时光: to spend time in **aimless activity**

例 I plan to spend the entire vacation just doodling. 我打算整个假期就随便做点事打发时间。

近 dawdle, trifle

dormant [ˈdɔːrmənt]

【考法】 *adj.* 静止的，不活跃的: in a state of rest or **inactivity; inoperative; in abeyance**

例 dormant volcanoes 静止的火山

近 dead, latent, lurking, abeyant, quiescent, inert

反 active, busy, operating 活跃的

dour [ˈdaʊər]

【考法】 *adj.* 严厉的: **harsh** and threatening in manner or appearance

例 a dour, taciturn man 一个严厉沉默的男人

近 strict, sharp, austere, exacting, fierce, gruff, intimidating, rough, stark, stern

反 benign, gentle, mild, tender 温和的

douse [daʊs]

【考法】 *vt.* 熄灭: to put out (a light or fire)

例 douse a fire with water 用水熄灭火焰

近 quench, extinguish, put out

反 kindle, ignite, inflame 点燃

downplay [ˌdaʊnˈpleɪ]

【考法】 *vt.* 轻描淡写，不予重视: to **minimize** the **significance** of, play down

例 downplay the bad news 对坏消息轻描淡写

近 de-emphasize, disregard, ignore, overlook, neglect, understate, play down

反 address, emphasize, underscore 强调

doom	[du:m]
【考法】	*v.* 注定(倒霉): to **determine the fate** of suffering in advance
例	That argument was the turning point for their marriage, and the one which doomed it to failure . 那次争吵是他们婚姻的一个转折点，它注定了他们婚姻的失败。
近	fate, foredoom, foreordain, predestine, predetermine

doyen	[ˈdɔɪən]
【考法】	*n.* 有经验的人，资深人士，老司机: a person considered to be **knowledgeable** or uniquely skilled as a result of long **experience** in some field of endeavor
例	a doyen in the industry 业界的元老
近	authority, expert, master, maven, veteran, virtuoso
反	amateur, layman 业余爱好者，门外汉; tyro, novice, neophyte, rookie, fledgling 新手

doze	[douz]
【考法】	*vi./n.* 小憩: to sleep **lightly** or briefly
例	He dozed off during the lecture . 他在讲座上睡着了。
近	drowse, nap, wink, slumber
反	wake 醒来

draconian	[drəˈkouniən]
【考法】	*adj.* 极其残酷的；十分严厉的: exceedingly **harsh**; very severe
例	draconian measures to solve the problem 解决这个问题的严厉措施
近	rigid, ironhanded, strict, stringent
反	mild, genial, lenient 温和的

drawl	[drɔ:l]
【考法】	*v.* 慢吞吞地说: to **speak slowly** with vowels greatly prolonged
例	The old woman was drawling on and on . 老太太慢吞吞说个没完。
近	extend, lengthen, prolong, protract, draw out
反	drivel, gibber 快速(而模糊)地说

Unit 3

■ DREARY	■ DRENCH	■ DRIVEL	■ DIMINUTIVE	■ DROLLNESS
■ DRONE	■ DRUDGERY	■ DUBIOUS	■ DUCTILE	■ DULCET

dreary	[ˈdrɪri]
【考法】	*adj.* 单调乏味的: having **nothing** likely to provide **cheer**, comfort, or interest
例	a dreary English lecture 一个无聊的英语讲座
近	desolate, gloomy, sullen, dull, monotone, pedestrian, somber
反	jocund 令人欢乐的

drench	[drentʃ]
【考法】	*vt.* 使湿透，浸透: to **wet thoroughly**
例	The thunderstorm drenched us to the skin . 雷雨把我们浇了个透。
近	bathe, deluge, douse, soak, saturate, sodden, sop, wet
反	dehydrate, desiccate, dry 脱水，干燥; parch, scorch, sear 烧焦，烤焦

drivel	[ˈdrɪvl]
【考法】	*n.* 胡言乱语: unintelligible or **meaningless** talk *v.* 胡言乱语，说傻话: to **talk stupidly** and carelessly
例	His writing is just meaningless drivel . 他的文章只是一些无意义的胡言乱语。
近	abracadabra, nonsense, prattle, gabble; babble, gabble, gibber, jabber

diminutive	[dɪˈmɪnjətɪv]
【考法】	*adj.* 极小的: of a size that is **less than average**
例	She noticed a diminutive figure standing at the entrance. 她注意到入口处站着一个小小的身影。
近	minuscule, small, pocket, slight, smallish, subnormal, undersized
反	considerable, grand, outsized, oversized, substantial, whopping 大的

drollness	[ˈdroulnəs]
【考法】	*n.* 搞笑，逗逼: the **amusing** quality or element in something

例 The professor's drollness endeared him to his students. 教授的幽默使他备受学生欢迎。
近 comedy, comic, funniness, hilariousness, humorousness
反 pathos 悲伤

drone [droʊn]
【考法】 v. 低沉单调地说；嗡嗡地叫：to talk in a persistently dull or monotonous tone
例 droning bees 嗡嗡作响的蜜蜂
近 hum, buzz, bumble

drudgery ['drʌdʒəri]
【考法】 n. 苦工；单调、卑贱或无趣的工作：tedious, menial, or unpleasant work
例 reduce drudgery and enhance people's quality of life 减少单调苦工并提高人们的生活质量
近 labor, slavery, toil, travail, grind
反 sinecure 闲职，美差；fun, play 玩耍，娱乐

dubious ['duːbiəs]
【考法】 adj. 充满不定性的，值得怀疑的：giving rise to uncertainty; questionable or suspect as to true nature or quality
例 his dubious testimony 他值得怀疑的证词
近 debatable, doubtful, disputable, equivocal, problematic, questionable, shaky
反 certain, incontestable, undeniable 确定的，毋庸置疑的；reliable 可靠的

ductile ['dʌktaɪl]
【考法】 adj. 易受影响的：easily led or influenced
例 a ductile personality 易受他人影响的性格
近 pliant, yielding, supple
反 adamant, intractable, refractory, obdurate 倔强的，不易改变立场的

dulcet ['dʌlsɪt]
【考法】 adj. 悦耳的，令人愉悦的：pleasing to the ear; melodious; generally pleasing or agreeable
例 dulcet tones from harps and flutes 竖琴和长笛发出的悦耳音调
近 sweet, agreeable, delightful, euphonic, mellifluous, tuneful, winsome
反 cacophonous, grating 刺耳的

Unit 4

■ DULLARD	■ DUPE	■ DUPLICITOUS	■ DWINDLE	■ DYSPEPTIC
■ EARNEST	■ EMBRYONIC	■ EARSPLITTING	■ EAVESDROP	■ EBULLIENT

dullard ['dʌlɑːrd]
【考法】 n. 笨蛋：a stupid or unimaginative person
例 A dullard alway distains knowledge. 一个笨蛋永远鄙视知识。
近 moron, simpleton, idiot, fool
反 wit 机智的人；genius 天才
派 dull adj. 愚笨的

dupe [duːp]
【考法1】 n. 易受骗的人：one that is easily deceived or cheated
例 The swindler was able to escape with all of the dupe's money. 骗子带着受骗人的财产成功逃跑了。
近 fool, victim, gull
反 connoisseur 行家，鉴赏家
【考法2】 vt. 欺骗：to deceive (an unwary person)
例 dupe stamp collectors into buying fake goods 欺骗集邮者买假货
近 bamboozle, beguile, cheat, cozen, delude, gull, hoax, hoodwink
派 dupable adj. 易受骗的

duplicitous [djuː'plɪsɪtəs]
【考法】 adj. 两面派的，奸诈的：given to or marked by cheating and deception
例 Paris had been duplicitous in its dealings with the European authorities. 法国在此事的处理上对欧盟大搞两面派。
近 crooked, deceptive, dishonest, fraudulent, guileful, shifty, underhanded
反 aboveboard, honest, straight 光明正大的
派 duplicity n. 欺骗，口是心非

dwindle [ˈdwɪndl]
【考法】 *vi.* 逐渐减少: to become **gradually less** until little remains
例 His vast fortune is dwindling away . 他的巨额财富正在慢慢缩水。
近 abate, decrease, drop, diminish, reduce, shrink, taper, wane, knock down
反 aggrandize, balloon, burgeon, increase 增加; accumulate 累积
派 dwindling *adj.* 减少的

dyspeptic [dɪsˈpeptɪk]
【考法】 *adj.* 脾气坏的: **bad-tempered**
例 in a dyspeptic mood 情绪暴躁
近 cantankerous, disagreeable, irritable, fretful, irascible, peevish, splenetic, surly
反 amiable, easygoing, genial, good-humored, good-natured, good-tempered 随和的, 和蔼的

earnest [ˈɜːrnɪst]
【考法】 *adj.* 严肃认真的: characterized by or proceeding from an intense and **serious** state of mind, **grave**
例 an earnest machine operator 一丝不苟的机器操作员
近 grave, serious, solemn, staid, sober
反 facetious, frivolous, flip, flippant, playful 轻浮的

embryonic [ˌembriˈɑːnɪk]
【考法】 *adj.* 初期的, 萌芽阶段的: being in an **early stage** of development
例 He does not have much faith in the embryonic European central bank. 他对于处于萌芽阶段的欧洲中央银行并不看好。
近 aborning, beginning, inceptive, incipient, inchoate, initial, nascent, rudimentary
反 adult, full-blown, full-fledged, mature, ripe 成熟的, 成形的; moribund 将死的

earsplitting [ɪrˈsplɪtɪŋ]
【考法】 *adj.* 震耳欲聋的: **distressingly loud** or shrill
例 earsplitting noise of airplane engines 飞机引擎的巨大噪音
近 blaring, blasting, deafening, loud, piercing, plangent, resounding, roaring, stentorian, thunderous
反 gentle, soft (音乐)轻柔的

eavesdrop [ˈiːvzdrɑːp]
【考法】 *vi.* 偷听: to **listen secretly** to the private conversation of others
例 eavesdrop on the conversation 偷听谈话
近 overhear, wiretap

ebullient [ɪˈbʌliənt]
【考法】 *adj.* 热情奔放的: **zestfully** enthusiastic
例 an ebullient and energetic president 一个热情、充满活力的总统
近 boiling, exuberant, effervescent, vivacious
反 tepid, torpid 无精打采的
派 ebullience *n.* 热情洋溢

Unit 5

| ■ ECCENTRIC | ■ ÉCLAT | ■ ECLIPSE | ■ ECSTASY | ■ ECUMENICAL |
| ■ EDIBLE | ■ EDIFICE | ■ EFFACE | ■ EFFERVESCE | ■ EFFETE |

eccentric [ɪkˈsentrɪk]
【考法】 *adj.* 行为出格的, 不循规蹈矩的: **deviating** from **conventional** or accepted usage or conduct
例 eccentric speech patterns 古怪的演讲模式
近 strange, bizarre, erratic, idiosyncratic, odd, offbeat, outlandish, quaint, weird
反 ordinary, regular 常规的
派 eccentricity *n.* 古怪

éclat [eɪˈklæ]
【考法】 *n.* 辉煌成就: brilliant or conspicuous **success**
例 The premier of Mozart's *Le Nozze di Figaro* enjoyed a great éclat in 1786. 莫扎特歌剧《费加罗的婚礼》于 1786 年的首演获得了极大的成功。
近 fame, renown, brilliance, triumph
反 debacle, fiasco 惨败

eclipse [ɪˈklɪps]
- 【考法】 *vt.* 使声望下降，使黯然失色：to obscure or **diminish** in **importance**, fame, or reputation
- 例 Her score eclipsed the old record . 她的分数使旧的纪录黯然失色。
- 近 adumbrate, obscure, overshadow

ecstasy [ˈekstəsi]
- 【考法】 *n.* 狂喜：**intense joy** or delight
- 例 be in ecstasy over the offer from Harvard University 因被哈佛录取而欣喜若狂
- 近 delight, elation, euphoria, exhilaration, rapture, transport
- 反 depression, melancholy 沮丧

ecumenical [ˌiːkjuːˈmenɪkl]
- 【考法】 *adj.* 世界范围的，普遍性的：**worldwide** or general in extent, influence, or application
- 例 an ecumenical scope 国际视野
- 近 universal, cosmopolitan, global, planetary, worldwide
- 反 provincial, insular 狭隘的

edible [ˈedəbl]
- 【考法】 *adj.* 可食用的：fit to be **eaten**
- 例 No chemicals in the laboratory is edible . 实验室中的任何化学试剂都不能食用。
- 近 eatable, comestible, consumable, digestible, esculent
- 反 inedible 不可食用的
- 派 edibility *n.* 可食用

edifice [ˈedɪfɪs]
- 【考法 1】 *n.* 大厦；大建筑物：a large or **massive structure**
- 例 The Capitol is one of the most impressive edifices in the United States. 国会山是美国最令人印象深刻的建筑之一。
- 近 building, erection, palace
- 反 cottage 小棚舍
- 【考法 2】 *n.* 基础，基本构架：the arrangement of parts that gives something its **basic form**
- 例 The edifice of the argument is quite simple, once you get past the fancy language. 只要你看透了表面花哨的语言，你会发现这段论证的基本构架是非常简单的。
- 近 architecture, configuration, framework, skeleton, structure

efface [ɪˈfeɪs]
- 【考法】 *vt.* 擦掉，抹去；使不明显：to eliminate or **make indistinct** by or as if by wearing away a surface
- 例 efface those unpleasant memories 抹去那些不快的记忆
- 近 eradicate, erase, expunge, exterminate, extirpate, liquidate, eclipse, obliterate, wipe, root out
- 反 blazon, decorate 装饰；emboss 使凸起，使显现
- 派 self-effacing *adj.* 谦卑的，低调的

effervesce [ˌefərˈves]
- 【考法】 *vi.* 兴奋，热情洋溢：to show **high spirits** or animation
- 例 effervesce over the news of victory 因胜利的消息而兴奋
- 近 rejoice, exult, jubilate, triumph
- 反 grieve 感到极度悲伤
- 派 effervescent *adj.* 热情洋溢的；effervescence *n.* 热情洋溢

effete [ɪˈfiːt]
- 【考法】 *adj.* 衰弱的，衰落的：**depleted** of vitality, force, or effectiveness
- 例 Effete heart needs a moment rest . 衰弱的心灵需要片刻的停歇。
- 近 consumed, debilitated, decadent, degenerate, depleted, drained, exhausted, feeble
- 反 hale, sound, robust 强健的，充满活力的
- 派 effetely *adv.* 衰弱地

Unit 6

effluvium [ɪˈfluːvɪəm]

【考法】 *n.* 难闻的气味：an **offensive** exhalation or **smell**

例 Repulsive effluvia made us vomit. 这恶臭让我们作呕。

近 malodor, stink, stench

反 fragrance, aroma 芳香

派 effluvial *adj.* 恶臭的

effrontery [ɪˈfrʌntəri]

【考法】 *n.* 厚颜无耻，放肆大胆：flagrant **disregard** of **courtesy** or propriety and an arrogant assumption of privilege

例 The man had the effrontery to insult her father. 这个男人胆敢辱骂她的父亲。

近 audacity, brashness, brazenness, insolence, nerve, presumption, temerity

反 decorum, propriety, courtesy, grace 得体；timidity 胆小

effulgent [ɪˈfʌldʒənt]

【考法】 *adj.* 光辉灿烂的：shining brilliantly; **resplendent**

例 an effulgent sunset on the Atlantic 大西洋上壮丽辉煌的日落

近 bright, beaming, glorious, luminous, radiant, splendid

反 dim, murky, dull 模糊的，黯淡的

派 effulgence *n.* 光辉

effusive [ɪˈfjuːsɪv]

【考法】 *adj.* 感情泛滥的/溢于言表的；感情表达不节制的/过度的；过分多情的：**unrestrained** or excessive **in emotional expression**

例 The principal delivered an effusive address at the commencement ceremony. 校长在毕业典礼上做了充满感情的演讲。

近 emotional, expansive, demonstrative, gushy, passionate

反 inhibited, reserved, restrained 节制的；undemonstrative, unemotional 不易动情的；numb, torpid 麻木不仁的

派 effusion *n.* 流出，溢出

egalitarian [iˌɡælɪˈterɪən]

【考法】 *adj.* 平等主义的：affirming, **promoting**, or characterized by belief in **equal** political, economic, social, and civil **rights** for all people

例 the notion of an egalitarian society 平等主义社会的理念

近 disinterested, impartial, unprejudiced, unbiased, objective

反 inequitable, discriminating, unfair 有偏见的，不公平的

派 egalitarianism *n.* 平等主义

egoistic [ˌiːɡoʊˈɪstɪk]

【考法】 *adj.* 利己的，以自我为中心的：being **centered in** or preoccupied with **oneself** and the gratification of one's own desires

例 egoistic behaviors others detest 令人厌恶的利己行为

近 egocentric, self-centered, individualistic, navel-gazing

反 altruistic, selfless 利他的，无私的

派 ego *n.* 自大，自我；egoism *n.* 利己主义；egoist *n.* 以自我为中心的人

elaborate

【考法】 [ɪˈlæbərət] *adj.* 详细的，复杂的：marked by **complexity**, fullness of detail, or ornament

[ɪˈlæbəreɪt] *vt.* 详细阐述：to expand something **in detail**

例 an elaborate manual 内容详尽的使用手册 ‖ elaborate on a statement 详细阐述一份声明

近 circumstantial, complex, complicated, intricate, knotty, minute, particular, particularized, sophisticated; develop, expand, amplify, explain

反 sketchy, brief, compendious, summary 概要性的；abstract, abbreviate, condense, simplify 简化；downplay, ignore, neglect, overlook 忽视，忽略

elastic	[ɪ'læstɪk]
【考法 1】	*adj.* 有弹性的：easily **resuming** original **shape** after being stretched or expanded
例	elastic rubber band 弹性橡胶圈
近	bouncy, flexible, malleable, resilient, stretchable, supple
反	rigid, stiff 僵化的
派	inelastic *adj.* 无弹性的，非弹性的
【考法 2】	*adj.* 能（迅速从伤痛中）恢复的：capable of **recovering** quickly especially **from depression** or disappointment
例	owe her success to an elastic optimistic nature 将她的成功归因于能迅速走出悲伤的乐观品质
近	adaptable, adjustable, buoyant, pliable, volatile
反	established, fixed, immutable 不变的

elate	[i'leɪt]
【考法】	*vt.* 使开心，使自豪：to **fill with joy** or pride
例	The phenomenal sales record elated him. 卓越的业绩让他高兴不已。
近	cheer, excite, exhilarate, inspire, stimulate
反	depress, dishearten, sadden 使沮丧
派	elated *adj.* 高兴的；elation *n.* 高兴

eleemosynary	[ˌelɪɪ'mɑːsɪˌneri]
【考法】	*adj.* 慈善的：of, relating to, or supported by **charity**
例	an eleemosynary foundation funded by the Bill Gates 由比尔·盖茨夫妇资助的慈善基金
近	benevolent, charitable, humane, humanitarian, philanthropic
反	parsimonious 吝啬的

Unit 7

■ ELEGY	■ ELEPHANTINE	■ ELEVATE	■ ELICIT	■ ELLIPTICAL
■ ELUCIDATE	■ EMACIATE	■ EMANCIPATE	■ EMBARGO	■ EMBARK

elegy	['elədʒi]
【考法】	*n.* 哀歌(诗)，挽歌(诗)：a song or poem **expressing sorrow** or lamentation
例	a moving elegy played at the funeral 葬礼上演奏的催人泪下的挽歌
近	dirge, lamentation, requiem
反	ode 颂歌，颂词

elephantine	[ˌelɪ'fæntiːn]
【考法 1】	*adj.* 巨大的：having **enormous size** or strength
例	an elephantine meteor crate 巨大的陨石坑
近	huge, colossal, enormous, gargantuan, gigantic, massive, prodigious, tremendous
反	microscopic, minute, tiny, infinitesimal 细微的，微小的
【考法 2】	*adj.* 笨拙的：**clumsy**, ponderous
例	elephantine movements 笨拙的行动
近	awkward, graceless, maladroit
反	graceful 优雅的

elevate	['elɪveɪt]
【考法 1】	*vt.* (在道德、智力、文化水平上)提升：to **improve** morally, intellectually, or culturally
例	a novel that both entertains and elevates readers 一本寓教于乐的小说
近	advance, boost, enhance, ennoble, raise, upgrade
反	abase, debase, demote, degrade 贬低
派	elevation *n.* 提升
【考法 2】	*vt.* 使兴奋：to **raise** the **spirits** of
例	one of the most elevating moments in their lives 生命中最让人兴奋的时刻之一
近	elate, enrapture, exhilarate, intoxicate, transport
反	depress 使沮丧

elicit	[i'lɪsɪt]
【考法】	*vt.* 激起，唤起：to draw forth or **bring out**
例	The king's speech elicited lasting cheer and applause. 国王的演讲激起了持续的欢呼和掌声。
近	arouse, evoke, excite, inspire, provoke, raise
反	appease, placate, mollify, pacify 平息

elliptical	[ɪ'lɪptɪkl]

【考法 1】 *adj.* 含糊不清的：of or relating to deliberate **obscurity**（as of literary or conversational style）

例 give an elliptical response to the inquiry 就问题给出一个含糊其辞的回答

近 ambiguous, arcane, cryptic, enigmatic, equivocal, inscrutable, murky, nebulous, occult, opaque, vague

反 clear, explicit, unambiguous, unequivocal 清晰明确的

【考法 2】 *adj.* 椭圆的：of, relating to, or shaped like an **ellipse**

近 oval, ovate

反 circular, round 圆形的

派 ellipse *n.* 椭圆

elucidate	[i'luːsɪdeɪt]

【考法】 *v.* 阐明：to **make lucid** especially by explanation or analysis

例 elucidate an abstruse equation in quantum mechanics 阐明一个深奥难懂的问题

近 clarify, clear, construe, explain, explicate, expound, illustrate

反 confuse, obfuscate, obscure 使困惑；garble 曲解

派 elucidation *n.* 阐释，阐明

emaciate	[ɪ'meɪʃieɪt]

【考法】 *vt.* 削弱：to make **feeble**

例 His hesitation emaciated the force of his argument. 他的迟疑削弱了他论证的力度。

近 droop, flag, sag, decay, enfeeble, enervate, languish, wane, wither

emancipate	[ɪ'mænsɪpeɪt]

【考法】 *vt.* 解放，解除束缚：to **free** from bondage, oppression, or restraint

例 emancipate the slaves 解放奴隶

近 discharge, enfranchise, free, liberate, loose, manumit, release

反 bind, shackle 束缚；enslave, enthrall 奴役

派 emancipation *n.* 解放，获得自由

embargo	[ɪm'bɑːrɡoʊ]

【考法】 *n.* 贸易禁止令：a legal **prohibition on commerce**

例 a trade embargo on luxuries 对奢侈品的禁运令

近 ban, interdiction, proscription, sanction, veto

反 approval, license, permission, prescription 许可

embark	[ɪm'bɑːrk]

【考法】 *vi.* 开始从事：to make a **start**

例 embark on one's career 开始某人的职业

近 begin, commence, launch, initiate, start

反 conclude, end, finish, terminate 结束

Unit 8

■ EMBARRASS	■ EMBED	■ EMBEZZLE	■ EMBOLDEN	■ EMBOSS
■ EMBRACE	■ EMBROIDER	■ EMIGRATE	■ EMINENT	■ EMOLLIENT

embarrass	[ɪm'bærəs]

【考法】 *vt.* 使尴尬：to cause to **experience** a state of self-conscious **distress**

例 bawdy jokes that embarrassed her 让她尴尬的荤段子

近 abash, discomfit, disconcert, faze, fluster, mortify, nonplus

派 embarrassing *adj.* 令人窘迫的；embarrassment *n.* 尴尬

embed	[ɪm'bed]

【考法】 *vt.* 嵌入：to **enclose** closely in or as if in a matrix

例 The thorn was embedded in her thumb. 刺扎入了她的拇指。

近 entrench, fix, ingrain, root

反 extract, dislodge, uproot 取出，移出

派 embedded *adj.* 嵌入（式）的

embezzle	[ɪmˈbezl]
【考法】	*vt.* 盗用：to **appropriate**（as property entrusted to one's care）fraudulently to one's own use
例	limitations on the right of the state to embezzle private property 限制政府挪用私人财产的权利
近	appropriate, peculate
反	confiscate 没收充公
派	embezzlement *n.* 挪用，盗用

embolden	[ɪmˈbəʊldən]
【考法】	*vt.* 鼓励，使大胆：to **instill** with boldness or **courage**
例	be emboldened by the wine 借酒壮胆
近	encourage, animate, cheer, hearten, strengthen
反	daunt, discourage, dishearten, dispirit 使沮丧，使丧失信心

emboss	[ɪmˈbɔːs]
【考法】	*vt.* 装饰：to raise the surface of into bosses; especially to **ornament with raised work**
例	embossed with a design of Shanghai skyline 用刻有上海城市轮廓的浮雕图案进行装饰
近	adorn, beautify, bedeck, blazon, ornament, garnish
反	flatten, efface 抹平，抹去

embrace	[ɪmˈbreɪs]
【考法】	*vt.* 乐于接受：to take up **willingly** or **eagerly**
例	embrace the new information age 乐于接受新的信息时代
近	accept, adopt, espouse, welcome
反	abjure, abrogate, renounce, spurn 废除，摒弃，放弃

embroider	[ɪmˈbrɔɪdər]
【考法】	*v.*（时常伴有夸张和想象内容地）详细说明：to **give** an **elaborate account** of, often with florid language and fictitious details
例	tell a lie by embroidering a truth 以夸大事实的方式说谎
近	elaborate, embellish, exaggerate, magnify, overstate, hyperbolize
反	downplay, de-emphasize 轻描淡写

emigrate	[ˈemɪgreɪt]
【考法】	*vi.* 移民，移居海外：to **leave** one's place of residence or country to live elsewhere
例	have to emigrate to the United States due to political persecution 因政治迫害而不得不移民美国
近	migrate
反	immigrate 移入，入境；repatriate 遣返
派	emigrant *n.*（向外的）移民；emigration *n.*（向外）移居，迁徙

eminent	[ˈemɪnənt]
【考法】	*adj.* 杰出的：exhibiting eminence especially in standing **above others** in some quality or position
例	an eminent young scientist 一名杰出的青年科学家
近	famous, celebrated, distinguished, famed, notable, prominent, renowned
反	mediocre, undistinguished 中庸的，平凡的
派	eminence *n.* 杰出，显赫

emollient	[iˈmɑːliənt]
【考法】	*adj.* 起缓和作用的：making **less intense** or harsh
例	soothe us in our grieves with emollient words 用安慰的话语抚平我们的悲伤
近	appeasing, assuaging, mollifying, mitigating, relieving
反	aggravating, intensifying 使（局势、情况）加剧恶化的

Unit 9

■ EMULATE	■ ENACT	■ ENAMEL	■ ENCOMIUM	■ ENCOMPASS
■ ENCUMBER	■ ENDEMIC	■ ENDORSE	■ ENERVATE	■ ENFRANCHISE

emulate	[ˈemjuleɪt]
【考法】	*vt.* 效仿：to strive to equal or **excel**, especially **through imitation**
例	a role model worthy emulating 值得效仿的榜样
近	copy, imitate, mimic, mime
派	emulation *n.* 模仿

enact [ɪˈnækt]

【考法】 *vt.* 制定或颁布(法律)：to **establish** by legal and authoritative act

例 Congress enacted the tax reform bill . 国会颁布了税法改革案。

近 constitute, establish, legislate, pass, ratify, ordain, lay down

反 abolish, repeal, rescind, revoke 废除

派 enactment *n.* 颁布

enamel [ɪˈnæml]

【考法】 *vt.* 装饰：to **adorn** with a brightly colored surface

近 adorn, beautify, bedeck, decorate, embellish, garnish, ornament

反 disfigure 破坏…的外形

encomium [enˈkoʊmiəm]

【考法】 *n.* 赞颂之词：glowing and warmly enthusiastic **praise**

例 receive encomiums from literary critics 受到文学评论家的好评

近 accolade, applause, compliment, eulogy, laud, panegyric, salutation, tribute

反 criticism 批评；abuse, invective, vituperation 辱骂

encompass [ɪnˈkʌmpəs]

【考法】 *vt.* 组成，包含：to constitute or **include**

例 a plan that encompasses multiple aims 一项包含了多个目标的计划

近 contain, comprehend, embody, entail, involve, subsume

反 exclude 排除

encumber [ɪnˈkʌmbər]

【考法】 *vt.* 阻碍；妨碍：to **impede** or hamper the function or activity of

例 encumber their progress 妨碍他们的进步 ‖ encumber myself with unnecessary luggage 受不必要的行李防碍

近 hamper, hinder, impede, obstruct, retard, stymie

反 promote, further 推动；aid, assist, facilitate, help 帮助

endemic [enˈdemɪk]

【考法】 *adj.* 地方性的：prevalent in or peculiar **to a particular** locality, **region**, or people

例 an endemic disease 地方性疾病

近 aboriginal, indigenous, native, domestic

反 exotic, foreign, nonindigenous, nonnative 国外的，外来的

endorse [ɪnˈdɔːrs]

【考法】 *vt.* 公开支持：to **express** support or **approval** of publicly and definitely

例 endorse a presidential candidate 公开支持一名总统候选人

近 advocate, back, approve, certify, champion, sanction, support, uphold

反 deprecate, impugn, oppose 反对

派 endorsement *n.* 支持，赞同

enervate [ˈenərveɪt]

【考法】 *vt.* 使衰弱：to **weaken** or destroy the strength or vitality of

例 an enervating disease 使人衰弱的疾病

近 debilitate, disable, enfeeble, fatigue, sap

反 fortify, strengthen 强化；energize, invigorate, vitalize 给…注入活力

派 enervation *n.* 虚弱

enfranchise [ɪnˈfræntʃaɪz]

【考法 1】 *vt.* 给予…权利(例如选举权)：to **endow** with the **rights** of citizenship, especially the right to vote

例 enfranchise women 给予妇女选举权

反 disenfranchise, disempower 剥夺权利

【考法 2】 *vt.* 解放：to **set free** (as from slavery)

例 enfranchise slaves 解放奴隶

近 discharge, emancipate, free, liberate, manumit, rescue, unfetter

反 bind, confine, enfetter 束缚；subjugate, subdue；enthrall 使臣服；使成为奴隶

Unit 10

engender ［ɪn'dʒendər］
【考法】 *vt.* 引起，使发展: to **cause** to exist or to develop
例 Her latest book has engendered a lot of controversy. 她的新书引发了很多争议。
近 beget, cause, catalyze, generate, induce, invoke, produce, spawn

engross ［ɪn'groʊs］
【考法】 *vt.* 使全神贯注: to **occupy exclusively**
例 an engrossing problem 使人全神贯注的问题
近 absorb, engage, enthrall, fascinate, grip, immerse
派 engrossed *adj.* 全神贯注的

enigma ［ɪ'nɪgmə］
【考法】 *n.* 难以理解或解释的事物，谜: something **hard to understand** or explain
例 the enigma of Mona Lisa smile 《蒙娜丽莎》的微笑之谜
近 mystery, conundrum, puzzle, riddle
派 enigmatic *adj.* 谜一般的

enlighten ［ɪn'laɪtn］
【考法】 *vt.* 使知道，启发: to give information to; **inform** or **instruct**
例 enlighten us about the thorny problem 启发我们思考这个棘手的问题
近 apprise, instruct
反 bewilder, confuse, confound, perplex 使疑惑

enmity ［'enməti］
【考法】 *n.* 敌意: positive, active, and typically **mutual hatred** or ill will
例 an unspoken enmity between two factions 两个派系间心照不宣的仇恨
近 animosity, animus, antagonism, antipathy, feud, gall, hostility, rancor
反 amity, comity 友好; concord 和睦

ennoble ［ɪ'noʊbl］
【考法】 *vt.* 使尊贵: to make **noble**
例 Her skill and talent ennoble her profession. 技能和天赋使她成为业界领军人物。
近 aggrandize, canonize, deify, dignify, glorify, magnify
反 debase, abase, degrade, demean, humble, humiliate 贬低

ennui ［ɑːn'wiː］
【考法】 *n.* 倦怠；缺乏兴趣: **listlessness** and dissatisfaction resulting from **lack of interest**
例 the ennui of the pedestrian world 平凡世界的倦怠
近 doldrums, listlessness, tedium, weariness
反 keen interest, energy, enthusiasm, exuberance 强烈的兴趣，生机盎然

expostulate ［ɪk'spɑːstʃuleɪt］
【考法】 *vi.* 争论，辩驳: **to reason** earnestly with a person for purposes of **dissuasion** or remonstrance
例 The concerned parents tried to expostulate with their daughter when she announced her intention to live on her own in Los Angeles. 当获知女儿想独自在洛杉矶生活的想法时，她的父母很担心试图劝阻她。
近 demur, inveigh (against), object, protest, remonstrate
反 accede, agree, approve, assent, sanction 同意，批准

ensconce ［ɪn'skɑːns］
【考法】 *vt.* 隐藏: to put in a **hiding** place
例 ensconce the spare house key in a place where no thief would think to look 把备用钥匙藏在小偷根本不会注意的地方
近 bury, cache, conceal, secrete
反 display, exhibit 展示

ensue ［ɪn'suː］
【考法】 *vi.* 紧随其后: take place **afterward** or as a result
例 A brief but embarrassing silence ensued. 一阵短暂且令人尴尬的沉默随之而来。
近 follow
派 ensuing *adj.* 随后发生的

List 9

"GRE，我愿意将它解释成 Glorious and Rewarding Experience。或许正如真爱是用来怀念的，青春就是用来追忆的——希望以及为了希望所付出的醉生梦死般的努力，才是我们青春存在的意义。"

（王彦妮，2008 年 6 月，Verbal 710, Quantitative 800, AW 5.0，现任职于北京新东方学校北美项目部）

Unit 1

■ ENTANGLE	■ EPISODIC	■ ENTICE	■ ENTRANCE	■ ENTRAP
■ ENTREAT	■ ENUNCIATE	■ EPHEMERAL	■ EPIC	■ EPICURE

entangle [ɪnˈtæŋgl]
【考法】 *vt.* 使变复杂或困难：to make **complex or difficult**
例 The history of Alexander the Great is entangled by variant accounts of his exploits. 亚历山大大帝的生平历史被不同版本的记录搞得很纠结。
近 complexify, perplex, sophisticate
反 simplify, streamline 简化

episodic [ˌepɪˈsɑːdɪk]
【考法】 *adj.* 片段的，断断续续的：**lacking in steadiness** or regularity of occurrence
例 episodic attacks of fever 断断续续的发烧
近 aperiodic, discontinuous, fitful, intermittent, sporadic
反 constant, continuous, habitual, periodic, steady 持续不变的

entice [ɪnˈtaɪs]
【考法】 *vt.* 诱使：to attract artfully or adroitly or by arousing hope or desire: **tempt**; **lure**
例 entice sb into doing sth 诱使某人做某事
近 allure, bait, beguile, decoy, seduce, solicit, tempt, lead on
派 enticing *adj.* 诱人的
反 formidable 可怕的

entrance [ɪnˈtræns]
【考法】 *vt.* 使入迷：to fill with delight, **wonder**, or **enchantment**
例 be entranced by the view 陶醉于景色
近 enrapture, enthrall, ravish, transport, carry away
反 bore, disappoint, disgust, repel, repulse 使厌烦
派 entrancing *adj.* 使人欣喜的
反 unprepossessing 不讨人喜欢的

entrap [ɪnˈtræp]
【考法】 *vt.* 诱骗：to **lure** into a compromising statement or act
例 A string of inconsistent statements finally entrapped the witness. 一系列不一致的陈述最终蒙骗了目击者。
近 ensnare, ensnarl, entoil, mesh, net, snare, catch up
反 disentangle, untangle 使解脱

entreat [ɪnˈtriːt]
【考法】 *vt.* 恳求：to **plead** with especially in order to **persuade**, **ask urgently**
例 He entreated his boss for another chance. 他恳求老板再给他一次机会。
近 beseech, besiege, conjure, implore, importune, solicit, supplicate, plead to, appeal to

enunciate [ɪˈnʌnsieɪt]
【考法 1】 *v.* 清晰地说：to utter **articulate** sounds
例 She enunciates very slowly and carefully. 她缓慢仔细清晰地说。
近 articulate
【考法 2】 *vt.* 公开宣布，宣称：to make known **openly or publicly**
例 Today the President enunciated a new foreign policy. 总统在今天宣布了一项新的对外政策。
近 annunciate, broadcast, declare, herald, proclaim, promulgate, publicize, release, give out

ephemeral	[ɪˈfemərəl]
【考法】	*adj.* 短暂的：lasting a **very short time**
例	ephemeral pressures 暂时的压力
近	evanescent, fleeting, impermanent, temporary, transient, transitory, fugacious, fugitive
反	eternal, permanent, perpetual, enduring, everlasting, ceaseless, immortal, undying 永久的

epic	[ˈepɪk]
【考法】	*adj.* 宏大的，超凡脱俗的：**surpassing the usual** or ordinary, particularly in scope or size
例	an epic journey 一次宏大的旅程
近	august, grandiose, imposing, magnificent, majestic, monumental
反	humble, unheroic, unimpressive, modest 适度的，印象不深的

epicure	[ˈepɪkjʊr]
【考法】	*n.* 美食家：one with sensitive and **discriminating tastes** especially in food or wine
例	Thomas Jefferson was one of America's first great epicures. 托马斯·杰斐逊算得上是美国早期美食家一枚。
近	bon vivant, gastronomist, gourmand, gourmet

Unit 2

■ EPIGRAM	■ EPILOGUE	■ EPITHET	■ EPITOMIZE	■ EQUABLE
■ EQUITY	■ EQUIVALENT	■ EQUIVOCATE	■ EMPIRICAL	■ ERRANT

epigram	[ˈepɪɡræm]
【考法】	*n.* 机智的短诗，警句：a **short**, **witty** poem expressing a single thought or observation
例	Benjamin Franklin's most famous epigram, "Remember that time is money." 本杰明·富兰克林最著名的警句就是，时间就是金钱。
近	adage, aphorism, apothegm, byword, maxim, proverb

epilogue	[ˈepɪlɔːɡ]
【考法】	*n.* 文学作品的结局：a **concluding section** that rounds out the design of a **literary** work
例	the epilogue of this novel 小说的结局
反	preface 序文

epithet	[ˈepɪθet]
【考法】	*n.* 外号，绰号：a **descriptive** or familiar **name** given instead of or in addition to the one belonging to an individual; a disparaging or abusive word or phrase
例	King Richard I of England was given the very laudatory epithet "the Lion-Hearted". 英王理查一世因英勇大胆被赞誉为"狮心理查"。
近	alias, cognomen, sobriquet

epitomize	[ɪˈpɪtəmaɪz]
【考法】	*vt.* 代表，体现，是…的典型范例：to **represent** in visible form; to be **a typical example of**
例	The Parthenon in Athens epitomizes the ancient Greek ideal of architectural beauty. 雅典的巴特农神庙体现了古希腊对于建筑美感的理念。‖ behavior that epitomizes selfishness 典型的自私行为
近	body, express, externalize, incarnate, incorporate, instantiate, manifest, materialize, substantiate

equable	[ˈekwəbl]
【考法】	*adj.* (脾气、性情)温和的：not easily disturbed; **serene**
例	equable temperament 温和的性情
近	balmy, genial, gentle, moderate, temperate
反	harsh, inclement, intemperate, severe 严厉的
派	equanimity *n.* 温和
反	agitation, excitability 激动

equity	[ˈekwəti]
【考法】	*n.* 不偏不倚，公平：**lack of favoritism** toward one side or another
例	a society run on the principle of equity 一个基于公平原则运转的社会
近	disinterestedness, evenhandedness, fairness, impartiality, neutrality, nonpartisanship
反	bias, favoritism, nonobjectivity, one-sidedness, partiality, partisanship, prejudice 歧视，偏见；偏爱
派	equitable *adj.* 公平的
反	biased, discriminatory 偏袒的，差别对待的

equivalent	[ɪ'kwɪvələnt]
【考法】	*adj./n.* 等价的，相等的：**equal** in force, amount, or value
例	A is the equivalent of B A 与 B 是等价的
近	coequal, coordinate, counterpart, peer, rival, parallel

equivocate	[ɪ'kwɪvəkeɪt]
【考法】	*vi.* (带有欺骗目的地)模棱两可地说，说谎话：to use **equivocal** language especially with intent to deceive
例	She equivocated about her finances. 她对自己的财务状况模棱两可。
近	fudge, hedge, weasel, prevaricate, palter
反	communicate straightforwardly 直率地说
派	equivocal *adj.* 模棱两可的：open to two or more interpretations and often intended to mislead; ambiguous; equivocation *n.* 模棱两可的话
反	clarity 清楚

empirical	[ɪm'pɪrɪkl]
【考法】	*adj.* 基于观察、实验的：**based on observation** or experiment
例	There is no empirical evidence to support his thesis. 他的论文缺乏实验证据的支持。
近	existential, experiential, experimental, objective, observational
反	nonempirical, theoretical, unempirical 非实证的

errant	['erənt]
【考法】	*adj.* 误入歧途的，犯错误的：**straying** from the **proper course or standards**
例	errant youngsters 误入歧途的青少年
近	misbehaving, mischievous
反	behaved, behaving, nice, orderly 行为规矩的

Unit 3

■ ERRATIC	■ ERUDITE	■ ESCALATE	■ ESCHEW	■ ESOTERIC
■ ESPOUSE	■ ESTEEM	■ ESTIMABLE	■ ESTRANGE	■ ETCH

erratic	[ɪ'rætɪk]
【考法】	*adj.* 善变的：**not** staying **constant**
例	erratic inflation rate 动荡的通胀率
近	changing, fluctuating, irregular, unequal, unstable, unsteady, varying
反	changeless, constant, stable, steady, unchanging, unvarying 不变的

erudite	['erudaɪt]
【考法】	*adj.* 博学的：characterized by erudition; **learned**
例	an erudite scholar 渊博的学者
近	knowledgeable, learned, lettered, literate, scholarly, well-read
反	ignorant, unlettered, benighted, illiterate, uneducated, unscholarly 无知的

escalate	['eskəleɪt]
【考法】	*v.* (使)(战争等)升级，扩大：to **increase** in extent, volume, number, amount, intensity, or scope
例	We don't want to escalate the war. 我们不想使战争扩大。
近	aggrandize, amplify, augment, boost, expand, pump up, build up
反	wane, diminish 减弱

eschew	[ɪs'tʃuː]
【考法】	*vt.* 刻意避开；戒绝：to **avoid** habitually especially on moral or practical grounds
例	The minister eschews involvement in local politics, since he doesn't want to diminish his moral authority in the community. 首相回避参与当地政治，因为他不想降低其道德权威。
近	dodge, elude, evade, shirk, shun, weasel out of
反	embrace, greet, welcome, habitually indulge in, seek 乐于接受，寻觅

esoteric	[ˌesə'terɪk]
【考法】	*adj.* 深奥难懂的：**difficult** for one of ordinary knowledge or intelligence **to understand**
例	esoteric terminology 深奥难懂的专业术语
近	abstruse, arcane, hermetic, recondite
反	shallow, superficial 肤浅的

espouse [ɪˈspaʊz]
【考法】 *vt.* 支持；拥护：to take up and **support** as a cause
例 espouse the revolutionary cause 支持革命事业
近 embrace, take on, take up
反 abjure, repudiate 誓绝

esteem [ɪˈstiːm]
【考法】 *n./v.* 尊重：to regard with **respect**; **prize**
例 be held in high esteem 被高度敬仰
近 appreciation, estimation, favor, regard, respect
反 disfavor, odium 不喜欢，憎恶

estimable [ˈestɪməbl]
【考法】 *adj.* 值得尊敬的：deserving of esteem; **admirable**
例 an estimable adversary 一位值得尊敬的对手
近 prestigious, reputable, applaudable, commendable, creditable, meritorious, praiseworthy
反 contemptible, infamous, censurable, discreditable, illaudable, reprehensible 令人鄙视的

estrange [ɪˈstreɪndʒ]
【考法】 *vt.* 使疏远，离间，使感情失和：to arouse especially mutual **enmity** or **indifference** in where there had formerly been love, affection, or **friendliness**
例 He estranged several of his coworkers. 他和好多同事疏远了。
近 alienate, disaffect, disgruntle, sour
反 reconcile 使和好

etch [etʃ]
【考法】 *v.* 留下深刻印象，铭记：to **produce a vivid impression** of
例 In just a few pages the writer etched an unforgettable portrait of one of the more remarkable First Ladies. 仅用数页，作者刻画出了令人难忘的形象。
近 impress, imprint, infix, ingrain

Unit 4

| ■ ETERNAL | ■ ETHEREAL | ■ ETHICS | ■ EULOGIZE | ■ EUPHEMISM |
| ■ EUPHONIOUS | ■ EUPHORIA | ■ EVACUATE | ■ EVANESCENT | ■ ENTAIL |

eternal [ɪˈtɜːrnl]
【考法】 *adj.* 永恒的：having **infinite duration**; **everlasting**; **perpetual**
例 eternal love 永恒的爱
近 ageless, everlasting, immortal, imperishable, perennial, perpetual, undying
反 ephemeral 短暂的

ethereal [iˈθɪriəl]
【考法 1】 *adj.* 轻巧精致的：resembling air in **lightness**, **highly refined**; **delicate**
例 The bakery's scrumptious pastries have a wonderfully ethereal consistency. 面包师可口的糕点有着一种奇妙的蓬松轻巧的质感。
近 fluffy, gossamer, light
反 heavy, leaden, ponderous 沉重的
【考法 2】 *adj.* 非物质的，精神(上)的：not of this world; **spiritual**; **not composed of matter**
例 that ethereal attribute that every performer should have——charisma 每位演奏者都应该具有一种精神上的特质——个人魅力
近 bodiless, formless, incorporeal, insubstantial, nonmaterial, nonphysical, spiritual
反 bodily, corporeal, material, physical, substantial 物质的，有实体的

ethics [ˈeθɪks]
【考法】 *n.* 道德规范：rules or standards **governing** the **conduct** of a person or the members of a profession
例 an old-fashioned work ethics 传统的工作行为规范
近 ethos, morality, morals, norms, principles, standards

eulogize [ˈjuːlədʒaɪz]
【考法】 *vt.* 称赞；颂扬：to **speak** or write **in high praise of**
例 The boss eulogized about his versatility. 老板称赞了他的多才多艺。
反 defame, pan 诬蔑，指责

euphemism [ˈjuːfəmɪzəm]

【考法】 *n.* 婉言，委婉的说法：the substitution of an agreeable or **inoffensive expression** for one that may offend or suggest something unpleasant

例 using "eliminate" as a euphemism for "kill" "杀死"的委婉说法是"灭掉"

euphonious [juːˈfoʊniəs]

【考法】 *adj.* 悦耳的：**pleasing** or agreeable to the ear

例 euphonious music 悦耳的音乐

近 mellifluous, melodious, canorous, harmonizing, symphonious, tuneful

反 cacophonous, discordant, disharmonious, dissonant, tuneless, unmelodious 刺耳的

euphoria [juːˈfɔːriə]

【考法】 *n.* 感觉极其愉快：a state of **overwhelming usually pleasurable** emotion

例 There was euphoria after election. 选举之后是一阵狂喜。‖ the euphoria of her victory 她胜利的喜悦

近 elation, exhilaration, intoxication, transport, rapture, rhapsody

反 depression 沮丧

evacuate [ɪˈvækjueɪt]

【考法】 *vt.* 撤离：to **empty or remove** the contents of

例 They were ordered to evacuate the building. 他们被命令搬出大楼。

近 clear, vacate, void

反 fill up, occupy, load 填满

evanescent [ˌevəˈnesnt]

【考法】 *adj.* 逐渐消失的，短暂的：tending to **vanish** like vapor

例 the evanescent economic boom 短暂的经济繁荣

近 ephemeral, fleeting, impermanent, temporary, transient, transitory

反 ceaseless, endless, enduring, eternal, everlasting, immortal, permanent, perpetual, timeless, undying, unending, abiding, lasting 持久的

entail [ɪnˈteɪl]

【考法】 *v.* 牵连；导致：If one thing entails another, it **involves** it or **causes** it.

例 Such a decision would entail a huge political risk in the midst of the presidential campaign. 这样的决定会在总统大选之际导致一个巨大的政治风险。

近 contain, embrace, encompass, include, involve

反 exclude, miss out, omit 排除，遗漏

Unit 5

■ EVERLASTING	■ EVICT	■ EVINCE	■ EVOKE	■ EXACERBATE
■ EXACTING	■ EXALT	■ EXASPERATE	■ EXCAVATE	■ EXCEPTIONAL

everlasting [ˌevərˈlæstɪŋ]

【考法】 *adj.* 永恒的，持久的：lasting **forever**; eternal

例 an everlasting love 永恒的爱情

近 ageless, enduring, eternal, immortal, imperishable, perennial, perpetual, undying

反 impermanent, mortal, temporary, transient, ephemeral 短暂的

evict [ɪˈvɪkt]

【考法】 *vt.* 赶出，逐出：to put out (a tenant, for example) by legal process; **expel**

例 She was evicted from the house. 她被从房子中逐出。

反 harbor 收容

evince [ɪˈvɪns]

【考法】 *vt.* 表明：to **make known** (something abstract) through outward signs

例 evince a strong desire 明显地表现出强烈的欲望

近 bespeak, betray, declare, demonstrate, expose, manifest, reveal, give away

反 conceal, keep hidden 隐藏

evoke [ɪˈvoʊk]

【考法】 *vt.* 唤起，引发：to **call** forth or **up**

例 evoke memories 唤起回忆

近 elicit, inspire, raise

派 evocative *adj.* 引发共鸣的

---

exacerbate [ɪɡˈzæsərbeɪt]

【考法】 *vt.* 使加剧，使恶化：to make more violent, bitter, or **severe**

例 a heavy rainfall that exacerbated the flood problems 大雨恶化了洪水问题

近 aggravate, complicate, worsen

反 allay, alleviate, assuage, mitigate, relieve, palliate 缓和

---

exacting [ɪɡˈzæktɪŋ]

【考法 1】 *adj.* 严格的，苛求的：making severe demands; **rigorous**

例 an exacting instructor 一位严苛的导师

近 choosy, demanding, fastidious, finical, fussy, pernickety, persnickety, picky

派 exact *vt.* 强求，索取：to force the payment or yielding of

例 exact tribute from a conquered people 从征服的人民手中强取贡品

反 condone, forgive 赦免，免除（债务）

【考法 2】 *adj.* 费时间花心思的：**requiring** much **time**, **effort**, or careful **attention**

例 Editing and proofreading will always be an exacting task. 编辑和校对是花时间花心思的工作。

近 arduous, burdensome, challenging, grueling, killing, laborious, onerous, taxing, toilsome

反 light, unchallenging, undemanding 要求不高的

---

exalt [ɪɡˈzɔːlt]

【考法】 *vt.* 赞扬：to glorify, **praise**, or honor

近 emblazon, extol, glorify, laud, magnify

反 condemn 谴责

---

exasperate [ɪɡˈzæspəreɪt]

【考法】 *vt.* 激怒：to **excite** the anger of

例 I was exasperated by the flight delays. 我被飞机延误激怒了。

近 aggravate, gall, nettle, peeve, rile, ruffle, vex, burn up

反 mitigate, mollify 平息

---

excavate [ˈekskəveɪt]

【考法】 *v.* 挖掘，挖空：to **dig out** and remove

例 excavate soil from one area 从某处挖土出来

反 fill in 填满

---

exceptional [ɪkˈsepʃənl]

【考法】 *adj.* 例外的，特别的，非凡的：being an exception; **uncommon**; **extraordinary**

例 children with exceptional ability 能力非凡的孩子们

近 aberrant, abnormal, anomalous, exceeding, extraordinary, peculiar, unwonted

反 commonplace, prosaic, customary, normal, ordinary, typical, unextraordinary, usual 平凡常见的

Unit 6

■ EXCORIATE	■ EXCRETE	■ EXCRUCIATE	■ EXCULPATE	■ EXCURSIVE
■ EXECRATE	■ EXEMPLARY	■ EXEMPT	■ EXHAUST	■ EXHILARATE

excoriate [ˌeksˈkɔːrieɪt]

【考法】 *vt.* 严厉批评：to **criticize harshly** and usually **publicly**

例 She was excoriated as a racist. 她被指责是一个种族歧视者。

近 abuse, assail, belabor, castigate, lambaste, vituperate

反 accolade, extol, flatter, praise lavishly 赞扬

---

excrete [ɪkˈskriːt]

【考法】 *vt.* 排泄：to separate and **discharge**（waste matter）from the blood, tissues, or organs

例 excrete sweat 排汗

反 absorb, ingest 吸收

excruciate [ɪkˈskruːʃieɪt]

【考法】 *vt.* 折磨，使痛苦：to inflict severe **pain** on; torture

例 She has long been excruciated by a persistent pain. 她长久以来被痛折磨。

近 agonize, anguish, plague, rack, torment, torture, harrow

反 exult 使欢跃

exculpate [ˈekskʌlpeɪt]

【考法】 *vt.* 声明无罪；开脱，使无罪：to **clear** from alleged **fault** or **guilt**

例 I have gathered evidence that will exculpate my client. 我已经搜集到能够证明委托人无罪的证据了。

近 absolve, acquit, clear, exonerate, vindicate

反 attribute guilt, inculpate, indict, criminate, incriminate 归罪，控告

excursive [ɪkˈskɜːrsɪv]

【考法】 *adj.* 离题的；散漫的：**passing** from one topic to another

例 an excursive story line that some readers of Melville's novel find very rewarding 梅尔维尔小说的一些读者非常喜欢松散的故事主线

近 desultory, digressive, meandering, rambling, wandering

execrate [ˈeksɪkreɪt]

【考法】 *v.* 痛恨：to **dislike strongly**

例 execrate the hideous side of religion 痛恨宗教丑恶的一面

近 abhor, abominate, despise, detest, loathe

反 love 爱

exemplary [ɪgˈzempləri]

【考法】 *adj.* 榜样的，值得效仿的：constituting, serving as, or worthy of **being a pattern** to be **imitated**

例 an exemplary innovation 榜样的创新

近 archetypal, imitable, paradigmatic, quintessential

派 exemplify *vt.* (通过榜样)示范，显示：to show or illustrate by example

exempt [ɪgˈzempt]

【考法】 *vt.* 使免除：to **release** or deliver from some **liability** or requirement to which others are subject

例 a man exempted from military service 免服军役的人

exhaust [ɪgˈzɔːst]

【考法】 *vt.* 耗尽：to **consume entirely**: to make **complete use of**

例 We exhausted our funds in a week. 我们在一周内就耗尽了经费。

近 consume, devour, drain, expend, spend, use up

派 exhaustive *adj.* 彻底的，完整的，详尽的：testing all possibilities; thorough; complete

例 conduct an exhaustive investigation 做详尽的调查

反 incomplete, partial 不完全的

exhilarate [ɪgˈzɪləreɪt]

【考法】 *vt.* 使高兴；使兴奋：to make **cheerful** and **excited**

例 be exhilarated by her success 为她的成功感到兴奋

近 electrify, galvanize, intoxicate, pump up, turn on

反 sadden, depress 使悲哀，使沮丧

派 exhilarating *adj.* 令人兴奋的

反 soporific 昏昏欲睡的

Unit 7

■ EXHORT	■ EXIGENT	■ EXODUS	■ EXONERATE	■ EXORBITANT
■ EXOTIC	■ EXPANSIVE	■ EXPEDITE	■ EXPEDIENCY	■ EXPIATE

exhort [ɪgˈzɔːrt]

【考法】 *vt.* 敦促，力劝：to **urge** by **strong**, often stirring argument, admonition, advice, or appeal

例 The speaker exhorted the graduating students to go forth and try to make a difference in the world. 演讲者鼓励毕业生们向广阔天地前进，有所作为。

近 encourage, goad, nudge, prod, prompt, egg on

exigent [ˈeksɪdʒənt]

【考法】 *adj.* 紧急的: requiring **immediate** aid or action

例 exigent circumstances 紧急情况

近 compelling, dire, emergent, imperative, importunate, necessitous, pressing, urgent

反 deferrable, noncritical, nonurgent 可拖延的，不紧急的

exodus [ˈeksədəs]

【考法】 *n.* 大批离去: a mass **departure**

例 an exodus of doctors 医生大批离去

近 gush, outpour, outpouring

反 influx, flux, inflow, inrush 涌入

exonerate [ɪɡˈzɑːnəreɪt]

【考法】 *vt.* 免除责备: to **free from blame**

例 An investigation exonerated the school from any blame. 一项调查使该学校免受责备。

近 absolve, acquit, clear, vindicate

反 censure, incriminate, inculpate, prove guilty 责难，证明有罪

exorbitant [ɪɡˈzɔːrbɪtənt]

【考法】 *adj.* 过度的: **exceeding the customary or appropriate limits** in intensity, quality, amount, or size

例 exorbitant prices 过高的价格

近 extravagant, intolerable, lavish, overdue, overweening, unconscionable

反 middling, moderate, modest, reasonable, temperate 适度的，合适的

exotic [ɪɡˈzɑːtɪk]

【考法】 *adj.* 外来的，不同寻常的: excitingly or mysteriously **unusual**

例 She's famous for her exotic tastes. 她以有异域风情著称。

近 outlandish, strange

反 indigenous, familiar, nonglamorous, plain-Jane, unexotic 本地的；平常的

expansive [ɪkˈspænsɪv]

【考法】 *adj.* 话多的，健谈的: characterized by high spirits, generosity, or **readiness to talk**

例 an expansive and relaxed man 一个话多轻松的人

近 communicative, eloquent, garrulous, glib, loquacious, talkative, vocative, voluble

反 laconic, reserved, reticent, taciturn 话少的，沉默寡言的

expedite [ˈekspədaɪt]

【考法】 *vt.* 加快进程: to **speed up the progress** of; accelerate

例 expedite your plans 加快你的计划

反 retard 减速，阻碍

派 expedition *n.* 动作迅速: speed in performance; promptness

例 deal with the order with the greatest possible expedition 以可能的最快的速度处理订单

近 haste, celerity, dispatch

反 foot-dragging 拖拉

expediency [ɪkˈspiːdiənsi]

【考法】 *n.* 应急手段，权宜之计: doing what is **convenient** rather than what is morally right

例 This was a matter less of morals than of expediency. 此举主要是权宜之计，而非道德问题。

近 advisability, desirability, judiciousness, makeshift

反 imprudence, inadvisability, inexpediency, injudiciousness 不明智

expiate [ˈekspieɪt]

【考法】 *vt.* 赎罪，纠正: to **extinguish the guilt** incurred by

例 expiate one's sin 赎罪

近 mend, redeem, atone for

Unit 8

■ EXPIRE	■ EXPLICIT	■ EXPLOIT	■ EXPONENT	■ EXPURGATE
■ EXQUISITE	■ EXTANT	■ EXTEMPORIZE	■ EXTENUATE	■ EXTINCT

expire [ɪkˈspaɪər]

【考法 1】 *v.* 断气，死亡: to breathe one's last breath; **die**

例 The patient expired early this morning. 病人今早逝世了。

近 conclude, elapse, terminate, decease, leave off, let up

反 come to life 出生

【考法 2】 *v.* 到期：to **come to an end**

例　My membership in the club has expired . 我的会员资格到期了。

近　discontinue, elapse, end, finish, terminate, wind up, wink out

反　continue, persist, hang on 持续，续期

explicit ［ɪkˈsplɪsɪt］

【考法 1】 *adj.* 表达清晰的：**fully revealed or expressed** without vagueness, implication, or ambiguity

例　explicit instructions 表达清晰的指示说明

近　clear-cut, definite, specific, unambiguous, unequivocal, univocal

反　obscure, implicit, implied, inferred, ambiguous, circuitous, equivocal, indefinite, unspecific, vague 模糊的

【考法 2】 *adj.* 成熟的，完全形成的：**fully developed** or formulated

例　an explicit plan 成熟的计划

反　inchoate 未完成的，未形成的

exploit

【考法 1】 ［ˈeksplɔɪt］ *n.* 英雄行为：a **notable** or heroic **act**

例　his wartime exploits 他在战争期间的英勇行为

【考法 2】 ［ɪkˈsplɔɪt］ *vt.* 最大程度地利用：to **employ** to the greatest possible advantage

例　exploit your opponent's weakness 利用你对手的弱点

近　abuse, leverage, play on, capitalize on, impose on

exponent ［ɪkˈspoʊnənt］

【考法】 *n.* 倡导者，支持者：one that speaks for, represents, or **advocates**

例　Exponents of space exploration earnestly called for more missions to the outer reaches of the solar system. 太空探险的支持者强烈要求对太阳系的外边缘进行探索。

近　advocator, backer, booster, champion, espouser, friend, promoter, proponent

反　adversary, antagonist, opponent 反对者

expurgate ［ˈekspərɡeɪt］

【考法】 *vt.* 净化（书等），删去（不当处）：to **remove** erroneous, vulgar, obscene, or otherwise objectionable material from（a book, for example）before publication

例　an expurgated edition of the letters 信件的删减版

近　bowdlerize, obliterate, launder, red-pencil, clean up

exquisite ［ɪkˈskwɪzɪt］

【考法】 *adj.* 精致精巧的：having qualities that appeal to a **refined taste**

例　exquisite food and service 精致的食物和服务

近　dainty, delicate, elegant, recherché, select

extant ［ekˈstænt］

【考法】 *adj.* 现存的：still in existence; **not destroyed**, **lost**, or **extinct**

例　the most charming writer extant 目前活着的作家中最有魅力的一位 ‖ extant manuscripts 未毁坏的手稿

近　current, immediate, ongoing, present-day, existent

反　destroyed, extinct, lost, missing, dead, nonextant 丢失的，不存在的

extemporize ［ɪkˈstempəraɪz］

【考法】 *v.* 即兴表现：to do or perform（something）**without prior preparation** or practice

例　A good talk show host has to be able to extemporize the interviews when things don't go as planned. 一个好的脱口秀主持人要能够在计划之外即兴表现。

反　follow a script 参考草稿

派　extemporaneous *adj.* 即席的

反　planned 有计划的

extenuate ［ɪkˈstenjueɪt］

【考法】 *vt.* 减轻罪行：to lessen or to try to **lessen the seriousness** or extent of by making partial excuses

例　Try to extenuate their vandalism with the old refrain of "Boys will be boys." 企图用"江山易改本性难移"的俗语为他们的暴行开脱。

近　deodorize, excuse, explain away, gloss over, gloze over

extinct ［ɪkˈstɪŋkt］

【考法】 *adj.* 灭绝的：**no longer existing** or living

例　extinct species 灭绝的物种

近　bygone, bypast, defunct, expired, nonextant, vanished

反　alive, extant, existing, living, resuscitated 现存的

派　extinction *n.* 灭绝

反　perpetuation 永存

Unit 9

extinguish [ɪkˈstɪŋgwɪʃ]
【考法】 *vt.* 熄灭：to **put out** (a fire, for example); quench
例 The fire in the skillet was quickly extinguished by slamming the lid on. 盖上锅盖后，平底锅的火苗很快熄灭了。
近 blanket, douse, quench, put out, snuff out
反 ignite, rekindle 点燃

extol [ɪkˈstoʊl]
【考法】 *vt.* 赞美；吹捧：to **praise** highly; glorify
例 extol the virtues of... 赞美……的优点
近 carol, exalt, glorify, laud, magnify, resound
反 censure, impugn, malign, deprecate, detract, rail, vilify, excoriate 批评

extort [ɪkˈstɔːrt]
【考法】 *vt.* 勒索：to obtain from a person by **force**, **intimidation**, or undue or illegal power
例 The criminals extorted large sums of money from their victims. 绑匪向受害者勒索大笔钱财。
近 wrest, wring

extract [ɪkˈstrækt]
【考法】 *vt.* 用力拔出：to pull or **take out** forcibly
例 extract a wisdom tooth 拔出一颗智齿
近 pull, uproot, wrest, wring, yank, root out, tear out
反 embed 嵌入
派 extraction *n.* 血统：origin; lineage; ancestry
例 a family of French extraction 有法国血统的家族
近 bloodline, breeding, descent, genealogy, lineage, origin, family tree

encyclopedic [ɪnˌsaɪkləˈpiːdɪk]
【考法】 *adj.* 全面的，百科全书式的：covering **everything** or all important points
例 Museums should be encyclopedic; they should strive to present art from many different cultures. 博物馆应当是百科全书式的；它们应当努力呈现源自诸多不同文化的艺术。
近 complete, comprehensive, exhaustive, inclusive, panoramic, thorough, universal

extraneous [ɪkˈstreɪniəs]
【考法】 *adj.* 无关的，不重要的：having **no relevance**
例 extraneous matters 不重要的事
近 impertinent, inapplicable, irrelative, accidental, adventitious, external
反 applicable, apposite, apropos, germane, pertinent, relative, relevant 相关的

extravagant [ɪkˈstrævəgənt]
【考法1】 *adj.* 挥霍的：given to **spending money freely** or foolishly
例 She has always been extravagant with her money. 她总是挥金如土。
近 profligate, spendthrift, squandering, thriftless, unthrifty, wasteful
反 frugal, conserving, economical, penny-pinching, scrimping, skimping, thrifty 节省的
【考法2】 *adj.* 过度的，不必要的：going **beyond** a **normal** or **acceptable limit** in degree or amount
例 The book doesn't quite merit the extravagant praise that it has received. 这本书被盛赞过度。
近 baroque, exorbitant, immoderate, inordinate, lavish, overdue, overmuch, overweening, plethoric, unconscionable, unmerciful
反 middling, moderate, modest, reasonable, temperate 适当的，适度的

extricate [ˈekstrɪkeɪt]
【考法】 *vt.* 使解脱，救出：to **free** or remove from an **entanglement** or difficulty
例 extricate himself from financial difficulties 使他摆脱财政困境
近 disengage, disentangle, free, liberate, release, untangle
反 enmesh, entangle, embroil 使卷入

exuberant [ɪgˈzuːbərənt]
【考法】 *adj.* 非常高兴的，热情洋溢的：**joyously unrestrained** and enthusiastic
例 the exuberant young girl 这个热情洋溢的年轻女孩
近 ebullient, effervescent, frolic, buoyant, bouncy, vivacious
反 austere 克制的；sullen 闷闷不乐的

exude [ɪgˈzuːd]
【考法】 *v.* 分泌，流出：to **flow forth** slowly through small openings
例 a sticky resin exuded from the bark 从树皮中分泌出来的黏稠的树脂
近 bleed, ooze, seep
反 absorb 吸收

Unit 10

■ EXULT	■ FABLE	■ FABRICATE	■ FACETIOUS	■ FACILE
■ FACILITATE	■ FACTION	■ FALLACIOUS	■ FALLOW	■ FAIL-SAFE

exult [ɪgˈzʌlt]
【考法】 *vi.* 感到欢喜：to **rejoice** especially with feelings or display of triumph or self-satisfaction
例 exult in a triumph 沉浸在胜利的欢喜当中
近 delight, glory, jubilate, joy, rejoice, triumph
反 lament, mourn 哀悼；bemoan 叹息，悲伤
派 exultant *adj.* 狂喜的

fable [ˈfeɪbl]
【考法 1】 *n.* 神话，传说：a legendary **story of supernatural happenings**
例 According to an ancient fable, the waters of the mountain spring are the tears of a woman weeping for her lost children. 根据一个古老的传说，山中的这眼泉水是一名失去孩子的母亲所流下的眼泪。
近 legend, mythos, tale
【考法 2】 *n.* 谎言，虚构：a **statement** known by its maker to be untrue and made **in order to deceive**
近 fabrication, falsehood, lie, mendacity, prevarication, story
反 fact 事实；truth 真相

fabricate [ˈfæbrɪkeɪt]
【考法】 *vt.* 捏造：to **make up** for the purpose of deception
例 be accused of fabricating evidence 被指控有捏造证据的行为
近 concoct, coin, devise, forge, fake, feign, invent

facetious [fəˈsiːʃəs]
【考法】 *adj.* 喜欢开玩笑的，轻浮的：**joking** or jesting often inappropriately
例 with a breezy and facetious tone 以活泼爱开玩笑的语调
近 humorous, jocose, jocular, waggish, witty
反 earnest, sincere 真挚的，真诚的；lugubrious 哀怨的

facile [ˈfæsl]
【考法】 *adj.* 表面的，浅尝辄止的：having or showing a **lack of depth** of understanding or character
例 a facile slogan devised by politicians 政客们肤浅的宣传口号
近 cursory, shallow, simplistic, superficial
反 deep, profound 深刻的；comprehensive, exhaustive 全面的，详尽的

facilitate [fəˈsɪlɪteɪt]
【考法】 *vt.* 使变容易，促进：to **make easy** or easier
例 The new airport will facilitate the development of tourism. 新建机场将促进旅游业的发展。
近 ease, expedite, forward, further, help
反 check, hamper, handicap, hinder, impede, obstruct, thwart, retard 阻碍，阻止；complicate 使复杂化
派 facility *n.* 设施；容易，方便

faction [ˈfækʃn]
【考法】 *n.* 派系：a **party** or group (as within a government) **that is often contentious** or self-seeking
例 affiliated with one faction 附属于某个党派 || North-Ocean Faction 北洋派
近 bloc, body, clique, coalition, sect, wing
派 factional *adj.* 派系的，派别的；factious *adj.* 内的，分派系的

fallacious	[fə'leɪʃəs]

【考法】 *adj.* 谬误的，不合逻辑的：**containing** or based on a **fallacy**

例　The once-common fallacious claim that girls just weren't any good at math. 曾经广为流传的一个谬论：女孩子无论如何就是学不好数学。

近　illogical, invalid, irrational, mad, reasonless, sophistic, unreasonable

反　sound 论证有力的；valid 合乎逻辑的

派　fallacy *n.* 逻辑谬误

fallow	['fælou]

【考法】 *adj.* 休耕的：left **untilled** or unsown after plowing

例　The field was lying fallow. 那田地正在休耕中。

近　untilled, uncultivated

fail-safe	[feɪl-seɪf]

【考法1】 *n.* 保险措施：a measure taken **to preclude loss or injury**

例　There are so many fail-safes built into the system that a highly unlikely series of mistakes would have to be made before failure could occur. 系统中嵌入了大量的保险措施，因此在系统崩溃之前，必须要发生一系列几乎不可能出现的错误。

近　caution, palladium, preventive, safeguard

【考法2】 *adj.* 万无一失的：having **no chance of failure**

例　a fail-safe device 自动防故障装置 || Men have traditionally regarded flowers as the fail-safe gift for Valentine's Day. 男士们长期以来认为鲜花是情人节永远不会错的礼物。

近　certain, foolproof, sure, unfailing

反　fallible 容易犯错的

Trouble is only opportunity in work clothes.

困难只是穿上工作服的机遇。

——美国实业家 凯泽（H.J. Kaiser, American businessman）

List 10

"背 GRE 单词的过程, 让我们铭记的不仅仅是单词, 更是周围人的关爱。
我们刷的不是单词, 而是关爱。"　　　　　　　　（底骞, 2009 年 10 月, Verbal 730, Quantitative 800,
录取院校: The Pennsylvania of State University, Department of Geography）

Unit 1

| ■ FALSEHOOD | ■ FALTER | ■ FANATIC | ■ FANTASY | ■ FARCE |
| ■ FASCINATE | ■ FAST | ■ FASTIDIOUS | ■ FATEFUL | ■ FATHOM |

falsehood ['fɔːlshʊd]
【考法】 *n.* 谎言: a statement known by its maker to be **untrue** and **made in order to deceive**
例 Truth always rise above falsehood, as oil rise above water. 油脂水面浮, 真理胜谎言。
近 deception, fable, lie, mendacity, prevarication, untruth
反 truth, verity 真相, 实话

falter ['fɔːltər]
【考法 1】 *vi.* 蹒跚: to **walk unsteadily**
近 lurch, stagger, stumble, teeter, totter, wobble
【考法 2】 *vi.* 犹豫, 踌躇: to be **unsteady in purpose or action**, as from loss of courage or confidence
例 Mr. Garrison never once faltered in his demand that slavery be unconditionally abolished. 盖瑞森先生从不对他废除奴隶的要求存有任何的犹豫。
近 balance, halt, hesitate, vacillate, waver
派 faltering *adj.* 犹豫的

fanatic [fəˈnætɪk]
【考法】 *n.* 狂热者: a person marked or motivated by an extreme, **unreasoning enthusiasm**, as for a cause
adj. 狂热的; 盲信的: marked by excessive enthusiasm and often **intense uncritical devotion**
例 a soccer fanatic 一个足球迷 ‖ fanatic about golf/GRE 对高尔夫/GRE 狂热
近 bigot, devotee, enthusiast, fiend, freak, maniac, partisan, zealot; extreme, rabid, radical, revolutionary, ultra
反 nonfan 非爱好者; conservative 保守的; rational 理性的
派 fanatical *adj.* 狂热的; 盲信的

fantasy ['fæntəsi]
【考法】 *n.* 幻想: **imaginative fiction** featuring especially strange settings and grotesque characters
vt. 产生幻想: to **form a mental picture** of
例 indulge in a fantasy 沉迷于幻想 ‖ He regularly fantasies romantic encounters that he knows will never happen. 他会定期意淫一些永远不可能发生的浪漫邂逅。
近 chimera, conceit, daydream, delusion, dream, hallucination, illusion, vision; dream, envisage, envision, fantasize, imagine, picture
反 actuality, fact, reality, truth 事实, 现实
派 fantastic *adj.* 梦幻般的, 极好的

farce [fɑːrs]
【考法】 *n.* 闹剧: **ridiculous** or empty show
例 be reduced to a force 沦为闹剧
近 joke, mockery, nonsense
派 farcical *adj.* 荒谬的

fascinate ['fæsɪneɪt]
【考法】 *vt.* 强烈吸引, 使入迷: to **hold an intense interest** or attraction for
例 fascinated by his charm/chinese food/stories in USA 被他的魅力/中餐/美国故事所吸引
近 allure, arrest, attract, bewitch, captivate, charm, enchant, enthrall, grip
反 disgust, repel 使厌恶, 使反感
派 fascinating *adj.* 引人入胜的

fast [fæst]

【考法 1】 *n.* 绝食；斋戒：an act of **abstaining from food**
例 fast to death 绝食而死
近 hunger strike

【考法 2】 *adj.* 忠诚的：**firm in one's allegiance** to someone or something
例 inseparable and fast friends 不离不弃的忠实好友
近 constant, dedicated, devoted, devout, loyal, pious
反 disloyal, perfidious 不忠诚的；treacherous 背叛的

fastidious [fæˈstɪdɪəs]

【考法】 *adj.* 挑剔的，极仔细的，追求完美的：possessing or displaying careful, **meticulous attention to detail**
例 be fastidious about personal appearance and hygiene 极其注意个人外表和卫生
近 demanding, exacting, fussy, hypercritical, squeamish
反 undemanding 不挑剔的；cursory 粗略的，敷衍的；indiscriminate, uncritical 不加区分的

fateful [ˈfeɪtfl]

【考法】 *adj.* 意义重大的：involving **momentous** consequences
例 make a fateful decision to declare war 做出了宣战的重大决定
近 critical, crucial, important, momentous, significant
反 inconsequential, insignificant, petty, paltry, trivial, unimportant 不重要的

fathom [ˈfæðəm]

【考法】 *vt.* 彻底理解，弄懂：to penetrate and **come to understand**
例 fathom his attitude / her meaning/the great truth of life. 理解他的态度 /她的含义/生活的真相
近 apprehend, cognize, comprehend, grasp, know, understand
反 misunderstand 误解
派 fathomable *adj.* 可测量的；可知晓的

Unit 2

■ FATIGUE ■ FATUOUS ■ FAULTFINDER ■ FAVORABLE ■ FAWN
■ FAZE ■ FECKLESS ■ FECUND ■ FEEBLE ■ FEIGN

fatigue [fəˈtiːg]

【考法】 *n.* 疲惫：**weariness or exhaustion** from labor, exertion, or stress
例 The day-long battle against the blaze left firefighters in a state of utter fatigue. 与大火一整天的斗争使得消防员们处于极度疲惫的状态。
近 collapse, exhaustion, lassitude, tiredness, weariness
反 refreshment, rejuvenation, revitalization 恢复活力

fatuous [ˈfætʃuəs]

【考法】 *adj.* 愚笨的，昏庸的：complacently or inanely **foolish**
例 a fatuous remark/performance/tyrant 愚笨的评论/表现/暴君
近 asinine, brainless, foolish, obtuse, silly, simple, stupid, unwitty, witless
反 sagacious, sapient 聪明的，睿智的；judicious, prudent, sensible, wise 谨慎的，明智的

faultfinder [ˈfɔːlt ˈfaɪndər]

【考法】 *n.* 吹毛求疵的人：one who is given to **petty criticism** and constant complaint
例 a querulous faultfinder 一个爱抱怨、吹毛求疵的人
近 carper, castigator, caviler, censurer, critic, disparager, hypercritic, nitpicker

favorable [ˈfeɪvərəbl]

【考法】 *adj.* 有利的：tending to **promote** or facilitate
例 mild climate favorable to his health 有利于他健康的温和气候
近 advantageous, benefic, beneficial, favoring, good, helpful, salutary
反 unfavorable, disadvantageous, untoward, unpropitious 不利的

fawn [fɔːn]

【考法】 *vi.* 阿谀奉承：to **seek favor** or attention **by flattery** and obsequious behavior
例 fawn on one's superior 向上司谄媚

近 cower, cringe, flatter, grovel, toady, truckle
反 domineer 统治；专横跋扈
派 fawning *adj.* 阿谀奉承的，讨好的

faze [feɪz]

【考法】 *vt.* 打扰，使尴尬：to **disturb the composure** of: disconcert, dismay
例 Nothing can faze her . 没有什么可以使她气馁。
近 abash, annoy, bother, disconcert, dismay, disturb, discomfit, embarrass, fluster, rattle
反 calm, lull 使平静，使镇定

feckless [ˈfekləs]

【考法 1】 *adj.* 无成果的，没有价值的：**having no** real **worth** or purpose
例 years of feckless negotiations 长达数年的毫无成果的谈判
近 bootless, fruitless, futile, meaningless, purposeless, useless, worthless
反 effective, effectual, efficacious 有成效的
【考法 2】 *adj.* 粗心不负责任的：**careless** and irresponsible
例 a feckless young man 一个极不负责的年轻人
近 careless, heedless, inadvertent, irresponsible, slipshod, sloppy
反 careful, cautious, circumspect, discreet, wary 谨慎小心的

fecund [ˈfiːkənd]

【考法】 *adj.* 多产的，肥沃的：**fruitful** in offspring or vegetation
例 fecund black soil 肥沃的黑土地
近 cornucopian, fertile, fruitful, lush, luxuriant, productive, prolific, rich
反 barren, infertile, sterile 贫瘠的
派 fecundity *n.* 多产，丰饶

feeble [ˈfiːbl]

【考法】 *adj.* 衰弱的：markedly **lacking in strength**
例 feeble link/heartbeat/economic recovery 衰弱的联接/心跳/经济发展
近 debilitated, effete, enervated, faint, fragile, frail, infirm, languid, sapped
反 mighty, powerful, robust, stalwart, stout, strong 强壮的，强健的
派 enfeeble *vt.* 使衰弱

feign [feɪn]

【考法】 *vt.* 制造假象，装出…的样子：to **give a false appearance** of
例 feign illness/death 假装生病/死亡
近 affect, assume, counterfeit, dissemble, pretend, profess, sham, simulate
派 unfeigned *adj.* 没有伪装的，真诚的

Unit 3

■ FORESHADOW　　■ FERAL　　　　■ FERTILIZE　　■ FERVID　　　■ FORTE
■ FESTER　　　　■ FETID　　　　■ FETTER　　　■ FIASCO　　　■ FICKLE

foreshadow [fɔːrˈʃædoʊ]

【考法】 *vt.* 预示：to represent, indicate, or typify beforehand; **prefigure**
例 Dark clouds foreshadow a storm . 乌云预示暴风雨的来临。
近 adumbrate, augur, betoken, forebode, foreshow, omen, portend, prefigure, presage

feral [ˈferəl]

【考法】 *adj.* 野生的：**not domesticated** or cultivated
例 Animal experts discourage homeowners from trying to adopt feral animals as pets. 动物专家们不建议户主们将野生动物收养为宠物。
近 undomesticated, untamed, wild
反 cultivated 人工培养的；domestic, tame 家养的，被驯化的

fertilize [ˈfɜːrtəlaɪz]

【考法】 *vt.* 使肥沃，使多产：to **make fertile**
例 Reading will fertilize vocabulary . 阅读丰富词汇。
近 enrich, manure
反 deplete, drain, exhaust 消耗，耗尽
派 fertilizer *n.* 化肥

fervid [ˈfɜːrvɪd]

【考法 1】 *adj.* 酷热的：having a notably **high temperature**

例 Set out when the fervid heat subsides . 当酷热消散之后出发。

近 boiling, hot, scorching, searing, sultry, sweltering, torrid

反 arctic, chilling, cold, freezing, frigid, frozen, glacial, icy 冰冷的，寒冷的

【考法 2】 *adj.* 热情的：marked by **great passion** or zeal

例 fervid call/service/patriot 热情洋溢的号召/服务/爱国者

近 ardent, fervent, impassioned, passionate, perfervid

反 cold, cool, dispassionate, emotionless, impassive, unemotional 淡定的，不为所动的

派 fervor *n.* 热情，狂热

---

forte [fɔːrt]

【考法】 *n.* 优势，长处：something for which a person shows a **special talent**

例 You are expected to demonstrate your strongest forte in the Statement of Purpose. 在个人陈述中，你应该展示自己最大的优势。

近 advantage, eminency, knack, medium, métier, oyster, talent

反 inadequacy, incapability, incompetence, inefficiency 不足，弱势

---

fester [ˈfestər]

【考法】 *v.* 感染，溃烂，腐烂：to infect, inflame, or **corrupt**

例 cause the wound to fester 导致伤口感染

近 corrupt, decompose, putrefy, rot, spoil

反 heal, cure 愈合

派 festering *adj.* 更加恶化的

例 festering dispute over sth 关于某事的争论更加恶化

---

fetid [ˈfetɪd]

【考法】 *adj.* 恶臭的：having a heavy **offensive smell**

例 Ammonia has a fetid odor that sickened the people. 氨气有着令人作呕的气味。

近 foul, fusty, malodorous, noisome, reeking, smelly, stinky

反 ambrosial, aromatic, balmy, fragrant, redolent, scented 芳香的

---

fetter [ˈfetər]

【考法】 *vt.* 束缚：to **restrain from motion**, action, or progress

例 be fettered by family responsibilities 被家庭责任所束缚

近 chain, clog, enfetter, hamper, manacle, restrain, shackle, trammel

反 enfranchise, free, liberate, unbind, unfetter, unshackle 解放；facilitate 促进

派 enfetter *vt.* 束缚

---

fiasco [fiˈæskoʊ]

【考法】 *n.* 大失败：a **complete failure**

例 The Hitler's plot ended in a fiasco . 希特勒的阴谋最终以彻底失败告终。

近 catastrophe, debacle, disaster, failure

反 blockbuster, éclat, success 成功

---

fickle [ˈfɪkl]

【考法】 *adj.* 易变的：**likely to change** frequently, suddenly, or unexpectedly

例 a fickle lover/customer/group 易变的情人/顾客/组织

近 capricious, fluid, mercurial, mutable, temperamental, volatile

反 constant, immutable, invariable, stable, steady 稳定的，不变的

Unit 4

■ FICTITIOUS	■ FIDELITY	■ FIGURATIVE	■ FRACTIOUS	■ FILIBUSTER
■ FILTER	■ FINALE	■ FINESSE	■ FINICKY	■ FLACCID

fictitious [fɪkˈtɪʃəs]

【考法】 *adj.* 虚构的：**not real** and existing only in the imagination

例 fictitious rumor/exploits/characters 建构的谣言/英雄事迹/角色

近 chimerical, fabricated, fabulous, fictional, imagined, invented

反 actual, existing, real 事实的

fidelity	[fɪˈdeləti]

【考法】 *n.* 忠诚：the quality or state of **being faithful**
例 promise fidelity to the king 宣誓效忠国王
近 adherence, allegiance, commitment, devotion, faith, loyalty, piety
反 disloyalty, infidelity, perfidy 不忠；treachery 背叛
派 infidel *n.* 异教徒

figurative	[ˈfɪɡərətɪv]

【考法】 *adj.* 比喻的：expressing one thing in terms normally **denoting another** with which it may be regarded as analogous
例 The word here is used in its figurative sense . 这个词在这里取它的比喻义。
近 extended, metaphorical
反 literal 字面上的，逐字逐句的

fractious	[ˈfrækʃəs]

【考法】 *adj.* 难以管束的：tending to be troublesome; **unruly**
例 a fractious rebel that would not submit to the authority 一名绝不向当局屈服的顽固的反叛分子
近 balky, contumacious, defiant, perverse, intractable, obstreperous, refractory, unruly, untoward, wayward. willful
反 compliant, docile, subdued, submissive, tractable 顺从的

filibuster	[ˈfɪlɪbʌstər]

【考法】 *n./v.* 拖延议事：the use of obstructionist tactics, especially prolonged speechmaking, **for the purpose of delaying legislative action**
例 filibuster a bill 拖延了一项法案
近 delay, hindrance, impediment, obstruction, postponement, procrastination

filter	[ˈfɪltər]

【考法】 *v.* 过滤：to **pass through a filter**
例 filter the drinking water 过滤饮用水
近 screen

finale	[fɪˈnæli]

【考法】 *n.* 终场，结局：the **closing part**, scene, or number in a public performance
例 Didier Drogba pulled one back for Chelsea in a finale . 德罗巴在终场结束时为切尔西扳回一球。
近 close, coda, conclusion, end
反 prologue 开场白；overture 序曲

finesse	[fɪˈnes]

【考法 1】 *n.* 娴熟技巧：mental **skill** or quickness
例 The musician shows wonderful finesse . 那位音乐家展现出了非凡的技艺。
近 adeptness, adroitness, cleverness, dexterity, proficiency
反 awkwardness, ineptitude, gaucherie, ungainliness 笨拙
【考法 2】 *v.* (巧妙地)躲避：to get or **keep away from** (as a responsibility) through cleverness or trickery
例 He tried to finesse the blame for the foreign policy fiasco, even though he was Secretary of State at the time. 他竭尽所能躲避因失败的对外政策而可能遭到指责，尽管他时任国务卿。
近 avoid, dodge, eschew, evade, shun
反 confront 直面

finicky	[ˈfɪnɪki]

【考法】 *adj.* 过分讲究的，挑剔的：**extremely** or excessively particular, exacting, or **meticulous** in taste or standards
例 have a reputation for being finicky eater 有着挑食的名声
近 demanding, exacting, fastidious, fussy, nice, particular
反 undemanding, unfussy 不挑剔的

flaccid	[ˈflæsɪd]

【考法】 *adj.* 不结实的，松弛的：not firm or stiff; **lacking** normal or youthful **firmness**
例 flaccid muscles 松弛的肌肉
近 droopy, floppy, lank, loose, slack, yielding
反 stiff, sturdy 结实的，坚硬的；resilient 有弹性的

图书在版编目(CIP)数据

GRE核心词汇考法精析 / 陈琦主编. —2版. —北京：群言出版社，2016（2018.7重印）
ISBN 978-7-5193-0169-9

Ⅰ.①G… Ⅱ.①陈… Ⅲ.①GRE—词汇—自学参考资料 Ⅳ.①H313

中国版本图书馆CIP数据核字（2016）第210995号

责任编辑：张　茜
封面设计：大愚设计

出版发行：群言出版社
地　　址：北京市东城区东厂胡同北巷1号（100006）
网　　址：www.qypublish.com（官网书城）
电子信箱：dywh@xdf.cn　qunyancbs@126.com
联系电话：010-62418641　65267783　65263836
经　　销：全国新华书店

印　　刷：廊坊十环印刷有限公司
版　　次：2017年10月第2版　2018年7月第7次印刷
开　　本：787mm×1092mm　1/16
印　　张：25.5
字　　数：758千字
书　　号：ISBN 978-7-5193-0169-9
定　　价：55.00元

GRE
核心词汇
考法精析
第2版

陈琦 周书林 / 主编

颜余真、戈弋、肖雪 编著

群言出版社
QUNYAN PRESS

· 北 京 ·

GRE考试最强词表

方程等号	描述
句间关系	
but/yet/however/nevertheless	取反
. 句号	取同。如果没有句间转,用句号表顺承,三空题、阅读中大量使用
句内关系	
although/though/while/despite/even (if/though)	取反
surprising/startling/astonishing/ironic/contradictory/paradoxical	取反,在句中找一组反义词
belie/mask/veil/hide	取反,A 掩盖 B,在句中找一组反义词
because/since/so/consequently/therefore/so...that/so that	取同
and/not only...but also/or	取同,平行结构,方向一致
, 逗号	取同。如果找不到方程等号,就找逗号
: 冒号	取同
; 分号	取同
局部关系	
not/no/never/less/rarely/hardly/scarcely/unless/without	取反,否定词
refuse/decline/reluctant/compelled+to do	取反,相当于 not
～／for beyond/transcend	取反,表示"不仅仅"
～oth	取同,指示词+名词,该名词一定要在前文出现

 List 28

"如果出国是一种信念，那GRE便是是否能坚守的第一道考验。"
（陈曦，录取院校：University of Pennsylvania 材料科学与工程系）

Unit 1

| ■ ABREAST | ■ APPURTENANCE | ■ ACCLAIM | ■ APOSTLE | ■ ACCORD |
| ■ ACCUSTOM | ■ ACQUIRE | ■ ACQUISITIVE | ■ ADJUDICATE | ■ ADVERSITY |

abreast [əˈbrest]
【考法】 *adj.* 熟知的：up to a particular standard or level especially of **knowledge of recent developments**
例 She tried to keep abreast of the latest fashion trends. 她总是尽可能地跟上时尚的潮流。
近 acquainted, conversant, informed, knowledgeable, versed, well-informed
反 ignorant, unacquainted, unfamiliar, uninformed, unknowledgeable 无知的，不熟悉的

appurtenance [əˈpɜːrtməns]
【考法】 *n.* 附属物：a **subordinate** part or adjunct
例 It is rather difficult, if not impossible, to determine how large the management consulting industry is mainly because there is so little agreement on its appurtenance. 由于对其附属产业的看法不统一，大家很难确定管理咨询产业的规模究竟有多大。
近 accessory, adjunct, affiliate, appendage, appendix, attachment

acclaim [əˈkleɪm]
【考法】 *n.* 称赞：**public acknowledgment or admiration** for an achievement
vt. 赞扬，赞颂：to declare enthusiastic **approval** of
例 Many people were involved in the search, but the person who actually found the missing girl got all the acclaim. 许许多多的人都参与了搜救行动，但是只有真正找到那个迷失的小女孩的人才受到了称赞。
He was acclaimed as the country's greatest modern painter. 他被盛赞为国内最优秀的现代画家。
近 accolade, applause, credit, distinction, homage, honor, kudos, laud, laurels; accredit, applaud, cheer, commend, endorse, exalt, hail, praise, salute, tout
反 castigate, excoriate, lambaste, pan, slam 猛烈抨击

apostle [əˈpɑːsl]
●【考法】 *n.* (政策或思想等的)信奉者，支持者：a person who **actively supports** or favors a cause
例 Her mother was a dedicated apostle of healthy eating. 她母亲是健康饮食矢志不渝的倡导者。
近 advocate, champion, crusader, expounder, espouser, exponent, partisan, promoter, proponent, protagonist, supporter, zealot
反 adversary, antagonist, opponent 反对者

accord [əˈkɔːrd]
【考法 1】 *n.* 一致：a state of **consistency** *vi.* 相符合，相一致：to be consistent or **in harmony**
例 These results accord with our predictions. 这些结果和我们的预测一致。
近 accordance, agreement, conformity, congruence, congruity, consensus, consonance, harmony, tune; agree, chord, cohere, coincide, conform, correspond, fit, harmonize, jibe, sort, square, tally
反 conflict, disagreement, incongruence, incongruity, incongruousness 不一致；differ, disagree 不相同，不一致
派 accordance *n.* 一致，和谐
【考法 2】 *vt.* 授予，给予：to **grant or give** especially as appropriate, due, or earned
例 accord women the right to vote 给予妇女投票权 ‖ accord a tumultuous welcome 给予热烈欢迎
近 accord, award, grant, vest, vouchsafe
反 withhold 保留，不给予；recant, retract, withdraw 撤回，收回

accustom [əˈkʌstəm]
【考法】 *vt.* 使习惯：to **make familiar with** something through use or experience
例 As a kid from Southern California, the first challenge in his PhD life is to accustom himself to the harsh winter climate in Boston. 身为来自南加州的小孩，他博士生涯的第一道挑战就是习惯波士顿寒冷的冬天。
近 familiarize, habituate, inure, orient, wont
反 alienate, estrange, wean 使疏远

关于本书的用法，在此做如下说明：

本书收录的是历次 GRE 考试中的超高频词汇，掌握好这些单词是考生取得理想分数的必要条件。学习这些词，考生需要在认知方面具有一定的深度。如果能够掌握好本书中的单词考法(本书在英文词条中加粗带下划线的形式突出了单词的"特征点"，即"考法")，考生的词汇知识和能力将达到一个新的水平，可以在新 GRE 考试中取得优异成绩。但如果背诵本书单词后，在练习中依然遇到大量生词，请考生选择四六级以及托福的单词书，做好基础单词的巩固工作。

关于本书和其他"再要你命 3K 系列"丛书的配合使用。本书应该与《GRE 核心词汇助记与精练：第 2 版》配合使用，以达到最佳效果。希望各位考生在备考中遵循"3000—精练—3000"的步骤(具体操作步骤参见下表)，充分掌握单词的核心考法。

前 3 遍 3000 背诵与精练配套任务

	3000 任务	精练任务	3000 任务
第一遍	单词 + 中文释义	词义连线题	回看英文释义，特别关注加粗下划线部分
第二遍	单词 + 中文释义 + 英文释义加粗下划线部分	单词填空题	回看【例】部分
第三遍	单词 + 中文释义 + 英文释义加粗下划线部分 + 【例】	找同义词题	回看【近】【反】部分

注：

在前 3 遍背诵 3000 的时候，可以采取表格中的学习方式。

例如，在第一遍记忆 3000 的时候，可以先单纯看单词的形状以及其中文释义，每看完 1 个 Unit 的 10 个单词(3000 任务)，就对应完成精练部分词义连线题的相关部分(精练任务)，做之后立刻回到 3000 中，再去看 3000 书中的英文解释(3000 任务)，就可以更充分地理解加粗下划线部分。

之后两遍，按照表格所给出的建议，从上到下，从左到右，循序渐进，每一遍各有侧重点，层层递进，也会更加有成就感。完成这 3 遍之后，相当于考生已经刷了 9 遍 3000。此后可以进入到简单语境的 GRE 填空题目训练——使用《GRE 基础填空 24 套精练与精析》一书，通过与 GRE 出题思路一致但是更加简单的题目进一步理解单词的考法，提升实力。

此外，针对 GRE 考试的填空部分，我们为同学们整理了 GRE 考试中的常见"方程等号"(逻辑关系指示词)，分为句间关系、句内关系和局部关系三类。本表放置在书籍正文之前，这部分的词汇以及符号在考试中出现的频率要远高于本书的主词条，是名副其实的 GRE 高频，更重要的是，它们是所有题目解题的突破口。所以这张词表被我们称之为"GRE 考试最强词表"，希望同学们能在日后背好 3000 做题的过程中，感受它们在解题中发挥的重大作用。

最后我们要感谢微臣的王耕伟、张禄、朱思宁三位老师在例句修订调整部分做出的贡献，因为微臣团队的力量，让这本书得以快速出版。我们还要感谢本书的读者们。3K 系列的与时俱进离不开大家的信任与反馈。

祝各位读者在 GRE 考试中取得理想的成绩。

前　言

2011 年 8 月新 GRE 改革之后，由琦叔所带领的 3000 团队第一时间针对新 GRE 考试的特点，对之前的老 G 时代的《GRE 核心词汇考法精析》(要你命 3000)进行大换血。同年，"再要你命 3000"面世，为新 GRE 考生的单词准备提供了帮助。

2013 年，新 GRE 考试改革2 年多时间，3000 词汇的单行本面世，5 个 Unit，50 个增补单词，全新的增补形式，再一次展现了 3000 的与时俱进。同时我们发现，自 3000 以后，后续上市的新 GRE 词汇书都出现了对单词解释粗体、下划线的标记；同时，更多的单词书，开始走收词精准，而不是收词全面的编写模式。对于这种效仿，既是对 3000 的认可，更是对 3000 团队的激励，激励我们要在书籍的创作上有更多创新。

2014 年，琦叔离开新东方创办微臣教育，专注于 GRE 的内容生产。在微臣创办的 2 年中，一线的教学，团队的教研，以及我们追踪的大量新 GRE 题目，丰富了我们对新 GRE 考试的理解。促成了针对新 GRE 考试的《GRE 核心词汇助记与精练》、《GRE 高分必备短语搭配》、《GRE 基础填空 24 套精练与精析》、《GRE/GMAT/LSAT 长难句 300 例精讲精练》等"再要你命 3K 系列"书籍。

在教学、教研、书籍编写的过程中，我们对新 GRE 考试相比于之前有了越发深入的认识，也从更加宏观的视角来看待考试中的各个部分。但是我们深知，词汇依旧是 GRE 考试的重要基石，是 GRE 考试的第一道门槛，是 GRE 备考者们接触考试的第一步。在 2016 年的春季，我们对近 5 年来承载了无数光荣和赞誉，历经多次更新的《GRE 核心词汇考法精析》进行了全面调整。

这次主要的调整有 4 个方面：
1. 将部分考试频率过低的词汇进行删除，增补近 2 年考试中常见的高频真题词汇；
2. 针对部分单词考法，根据近 2 年考试的实际情况，删除并进行合并，大大减轻记忆负担；
3. 将部分单词释义调整得更为通俗易懂，更符合考试要求，方便同学们理解记忆；
4. 调整以往例句，将其替换为以单词为核心的用法搭配，将体现单词使用的核心语境部分用方框和下划线的方式标记出来。通过熟悉单词使用语境，不仅让考生更关注例句，防止孤立单词的死记硬背，更可以在未来把 GRE 词汇运用到写作中。

调整后，《GRE 核心词汇考法精析：第 2 版》共收录 GRE 考试中最常做主考的 3041 个单词，相比于上一版（包含增补），我们共替换 201 个单词词条，删除 282 个单词词条，删除、合并大量单词考法，精简 60 页篇幅。给出每个单词常考的中英文释义，配有精选例句、同义词群以及反义词群，部分单词还增加了派生词汇。

本书特色具体如下：
结构科学：本书共有 31 个 List，每个 List 包含 10 个 Unit，每个 Unit 的单词量为 10 个，考生可以以 Unit 为单位，循序渐进地进行学习。避免以 List 为单位学习，背不了几个单词就急于翻看这个 List 还剩多少单词。

收词精准：本书针对新 GRE 考试再度修订，删除在上一版中不常考查的词汇与考法，同时增补了近 2 年考试中出现的主考词，做到与时俱进。

释义权威：所有单词的解释均结合 GRE 考试的常考含义进行筛选。英文释义出自《美国传统词典》(*American Heritage Dictionary*)及 GRE 官方指定的《韦氏大学词典》(*Merriam-Webster's Collegiate Dictionary*)。同时辅以例句，将例句部分调整为常见的语境表达，并作出重点标识，方便用于写作表达。

结合实战：每条英文解释中均以加粗和下划线标记出单词考点所在，便于考生迅速把握单词的特征，在平时背诵的过程中逐步由中式思维转换为英式思维。

词汇延展：词条中给出派生词汇，扩大了横向词汇，达到举一反三的效果。

序二（2010年版）

"我不去想是否能够成功/既然选择了远方/便只顾风雨兼程"

——《热爱生命》，汪国真

2008年的冬天，在和Jason的一次聊天中，谈起市面上几乎人手一本的GRE红宝书。这本厚厚的红宝书收录了8000多词条，而GRE考试中类比、反义、填空常考词汇只占其中的一部分。为了能让同学们节省备考时间，提高备考效率，Jason和我决定开始合作写一本赋予全新理念的GRE考试词汇书。在这本词汇书中，我们只收录GRE考试类反、填空部分的核心词汇，并对每个词汇的词义解释和考点考法进行详尽的分析。

经济学十大原理之一就是，某种东西的成本是为了得到它所放弃的东西。于我而言，这本词汇书的成本就是在工作辛苦忙碌之余仅有的那一点休息时间。工作日每天上午7点起床，晚上9点多到家，从10点一直编写到12点然后睡觉。每个周末不睡懒觉并不是为了看心爱的NBA，而是为了从上午9点一直到晚上1点的编写工作。就这样，在把几乎所有的闲暇时间挤出来以后，经历了3个多月的努力，把陈琦精心筛选出来的3000多个词在《韦氏大学词典》和《美国传统词典》里统统查了一遍，对照着曾经考过的题，将一个个对应的词汇意思摘录出来，终于初步完成了词义筛选工作。Jason对初稿进行校稿，添加和删除一些内容。由于种种原因，这本词汇书曾一度搁浅。电脑里所有的初稿被我堆进一个文件夹，之后，又被我扔进了移动硬盘的某个角落。

过了许久，我和Jason重提这本词汇书的事。毕竟这本书对于每一位考G人来说是那么的重要，而且我们也花了那么多心血，不能就这么轻易放弃。这时，幸得几位同学以及Jason的同事也一起参与进来，形成了一个编辑团队。大家对初稿所有词条又重新校一遍，并补充了很多新的内容。2009年夏天，Jason忙着新东方的暑假GRE班，我亦被派到外地出差，这一去就是几个月，这本词汇书又被耽搁了下来。2009年12月31日的晚上，Jason跟我说，他教了这么多年的GRE类反，有必要为每一个考GRE的同学做一点事情了，于是我们决定将这本词汇书完成，并放到网上，让更多人能自由地获取，免费地阅读这本电子书。

在2010年年初的寒假班中，Jason对同学们做出了承诺，一定会让这本书上线。这是男人的承诺。Jason每天晚上9点下课后，从京郊的房山、琉璃河赶到家编写，第二天上午6点继续赶去上课。我将Jason编写的内容进行审阅并站在阅读者的角度提出修改意见，Jason再进行二次修稿。这样来来回回地斟酌敲定，只为将这本"用心良苦"的词汇书付诸实现。Jason是一个典型的完美主义者，我也喜欢flawless的东西，于是从内容到排版，从字体到颜色，Jason和我都反复商量，终于在2月的最后一天，将这本词汇书的第一个List终稿完成并上传到网上。本书一共有30个List，我戏谑地称之为"要你命三千"。搞定这些词，"你"就是ETS；搞不定，"你"就只是你自己。

就在我们逐步将终稿完成的时候，ETS正式宣布将于2011年8月对GRE考试进行改革。于是我们在保证质量的前提下加快了进度，只为能让那些在GRE改革前参加考试的同学们可以尽早获取到这本书。在这个艰难的时刻，我们非常感谢北京新东方大愚文化传播有限公司对出版这本"短命"的词汇书的肯定和支持，若没有他们，这本词汇书将永远停留在0和1的世界里。针对改革后的GRE，我和Jason已决定将在第一时间为广大考生编写出一本应对全新GRE考试的全新词汇书。

最后，谨以此书献给所有看过这本书，考完GRE，出国深造的同学，希望你们能够披荆斩棘，实现自己的梦想，和心中所爱的人一起创造人生的辉煌。同时，我也要把这本书献给那些在我遭遇挫折困苦的时候，在我人生低谷中给我鼓励和帮助的每一位朋友，以及我心中所爱的人。谢谢你们！

周书林

Franklin Chow

于杭州

够坚持。毕竟这一路走过来，你必须学会承受各种挫败与打击。背单词的过程是需要积累的，是爆发式的增长。如果你不想坚持了，请参看本段第一句话。

悉数从 2003 年 3 月份第一次参加GRE考试，到 2009 年的 10 月，我总共参加了 11 次 GRE 考试，Verbal 部分平均分 700+。我在课上总跟学生说我的词汇量不大。除了那些基础的四、六级词汇，我能记得的 GRE 单词只是 GRE 考试里主考的那些高频词，只不过对这些高频词，我太熟悉——不是简单的只知道意思，而是对于它们的种种考法了如指掌。

和 GRE 纠结了这么多年，我决定把自己花了六年时间精心分析筛选的 GRE 高频词和大家分享一下了。于是，我和我的团队成员们共同编写了这本用心良苦的 GRE 词汇书。在这本书中，我们对 GRE 考试中最常做主考的 3000 多个单词的考法进行了全新的演绎，让那些想花最少的时间和精力在 Verbal 部分取得 600 分以上的同学，免去大量无意义单词的背诵，免去大量无用处题目的反复，免去与《韦氏大学词典》以及《美国传统词典》之间的磨磨唧唧。

感谢为本书倾注时间与精力的团队成员们，因为你们，那些备受 GRE 单词煎熬的同学们可以在备考时大大减负；

感谢为了本书的出版付出心血和努力的所有编辑，因为你们，这本书可以如此快地出版；

感谢为本书题词的小牛人俱乐部的 25 位同学和 5 位名校录取的学员（曹楚楠、金宇航、朱晨光、蒋喆、罗弥、武阳乐、童心、卢璐、王彦妮、底骞、温韬、刘琮、周慧杰、汪洋、刘宜君、赵禾、徐碧慧、宋歆怡、赵墨非、杨璐、吕秋莹、相舒、蔺琳、周晟茹、姚佳雄、李丹、刘栩志、陈曦、翟冰、薄瓜瓜），因为你们，阅读本书的读者可以看到他们美好的将来；

感谢新东方曾经影响过我的老师（王鹏、王海波、黄顺、戴云、张晓楠、孙继军、张旭、宋昊、郭行），你们的智慧、才华、洒脱是当年吸引我来新东方的主要动因；

感谢新东方正在影响我的同事，与你们的碰撞是我在新东方快乐工作的原因；

感谢我所有的学生，因为你们，我有了被需要的理由；

感谢我的爸爸妈妈，我永远爱你们！

最后，祝各位同学在 GRE 之旅中一切顺利。为了享受明天美好的生活，也希望你学会享受当下的艰辛与感动。

陈 琦
Jason Chen

序一（2010年版）

> 提着昨日种种千辛万苦，向明天换一些美满和幸福。
>
> ——周华健《风雨无阻》

2004年，我第一次踏上北京新东方学校GRE类比/反义课堂的讲台，这一讲就是六年。GRE的类比/反义对于单词量的要求是迄今为止所有以英语为载体的能力测试中最高的。在课上，我要求学生们把俞敏洪老师的《GRE词汇精选》背诵50遍。我深知背单词是一件苦差事，要想背好海量单词，没有捷径，只能反复重复。但是既然选择去美国深造，我们终究逃不过单词这一关。

记得在大二备考GRE的那个学期，我每天背着双肩书包，手里拿着富光杯的透明水壶，耳朵上塞着耳机听俞敏洪老师的GRE词汇串讲，匆匆地走在去自习教室的路上。那段时间，我的生活重心就在自习教室。用现在流行的话来描述我的生活轨迹应该是"要么我在自习教室，要么我在去自习教室的路上"。每晚将近1点钟才能完成一天的学习任务，而11点时，北航教学区的门就被锁上了。为了能够尽早回到宿舍休息而不走远路，我需要从北航教学区大门旁3米高的铁栏杆翻出教学区。一开始翻的时候，心里会很心酸，但是日子久了，我告诉自己每翻一次就距离我的美国梦又近了一步。有一天我发现那个经常翻的栏杆断了，我意识到在学校里有很多我未曾谋面的同学，他们也为了自己的梦想，每天下自习很晚而走捷径翻这个栏杆。在那个学期，我目睹栏杆断了多次，但后来都被学校的后勤及时地焊上了。毕业的时候，我除了去学校的图书馆拍了毕业照，也去当年翻的这个栏杆拍了我大学四年里最有意义的一张照片。因为这个栏杆，我不是北航里的匆匆过客，它时常让我想起我曾经像一个骄傲的英雄一样每天执着地追逐着自己的梦想。有事做本身就是一件幸福的事，在那段准备GRE的日子里，GRE是我的第二次高考，我有幸能够在大二的时候就接触到它，因为这个考试，我拥有了新东方的工作，让我过上了自己当年想都不敢想的生活。

在新东方讲课除了可以大大改善自己的生活，还可以去影响别人的生活。我曾经将自己备考GRE的经历讲给学生听，这些可爱的学生们也会把他们的故事说给我听。北大光华管理学院的卢璐在2006年10月的GRE考试中取得了Verbal 750的高分，她的高分是每天自习到凌晨3点多，坚持两个月换来的。这个女孩和我提及这段经历的时候告诉我，"每天晚上下了自习，自习所在的北大老4教的楼门都锁了，我每晚是从一层的男厕所开着的窗户翻出来的。每当我翻的时候，我就想到当时课上老师讲的翻栏杆的故事，我觉得我也应该坚持下来。只不过我要是毕业的话，拍毕业照的地方就不是特别合适了"。当我听到卢璐的描述后，当我知道她是北京四中的理科高考状元后，当我知道她家庭背景非常好，全身都是Prada的时候，我意识到有些人的存在就是让你不舒服的。他们既聪明又有好的出身，但和别人一样甚至比别人还要勤奋。当我们面对这样的人的时候，我们没有任何懈怠的借口。每当我们看到他人成功的时候，不要只看结果，多问问他们都吃了哪些苦。因为要吃的苦很多，所以成功走下来的人并不多。

吃苦是守恒的，早吃苦总比晚受苦要好得多。在各位考生背单词受挫的时候，请学会调整自己的心态。唐僧当年也是经过九九八十一难才成功到达西天取得真经的，而背诵GRE单词也只是我们去西方发达国家取经道路中的小小一步。我们不妨将每次挫折都当成一次锻炼自己的机会，熬过它，我们就距离我们的梦想更近一些。

成功的人经常毅然地选择去做他们不喜欢的事情。如果只愿意挑喜欢的、容易做的事情，我们就好比在跑步机上跑步，即使努力很多，在距离上还是原地踏步。如果说你现在想要开始GRE单词的征程，你一定要能

迎接改变

2011 年 2 月，万泉河教学区 101 的讲台上，我在新东方最后一节 GRE 强化班的类反课因为 GRE 考试改革而正式落幕。之前的"要你命 3000"也被 GRE 改革要了命。面对新 GRE 的变化，我多次犹豫是否还有必要做本书的改编。倘若改编，耗时耗力。恰逢这个时期，我从新东方的北美部调岗至多语种部了。面对一个新的部门，面对多语种部六门自己一窍不通的语言，我诚惶诚恐，不知所措。岗位上的巨变，对于缺乏管理经验的我来说，无异于七年前一个内向木讷的理工男双腿发抖地在四百多学生面前讲课时的巨大挑战。但是面对改变，面对新的事物，我们需要将对它本能的恐惧转化成进步的动力。在多语种部的工作，自己成长了很多，认识了很多朋友，喝了很多酒。虽然每天过得很辛苦，但是刻骨铭心。因为我相信如果我们能够把每天的艰辛、痛苦、委屈当作生活的常态，我们的内心就会更加丰富。

每晚拖着疲惫的身躯回到家，想想当年讲台上的日子，百感交集。怀念讲台下那些渴望知识、渴望美好生活的学生；怀念讲台上同台搭档的好朋友。与其怀念，不如行动。最终，我还是决定做这本书的改编。因为这本书对我来说最大的意义，就是永远留在我逝去青春中的——陪我一路走过的学生和朋友。

在此，我要感谢刘宜君、路鹭，因为你们的爬虫程序，使得"新 3000"的编写效率大增；感谢颜余真和肖雪，我能理解每个夜晚你们泪眼婆娑地看着屏幕仔细做修订的辛苦；恭喜小牛人俱乐部今年申请的同学，你们持之以恒的努力，让读者在 list 题词中见证了你们申请的成功！

最后，感谢老 GRE，让我的青春那么美好。

新 GRE 来了，让我们洒脱地迎接它！

琦叔
Jason Chen
于北京

序言（2016 年版）

2014 年 2 月，我从工作了十年的岗位辞职，创立了专注于 GRE 培训的北京市海淀区微臣培训学校。迈出这一步需要极大的勇气，尤其是在过去的生活状态还不至于走投无路的情况下。上大学时候的我，想的只是将来能在北京找一份工作，打好这份工，如果能月赚 8000 就真是人生赢家了（当时我们北航机械学院的辅导员说过，我们机械学院的研究生毕业一个月不给 6000 的工作是不会去干的！我那时还是本科）。那时的我，从未想过有一天，会成立一所学校，会成为一名所谓的创业者。这就好像在我早先 3000 的序中所提及的，我万万没想到自己作为一名理工男，会成为一名培训教师，后来还可以接管并运营一个部门。不过，生活就是这样充满意外而又让人期待。

在微臣创立的第一年，我们做了大量提升教学水平的工作。通过组织老师教研，内部测试，外教答疑，写微信文章，写书，批课，来调动整个团队的积极性，激发大家的潜力。白天除了上课以外的时间，我就会找老师当面给我讲题目，进行辅导。回到家后，我会穿梭在不同的微信群里，听各位老师的讲解。一遍不行就再重复一遍，直到达到规范，而那时往往都已经过了凌晨。而合格并不是完结。因为微臣的课程要依据每次 GRE 考试进行备课，所以备课的压力非常巨大，需要快速迭代更新。一些非常时效性的课程内容甚至讲一遍以后就不再用了。记得一位国内考研的老师发朋友圈，说今天考研结束，他在熬夜解析今天的题目感觉非常辛苦。我只是想，GRE 考试每年考约 30 次，我们每月都至少有两次类似的体验，整个微臣团队早已经习以为常。我经常和微臣的老师说，大家在微臣一年的锤炼至少相当于我过去三年的摸爬滚打。这样的努力，不仅练出了队伍，更让老师们在年轻的时候就体验到了一条非常简单的道理——坚持做事情就会有源源不断的灵感，生活就会变得越来越好。

在这样的努力下，我们获得了同学们广泛的认可。在各大 GRE 网络论坛的版面上，会发现至少一半都是网友们分享的微臣的备考材料。在各个贩卖二手备考材料的交易平台上，遍布着微臣过往淘汰的课程的盗版。一位在同济大学姓赵的盗版淘宝卖家曾经邮件我说"琦叔，你以前在新东方录制的《GRE 核心词汇考法精析》的课程讲得太好了，是我所有课程里卖得最好的。只有你自己才能超越你自己，请你录制更多精彩的课程"。面对盗版卖家如此的肯定，起初对于盗版的愤怒转化成了对自己的一种督促。恰是因为他的这封邮件，提醒了我，微臣需要更多的内容生产，盗版卖家都在催稿了。同学们现在在网络上看到的一门新的课程《GRE Verbal 方法与高频题目精讲》就是在这封邮件的提醒下录制的。

大家的认可激励着微臣团队更多的努力。在过去这两年中，我们因为只专注于 GRE 培训，每位老师的年平均授课多达 1200 小时，教研多达 1500 小时。大家的生活里 GRE 占了最重的分量。在学校成立的这两年间里，我们的教研成果转化成了四本正式出版物。接下来我们还会有六本 GRE 书籍陆续出版。到此为止，微臣的 GRE 出版物基本覆盖了 GRE 所有的科目。而在这个过程中，我们一直没有忘记 3000 系列的开山之作——再要你命 3000。所以，结合这两年 GRE 的变化，我们将 3000 再次改版。

感谢优秀的同行们对此书的推荐，感谢老东家的很多同事将自己的孩子们推荐到微臣学习。感谢一切以各种方式帮助微臣进步的人们。微臣恐怕做不大，但是一定会认真做好自己现有分内的事情。

陈 琦

于微臣培训学校

献给所有为 GRE 奋斗的人以及那逝去的青春。

Unit 5

flag [flæg]

【考法】 *vi.* 变得衰弱：to **become** unsteady, **feeble**, or spiritless

例 revive the flagging enthusiasm/career 恢复逐渐衰弱的热情/职业

近 decay, decline, deteriorate, emaciate, fade, fail, languish, sag, waste, wilt, wither

反 thrive 繁荣；revitalize, revive 恢复活力

派 unflagging *adj.* 坚持不懈的

flamboyant [flæm'bɔɪənt]

【考法】 *adj.* 艳丽夺目的，炫耀的，充满装饰的：marked by or given to **strikingly elaborate** or colorful display or behavior; ornate

例 flamboyant dressing/wedding/writing style 炫耀的穿着/婚礼/写作风格

近 flaring, florid, garish, ornate, ostentatious, showy

反 natural 自然的；conservative, quiet, understated 低调的

派 flamboyance *n.* 炫目，炫耀

flatter ['flætər]

【考法】 *vt.* 拍马屁，奉承，讨好：to **praise excessively** especially from motives of self-interest

例 flatter your readers/monarch 讨好读者/君主

近 adulate, blandish, compliment, court, massage, overpraise, stroke, wheedle

反 abuse 辱骂；censure, criticize 批评

flaw [flɔː]

【考法1】 *n.* 瑕疵，缺点：an **imperfection**, often concealed, that impairs soundness

例 The absence of flaw in beauty is itself a flaw. 完美无瑕本身就是瑕疵。

近 blight, blotch, defect, fault, imperfection, mar, scar, spot

【考法2】 *v.* 降低，破坏，使不完美：to **reduce** the soundness, effectiveness, or **perfection** of

例 That crack has flawed the vase to the extent that its value in the antiques market is greatly reduced. 那道裂缝让这个花瓶在古董市场上大大地掉价。

近 blemish, break, compromise, cripple, harm, hurt, impair, injure, spoil, vitiate

反 fix, mend, repair, revamp 修复，改造

派 flawed *adj.* 有瑕疵的；flawless *adj.* 完美无瑕的；flawlessness *n.* 完美

fledgling ['fledʒlɪŋ]

【考法】 *n.* 新手：a person who is just **starting out in a field** of activity

例 fledgling experience/market 新手经验/市场

近 apprentice, beginner, freshman, neophyte, novice, tyro, recruit, rookie

反 veteran 老兵，身经百战的人

派 fledge *v.* (鸟类)长羽毛

fleet [fliːt]

【考法】 *adj.* 迅速的：moving, proceeding, or acting **with great speed**

例 fleet move 迅速行动

近 brisk, expeditious, fast, hasty, nimble, quick, rapid, rattling, speedy, swift

反 slow 缓慢的

flexible ['fleksəbl]

【考法1】 *adj.* 灵活的，可变的：capable of being **readily changed**

例 flexible schedules/working hours 灵活的时间表/工作时间

近 adaptable, adjustable, alterable, changeable, elastic, fluid, malleable, modifiable, pliable, variable

反 fixed, immutable, inflexible, invariable 确定的，不可变的；stiff, rigid 僵化的

派 flexibility *n.* 灵活性

【考法2】 *adj.* 易受影响的：**susceptible to influence** or persuasion

例 a flexible boss 易受影响的老板

近 docile, manageable, tractable

反 adamant, headstrong, intractable, mulish, recalcitrant, refractory, stubborn, obstinate 倔强的

flinch	[flɪntʃ]
【考法】	vi. 畏缩；退缩：to **draw back** in fear, pain, or disgust
例	He met my gaze without flinching. 他毫不畏缩地与我对视。
近	cringe, quail, recoil, shrink, wince
反	face, meet 面对；confront 直面

flippancy	[ˈflɪpənsi]
【考法】	n. 轻率，无礼：**unbecoming levity** or pertness especially in respect to grave or sacred matters
例	The flippancy of your answer annoyed me. 你轻率的回答让我很恼火。
近	facetiousness, flightiness, frivolousness, frothiness, levity, silliness
反	earnestness, gravity, seriousness, soberness, solemnity, solemnness 严肃，认真

flirt	[flɜːrt]
【考法】	vi. 调情：to **behave amorously** without serious intent
例	The waitress at that restaurant flirts with all single male customers. 这家餐厅的女服务员对所有的男性单身顾客都暗送秋波。
近	coquet, dally, frivol, toy, trifle

Unit 6

■ FLIT ■ FLOCK ■ FLORID ■ FLOUNDER ■ FLOURISH
■ FLOUT ■ FLABBY ■ FLUENT ■ FLUKY ■ FLUSH

flit	[flɪt]
【考法】	vi. 快速或突然地经过：to **pass quickly** or abruptly from one place or condition to another
例	Memories of the evening flitted through her mind. 关于那一晚的记忆在她脑海中一掠而过。
近	dance, dart, fleet, flick, flirt, flutter, hurry, rush, zip
反	plod 沉重缓慢地走

flock	[flɑːk]
【考法】	vi. 聚集，集体行动：to congregate or **travel in a flock** or crowd
例	Vacationers flocked to the towns along the shore in order to escape the August heat. 度假的人们一起涌向海岸，以躲避八月里的热浪。
近	mob, swarm, throng

florid	[ˈflɔːrɪd]
【考法】	adj. 辞藻华丽的，花哨的：**full of** fine words and **fancy expressions**
例	florid speech/language/prose style 华丽的演讲/语言/文风
近	bombastic, flowery, grandiloquent, magniloquent, rhetorical

flounder	[ˈflaʊndər]
【考法】	vi. 笨拙地行动，挣扎：to proceed or **act clumsily** or ineffectually
例	flounder through the desert 步履蹒跚地穿越沙漠
近	blunder, fumble, lumber, plod, struggle, trudge
反	glide, slide 滑行；breeze, waltz 轻松地行动

flourish	[ˈflɜːrɪʃ]
【考法】	vi. 茂盛；繁荣：to grow luxuriantly; to **achieve success**
例	innovation/art flourish 发明/艺术繁荣
近	bloom, burgeon, prosper, thrive
反	languish, wane 变得衰弱，衰败；fail 失败

flout	[flaʊt]
【考法】	n./v. 嘲弄性不理会，蔑视：to **treat with** contemptuous **disregard**
例	flout the academic norm by plagiarizing 通过抄袭来蔑视学术规范
近	despise, disregard, gibe, sneer, taunt
反	respect, revere, venerate 尊敬

flabby	[ˈflæbi]
【考法】	adj. 疲软的，无力的：**lacking strength** or determination; weak and ineffective; feeble
例	You can always hear talk about American business being flabby. 你总会听到有关美国经济发展疲软、后劲乏力的议论。
近	debilitated, effete, enervated, faint, feeble, fragile, frail, infirm, languid, sapped
反	mighty, powerful, robust, stalwart, stout, strong 强壮的，强健的

fluent	['fluːənt]
【考法】	*adj.* 表达流利的：**able to express** oneself clearly and **well**
例	a fluent speaker 表达清楚的演说家
近	eloquent, silver-tongued, well-spoken
反	inarticulate, ineloquent, unvocal 说话不清楚的
派	fluency *n.* 流畅，流利

fluky	['fluːki]
【考法】	*adj.* 侥幸的：coming or **happening by good luck** especially unexpectedly
例	a fluky coincidence that kept me safely at home when the blizzard hit 一个侥幸的巧合让我在暴风雪来袭时安全地待在家里
近	fortuitous, lucky, providential
反	hapless, unfortunate, unlucky, ill-fated 不幸的

flush	[flʌʃ]
【考法 1】	*adj.* 大量的：marked by **abundance**
例	a field flush with flowers 长满了鲜花的原野
近	abounding, abundant, awash, fraught, lousy, replete, swarming, teeming, thronging
反	inadequate, insufficient, scant, scarce, short 匮乏的，不足的
【考法 2】	*vi.* 冲洗：to **pour liquid** over or through in order to cleanse
例	flush a wound with iodine 用碘酒冲洗伤口
近	irrigate, rinse, sluice, wash

Unit 7

■ FLUSTER	■ FOIBLE	■ FOIL	■ FOMENT	■ FOOLPROOF
■ FOOTLOOSE	■ FORBEARANCE	■ FOREBEAR	■ FORESTALL	■ FOREWORD

fluster	['flʌstər]
【考法】	*vt.* 使慌乱：to **put into** a state of **agitated confusion**
例	refused to be flustered 不慌乱
近	abash, confound, confuse, discomfit, disconcert, discountenance, faze, mortify, nonplus, rattle
反	calm, quiet, settle, soothe, tranquilize 安抚，使情绪稳定

foible	['fɔɪbl]
【考法】	*n.* 小缺点：a **minor flaw** or shortcoming in character or behavior
例	tolerate each other's foible 指出他人缺点
近	demerit, dereliction, failing, fault, frailty, shortcoming, sin, vice, want, weakness
反	merit, virtue 优点，美德

foil	[fɔɪl]
【考法】	*vt.* 挫败：to **prevent from being successful**; defeat
例	foil her enemy by pulling some strings 通过一些关系和手段挫败了她的对手
近	baffle, balk, beat, checkmate, discomfit, frustrate, thwart
反	forward, foster, further, promote 帮助，促进

foment	[foʊ'ment]
【考法】	*vt.* 助长，煽动：to **promote the growth** or development of
例	He was accused of fomenting violence. 他被指控煽动暴力行为。
近	abet, brew, ferment, incite, instigate, provoke, raise, stir
反	quash, quell, quench, squash 平息，镇压

foolproof	['fuːlpruːf]
【考法】	*adj.* 十分简单以至于不会失败的：so simple, plain, or reliable as to **leave no opportunity for error, misuse, or failure**
例	a fool proof system/plan 一个不会失败的系统/计划
近	guaranteed, infallible, safe, unfailing, fail-safe
反	fallible 容易出错的

footloose [ˈfʊtluːs]

【考法】 *adj.* 无拘无束的，自由的：**having no attachments** or ties; free to do as one pleases

例 the footloose dog/people 自由的狗/人

近 loose, unbound, unconfined, unfettered, unrestrained, untrammeled

反 bound, confined, restrained, tied 有束缚的

forbearance [fɔːrˈberəns]

【考法】 *n.* 克制；忍耐：**tolerance and restraint** in the face of provocation; patience

例 reach the end of my forbearance 到了让我忍无可忍的地步

近 patience, temperance, tolerance, toleration

反 impatience 不耐烦

forebear [ˈfɔːrber]

【考法】 *n.* 祖先：a person from whom one is descended; **an ancestor**

例 the land of my forebears 祖先的土地

近 ancestor, antecedent, ascendant, father, grandfather, primogenitor, progenitor

反 descendant, offspring 后代

forestall [fɔːrˈstɔːl]

【考法】 *vt.* 预先阻止：to delay, hinder, or **prevent** by taking precautionary measures **beforehand**

例 forestall a crisis/demonstration/aging 预先阻止危机/示威/老化

近 avert, deter, obviate, preclude, prevent

反 abet, assist, facilitate, further, precipitate, promote 帮助，促进

foreword [ˈfɔːrwɜːrd]

【考法】 *n.* 前言：a **preface** or an introductory note, as for a book, especially by a person other than the author

例 The foreword of this book is co-written by Jason and Franklin. 这本书的序 Jason 和 Franklin 共同写成。

近 beginning, introduction, overture, preamble, preface, prelude, prologue

反 epilogue, coda 尾声；finale 终场

Unit 8

■ FORGE	■ FORMIDABLE	■ FORTHRIGHT	■ FORTIFY	■ FOSTER
■ FOUNDER	■ FRACAS	■ FRACTURE	■ FRAGILE	■ FRAIL

forge [fɔːrdʒ]

【考法 1】 *v.* 伪造：to make or **imitate falsely** especially with intent to defraud

例 The boy forged his father's signature on his transcript. 小男孩在他的成绩单上伪造了父亲的签名。

近 coin, counterfeit, fabricate, fake

【考法 2】 *v.* 锻造，铸就：to **form** (as metal) by or as if by heating and hammering

例 a real man forged by adversity 一个经磨难考验而成的纯爷们 ‖ They agreed to forge closer economic and political ties. 他们就打造双边的紧密政治经济联系达成了共识。

近 build, construct, form, make, manufacture, mold, shape

派 forger *n.* 打铁匠

formidable [ˈfɔːrmɪdəbl]

【考法】 *adj.* 艰难的：**requiring** considerable physical or mental **effort**

例 Running a marathon is a formidable undertaking. 跑马拉松是个困难的任务。‖ They have recently made a formidable decision. 他们最近做出了一个艰难的决定。

近 arduous, challenging, demanding, exacting, grueling, heavy, laborious, sweaty, toilsome, tough, strenuous

反 easy, effortless, facile, mindless, simple 轻松的，简单的

forthright [ˈfɔːrθraɪt]

【考法 1】 *adj.* 直率的，说话率真的：**free in expressing** one's true feelings and **opinions**

例 her forthright way of dealing with people 她率真的为人处事方式

近 candid, forthcoming, frank, honest, open, outspoken, straightforward

反 dissembling 虚伪的

【考法 2】 *adj.* 直接的，不绕弯子的：free from ambiguity or evasiveness: **going straight to the point**

例 forthright reply/appraisal 直接的回答/评价

近 direct, plain, straight

反 circuitous, indirect, roundabout 不直接的，绕弯子的

fortify ['fɔːrtɪfaɪ]
【考法】 *vt.* 加固，鼓励：to **give physical strength**, courage, or endurance to
例 This country will fortify the coastal areas. 这个国家将加强沿海地区的防御。
近 energize, harden, invigorate, reinforce, strengthen, toughen
反 debilitate, enervate, enfeeble, vitiate, weaken 使衰弱，削弱

foster ['fɔːstər]
【考法】 *vt.* 促进，鼓励，培养：to **help the growth** or development of
例 detect and foster artistic talent 发现并培养艺术天分
近 advance, encourage, forward, further, incubate, promote
反 discourage, frustrate, inhibit 阻碍，妨碍

founder ['faʊndər]
【考法1】 *n.* 建立者：**one** that founds or **establishes**
例 founders of the nation 国父们
近 architect, author, creator, father, generator, initiator, originator, sire
反 terminator 终结者
【考法2】 *vi.* 完败：to **fail utterly**
例 a foundering talk/career/company 一个彻底失败的对话/职业/公司
近 collapse, flunk, miss, strike out, wash out
反 succeed, work out 成功

fracas ['freɪkəs]
【考法】 *n.* 争吵，吵闹：a **physical dispute** between opposing individuals or groups; a rough and often **noisy fight** usually involving several people
例 The police were called in to break up the fracas. 警察奉命去制止骚乱。
近 battle, clash, combat, conflict, contest, hassle, skirmish, struggle, tussle

fracture ['fræktʃər]
【考法】 *n.* 破裂：the act or process of **breaking** *vt.* 打碎，破坏：to cause to **separate into pieces** usually suddenly or forcibly
例 a sudden fracture of the established order 已建立起的秩序被突然打破 ‖ Their happiness was fractured by an unforeseen tragedy. 他们的幸福生活被突如其来的悲剧打破了。
近 breach, break, rupture, schism, split; disrupt, fragment, rive
反 unity 统一；cement 接合

fragile ['frædʒl]
【考法】 *adj.* 易碎的：easily **broken** or destroyed
例 a fragile piece of glass 一块易碎的玻璃
近 breakable, feeble, frail, friable, frangible, infirm, unsound, weak
反 tough, durable 抗打击的

frail [freɪl]
【考法1】 *adj.* 虚弱的：physically **weak**
例 frail patients 虚弱的病人
近 weak, effete, enervated, feeble, fragile, infirm, languid, unsubstantial
反 robust 充满活力的；hale, sturdy 健壮的
【考法2】 *adj.* (意志)薄弱的：easily led astray; morally **weak**
例 frail and pathetic humanity 容易误入歧途的可悲人性
近 characterless, invertebrate, nerveless, spineless
反 faithful, resolute 意志坚定的，有坚定信念的
派 frailty *n.* 虚弱；(意志)脆弱

Unit 9

| ■ FRAUDULENT | ■ FRAUGHT | ■ FRENZY | ■ FAR-FETCHED | ■ FRETFUL |
| ■ FRIABLE | ■ FRICTION | ■ FRIGID | ■ FRINGE | ■ FRIVOLOUS |

fraudulent ['frɔːdʒələnt]
【考法】 *adj.* 欺诈的：characterized by, based on, or done by **fraud**
例 a fraudulent interpretation of experimental data 对实验数据的欺骗性解释
近 deceitful, deceptive, dishonest, duplicitous, guileful, underhanded
反 reliable, trustworthy 可信的；authentic 真实的；honest, straight 诚实的
派 fraudulence *n.* 欺骗

fraught [frɔːt]

【考法】 *adj.* 充满的：**full** of or accompanied by something

例 an experience fraught with peril 充满危险的经历

近 abounding, abundant, awash, flush, replete, thronging

反 scarce 稀缺的

frenzy ['frenzi]

【考法】 *n.* 疯狂，狂怒：a violent **mental** or emotional **agitation**

例 She is subject to these frenzies several times a year. 她每年都要暴怒几次。

近 delirium, fever, furor, fury, hysteria, insanity, rage, rampage, uproar

反 sanity 理智

派 frenetic *adj.* 疯狂的

far-fetched ['fɑːr fetʃt]

【考法】 *adj.* 牵强的，不可信的：**not likely to be true** or to occur

例 an exciting thriller, but one with a far-fetched plot that no sensible person could believe 一部刺激的恐怖片，但是有着任何理智的人都不会相信的牵强的剧情

近 doubtful, dubious, questionable, unapt, unlikely

fretful ['fretfl]

【考法】 *adj.* 易怒的，烦躁的：inclined to be **vexed** or troubled

例 fretful stage/public 烦躁的阶段/公众

近 irritable, fractious, peevish, pettish, petulant

反 easygoing 随和的

派 fret *v.* (使)烦躁

friable ['fraɪəbl]

【考法】 *adj.* 易碎的：**easily crumbled** or pulverized

例 friable mineral rock 易碎的矿石

近 crumbly, delicate, feeble, fragile, frail, infirm, weak

反 sturdy, substantial 坚固的

friction ['frɪkʃn]

【考法 1】 *n.* 摩擦：the **rubbing** of one object or surface against another

例 lubricant that significantly reduces friction 能显著减少摩擦的润滑剂

近 abrasion

【考法 2】 *n.* 冲突，不和：the **clashing** between two persons or parties of opposed views

例 There is a friction between the professor and students. 教授和学生之间存在不和。

近 disagreement, conflict, contention, dissidence, schism, war

反 accord, harmony, peace, concord 和谐

派 frictional *adj.* 产生摩擦的

frigid ['frɪdʒɪd]

【考法 1】 *adj.* 严寒的：extremely **cold**

例 an unusually frigid winter of Wuhan 武汉一个反常的寒冬

近 cold, arctic, chilling, freezing, frosty, glacial

反 roasting, scalding, scorching, searing, seething, sizzling, sultry, sweltering, torrid 炎热的

【考法 2】 *adj.* 冷漠的：**lacking warmth** or ardor

例 a formal but frigid welcome 一个正式但冷漠的招呼

近 indifferent, cold, emotionless, passionless, unresponsive

反 ardent, amorous, cordial 饱含感情的

派 frigidity *n.* 严寒；冷漠

fringe [frɪndʒ]

【考法】 *n.* 边缘：something that resembles such a **border** or edging

例 "Don't act on the fringes of the law," warns the customs officer. 海关人员警告说："不要打法律的擦边球"。

近 border, boundary, circumference, edge, margin, perimeter, periphery, skirt

反 center, core 中心，核心

frivolous ['frɪvələs]

【考法 1】 *adj.* 轻浮的：marked by **unbecoming levity**

例 a frivolous young woman 一个举止轻浮的年轻女子

近 giddy, shallow, superficial

反 earnest, sober, serious 严肃的

派 frivolity *n.* 轻浮，轻佻

【考法 2】 *adj.*不重要的：of **little** weight or **importance**
例　The frivolous comment was soon forgotten. 那个不值一提的评论很快就被遗忘了。
近　trivial, flimsy, light, petty, trifling
反　consequential, eventful, meaningful, momentous, weighty 重要的

Unit 10

■ FROTHY　　　■ FROWSY　　　■ FRUGAL　　　■ FUNGIB LE　　　■ FULL-BODIED
■ FULMINATE　　■ FUMBLE　　　■ FUROR　　　■ FURTIVE　　　■ FURY

frothy ['frɔːθi]
【考法】 *adj.*(内容等)欢乐轻佻、不严肃的：**gaily frivolous** or light in content or treatment
例　a frothy movie 一部有喜感的电影
近　flighty, frivolous, puerile
反　earnest, serious, sober 严肃的

frowsy ['frauzi]
【考法】 *adj.*邋遢的：having a **slovenly** or uncared-for appearance
例　frowsy hair 邋遢的头发
近　slovenly, unkempt, untidy
反　dapper, neat, tidy, spruce 整洁的

frugal ['fruːɡl]
【考法】 *adj.*节约的：characterized by or reflecting **economy** in the use of resources
例　be frugal in her expenditures 节约她的开销
近　sparing, economical, provident, stingy
反　extravagant, prodigal, sumptuous 奢侈浪费的
派　frugality *n.* 节俭

fungible ['fʌndʒəbl]
【考法】 *adj.*可互换的：capable of being **substituted in place of one another**
例　The important thing about crude oil is that it is fungible. 原油重要的一点是它是可以被替换的。
近　interchangeable, commutable, substitutable, switchable

full-bodied [fʊl'bɑːdid]
【考法】 *adj.*重要的：having **importance**, significance, or meaningfulness
例　a full-bodied study of genetic engineering 一项基因工程的重要研究
近　important, consequential, momentous, significant, weighty
反　trivial 不重要的

fulminate ['fʊlmɪneɪt]
【考法】 *v.*大声斥责：to issue a **thunderous** verbal attack or **denunciation**
例　fulminate the so-called curricular reform 痛斥所谓的课程改革
近　criticize, blame, censure, condemn, denounce, denunciate, lambaste, reprehend, reprobate
反　applaud, compliment, praise 赞美
派　fulmination *n.* 训斥

fumble ['fʌmbl]
【考法】 *v.*笨拙地做：to make **awkward attempts** to do or find something
例　fumble through a speech 笨拙地发表演讲
近　botch, flounder, mess, stumble

furor ['fjʊrɔːr]
【考法】 *n.*喧闹，狂怒；激动，狂热：a general commotion; public disorder or uproar; a state of **intense excitement** or ecstasy
例　The decision to raise tax has caused a great furor among the working class. 提高税收的决定引起了工人阶级的强烈骚动。
近　delirium, frenzy, fever, fury, hysteria, outrage, rage, uproar, wrath
反　serenity, tranquility 平静，宁静；delight, pleasure 愉悦

furtive ['fɜːrtɪv]
【考法】 *adj.*鬼鬼祟祟的；秘密的：done by **stealth**
例　a furtive glance at her 朝她投去的隐秘一瞥
近　secret, clandestine, covert, stealthy, surreptitious
反　aboveboard 光明正大的；candid, forthright 坦率的
派　furtively *adv.* 秘密地

125

fury [ˈfjʊri]

【考法】 *n.* 暴怒：intense, disordered, and often destructive **rage**

例 react in a fury 暴怒下行动

近 anger, indignation, ire, mad, rage, wrath

反 forbearance 容忍；delight, pleasure 快乐，愉悦

派 furious *adj.* 狂暴的，暴怒的

If you would go up high, then use your own legs! Do not let yourselves carried aloft; do not seat yourselves on other people's backs and heads.

如果你想要走到高处，就要使用自己的两条腿！不要让别人把你抬到高处；不要坐在别人的背上和头上。

——德国哲学家 尼采（F. W. Nietzsche, German philosopher）

List 11

Unit 1

■ FUSSY	■ FUSTY	■ FUTILE	■ GADFLY	■ GAFFE
■ GAINSAY	■ GALL	■ GALLANT	■ GALVANIZE	■ GAMBLE

fussy ['fʌsi]
【考法 1】 *adj.* 谨慎的：taking, showing, or **involving great care** and effort
例 a fussy actuarial problem 需要谨慎处理的保险计算问题
近 careful, exact, meticulous, punctilious
反 careless 粗心大意的
【考法 2】 *adj.* 挑剔的：**hard to please**
例 fussy eater/matter 挑剔的食客/事情
近 choosy, delicate, demanding, exacting, fastidious, nice, particular, persnickety, picky
反 undemanding, unfussy 不挑剔的

fusty ['fʌsti]
【考法 1】 *adj.* 过时的：rigidly **old-fashioned** or reactionary
例 fusty old carpets 过时的旧地毯
近 antiquated, archaic, bygone, moldy, outdated
【考法 2】 *adj.* 腐臭的：saturated with dust and **stale odors**
例 the fusty odor of a damp cellar 潮湿的地下室里的腐臭味道
近 malodorous, fetid, musty, noisome, smelly, stale
反 ambrosial, aromatic, fragrant, perfumed, redolent, savory, scented, sweet 有香味的，芳香的

futile ['fjuːtl]
【考法】 *adj.* 无效的，无用的：serving no useful purpose; completely **ineffective**
例 It would be an undoubtedly futile effort to persuade him. 想说服他毫无疑问是徒劳。
近 abortive, bootless, fruitless, ineffective, useless, vain
反 effectual, efficacious 有效的
派 futility *n.* 徒劳，无益

gadfly ['gædflaɪ]
【考法】 *n.* 刺激物：one that acts as a **provocative stimulus**
近 goad, impetus, impulse, incentive, irritant, spur, stimulus
反 balm 安抚，慰藉

gaffe [gæf]
【考法】 *n.* (社交上)失礼，失态：a **social** or diplomatic **blunder**
例 social gaffes committed by high-ranking individuals 高层人士在社交场合的失态行为
近 impropriety, indecorum, indiscretion
反 decency, decorum, propriety 举止得体

gainsay [ˌgeɪn'seɪ]
【考法】 *vt.* 否认：to **declare false**
例 gainsay the truth of my statement 否认我声明的真实性
近 deny, contradict, contravene, naysay
反 acknowledge, admit, avow, concede 承认；affirm 证实

gall	[gɔːl]
【考法】	*vt.* (使)焦躁，激怒：**irritate**, vex
例	The sarcastic applause from the audience galled her . 观众反讽的掌声激怒了她。
近	aggravate, exasperate, grate, inflame, provoke, pique, roil
反	appease, assuage, calm, lull, pacify, placate 使平静，使平息

gallant	[ˈɡælənt]
【考法】	*adj.* 英勇的：**brave**, spirited; nobly **chivalrous** and often self-sacrificing
例	Gallant paratroopers jumped out of the plane without hesitation. 英勇的伞兵们毫不犹豫地跳出了飞机。
近	bold, courageous, dauntless, heroic, stouthearted, valorous
反	craven, pusillanimous 胆小的
派	gallantly *adv.* 英勇地

galvanize	[ˈɡælvənaɪz]
【考法】	*vt.* (好似用电击)刺激：to **stimulate** or **excite** as if by an electric shock
例	an issue that would galvanize public opinion 激起大众评论的问题
近	provoke, agitate, excite, intoxicate, motivate, stimulate, pump up
反	allay, lull, pacify 使平静
派	galvanizing *adj.* 刺激的

gamble	[ˈɡæmbl]
【考法】	*v.* 赌博，孤注一掷：to **bet** on an uncertain outcome, as of a contest
例	gamble on the train being late 赌火车晚点
近	bet, adventure, chance, risk, stake, venture
派	gambling *n.* 赌博

Unit 2

■ GAMBOL	■ GAG	■ GARBLE	■ GARGANTUAN	■ GARISH
■ GENERIC	■ GARRULOUS	■ GUARDIAN	■ GLEAM	■ GAUCHE

gambol	[ˈɡæmbl]
【考法】	*vi.* 欢跳，雀跃：to leap about **playfully**
例	They gamboled down the passage way . 他们沿着走廊跳跃着走过来。
近	frolic, caper, cavort
反	plod, trudge 沉重缓慢地走

gag	[ɡæɡ]
【考法】	*n.* 笑话；玩笑之举：a laugh-provoking remark or act; **a joke**
例	a running gag 一个流传的笑话 ‖ gag reels 幕后花絮
近	crack, drollery, giggle, jape, jest, quip, sally, waggery, wisecrack, witticism

garble	[ˈɡɑːrbl]
【考法】	*vt.* 曲解，篡改，混淆(以至使无法理解)：to mix up or **distort** to such an extent as to make **misleading** or incomprehensible
例	The summary totally garbles the results of the investigation . 这份摘要完全曲解了调查结果。
近	misrepresent, belie, color, distort, falsify, twist, warp
反	clarify, elucidate 阐明

gargantuan	[ɡɑːrˈɡæntʃuən]
【考法】	*adj.* 巨大的：**tremendous** in size, volume, or degree
例	a gargantuan waterfall in the rainforest 热带雨林中的巨大瀑布
近	huge, astronomical, colossal, elephantine, enormous, gigantic, immense, mammoth, monstrous, titanic
反	infinitesimal, minuscule 微小的

garish	[ˈɡerɪʃ]
【考法】	*adj.* 过于鲜艳的，过于张扬的：marked by **strident color** or excessive ornamentation
例	With garish makeup on, she looks exceedingly frivolous. 浓妆艳抹之下的她显得格外轻佻。
近	gaudy, blatant, brazen, flamboyant, glaring, ostentatious
反	dim, gloomy, murky, somber 黯淡的；conservative, quiet 不张扬的

generic [dʒə'nerɪk]

【考法】 *adj.* 无差别的，普遍的：having **no particularly distinctive quality** or application

例 A love of big things-big houses, big cars, big meals-seems to be a generic trait of the American people. 热衷于大的事物——大房、大车、大餐——似乎是美国人的普遍特征。

近 blanket, common, general, universal

反 concrete, distinct, peculiar, precise, specific, unique 特有的，独特的

garrulous ['gærələs]

【考法】 *adj.* 啰嗦的，话多得令人厌烦的：given to excessive and often trivial or rambling talk; **tiresomely talkative**

例 garrulous traveling companions 多话的旅伴

近 talkative, chatty, loquacious, verbose, voluble

反 laconic, reserved, reticent, taciturn 缄默的

派 garrulity *n.* 啰嗦

guardian ['gɑːrdiən]

【考法】 *n.* 保护者，捍卫者：The guardian of something is someone who defends and protects it.

例 an institution acting as the guardian of democracy in Europe 一个在欧洲扮演民主捍卫者的机构

近 custodian, defender, protector

gleam [gliːm]

【考法】 *v.* 闪光：to shoot forth bursts of **light**

例 fine china gleaming in the candlelight 精美的瓷器在烛光下闪闪发光

近 flame, flash, glisten, glitter, luster, scintillate, sparkle, twinkle, winkle

gauche [ɡoʊʃ]

【考法】 *adj.* 笨拙的，缺乏社交经验的：**lacking** social experience or **grace**

例 a gouche countryman 一个笨拙的乡下人

近 awkward, clumsy, crude, inept, maladroit, rustic, tactless

反 graceful 优雅的；polished, refined, urbane 有教养的

派 gaucheness *n.* 笨拙

Unit 3

| ■ GAUDY | ■ GAUGE | ■ GEAR | ■ GENIAL | ■ GENTEEL |
| ■ GERMANE | ■ GIBE | ■ GIDDY | ■ GILD | ■ GIST |

gaudy ['ɡɔːdi]

【考法】 *adj.* 俗丽的：ostentatiously or tastelessly ornamented, **excessively showy**

例 gaudy movie posters 俗丽的电影海报

近 blatant, brazen, flashy, garish, glaring, meretricious, tawdry, flamboyant

反 austere, homely, plain 朴素的；conservative, understated, unflamboyant, unflashy 不张扬的

gauge [ɡeɪdʒ]

【考法1】 *n.* 测量标准：a **measurement** (as of linear dimension) according to some **standard** or system

例 polls as a gauge of voter satisfaction 用以衡量选民满意度的投票选举

近 standard, benchmark, criterion, measure, touchstone, yardstick

【考法2】 *vt.* 判定：to **determine** the capacity or contents of

例 It is hard to gauge his mood. 要判断他的情绪很困难。

近 assess, determine, evaluate, figure, measure, scale

gear [ɡɪr]

【考法】 *v.* 调整（以配合）：to **adjust** or adapt so as to make suitable

例 gear the speech towards a conservative audience 调整演讲以适应保守的观众

近 adapt, adjust, fit, suit, tailor

genial ['dʒiːniəl]

【考法】 *adj.* 和蔼亲切的：having an **easygoing** and pleasing manner especially in social situations

例 a genial host who makes a point of speaking personally to each and every guest 一个重视与每个客人私下交流的亲切的主人

近 affable, agreeable, gracious, mellow, nice, pleasant, sweet

反 caustic, mordant 尖酸刻薄的；truculent 凶残的

派 geniality *n.* 和蔼

genteel	[dʒen'tiːl]
【考法】	*adj.* 有教养的，不粗俗的：**free from vulgarity** or rudeness
例	Her genteel behaviors at the ball make others conjecture that she must come from a distinguished noble family. 舞会上她极有教养的举止让他人纷纷猜测她一定来自名门望族。
近	courteous, decent, decorous, mannerly, polite, polished, respectable, urbane, couth, cultured, refined
反	churlish 粗暴的；loutish 蠢笨的

germane	[dʒɜːr'meɪn]
【考法】	*adj.* 有关的，适当的：being at once **relevant** and appropriate
例	details not germane to the discussion 与讨论无关的细节
近	applicable, apropos, apposite, pertinent, relevant
反	extraneous, irrelevant 无关的；inappropriate 不适当的

gibe	[dʒaɪb]
【考法】	*v.* 嘲弄：to deride or tease with **taunting words**
例	gibe at the umpire 嘲弄裁判员
近	deride, jeer, ridicule, mock, scoff, sneer, taunt
反	respect, revere, venerate 尊敬

giddy	['gɪdi]
【考法】	*adj.* 轻率不严肃的：**lacking in seriousness** or maturity
例	teach a bunch of giddy Girl Scouts how to make a fire 教一群漫不经心的女童子军如何生火
近	flighty, frivolous, frothy
反	grave, serious 严肃的；earnest 认真的

gild	[gɪld]
【考法】	*vt.* （带欺骗性地）修改，润色：to give an often **deceptively attractive** or improved appearance to
例	Any further retouch would be gilding the lily. 任何形式的润色都会是画蛇添足。
近	polish, refine, smooth

gist	[dʒɪst]
【考法】	*n.* 要点：the **main point** or part
例	the gist of the argument 论证的要点
近	core, essence, kernel, pivot, quintessence, substance
反	divergence 偏离（主旨）

Unit 4

■ GIGANTIC	■ GLAZE	■ GLIB	■ GLISTEN	■ GLITCH
■ GLOAT	■ GLOOMY	■ GLOSS	■ GLOSSY	■ GLUT

gigantic	[dʒaɪ'gæntɪk]
【考法】	*adj.* 巨大的：unusually **large**
例	Stars glittered in the gigantic sky. 星星在庞大的空中闪耀。
近	colossal, elephantine, enormous, gargantuan, giant, grand, immense, mammoth, massive, titanic, tremendous, vast
反	diminutive, infinitesimal, microscopic, minuscule, minute, pocket, tiny 小的

glaze	[gleɪz]
【考法】	*vt.* 给…上釉，妆点：to **coat** with or as if with a **glaze**
例	The storm glazed trees with ice. 暴风雪给树木镀上了一层冰装。
近	adorn, bedeck, decorate, embellish, garnish
反	strip, uncover 剥去

glib	[glɪb]
【考法 1】	*adj.* 流利圆滑的（常含有不真诚或欺诈的成分），油腔滑调的：marked by ease and **fluency** in speaking or writing often to the point of being **insincere** or **deceitful**
例	a glib politician 油嘴滑舌的政客
近	nonchalant, oily
反	taciturn 沉默寡言的；awkward 笨拙的

【考法2】 *adj.* 缺乏深度的，肤浅的：**lacking depth** and substance
例 glib solutions to the knotty problem 对复杂难解问题的肤浅的解决方案
近 cursory, shallow, superficial
反 abstruse, deep, profound 深奥的，深刻的

glisten [ˈɡlɪsn]
【考法】 *vi.* 闪光：to **shine** by reflection with a **sparkling** luster
例 the glistening lake in the sunset 在落日中闪光的湖
近 flash, scintillate, sparkle, twinkle, winkle
反 dim 变得黯淡

glitch [ɡlɪtʃ]
【考法】 *n.* 小故障：a **minor malfunction**, mishap, or technical problem
例 a computer/navigational glitch 一个电脑/航行的小故障
近 bug, defect, fault, lapse, imperfection, peccadillo
反 fatal error 致命错误

gloat [ɡloʊt]
【考法】 *vi.* 幸灾乐祸，自鸣得意：a feeling of great, often malicious, pleasure or **self-satisfaction**
例 gloat over his enemy's misfortune 为敌人的不幸而幸灾乐祸
近 crow, relish, triumph
反 mourn 哀悼

gloomy [ˈɡluːmi]
【考法】 *adj.* 忧郁的：**low** in **spirits**
例 feel gloomy about future career 对未来的职业生涯倍感忧心
近 sullen, dejected, dour, melancholy, morose, saturnine, surly
反 frothy 欢乐轻佻的；buoyant, cheerful, jubilant 高兴的

gloss [ɡlɑːs]
【考法1】 *n.* 简短解释：a **brief explanation** of a difficult or **obscure** word or expression
近 abstract, annotation, brief, epitome, synopsis
反 amplification 详解
派 glossary *n.* 术语表
【考法2】 *v.* 敷衍潦草做事（甚至忽略）：to deal with（a subject or problem）**too lightly** or not at all
例 gloss over the problems 不怎么理会这些问题
近 disregard, ignore, neglect, overlook
反 scrutinize 仔细研究

glossy [ˈɡlɑːsi]
【考法】 *adj.* 平滑的，有光泽的：having a **smooth**, shiny, lustrous **surface**
例 glossy surface of the floor 平整光亮的地板
近 lustrous, burnished, glistening, polished, shining
反 coarse 粗糙的；dull, dim 无光泽的

glut [ɡlʌt]
【考法】 *vt.* 使过量，使充满：to fill **beyond capacity**, especially with food
例 glut himself with Sushi 吃寿司吃撑了
近 cloy, cram, fill, satiate, surfeit, oversupply, sate
反 lack 缺乏
派 glutted *adj.* 饱和的

Unit 5

| ■ GLUTINOUS | ■ GLUTTON | ■ GOAD | ■ GOBBLE | ■ GOGGLE |
| ■ GOLDBRICK | ■ GORGE | ■ GOSSAMER | ■ GRIMY | ■ GOURMET |

glutinous [ˈɡluːtənəs]
【考法】 *adj.* 胶状的，粘的：of the nature of or resembling **glue**
例 glutinous liquid 胶状液体
近 adherent, adhesive, cloggy, gluey, sticky, tenacious, viscid
反 fluid 流体的

glutton	[ˈɡlʌtn]

【考法】 *n.* 贪吃者：a person who eats or consumes **immoderate** amounts of **food** and drink
例 a glutton for work 工作狂
近 gorge, gourmand
派 gluttony *n.* 暴饮暴食

goad	[ɡoʊd]

【考法】 *vt.* 刺激，驱使，激发：to **incite** or **rouse** as if with a goad
例 goad someone to do something 激励某人做某事
近 urge, abet, exhort, instigate, prod, prompt, propel, spur, stimulate
反 check, curb 阻止；lull 使安静

gobble	[ˈɡɑːbl]

【考法】 *vt.* 狼吞虎咽：to swallow or **eat greedily**
例 Lions gobble their prey. 狮子狼吞虎咽地啃食它们的猎物。
近 devour, gorge, guzzle, quaff, raven, swill
反 nibble 小口咬

goggle	[ˈɡɑːɡl]

【考法】 *vi.* 凝视：to **look** long and hard in wonder or surprise
例 goggle at the characters on the stele 凝视石碑上的文字
近 blink, gawk, gaze, peer, stare
反 glance, glimpse 瞥视

goldbrick	[ˈɡoʊldbrɪk]

【考法】 *v.* 逃避工作和责任：to **shirk** one's assigned duties or **responsibilities**
例 goldbrick his duty as a citizen 逃避他作为公民的义务
近 idle, parry, shirk, sidestep
反 dedicate, devote 致力于

gorge	[ɡɔːrdʒ]

【考法 1】 *n.* 峡谷：a narrow steep-walled **canyon** or part of a canyon
例 Wenchuan earthquake is said to have no detrimental effect on Three-Gorge dam . 汶川地震据称对三峡大坝没有破坏性影响。
近 gap, gulch, notch, ravine
【考法 2】 *v.* 狼吞虎咽：to **eat greedily** or to repletion
例 He gorged himself at the party. 他在聚会上狼吞虎咽。
近 cram, devour, gobble, guzzle, quaff, sate, swill
反 nibble 小口咬

gossamer	[ˈɡɑːsəmər]

【考法 1】 *n.* 虚无缥缈的东西：something light, delicate, or **insubstantial**
例 the gossamer of youth's dreams 年少时缥缈的梦想
近 ether, delicacy
反 substance, entity 实体
【考法 2】 *adj.* 轻薄的；薄弱的：extremely **light**, delicate, or tenuous
例 a gossamer explanation 站不住脚的解释
近 diaphanous, ethereal, filmy, light, insubstantial, tenuous
反 heavy, leaden, ponderous 沉重的

grimy	[ˈɡraɪmi]

【考法】 *adj.* 肮脏的：**not clean**
例 a grimy mirror 一个脏镜子
近 besmirched, dingy, dusty, filthy, dirty, mucky, muddy, sordid, stained, unclean
反 clean, immaculate, spotless, stainless, unsoiled, unstained 干净的

gourmet	[ˈɡʊrmeɪ]

【考法】 *n.* 美食家：a **connoisseur** of **food** and drink
例 a gourmet of Chinese food 中餐美食家
近 bon vivant, connoisseur, epicure
反 layman 门外汉

Unit 6

■ GRANDEUR ■ GRANDILOQUENT ■ GRANDIOSE ■ GRANDSTAND ■ GRATE
■ GRATIFY ■ GRATUITOUS ■ GREEN ■ GREGARIOUS ■ GRIEVE

grandeur ['grændʒər]
【考法】 *n.* 宏伟，壮丽：the quality or condition of being **grand**; magnificence
例 the glory that was Greece and the grandeur that was Rome 希腊的荣耀和罗马的辉煌
近 magnificence, augustness, brilliance, glory, majesty, nobility, resplendence, splendor
反 frivolousness 无关紧要
派 grand *adj.* 宏伟壮观的

grandiloquent [græn'dɪləkwənt]
【考法】 *adj.* (语言等)浮夸的：a lofty, **extravagantly** colorful, pompous, or **bombastic** style, manner, or quality especially in language
例 feel disgusted with his grandiloquent speech 对他浮夸的演讲表示厌恶
近 rhetorical, bombastic, inflated, magniloquent, pretentious
反 secretive 低调的，隐秘的；simple 简单的
派 grandiloquence *n.* 夸张的话语

grandiose ['grændioʊs]
【考法】 *adj.* 自命不凡的，浮夸的：characterized by feigned or affected **grandeur**
例 grandiose words 自命不凡的话语
近 extravagant, flamboyant, pompous, pretentious
反 humble 谦逊的

grandstand ['grænstænd]
【考法】 *vi.* 为了给人留下印象而表演，哗众取宠：to play or act so as to **impress** onlookers
例 grandstand on the stage 在舞台上哗众取宠
近 act, perform, pretend

grate [greɪt]
【考法1】 *v.* 刮擦(以发出刺耳的声音)：to make a **rasping** sound
例 The sled grated along the bare pavement. 雪橇与裸露的路面刮擦发出刺耳声。
近 abrade, rasp, scratch, scrape
派 grating *adj.* 刺耳的
【考法2】 *v.* 骚扰，惹恼：to **irritate** or annoy persistently
例 a noise that grates on one's nerves 使人烦躁的噪音
近 irritate, aggravate, gall, nettle, peeve, plague, provoke, vex
反 soothe 使平静，安抚

gratify ['grætɪfaɪ]
【考法】 *vt.* 使满足：to give what is **desired** to, to **please** or satisfy
例 gratify her curiosity 满足她的好奇心 || Her praise will gratify all who worked so hard to earn it. 她的表扬会使所有辛勤工作的人们高兴。
近 appease, cater, content, satisfy
反 displease 使不满；grieve 使悲痛
派 gratification *n.* 满意

gratuitous [grə'tuːɪtəs]
【考法1】 *adj.* 无根据的，无理由的：unnecessary or **unwarranted**
例 a dubious request based on a gratuitous assumption 基于无根据假设的可疑要求
近 unfounded, unjustified, unreasonable, baseless, groundless
反 justified, warranted 有理有据的
【考法2】 *adj.* 无报酬的，免费的：given or granted **without return** or recompense
例 a gratuitous ticket 免费的门票
近 free, complimentary, unearned, voluntary
反 merited 应得的
派 gratuity *n.* 报酬，小费

green	[griːn]
【考法】	*adj.* 无经验的：**deficient** in training, knowledge, or **experience**
例	lead a squad of green recruits 带领一队没有经验的新兵
近	inexperienced, callow, fresh, raw, unfledged, young
反	experienced, versed 经验丰富的

gregarious	[grɪˈgeriəs]
【考法 1】	*adj.* 爱社交的: likely to seek or **enjoy the company** of others
近	convivial, extroverted, genial, outgoing, sociable, outgoing
反	aloof 疏远的；antisocial 不合群的；introverted, reclusive 内向的
【考法 2】	*adj.* 群居的: tending to **group with others** of the same kind
例	ecologically define human as gregarious carnivore 从生态学上将人类定义为群居类肉食动物
近	social
反	solitary 独自的

grieve	[griːv]
【考法】	*vt.* (使)感到悲伤: to (cause to) feel **deep sadness** or mental pain
例	grieve over sth. 为某事感到悲伤
近	agonize, anguish, suffer, bemoan, bewail, deplore
反	delight, exult in, glory in, joy, rejoice in 感到高兴

Unit 7

■ GLAMOROUS	■ GRIN	■ GRIPE	■ GRISLY	■ GROOVE
■ GROTESQUE	■ GROVEL	■ GRUELING	■ GUILE	■ GLEAN

glamorous	[ˈglæmərəs]
【考法】	*adj.* 迷人的: having an often mysterious or **magical power to attract**
例	Every glamorous puss knows that lack of competition is the key to success. 每个迷人的姑娘都清楚地知道想要成功的关键就是减少竞争。
近	alluring, appealing, attractive, bewitching, captivating, charismatic, charming, enchanting, engaging, entrancing, fascinating
反	repellent, repelling, repugnant, repulsive, revolting 令人厌恶的

grin	[grɪn]
【考法】	*v.* 咧嘴笑，咧嘴笑着表示: to **express an emotion** (as amusement) by curving the lips upward
例	The boss grinned his approval. 老板咧嘴一笑表示赞许。
近	beam
反	pout 噘嘴生气

gripe	[graɪp]
【考法】	*vi.* 抱怨: to express **dissatisfaction**, pain, or resentment usually tiresomely
例	All workers were griping about the new regulations. 所有的工人都在抱怨新规章。
近	carp, fuss, grouch, grouse, grumble, wail
反	crow, delight, rejoice 欢快，喜悦

grisly	[ˈgrɪzli]
【考法】	*adj.* 令人反感的，令人恐惧的: inspiring **repugnance**; gruesome
例	a series grisly murders 一系列令人恐惧的谋杀
近	appalling, dreadful, ghastly, gruesome, hideous, horrifying, macabre

groove	[gruːv]
【考法】	*v.* 享受，极其满意，过得快活: to **take pleasure in**
例	Thrill-seekers who groove on skiing will love snowboarding. 那些乐在滑雪中的追求刺激的人们也会喜欢滑雪板的。 Il just sitting around, grooving on the music 随便坐坐，在音乐中享受一下
近	adore, fancy, savor, relish, get off on, rejoice in, revel in, delight in

grotesque	[groʊˈtesk]
【考法】	*adj.* 难看的: **unpleasant** to look at
例	That bloody Halloween mask is grotesque. 那个血腥的万圣节面具丑死了。
近	hideous, homely, ill-favored, monstrous, unappealing, unattractive, uncomely, unsightly
反	aesthetic, attractive, beautiful, bonny, comely, fetching, gorgeous, knockout, ravishing, seemly, sightly, stunning, taking, well-favored 悦目的，吸引人的

	grovel	[ˈɡrɑːvl]
【考法】		*vi.* 卑躬屈膝：to **draw back** or crouch down in **fearful submission**
例		He made a groveling apology to the girl. 他放下身段，给那姑娘道歉。
近		cringe, creep, slither, wriggle
派		groveler *n.* 卑躬屈膝者：the one who lies with the body prostrate in token of subservience or abasement

	grueling	[ˈɡruːəlɪŋ]
【考法】		*adj.* 费时间花心思的：**requiring** much time, effort, or careful attention
例		Cutting diamonds can be grueling work. 切割钻石是项劳神的活儿。
近		arduous, burdensome, laborious, onerous, taxing, toilsome
反		undemanding, facile 不费力气的

	guile	[ɡaɪl]
【考法】		*n.* 狡猾，狡诈：the inclination or practice of **misleading** others through lies or trickery
例		A person so full of guile he can't even be trusted to give you the correct time of day. 他这个人狡诈成性，说的话都不足为信。
近		artfulness, canniness, craft, cunningness, deviousness, slyness, subtleness, wiliness
反		artlessness, forthrightness, ingenuousness, sincerity 朴实
派		guileless *adj.* 朴实的：free of guile; artless
反		manipulative 操纵的

	glean	[ɡliːn]
【考法】		*v.* 收集：to **collect** bit by bit
例		records from which historians glean their knowledge 历史学家们从记录资料中收集信息
近		accumulate, amass, assemble, collect, congregate, garner

Unit 8

■ GULL	■ GROUNDLESS	■ GUSH	■ GUST	■ GUZZLE
■ HACK	■ HACKNEYED	■ HALCYON	■ HALE	■ HALF-BAKED

	gull	[ɡʌl]
【考法】		*vt.* 欺骗：to cause to believe what is **untrue**
例		gull the old woman out of her money 骗取老妇的钱财
近		bamboozle, beguile, cozen, delude, dupe, fake out, gaff, hoax, hoodwink, snooker, string along, take in
反		undeceive 使醒悟

	groundless	[ˈɡraʊndləs]
【考法】		*adj.* 没有依据的：having **no basis in reason** or fact
例		groundless fear/evidence 没有根据的恐惧/证据
近		baseless, foundationless, unfounded, unreasonable, unsubstantiated, unwarranted
反		justified, reasonable, reasoned, substantiated, valid, well-founded, well-grounded 有依据的

	gush	[ɡʌʃ]
【考法】		*v.* (使)感情强烈外溢：to make an **exaggerated display** of affection or enthusiasm
例		an aunt gushing over the baby 对着婴儿母爱泛滥的姑姑
近		drool, effuse, enthuse, fuss, rave, slobber

	gust	[ɡʌst]
【考法】		*n.* 情感爆发：a **sudden intense expression** of strong feeling
例		The stressed-out coworker cried out with a gust of emotion. 压力巨大的同事开始嚎啕大哭。
近		burst, ebullition, eruption, explosion, flush, gush

	guzzle	[ˈɡʌzl]
【考法】		*v.* 狂饮：to **drink** especially liquor **greedily**, continually, or habitually
例		guzzle beer 狂饮啤酒
近		gulp, quaff, swig, booze, soak, tipple

	hack	[hæk]
【考法 1】		*n.* 雇佣文人：a **writer** who aims solely for **commercial** success
【考法 2】		*v.* 乱砍；开辟：to cut or chop with repeated and **irregular blows**
例		hacking out new election districts 开辟新的选区

hackneyed	[ˈhæknɪd]
【考法】	*adj.* 陈腐的，缺乏创新的：**lacking** in **freshness** or **originality**
例	hackneyed slogans 老掉牙的口号
近	banal, cliché, commonplace, hack, threadbare, trite, well-worn, stereotyped
反	fresh, offbeat, original, novel 新鲜的

halcyon	[ˈhælsɪən]
【考法】	*adj.* 宁静的，平静的：**free from** storms or physical disturbance
近	hushed, peaceful, placid, serene, tranquil, untroubled
反	tempestuous, stormy, agitated, inclement, restless, rough, turbulent, unquiet, unsettled 暴风雨的；暴躁的

hale	[heɪl]
【考法】	*adj.* 强壮的，健壮的：**free from infirmity or illness**; sound
例	a hale and hearty old lady 硬朗矍铄的老奶奶
近	bouncing, fit, robust, sound, well-conditioned, wholesome
反	effete, infirm, anemic, wan, decrepit, blighted 衰弱的，衰老的

half-baked	[ˌhæf ˈbeɪkt]
【考法】	*adj.* 不明智的：showing or marked by a **lack of good sense or judgment**
例	a half-baked scheme 不明智的计划
近	daffy, daft, dippy, harebrained, half-witted, preposterous
反	judicious, prudent, sagacious, sapient, sensible, sound, wise 明智的

Unit 9

■ HALLMARK	■ HALLOW	■ HALLUCINATION	■ HAM-HANDED	■ HAMMER
■ HAMPER	■ HAMSTRING	■ HANGDOG	■ HANKER	■ HAPHAZARD

hallmark	[ˈhɔːlmɑːrk]
【考法】	*n.* 典型的特征：a **conspicuous feature** or characteristic
例	The sense of guilt is the hallmark of civilized humanity . 内疚是人类文明的特征。
近	ensign, impresa, logo, symbol, totem, trademark
反	uncharacteristic feature 不典型的特征

hallow	[ˈhæloʊ]
【考法】	*vt.* 尊敬，把…视为神圣：to **respect** or honor greatly; revere
近	consecrate, sacralize, sanctify
反	desecrate, deconsecrate, desacralize, desanctify 亵渎

hallucination	[həˌluːsɪˈneɪʃn]
【考法】	*n.* 错觉：a **false idea** or belief
例	a hallucination not a real thing 是幻觉而不是现实
近	chimera, daydream, delusion, fancy, figment, illusion
反	truth, verity

ham-handed	[ˈhæmhændɪd]
【考法】	*adj.* 笨手笨脚的：**lacking dexterity** or grace
例	too ham-handed to use one of those tiny cell phones 手指太不灵活了，用不了那种迷你型手机
近	awkward, handless, heavy-handed, maladroit, unhandy
反	deft, dexterous, handy, sure-handed, adroit 敏捷的

hammer	[ˈhæmər]
【考法】	*v.* 屡次重申：to make **repeated** efforts especially: to reiterate an opinion or attitude
例	The lectures all hammered away at the same points . 整场讲座都是在阐述相同的论点。‖ hammer the information into the students' heads 反复向学生们强调这条信息

hamper	[ˈhæmpər]
【考法】	*vt.* 阻碍：to **restrict the movement** of by bonds or obstacles: **impede**
例	Construction is hampering traffic on the highway . 高速路上的建设阻碍了正常交通。
近	cramp, encumber, fetter, handicap, hinder, impede, stymie, trammel
反	facilitate, aid, assist, help 促进

hamstring	[ˈhæmstrɪŋ]
【考法】	*vt.* 使无效，使无力：to make **ineffective** or powerless
例	The downtown development committee claims that it's hamstrung by city ordinances . 市中心发展委员会声称它受到了城市法令的阻碍。
近	cripple, immobilize, incapacitate, prostrate

hangdog	[ˈhændɔːɡ]
【考法】	*adj.* 伤心的，沮丧的：**sad**, **dejected**
例	She came home with a hangdog expression on her face . 她一脸沮丧地回到了家。
近	crestfallen, dejected, despondent, disconsolate, doleful, melancholy, sorrowful
反	buoyant, elated, sprightly, blissful, delighted, joyous, jubilant, upbeat 热情高涨的

hanker	[ˈhæŋkər]
【考法】	*v./n.* 向往，渴望：to have a strong or persistent **desire**: **yearn**
例	hanker for adventure 渴望冒险
近	appetite, craving, hunger, itch, longing, lust, passion, thirst, yearning
反	odium, lack of desire 讨厌

haphazard	[hæpˈhæzərd]
【考法】	*adj.* 无秩序的，无目标的：marked by **lack of plan, order, or direction**
例	We were given a haphazard tour of the city . 我们进行了一次城市漫游。
近	aimless, arbitrary, desultory, erratic, scattered, stray
反	methodical, systematic, nonrandom, orderly, organized, regular 系统的，有序的

Unit 10

◼ HARANGUE	◼ HARASS	◼ HARBINGER	◼ HARBOR	◼ HARD-BITTEN
◼ HARDY	◼ HARMONIOUS	◼ HARNESS	◼ HARROW	◼ HARRY

harangue	[həˈræŋ]
【考法】	*v./n.* （发表）长篇大论：a **long pompous** speech, especially one delivered before a gathering
例	She harangued us for hours about the evils of popular culture. 她向我们絮叨了好几小时，批判流行文化的堕落。
近	diatribe, jeremiad, philippic, rant
反	speak temperately 有节制地说话

harass	[həˈræs]
【考法】	*vt.* 烦扰：to **irritate** or torment **persistently**
例	The troops harassed the defeated army throughout its retreat. 战胜的队伍在撤退过程中还不忘突袭一下败北的队伍。

harbinger	[ˈhɑːrbɪndʒər]
【考法】	*n.* 预言者：one that **presages** or foreshadows what is to come
例	The October air stung my cheeks, a harbinger of winter . 十月的寒风凛冽地吹在脸上，这是冬天的预兆。
近	foregoer, herald, outrider, precursor

harbor	[ˈhɑːrbər]
【考法】	*vt.* 心怀，牢记：to **keep in one's mind** or heart
例	He had long harbored a grudge against his old employer , who had fired him without cause. 他对前老板一直耿耿于怀，因为他无缘无故炒了他。
近	bear, cherish, entertain, hold, nurse

hard-bitten	[hɑːrd ˈbɪtn]
【考法】	*adj.* 顽强的，经受得住困境、压力的：**able to withstand** hardship, strain, or exposure
例	Hard-bitten Chinese people could endure both the scorching heat and the freezing cold. 坚强勇敢的中国人民既能受得住酷暑，又能受得住严寒。
近	hardened, sturdy, tough, cast-iron, inured, rugged, stout, vigorous, hardy
反	delicate, nonhardy, soft, tender, weak 柔弱的

hardy	[ˈhɑːrdi]
【考法】	*adj.* 顽强的：**able to withstand** hardship, strain, or exposure
例	Chrysanthemums are hardy enough to survive a light frost . 菊花能够经受霜打。
近	hardened, sturdy, tough, cast-iron, inured, rugged, stout, vigorous, hard-bitten
反	delicate, nonhardy, soft, tender, weak 柔弱的

harmonious [hɑːrˈmoʊniəs]

【考法】 *adj.* 和谐一致的：having the parts **agreeably related**

例 a harmonious arrangement of archways and doorways in the palace courtyard 宫殿的庭院、拱门和门廊排列有序协调

近 balanced, congruous, consonant, eurythmic, harmonic, accordant, coherent, compatible, concordant, conformable, congruent, consonant, correspondent, nonconflicting

反 disharmonic, disharmonious, incongruous, unbalanced 不协调的；conflicting, incompatible, incongruous, inconsistent 冲突的

harness [ˈhɑːrnɪs]

【考法】 *vt.* 利用：**utilize**

例 harness the sun's rays as a source of energy 利用阳光作为一种能源

近 apply, employ, exercise, exploit, operate, utilize

反 fail to utilize 没能够利用

harrow [ˈhæroʊ]

【考法】 *vt.* 折磨，使苦恼：to inflict great **distress** or **torment** on

例 The villagers were gaunt and sickly, harrowed by years of disease and starvation. 村民们枯瘦如柴，体弱多病，都是被多年的疾病和饥饿折磨的。

近 agonize, beset, besiege, torment, torture, excruciate, plague

反 assuage 减轻(苦恼)

harry [ˈhæri]

【考法】 *vt.* 不断烦扰，骚扰：to disturb or **distress** by or as if by repeated attacks; **harass**

例 harry the government 不断烦扰政府

反 comfort, mollify 安慰

Every man's work, whether it be literature of music of pictures or architecture of anything else, is always a portrait of himself.

每个人的工作，不管是文学、音乐、美术、建筑还是其他工作，都是自己的一幅画像。

——美国教育家 勃特勒(Samuel Brtler, American educator)

List 12

"真正努力过才能发现自己的潜能有多大。不要给自己犹豫后退的借口，让小宇宙爆发吧！"
（刘琼，2009 年 6 月，Verbal 720，Quantitative 800，录取院校：University of Southern California, Annenberg School of journalism and Communication, Public Diplomacy）

Unit 1

■ HARSH	■ HASTEN	■ HASTY	■ HAUNT	■ HAUTEUR
■ HAVEN	■ HAVOC	■ HEADLONG	■ HEARKEN	■ HEARTEN

harsh [hɑːrʃ]
【考法】 *adj.* 严厉的：unduly **exacting**, given to exacting standards of discipline and self-restraint
例 a harsh judge when it comes to drug users and especially drug dealers 对瘾君子特别是毒贩处罚格外严厉的法官
近 afflicting, agonizing, cruel, excruciating, galling, grievous, harrowing
反 clement, forbearing, gentle, indulgent, lax, lenient, tolerant 温和的，宽松的

hasten [ˈheɪsn]
【考法】 *vt.* 促进：to **speed up**; **accelerate**
例 The man's death was hastened by alcohol abuse. 酗酒加速了这个人的死亡。
近 accelerate, bundle, fast-track, rush, speed up
反 slow the progress of, check, retard, brake, decelerate, retard, slow down 阻碍，放慢

hasty [ˈheɪsti]
【考法】 *adj.* 轻率的：fast and typically **superficial**; acting or done with **excessive or careless speed**
例 a hasty decision 轻率的决定
近 cursory, headlong, precipitate, rash, rushed, pell-mell
反 deliberate, well-considered, unhurried, unrushed 深思熟虑的，不慌不忙的

haunt [hɔːnt]
【考法 1】 *vt.* 常去拜访：to visit often; **frequent**
例 haunt the movie theater 常去影院
近 affect, habituate, visit, hang at, resort to
反 avoid, shun 避开
派 haunted *adj.* 闹鬼的
【考法 2】 *vt.* 不断地想起，萦绕心头：to come to mind continually; **obsess**
例 a riddle that haunted me all morning 整个早上萦绕在我心头的谜

hauteur [hɔːˈtɜːr]
【考法】 *n.* 傲慢，自大：haughtiness in bearing and attitude; **arrogance**
例 behave with hauteur 举止傲慢
近 bumptiousness, imperiousness, peremptoriness, pomposity, presumptuousness, pretentiousness, superciliousness, superiority
反 humility, humbleness, modesty, unassumingness, unpretentiousness 谦虚

haven [ˈheɪvn]
【考法】 *n.* 安全的地方：a **place of safety**
例 a haven for artists 艺术家们的圣地
近 asylum, harbor, refuge, retreat, sanctuary
反 unsafe place, dangerous place 不安全的地方

havoc [ˈhævək]
【考法】 *n.* 大混乱：a state in which everything is **out of order**
例 The blackout caused havoc in the city. 断电造成了城市一片混乱。
近 disarrangement, disarray, dishevelment, muddle, muss, tumble, welter
反 order, orderliness 有序

headlong [ˈhedlɔːŋ]

【考法】 *adj.* 鲁莽的，草率的：without deliberation

例 terrified forest creatures in a headlong retreat from the rapidly spreading fire 受惊的动物们惊慌失措地从不断蔓延的森林大火中逃离出来

近 cursory, overhasty, precipitate, precipitous, rash, pell-mell, helter-skelter

反 deliberate, unhurried, unrushed 深思熟虑的

hearken [ˈhɑːrkən]

【考法】 *vi.* 倾听，关注：to give respectful **attention**

近 attend, harken, heed, mind

反 ignore 不理睬

hearten [ˈhɑːrtn]

【考法】 *vt.* 给予鼓励，鼓舞：to **give strength**, **courage**, or hope to; **encourage**

例 Thinking we were hopelessly lost, we were heartened by the sight of a familiar farmhouse. 悲催地以为我们完全迷路了时，前方一座熟悉的农场给了我们新的希望。

近 embolden, inspire, inspirit, buck up, buoy up, cheer up

反 daunt, dismay, discourage, dishearten, dispirit 使胆怯

Unit 2

■ HEARTRENDING　　■ HEDONISM　　■ HEGEMONY　　■ HEINOUS　　■ HEW
■ HERALD　　　　　■ HERESY　　　■ HERETICAL　　■ HERMETIC　　■ HAGIOGRAPHIC

heartrending [ˈhɑːrtˌrendɪŋ]

【考法】 *adj.* 令人心碎的：causing intense **sorrow** or **distress**

例 a heartrending choice between saving his mother or his wife 先救老妈还是先救老婆的纠结选择

hedonism [ˈhiːdənɪzəm]

【考法】 *n.* 享乐主义：the **doctrine** that **pleasure** or happiness is the sole or chief good in life

例 Their spring break trip to Mexico became an exercise in heedless hedonism. 他们春季的墨西哥之行成为了一次未加注意的享乐之旅。

近 carnality, debauchery, sybaritism, voluptuousness

反 abstinence, asceticism, sobriety, temperance 禁欲，节制

hegemony [hɪˈdʒemoʊni]

【考法】 *n.* 霸权，统治权：**preponderant** influence or **authority** over others

例 battle for hegemony in Asia 争夺在亚洲地区的霸权地位

近 ascendancy, dominance, dominion, predominance, preeminence

反 lack of authority 缺少权利

heinous [ˈheɪnəs]

【考法】 *adj.* 可憎的，十恶不赦的：**hatefully** or shockingly evil, abominable

例 a heinous crime 十恶不赦的罪行

反 commendable 值得赞美的

hew [hjuː]

【考法】 *vi.* 遵守：**confirm**, adhere, to **hold to something firmly** as if by adhesion

例 hew to tradition 遵守传统

近 adhere, cling, conform

herald [ˈherəld]

【考法】 *vt.* 预示，预兆：to give a slight **indication of beforehand**

例 The reshuffle of the company's management heralded the sweeping changes to come. 公司管理层的重新洗牌预示着即将到来的巨大变革。

近 adumbrate, forerun, harbinger, prefigure

heresy [ˈherəsi]

【考法】 *n.* 异教，和普遍观点相悖的说法：a **controversial or unorthodox opinion** or doctrine, departure from a generally accepted theory, opinion, or practice

例 be convicted of heresy 被判信奉异教罪

近 dissent, dissidence, heterodoxy, nonconformity

反 dogma, conformity, orthodoxy 正教，正统

heretical	[həˈretɪkl]
【考法】	*adj.* 异教的，异端邪说的：**departure** from established beliefs or **standards**
例	heretical opinions on theology 关于神学的异教观点
近	heterodox, nonconformist, unconventional, unorthodox
反	conforming, conformist, conventional, orthodox 正统的

hermetic	[hɜːrˈmetɪk]
【考法】	*adj.* 深奥的：relating to or characterized by occultism or **abstruseness**
例	wrote hermetic poetry 写晦涩难懂的诗歌
近	abstruse, arcane, esoteric, recondite
反	easily comprehended, shallow, superficial 容易理解的，肤浅的

hagiographic	[ˌhæɡiˈɑːɡrəfɪk]
【考法】	*adj.* 捧为圣人一般的，过分诡媚的：of, relating to, or being hagiogra-phy; **overly or insincerely flattering**
例	He deserves more careful and more objective scrutiny rather than the hagiographic portrayal he has generally received from the press. 比起媒体对他惯用的诡媚描绘，他的一生值得我们更为仔细和客观地研究。
近	adulatory, flattering, gushy, ingratiating, oily, oleaginous, soapy, toady, unctuous
反	artless, earnest, genuine, heartfelt, ingenuous, sincere, unfeigned 真挚的，真诚的

Unit 3

■ HETERODOX	■ HIDEBOUND	■ HIDEOUS	■ HIE	■ HUMBUG
■ HILARIOUS	■ HISTRIONIC	■ HIVE	■ HOARD	■ HOARY

heterodox	[ˈhetərədɑːks]
【考法】	*adj.* 非正统的，异端的：holding **unorthodox opinions** or doctrines, not rigidly following established form, custom, or rules
例	Her heterodox approach to teaching science initially met with some resistance from her peers. 她对于教学的一些非正统方法最开始受到了同辈的抵触。
近	dissenting, out-there, unconventional, unorthodox
反	conforming, conventional, orthodox, regular, routine 正常的，正统的

hidebound	[ˈhaɪdbaʊnd]
【考法】	*adj.* 死板的，极度保守的：**tending to favor** established ideas, conditions, or institutions
例	The hidebound innkeeper refused to see the need for a Web site. 死板的旅店老板坚决不肯装宽带。
近	archconservative, brassbound, die-hard, old-fashioned, standpat, ultraconservative
反	broad-minded, large-minded, liberal, nonconservative, nonconventional, nonorthodox, nontraditional, open-minded, progressive 进步的，开放包容的

hideous	[ˈhɪdiəs]
【考法】	*adj.* 非常丑陋的：exceedingly **ugly**
例	The old man wore a hideous Halloween mask that made the kids all jump with fright. 老头戴着一个丑陋的万圣节面具，把小孩子全都吓跑了。
近	homely, ill-favored, monstrous, uncomely, unsightly
反	pulchritudinous, aesthetic, attractive, comely, gorgeous, handsome, knockout, ravishing, seemly, stunning, taking, well-favored 美丽的，有吸引力的
派	hideousness *n.* 丑陋
反	affinity 吸引力

hie	[haɪ]
【考法】	*vi.* 匆匆忙忙：to go quickly, **hasten**
例	We had best hie home before the rain gets worse. 我们最好在雨下大之前赶快回家。
近	bustle, dash, hustle, scoot, scurry, scuttle, shoot, trot
反	dawdle, crawl, creep, poke 闲荡，爬行

humbug	[ˈhʌmbʌɡ]
【考法】	*n.* 骗子：a willfully false, **deceptive**, or insincere person
例	To blame the dam for environmental destruction which has already occurred is a plot of political humbugs. 把先前已经出现的环境破坏归罪于大坝是政治骗子们的一个阴谋。
近	charlatan, fake, fraud, hoaxer, imposter, mountebank, phony, pretender, quack, quacksalver, ringer, sham
反	humbuggery *n.* 欺骗

hilarious	[hɪ'leriəs]
【考法】	*adj.* 非常好笑的：marked by or causing hilarity: **extremely funny**
例	hilarious cartoons that the whole family can enjoy 适合全家观看的搞笑动画片
近	hysterical, ludicrous, ridiculous, screaming, sidesplitting, uproarious
反	humorless, lame, unamusing, uncomic, unfunny 不好笑的

histrionic	[ˌhɪstri'ɑːnɪk]
【考法】	*adj.* 夸张做作的：**dramatic**, exaggerated, and insincere
例	Obama and McCain avoided a histrionic debate about China during the 2008 campaign and Obama probably thought he had a free hand on China policy. 奥巴马和麦凯恩在 2008 年的选战中没有就中国进行做秀似的辩论，也许奥巴马就此认为他在对华政策上可以随心所欲。
近	dramatic, melodramatic, operatic, stagy, theatrical, affected
反	undramatic 没有戏剧化的

hive	[haɪv]
【考法 1】	*n.* 忙碌之地：a place swarming with **activity**
例	The house was a hive of activity as we prepared for the party. 我们筹备派对时，房子里很是熙熙攘攘。
【考法 2】	*v.* 储备，积累：to **store up**; accumulate

hoard	[hɔːrd]
【考法】	*v.* 贮藏，秘藏：to **keep hidden** or private
例	He's been hoarding empty yogurt containers all winter. 他整个冬天都在攒空酸奶瓶。
近	cache, stash, stockpile, store, squirrel, stockpile
反	lavish 挥霍

hoary	['hɔːri]
【考法】	*adj.* 极老的：**extremely old**
例	hoary legends 上古的传说故事
近	aged, antique, dateless, immemorial, antediluvian
反	modern, new, recent 新的

Unit 4

■ HOAX	■ HODGEPODGE	■ HOMAGE	■ HOMELY	■ HOMILY
■ HOMOGENIZE	■ HONE	■ HOODWINK	■ HORTATIVE	■ HEARTFELT

hoax	[hoʊks]
【考法】	*n./vt.* 欺骗：to **cause to believe** what is **untrue**
例	a skilled forger who hoaxed the art world into believing that the paintings were long-lost Vermeers 一个老道的骗子成功让艺术界相信那些画作是遗失多年的维米尔的真迹
近	bamboozle, beguile, bluff, con, cozen, delude, dupe, fake out, gull, hoodwink, take in

hodgepodge	['hɑːdʒpɑːdʒ]
【考法】	*n.* 大杂烩：a **mixture** of **dissimilar** ingredients; a jumble
例	a hodgepodge of styles 混搭风格 ‖ The exhibit was a hodgepodge of mediocre art, bad art, and really bad art. 整场展览就是中庸、烂和非常烂的艺术作品的大杂烩。
近	agglomeration, assortment, collage, medley, mishmash, pastiche, potpourri

homage	['hɑːmɪdʒ]
【考法】	*n.* 尊敬，敬意：expression of high regard: **respect**
例	Homage to Catalonia 向加泰罗尼亚致敬
近	commendation, eulogy, hymn, paean, panegyric, salutation, tribute, dithyramb
反	disrespect 不尊敬

homely	['hoʊmli]
【考法】	*adj.* 其貌不扬，朴素简单的：**not attractive** or good-looking
例	homely truth 朴素的真理
近	hideous, unappealing, unattractive, uncomely, unsightly
反	pulchritudinous, aesthetic, attractive, beautiful, comely, gorgeous, handsome, knockout, lovely, pretty, ravishing, seemly, sightly, stunning, taking, well-favored 美丽的

homily	[ˈhɑːməli]
【考法】	n. 冗长乏味的道德讲演或训诫: a tedious moralizing lecture or **admonition**
例	a solemn homily on life 关于生活的严肃说教
近	banality, bromide, chestnut, cliché, groaner, platitude, shibboleth

homogenize	[həˈmɑːdʒənaɪz]
【考法】	vt. 使统一化: to **make agree** with a **single established standard** or model
例	plans to homogenize the science curriculum in public high schools throughout the state 计划将全州的公立高中的课程安排统一化
近	formalize, normalize, regularize

hone	[hoʊn]
【考法】	vt. 提升，改进: to make more acute, intense, or effective; **improve**
例	The expedition enables participants to explore backcountry terrain and hone survival skills. 远征能够让参与者尽情探索尚未开化的地区，同时也锻炼了他们的求生能力。
近	ameliorate, cultivate, improve, meliorate, perfect, polish, refine
反	aggravate, deteriorate, worsen 恶化，降低

hoodwink	[ˈhʊdwɪŋk]
【考法】	vt. 欺骗: to take in by **deceptive** means; deceive
例	Don't let yourself be hoodwinked into buying things you don't need. 别被忽悠着去买用不着的东西。
近	beguile, con, delude, dupe, fool, hoax, humbug
反	disabuse 消除…的错误念头

hortative	[ˈhɔːrtətɪv]
【考法】	adj. 鼓励的: giving **exhortation**

heartfelt	[ˈhɑːrtfelt]
【考法】	adj. 真心实意的: **genuine** in feeling
例	My heartfelt sympathy goes out to all the relatives. 我对所有的亲属表示衷心的慰问。
近	sincere, unfeigned
反	affected, artificial, false, feigned, insincere 不真诚的

Unit 5

■ HUBRIS	■ HUMBLE	■ HEDGE	■ HUMOR	■ HURRICANE
■ HUSBAND	■ HUSK	■ HUSKY	■ HYBRID	■ HYMN

hubris	[ˈhjuːbrɪs]
【考法】	n. 狂妄自大: **exaggerated pride** or **self-confidence**
例	His failure was brought on by his hubris. 就是他的狂妄自大才导致了失败。
反	humility 谦逊

humble	[ˈhʌmbl]
【考法1】	adj. 谦逊的: marked by **meekness** or **modesty** in behavior, attitude, or spirit; not arrogant or prideful
例	a medical scientist who remained remarkably humble even after winning the Nobel Prize 获得诺贝尔奖之后仍然保持谦逊的医学家
近	modest, unassuming, unpretentious, demure, down-to-earth
反	arrogant, bumptious, conceited, egotistic, haughty, high-and-mighty, imperious, lordly, overweening, peremptory, pompous, presuming, presumptuous, pretentious, self-assertive, supercilious, superior, toplofty, uppish, uppity 傲慢的
【考法2】	adj. 顺从的，谦卑的: showing, expressing, or offered in a spirit of **humility or unseemly submissiveness**
例	Please accept my humble thanks. 请接受我的卑微的感谢。
近	base, humble, menial, servile, slavish
派	humility n. 谦卑，谦逊: the absence of any feelings of being better than others
例	Haughtiness invites disaster; humility receives benefit. 满招损，谦受益。
近	demureness, humbleness, lowliness, meekness, modesty
反	arrogance, assumption, bumptiousness, hauteur, pomposity, presumption, superciliousness 傲慢，自大

hedge [hedʒ]

【考法】 *v.* 闪烁其词：to **avoid** giving a **definite answer** or position

例 She kept hedging whenever he asked her to go on a date with him. 每当他问她什么和他出去约的时候，她都闪烁其词。

近 fudge, equivocate, waffle, weasel

humor [ˈhjuːmə]

【考法】 *vt.* 迎合，迁就：to **comply with** the wishes or ideas of

例 Parents need to know how to humor kids when they are upset. 父母需要知道当孩子烦躁的时候怎么哄孩子。

近 cater, gratify, indulge

hurricane [ˈhɜːrəkən]

【考法】 *n.* 飓风般的事物，引起动荡的事物：something **resembling a hurricane** especially in its turmoil

例 economic news that unleashed a hurricane on the trading floor 在交易大厅掀起轩然大波的经济新闻

近 disturbance, furor, pandemonium, tumult, turmoil, uproar

husband [ˈhʌzbənd]

【考法】 *vt.* 节俭，勤俭持家：to **use** sparingly or **economically**

例 Husbanding precious resources was part of rural life. 节俭使用珍贵的资源是农村生活的一部分。

近 budget, conserve, economize

反 dissipate, lavish, prodigalize, squander, waste 挥霍，浪费

派 husbandly *adj.* 节俭的；husbandry *n.* 节俭

husk [hʌsk]

【考法】 *vt.* 剥去：to **remove** the natural covering of

例 the tedious task of husking coconuts 无聊的任务——剥椰子

近 bark, flay, hull, shell, shuck, skin

husky [ˈhʌski]

【考法】 *adj.* (尤指声音)沙哑的，粗糙的：hoarse or **rough** in quality

例 a voice husky with emotion 富有感情的沙哑声音

近 coarse, grating, gravelly, harsh, rasping, rusty, scratchy, throaty

反 mellifluous (声音)甜蜜的，甜美的

hybrid [ˈhaɪbrɪd]

【考法】 *n.* 杂交品种，混合品种：something of **mixed origin** or composition

adj. 杂交的：being offspring produced by **parents of different races**, breeds, species, or genera

例 a hybrid of medieval and Renaissance styles 中世纪和文艺复兴的混搭风 ‖ a hybrid rose called "American Beauty" 一种被称为"美国丽人"的杂交玫瑰

近 amalgam, bastard, compound, mixture, mule; crossbred, mongrel

反 purebred 纯种的

hymn [hɪm]

【考法】 *n.* 赞歌，赞美诗：a **song of praise** or joy *v.* 赞美：to **proclaim the glory** of

例 They sang a hymn of praise to God. 他们唱赞歌赞美上帝。‖ During the honeymoon following the inauguration, newspaper articles seemed to hymn the president's every move. 在上任后的"蜜月期"之中，报纸新闻似乎在赞美总统的每一项措施。

近 eulogy, homage, hymn, ode, paean, panegyric, psalm, salutation, tribute; bless, carol, celebrate, emblazon, exalt, extol, glorify, laud, magnify, resound

反 dirge, elegy 哀诗，挽歌；blame, censure, reprehend, reprobate 责难，斥责

Unit 6

■ HYPERBOLE   ■ HYPNOTIC   ■ HYPOCRITICAL   ■ ICONOCLAST   ■ IDOLATRIZE
■ IDYLL   ■ IGNITE   ■ IGNOMINY   ■ ILLITERACY   ■ ILLUMINATI

hyperbole [haɪˈpɜːrbəli]

【考法】 *n.* 夸张：a figure of speech in which **exaggeration** is **used for emphasis** or effect

例 The debate was carried on with increasing rhetorical hyperbole. 随着辩论的进行，双方修辞当中的夸张越来越多。

近 coloring, embellishment, embroidering, exaggeration, magnification, overstatement

反 understatement 有节制的陈述

hypnotic [hɪp'nɑːtɪk]

【考法】 *adj.* 催眠的：tending to **cause sleep**

例 Her eyes soon grew heavy from the hypnotic rhythm of the train's wheels . 伴随着催眠的铁轨声，她很快就有了睡意。

近 drowsy, narcotic, opiate, sleepy, slumberous, soporific

反 stimulating 刺激性的；refreshing 使人精神焕发的

hypocritical [ˌhɪpə'krɪtɪkl]

【考法】 *adj.* 虚伪的：**not being** or expressing **what one appears to be** or express

例 hypocritical behaviors 虚伪的行为

近 artificial, backhanded, feigned, mealy-mouthed, phony, pretended, unctuous

反 artless, candid, genuine, honest, sincere, undesigning, unfeigned 真诚的，诚实的

派 hypocrite *n.* 虚伪的人，伪君子

iconoclast [aɪ'kɑːnəklæst]

【考法】 *n.* 特立独行的人：a person who does **not conform** to generally **accepted standards** or customs

例 an eccentric iconoclast 一个古怪的特立独行者

近 bohemian, deviant, heretic, maverick, non-conformer

反 conformer, conformist 循规蹈矩的人

派 iconoclastic *adj.* 特立独行的

idolatrize [aɪ'dɑːlətraɪz]

【考法】 *vt.* (通常盲目)崇拜：**admires intensely** and often blindly

例 Some teenagers idolatrized Hitler more than their own parents. 曾经有一些青少年崇拜希特勒超过自己的父母。

近 adore, adulate, canonize, deify, dote, worship

反 abhor, abominate, detest, dislike, hate, loathe 痛恨，憎恶

派 idolatry *n.* 崇拜

idyll ['aɪdl]

【考法】 *n.* 无忧无虑的生活：a **carefree episode** or experience

例 a summer idyll on the coast of the Mediterranean 地中海岸的悠闲夏日

近 frisk, frolic, gambol, revel, lark

ignite [ɪg'naɪt]

【考法】 *vt.* 激起，唤起(感情等)：to **arouse the passions** of

例 The insults ignited my anger . 那些侮辱让我倍感愤怒。

近 arouse, incite, instigate, pique, spark, stimulate, stir

反 appease, assuage, calm, conciliate, mollify, pacify, placate, propitiate, soothe 平息怒火，安抚

ignominy ['ɪgnəmɪni]

【考法】 *n.* 耻辱：the state of having **lost the esteem** of others

例 He spent the remainder of his life in ignominy after being involved in a bribery scandal. 因为卷入了受贿丑闻当中，他在耻辱中度过余生。

近 discredit, disesteem, dishonor, disrepute, infamy, obloquy, odium, opprobrium, reproach, shame

反 glory, honor 荣耀；esteem, respect 敬意

派 ignominious *adj.* 可鄙的

illiteracy [ɪ'lɪtərəsi]

【考法】 *n.* 文盲：the condition of being **unable to read and write**

例 a nationwide campaign against illiteracy 全国扫盲运动

近 ignorance

反 learning, literacy 受过教育

派 illiterate *adj.* 不识字的

illuminati [ɪˌluːmiː'nɑːtiː]

【考法】 *n.* 智者：persons who claim to be unusually **enlightened**

近 clerisy, intellectual, intelligentsia, literati

反 fool, dolt, dullard, idiot, simpleton 傻子

Unit 7

illuminate [ɪˈluːmɪneɪt]
【考法】 *vt.* 阐明：to **make plain** or understandable
例 a theory illuminated by facts 被事实说明的理论
近 clarify, clear, construe, demonstrate, demystify, elucidate, explicate, expound, illustrate, interpret
反 obscure 使费解

illusory [ɪˈluːsəri]
【考法】 *adj.* 幻觉的，虚幻的：produced by, based on, or having the nature of an **illusion**
例 the illusory definition of nationhood 国家的虚幻定义
近 chimerical, fanciful, fantastic, fictional, fictitious, imaginary, supposititious, unreal
反 factual 事实的
派 illusion *n.* 幻觉

imbibe [ɪmˈbaɪb]
【考法】 *v.* 喝水，摄取水分：to **take in** (something **liquid**) through small openings
例 Plants can imbibe water through their roots. 植物可以通过它们的根摄取水分。
近 drink, guzzle, hoist, quaff, sip, sponge
反 urinate 排尿

imbroglio [ɪmˈbroʊliou]
【考法】 *n.* 困境，复杂的局面：an intricate or **complicated situation**
例 What investor would willingly become involved in this imbroglio? 怎样的投资者才会像这样宁愿身陷困境吗？
近 complexity, complication, embarrassment, entanglement, involvement, misunderstanding, quandary

imitation [ˌɪmɪˈteɪʃn]
【考法】 *n.* 仿制品：something that is made to look exactly **like something else**
例 She usually wore imitations of her costly jewels. 她通常只戴她那些贵重珠宝的仿制品。
近 clone, copy, dupe, duplication, facsimile, mock, reduplication, replica, replication, reproduction
反 archetype, original, prototype 原型
派 imitating *adj.* 仿制的

immaculate [ɪˈmækjələt]
【考法】 *adj.* 完美的，没有任何错误的：being entirely **without fault** or flaw
例 an immaculate rendering of the Queen of the Night's aria 《魔笛之夜后》咏叹调的完美演绎
近 absolute, faultless, flawless, impeccable, indefectible, irreproachable, perfect, seamless, unblemished
反 amiss, defective, faulty, flawed, imperfect 有错误的，有误差的

immanent [ˈɪmənənt]
【考法】 *adj.* 内在的：being a part of the **innermost** nature of a person or thing
例 Beauty is not something imposed but something immanent. 美丽是内在的品格而非外外加的东西。
近 constitutional, essential, inborn, inbred, indigenous, ingrained, innate, integral, intrinsic, natural
反 adventitious, extrinsic, extraneous 外在的，非本源的

immaterial [ˌɪməˈtɪriəl]
【考法】 *adj.* 无关的，不重要的：of **no** importance or **relevance**
例 While undoubtedly upsetting, that story is immaterial to the question of why you are late. 尽管那个故事的确很让人遗憾，但是和你为什么迟到没有半点关系。
近 extraneous, impertinent, inapplicable, inapposite, irrelevant
反 applicable, apposite, apropos, germane, pertinent, relevant 相关的；crucial, important, significant 重要的

immature [ˌɪməˈtʃʊr]
【考法】 *adj.*（生理、心理）未完全发展的，未发育成熟的：**lacking complete growth**, differentiation, or development
例 Immature frogs are called "tadpoles". 未发育成熟的青蛙被称为"蝌蚪"。
近 adolescent, juvenile, youngish, youthful

immemorial	[ˌɪmə'mɔːriəl]
【考法】	*adj.* 古老的：dating or surviving **from the distant past**
例	a modern version of an immemorial myth 一个远古传说的现代版本
近	aged, age-old, antediluvian, antique, dateless, hoary, old, venerable
反	contemporary, modern 当代的，现代的；recent 近来的

Unit 8

immune	[ɪ'mjuːn]
【考法1】	*adj.* 不易被感染的，有免疫力的：of, relating to, or **having resistance to infection**
例	The blood test will tell whether you are immune to the disease. 验血可以判断你是否对这种疾病免疫。
近	resistant
反	susceptible, vulnerable 易感染的，易受攻击的
派	immunity *n.* 免疫性
【考法2】	*adj.* 不受影响的：**not affected by** a given **influence**
例	immune to persuasion 不听劝
近	insusceptible, unaffected, unresponsive
反	ductile, pliable, pliant, yielding 易受影响的

immure	[ɪ'mjʊr]
【考法】	*vt.* 监禁，禁闭；使闭门不出：to **confine** within or as if within walls
例	immure oneself for GRE 闭门苦读 GRE
近	confine, constrain, incarcerate, intern, jail, imprison
反	discharge, release 释放；enfranchise, free, liberate 解放

immutable	[ɪ'mjuːtəbl]
【考法】	*adj.* 不可变的：**not capable of changing** or being changed
例	One of the immutable laws of television is that low ratings inevitably lead to cancellation. 电视行业中一个不变的原则就是：低收视率的节目必然会被撤掉。
近	constant, fixed, inalterable, inflexible, invariable, unalterable, unchangeable
反	alterable, changeable, elastic, flexible, mutable, variable 可变的
派	immutability *n.* 不变性

impassive	[ɪm'pæsɪv]
【考法】	*adj.* 冷漠的，无感情的：giving **no sign of feeling** or emotion
例	She remained impassive as the officers informed her of her son's death. 她面不改色地听着警官宣读她儿子的死讯。
近	affectless, apathetic, cold-blooded, deadpan, emotionless, numb, phlegmatic, stoic, undemonstrative
反	demonstrative, emotional, fervent, fervid, impassioned, passionate, vehement 充满感情的

impeccable	[ɪm'pekəbl]
【考法】	*adj.* 无瑕的，无可挑剔的：**free from fault** or blame
例	She had impeccable taste in clothes. 她有着无可挑剔的穿衣品味。
近	absolute, faultless, flawless, immaculate, indefectible, irreproachable, perfect, seamless, unblemished
反	amiss, defective, faulty, flawed, imperfect 有错误的，有误差的

impecunious	[ˌɪmpɪ'kjuːniəs]
【考法】	*adj.* 贫穷的：having very little or **no money**
例	impecunious village children 贫困的乡村小孩
近	beggared, destitute, impoverished, indigent, necessitous, needy, penniless, penurious, threadbare
反	affluent, flush, opulent, rich, wealthy 富有的

impede	[ɪm'piːd]
【考法】	*vt.* 妨碍，阻碍：to interfere with or **slow the progress of**
例	Storms at sea impeded our expedition. 海上的风暴阻碍了我们的远征。
近	clog, embarrass, encumber, fetter, hinder, inhibit, obstruct, retard, shackle, stymie, trammel
反	aid, assist, facilitate, help 促进，帮助
派	impediment *n.* 障碍，阻碍

impending [ɪmˈpendɪŋ]
【考法】 *adj.* 即将发生的：being **soon to** appear or **take place**

例 an impending celebration 即将来临的庆祝

近 approaching, coming, imminent, nearing, pending, proximate, upcoming, around the corner

反 late, recent 最近发生的；distant, remote 遥远的

impenetrable [ɪmˈpenɪtrəbl]
【考法1】 *adj.* 不可渗透的，不可穿透的：**impossible to get through** or into

例 The ancient temple was surrounded by vast stretches of impenetrable jungle. 包围着古老的神庙的是密不可穿的灌木丛。

近 impassable, impermeable, impervious, impregnable

反 passable, penetrable, permeable, pervious 可通过的

【考法2】 *adj.* 难以理解的：**incapable of being comprehended**

例 The textbook's language is completely impenetrable, at least to me. 至少在我看来，这个教材就是天书。

近 arcane, cryptic, enigmatic, incomprehensible, inscrutable, unfathomable, ungraspable, unintelligible

反 fathomable, intelligible, understandable 可以理解的

impenitent [ɪmˈpenɪtənt]
【考法】 *adj.* 不悔悟的：**not** feeling or expressing humble or **regretful** pain or sorrow for sins or offenses

例 remain impenitent about her criminal past 对她过去所犯罪行执迷不悟

近 remorseless, regretless, shameless, unashamed, unrepentant

反 contrite, regretful, remorseful, rueful, penitent 感到悔恨的

Unit 9

■ IMPERATIVE	■ IMPERIAL	■ IMPERIOUS	■ IMPERTINENT	■ IMPERTURBABLE
■ IMPERVIOUS	■ IMPETUOUS	■ IMPIOUS	■ IMPLACABLE	■ IMPLEMENT

imperative [ɪmˈperətɪv]
【考法1】 *adj.* 命令的，强制性的：**forcing one's compliance** or participation by or as if by law

例 requests that grew more and more imperative 命令性越来越强的请求

近 compulsory, forced, involuntary, obligatory, peremptory, required

反 optional 可选择的；voluntary 志愿性的

【考法2】 *adj.* 迫切的：**needing immediate attention**

例 an imperative need for medical supplies in the earthquake-ravaged country 地震灾区国家对于医疗物资的迫切需求

近 clamant, compelling, critical, crying, emergent, exigent, imperious, importunate, pressing, urgent

反 noncritical, unimportant 不重要的

imperial [ɪmˈpɪriəl]
【考法】 *adj.* 巨大的，令人惊叹的：large and **impressive in size**, grandeur, extent, or conception

例 People envisioned an imperial city that would rival the capitals of Europe for beauty and magnificence. 人们幻想着一个比欧洲各国首都更为动人和壮丽的巨大城市。

近 august, epic, glorious, grand, imposing, magnificent, monumental, noble, splendid

反 common, humble, inferior, low 低下的，平凡的

imperious [ɪmˈpɪriəs]
【考法】 *adj.* 傲慢的，专横的：**arrogantly domineering** or overbearing

例 an imperious movie star who thinks she's some sort of goddess 一个把自己当成某种女神的傲慢的影星

近 arrogant, bumptious, haughty, lofty, lordly, peremptory, pompous, presumptuous, supercilious, superior

反 humble, lowly, modest 谦逊的

impertinent [ɪmˈpɜːrtnənt]
【考法1】 *adj.* 无关紧要的：**not having** a clear decisive **relevance** to the matter in hand

例 Your résumé needlessly lists extracurricular experiences that are impertinent to the PhD program for which you are applying. 你的简历里列出的一些课外活动和你申请的博士项目是毫不相关的。

近 extraneous, immaterial, inapplicable, inapposite, irrelevant

反 germane, pertinent, relevant 相关的；crucial, important, significant 重要的

【考法2】 *adj.* 粗鲁无礼的，大胆的：given to or characterized by **insolent rudeness**

例 I don't like strangers who ask impertinent questions. 我很讨厌那些问无礼问题的陌生人。

近 audacious, bold, brash, brassbound, brassy, brazen, impudent, insolent

反 meek, mousy, retiring, shy, timid 内敛的，胆小的

imperturbable [ˌɪmpərˈtɜːrbəbl]

【考法】 *adj.* 沉着冷静的，淡定的：marked by **extreme calm**, impassivity, and steadiness

例 The chef was absolutely imperturbable—even when the kitchen caught on fire. 这个厨师可谓淡定到了极致——他连厨房着火的时候都依然沉着。

近 collected, composed, cool, disimpassioned, nonchalant, unflappable, unruffled

反 choleric, touchy 暴躁的，易怒的

impervious [ɪmˈpɜːrviəs]

【考法 1】 *adj.* 不可渗透的，不可穿透的：**not allowing entrance** or passage

例 The material for this coat is supposed to be impervious to rain. 这件大衣的材料应该是能防雨的。

近 impassable, impenetrable, impermeable, impregnable

反 passable, penetrable, permeable, pervious 可渗透的

【考法 2】 *adj.* 不能被破坏的：**not capable of being damaged** or harmed

例 a carpet impervious to rough treatment 耐用的地毯

近 bulletproof, imperishable, indestructible, inextinguishable, invulnerable

反 delicate, sensitive, vulnerable 脆弱的，敏感的

【考法 3】 *adj.* 不为所动的：**not capable of being affected** or disturbed

例 These sailors are impervious to fear. 这些水手无所畏惧。

近 immune, insusceptible, unaffected, unresponsive

反 ductile, pliable, pliant, yielding 易受影响的

impetuous [ɪmˈpetʃuəs]

【考法】 *adj.* 冲动的，性急的，轻率的：marked by **impulsive vehemence** or passion

例 He is young and impetuous. 他年轻易冲动。

近 ardent, hasty, headlong, impassioned, impulsive, passionate, rash, vehement

反 cautious, circumspect, wary 谨慎的，小心的

impious [ɪmˈpaɪəs]

【考法】 *adj.* 不敬神的：**lacking reverence** for holy or sacred matters

例 make impious remarks about the church 对教会做出不敬的评论

近 blasphemous, irreverent, profane, sacrilegious

反 pious 虔诚的；reverent 敬神的

派 impiety *n.* (对神的)不敬

implacable [ɪmˈplækəbl]

【考法 1】 *adj.* 固执的：**sticking to an opinion**, purpose, or course of action in spite of reason, arguments, or persuasion

近 adamant, dogged, headstrong, intransigent, mulish, obdurate, pertinacious, stubborn, unyielding

反 acquiescent 默认的；compliant, flexible, pliable, pliant, yielding 易受影响的

【考法 2】 *adj.* 无法平息的：**not capable of being appeased**, significantly changed, or mitigated

例 an implacable enemy 无法与之和解的敌人

近 determined, grim, relentless, unappeasable

反 placable 可平息的，可缓和的

implement [ˈɪmplɪment]

【考法】 *vt.* 执行，实施：to put into practical effect; **carry out**

例 implement the new online application procedures 实行新的网申程序

近 administer, apply, effect, enforce, execute, invoke, perform

反 cancel, repeal, rescind, revoke 撤销

派 implementation *n.* 执行，履行

Unit 10

■ IMPLODE   ■ IMPORTUNE   ■ IMPOSING   ■ IMPOSTOR   ■ IMPOTENT
■ IMPRECISE   ■ IMPROMPTU   ■ IMPROVISE   ■ IMPRUDENT   ■ IMPUDENT

implode [ɪmˈploʊd]

【考法】 *v.* (使)剧烈收缩，(使)坍缩，(使)内爆：to (cause to) **collapse inward** violently

例 The flask imploded during the vacuum distilling. 做低压蒸馏的时候烧瓶发生了内爆。

近 buckle, founder, tumble, yield

反 explode 外爆，爆炸

importune [ˌɪmpɔːrˈtuːn]

【考法】 *vt.* 恳求，迫切请求：to make a request to（someone）in an earnest or **urgent manner**

例 beggars importuning passers-by 在恳求着过路人的乞丐

近 appeal, beseech, besiege, conjure, entreat, impetrate, implore, petition, plead, pray, solicit, supplicate

反 demand 要求，强求

imposing [ɪmˈpoʊzɪŋ]

【考法】 *adj.* 宏伟壮丽的：**impressive** in size, bearing, dignity, or grandeur

例 The corporation's imposing headquarters were designed by one of the nation's cutting-edge architects. 这家公司宏伟壮丽的总部是由该国最优秀的建筑师之一设计的。

近 august, epic, glorious, grand, imperial, magnificent, monumental, noble, splendid

反 common, humble, inferior, low 低下的，平凡的

impostor [ɪmˈpɑːstər]

【考法】 *n.* 冒充者，骗子：one that **assumes false identity** or title for the purpose of deception

例 an unforgivable impostor 一个不可原谅的冒充者

近 charlatan, fake, fraud, hoaxer, mountebank, phony, pretender, quack, sham

impotent [ˈɪmpətənt]

【考法】 *adj.* 无力的，无能的：**lacking in power**, strength, or vigor

例 an impotent ruler who was just a figurehead 一个无能的傀儡统治者

近 hamstrung, handcuffed, helpless, impuissant, paralyzed, weak

反 mighty, potent, powerful, puissant, strong 强大的，有能力的

imprecise [ˌɪmprɪˈsaɪs]

【考法】 *adj.* 不精确的：**not precise**

例 incomplete and imprecise satellite data 既不完整又不精确的卫星数据

近 approximate, inaccurate, loose, squishy

反 accurate, exact, precise, veracious 精确的，准确的

派 imprecision *n.* 不准确，不精确

impromptu [ɪmˈprɑːmptuː]

【考法1】 *n.* 即席的表演：something, such as a speech, that is made or **done extemporaneously**

近 improvisation, extemporization

【考法2】 *adj.* 即席的，即兴的：composed **without previous preparation**

例 Our dinner guest thanked us with an impromptu song. 客人们即兴高歌一首以表达谢意。

近 ad-lib, extemporary, improvised, offhand, unplanned, unpremeditated, unprepared, unrehearsed

反 considered, planned, premeditated, prepared, rehearsed 事先有所准备的

improvise [ˈɪmprəvaɪz]

【考法】 *v.* 即兴而作：to invent, compose, or **perform with little or no preparation**

例 Since the award was a complete surprise, I improvised an acceptance speech. 因为那个奖项完全是个惊喜，所以我即兴发表了一个获奖演说。

近 ad-lib, extemporize

反 plan, premeditate 计划，预先考虑

imprudent [ɪmˈpruːdnt]

【考法】 *adj.* 不明智的：**lacking** discretion, wisdom, or **good judgment**

例 an imprudent investment he made many years ago 他许多年前做的一笔不明智的投资

近 impolitic, inadvisable, indelicate, injudicious, tactless, undiplomatic, unwise

反 advisable, politic, prudent, tactical, wise 明智的

impudent [ˈɪmpjədənt]

【考法】 *adj.* 放肆大胆的，无礼的：marked by contemptuous or cocky **boldness or disregard** of others

例 impudent children 无礼的孩子

近 audacious, barefaced, bold, brash, brazen, impertinent, insolent, shameless

反 courteous, genteel, mannerly, polite, proper 举止得体的

派 impudence *n.* 放肆无礼

List 13

"无论多久后的将来，无论当我遇到什么困难险阻，每当我回想起当年奋战GRE的日子，我的血液中仍然迸发着那种不安分的激情和冲劲，让我继续舔着伤口，在荆棘丛中勇往直前。"

（周慧杰，2006年10月，Verbal 720，Quantitative 800，AW 5.5，现就职于凯雷投资集团，中国香港）

Unit 1

■ IMPUGN	■ IMPUISSANCE	■ INADVERTENT	■ INALIENABLE	■ INANE
■ INANIMATE	■ INAUGURATE	■ INCANDESCENT	■ INCANTATION	■ INCARNATE

impugn [ɪmˈpjuːn]
【考法】 *vt.* 责难，抨击：to **attack as false** or questionable; challenge in argument
例 impugn a political opponent's character 就政治对手的人品发难
近 attack, assail, contradict, contravene, cross, disaffirm, deny, gainsay, negate, negative, traverse
反 advocate, back, support, uphold 支持；authenticate 证实，证明

impuissance [ɪmˈpjuːɪsns]
【考法】 *n.* 无权，虚弱：**lack of power** or effectiveness
例 conspicuous impuissance 显而易见的虚弱
近 impotence, powerlessness, weakness
反 clout, potency, power, puissance 权势
派 impuissant *adj.* 无权无势的，无能的

inadvertent [ˌɪnədˈvɜːrtənt]
【考法 1】 *adj.* 偶然发生的：happening **by chance**
例 an inadvertent encounter with a rattlesnake 偶遇响尾蛇
近 casual, fluky, incidental, unintentional, unplanned, unpremeditated, unwitting
反 calculated, deliberate, intended, intentional, planned, premeditated 有计划的，有预谋的
【考法 2】 *adj.* 疏忽的，不留意的：marked by **unintentional lack of care**
例 The military has said it was an inadvertent error. 军方表示这是个疏忽大意的错误。
近 careless, feckless, heedless, irreflective, thoughtless, uncaring
反 advertent, careful, heedful, mindful 留意的，小心的

inalienable [ɪnˈeɪliənəbl]
【考法】 *adj.* 不可剥夺的，不能让与的：**cannot be transferred** to another or others
例 inalienable rights of the citizen 公民不可予夺的权利
近 untransferable
反 alienable 可让与的

inane [ɪˈneɪn]
【考法】 *adj.* 空洞的：**lacking significance**, meaning, or point
例 inane comments 空洞的评论
近 empty, insubstantial, pointless, senseless
反 meaningful, significant 有意义的；deep, profound 深刻的

inanimate [ɪnˈænɪmət]
【考法】 *adj.* 无生命的：**not** having the qualities associated with active, **living** organisms
例 He thinks that inanimate objects have a life of their own. 他认为无生命的事物其实也是有生命的。
近 dead, lifeless, insensible, insentient, senseless, unfeeling
反 animate, living 有生命的

inaugurate [ɪˈnɔːɡjəreɪt]
【考法】 *vt.* 开始：to cause to **begin**, especially officially or formally
例 inaugurate a new immigration policy 实施新的移民政策
近 begin, commence, establish, institute, introduce, launch, open, plant, start
反 cease, close, end, terminate 结束
派 inauguration *n.* 就职；开始

incandescent [ˌɪnkænˈdesnt]

【考法 1】 *adj.* 明亮灿烂的: strikingly **bright**, radiant, or clear

例 incandescent light bulbs 明亮的灯泡

近 beaming, brilliant, dazzling, effulgent, glowing, lucent, luminous, lustrous, radiant, refulgent, shining

反 dim, dull, lackluster 黯淡的

【考法 2】 *adj.* 热情饱满的, 感情强烈的: characterized by glowing **zeal**

例 It makes me incandescent with fury. 它让我愤怒不已。

近 ardent, demonstrative, emotional, fervid, impassioned, passionate, torrid, vehement

反 cold, cool, dispassionate, emotionless, impassive, unemotional 无感情的, 漠然的

incantation [ˌɪnkænˈteɪʃn]

【考法】 *n.* 咒语: a spoken word or set of words believed to have **magic power**

例 Hovering over the sick child, the witch doctor muttered mysterious incantations. 巫医在生病的小孩子身边走来走去, 嘴里念着神秘的咒语。

近 abracadabra, bewitchment, charm, conjuration, enchantment, glamour, hex, invocation

incarnate [ɪnˈkɑːrneɪt]

【考法】 *vt.* 使(思想、理论)具化, 体现: to **constitute an embodiment** or type of

例 the general view that Hitler incarnated extreme egotism 通常认为希特勒代表了极端的以自我为中心

近 epitomize, incorporate, manifest, materialize, personalize, personify, substantiate, symbolize

反 disembody 使(灵魂等)脱离躯体

派 incarnation *n.* 化身

Unit 2

■ INCENDIARY	■ INCENSE	■ INCEPTION	■ INCESSANT	■ INCH
■ INCHOATE	■ INCINERATE	■ INCIPIENT	■ INCITE	■ INCLEMENT

incendiary [ɪnˈsendieri]

【考法】 *n.* 煽动者: a **person who stirs up** public feelings especially of discontent

adj. 煽动性的: **tending to inflame**

例 behind-the-scenes incendiaries who were intending to overthrow the government 企图推翻政府的幕后煽动者 ‖ an incendiary speech 煽动性的演说

近 demagogue, exciter, firebrand, fomenter, inciter, instigator, kindler, provocateur; agitational, instigative, provocative, seditious

反 conciliatory, pacific 安抚性的

incense [ɪnˈsens]

【考法】 *vt.* 激怒: to cause to be **extremely angry**

例 This proposal will certainly incense female activists. 这个提案肯定会激怒女权主义者。

近 aggravate, enrage, exasperate, inflame, infuriate, madden, outrage, rankle, rile, roil

反 delight, gratify, please 取悦; appease, conciliate, mollify, pacify, placate, propitiate, soothe 缓和

inception [ɪnˈsepʃn]

【考法】 *n.* 开端, 开始: an act, process, or instance of **beginning**

例 This seemed like a good program at its inception, but it isn't working out as planned. 一开始这像是个不错的项目, 但是它没有按照我们的预期发展。

近 beginning, birth, commencement, dawn, genesis, kickoff, launch, nascence, onset, outset, start, threshold

反 close, conclusion, end, termination, omega 结束, 终止

派 inceptive *adj.* 开端的, 初生的

incessant [ɪnˈsesnt]

【考法】 *adj.* 无间断的: continuing or following **without interruption**

例 The incessant noise from an outside repair crew was a real distraction during the test. 考试时, 窗外维修工发出的持续不断的噪音着实让人分心。

近 ceaseless, continual, nonstop, perpetual, running, unbroken, unceasing, uninterrupted, unremitting

反 interrupted 中断的; discontinuous, intermittent 有间断的

inch	[ɪntʃ]
【考法】	v. (使)慢慢移动：to move or cause to **move slowly** or by small degrees
例	The car inched carefully across the snow-covered bridge. 汽车慢慢地通过被大雪覆盖的桥梁。
近	crawl, creak, creep, limp, plod, slouch, snail
反	dart, fleet, flit, scurry 飞奔，疾行

inchoate	[ɪnˈkoʊət]
【考法】	adj. 新生的，才开始的：in an initial or **early stage**
例	inchoate feelings of affection 刚刚产生的好感
近	aborning, beginning, inceptive, incipient, initial, nascent
反	adult, full-blown, full-fledged, mature, ripe 成熟的，成型的；moribund 将死的

incinerate	[ɪnˈsɪnəreɪt]
【考法】	v. 将…烧成灰烬：to cause to **burn to ashes**
例	The government is trying to stop farmers incinerating their own waste. 政府开始阻止农民们焚烧垃圾的行为。
近	burn, carbonize
反	douse, extinguish, quench, put out 扑灭
派	incineration n. 焚化 incinerator 焚化炉

incipient	[ɪnˈsɪpiənt]
【考法】	adj. 起初的，初现的：**beginning to come into being** or to become apparent
例	an incipient economic recovery 刚刚出现的经济复苏
近	aborning, beginning, inceptive, inchoate, initial, nascent
反	adult, full-blown, full-fledged, mature, ripe 成熟的，成型的；moribund 将死的

incite	[ɪnˈsaɪt]
【考法】	vt. 煽动，激起：to **provoke** and urge on
例	incite workers to strike 煽动工人罢工
近	arouse, abet, foment, instigate, pick, provoke, raise, stir
反	dampen, deter, discourage, dishearten, dissuade 劝阻

inclement	[ɪnˈklemənt]
【考法1】	adj. (天气等)恶劣的：**lacking mildness**
例	inclement weather conditions 恶劣的气象条件
近	bleak, harsh, severe, stormy, tempestuous
反	bright, clear, cloudless, fair, sunny, sunshiny, unclouded 天气晴好的
【考法2】	adj. 无情的，严酷的：showing no clemency; **unmerciful**
近	bitter, brutal, intemperate, rigorous
反	charitable, clement, lenient, merciful 仁慈的
派	inclemency n. 严酷无情

Unit 3

■ INCOGITANT ■ INCONGRUENT ■ INCONSEQUENTIAL ■ INCONTROVERTIBLE ■ INCORRIGIBLE
■ INCRIMINATE ■ INCUBATE ■ INCULPATE ■ INCURSION ■ INDELIBLE

incogitant	[ɪnˈkɑːdʒɪtənt]
【考法】	adj. 考虑不周的，不体谅的：thoughtless; **inconsiderate**
例	an incogitant litterbug 不体谅人的乱扔垃圾者
近	discourteous, disrespectful, ill-mannered, impertinent, inconsiderate, rude, thoughtless, ungracious
反	civil, considerate, courteous, genteel, gracious, thoughtful 体谅他人的，举止得体的

incongruent	[ɪnˈkɑːŋgruənt]
【考法】	adj. 不全等的；不一致的：not coinciding exactly when superimposed; **not conforming** to the circumstances or requirements of a situation
例	two incongruent triangles 两个不全等的三角形
近	conflicting, discordant, discrepant, dissonant, incompatible, incongruous, inconsonant
反	congruent, congruous, consistent 一致的

inconsequential [ˌɪnˌkɑːnsɪˈkwenʃl]

【考法】 *adj.* 不重要的：of **no significance**

例 That's an inconsequential problem compared to the other issues. 和其他问题相比，这就是一个无关痛痒的小事。

近 fiddling, frivolous, inconsiderable, insignificant, minor, minute, negligible, nugatory, petty, slight, trivial

反 consequential, eventful, important, meaningful, momentous, significant, substantial, weighty 重要的

incontrovertible [ˌɪnkɑːntrəˈvɜːrtəbl]

【考法】 *adj.* 无可争议的：**not open to question**

例 incontrovertible facts 无可非议的事实

近 certain, inarguable, incontestable, indisputable, indubitable, positive, sure, undeniable, unquestionable

反 arguable, controversial, debatable, disputable, problematic, questionable, refutable 有争议的

派 incontrovertibility *n.* 无可争议

incorrigible [ɪnˈkɔːrɪdʒəbl]

【考法 1】 *adj.* 不可救药的，积习难改的：**incapable of being corrected** or amended

例 an incorrigible criminal deserving death penalty 一个应该被判死刑的恶习难改的罪犯

近 incurable, irrecoverable, irredeemable, irremediable, irretrievable, unrecoverable, unredeemable

反 curable, reclaimable, recoverable, redeemable, remediable, retrievable, savable 可以拯救的

【考法 2】 *adj.* 无法管制的：difficult or **impossible to control** or manage

例 an incorrigible, spoiled child 被宠坏了的难管的孩子

近 headstrong, intractable, obstinate, refractory, stubborn, unmanageable, unruly, willful

反 compliant, docile, manageable, obedient, submissive, tractable 顺从的

incriminate [ɪnˈkrɪmɪneɪt]

【考法】 *vt.* 归罪于：to **accuse of a crime** or other wrongful act

例 incriminate innocent people 诬陷好人

近 charge, criminate, impeach, indict

反 absolve, acquit, exculpate, exonerate, vindicate 免罪

incubate [ˈɪŋkjubeɪt]

【考法 1】 *vt.* 孵化：to **cover and warm eggs** as the young inside develop

例 The hen incubated her eggs for two weeks. 母鸡孵蛋两周。

近 brood, hatch, sit

派 incubator *n.* 恒温箱；incubation *n.* 孵化，孵卵

【考法 2】 *vt.* 帮助，培养，促进：to cause or **aid** the development of

例 Hopefully, these youthful visits to the museum will incubate an enduring love of art. 我们希望年轻时参观博物馆能够培养人们对于艺术的持久热爱。

近 advance, cultivate, encourage, forward, further, nourish, nurse, nurture, promote

反 check, discourage, frustrate, hinder, impede, inhibit, obstruct, retard, shackle 妨碍，阻碍

inculpate [ɪnˈkʌlpeɪt]

【考法】 *vt.* 归罪于：**incriminate**

近 charge, criminate, incriminate, indict

反 absolve, acquit, exculpate, exonerate, vindicate 免罪

incursion [ɪnˈkɜːrʒn]

【考法】 *n.* 入侵：a **hostile entrance** into a territory

例 homes damaged by the incursion of floodwater 被洪水入侵破坏的房屋

近 foray, inroad, invasion, irruption, raid

反 retreat, withdrawal 撤退

indelible [ɪnˈdeləbl]

【考法】 *adj.* 无法忘怀的：**not easily forgotten**

例 most indelible experiences 最难以磨灭的经历

近 impressive, memorable, unforgettable

反 forgettable 容易被忘记的

Unit 4

■ INDEMNITY　　　■ INDICT　　　■ INDIFFERENT　　　■ INDIGENOUS　　　■ INDIGENT
■ INDISPENSABLE　■ INDOCTRINATE　■ INDOLENT　　　■ INDUCE　　　■ INDULGENT

indemnity [ɪnˈdemnəti]
【考法】 *n.* (损害、伤害等的)保险补偿: **compensation** for damage, loss, or injury suffered
例　The widow now lives on a pension and an indemnity from her late husband's company. 这个寡妇如今依靠社保和前夫公司的保险赔偿过日。
近　compensation, indemnification, quittance, recompense, redress, remuneration, reparation, requital

indict [ɪnˈdaɪt]
【考法】 *vt.* 起诉,控告: to **accuse** of wrongdoing; charge
例　indict the mayor for fraud and embezzlement 起诉市长受贿和挪用公款
近　charge, criminate, impeach, incriminate
反　absolve, acquit, exculpate, exonerate, vindicate 免罪

indifferent [ɪnˈdɪfrənt]
【考法】 *adj.* 不感兴趣的,冷漠的: marked by a **lack of interest**, enthusiasm, or concern for something
例　indifferent about the result of CET-4 对四级成绩不感兴趣
近　aloof, apathetic, detached, incurious, nonchalant, numb, pococurante, remote, unconcerned, uninterested
反　attentive, concerned, interested 关切的,有兴趣的
派　indifference *n.* 漠然

indigenous [ɪnˈdɪdʒənəs]
【考法1】 *adj.* 土产的,本地的: **originating** and living or occurring naturally in an area or environment
例　the culture of the indigenous people of that country 那个国家原住民的文化
近　aboriginal, endemic, native
反　exotic, extraneous, foreign 外来的; nonnative 非本地的
【考法2】 *adj.* 与生俱来的,先天的: being a part of the **innermost nature** of a person or thing
例　indigenous abilities 天生的能力
近　constitutional, essential, immanent, inborn, inbred, ingrained, innate, integral, intrinsic, natural
反　adventitious, extrinsic 外在的; acquired, studied 后天习得的

indigent [ˈɪndɪdʒənt]
【考法】 *adj.* 贫穷的: **lacking money** or material possessions
例　indigent people who require some outside assistance 需要外来援助的贫苦人民
近　beggared, destitute, impecunious, impoverished, necessitous, needy, penniless, penurious, threadbare
反　affluent, opulent, rich, wealthy 富裕的
派　indigence *n.* 贫穷

indispensable [ˌɪndɪˈspensəbl]
【考法】 *adj.* 必不可少的,不可或缺的: **impossible to do without**
例　indispensable resources 必不可少的资源 ‖ 3K is indispensable to GRE preparation 3千对GRE备考必不可少
近　critical, crucial, imperative, necessary, necessitous, needed, required, requisite, vital
反　dispensable 可替代的; redundant, superfluous, surplus 多余的

indoctrinate [ɪnˈdɑːktrɪneɪt]
【考法】 *vt.* 教育,灌输思想: to **instruct** especially in fundamentals or rudiments
例　indoctrinate students with the notion of egalitarianism 向学生灌输平等主义的思想
近　educate, instruct, lesson, teach, train, tutor
反　learn, study 学习

indolent [ˈɪndələnt]
【考法】 *adj.* 懒惰的: **averse to activity**, effort, or movement
例　an indolent student 一个懒学生
近　lazy, idle, shiftless, slothful, sluggish
反　diligent, industrious 勤奋的
派　indolence *n.* 懒惰

induce	[ɪnˈdjuːs]

【考法】 *v.* 引发,导致: to be the **cause** of (a situation, action, or state of mind)

例 Doctors said surgery could induce a heart attack . 医生们说手术可能导致心脏病。

近 engender, beget, bring about, cause, generate, produce, yield

indulgent	[ɪnˈdʌldʒənt]

【考法】 *adj.* (对己)放纵的,(对他人)纵容的: showing, characterized by, or **given to indulgence**

例 indulgent aristocrats 生活放纵的贵族

近 decadent, forbearing, lenient, luxurious, tolerant, sybaritic

反 ascetic 禁欲的; draconian 严酷的

派 indulgence *n.* 放纵

Unit 5

■ INDURATE	■ INDUSTRIOUS	■ INEFFABLE	■ INELUCTABLE	■ INEPT
■ INERT	■ INEVITABLE	■ INEXORABLE	■ INFAMOUS	■ INFATUATE

indurate	[ˈɪndjʊreɪt]

【考法1】 *adj.* 铁石心肠的,冷酷无情的: having or showing **a lack of sympathy** or tender feelings

例 an indurate heart that admits no love or mercy 一颗不认可爱或仁慈的冷酷心灵

近 affectless, callous, heartless, inhumane, merciless, obdurate, pitiless, ruthless, unsparing, cold-blooded

反 charitable, compassionate, humane, kindhearted, merciful, tender 仁慈的

【考法2】 *vt.* 使变硬: to become **physically firm** or solid

例 Great heat indurates clay . 高温使黏土变硬。

近 concrete, congeal, firm, freeze, set, solidify

反 liquefy 液化; soften 柔化

industrious	[ɪnˈdʌstriəs]

【考法】 *adj.* 勤勉的: constantly, regularly, or habitually occupied, **diligent**

例 The industrious PhD spends all his summer holiday in the laboratory. 勤奋的博士整个暑假都在做实验。

近 assiduous, busy, diligent, sedulous

反 indolent, lazy, slothful 懒惰的

派 industriousness *n.* 勤奋

ineffable	[ɪnˈefəbl]

【考法】 *adj.* 难以表达的: **incapable** of being **expressed**

例 ineffable ecstasy 无法用语言表达的狂喜

近 indefinable, indescribable, inexpressible, unspeakable, unutterable

反 communicable 可传达的; expressible 可描述的

派 ineffability *n.* 不可描述性

ineluctable	[ˌɪnɪˈlʌktəbl]

【考法】 *adj.* 无法逃避的,必然的: **not to be avoided**, changed, or resisted

例 Although death is an ineluctable fate for any and every individual organism, it lays the foundation of the metabolism that perpetuates the planetary ecosystem. 尽管死亡对于任何单个的有机体而言是不可避免的宿命,但它奠定了能使整个行星生态系统永不衰竭的新陈代谢的基础。

近 certain, inescapable, inevasible, inevitable, unavoidable

反 avoidable, evadable 可避免的; uncertain, unsure (结果等)不确定的

派 ineluctability *n.* 不可避免

inept	[ɪˈnept]

【考法1】 *adj.* 愚笨的,荒谬的: displaying a **lack of judgment**, sense, or reason

例 an inept and irresponsible remark on his paper 对他文章的荒谬而不负责任的评论

近 absurd, foolish, fatuous, preposterous, stupid, witless, unwise

反 judicious, prudent, sagacious, sapient, smart, wise 聪明的,明智的

【考法2】 *adj.* 不称职的,无能力的: generally **incompetent**

例 a hopelessly inept defense attorney 严重不靠谱的辩护律师

近 incapable, inexpert, unfitted, unskillful, unqualified

反 capable, competent 有能力的; proficient, masterful 精通的,技艺精湛的

派 ineptitude *n.* 不合适

inert	[ɪ'nɜːrt]
【考法】	*adj.* (人)懒惰缺乏活力的；(物品)惰性的：**sluggish** in action or motion; **deficient** in active properties
例	inert ingredients in drugs 药品中的惰性成分
近	dead, dormant, lethargic, idle, inactive, passive, torpid
反	active, dynamic 充满活力的；passionate 饱含激情的
派	inertia *n.* 惰性

inevitable	[ɪn'evɪtəbl]
【考法】	*adj.* 不可避免的，必然的：**incapable** of being **avoided** or evaded
例	inevitable consequence 不可避免的结果
近	certain, ineluctable, inescapable, inevasible, sure, unalterable, unavoidable
反	evitable, avoidable 可避免的；uncertain, unsure 不确定的
派	inevitability *n.* 必然性

inexorable	[ɪn'eksərəbl]
【考法】	*adj.* 无法劝阻的，不为所动的：**not** to be **persuaded**, moved, or stopped
例	the seemingly inexorable rise in unemployment 看起来无法阻止其高攀的失业率
近	inflexible, adamant, obdurate, relentless, rigid, unyielding
反	flexible 易受影响的；yielding 屈服的
派	inexorably *adv.* 势不可挡地

infamous	['ɪnfəməs]
【考法】	*adj.* 臭名昭著的：having an extremely and deservedly **bad reputation**
例	an infamous city for smuggling and prostitution 因走私和卖淫而臭名昭著的城市
近	notorious, opprobrious
反	distinguished, esteemed, prestigious, reputable 声名显赫的，受尊敬的
派	infamy *n.* 声名狼藉

infatuate	[ɪn'fætʃueɪt]
【考法】	*vt.* 使迷恋：to **inspire** with **unreasoning love** or attachment
例	a naïve girl infatuated by cajolery 被甜言蜜语冲昏头脑的天真女孩
近	allure, captivate, bewitch, enchant, fascinate
反	disgust 使反感
派	infatuation *n.* 迷恋

Unit 6

■ INCOMMENSURATE	■ INFILTRATE	■ INFINITE	■ INFIRM	■ INFLAME
■ INFELICITOUS	■ INFLUX	■ INFURIATE	■ INFUSE	■ INGENIOUS

incommensurate	[ˌɪnkə'menʃərət]
【考法】	*adj.* 不相称的 **too large or too small** in relation to something
例	a reward incommensurate with their efforts 与他们的努力不相称的奖励
近	disproportionate

infiltrate	['ɪnfɪltreɪt]
【考法】	*vt.* 秘密潜入：to **enter** or take up positions in gradually or **surreptitiously**, as for purposes of espionage or takeover
例	The intelligence staff had been infiltrated by spies . 情报工作人员已经被间谍渗透了。
近	creep, insinuate, penetrate, sneak, slip
反	abscond 潜逃
派	infiltration *n.* 潜入，渗透

infinite	['ɪnfɪnət]
【考法】	*adj.* 无尽的，无限的：having **no boundaries** or limits
例	the idea of an infinite universe 无限宇宙的概念
近	endless, boundless, limitless, immeasurable, unfathomable
反	finite 有限的；bounded, circumscribed, confined, definite, limited, restricted 有界限的，受限的
派	infinity *n.* 无限

infirm [ɪnˈfɜːrm]

【考法 1】 *adj.* 虚弱的：**weak in body**, especially from old age or disease

例 her aging, infirm husband 她上了年纪、身体虚弱的丈夫

近 debilitated, effete, enervated, feeble, frail, languid, sapped, unsubstantial

反 hale, mighty, powerful, rugged, stalwart, stout, strong 强壮的，有力的

【考法 2】 *adj.* 不果断的，优柔寡断的：**lacking firmness of will**, character, or purpose

例 She has little patience with the "infirm of purpose". 她对那些优柔寡断的人没什么耐心。

近 faltering, irresolute, vacillating, wavering

反 resolute 果断的

inflame [ɪnˈfleɪm]

【考法】 *vt.* 使加剧：to make **more violent**

例 Retaliation served only to inflame the feud. 冤冤相报何时了。

近 aggravate, enrage, exacerbate, intensify, ire, irritate, provoke, rile, vex

反 assuage, mitigate, mollify, pacify, placate, subdue 平息

infelicitous [ˌɪnfɪˈlɪsɪtəs]

【考法 1】 *adj.* 不愉快的，不幸的：not happy; **unfortunate**

例 an infelicitous moment 不幸的时刻

近 hapless, ill-fated, luckless, unfortunate, unhappy

反 lucky, happy 幸运的，令人高兴的

【考法 2】 *adj.* 不适当的，不合时宜的：**not appropriate** or well-timed

例 make a very infelicitous remark 做出极不恰当的评价

近 inappropriate, indecorous, inept, malapropos, unfit, unseemly

反 apt, appropriate, becoming, proper 合适的

派 infelicity *n.* 不恰当

influx [ˈɪnflʌks]

【考法】 *n.* 涌入：a **coming in**

例 They anticipated an influx of tourists next month. 他们预期下个月会有大批游客涌入。

近 affluence, flux, income, inflow, inpouring, inrush

反 exodus 大批离去；outflow, outpouring 流出

infuriate [ɪnˈfjʊrieɪt]

【考法】 *vt.* 激怒：to make **furious**

例 be infuriated by the deliberate insults 被蓄意的中伤激怒

近 aggravate, enrage, exasperate, incense, ire, madden

反 appease, assuage, pacify, placate, propitiate 平息，安抚；delight, gratify, please 取悦，讨好

派 infuriated *adj.* 被激怒的

infuse [ɪnˈfjuːz]

【考法】 *vt.* 灌输，使…充满：to **fill** or cause to be filled with something

例 New members infused enthusiasm into the club. 新成员为俱乐部注入了激情。

近 endue, imbue, implant, ingrain, instill, permeate, suffuse, steep

反 extract 提取

派 infusion *n.* 注入

ingenious [ɪnˈdʒiːniəs]

【考法】 *adj.* 聪明的，有创造才能的：marked by originality, **resourcefulness**, and **cleverness** in conception or execution

例 Ingenious designers soon came up with a solution to the battery problem. 聪明的设计者们很快便提出了电池问题的解决方案。

近 artful, clever, imaginative, innovative, inventive, original

反 awkward 笨拙的；uncreative, unimaginative 无创造力或想象力的

派 ingenuity *n.* 独创性，创新性

Unit 7

intermediary [ˌɪntərˈmiːdieri]

【考法】 *n.* 中间人：one who works with opposing sides in order to **bring about an agreement**

例 She wanted him to act as an intermediary in the dispute with Moscow. 她想让他在与莫斯科的争端中担当中间人。

近 broker, conciliator, intercessor, mediator

ingenuous [ɪnˈdʒenjuəs]

【考法】 *adj.* 天真淳朴的：**lacking** in **cunning**, guile, or worldliness

例 Photographs captured the ingenuous smiles of young children at play. 摄影家捕捉到了演出中孩子们天真无邪的笑脸。

近 artless, innocent, guileless, naïve, simple, unaffected, unpretending, unsophisticated

反 artful, cunning, sly 狡猾的；assuming, hypocritical 虚伪做作的；sophisticated, worldly 世故的，老练的

ingest [ɪnˈdʒest]

【考法】 *vt.* 摄入，咽下：to **take into** the **body** by the mouth for digestion or absorption

例 An expert claims that the average person ingests considerably more calories than is necessary or desirable. 一位专家宣称每个人平均摄取的卡路里大大超出了必要或者所需的范围。

近 eat, consume, devour, intake

反 evacuate, expel 排出；vomit 呕吐

派 ingestion *n.* 摄取

ingrained [ɪnˈɡreɪnd]

【考法】 *adj.* 本质的，根深蒂固的：forming a part of the essence or inmost being; **firmly established**

例 ingrained prejudice against foreigners 对外国人根深蒂固的偏见

近 constitutional, immanent, inborn, indigenous, inherent, innate, intrinsic

反 adventitious 外来的，偶然的；extraneous, extrinsic 非本质的，外在的

派 ingrain *vt.* 灌输，使根深蒂固

ingratiating [ɪnˈɡreɪʃieɪtɪŋ]

【考法1】 *adj.* 讨人喜欢的：capable of **winning favor**

例 They adopted the orphan who had a most ingratiating smile. 他们收养了那名有着最惹人喜欢的笑容的孤儿

近 disarming, endearing, winsome

反 disagreeable 令人厌恶的

【考法2】 *adj.* 逢迎的，意在奉承的：intended or adopted in order to **gain favor**

例 an repulsive ingratiating smile 令人反感的阿谀奉承的微笑

近 adulatory, deferential, fawning, flattering, toady, insinuating

派 ingratiate *vt.* 讨好

inherent [ɪnˈhɪrənt]

【考法】 *adj.* 内在的，本质的：involved in the constitution or **essential** character of something

例 a disposition inherent in human nature 人性内在的倾向

近 constitutional, elemental, essential, inborn, ingrained, innate, intrinsic

反 adventitious 外来的，偶然的；extraneous, extrinsic 外在的

派 inherently *adv.* 内在地

inimical [ɪˈnɪmɪkl]

【考法】 *adj.* 带有敌意的：reflecting or indicating **hostility**

例 a cold, inimical voice 冰冷而不友好的声音

近 antagonistic, hostile, opposing, unfriendly

反 amiable, amicable, friendly, hospitable 友好的；amenable 服从的

inimitable [ɪˈnɪmɪtəbl]

【考法】 *adj.* 无法仿效的，独特的：**not** capable of being **imitated**

例 her own inimitable style 她特立独行的作风

近 incomparable, matchless, peerless, unique, unparalleled

反 commonplace, ordinary 平凡的

派 inimitability *n.* 独特性

iniquity	[ɪˈnɪkwəti]

【考法】 *n.* 邪恶，不公正：gross **immorality** or **injustice**

例 The use of illegal narcotics is not only a destroyer of personal health but also an iniquity that undermines our society. 非法的毒品不仅仅摧残着个人健康，还是一颗危害社会的毒瘤。

近 corruption, depravity, debauchery, evil, infamy, sin, unfairness, wickedness

反 integrity, rectitude 正直；virtue 美德；disinterestedness 公正

initiate	[ɪˈnɪʃieɪt]

【考法】 *vt.* 创始，发动促进：to **cause** or facilitate the **beginning** of

例 initiate a new school 创立一个新的学派

近 begin, start, commence, inaugurate, introduce, launch

反 terminate 终止

派 initiative *n.* 主动性，首创精神

Unit 8

■ INKLING	■ INNOCUOUS	■ INNOVATIVE	■ INQUISITIVE	■ INSENSIBLE
■ INCONSISTENT	■ INSENTIENT	■ INCONCLUSIVE	■ INSIPID	■ INSOLENT

inkling	[ˈɪŋklɪŋ]

【考法】 *n.* 轻微暗示，小提示：a **slight indication** or suggestion

例 They hadn't given us an inkling of what was going to happen. 他们不给我们任何暗示将会发生什么。

近 clue, cue, hint

innocuous	[ɪˈnɑːkjuəs]

【考法1】 *adj.* 无害的：producing **no injury**

例 The government enacted a more strict regulation on innocuous preservatives. 政府对无害防腐剂制定了更为严格的规定。

近 anodyne, benign, harmless, inoffensive, nontoxic, safe

反 damaging, detrimental, harmful, injurious, noxious, pernicious, invasive 有害的

【考法2】 *adj.* 不会引起敌意的：**not** likely to give offense or to **arouse** strong feelings or hostility

例 He made an innocuous remark to avoid conflict. 为了避免冲突，他做了一个中庸的评价。

近 bland, inoffensive, insipid, neutral, sapless

反 provoking 刺激性的

innovative	[ˈɪnəveɪtɪv]

【考法】 *adj.* 创新性的：characterized by, tending to, or **introducing innovations**

例 an innovative macro-economic strategy 创新性的宏观经济战略

近 creative, ingenious, inventive, original

反 conservative, hidebound 保守的

派 innovation *n.* 创新

inquisitive	[ɪnˈkwɪzətɪv]

【考法】 *adj.* 过分好奇的：**inordinately** or improperly **curious** about the affairs of others

例 big sunglasses to frustrate inquisitive journalists 让狗仔队的企图无法得逞的大墨镜

近 curious, inquiring, investigative, prying

反 indifferent, unconcerned, uninterested 不感兴趣的；incurious 无好奇心的

派 inquisitiveness *n.* 好奇

insensible	[ɪnˈsensəbl]

【考法】 *adj.* 无知觉的：having **lost consciousness**, especially temporarily

例 The security guard was knocked insensible by a sudden blow. 保安被突如其来的一击敲晕了。

近 anesthetic, insensate, senseless, unfeeling, unconscious

反 conscious 神志清醒的

inconsistent	[ˌɪnkənˈsɪstənt]

【考法】 *adj.* 不一致的，矛盾的 **not being in agreement** or harmony

例 inconsistent theories make it difficult to settle on one explanation 矛盾的理论使得很难确定一个解释

近 conflicting, disagreeing, discordant, incompatible, incongruous, inconsonant, inharmonious

反 accordant, agreeing, compatible, congruent, consistent, harmonious 一致的

派 inconsistency *n.* 矛盾

insentient [ɪnˈsentɪənt]

【考法 1】 *adj.* 无感觉的，无知觉的：**lacking perception**, consciousness, or animation

例 He refused to believe that the universe as we know it evolved from the random interactions of insentient particles of matter. 他拒绝相信我们所知的宇宙是经由无生命的粒子间的相互作用演化而来的。

近 impassive, insensate, insensible, senseless, unresponsive

反 perceiving, sensible, sensitive 有知觉的

【考法 2】 *adj.* 一知半解的，略懂的：**not having** or showing **a deep understanding** of something

例 an insentient therapist who failed to see what the teenager's real problem was 一个对这名青少年的真正问题所在一知半解的医生

近 impercipient, unwise

反 discerning, insightful 深邃的，有洞察力的；sagacious, sage, sapient 睿智的

inconclusive [ˌɪnkənˈkluːsɪv]

【考法】 *adj.* 没有定论的：**not** showing that something is **certainly true**

例 inconclusive vote 无定论的表决

近 inconclusive, indecisive, unclear

反 absolute, clear, conclusive, decisive, definitive 确凿无疑的

insipid [ɪnˈsɪpɪd]

【考法】 *adj.* 平淡的，无聊的：**lacking** in qualities that **interest**, stimulate, or challenge

例 an insipid story of the prince and the princess 一个关于王子和公主的无聊故事

近 banal, bland, driveling, prosaic, tedious, uninteresting, vapid

反 enchanting 引人入胜的

insolent [ˈɪnsələnt]

【考法】 *adj.* 粗野的，无礼的：audaciously **rude** or disrespectful

例 an insolent child with no respect or regard for anyone 对他人不敬的无礼的小孩

近 arrogant, audacious, bold, haughty, supercilious, impertinent, impudent

反 courteous, polite 有礼貌的；respectful 恭敬的；meek, mousy, timid 胆小的

派 insolence *n.* 无礼

Unit 9

■ INSOUCIANT	■ INSTATE	■ INSTIGATE	■ INSTILL	■ INSTITUTE
■ INSUBORDINATE	■ INSULAR	■ INSULATE	■ INSURGENT	■ INTANGIBLE

insouciant [ɪnˈsuːsɪənt]

【考法】 *adj.* 无忧虑的，不在乎的：**free from concern**, worry, or anxiety

例 an insouciant shrug 无所谓地耸耸肩

近 carefree, casual, indifferent, nonchalant, unconcerned

反 anxious, careworn 焦虑的；concerned, worried 关注的，担心的

派 insouciance *n.* 不在乎

instate [ɪnˈsteɪt]

【考法】 *vt.* 任命：to set or **establish** in a **rank** or office

例 The new Secretary of the Treasury was instated on Monday. 新的财政部长于星期一被任命。

近 appoint, designate, inaugurate, induct, install, nominate

反 dismiss, oust 罢免

instigate [ˈɪnstɪɡeɪt]

【考法】 *vt.* 煽动，激起：to goad or **urge forward**; to **stir up**

例 instigate his flame 激起他的热情

近 abet, arouse, excite, foment, goad, incite, inflame, provoke, stir

反 assuage, allay, mitigate, mollify, pacify, soothe 平息，缓和

派 instigation *n.* 煽动

instill [ɪnˈstɪl]

【考法】 *vt.* 灌输：to **impart** gradually

例 instill a sense of responsibility to the young 向年轻人灌输一种责任感

近 breed, enroot, implant, inculcate, infix, infuse, ingrain, plant, sow

反 remove 移除

派 instillation *n.* 滴入；灌输

institute [ˈɪnstɪtuːt]

【考法】 *vt.* 创立，制定：to **establish**, organize, and set in operation

例 institute a new department 创建一个新的部门

近 begin, constitute, create, found, inaugurate, launch, start, set up

反 abrogate, efface, rescind 废除；close, shut 关闭；phase out 淘汰

insubordinate [ˌɪnsəˈbɔːrdɪnət]

【考法】 *adj.* 不服从权威的：**not submissive** to authority

例 Insubordinate soldiers are court-martialed. 抗命的士兵被送上了军事法庭。

近 balky, contumacious, intractable, mutinous, recalcitrant, rebellious, refractory

反 amenable, docile, obedient, ruly, submissive, tractable 顺从的

insular [ˈɪnsələr]

【考法】 *adj.* (观念、想法等)孤立狭隘的：being, having, or reflecting a **narrow provincial viewpoint**

例 the insular thinking of peasant communities 农民阶级的狭隘思想

近 confined, local, narrow, parochial, provincial, regional, restricted

反 cosmopolitan, ecumenical 有国际视野的；catholic (兴趣等)广泛的；receptive 善于接受的

insulate [ˈɪnsəleɪt]

【考法】 *vt.* 使绝缘，使隔离，不受外界影响：to place in a **detached situation**

例 greenhouse gas that insulates ground infrared radiation 能阻碍地表红外辐射的温室气体

近 block, isolate, quarantine, seclude, segregate, separate, sequester

反 connect, link, unite 连结；integrate 使成一体

派 insulation *n.* 隔绝，绝热

insurgent [ɪnˈsɜːrdʒənt]

【考法】 *n.* 叛乱分子：one who breaks with or **opposes** constituted **authority** or the established order

例 Insurgents armed with assault rifles and grenades ambushed a US convoy, resulting in heavy casualties. 持有突击步枪和手榴弹的叛乱分子偷袭了美军车队，造成重大伤亡。

近 rebel, anarchist, antagonist, malcontent, mutineer

派 insurgency *n.* 叛乱

intangible [ɪnˈtændʒəbl]

【考法】 *adj.* 无法感知的，无形的：**incapable** of being **perceived** by the senses

例 intangible value of a good reputation 良好声誉的无形价值

近 impalpable, imperceptible, imponderable, inappreciable, indiscernible, insensible, invisible

反 corporeal 肉体的，有形的；palpable, tactile, tangible, touchable 可感知的

Unit 10

■ INTEGRAL	■ INTEGRITY	■ INTELLIGIBLE	■ INTEMPERATE	■ INTENSIFY
■ INTER	■ INTERCESSOR	■ INTERDICT	■ INTERIM	■ INTERLOCK

integral [ˈɪntɪgrəl]

【考法】 *adj.* 完整的：**not lacking any part** or member that properly belongs to it

例 the belief that athletics are essential to an integral life 坚信运动是完整的人生所不可或缺的一部分

近 comprehensive, entire, full, grand, intact, perfect, plenary, total, whole

反 imperfect, incomplete 不完美的，不完整的；partial 部分的

integrity [ɪnˈtegrəti]

【考法1】 *n.* 正直：steadfast **adherence** to a strict **moral** or ethical code, devotion to telling the truth

例 After a thorough investigation into "Climategate", the panel concluded that the integrity of scientific community is still sound. 经过对"气候门事件"的彻底调查，专家组认为学术界的信誉和道德仍然是值得信赖的。

近 conscience, honesty, incorruptibility, rectitude, righteousness, scrupulousness

反 baseness 卑鄙；deceit, deceitfulness, dishonesty, lying, mendacity, untruthfulness 欺骗

【考法2】 *n.* 完整性：the quality or condition of **being whole** or undivided
例 try to maintain the integrity of the falling empire 尽力维持日趋西山的帝国的统一
近 completeness, entireness, perfection, wholeness

intelligible [ɪnˈtelɪdʒəbl]
【考法】 *adj.* 可理解的：capable of **being understood**
例 intelligible literature 可以理解的文学作品
近 accessible, apprehensible, comprehensible, fathomable, lucid, understandable
反 abstruse, recondite, inscrutable, insensible 难以理解的
派 intelligibility *n.* 可理解性

intemperate [ɪnˈtempərət]
【考法】 *adj.* 无节制的，极端的，不温和的：**not temperate** or moderate
例 an intemperate demand 无节制的要求
近 excessive, extreme, immoderate, inordinate, overindulgent, unrestrained
反 equable 温和的；bridled, checked, constrained, controlled, curbed, governed, hampered, hindered, trammeled 受限制的，节制的

intensify [ɪnˈtensɪfaɪ]
【考法】 *vt.* 加强，激化：to **make intense** or more intensive
例 Both companies intensified their efforts to win the contract. 为了获得这份合同，两家公司都加大了投入。
近 accentuate, aggravate, amplify, deepen, enhance, magnify, redouble, strengthen
反 abate, assuage, attenuate, mitigate, moderate 减缓，降低(程度)
派 intensity *n.* 强度

inter [ɪnˈtɜːr]
【考法】 *vt.* 埋葬：to **place in** a **grave** or tomb
例 The infamous terrorist leader Bin Laden was interred at sea. 臭名昭著的恐怖分子本·拉登被葬于海中。
近 bury, entomb, inhume
反 dig, disinter, excavate, exhume, unearth 掘出

intercessor [ˌɪntərˈsesər]
【考法】 *n.* 调停者：one that **mediates**
例 attend the meeting as the intercessor 作为调停人出席会议
近 broker, buffer, conciliator, intermediate, mediator, peacemaker
反 flame-fanner 煽风点火的人
派 intercession *n.* 调停，斡旋

interdict [ˈɪntərdɪkt]
【考法】 *vt.* 禁止：to **forbid** in a usually formal or authoritative manner
例 Though not interdicted by law, such an action is morally wrong. 尽管这种行为不被法律所禁止，但是道德上来说是不对的。
近 ban, forbid, prohibit, proscribe
反 authorize 授权；allow, permit, suffer 允许；approve, endorse, ratify, sanction 批准
派 interdiction *n.* 禁止，封锁

interim [ˈɪntərɪm]
【考法1】 *n.* 中间过渡时期，间隔：an interval of **time between** one **event**, process, or period and another
例 Richard Wagner's operas usually require an interim of more than 30 minutes for performers to have a break. 理查德·瓦格纳的歌剧通常需要长达30多分钟的幕间休息时间以供演员调整。
近 breach, break, gap, interruption, interval, interlude, parenthesis
反 continuation, continuity 持续
【考法2】 *adj.* 暂时的：serving in a position **for the time being**
例 an interim government to maintain social stability 维持社会稳定的临时政府
近 acting, provisional, temporary
反 eternal, permanent 永恒的

interlock [ˌɪntərˈlɑːk]
【考法】 *vi.* 连锁，连结：to become united or **joined closely**, as by hooking or dovetailing
例 interlocking branches of trees 纠缠盘错的树干
近 associate, connect, join, link, unite
反 sunder 拆散
派 interlocking *adj.* 连锁的

List 14

> "未曾想与雄鹰争锋，来赢得他人艳羡的目光，我却凭着志在四方的信念和风雨兼程的决心，成为站在金字塔尖的蜗牛，沐浴着清风，唱响青春无悔的乐章！"
>
> （汪洋，2009年10月，Verbal 710, Quantitative 800）

Unit 1

■ INTERMINABLE　　■ INTERMITTENT　　■ INTERREGNUM　　■ INTERROGATE　　■ INTIMATE
■ INTIMIDATE　　■ INTOXICANT　　■ INTRANSIGENT　　■ INTREPID　　■ INTRIGUE

interminable ［ɪn'tɜːrmɪnəbl］
【考法】 *adj.* 无尽头的：having or seeming to have **no end**
例 A large audience fell asleep during the interminable sermon . 许多观众都在冗长的布道演说中睡着了。
近 continual, ceaseless, endless, everlasting, perpetual
反 completed 完成的

intermittent ［ˌɪntər'mɪtənt］
【考法】 *adj.* 断断续续的：coming and going at intervals, **not continuous**
例 intermittent rain in June 六月里断断续续的梅雨
近 episodic, erratic, occasional, periodical, recurrent, recurring
反 constant, continuous, incessant, unceasing 持续不断的

interregnum ［ˌɪntə'regnəm］
【考法】 *n.* 过渡期：**break** in continuity
例 The democratic regime proved to be a short-lived interregnum between dictatorships. 这个民主政权被证明只不过是两个独裁政权之间的短暂过渡罢了。
近 breach, break, gap, interim, interruption, interval, interlude, parenthesis
反 continuation, continuity 持续

interrogate ［ɪn'terəgeɪt］
【考法】 *vt.* 质问，审问：to **question formally** and systematically
例 interrogate the prisoner of war for valuable intelligence 审问战俘以获取有价值的情报
近 ask, grill, inquire, milk, question
反 answer, reply, respond 回答，回复
派 interrogation *n.* 审讯

intimate
【考法 1】 ［'ɪntɪmət］*adj.* 有紧密联系的，亲密无间的：marked by very **close association**, contact, or familiarity
例 intimate friends since childhood 孩童时期以来的密友
近 familiar, close, confidential
反 distant, remote 疏远的
【考法 2】 ［'ɪntɪmeɪt］ *v.* 间接地沟通：to **communicate** delicately and **indirectly**
例 intimate a wish to leave 暗示想离开
近 allude, connote, hint, imply, indicate, infer, suggest
反 articulate 清晰明确地说

intimidate ［ɪn'tɪmɪdeɪt］
【考法】 *vt.* 威吓：to make timid or fearful, **frighten**
例 He refused to be intimidated by the manager. 他对经理的恐吓不为所动。
近 browbeat, bully, coerce, cow, frighten, hector, terrify
反 blandish, cajole, coax 用花言巧语讨好
派 intimidation *n.* 恐吓

intoxicant ［ɪn'tɑːksɪkənt］
【考法】 *n.* 使人陶醉的东西（尤指酒精饮料）：an agent that **intoxicates**, especially an alcoholic beverage
近 alcohol, liquor, stimulant
反 refresher 使人清醒的东西
派 intoxicating *adj.* 使人陶醉的

intransigent	[ɪnˈtrænzɪdʒənt]

【考法】 *adj.* 不妥协的，固执的：characterized by **refusal to compromise** or to abandon an extreme position

例 an intransigent attitude 不妥协的态度

近 adamant, headstrong, intractable, obstinate, pertinacious, stubborn, uncompromising, unyielding

反 compliant, pliable 易受影响的；tractable, yielding 容易驾驭的

派 intransigence *n.* 顽固

intrepid	[ɪnˈtrepɪd]

【考法】 *adj.* 大胆的：characterized by **resolute fearlessness**, fortitude, and endurance

例 an intrepid explorer 大胆的探险家

近 audacious, brave, bold, courageous, dauntless, fearless, gallant, valiant, valorous

反 apprehensive 恐惧的；cowardly, craven, gutless, pusillanimous, timorous 怯懦的，胆小的

派 intrepidity *n.* 无所畏惧

intrigue	

【考法1】 [ˈɪntriːg] *n.* 阴谋：**a secret plan** for accomplishing evil or unlawful ends

例 The intrigue was quickly discovered, and the would-be assassins were arrested. 随着阴谋的迅速识破，未得手的刺客被逮捕了。

近 conspiracy, design, intrigue, machination, scheme

【考法2】 [ɪnˈtriːg] *vt.* 激起…的兴趣：to **arouse** the interest, desire, or **curiosity** of

例 The children are apparently intrigued by the tale. 孩子们很明显被这个传奇故事吸引了。

近 appeal, attract, enthrall, entice, excite, fascinate, interest, occupy

反 ennui, pall 使厌倦

派 intriguing *adj.* 有趣的

Unit 2

■ INTRINSIC	■ INTUITIVE	■ INUNDATE	■ INURE	■ INVECTIVE
■ INVEIGH	■ INVEIGLE	■ INVENTORY	■ INVETERATE	■ INVIDIOUS

intrinsic	[ɪnˈtrɪnsɪk]

【考法】 *adj.* 固有的，内在的：of or relating to the **essential** nature of a thing

例 the intrinsic worth of a gem 宝石的内在价值

近 congenial, constitutional, immanent, inborn, inherent, innate, native, natural

反 adventitious, extraneous, extrinsic 外在的

intuitive	[ɪnˈtuːɪtɪv]

【考法】 *adj.* 直觉的：knowing or perceiving **by intuition**

例 The twins have an intuitive awareness of each other's feelings. 这对双胞胎天生就能感知彼此的感受。

近 instinctive

反 acquired 后天习得的

派 intuition *n.* 直觉

inundate	[ˈɪnʌndeɪt]

【考法】 *vt.* 淹没：to **cover with** or as if with **flood**

例 inundated with trash e-mails 被垃圾邮件所淹没

近 avalanche, deluge, drown, engulf, overflow, overwhelm, submerge

反 drain 排空

派 inundation *n.* 淹没

inure	[ɪˈnjʊr]

【考法】 *vt.* 使习惯接受不好的东西：to **accustom** to accept something undesirable

例 children inured to violence 习惯了暴力的孩子们

近 accustom, familiarize, habituate

派 inured *adj.* 习惯的

invective	[ɪnˈvektɪv]

【考法】 *adj.* 侮辱性的：of, relating to, or **characterized by insult** or abuse

例 invective comments on female activists 对女权主义者的侮辱性评论

近 abusive, opprobrious, scurrile, scurrilous, truculent, vitriolic, vituperative

反 adulatory, flattery 阿谀奉承的；complimentary 称赞的

inveigh	[ɪnˈveɪ]	

inveigh [ɪnˈveɪ]

【考法】 *vi.* 激烈抗议，表示强烈不满：to **protest** or complain bitterly or **vehemently**

例 inveigh against the bank industry 对银行行业表示强烈不满

近 gripe, grouse, object, protest, remonstrate, repine

反 support 支持；delight, rejoice 感到高兴

inveigle [ɪnˈveɪgl]

【考法】 *vt.* 诱骗：to **win over by coaxing**, flattery, or artful talk

例 inveigle consumers into buying the item 诱骗顾客购买商品

近 allure, bait, decoy, entice, entrap, seduce, tempt

反 demand 强求

派 inveigling *adj.* 诱骗性的

inventory [ˈɪnvəntɔːri]

【考法】 *n.* (包含要点的)简介：a **short statement** of the main points

例 They decided to offer the public an informative inventory of everything that is known about the virus at this time. 他们决定向公众提供一份极富价值的报告，它涵盖了目前为止关于这种病毒的所有认识。

近 abstract, brief, epitome, outline, résumé, summarization, synopsis

inveterate [ɪnˈvetərət]

【考法】 *adj.* 根深蒂固的：**firmly established** by long persistence

例 the inveterate tendency to overlook the obvious 总是忽视显而易见事物的习惯

近 chronic, entrenched, ingrained, rooted, settled, hard-cored

反 adventitious 偶然的

invidious [ɪnˈvɪdiəs]

【考法1】 *adj.* 惹人反感的：tending to **cause discontent**, animosity, or envy

例 the invidious task of arbitration 令人反感的仲裁任务

近 abhorrent, detestable, obnoxious, odious, repugnant, repellent

反 agreeable, gratifying, pleasant 令人高兴的

【考法2】 *adj.* 羡慕嫉妒恨的：having or showing mean **resentment of another's possessions** or advantages

例 Inevitably, his remarkable success attracted the invidious attention of the other sales representatives. 不可避免地，他的巨大成功引来了其他销售代表羡慕嫉妒恨的眼光。

近 covetous, envious, jaundiced, jealous, resentful, green-eyed

Unit 3

■ INVIGORATE	■ INVINCIBLE	■ INVOKE	■ IRASCIBLE	■ IRATE
■ IRIDESCENT	■ IRK	■ IRONCLAD	■ IRRADICABLE	■ ITINERANT

invigorate [ɪnˈvɪgəreɪt]

【考法】 *vt.* 使精神，使强壮，鼓舞激励：to **impart vigor**, strength, or vitality to

例 news that invigorates the public 给大众打鸡血的新闻

近 animate, energize, fortify, reinforce, strengthen, vitalize

反 dampen, deaden, debilitate, emaciate, sap 使衰弱；demoralize 使士气衰落

派 invigorated *adj.* 精力充沛的

invincible [ɪnˈvɪnsəbl]

【考法】 *adj.* 不可战胜的，不可超越的：**incapable** of being **conquered**, overcome, or subdued

例 The soccer team proved to be invincible. 这支球队证明了自己是不可战胜的。

近 bulletproof, impregnable, invulnerable, unbeatable, unconquerable

反 conquerable 可被征服的；surmountable 可超越的；vulnerable 脆弱的，敏感的

派 invincibility *n.* 无敌

invoke [ɪnˈvoʊk]

【考法1】 *vt.* 实施：to **put into effect** or operation

例 New train timetable has been invoked. 新的火车时刻表已经生效。

近 enforce, effect, execute, implement, perform

反 suspend 暂停，搁置

【考法2】 *vt.* 产生，造成：to **be the cause** of (a situation, action, or state of mind)

例 We should be prepared for the possibility that any solution may invoke another set of problems. 我们必须要为这样一种可能做好心理准备：任何解决方案都可能带来一系列新的问题。

近 beget, bring, catalyze, cause, create, engender, generate, induce, produce, result

irascible	[ɪˈræsəbl]
【考法】	*adj.* 易怒的：marked by hot temper and **easily provoked anger**
例	an irascible temper 易怒的脾气
近	choleric, irritable, peevish, petulant
反	affable 和蔼的

irate	[aɪˈreɪt]
【考法】	*adj.* 极其愤怒的：**extremely angry**
例	an irate taxpayer 极为愤怒的纳税人
近	aggravated, apoplectic, choleric, enraged, exasperated, infuriated, ireful, mad, wrathful
反	calm, halcyon 平静的；delighted, pleased 高兴的，满意的

iridescent	[ˌɪrɪˈdesnt]
【考法】	*adj.* 五颜六色的：displaying a play of **lustrous colors** like those of the rainbow
例	an iridescent soap bubble 一个五颜六色的肥皂泡
近	nacreous, opalescent, pearlescent
反	monochromatic 单色的
派	iridescence *n.* 五彩斑斓

irk	[ɜːrk]
【考法】	*vt.* 使烦恼，使厌倦：to cause to be **irritating**, wearisome, or vexing to
例	She irked her friends by chewing her gum loudly during the movie. 她因为看电影时嚼口香糖弄出声响而惹怒了她的朋友们。
近	annoy, bother, fret, gall, provoke, ruffle, vex
反	appease, assuage, pacify, placate, propitiate, soothe 安抚，平息
派	irksome *adj.* 令人厌烦的

ironclad	[ˈaɪərnklæd]
【考法】	*adj.* 非常坚固的，坚不可摧的：so firm or secure as to be **unbreakable**
例	pride on their ironclad fleet 对他们坚不可摧的舰队感到自豪
近	firm, invulnerable, secure, sound, tenacious, tough
反	fragile 脆弱的

irradicable	[ɪˈrædɪkəbl]
【考法】	*adj.* 不能根除的：**impossible** to uproot or **destroy**
例	Smoking has become an irradicable bad habit for him. 吸烟已成了他不能根除的恶习。
近	entrenched, ineradicable, ingrained, inveterate, rooted
反	eradicable 可根除的

itinerant	[aɪˈtɪnərənt]
【考法】	*adj.* 巡游的，巡回的：**traveling from place to place**
例	An itinerant musician can see a lot of the world. 一位巡游音乐家可以看到大千世界。
近	ambulant, errant, nomadic, peripatetic, roaming, wandering

Unit 4

■ IRRIGATE	■ IRRITATE	■ ISSUE	■ JABBER	■ JADED
■ JAPE	■ JARGON	■ JARRING	■ JAUNDICE	■ JAUNTY

irrigate	[ˈɪrɪɡeɪt]
【考法 1】	*vt.* 灌溉：to supply (dry land) with **water** by means of ditches, pipes, or streams; water artificially
例	irrigate crops periodically 定期灌溉农作物
近	water
派	irrigation *n.* 灌溉
【考法 2】	*vt.* 冲洗：to **flush** (a body part) with a stream of liquid (as in removing a foreign body or medicating)
例	irrigate the wound 冲洗伤口
近	flush, rinse, wash

irritate	[ˈɪrɪteɪt]
【考法】	*vt.* 刺激，惹恼：to **provoke** impatience, **anger**, or displeasure in
例	His rude interruptions really irritated her. 他粗鲁的打断激怒了她。
近	aggravate, annoy, exasperate, gall, inflame, nettle, peeve, provoke, rile, roil
反	appease, assuage, pacify, placate, propitiate, soothe 安抚，平息
派	irritant *n.* 刺激物

issue [ˈɪʃuː]

【考法 1】 *n.*（有争议的）话题，议题：**a matter that is in dispute** between two or more parties

例 focused on economic and political issues 重点关注经济和政治话题

近 nut, problem, question

【考法 2】 *v.*（使）流出：to (cause to) go, come, or **flow out**

例 strange sound issued from the abandoned house 废弃房中传来的奇怪声音

近 discharge, emit, exude, release, vent

反 withdraw 撤回

jabber [ˈdʒæbər]

【考法】 *vi.* 快而不清楚地说：to **talk rapidly, indistinctly**, or unintelligibly

例 monkeys jabbering at each other in their cages 在笼子里唧唧歪歪的猴子

近 babble, blabber, drivel, gabble, gibber, mumbo jumbo

反 speak slowly 慢慢地说

jaded [ˈdʒeɪdɪd]

【考法】 *adj.* 厌倦的，没兴趣没热情的：having one's **patience**, interest, or pleasure **exhausted**

例 Even jaded sci-fi fans are finding this new space adventure fresh and exciting. 即使是没热情的科幻小说粉也觉得这次的太空探险非常新鲜有趣。

近 bored, tired, wearied, fed up

反 absorbed, engaged, engrossed, interested, intrigued, rapt 有兴趣的

jape [dʒeɪp]

【考法】 *v.* 嘲弄：to say or do something jokingly or **mockingly**

例 The characters in Oscar Wilde's plays jape with a sophistication that is rarely encountered in real life. 奥斯卡·王尔德戏剧作品中的角色用一种十分世故的态度进行嘲讽，而这种态度在真实生活当中是很少见的。

近 jest, quip, wisecrack, banter, chaff, gag, jive, jolly, josh

反 revere 尊敬

jargon [ˈdʒɑːrgən]

【考法】 *n.* 行业术语：the **specialized or technical language** of a trade, profession, or similar group

例 medical jargon that the layman cannot understand 外行不理解的医学术语

近 argot, cant, dialect, jive, lingo, patois

jarring [ˈdʒɑːrɪŋ]

【考法】 *adj.* 刺耳的：harsh or **discordant**

例 The final chord of that song is too jarring for me. 那首歌最后的合声部分太刺耳了。

近 grating, cacophonous, strident

反 melodious 音调优美的

jaundice [ˈdʒɔːndɪs]

【考法】 *n.*（因嫉妒或厌世而产生的）偏见：to affect with the negativity or bitterness of jaundice; **bias**

例 the jaundice in the eyes of the two feuding neighbors 两个有积怨的邻居之间的偏见

近 animosity, animus, antagonism, antipathy, gall, hostility, rancor

反 amity 和睦，好感

jaunty [ˈdʒɔːnti]

【考法】 *adj.* 轻快的，活泼的：**sprightly** in manner or appearance: lively

例 a jaunty stroll 轻快的散步

近 animate, brisk, energetic, frisky, perky, racy, spirited, vivacious

反 staid, dead, inactive, inanimate, lackadaisical, languid, languishing, leaden, limp, listless, spiritless, vapid 无生气的

Unit 5

■ JEJUNE	■ JETTISON	■ JEOPARDY	■ JEST	■ JIBE
■ JINGOIST	■ JITTERS	■ JOCULAR	■ JOCUND	■ JOG

jejune [dʒɪˈdʒuːn]

【考法】 *adj.* 无趣乏味的：**not interesting**; dull

例 jejune lectures 无聊的讲座

近 arid, drab, dreary, leaden, monotonous, ponderous, tedious, weary

反 absorbing, engaging, engrossing, gripping, interesting, intriguing, involving, riveting, thought provoking 促人深思的，吸引人的

jettison ['dʒetɪsn]

【考法】 *vt.* 放弃，拒绝接受（想法、计划等）：to **get rid of** as superfluous or encumbering; omit or forgo as part of a plan or as the result of some other decision

例 The Government seems to have jettisoned the bail-out plan . 政府似乎已经放弃了这个救市计划。

近 abandon, abdicate, discard, junk, reject, scrap, shed, slough, throw away

反 rescue, salvage 救援，拯救

jeopardy ['dʒepərdi]

【考法】 *n.* 危险：**risk** of loss or injury; peril or **danger**

例 The city's firefighters routinely put their lives in jeopardy . 消防队员们早就把生命置于危险之中。

近 distress, endangerment, imperilment, peril

反 safeness, safety, secureness, security 安全

jest [dʒest]

【考法】 *n.* 轻浮的态度，戏谑：a **frivolous** mood or manner

例 spoken in jest 戏谑地说

近 butt, derision, mockery

反 solemnity, solemn utterance 严肃

jibe [dʒaɪb]

【考法】 *vi.* 意见一致：to be in accord: **agree**

例 Your figures jibe with mine . 你的数据与我的数据一致。

近 accord, cohere, conform, correspond, harmonize, tally

反 conflict 冲突

jingoist ['dʒɪŋɡoʊɪst]

【考法】 *n.* 极端爱国激进分子（通常表现为好战的对外政策）：**extreme** chauvinism or **nationalism** marked especially by a **belligerent** foreign policy

例 jingoists who cry for war 叫嚣着鼓吹开战的激进分子

近 chauvinist, nationalist, superpatriot, war hawk

反 dove, pacifist, peacenik 反战派人士

jitters ['dʒɪtərz]

【考法】 *n.* 紧张，不安：a sense of **panic** or extreme **nervousness**

例 She suffered pre-wedding jitters . 她有婚前恐惧。

近 butterflies, dither, jimjams, nerves, shakes, shivers, willies

反 aplomb, calm, composure, equanimity, imperturbability, self-possession, tranquility 镇定，冷静

jocular ['dʒɑːkjələr]

【考法】 *adj.* 搞笑的，欢乐的：characterized by **joking, playful**

例 jocular manner/mood 搞笑的方式/心情

近 blithesome, festive, gleeful, jocund, jovial, mirthful

反 lachrymose, saturnine 悲哀的；dour, dreary, morose, serious 阴郁的

jocund ['dʒɑːkənd]

【考法】 *adj.* 欢快的，高兴的：**sprightly** and **lighthearted** in disposition, character, or quality

例 old friends engaged in jocund teasing 老朋友相见，互相打趣调侃

近 blithesome, jocose, jocular, jolly, jovial, mirthful, sunny

反 lachrymose, saturnine 悲哀的；dour, dreary, morose, serious 阴郁的

jog [dʒɑːɡ]

【考法】 *vt.* 唤起：to **rouse** or stimulate

例 an old photo that might jog your memory 一张也许会唤起你回忆的老照片

近 arouse, excite, incite, instigate, pique, remind, stimulate, stir

反 allay, alleviate, assuage, ease, mitigate, mollify, palliate, relieve, soothe 缓和

Unit 6

jolt [dʒoʊlt]

【考法】 *vt.* 惊吓：to cause an **unpleasant surprise** for

例 The sneak terrorist attack jolted the country out of its indolence and indifference. 偷偷摸摸的恐怖袭击将该国从懒惰和冷漠无情中惊醒。

近 appall, floor, shake up

jot [dʒɑːt]

【考法】 *vt.* 简要记录：to **write briefly** or hurriedly

例 jot down an address 简要地记下地址

近 log, mark, put down, register, report, set down, take down, write down

jovial ['dʒoʊviəl]

【考法】 *adj.* 愉快的：markedly **good-humored** especially as evidenced by **jollity** and **conviviality**

例 a jovial host 快活的主人

近 blithesome, festive, gay, gleeful, jocular, jocund, jolly, mirthful

反 lachrymose, saturnine 悲哀的；dour, dreary, morose, serious 阴郁的

jubilant ['dʒuːbɪlənt]

【考法】 *adj.* 喜悦的：exultingly **joyful**

例 The nominee delivered a jubilant speech before the cheering crowd. 在欢呼的人群面前，被提名人发表了充满喜悦的演说。

近 exulting, glorying, rejoicing, triumphant

反 lachrymose, saturnine 悲哀的；dour, dreary, morose, serious 阴郁的

judicious [dʒuˈdɪʃəs]

【考法】 *adj.* 明智的，慎重的：having or exhibiting sound **judgment**; **prudent**

例 a judicious choice 明智的抉择

近 intelligent, judgmatic, prudent, tactical, wise

反 daft, imprudent, inadvisable, inexpedient, indiscreet, impolitic, unwise 愚蠢的，轻率的

juggernaut ['dʒʌɡərnɔːt]

【考法】 *n.* 无法阻挡的力量，摧毁一切的强大力量：an **overwhelming**, advancing **force** that crushes everything in its path

例 the juggernaut of industrialization 工业化无法阻挡的力量

近 steamroller

ken [ken]

【考法】 *n.* 视野范围：the range of **vision**

例 abstract words that are beyond the ken of children 超出孩子们理解范围的单词

近 sight

kidnap ['kɪdnæp]

【考法】 *vt.* 绑架勒索：to seize and **detain** by **unlawful force** or fraud and often with a demand for ransom

例 The child was kidnapped and held for ransom. 歹徒绑架了孩子，并且向家属勒索赎金。

近 abduct

反 release, set free 释放

kindle ['kɪndl]

【考法】 *vt.* 点燃：to build or fuel (a fire); to **set fire** to; **ignite**

例 kindle interest 激发兴趣

近 enkindle, ignite, inflame, torch

反 douse, extinguish, quench, put out, snuff out 熄灭

kindred ['kɪndrəd]

【考法】 *adj.* 类似的；具有相似或相近的起源、本性或性质的：having a **similar** or related **origin**, nature, or character

例 She finally found people who were kindred spirits when she joined the hiking club. 她加入登山俱乐部的时候终于发现了志向相同的人。

近 agreeable, amicable, compatible, congenial, frictionless, unanimous, united

反 disagreeable, discordant, disharmonious, disunited, incompatible, inharmonious, uncongenial 不一致的，不和谐的

Unit 7

■ KNACK	■ KILTER	■ KNIT	■ KNOTTY	■ KUDOS
■ LABILE	■ LABORIOUS	■ LABYRINTH	■ LACERATE	■ LACKLUSTER

knack [næk]

【考法】 *n.* 诀窍，聪明的做法：a **clever** trick or stratagem; a clever way of doing something

例 She's tried every knack in Cupid's book to get her guy to marry her. 她试过了所有爱情三十六计，希望那男人娶她。

近 artifice, device, gambit, ploy, scheme, sleight, stratagem

反 foolishness 愚蠢

kilter ['kɪltər]

【考法】 *n.* 平衡：state of being or **fitness**

例 Her lifestyle was out of kilter with her politics. 她的生活方式与她的政治活动格格不入。

近 form, keeping, order, shape

knit [nɪt]

【考法】 *vt.* 连接，联系：to **join closely**; unite securely

例 Sport knits the whole family close together. 体育将整个家庭紧紧地联系在一起。

近 bind, bond, combine, connect, fasten, join, link, meld, merge, tie, secure, unite

反 disassociate, disconnect, disjoin, divide, sever, split, sunder 分开

knotty ['nɑːti]

【考法】 *adj.* 复杂的，困难的：marked by or full of knots especially: so **full of difficulties** and **compli-cations** as to be likely to defy solution

例 The candidates cautiously gave their views on an array of knotty issues. 候选人就一系列困难问题谨慎地给出了自己的看法。

近 baroque, byzantine, complicated, convoluted, intricate, involved, labyrinthine, sophisticated, tangled

反 easy, effortless, plain, simple 容易的，明显的

kudos ['kuːdɑːs]

【考法1】 *n.* 名望，名声：**fame** and renown resulting from an act or achievement

例 Employees enjoy the kudos that the job brings as much as the financial rewards. 正如同喜欢工作带来的经济回报一样，雇员们也很享受工作所带来的名声和荣誉。

近 credit, distinction, homage, honor, laurels

反 infamy, notoriety 不好的名声

【考法2】 *n.* 夸奖，赞扬：**acclaim or praise** for exceptional achievement

例 The attorney did pro bono work because it was the right thing to do, and not for any future kudos that it might bring. 这名律师之所以为慈善机构和穷人提供免费服务，是因为他觉得这是正确的事情，而非为了任何可能因此而产生的赞扬。

近 acclaim, accolade, applause, credit, distinction, homage, honor, laud, laurels

反 belittlement, denigration, deprecation, derogation, diminishment, disparagement 贬损

labile ['leɪbaɪl]

【考法】 *adj.* 易变的，不稳定的：continually undergoing chemical, physical, or biological change; **unstable**

例 labile mineral 不稳定的矿物质 || an emotionally labile person 一个多愁善感的人

近 capricious, fluctuating, fluid, inconstant, mercurial, temperamental, unsettled, unsteady, variable, volatile

反 constant, immutable, invariable, stable, stationary, steady 稳定的

laborious [ləˈbɔːriəs]

【考法 1】 *adj.* 勤奋的：hard-working; **industrious**

例 The volunteers have been commendably laborious in their cleanup of the beach. 清理海滩的志愿者们的勤奋努力值得赞扬。‖ He was gentle and kindly, living a laborious life in his Paris flat. 他是一个温柔、好心的人，住在巴黎的公寓里，过着勤奋的生活。

近 active, assiduous, bustling, diligent, engaged, industrious, occupied, sedulous

反 idle, inactive, indolent, inert, slothful 懒散的

【考法 2】 *adj.* 费力的：marked by or requiring **long, hard work**

例 the laborious task of cleaning up the oil spill 清除泄露石油的艰苦工作

近 arduous, challenging, demanding, difficult, exacting, formidable, grueling, heavy, labored, rigorous, rough, rugged, severe, strenuous, sweaty, toilsome, tough

反 easy, effortless, facile, light, mindless, simple, undemanding 轻松的，容易的

labyrinthine [ˌlæbəˈrɪnθaɪn]

【考法】 *adj.* 迷宫似的，复杂曲折的：of, relating to, resembling, or constituting a labyrinth; **extremely complex** or tortuous in **structure**

例 The labyrinthine political situation of Middle East left us totally befuddled. 中东地区复杂迷离的政治局势让我们彻底迷惑了。

近 baroque, byzantine, complicate, complicated, convoluted, intricate, involved, knotty, sophisticated, tangled

反 easy, effortless, plain, simple 容易的，明显的

lacerate [ˈlæsəreɪt]

【考法】 *vt.* 使非常痛苦：to **cause** deep emotional **pain** to; distress

例 He was born into a family already lacerated with tensions and divisions. 他出生在一个已经被冲突和分裂折磨不堪的家庭当中。

近 afflict, distress, harrow, hurt, rend, torment, torture, wound

反 allay, alleviate, assuage, ease, mitigate, mollify, palliate, relieve, soothe 减轻(痛苦等)

lackluster [ˈlæklʌstər]

【考法】 *adj.* 黯淡无光泽的：**lacking brightness**, luster, or vitality

例 lackluster hair 黯淡无光的头发

近 dim, dull, flat, lusterless

反 burnished, glistening, glossy, lustrous, polished, shiny, sleek 光亮的

Unit 8

| ■ LACONIC | ■ LACHRYMOSE | ■ LAMBASTE | ■ LAMENT | ■ LIBELOUS |
| ■ LAMPOON | ■ LANGUID | ■ LANGUISH | ■ LANGUOR | ■ LANK |

laconic [ləˈkɑːnɪk]

【考法】 *adj.* 简洁(以至于显得粗鲁或难以理解)的：using or involving the use of a **minimum of words**: **concise** to the point of seeming rude or mysterious

例 His mentor's comment tends to be laconic but very much to the point. 他导师的点评很简短，但是却总能说到点子上。

近 apothegmatic, brief, capsule, compact, compendious, curt, pithy, succinct, summary, telegraphic, terse

反 circuitous, circumlocutory, diffuse, prolix, rambling, verbose, windy, wordy 冗长的

lachrymose [ˈlækrɪmoʊs]

【考法】 *adj.* 催人泪下的，悲伤的：tending to cause tears, **mournful**

例 The lachrymose mourners at the funeral required a steady supply of tissues. 葬礼上多愁善感的哀悼者对纸巾有稳定的需求。

近 doleful, lamentable, lugubrious, melancholy, mournful, tearful, teary, weepy, woeful

反 cheerful, delighted, jocund, jovial 欢乐的，快乐的

lambaste [læmˈbeɪst]

【考法】 *vt.* 严厉斥责：to **scold sharply**; berate

例 Critics lambasted his performance. 评论家严厉斥责了他的表演。

近 assail, baste, belabor, berate, castigate, excoriate, reprimand, reproach, scathe, slam, upbraid, vituperate

反 carol, extol, glorify, hymn, laud, magnify, praise 表扬，赞美

lament	[lə'ment]
【考法】	v. 为…哀悼，表达痛苦或遗憾：to **express sorrow** or regret; mourn
例	lament an innocent death 为无辜的死者而悲痛
近	bemoan, deplore, grieve, moan, mourn, wail
反	delight, exult, joy, rejoice 感到高兴
派	lamentable *adj.* 值得惋惜的，悲哀的

libelous	['laɪbələs]
【考法】	*adj.* 恶意中伤的，诽谤的：constituting or including a **libel**；defamatory
例	The election campaign degenerated into an exchange of libelous remarks. 竞选活动已经沦为了双方互相的谩骂和诽谤。
近	backbiting, calumnious, defamatory, detractive, invidious, maligning, scandalous, slanderous, traducing, vilifying
反	adulatory, applauding, commendatory, eulogistic, eulogizing, laudatory, praising 说好话的，奉承的

lampoon	[læm'puːn]
【考法】	*n.* 讽刺：a **harsh satire** usually directed against an individual
例	a lampoon of the movie business at the time 对当时电影产业的一种讽刺
近	burlesque, caricature, farce, mockery, parody, ridicule, spoof, travesty
反	eulogy, ode, paean 颂歌

languid	['læŋgwɪd]
【考法】	*adj.* 没精打采的，虚弱的：**lacking energy** or vitality; weak
例	be languid for weeks after surgery 术后的几周都无精打采的
近	debilitated, effete, enervated, feeble, frail, infirm, lackadaisical, spiritless, sapped, enfeebled
反	animated, energetic, vehement, vivacious 有精力的；mighty, powerful, stalwart, stout, strong 强壮的

languish	['læŋgwɪʃ]
【考法】	*vi.* 变得衰弱：to be or **become feeble**, weak, or enervated
例	languish during the prolonged heat wave 在持续的热浪下变得虚弱
近	decay, droop, emaciate, fade, fail, flag, sag, wither
反	burgeon, flourish, thrive, prosper 旺盛生长

languor	['læŋgər]
【考法1】	*n.* 懒惰：physical or mental **inertness**
例	He enjoyed the languor brought on by a hot summer afternoon. 他很享受夏日午后的慵懒。
近	collapse, exhaustion, frazzle, lassitude, listlessness, stupor, torpor, prostration
反	verve, vim, animation, vitality 有活力
【考法2】	*n.* 衰弱：**weakness** or **weariness** of body or mind
例	The tropical heat sapped our strength, leaving us in a state of unaccustomed languor. 热带的炎热气候消磨着我们的精力，让我们感到一阵不适的虚弱。
近	debilitation, enervation, enfeeblement, fragility, infirmity
反	robustness, strength, vivacity 强壮，有力

lank	[læŋk]
【考法1】	*adj.* 细长瘦弱的：**long** and **lean**
例	lank cattle 瘦牲口
近	emaciated, lean, slender, svelte, tenuous, thin
反	fat, fleshy, gross, obese 肥胖的
【考法2】	*adj.* 不僵硬的，柔软松弛的：long, straight, and **limp**; **not stiff** in structure
例	a woman with long, lank hair 有着长而稀疏头发的女子 ‖ Right after a shower, her lank hair hung down to her shoulders. 出浴后，柔软的头发搭在她的肩上。
近	droopy, flaccid, floppy, yielding
反	inflexible, rigid, stiff, sturdy, tense 僵硬的；resilient 有弹性的

Unit 9

■ LAPSE	■ LARGESSE	■ LASH	■ LASSITUDE	■ LATENT
■ LATITUDE	■ LAUDATORY	■ LAVISH	■ LEAVEN	■ LEER

lapse	[læps]
【考法】	*n.* 小过失：a **slight error** typically due to forgetfulness or inattention
例	a lapse in table manner 餐桌礼仪的小过错
近	blunder, fumble, gaffe, miscue, oversight, peccadillo

largesse [lɑːrˈdʒes]
【考法】 *n.* 慷慨：**liberality** in giving or willingness to give
例 be noted for his largesse 因慷慨而闻名
近 bountifulness, generosity, munificence, openhandedness, philanthropy
反 miserliness, parsimony, penury, stinginess 小气

lash [læʃ]
【考法】 *v.* 猛击，撞击：to **strike** against **with force** or violence
例 All night long a barrage of rain lashed the windows. 倾盆大雨整夜敲击着窗户。
近 baste, hammer, lace, lambaste, punch

lassitude [ˈlæsɪtuːd]
【考法】 *n.* 乏力，没精打采：a state or feeling of weariness, **diminished energy**, or listlessness
例 Symptoms of anaemia include general fatigue and lassitude. 贫血的通常症状包括体虚和乏力。
近 collapse, exhaustion, frazzle, languor, listlessness, stupor, torpor, prostration
反 verve, vim, animation, vitality 有活力

latent [ˈleɪtnt]
【考法】 *adj.* 潜在的，不活跃的：present or **potential** but **not evident** or active
例 a latent infection 潜伏性传染病 ‖ He has a latent talent for acting that he hasn't had a chance to express yet. 他有着潜在的表演的天赋，只不过他还没有机会来表现这一才能。
近 dormant, fallow, inert, inoperative
反 apparent, evident, manifest, obvious, plain 明显的；active 活跃的
派 latency *n.* 潜伏期

latitude [ˈlætɪtuːd]
【考法】 *n.* (行动或言论)自由：**freedom** from normal restraints, limitations, or regulations
例 Students are allowed considerable latitude in choosing courses. 学生在选课时被给予相当大的自由度。
近 authorization, license, freedom, leeway, free hand
反 limitation 限制；custody 监护，拘留

laudatory [ˈlɔːdətɔːri]
【考法】 *adj.* 表示赞扬的：of, relating to, or expressing **praise**
例 a laudatory review of the new play 对新剧目的赞扬性评论
近 adulatory, commendatory, complimentary, extolling, eulogistic, panegyric
反 derogatory, depreciatory, disparaging, pejorative 贬低的
派 laudable *adj.* 值得赞扬的

lavish [ˈlævɪʃ]
【考法1】 *adj.* 奢侈的，大量的，无节制的：characterized by or produced with **extravagance and profusion**
例 lavish buffet 奢侈的自助餐
近 copious, exuberant, gushing, lush, luxuriant, opulent, profuse, riotous
反 moderate, modest, reasonable, temperate 适度的，合理的
【考法2】 *vt.* 挥霍，浪费：to **give readily** and in large quantities; to use up **carelessly**
例 a great actor who lavished his talent in lousy movies 将才华浪费在低劣电影上的影星
近 blow, dissipate, fritter, misspend, squander, waste
反 conserve 节约

leaven [ˈlevn]
【考法】 *vt.* 在…中加入轻松、活泼或变更的因素：to **mingle** or **permeate** with some modifying, alleviating, or vivifying element
例 He needs to leaven his speeches with more humor. 他需要在演讲中再加入点幽默元素。
近 imbue, infuse, ingrain, inoculate, inspire, permeate, steep, suffuse
反 extract 抽取

leer [lɪr]
【考法】 *vi.* 一瞥，斜眼看：to cast a **sidelong** glance
例 He gave her a leering look. 他瞥了她一眼。
近 squint
反 gape, gaze, glare, goggle, stare 盯着看

Unit 10

leery [ˈlɪri]
【考法】 *adj.* 怀疑的, 不信任的: **suspicious** or distrustful; wary
例 be leery of strangers 对陌生人存有怀疑
近 dubious, distrustful, skeptical, suspicious, wary
反 credulous 轻信的

legacy [ˈlegəsi]
【考法】 *n.* 遗产: something **handed down** from an **ancestor** or a predecessor or from the past
例 the legacy of the ancient philosophers 古代哲学家们的思想遗产
近 bequest, heritage, patrimony

lucrative [ˈluːkrətɪv]
【考法】 *adj.* 有利可图的: yielding a **profit**
例 a lucrative marketing strategy 一套赢利的市场策略
近 profitable, remunerative
反 unprofitable 不赚钱的

legion [ˈliːdʒən]
【考法】 *adj.* 大量的: many, **numerous**
例 The problems are legion. 问题不计其数。
近 beaucoup, multifold, multitudinous, numerous
反 few, lack in number 少量的

lenient [ˈliːniənt]
【考法】 *adj.* 宽大仁慈的: inclined not to be harsh or strict; **merciful**, generous, or indulgent
例 the lenient sentences 仁慈的审判
近 clement, gentle, merciful, mild, sparing, tender, tolerant
反 harsh, merciless, severe, strict 残酷的, 严厉的
派 lenience *n.* 仁慈

lethal [ˈliːθl]
【考法】 *adj.* 非常有害的, 致命的: **extremely harmful**; devastating
例 This dagger is lethal. 这把匕首是致命的武器。 ‖ launch a lethal attack 发动致命的进攻
近 baleful, deadly, deathly, fatal, mortal, murderous, pestilent, terminal, vital
反 innocuous 无害的; healthy, salubrious, wholesome 有益健康的

lethargic [ləˈθɑːrdʒɪk]
【考法】 *adj.* 没精打采的, 行动迟缓的: of, relating to, or characterized by lethargy, **sluggish**
例 A big nice meal always makes me feel lethargic and sleepy. 一顿大餐吃完总是让我既慵懒又想睡。
近 dull, inert, quiescent, sluggish, torpid
反 dynamic, energetic, robust, vigorous 有精力的; active 活跃的

levelheaded [ˌlevl ˈhedɪd]
【考法】 *adj.* 明智的: characteristically self-composed and **sensible**
例 a levelheaded assessment of the problem 对于问题的一个明智的评估
近 informed, justified, logical, rational, reasonable, sensible, sober, valid, well-founded
反 foolish 愚蠢的; groundless, invalid, unfounded, unjustified, unsound 没有根据的, 理由不充分的

levity [ˈlevəti]
【考法】 *n.* 轻浮: excessive or unseemly **frivolity**
例 The teachers disapprove of any displays of levity during school assemblies. 老师们不允许学生在学校聚会中表现出任何轻浮的态度。
近 facetiousness, flightiness, flippancy, frivolousness, frothiness, silliness
反 earnestness, gravity, seriousness, soberness, solemnity 严肃

liability [ˌlaɪə ˈbɪləti]
【考法】 *n.* 责任: the quality or state of being **liable**
例 The company is trying to reduce its liability in this case. 在这个案件中, 公司试图减少他们的责任。
近 accountability, answerability, responsibility
反 immunity 豁免权

List 15

"每当我们对未来充满了各种美好的期望与幻想时，就该反思一下自己现在的努力是否配得上这幻境中的将来。莫问收获，但问耕耘。"

（刘宜君，2009 年 10 月，Verbal 730，Quantitative 800，
录取院校：斯坦福大学，计算机系）

Unit 1

| ■ LIBERAL | ■ LIBERTINE | ■ LICENTIOUS | ■ LIKEN | ■ LIMBER |
| ■ LIMP | ■ LIMPID | ■ LINGER | ■ LISSOME | ■ LIST |

liberal ［ˈlɪbərəl］

【考法 1】 *adj.* 思想前卫的：**not bound** by traditional ways or beliefs
例 parents who take a very liberal attitude toward letting their children stay out late 思想开放，同意让他们的小孩晚归的家长们
近 nonconventional, nonorthodox, nontraditional, open-minded, progressive, radical
反 conservative, conventional, hidebound, old-fashioned, stodgy, traditional 守旧的，传统的

【考法 2】 *adj.* 慷慨的，大方的：marked by **generosity**
例 They were liberal in their help. 他们慷慨相助。
近 charitable, munificent, unselfish, unsparing, unstinting
反 closefisted, miserly, niggardly, parsimonious, stingy, tightfisted 吝啬的

libertine ［ˈlɪbərtiːn］

【考法】 *n.* 放荡不羁者：one who acts **without moral restraint**; a dissolute person
例 The legend of Don Juan depicts him as a playboy and libertine. 有关唐璜的传说把他描绘成一个放荡不羁的花花公子。
近 backslider, debaucher, decadent, deviate, pervert, profligate
反 ascetic 禁欲者

licentious ［laɪˈsenʃəs］

【考法】 *adj.* 放荡的，性欲强的：**lacking** legal or moral **restraints**; having a strong sexual, desire
例 a moralist who decried what she regarded as the licentious and corrupt culture of the entertainment industry 一个公开谴责在她看来无比堕落和放荡的娱乐圈文化的道德家
近 concupiscent, horny, lascivious, lecherous, libidinous, lubricious, salacious, wanton
反 frigid, undersexed 性冷淡的
派 licentiousness *n.* 放荡

liken ［ˈlaɪkən］

【考法】 *vt.* 显示相似，把…比作：to see, mention, or **show as similar**; compare
例 Life is often likened to a journey. 生活经常被比作一次旅行。
近 analogize, bracket, equate, equalize
反 contrast 对比，对照以产生反差

limber ［ˈlɪmbər］

【考法】 *adj.* 可塑的，柔软的：capable of being shaped: **flexible**
例 She shaped the basket out of limber branches. 她用柔软的树枝编了一个筐。
近 flexible, lissome, lithesome, pliable, pliant, supple
反 inflexible, rigid, stiff, stiffened 僵硬的

limp ［lɪmp］

【考法 1】 *adj.* 柔软的，松散的：**lacking firm** texture, substance, or structure
例 Her hair hung limp about her shoulders. 她的头发松散地垂在肩上。
近 droopy, flaccid, floppy, lank, yielding
反 firm, stiff, sturdy, tense 坚硬的；resilient 有弹性的

【考法2】 *vi.* 跛行，艰难地行走：to move or proceed **haltingly or unsteadily**

例 The project limped along with half its previous funding. 项目靠着之前一半的资金艰难地进行着。

近 blunder, bumble, lumber, plod, struggle, stumble, trudge

limpid [ˈlɪmpɪd]

【考法】 *adj.* 透明清澈的：characterized by **transparent clearness**

例 limpid streams 清澈的小溪

近 crystal, clear, lucent, pellucid, transparent

反 cloudy, murky, opaque, unclear, turbid 模糊不清的

linger [ˈlɪŋgər]

【考法】 *vi.* 磨蹭，闲荡：to **proceed slowly**; saunter

例 Fans lingered outside the door. 粉丝们在门外徘徊。

近 crawl, creep, dally, dawdle, lag, loiter

反 hurry, run, rush 飞奔

派 lingering *adj.* 闲荡的

lissome [ˈlɪsəm]

【考法1】 *adj.* 柔软的：**easily bent**; supple

例 Rattan is such a lissome material that it can be used for all manner of furniture and baskets. 藤是一种非常柔软的材料，可以被用于形形色色的家具和篮子之中。

近 flexible, limber, lithe, pliable, pliant, supple

反 solid 坚硬的；inflexible, rigid, stiff, stiffened 僵硬的

【考法2】 *adj.* 敏捷的，轻盈的：having the ability to **move with ease**; limber

例 a lissome ballerina 身姿轻盈的女芭蕾舞演员

近 agile, featly, feline, gracile, lithesome, nimble

反 awkward, clumsy, graceless, ungainly 笨拙的

list [lɪst]

【考法】 *v.* (使)倾斜：to set or cause to be **at an angle**

例 The sudden lift of the load on the deck listed the ship badly. 甲板上货物被突然提起，使船陡然倾斜。

近 angle, cant, heel, incline, pitch, slant, slope, tilt, tip

反 erect 竖立

Unit 2

■ LITHE	■ LOATH	■ LOATHE	■ LOFTY	■ LOLL
■ LOPSIDED	■ LOQUACIOUS	■ LOUTISH	■ LUBRICATE	■ LUCID

lithe [laɪð]

【考法1】 *adj.* 敏捷的，轻盈的：characterized by easy flexibility and **grace**

例 lithe dancers 轻盈优雅的舞者

近 agile, featly, feline, gracile, lightsome, nimble

反 awkward, clumsy, graceless, ungainly 笨拙的

【考法2】 *adj.* 柔软的：**easily bent** or flexed

例 lithe branches 柔软的枝条

近 flexible, limber, pliable, pliant, supple

反 solid 坚硬的；inflexible, rigid, stiff, stiffened 僵硬的

loath [loʊθ]

【考法】 *adj.* 不情愿的，讨厌的：unwilling or **reluctant**; disinclined

例 I was loath to accept the fact that he had been killed in a terrorist attack. 我极不情愿地接受了他在一场恐怖袭击中丧生的事实。

近 disinclined, indisposed, reluctant, reticent

反 eager 渴望的；disposed, inclined 有意向的

loathe [loʊð]

【考法】 *vt.* 厌恶：to **dislike** someone or something greatly; abhor

例 I loathe having to do this. 我鄙视不得不这样做。

近 abhor, abominate, despise, detest, execrate

反 adore, love 热爱

派 loathsome *adj.* 令人讨厌的

lofty [ˈlɔːfti]

【考法 1】 *adj.* 崇高的：**elevated** in character and spirit, noble

例 lofty ideals 崇高的理想

近 chivalrous, elevated, greathearted, high-minded, magnanimous, sublime

反 base, debased, ignominious, mean 可耻的

【考法 2】 *adj.* 自大的：having a feeling of **superiority** that shows itself in an overbearing attitude

例 lofty distain 自大的不满

近 assumptive, bumptious, haughty, lordly, peremptory, pompous, presumptuous, supercilious, superior

反 humble, lowly, modest 谦逊的，低调的

loll [lɑːl]

【考法】 *vi.* 偷懒，打发时间：to spend time **doing nothing**

例 Some members of the decorating committee were hard at work, and others were just lolling about. 装修队的一部分人在很努力地工作，另一些则在偷懒。

近 dally, dawdle, drone, laze

lopsided [ˌlɑːpˈsaɪdɪd]

【考法】 *adj.* 不平衡的，不协调的：**lacking in balance**, symmetry, or proportion

例 The arrangement of the furniture was lopsided. 家具的摆放太不协调了。‖ a lopsided score of 4-0 四比零的压倒性比分

近 asymmetric, disproportional, irregular, off-balance, unbalanced, unequal

反 balanced 平衡的；symmetrical 对称的

loquacious [ləˈkweɪʃəs]

【考法】 *adj.* 话多的：given to fluent or **excessive talk**

例 Sometimes the loquacious talk show host barely lets her guests get a word in. 有时候多话的脱口秀主持人让她的嘉宾一句话都插不进来。

近 chatty, conversational, gabby, garrulous, talkative, voluble

反 laconic, reserved, reticent, taciturn, uncommunicative 话少的

派 loquaciousness, loquacity *n.* 话多

loutish [ˈlaʊtɪʃ]

【考法】 *adj.* 粗鲁的：having the characteristics of a lout; **awkward, stupid, and boorish**

例 a boy with a loutish air 一个举止粗鲁的男孩

近 boorish, churlish, clumsy, crude, discourteous, uncouth, uncivilized, uncultured, unrefined

反 courteous, civilized, genteel, graceful, polished, refined, urbane 有教养的

派 lout *n.* 举止粗鲁的人

lubricate [ˈluːbrɪkeɪt]

【考法】 *vt.* 使润滑：to coat（something）with a slippery substance in order to **reduce friction**

例 lubricate the gears 给齿轮打润滑油

近 grease, oil, slick, smooth, wax

派 lubricant *n.* 润滑剂

lucid [ˈluːsɪd]

【考法】 *adj.* 表达清晰的，简单易懂的：**easily understood**

例 The teaching assistant tried to make his instructions as lucid as possible so that everyone would understand what to do. 助教努力使自己的指令容易理解，从而让所有人都知道应该要干什么。

近 apprehensible, clear, comprehensible, intelligible, palpable, patent, pellucid, plain, understandable

反 ambiguous, enigmatic, equivocal, indistinct, obfuscated, obscure, unclear 模糊不明确的

Unit 3

■ LUG　　　　■ LUGUBRIOUS　　　　■ LULL　　　　■ LULLABY　　　　■ LUMBER
■ LUMINARY　　　■ LURCH　　　　■ LURK　　　　■ LUSH　　　　■ LUSTROUS

lug [lʌg]

【考法】 *vt.* 费力搬运：to carry **laboriously**

例 I don't understand why he's always lugging all of his books around when his locker is right over there. 我真搞不懂为什么他总是明明在有锁柜的情况下还随身扛着所有的书。

近 bear, cart, convey, ferry, haul, pack, tote, transport

lugubrious [lə'ɡuːbrɪəs]

【考法】 *adj.* （故作夸张的）悲哀的：**mournful**, dismal, or gloomy, especially to an exaggerated or ludicrous degree

例 his lugubrious tear-stained face 他忧郁而带着泪痕的脸庞

近 deploring, doleful, dolorous, lamentable, melancholy, morose, plaintive, rueful, saturnine, sullen, woeful

反 cheerful, delighted, jocund, jovial 快乐的

lull [lʌl]

【考法1】 *n.* 相对平静时期，间隙：a **momentary halt** in an activity

例 the lull before the storm 暴风雨前的平静

近 break, breath, interruption, recess

【考法2】 *vt.* 使镇静，使安心：to **free from distress** or disturbance

例 The absence of attacks for such an extended period had lulled the nation into a false sense of security. 长期以来没有遭受攻击让这个国家产生了一种错误的安全感。

近 allay, balm, becalm, compose, lullaby, quiet, salve, settle, soothe, still, tranquilize

反 agitate, discompose, disquiet, disturb, perturb, upset, vex 打扰，扰乱

lullaby ['lʌləbaɪ]

【考法】 *vt.* 使镇静，使安心：to **free from distress** or disturbance

例 Reclining peacefully on the deck, he was lullabied by the gentle motion of the ship. 他躺卧在甲板上，随着船轻轻的颠簸放松下来。

近 allay, balm, becalm, compose, lull, quiet, salve, settle, soothe, still, tranquilize

反 agitate, discompose, disquiet, disturb, perturb, upset, vex 打扰，扰乱

lumber ['lʌmbər]

【考法1】 *vi.* 笨拙地行动：to walk or move with heavy **clumsiness**

例 The elephant lumbered through the jungle. 大象缓缓地穿越丛林。

近 flounder, plod, stumble, trudge

反 glide, slide 轻松地滑动

【考法2】 *vt.* 使负担（从而拖累）：to place a weight or **burden** on

例 lumber the expedition with unnecessary equipment and supplies 不必要的仪器和补给品给此次远征徒增了许多负担

近 burden, encumber, freight, lade, laden, saddle, weight

反 disburden, discharge, disencumber, unlade, unload 卸下，解脱

luminary ['luːmɪneri]

【考法】 *n.* 杰出人物：a person who has achieved **eminence** in a specific field

例 Buddhist luminary 佛学大师 || Luminaries from the worlds of sports, entertainment, and politics were at the gala. 全球体育界、娱乐圈和政界的名人都出席了此次盛会。

近 celebrity, eminence, figure, icon, notability, star, superstar

反 nobody, nonentity 小人物

lurch [lɜːrtʃ]

【考法】 *vi.* 蹒跚：to move forward while **swaying** from side to side

例 The ship lurched in the storm. 船在风暴中摇摆前行。

近 careen, dodder, falter, reel, stagger, stumble, teeter, totter, waddle

反 progress smoothly 平稳前进；march, stride, swagger 游行，大步走

lurk [lɜːrk]

【考法】 *vi.* 潜伏：to **lie in wait** in a place of concealment especially for an evil purpose

例 Dangers lurk in the path of wilderness. 在这条荒野的小路上隐伏着危险。

近 ambush, snake, steal

反 appear, come out 出来

lush [lʌʃ]

【考法】 *adj.* 多产的：**producing abundantly**

例 His lush fields were the envy of neighboring farmers. 他富饶多产的土地让邻居羡慕嫉妒恨。

近 cornucopian, fecund, fruitful, productive, prolific, rich

反 barren, dead, infertile, sterile, unproductive 贫瘠的

lustrous [ˈlʌstrəs]

【考法】 *adj.* 有光泽的：having a **shiny** surface or finish

例 lustrous black hair 乌黑光亮的头发

近 brilliant, burnished, gleaming, glistening, glossy, polished, refulgent, rubbed, shining, sleek, splendid

反 dim, dull, lackluster, lusterless 昏暗的

Unit 4

■ LUXURIOUS	■ LYRIC	■ MACABRE	■ MACERATE	■ MACULATE
■ MAELSTROM	■ MAGNIFICENT	■ MALADROIT	■ MALAISE	■ MALCONTENT

luxurious [lʌɡˈʒʊriəs]

【考法】 *adj.* 奢侈的：given to or marked by **excessive gratification** of one's desires

例 He squandered his family fortune in the relentless satisfaction of his luxurious tastes . 他为满足自己奢侈的品味而挥霍家族的财产。

近 decadent, indulgent, overindulgent, self-indulgent, sybaritic

反 abstemious, abstinent 克制的

派 luxury *n.* 豪华；奢侈，奢侈品

lyric [ˈlɪrɪk]

【考法】 *adj.* 如诗歌般流畅甜美的：having a pleasantly flowing quality **suggestive of poetry or music**

例 The film's lyric photography really enhanced its romantic mood. 电影中如诗歌般的图像效果着实增强了浪漫的氛围。

近 euphonious, lyrical, mellifluous, mellow, melodious, musical, poetical

反 prosaic, prose 无聊乏味的

派 lyrics *n.* 歌词

macabre [məˈkɑːbrə]

【考法】 *adj.* 恐怖的：suggesting the **horror of death** and decay; gruesome

例 Impressively, Plants vs. Zombies presented a supposedly macabre theme in such an enjoyable way. 令人难忘的是，《植物大战僵尸》将一个本应该十分恐怖的主题用一种如此欢乐的方式呈现出来。

近 appalling, atrocious, dreadful, ghastly, gruesome, hideous, horrific, nightmarish, terrific

反 agreeable, delightful, enjoyable, pleasant 令人愉悦的

macerate [ˈmæsəreɪt]

【考法】 *vt.* 浸泡(以软化)：to make soft by **soaking or steeping** in a liquid

例 macerate the sample in ethanol 用乙醇浸软试样

近 drench, drown, impregnate, saturate, sodden, sop, souse, steep

反 wring 拧干；dehydrate, desiccate, parch, sorch, sear 烤干，烤焦

maculate [ˈmækjəleɪt]

【考法】 *vt.* 使有斑点，弄脏；玷污，损坏：to **spot**; blemish

例 Her reputation was maculated after the affair with a married man. 自从被指与一个已婚男士有染之后，她的名声受到了影响。

近 besmirch, dot, dirty, soil, spot, stain

反 clean, cleanse, purify, wash 清洗，弄干净

派 maculated *adj.* 有斑点的

maelstrom [ˈmeɪlstrɑːm]

【考法】 *n.* 混乱、动荡的局势：a violent or **turbulent** situation

例 the maelstrom of war 战争带来的乱世

近 chaos, disorder, pandemonium, tumult, tumoil, upheaval, uproar

反 calm 风平浪静

magnificent [mæɡˈnɪfɪsnt]

【考法】 *adj.* 壮丽的：**strikingly** beautiful or **impressive**

例 a magnificent cathedral 宏伟壮观的大教堂

近 august, epic, glorious, grand, imperial, imposing, massive, monumental, noble, regal, splendid

反 humble, unimpressive 平凡的

派 magnificence *n.* 壮丽，壮观

| **maladroit** | [ˌmælə'drɔɪt] |

【考法】 *adj.* 笨拙的：lacking or showing a **lack of nimbleness** in using one's hands

例 a maladroit movement 笨拙的动作

近 awkward, bumbling, clumsy, fumbled, gauche, graceless, heavy-handed, inept, unhandy

反 adroit, ambidexterous, deft, dexterous, handy 灵巧的

| **malaise** | [mə'leɪz] |

【考法】 *n.* 不舒服：a vague feeling of **bodily discomfort**, as at the beginning of an illness

例 He complained of depression, headaches and malaise. 他抱怨说感到沮丧、头痛和身体不适。

近 debility, decrepitude, disease, feebleness, infirmity, infirmness, sickliness, unhealthiness

| **malcontent** | [ˌmælkən'tent] |

【考法】 *n.* 不满分子：one who is in active **opposition** to an established order or government

adj. 不满的：**dissatisfied** with the existing state of affairs

例 The chaos was caused by a handful of malcontents. 混乱是由一小撮不满分子引起的。 || The film follows three malcontent teenagers around Paris. 电影围绕着三个不满现实的青少年在巴黎展开。

近 complainer, faultfinder, grouch, rebel; discontented, discontent, disgruntled, displeased, dissatisfied, ungratified

反 contented, fulfilled, gratified, pleased, satisfied 满意的

Unit 5

| ■ MALICIOUS | ■ MALIGN | ■ MALINGER | ■ MALLEABLE | ■ MALODOROUS |
| ■ MANDATORY | ■ MANGLE | ■ MANGY | ■ MANIA | ■ MANIFEST |

| **malicious** | [mə'lɪʃəs] |

【考法】 *adj.* 恶意的：given to, marked by, or arising from malice; **deliberately harmful**

例 spread malicious gossips 散播恶意的流言蜚语

近 bad, cruel, despiteful, evil, malevolent, malign, mean, nasty, spiteful, vicious, virulent, wicked

反 benevolent, benign, benignant, charitable, kind, kindly 善良的，仁慈的

| **malign** | [mə'laɪn] |

【考法 1】 *adj.* 恶意的：having or showing a desire to **cause** someone pain or **suffering** for the sheer enjoyment of it

例 Both parties to the divorce showed a malign desire to make each other's future life utterly miserable. 离婚双方都表露出了恶毒的愿望，希望对方未来的生活陷入彻底的悲剧之中。

近 bad, cruel, despiteful, evil, malevolent, malicious, mean, nasty, spiteful, vicious, virulent, wicked

反 benevolent, benign, benignant, charitable, kind, kindly 善良的，仁慈的

【考法 2】 *vt.* 诽谤：to **utter injuriously** misleading or false reports about: speak evil of

例 the belief that it is possible to win an election without maligning anyone 一种信念，那就是不需要诽谤他人而赢得选举是可能的

近 asperse, blacken, calumniate, defame, libel, smear, traduce, vilify

反 acclaim, applaud, eulogize, extol, laud, praise 赞美；defend, vindicate 辩护

| **malinger** | [mə'lɪŋgər] |

【考法】 *vi.* 装病以逃避工作：to **pretend** or exaggerate incapacity or **illness** (as to avoid duty or work)

例 He claims he's ill, but I think he's just malingering. 他声称他病了，但我觉得他是装的。

近 goldbrick, shirk

反 confront, face, meet 面对

派 malingerer *n.* 装病以逃避工作的人

| **malleable** | ['mæliəbl] |

【考法】 *adj.* 可塑的：**capable of being** extended or **shaped** by beating with a hammer or by the pressure of rollers

adj. 易控制的：**capable of being** altered or **controlled** by outside forces or influences

例 a malleable metal 有延展性的金属 || The cult leader took advantage of the malleable, compliant personalities of his followers. 这个头目利用了他的信徒们容易被控制和顺从的特征。

近 moldable, waxy; ductile, elastic, fluid, modifiable, plastic, pliable, pliant, supple, variable

反 adamant, intractable, recalcitrant, refractory, ungovernable, unmanageable, unruly 难管制的

malodorous [ˌmælˈoʊdərəs]

【考法】 *adj.* 恶臭的：having an **unpleasant smell**

例 American musteline will eject a malodorous fluid when startled. 美洲鼬科动物在受到惊吓时会喷出有恶臭味的液体。

近 fetid, foul, frowsy, funky, fusty, musty, noisome, rank, reeky, smelly, stinking, stinky

反 ambrosial, aromatic, fragrant, perfumed, redolent, savory, scented, sweet 芳香的，有香味的

派 malodor *n.* 恶臭

mandatory [ˈmændətɔːri]

【考法】 *adj.* 强制的：**forcing** one's **compliance** or participation

例 GRE test is mandatory for all students , regardless of their nationality, who wish to apply for graduate schools in the United States. GRE 是每个申请美国研究生院的学生（无论国籍）所必须参加的考试。

近 compulsory, forced, imperative, incumbent, involuntary, necessary, obligatory, peremptory, required

反 elective, optional, voluntary 可自由选择的，选修的

mangle [ˈmæŋgl]

【考法】 *vt.* 弄砸：to **ruin** or spoil through ineptitude or ignorance

例 The orchestra had completely mangled Bach's music . 乐队彻底演砸了巴赫的音乐。

近 blow, bumble, bungle, butcher, fumble , mar, mess, ruin, foul up, screw up

mangy [ˈmeɪndʒi]

【考法】 *adj.* 卑劣的：mean; **contemptible**

例 a mangy trick 卑鄙的手段

近 base, contemptible, debased, despicable, detestable, execrable, mean, sordid, squalid

反 lofty, noble, upright, venerable, virtuous 正直的，有道德的

mania [ˈmeɪniə]

【考法】 *n.* 热衷，狂热：an excessively **intense enthusiasm**, interest, or desire; a craze

例 a mania for neatness 强烈的洁癖

近 ardor, craze, enthusiasm, fervor, obsession, passion, preoccupation, prepossession, zeal

反 apathy, indifference, nonchalance, torpor 冷漠，麻木

派 manic *adj.* 疯狂的

manifest [ˈmænɪfest]

【考法 1】 *adj.* 显然的，明显易懂的：clearly apparent to the sight or **understanding**; obvious

例 He is a manifest poseur . 他显然是个装模作样的人。

近 apparent, clear, distinct, evident, lucid, obvious, palpable, patent, perspicuous, plain, transparent

反 cryptic, enigmatic, indistinct, mysterious, obfuscated, obscure, unclear 晦涩的，难懂的

【考法 2】 *v.* 显现，显露：to **make evident** or certain by showing or displaying

例 His frustration is often manifested by a minor facial tic . 他的沮丧通常会从脸部的细微抽搐中表现出来。

近 bespeak, betray, demonstrate, display, evince, expose, reveal

反 conceal, hide 隐藏

派 manifesto *n.* 宣言，声明

Unit 6

| ■ MANIPULATE | ■ MANNERED | ■ MANUMIT | ■ MANUSCRIPT | ■ MAR |
| ■ MALFEASANCE | ■ MARTINET | ■ MARVEL | ■ MASH | ■ MASQUERADE |

manipulate [məˈnɪpjuleɪt]

【考法】 *vt.* 巧妙处理；暗中操控：to influence or manage shrewdly or **deviously**

例 He manipulated public opinion in his favor . 他巧妙地将大众观点导向了有利于他的一边。
manipulate a foreign language 熟练地掌握外语

近 machinate, maneuver

派 manipulation *n.* 操纵，控制

mannered [ˈmænərd]

【考法】 *adj.* 不自然的，做作的：having an **artificial** or stilted character

例 a mannered speech 做作的演讲

近 affected, artificial, assumed, factitious, fake, feigned, pretended, pseudo, sham, spurious

反 natural 自然的；artless, genuine, unfeigned 真诚的

manumit [ˌmænjuˈmɪt]

【考法】 vt. 解放（奴隶）：to **release from slavery** or bondage

例 Though he was an outspoken defender of liberty, this son of Virginia did not manumit his own slaves until he was on his deathbed. 尽管这位维吉尼亚之子公开地支持自由，但他直到临死前才释放自己的奴隶。

近 free, emancipate, enfranchise, liberate, loose, release, unbind, unchain, unshackle

反 detain 拘留；enchain, enfetter, enslave 奴役

manuscript [ˈmænjuskrɪpt]

【考法】 n. 手稿：a book, document, or other composition **written by hand**

例 beautiful Latin manuscript on the school's diplomas 学校毕业证书上美丽的手写拉丁文

近 calligraphy, penmanship, script

反 print, type, typewriting 打字稿

mar [mɑːr]

【考法】 vt. 破坏，削弱：to **impair** the soundness, perfection, or integrity of; spoil

例 The once flatroad surface is now marred by numerous potholes. 曾经平整的路面如今被坑洞所破坏。‖ an election marred by sexual scandal 被性丑闻蒙上阴影的选举

近 blemish, compromise, cripple, damage, deface, disfigure, harm, hurt, impair, injure, spoil, vitiate

反 doctor, fix, mend, patch, renovate, repair 修补；adorn, beautify, bedeck, embellish, garnish 装饰

malfeasance [mælˈfiːzns]

【考法】 n. 非法行为：improper or **illegal behavior**

例 administrative malfeasance 行政违法行为

近 misconduct, misbehavior, misdoing, wrongdoing

martinet [ˌmɑːrtnˈet]

【考法】 n. 纪律严明之人：a **strict** disciplinarian

例 He's a retired lieutenant and a bit of a martinet. 他是一个退役的中尉，并且是一个有点纪律严明的人。

近 disciplinarian, purist, stickler

反 reprobate 放纵的人

marvel [ˈmɑːrvl]

【考法 1】 n. 令人惊奇的事物：one that evokes **surprise, admiration, or wonder**

例 The robot is a marvel of modern engineering. 机器人是现代工程领域的奇迹。

近 flash, miracle, phenomenon, prodigy, splendor

【考法 2】 v. (因为壮观、美丽等而)表示惊讶：to **feel amazement** or bewilderment at or about

例 marvel at the tranquility of Chopin's nocturne 惊叹于肖邦夜曲中体现出来的宁静祥和

近 gape, gaze, goggle, wonder

派 marvelous adj. 令人惊奇的

mash [mæʃ]

【考法】 vt. 捣碎：to cause to become a **pulpy mass**

例 mash potatoes before adding it to the mixture 在混合之前捣碎土豆

近 crush, grind, smash, squeeze

反 agglomerate 聚集成团

masquerade [ˌmæskəˈreɪd]

【考法】 n. 面具，伪装：a **display** of emotion or behavior that is **insincere** or intended to deceive

vi. 伪装，掩饰：to **disguise** oneself

例 masquerade as a policeman 化装成警察

近 facade, guise, mask, pretense, semblance, show, veil; act, disguise, pose, pretend

反 betray, disclose, reveal, unmask 揭露

Unit 7

■ MASTERY　　　　■ MATRICULATE　　　■ MAUDLIN　　　　　■ MAVEN　　　　　■ MAVERICK

■ MAWKISH　　　　■ MEAGER　　　　　■ MEAN　　　　　　■ MEANDER　　　　■ MEASLY

mastery [ˈmæstəri]

【考法】 n. 技艺超群，精通：possession or display of **great skill** or technique

例 She has mastery of several languages. 她熟练掌握多种语言。

近 deftness, dexterity, finesse, prowess, virtuosity

反 amateurishness 业余

派 masterful adj. 精通的

matriculate [məˈtrɪkjuleɪt]

【考法】 *v.* 录取：to **admit or be admitted** into a group, especially a college or university

例 matriculate at Princeton 在普林斯顿入学

近 admit, enroll, inscribe, recruit, register

反 commence, graduate 毕业；delist 除名

派 matriculation *n.* 录取

maudlin [ˈmɔːdlɪn]

【考法】 *adj.* 过于感伤的：effusively or **tearfully sentimental**

例 Some naive students display an almost maudlin concern for the welfare of animals while ignoring basic social inequity. 一些幼稚的学生忽视根本的社会不公平问题，而对动物的权益表现出一种多愁善感的忧虑。

近 lachrymose, mawkish, mushy, overemotional, sentimental, tearful

反 blithe, cheerful, jocund, jovial, jubilant 高兴的；apathetic, impassive, indifferent 冷漠的

maven [ˈmeɪvn]

【考法】 *n.* 专家：one who is **experienced** or knowledgeable: expert

例 As an investment maven, he was doing well even when the market was doing poorly. 作为一名投资高手，他在市场不景气的时候也能赚钱。

近 ace, adept, connoisseur, expert, maestro, master, professional, proficient, virtuoso

反 amateur, dabbler, dilettante 业余爱好者

maverick [ˈmævərɪk]

【考法】 *n.* 特立独行之人：a person who **does not conform** to generally accepted standards or customs
adj. 标新立异的，不合常规的：**deviating** from commonly accepted beliefs or practices

例 a maverick view on marriage 关于婚姻的非传统看法

近 bohemian, deviant, heretic, iconoclast, nonconformist; dissentient, dissenting, dissident, heterodox, iconoclastic, unorthodox

反 conformer, conformist, conventionalist 遵从传统的人；conforming, conventional, orthodox 遵从传统的

mawkish [ˈmɔːkɪʃ]

【考法】 *adj.* 过度伤感的：excessively and objectionably **sentimental**

例 a mawkish love story 令人伤感的爱情故事

近 lachrymose, maudlin, mushy, overemotional, sentimental, tearful

反 blithe, cheerful, jocund, jovial, jubilant 高兴的；apathetic, impassive, indifferent 冷漠的

meager [ˈmiːɡər]

【考法】 *adj.* 贫乏的：**deficient** in quantity, fullness, or extent; scanty

例 meager cultural resources 贫乏的文化资源

近 exiguous, niggardly, poor, scanty, scarce, skimpy, slender, slim, sparing, sparse, stingy

反 abundant, ample, bountiful, copious, generous, liberal, plenteous, plentiful 大量的，富足的

mean [miːn]

【考法 1】 *adj.* 卑贱的：**ignoble**; base

例 a mean trick to play on a credulous person 要在一个轻信别人的人身上的卑劣诡计

近 base, contemptible, despicable, detestable, dirty, dishonorable, execrable, ignominious, sordid

反 lofty, noble, venerable, virtuous 高尚的

【考法 2】 *adj.* 吝啬的：giving or **sharing** as **little** as possible

例 a mean child who hoarded all her toys 一个把她的所有玩具都藏起来的小气孩子

近 closefisted, mingy, miserly, niggardly, parsimonious, penurious, tightfisted, ungenerous

反 generous, liberal, munificent 慷慨的；extravagant, lavish, prodigal, profligate, spendthrift 浪费的

meander [miˈændər]

【考法】 *vi.* 闲逛，漫步：to move **aimlessly and idly** without fixed direction

例 meander along the river 沿着河闲逛 ‖ vagabonds meandering through life 漂泊一生的浪子

近 amble, cruise, drift, float, ramble, roam, saunter, stroll, wander

measly [ˈmiːzli]

【考法】 *adj.* 少得可怜的，微不足道的：so **small** or unimportant as to warrant little or no attention

例 The stingy man gave the parking attendant a measly tip. 那个吝啬男给了停车保安少得可怜的小费。

近 inconsequential, inconsiderable, insignificant, minute, paltry, peanut, petty, slight, trifling, trivial

反 big, consequential, considerable, significant 大量的，重要的

Unit 8

measured ['meʒərd]
【考法】 *adj.* 深思熟虑的，审慎的：deliberated, **calculated**
例 a measured response to the terrorist attack 就恐怖袭击做出的深思熟虑的反应
近 advised, calculated, considered, knowing, reasoned, studied, thoughtful, weighed
反 casual 随意的；uncalculated, unconsidered, unstudied 没仔细考虑过的

meddle ['medl]
【考法】 *vi.* 干涉，管闲事：to **intrude** into other people's affairs or business; interfere
例 Please stop meddling in my marriage. 请不要来干涉我的婚姻。
近 interfere, interlope, intermeddle, intrude, obtrude, poke, pry, snoop
反 disregard, ignore, neglect, omit, overlook 忽略，不理会
派 meddlesome *adj.* 爱管闲事的

mediate ['miːdieɪt]
【考法】 *vt.* 调解，调停：to intervene between two or more disputants in order to **bring about an agreement**, a settlement, or a compromise
例 mediate a labor-management dispute 调解劳工纠纷
近 conciliate, intercede, intermediate, interpose
反 arouse, encourage, excite, foment, incite, inflame, instigate, pique, spark, stimulate, stir 煽动激起
派 mediator *n.* 调停人

mediocre [ˌmiːdi'oʊkər]
【考法】 *adj.* 平庸的；质量中等偏下的：**moderate** to inferior in quality; ordinary
例 Without a desire for success, life is at best mediocre. 没有对成功的强烈渴望，人生最多也就是碌碌无为。
近 average, common, commonplace, fair, indifferent, medium, ordinary
反 outstanding, excellent, exceptional, extraordinary, impressive, superior 优秀的
派 mediocrity *n.* 平庸者；平庸

medley ['medli]
【考法】 *adj.* 大杂烩，混合物：an unorganized collection or **mixture** of various things
例 a medley of snack foods available on the buffet table 自助餐桌上供应着各式各样的小吃
近 agglomerate, collage, hodgepodge, jumble, montage, motley, muddle, salad, shuffle, variety, welter

meek [miːk]
【考法】 *adj.* 顺从的：easily imposed on; **submissive**
例 He may be self-effacing, but he certainly isn't meek. 他可能是个很低调的人，但他绝非软骨头。
近 compliant, docile, manageable, obedient, submissive, tractable
反 adamant, headstrong, intractable, obstinate, refractory, stubborn, unruly, unyielding 倔强的，不顺从的

meet [miːt]
【考法】 *adj.* 合适的：precisely adapted to a particular situation, need, or circumstance: **very proper**
例 In this case, splitting the winnings of the contested lottery ticket seems like a meet solution. 在这种情况下，平分有争议的彩票奖金或许是个合适的解决方案。
近 applicable, appropriate, apt, becoming, befitting, felicitous, fitting, proper, right, suitable
反 improper, inapplicable, inapposite, inappropriate, inapt, infelicitous, malapropos 不合适的

mellifluous [me'lɪfluəs]
【考法】 *adj.* (曲调)优美的：**smooth and sweet**
例 a mellifluous voice 甜美的嗓音
近 dulcet, euphonious, mellifluent, mellow, melodious
反 cacophonous, raspy 刺耳的

melodramatic [ˌmelədrə'mætɪk]

【考法】 *adj.* 感情夸张的，伤感的：**exaggeratedly emotional** or sentimental; histrionic

例 Our office drama queen yet again made the melodramatic declaration that she was contemplating suicide. 我们办公室的"影后"又一次在危言耸听了：这回她说她准备自杀。

近 dramatic, hammy, histrionic, mannered, pretentious, stagy

反 nondramatic, nontheatrical 平淡无奇的，非戏剧性的

menace ['menəs]

【考法】 *vt.* 威胁，使处于危险：to make a show of **intention to harm**; to place in danger

例 Stockpiles of nuclear weapons continue to menace the inhabitants of this planet. 大量的核武器继续威胁着这个行星上的居民。

近 compromise, hazard, imperil, jeopardize, peril, risk, threaten

反 rescue, save 救出

派 menacing *adj.* 具有威胁性的

Unit 9

■ MENDACIOUS ■ MENTOR ■ MERCENARY ■ MERCURIAL ■ MERITED
■ MESH ■ MESMERIC ■ METAMORPHOSE ■ METAPHYSICAL ■ METEORIC

mendacious [men'deɪʃəs]

【考法】 *adj.* 撒谎的，虚假的：telling or containing **lies**

例 mendacious tales about his adventures 关于他冒险的虚假传说

近 dishonest, deceitful, fallacious, lying, spurious, untruthful

反 authentic, honest, truthful, veracious 真实的，诚实的

mentor ['mentɔːr]

【考法】 *vt.* 教导，指导：to **give advice** and instruction regarding the course or process to be followed

例 We're looking for volunteers to mentor students in career planning. 我们正在寻找能指导学生职业规划的志愿者。

近 coach, counsel, lead, pilot, shepherd, show, tutor

反 comply, follow, observe 遵从

mercenary ['mɜːrsəneri]

【考法】 *adj.* 唯利是图的，贪婪的：motivated solely by a desire for **monetary or material gain**

例 Virtue flies from the heart of a mercenary man. 唯利是图的人没有美德可言。

近 acquisitive, avaricious, avid, covetous, grasping, greedy, moneygrubbing, rapacious

反 benevolent, generous, liberal, philanthropic, munificent 慷慨的

mercurial [mɜːr'kjʊriəl]

【考法】 *adj.* (情绪)善变的：characterized by rapid and unpredictable **changeableness of mood**

例 his mercurial temperament 他善变的脾气

近 capricious, changeful, fluctuating, fluid, mutable, temperamental, uncertain, variable, volatile

反 certain, constant, immutable, invariable, settled, stable, steady, unvarying 稳定的，不变的

merited ['merɪtɪd]

【考法】 *adj.* 应得的，理所当然的：being **what is called for** by accepted standards of right and wrong

例 a merited bonus 应得的奖金 ‖ The punishment, although harsh, was entirely merited. 虽然惩罚很严厉，但的确是应该的。

近 condign, deserved, due, fair, justified, right, warranted

反 undeserved, undue 不应得的；gratuitous, unjustified, unwarranted 没有根据的，无正当理由的

mesh [meʃ]

【考法】 *v.* 诱捕：to **catch** or hold as if in a net

例 Dolphins sometimes become meshed in fishnets. 有时海豚也会被渔网缠住。

近 enmesh, ensnare, ensnarl, entoil, entrap, net, snare, tangle, trap

反 disentangle, untangle 解开，使解脱

mesmeric	[mezˈmerɪk]
【考法】	*adj.* 令人着迷的，难以抗拒的：**attracting** and holding interest as if by a spell
例	the mesmeric recital 迷人的独奏
近	attractive, alluring, captivating, charming, drawing, enchanting, riveting
反	disgusting, loathesome, repellent, repulsive 令人厌恶的；unappealing, unattractive 没有吸引力的
派	mesmerism *n.* 催眠术，难以抗拒的魅力；mesmerize *vt.* 催眠

metamorphose	[ˌmetəˈmɔːrfouz]
【考法】	*vt.* (使)变形：to **change** into a different physical form especially by supernatural means
例	a science fiction story in which radiation metamorphoses people into giant bugs 一个描绘辐射将人变成了巨大虫子的科幻小说
近	alchemize, transfigure, transform, transmute, transpose, transubstantiate
反	remain 保持

metaphysical	[ˌmetəˈfɪzɪkl]
【考法1】	*adj.* 哲学上的，理论上的：dealing with or expressing a quality or **idea**
例	a work that deals with such metaphysical questions as the very nature of knowledge 一部探讨诸如"知识的本质是什么"的理论问题的著作
近	conceptual, ideal, ideational, notional, theoretical
反	concrete 具体的，实实在在的
【考法2】	*adj.* 非尘世的：of, relating to, or being part of a reality **beyond** the observable physical **universe**
例	a metaphysical world beyond the one in which we live 在我们居住的世界之外的"超然世界"
近	ethereal, heavenly, otherworldly, paranormal, preternatural, transcendental, unearthly, unworldly
反	mundane 世俗的；natural 自然界的

meteoric	[ˌmiːtiˈɔːrɪk]
【考法】	*adj.* 流星般迅速而短暂的：similar to a meteor in speed, brilliance, or **brevity**
例	a meteoric rise to fame 一夜成名
近	ephemeral, evanescent, fleeting, momentary, rapid, transient, transitory
反	enduring, lasting, permanent, prolonged 持久的

Unit 10

■ METHODICAL	■ METICULOUS	■ METTLE	■ MIFF	■ MIGRATORY
■ MILK	■ MIME	■ MIMIC	■ MINATORY	■ MINISTRATION

methodical	[məˈθɑːdɪkl]
【考法】	*adj.* 井然有序的，有条理的：arranged or proceeding in regular, **systematic order**
例	a methodical summary that included lists of points to memorize 一份包含了记忆重点的有条理的总结
近	neat, orderly, organized, regular, systematic, systematized
反	disorganized, haphazard, irregular, unsystematic 杂乱的，混乱无序的

meticulous	[məˈtɪkjələs]
【考法】	*adj.* 极为谨慎的：marked by **extreme or excessive care** in the consideration or treatment of details
例	He was so meticulous about everything. 他对所有事都一丝不苟。
近	careful, conscientious, exact, fussy, heedful, painstaking, punctilious, scrupulous
反	careless, feckless, heedless, thoughtless 疏忽大意的

mettle	[ˈmetl]
【考法1】	*n.* 勇气：vigor and **strength of spirit** or temperament
例	troops who showed their mettle in combat 在战场上表现出坚强勇气的部队
近	bravery, courage, dauntlessness, fortitude, guts, nerve, pluck, spirit, spunk, valor
反	cowardice, cravenness, gutlessness, pusillanimity, spinelessness 胆小，怯懦
【考法2】	*n.* 毅力，耐力：staying quality: **stamina**
例	Those trucks had proved their mettle in army transport. 那些卡车通过在军队运输中的表现证明了它们的耐用性。
近	durability, endurance, stamina, persistence, resolution
派	mettlesome *adj.* 有毅力的

miff	[mɪf]
【考法】	*vt.* 使恼怒：to cause to become offended or **annoyed**
例	be miffed by her son's disobedience 被她儿子的叛逆惹恼
近	aggravate, annoy, enrage, exasperate, incense, infuriate, ire, madden, nettle, peeve, vex
反	appease, assuage, mollify, placate, propitiate 平息，安抚；delight, gratify, please 取悦，讨好

migratory ['maɪɡrətɔːri]

【考法】 *adj.* 迁移的：having a way of life that involves **moving from one region to another** typically on a seasonal basis

例 migratory birds heading south for the winter 为了越冬而往南飞的候鸟

近 migrant, mobile, nomad, nomadic, traveling

反 nonmigrant, resident, sedentary 常居一处的，不迁移的

milk [mɪlk]

【考法】 *vt.* 榨取（财富、信息等）：to draw or **coerce profit** or advantage from illicitly or to an extreme degree

例 milk the workers 从工人身上榨取好处 ‖ The interrogators milked the arrested spy, but he was dry. 审问者想尽办法套被捕间谍的话，但是无功而返。

近 drain, exploit

mime [maɪm]

【考法】 *v.* 模仿：to use（someone or something）as the **model** for one's speech, mannerisms, or behavior

例 mime a dog begging for food 模仿小狗乞食

近 ape, copy, copycat, emulate, mimic, simulate

mimic ['mɪmɪk]

【考法1】 *adj.* 仿真的，仿造的：being such **in appearance** only and made with or manufactured from usually cheaper materia

例 Police were concerned that the mimic gun, although intended only as a toy, might be confused with the real thing in certain situations. 尽管仿真枪只是玩具，但警方担忧在某些情况下它会被误认为是真枪。

近 artificial, bogus, factitious, fake, false, imitative, mock, sham, simulated, substitute, synthetic

反 genuine, natural, real 真实的

【考法2】 *vt.* 模仿：to use（someone or something）as the **model** for one's speech, mannerisms, or behavior

例 She began to learn their language by mimicking the sounds they made. 她开始通过模仿发音来学习他们的语言。

近 ape, copy, copycat, emulate, mimic, simulate

派 mimicry *n.* 模仿

minatory ['mɪnətɔːri]

【考法】 *adj.* 带来威胁的，有凶兆的：being or showing **a sign of evil** or calamity to come

例 The novel's protagonist is haunted by a minatory black specter. 这部小说的主人公被不祥的黑色幽灵所骚扰。

近 baleful, direful, doomy, foreboding, ill-boding, inauspicious, menacing, portentous, sinister, threatening

反 unthreatening 没有威胁的；reassuring 令人安心的

ministration [ˌmɪnɪ'streɪʃn]

【考法】 *n.* 帮助：the act or process of serving or **aiding**

例 assistance, aid, duty, service

List 16

"所谓抱负就是对现状的永不满足，有变化的生活才精彩，永远不要停下追逐梦想的脚步。"

（赵禾，2006 年 10 月，Verbal 700, Quantitative 800，
录取学校：Cornell University Ms. Financial Engineering）

Unit 1

■ MINGLE   ■ MINIMIZE   ■ MINT   ■ MINUSCULE   ■ MINUTE
■ MINUTIAE   ■ MIRAGE   ■ MIRE   ■ MIRTH   ■ MISANTHROPIC

mingle ['mɪŋgl]
- 【考法】 *vt.* 混合，结合：to **mix** so that the components become united
- 例 mingle the ingredients 将调料混合 ‖ mingle fact and fiction 糅杂了现实与幻想
- 近 mix, amalgamate, blend, commingle, immingle, intermix, merge
- 反 divide, separate, sunder 分开

minimize ['mɪnɪmaɪz]
- 【考法 1】 *vt.* 将…减到最少：to **reduce to** the **smallest** possible amount, extent, size, or degree
- 例 All striking forces are told to minimize civilian casualties. 所有攻击部队被要求尽可能减少平民伤亡。
- 近 deprecate, diminish, discount, reduce
- 反 inflate, magnify 膨胀，扩大；maximize 最大化
- 派 minimum *adj.* 最小的
- 【考法 2】 *vt.* 刻意低估：to **underestimate** intentionally
- 例 minimize losses in our own company while maximize those of the rival 低估我方损失而高估对手损失
- 近 underestimate, underrate, undervalue
- 反 overestimate 高估；exaggerate 夸张，夸大

mint [mɪnt]
- 【考法】 *adj.* 无损坏的：**unmarred** as if fresh from a mint
- 例 a second-handed laptop in mint condition 一台几乎全新的二手笔记本电脑
- 近 intact, original, perfect, pristine, unmarred, virginal
- 反 impaired, damaged 有损坏的；stale 陈腐的

minuscule ['mɪnəskju:l]
- 【考法】 *adj.* 极小的：**very small**
- 例 a minuscule progress 极小的进步
- 近 atomic, infinitesimal, microscopic, miniature, minute, tiny
- 反 colossal, elephantine, enormous, gargantuan, gigantic, huge, immense, mammoth, prodigious 巨大的

minute [maɪ'nju:t]
- 【考法 1】 *adj.* 仔细的，谨小慎微的：characterized by **careful scrutiny** and close examination
- 例 a minute description of the setting of the story 故事背景的详细介绍
- 近 circumstantial, elaborate, full, particular, particularized, thorough
- 反 brief, compendious, concise, succinct, summary, terse 摘要性的，简述的
- 【考法 2】 *adj.* 小的，不重要的：very small or **of small importance**
- 例 It is not sagacious to invest excessively in minute details. 过分投入到不重要的细枝末节上是不明智的。
- 近 frivolous, incidental, inconsiderable, insignificant, little, minor, negligible, nugatory, slight, trifling, trivial
- 反 consequential, critical, crucial, momentous, significant, vital, weighty 关键的，重要的
- 派 minutes *n.* 会议记录

minutiae [mɪ'nu:ʃii:]
- 【考法】 *n.* 次要的细节，小事：a minute or **minor detail**
- 例 plagued by minutiae 被不重要的细节困扰
- 近 triviality
- 反 gist 要点

mirage [mə'rɑːʒ]

【考法】 *n.* 海市蜃楼，幻想：something **illusory** and unattainable like a mirage

例 The boom is a mirage. 繁荣是一个幻想。

近 chimera, delusion, hallucination, illusion, phantom, vision

反 reality 现实

mire ['maɪər]

【考法】 *n.* 困境：a **difficult**, puzzling, or embarrassing **situation** from which there is no easy escape

vt. 使陷入困境，拖后腿：to hamper or **hold back** as if by mire

例 stuck in a mire of emotional dependency 陷于感情依赖的困境中 ‖ be mired in the past 陷于过去的回忆不能自拔

近 dilemma, hole, impasse, jam, pickle, quagmire, rattrap, swamp; bog, broil, delay, detain, entangle, entrap, retard

反 enfranchise, extricate, free, liberate, rescue 使解脱

mirth [mɜːrθ]

【考法】 *n.* 欢乐，欢笑：**gladness** or gaiety as shown by or accompanied with **laughter**

例 a man of little mirth 不苟言笑之人

近 cheer, festivity, gaiety, glee, happiness, hilarity, jocundity, joviality, lightheartedness

反 dejection, depression, desolation, despondence, doldrums, melancholy, oppression 沮丧，忧伤

派 mirthful *adj.* 高兴的

misanthropic [ˌmɪsən'θrɑːpɪk]

【考法】 *adj.* 反人类的：having or showing a **deep distrust of human** beings and their motives

例 a solitary and misanthropic artist 一个孤立的反人类艺术家

近 antisocial, cynical, pessimistic

反 philanthropic 博爱的；uncynical 不愤世嫉俗的

派 misanthrope *n.* 反人类分子

Unit 2

■ MISBEHAVING	■ MISCHIEVOUS	■ MISCONSTRUE	■ MISCREANT	■ MISDEMEANOUR
■ MISERLY	■ MANACLE	■ MISGIVING	■ MISHAP	■ MISREPRESENT

misbehaving [ˌmɪsbɪ'heɪvɪŋ]

【考法】 *adj.* 调皮的，行为不端的：engaging in or marked by **childish misbehavior**

例 a new approach for disciplining a chronically misbehaving child 一个教育调皮小孩的新方法

近 annoying, devious, errant, impish, mischievous, naughty, playful, wicked

反 decorous, urbane 举止得体的

mischievous ['mɪstʃɪvəs]

【考法】 *adj.* 调皮的，淘气的：playful in a **naughty** or **teasing** way

例 The mischievous child broke the vase. 那个调皮的孩子打碎了花瓶。

近 annoying, devious, errant, impish, misbehaving, naughty, playful, wicked

反 decorous, urbane 举止得体的

misconstrue [ˌmɪskən'struː]

【考法】 *vt.* 误解，曲解：to **mistake** the meaning of

例 An outsider might misconstrue the nature of the phenomenon. 局外者可能会曲解这个现象的本质。

近 garble, misapprehend, misinterpret, misperceive, misread, misrepresent, mistake

反 appreciate, apprehend, catch, comprehend, fathom, grasp, perceive, savvy, seize, understand 获知

miscreant ['mɪskriənt]

【考法】 *n.* 恶棍，罪犯：one who **behaves criminally** or viciously

例 financial miscreant 金融恶棍

近 brute, culprit, devil, felon, fiend, offender, rascal, reprobate, villain

反 cavalier, chevalier（尤指对女士）彬彬有礼的绅士

misdemeanour [ˌmɪsdɪ'miːnər]

【考法】 *n.* 轻罪：a **crime less serious** than a felony

例 charged with several misdemeanours 被指控几项轻罪

近 infraction, infringement, offense, peccadillo, violation

反 felony 重罪

miserly	[ˈmaɪzərli]
【考法】	*adj.* 吝啬的：marked by grasping meanness and **penuriousness**
例	He is miserly with both his time and money . 他对时间和金钱都非常吝啬。
近	closefisted, mean, niggard, parsimonious, penurious, stingy, tightfisted
反	lavish, prodigal, spendthrift, squandering 浪费的；generous, liberal, munificent, openhanded 慷慨的
派	miser *n.* 守财奴

manacle	[ˈmænəkl]
【考法】	*vt.* 限制，给…制造困难：to **confine or restrain** with or as if with chains; to **create difficulty** for the work or activity of
例	Some of the company's supporters charged that the negative report had been motivated by a broader political assault on the company that was designed to help market rivals who would like to see the company manacled . 一些该公司的支持者指责这份不利于该公司的报告背后有着更为巨大的政治阴谋，它旨在让该公司受到限制——而这正是该公司的市场竞争者们所期待的。
近	chain, check, clog, encumber, fetter, hamper, handicap, restrain, shackle, trammel
反	enfranchise, liberate, unbind, unfetter, unshackle 解放；aid, assist, facilitate, help 促进，帮助

misgiving	[ˌmɪsˈɡɪvɪŋ]
【考法】	*n.* 担忧，疑虑：a feeling of **doubt** or suspicion especially concerning a future event
例	No one can dispel his misgiving . 没有人能打消他的疑虑。
近	apprehension, distrust, doubt, dread, fear, foreboding, incertitude, skepticism, suspicion
反	assurance, belief, certainty, certitude, confidence, conviction, sureness, surety, trust 信心

mishap	[ˈmɪshæp]
【考法】	*n.* 不幸之事：an **unfortunate** accident
例	avoid the mishap 避免不幸
近	adversity, calamity, cataclysm, catastrophe, disaster, ill, mischance, misfortune, tragedy
反	fortune, luck, serendipity 幸事

misrepresent	[ˌmɪsˌreprɪˈzent]
【考法】	*vt.* 误传，篡改：to **give** an incorrect or **misleading representation** of
例	misrepresent the facts 篡改事实真相
近	belie, color, distort, falsify, garble, misinterpret, misrelate, misstate, pervert
反	clarify, explain, illuminate, illustrate 澄清，阐明
派	misrepresentation *n.* 篡改

Unit 3

■ MITE	■ MITIGATE	■ MAJESTIC	■ MOCKERY	■ MODERATE
■ MODICUM	■ MOLLIFY	■ MOLLYCODDLE	■ MOLT	■ MOMENTOUS

mite	[maɪt]
【考法】	*n.* 微小的东西，很少的钱：a very **small object**, creature, or particle, a very small sum of money
例	a mite of comfort 一点安慰
近	atom, bit, hint, iota, molecule, particle, pittance, trace
反	boodle, bundle, fortune 大笔(金钱)；colossus 巨大的事物

mitigate	[ˈmɪtɪɡeɪt]
【考法】	*vt.* 减轻痛苦，使缓和：to make **less severe** or painful
例	powerful drugs that mitigate pains 强力的镇痛剂
近	allay, alleviate, assuage, ease, mollify, palliate, relieve, soothe
反	aggravate, exacerbate, intensify 加剧
派	mitigation *n.* 缓和

majestic	[məˈdʒestɪk]
【考法】	*adj.* 宏伟壮丽的：large and **impressively beautiful**
例	majestic monuments 宏伟的纪念碑
近	august, epic, glorious, grandiose, imposing, magnificent, monumental, splendid
反	humble, unheroic, unimposing, unimpressive 没有留下深刻印象的

mockery ['mɑːkəri]

【考法 1】 *n.* 鄙视，嘲弄：scornfully contemptuous **ridicule**

例 Her deliberate mockery triggered a fierce fight. 她的蓄意嘲弄引起了一场激烈的打斗。

近 derision, joke, mock, ridicule, scoffing

反 respect, reverence, veneration 尊敬

【考法 2】 *n.* 以嘲笑为目的的模仿：a false, **derisive**, or impudent **imitation**

例 arbitrary methods that make a mockery of justice 专断的方式是对司法公正的嘲弄性模仿

近 burlesque, caricature, farce, parody, sham, travesty

派 mock *v.* 愚弄，嘲弄

moderate

【考法 1】 ['mɑːdəreɪt] *vt.* 使缓和：to **lessen** the **intensity** or extremeness of

例 Sopranos and tenors moderates their voices to fit the size of the theater. 女高音和男高音们根据剧场的大小调节他们的声音以创造合适的效果。

近 abate, diminish, dwindle, ease, lessen, lower, modulate, subside, taper, temper, wane

反 escalate, enhance, expand, heighten, intensify 扩大，升级，增强

【考法 2】 ['mɑːdərət] *adj.* 适度的，中庸的：being **within** reasonable **limits**; not excessive or extreme

例 The new proposals regarding defense budget were met with only moderate enthusiasm. 关于国防预算的新提案只获得了平淡的热情。

近 average, conservative, fair, intermediate, mediocre, modest, reasonable, temperate

反 exorbitant, excessive 过分的；extreme, radical 极端的

派 immoderate *adj.* 不适度的

modicum ['mɑːdɪkəm]

【考法】 *n.* 少量：a **small portion**; a limited quantity

例 a modicum of food quota 极少量的食物配额

近 atom, iota, mite, molecule, particle

反 abundance, affluence 大量

mollify ['mɑːlɪfaɪ]

【考法】 *vt.* 平息，抚慰，缓和：to **calm** in temper or feeling

例 mollify the angry customer 平息消费者的怒气

近 allay, alleviate, appease, assuage, conciliate, mitigate, placate, propitiate, soothe

反 aggravate, enrage, exasperate, incense, inflame, infuriate, ire, rankle, vex 激怒；antagonize 使敌对

派 mollification *n.* 安抚

mollycoddle ['mɑːlikɑːdl]

【考法】 *vt.* 宠爱，溺爱：to treat with an **excessive** or absurd degree of **indulgence** and attention

例 mollycoddle his only grandson 溺爱他唯一的孙子

近 coddle, cosset, indulge, pamper, spoil

反 abuse, ill-treat 虐待

molt [moʊlt]

【考法】 *vi.* 脱（羽、皮等）：to **shed** hair, **feathers**, shell, horns, or an outer layer periodically

例 molt the old skin 脱去老皮

近 exfoliate, exuviate, shed

反 fledge 长羽毛

momentous [moʊ'mentəs]

【考法】 *adj.* 极重要的：of **utmost importance**; of outstanding significance or consequence

例 Battle of Stalingrad is a momentous campaign in World War. II 斯大林格勒之战是第二次世界大战中具有重大意义的一次战役。

近 consequential, considerable, crucial, eventful, important, monumental, pivotal, significant, vital, weighty

反 inconsequential, negligible, slight, trifling, trivial 无关紧要的

Unit 4

| ■ MOMENTUM | ■ MONGREL | ■ MONOCHROMATIC | ■ MONOLOGUE | ■ MONOTONOUS |
| ■ MONTAGE | ■ MORATORIUM | ■ MORBID | ■ MORDANT | ■ MORIBUND |

momentum [moʊ'mentəm]

【考法】 *n.* 动力；势头：**impetus** of a physical object in motion; impetus of a nonphysical process, such as an idea or a course of events

例 Their luck began to pick up momentum . 他们的运气开始转旺。
近 boost, encouragement, goad, impetus, incentive, incitation, instigation, motivation, spur, stimulus
反 deterrent 阻碍物；obstruction, resistance 阻力

mongrel [ˈmʌŋɡrəl]
【考法】 *adj.* 杂种的，混血儿的：of **mixed origin** or character
例 homeless mongrel dogs on the streets 街上的流浪杂种狗
近 crossbred, hybrid
反 purebred 纯种的

monochromatic [ˌmɑːnəkroʊˈmætɪk]
【考法】 *adj.* 单调无聊的：**lacking variety**, creativity, or excitement
例 a monochromatic article eulogizing a hero 一篇无聊的赞颂英雄的文章
近 arid, dreary, drudging, dull, jejune, monotonous, pedestrian, ponderous, stale, stodgy, tiresome
反 absorbing, engaging, engrossing, gripping, interesting, intriguing, involving, riveting 吸引人的

monologue [ˈmɑːnəlɔːɡ]
【考法】 *n.* 独白：a dramatic sketch performed **by one actor**
例 deliver a tedious monologue 做了一个冗长的独白
近 soliloquy, solo, speech
反 dialogue 对话

monotonous [məˈnɑːtənəs]
【考法】 *adj.* 无聊的：**tediously** uniform or **unvarying**
例 a sparkle in the monotonous background 单调背景中的一个亮点
近 arid, dreary, drudging, dull, jejune, monochromatic, pedestrian, ponderous, stale, stodgy, tiresome
反 absorbing, engaging, engrossing, gripping, interesting, intriguing, involving, riveting 吸引人的

montage [ˈmɑːntɑːʒ]
【考法】 *n.* 大杂烩：an unorganized **collection** or mixture of various things
例 a montage of sth. 关于某事的大杂烩
近 agglomerate, collage, hodgepodge, medley, motley, salad, variety

moratorium [ˌmɔːrəˈtɔːriəm]
【考法】 *n.* 延期，暂缓施行：a **suspension** of activity
例 a moratorium on nuclear tests 暂缓核试验
近 abeyance, delay, doldrums, dormancy, latency, quiescence, postponement, suspension
反 resumption（从中断处）继续进行

morbid [ˈmɔːrbɪd]
【考法1】 *adj.* 疾病的，疾病所致的：affected with or induced **by disease**
例 a morbid condition 有疾病的状况
近 diseased, pathological
反 verdant 青翠的
【考法2】 *adj.* (思想性格)变态的：characterized by preoccupation with **unwholesome thoughts** or feelings
例 read the account of the murder with a morbid interest 怀着病态的心态读谋杀报告 ‖ exhibit a morbid fascination 展现出一种病态的迷恋
近 brainsick, crazy, deranged, lunatic, psychotic
反 hale, salubrious, wholesome 健康的
派 morbidity *n.* 病态

mordant [ˈmɔːrdnt]
【考法】 *adj.* 尖酸刻薄的：**biting** and **caustic** in thought, manner, or style
例 feel embarrassed about the mordant satire of the critics 对评论家刻薄的讽刺感到尴尬
近 acerbic, acid, acrid, barbed, caustic, corrosive, pungent, sardonic, satiric, scalding, scathing, tart
反 congenial, genial 和蔼的

moribund [ˈmɔːrɪbʌnd]
【考法】 *adj.* 即将过时的：on the verge of becoming **obsolete**
例 moribund social conventions 过时的社会习俗
近 antiquated, archaic, dated, fossilized, moth-eaten, outdated, outworn, rusty
反 fresh, new 崭新的；promising 充满希望的

Unit 5

■ MOROSE　　　　■ MOSAIC　　　　■ MONOLITHIC　　　　■ MOTH-EATEN　　　　■ MOTILE
■ MOTIVATE　　　　■ MOTLEY　　　　■ MOTTLE　　　　■ MULTIFARIOUS　　　　■ MOURNFUL

morose　[məˈroʊs]
【考法】 *adj.* 忧郁的：having a **sullen** and **gloomy** disposition
例　morose job seekers who are inured to rejection 习惯了被拒的郁郁寡欢的求职者
近　bleak, chill, dark, depressed, dire, dour, gloomy, lugubrious, saturnine, solemn, sulky, sullen, surly
反　bright, cheerful, festive, jovial, jocund, sanguine, lighthearted, rejoiced 高兴的，欢快的

mosaic　[moʊˈzeɪɪk]
【考法】 *n.* 综合物，马赛克般的东西：an unorganized **collection** or mixture of various things
例　a mosaic of testimony from various witnesses 从不同证人中得来的综合证词
近　agglomerate, collage, hodgepodge, jumble, montage, motley, muddle, salad, shuffle, variety, welter

monolithic　[ˌmɑːnəˈlɪθɪk]
【考法】 *adj.* 大一统的 constituting or acting as a **single**, often rigid, **uniform** whole
例　a monolithic worldwide movement 世界范围内的统一运动
近　homogeneous, uniform, alike, identical
反　motley, assorted, eclectic, heterogeneous, mixed, patchwork, piebald, varied

moth-eaten　[ˈmɔːθ ˌiːtn]
【考法】 *adj.* 过时的：having **passed its time** of use or usefulness
例　dressed in a moth-eaten style 过时的衣着
近　antiquated, archaic, dated, fossilized, moribund, outdated, outworn, rusty
反　fresh, new 崭新的；promising 充满希望的

motile　[ˈmoʊtl]
【考法】 *adj.* 能动的：exhibiting or capable of **movement**
例　Aircraft carriers are recognized as a motile combat platform. 航空母舰是一种移动作战平台。
近　mobile, movable, portable, transportable
反　immobile 不可移动的
派　motility *n.* 可运动性

motivate　[ˈmoʊtɪveɪt]
【考法】 *vt.* 刺激，激发：to **provide** with an **incentive**；move to action
例　motivate him to murder 刺激他杀人
近　excite, galvanize, impel, innervate, provoke, rouse, stimulate
反　discourage, dishearten 使泄气
派　motivation *n.* 动机；motivated *adj.* 被激励的

motley　[ˈmɑːtli]
【考法】 *adj.* 混杂的，富于变化的：(especially of colors) having elements of great **variety** or incongruity
例　an arrangement of motley flowers 多种不同花束的组合
近　assorted, chromatic, kaleidoscopic, heterogeneous, indiscriminate, magpie, piebald, variegated
反　homogeneous, monochromatic, monotonous, unvaried 单一的，同一性的

mottle　[ˈmɑːtl]
【考法】 *vt.* 标记上杂色斑点：to **mark** with **spots** or blotches of different shades or colors
例　a black horse mottled with white 身上带有白色斑点的黑马
近　blotch, dapple, dot, marble, splotch, spot, stain
反　blanch 漂白
派　mottled *adj.* 斑驳的

multifarious　[ˌmʌltɪˈferiəs]
【考法】 *adj.* 多种多样的：being of **many and various** kinds
例　the multifarious interests and activities in which Benjamin Franklin immersed himself 本杰明·富兰克林专心于多种多样的兴趣与活动
近　divers, manifold, myriad

mournful	[ˈmɔːrnfl]

【考法】 *adj.* 悲伤的：feeling or **expressing sorrow** or grief

例 The mournful survivors of the disaster were faced with the grim task of burying the dead. 悲伤的幸存者面临着掩埋灾难中死者尸体的可怕任务。 ‖ Mrs. Murphy fainted at the mournful news of her son's death. Murphy 太太听到她儿子的悲伤的消息死讯后晕了过去。

近 aching, agonized, anguished, doleful, dolorous, grievous, lamentable, lugubrious, melancholy, sad, woeful

反 cheerful, delighted, jocund, jovial, jubilant 快活的

派 mournfulness *n.* 悲伤

Unit 6

■ METAPHOR	■ MUDDY	■ MUFFLE	■ MULISH	■ MUMBLE
■ MUNDANE	■ MUNIFICENT	■ MURKY	■ MURMUR	■ MUTATE

metaphor	[ˈmetəfər]

【考法】 *adj.* 暗喻：a word or phrase for one thing that is **used to refer to another thing** in order to show or suggest that they are **similar**

例 "It's raining cats and dogs" is just a colorful metaphor. "it's raining cats and dogs"是一个丰富多彩的暗喻。

反 simile

muddy	[ˈmʌdi]

【考法1】 *adj.* 浑浊的，不清晰的：**lacking** in **clarity** or brightness

例 a muddy recording 嘈杂不清的纪录

近 cloudy, foul, murky, obscure, turbid

反 clear 清晰的

【考法2】 *vt.* 使难以理解：to **make** (something) **unclear** to the understanding

例 That point is irrelevant and will just muddy the issue we're trying to resolve. 那个观点和我们讨论的问题毫不相干，它只会妨碍我们对于问题的理解。

近 becloud, befog, blur, cloud, fog, obfuscate

反 clarify, illuminate 阐明

muffle	[ˈmʌfl]

【考法】 *vt.* 使消声：to wrap or pad in order to **deaden the sound**

例 close the window to muffle the outside noises 关上窗户以减少外界的噪音

近 attenuate, dampen, deaden, mute, soften, stifle, suppress

反 amplify, enhance, magnify 放大，增强

派 muffler *n.* 消音器

mulish	[ˈmjuːlɪʃ]

【考法】 *adj.* 固执的：unreasonably and inflexibly **obstinate**

例 a mulish determination to act on his own 铁了心要单打独斗

近 adamant, headstrong, immovable, intractable, obstinate, pertinacious, perverse, refractory, stubborn

反 flexible, pliable, pliant, yielding 易改变立场的，易受影响的

派 mulishly *adv.* 固执地

mumble	[ˈmʌmbl]

【考法】 *v.* 说话含糊：to **utter** words in a low **confused** indistinct manner

例 He mumbled an apology reluctantly. 他不情愿地咕哝了句抱歉。

近 grunt, murmur, mutter, whisper

反 articulate, enunciate 清楚地表达

mundane	[mʌnˈdeɪn]

【考法】 *adj.* 平凡的：relating to, characteristic of, or concerned with **commonplaces**

例 mundane concerns of day-to-day life 关于日常生活的一般顾虑

近 common, ordinary, prosaic

反 extraordinary 非凡的

munificent	[mjuːˈnɪfɪsnt]

【考法】 *adj.* 慷慨的：very **liberal in giving**

例 The university received a munificent foundation grant. 那所大学收到了一笔慷慨的基金资助。

近 bountiful, charitable, generous, liberal, openhanded, unsparing

反 closefisted, mean, miserly, niggardly, parsimonious, penurious, stingy, tightfisted 小气的

派 munificence *n.* 慷慨

murky ['mɜːrki]
【考法】 *adj.* 模糊的，晦涩的：**lacking clarity** or distinctness
例 He felt lost in the murky bureaucratic rhetoric . 他感觉自己被官僚主义的晦涩说辞弄晕了。
近 ambiguous, arcane, cloudy, equivocal, muddy, nebulous, obscure, occult, vague
反 clear, limpid, pellucid, plain 清晰的

murmur ['mɜːrmər]
【考法】 *vi.* 低声抱怨，发牢骚：to complain in low mumbling tones; **grumble**
例 No prisoner dared murmur out toud . 没有囚犯敢大声报怨。
近 carp, fuss, gripe, grizzle, grouch, grouse, grumble, moan, repine, whine
反 crow, delight, rejoice 欢呼，高兴

mutate ['mjuːteɪt]
【考法】 *v.* (使)改变，(使)变异：to undergo or cause to **undergo mutation**
例 Some chromosomes started to mutate after exposure to X-Ray. 经 X 光照射之后部分染色体开始发生变异。
近 alter, change, fluctuate, modify, shift, transfigure, transform, vary
反 remain 保持不变；plateau, stabilize 使稳定
派 mutation *n.* 改变；变异

Unit 7

| ■ MUTE | ■ MUTTER | ■ MYOPIC | ■ MYRIAD | ■ NADIR |
| ■ NAIVE | ■ NARCISSISTIC | ■ NASCENT | ■ NATTY | ■ NAUSEATE |

mute [mjuːt]
【考法】 *adj.* 不说话的，缄默的：deliberately **refraining from speech**
例 He always remained mute no matter how much we pleaded for an answer. 不论我们怎么恳求回答，他总是保持沉默。
近 dumb, inarticulate, speechless, uncommunicative, voiceless, wordless
反 communicative, expansive, loquacious, talkative 爱说话的，话多的

mutter ['mʌtər]
【考法】 *vi.* 低声抱怨：to **murmur complainingly** or angrily
例 mutter about the difficult assignment 抱怨作业太难
近 carp, fuss, gripe, grizzle, grouch, grouse, grumble, moan, murmur, repine, whine
反 crow, delight, rejoice 欢呼，高兴

myopic [maɪˈɑːpɪk]
【考法】 *adj.* 缺乏远见的，缺乏辨别能力的：a **lack of foresight** or discernment
例 a myopic view on climate change 关于气候变化缺乏远见的观点
近 shortsighted, narrow-minded
反 far-sighted, foreseeing, provident 有远见的；discerning 有辨别能力的
派 myopia *n.* 近视；鼠目寸光

myriad ['mɪriəd]
【考法】 *adj.* 无限的，大量的：constituting a very large, **indefinite number**
例 the myriad stars of a summer night 夏日夜空中的无尽繁星
近 innumerable, numerous, uncountable, untold
反 few, scarce, scanty 少的，缺乏的；countable, enumerable 可数清的

nadir ['neɪdɪr]
【考法】 *n.* 最低点：the **lowest point**
例 the nadir on the curve 曲线上的最低点
近 base, bottom, foot
反 acme, apex, climax, meridian, peak, pinnacle, summit, top, zenith 最高点

naïve [naɪˈiːv]
【考法】 *adj.* 天真纯朴的：**lacking worldly experience** and understanding, simple and guileless
例 a child with a naïve charm 天真无邪的孩子
近 artless, guileless, ingenuous, innocent, natural, simple, unaffected, unsophisticated
反 sophisticated, worldly 世故的；affected, artful, assuming, dishonest, dissembling, guileful 虚伪做作的
派 naivety *n.* 天真

narcissistic	[ˌnɑːrsɪ'sɪstɪk]
【考法】	*adj.* 自恋的：having an **undue fascination with oneself**
例	He tried to raise a sense of social consciousness of the normally narcissistic Hollywood community. 他试着在通常无比自恋的好莱坞圈子中激起一丝社会意识。
近	egotistical, self-absorbed, self-centered, self-infatuated, self-obsessed, self-preoccupied
反	altruistic, self-forgetting, selfless, unselfish 无私的

nascent	['næsnt]
【考法】	*adj.* 新生的：coming or having **recently come into existence**
例	The rise of the nascent middle class catalyzed a new economic boom. 新生中产阶级的崛起催生了一场新的经济繁荣。
近	beginning, emerging, inceptive, inchoate, incipient, initial, introductory
反	full-blown, full-fledged, mature, ripe 成熟的；moribund 将死的
派	nascence *n.* 新生的状态

natty	['næti]
【考法】	*adj.* 整洁的，时髦的：trimly neat and **tidy**
例	a natty young woman 整洁漂亮的年轻女子
近	dapper, smart, spruce
反	frowsy, sloppy, slovenly 邋遢的

nauseate	['nɔːzieɪt]
【考法】	*v.* (使)厌恶，(使)作呕：to feel or **cause** to feel loathing or **disgust**
例	The malodor of the rotten meat made us nauseate. 腐肉的恶臭让我们恶心。
近	disgust, repel, repulse, revolt, sicken
反	delight 使愉悦
派	nausea *n.* 恶心反胃

Unit 8

■ NAUTICAL	■ NAYSAY	■ NEBULOUS	■ NEEDY	■ NEFARIOUS
■ NEGATION	■ NEGLIGENT	■ NEGOTIATE	■ NEOPHYTE	■ NERVE

nautical	['nɔːtɪkl]
【考法】	*adj.* 航海的：of, relating to, or characteristic of ships, shipping, sailors, or navigation **on** a body of **water**
例	nautical mile 海里
近	marine, maritime, navigational
反	aeronautic 航空的；astronautic 航天的

naysay	['neɪseɪ]
【考法】	*vt.* 拒绝，否认：to **oppose**, **deny**, or take a pessimistic or negative view of
例	She naysayed she knew about the murder. 她否认她知道那件命案。
近	decline, deny, deject, disallow, gainsay, oppose, refuse, reject
反	accede, agree, concur, consent 同意
派	naysayer *n.* 反对者

nebulous	['nebjələs]
【考法】	*adj.* 模糊的：**indistinct**, vague
例	a nebulous description of the topic 对于主题的模糊描述
近	ambiguous, arcane, equivocal, hazy, indistinct, muddy, murky, obscure, occult, vague
反	distinct 明显的；clear, definite, unambiguous, unequivocal 明确的
派	nebula *n.* 星云

needy	['niːdi]
【考法】	*adj.* 贫困的：being in need; **impoverished**, poor
例	a needy and diffident child 一个贫困并且缺乏自信的小孩
近	destitute, impecunious, impoverished, indigent, penurious, poor, threadbare
反	affluent, opulent, wealthy 富有的

nefarious	[nɪ'feriəs]
【考法】	*adj.* 极坏的，邪恶的：flagrantly **wicked** or impious
例	a nefarious plan to kill the president 一个谋杀总统的邪恶计划
近	atrocious, degenerate, devious, evil, heinous, infamous, miscreant, vicious, villainous, wicked
反	ethical, righteous, upright, virtuous 品德高尚的；beneficial 有益的；exemplary 模范的

negation [nɪ'ɡeɪʃn]

【考法】 *n.* 否定：the **opposite** or absence of something regarded as actual, positive, or affirmative

例 negations of the charges 对这些指控的否认

近 contradiction, denegation, denial, gainsaying, rejection, repudiation

反 acknowledgement, affirmation, avowal 肯定，同意

派 negative *adj.* 否定的；负面的

negligent ['neɡlɪdʒənt]

【考法】 *adj.* 疏忽大意的：**failing** to give proper attention or **care**

例 negligent in taking care of the children 粗心大意地照顾孩子

近 careless, derelict, heedless, neglectful, remiss

反 attentive, careful, cautious, heedful 专心的，谨慎的

派 negligence *n.* 疏忽

negotiate [nɪ'ɡoʊʃieɪt]

【考法】 *v.* 商量，谈判：to arrange or settle **by** discussion and **mutual agreement**

例 negotiate the term of truce 共商停战事宜

近 arrange, bargain, concert, settle

反 break down (谈判等)失败，破产

派 negotiable *adj.* 可商量的；negotiation *n.* 商量，谈判

neophyte ['niːəfaɪt]

【考法】 *n.* 初学者，新手：a **beginner** or novice

例 a political neophyte 一个政治新手

近 abecedarian, apprentice, fledgling, freshman, novice, recruit, rookie, tyro

反 veteran 老兵，身经百战的人

nerve [nɜːrv]

【考法】 *n.* (坚强的)意志，勇气：**power of endurance** or control; strength of mind to carry on in spite of danger
vt. 给予勇气，鼓励：to **give** strength or **courage** to

例 nerves of steel 钢铁般的意志 ‖ He needs to nerve himself for the big game tomorrow . 他需要为明天的大赛给自己加油鼓劲。

近 bravery, fortitude, guts, intrepidity, resolution, stamina; animate, brace, cheer, embolden, encourage, inspirit, steel, strengthen

反 cowardice, pusillanimity 怯懦; appall 使胆寒; discourage, dishearten 使沮丧

派 nervy *adj.* 有勇气的

Unit 9

■ NETTLE	■ NEUTRALIZE	■ NEXUS	■ NIBBLE	■ NICETY
■ NIL	■ NIP	■ NITPICK	■ NOCTURNAL	■ NOISOME

nettle ['netl]

【考法】 *vt.* 惹怒：to **arouse** to sharp but transitory annoyance or **anger**

例 His pompous attitude nettled several people . 他自大的性格得罪了不少人。

近 aggravate, annoy, exasperate, inflame, infuriate, irritate, peeve, pique, provoke, roil, ruffle, vex

反 appease, assuage, conciliate, mollify, placate, propitiate 安抚

neutralize ['nuːtrəlaɪz]

【考法】 *vt.* 使无效：to **make inoperative or ineffective** usually by means of an opposite force, influ-ence, or effect

例 neutralize the bad influence 抵消坏影响

近 annul, cancel, counteract, frustrate, negate, nullify

反 activate, vitalize 激活

派 neutralization *n.* 中和；消除

nexus [ˈneksəs]

【考法 1】 *n.* 连结：a means of **connection**

例 Correlativity does not sufficiently lead to causal nexus. 相关性不是因果关联的充分条件。

近 bond, connection, link, tie

【考法 2】 *n.* 核心，最重要的地带：a thing or place that is of **greatest importance** to an activity or interest

例 the nexus for the religion 宗教核心

近 base, capital, center, core, focus, kernel, heart, hub, nucleus

反 margin, periphery 边缘

nibble [ˈnɪbl]

【考法】 *vt.* 小口咬：to eat with **small**, quick **bites** or in small morsels

例 waves nibbling the shore 缓慢侵蚀海岸的浪

近 bite, nip, peck, sip, tipple

反 gobble 狼吞虎咽

nicety [ˈnaɪsəti]

【考法】 *n.* 准确，精确：**careful** attention to **details**; delicate exactness

例 There's a nicety of detail in his meticulously painted landscapes. 在他精心绘制的景观图中，有着十分精准翔实的细节。

近 accuracy, delicacy, exactness, fineness, precision, veracity

反 coarseness, imprecision, inaccuracy, roughness 不准确，粗糙

nil [nɪl]

【考法】 *n.* 不存在，零：**nothing**; zero

例 reduced to nil 消失殆尽

近 nothing, nonentity, nullity, zip

反 existence 存在

nip [nɪp]

【考法 1】 *n.* 少量：a very **small amount**

例 I'll have just a nip of your sandwich. 我只吃一点点你的三明治。

近 bit, hint, little, mite, ounce, snap, trace

反 abundance, affluence, avalanche 大量

【考法 2】 *vi.* 小口吃喝：to sip (alcoholic liquor) **in small amounts**

近 nibble, sip, tipple

反 guzzle, quaff, swill 大口吃喝

nitpick [ˈnɪtpɪk]

【考法】 *v.* 吹毛求疵：to **criticize** by nit-picking

例 a peevish critic always ready to nitpick 一个总是吹毛求疵的古怪评论家

近 carp, cavil, fuss, niggle, quibble

派 nitpicker *n.* 吹毛求疵的人

nocturnal [nɑːkˈtɜːrnl]

【考法】 *adj.* 夜间的：of, relating to, or occurring **in the night**

例 a nocturnal raid 夜间突袭

近 nightly, nighttime

反 daily, diurnal 白昼的

noisome [ˈnɔɪsəm]

【考法 1】 *adj.* 恶臭的：**offensive** to the senses and especially to the sense of **smell**

例 noisome garbage 散发着恶臭的垃圾

近 fetid, foul, malodorous, smelly, stinky

反 ambrosial, aromatic, fragrant, perfumed, redolent, savory, scented, sweet 有香味的

【考法 2】 *adj.* 非常令人厌恶的：highly obnoxious or **objectionable**

例 noisome habits of littering 让人反感的随地乱扔垃圾的坏习惯

近 abhorrent, appalling, disgusting, hideous, loathsome, nauseating, offensive, repugnant, repulsive

反 appealing, captivating, enchanting, fascinating 有吸引力的；agreeable, pleasant 令人愉悦的

Unit 10

nomad ［ˈnoʊmæd］

【考法】 *adj./n.* 游牧的；居无定所的人：a member of a people who have **no fixed residence** but move from place to place usually seasonally and within a well-defined territory

例 a homeless nomad 一个无家可归、居无定所的人

近 ambulant, fugitive, gallivanting, perambulatory, peripatetic, ranging, roaming, vagabond, vagrant, wandering, wayfaring

反 settled 定居的

nominal ［ˈnɑːmɪnl］

【考法】 *adj.* 不重要的：so small or unimportant as to warrant little or no attention

例 play a nominal part in sth. 在某事中发挥不太重要的作用

近 inconsequential, inconsiderable, paltry, trifling, trivial

反 big, consequential, considerable, important, material, significant 重要的

nonchalant ［ˌnɑːnʃəˈlɑːnt］

【考法】 *adj.* 冷漠的：having an air of easy unconcern or **indifference**

例 hold a nonchalant attitude toward sth. 对某事态度冷漠

近 apathetic, disinterested, insensible, insouciant, perfunctory, unconcerned

反 concerned, interested 忧虑的，有兴趣的

nondescript ［ˈnɑːndɪskrɪpt］

【考法】 *adj.* 平凡的，不吸引人的：**lacking distinctive** or **interesting** qualities

例 hundreds of nondescript buildings 几百个平凡的建筑

近 beige, characterless, featureless, indistinctive, vanilla

反 conspicuous, remarkable, striking 明显的，惊人的

nonentity ［nɑːˈnentəti］

【考法】 *n.* 不重要的人：a person or thing of **little consequence** or significance

例 She was so quiet she was almost a nonentity at the meeting . 她非常沉默，在会议上是个边缘人物。

近 cipher, half-pint, insignificancy, lightweight, nullity, snippersnapper, twerp, whippersnapper, zero, zilch

反 mogul, big shot, big wheel, bigwig, eminence, figure, magnate, personage, somebody 显要人物

nonplus ［ˌnɑːnˈplʌs］

【考法】 *vt.* 使迷惑，使困窘：use to be at a loss as to what to say, think, or do: **perplex**

例 be nonplussed by the question/situation 被问题/局面弄得很困窘

近 confound, confuse, discomfit, disconcert, discountenance, mortify, abash, faze, fluster

numinous ［ˈnuːmɪnəs］

【考法】 *adj.* 神秘的,超自然的：having **supernatural and mysterious** qualities or powers

例 a numinous place 神秘的地方

近 magic, magical, mystic, occult, weird

notch ［nɑːtʃ］

【考法】 *vt.* 通过努力获得：to **obtain**（as a goal）through effort

例 a stunning performance that notched up a second Academy Award for the actor 出色的表演为该演员拿到了第二座小金人

近 attain, bag, chalk up, clock up, gain, hit, log, make, rack up, ring up, score, win

novel ［ˈnɑːvl］

【考法】 *adj.* 新奇的：strikingly **new**, unusual, or different

例 a novel method/gadget 一个新奇的方法/小玩意

近 original, unaccustomed, unfamiliar, unheard-of, unknown, unprecedented

反 banal, timeworn, familiar, hackneyed, time-honored, tired, warmed-over 陈腐的

noxious [ˈnɑːkʃəs]

【考法 1】 *adj.* 有害的，有毒的：**harmful** to living things; **injurious to health**

例 noxious waste 有害的废弃物

近 unwholesome, baneful, deleterious, detrimental, nocuous, pernicious, wicked

反 beneficial, salubrious, anodyne, benign, harmless, hurtless, innocent, innocuous, inoffensive, safe 有益的，无害的

【考法 2】 *adj.* 产生强烈厌恶的：**causing intense displeasure**, disgust, or resentment

例 a noxious smell of burning sugar 糖烧焦的让人厌恶的气味

近 abhorrent, abominable, appalling, awful, disgusting, distasteful, dreadful, foul, fulsome, gross, hideous, horrid, loathsome, nasty, nauseating, noisome, obnoxious, odious, repellent, repugnant, repulsive, revolting, scandalous

Education is a progressive discovery of our ignorance.

教育是一个逐步发现自己无知的过程。

——美国历史学家 杜兰特（Durant, American historian）

List 17

"敢于不断挑战极限的你将发掘拥有无限潜力的我。"

（徐碧慧，2010 年 2 月，Verbal 720，Quantitative 790，AW 4.5

录取院校：University of Oxford）

Unit 1

■ NUANCE　　　　■ NUDGE　　　　■ NUGATORY　　　　■ NURTURE　　　　■ OBTRUSIVE
■ OBDURATE　　　■ OBEDIENT　　　■ OBEISANCE　　　　■ OBFUSCATE　　　■ OBLIGATORY

nuance [ˈnuːɑːns]
【考法】 *n.* 细微的差异：a **subtle distinction** or variation
例 a poem of little depth and nuance 一首没有什么深度、没有什么辨识度的诗
反 patent difference, lack of subtlety, sharp distinction, patency 明显的差别

nudge [nʌdʒ]
【考法】 *vt.* 说服某人做某事：to try to **persuade** (someone) through earnest appeals to follow a course of action
例 nudge sb. into doing sth. 说服某人做某事
近 encourage, exhort, goad, press, prod, prompt

nugatory [ˈnuːgətɔːri]
【考法】 *adj.* 无关紧要的：of little or no **consequence; inconsequential**
例 The book is entertaining, but its contributions to Shakespearean scholarship are nugatory. 这本书娱乐性不错，但是对于莎士比亚研究的贡献微不足道。
近 incidental, inconsequential, inconsiderable, insignificant, negligible, trifling, trivial
反 consequential, eventful, important, major, meaningful, momentous, significant, substantial, unfrivolous, weighty 重要的

nurture [ˈnɜːrtʃər]
【考法】 *vt.* 培育，培养：to **provide** (someone) **with** moral or spiritual **understanding**
例 nurture great ambitions 培养雄心大志
近 edify, illuminate, inspire
反 impede, stunt, disregard 阻碍，漠视

obtrusive [əbˈtruːsɪv]
【考法】 *adj.* 扎眼的，难看显眼的：**noticeable in an unpleasant** way
例 the obtrusive behavior of a spoiled child 一个被宠坏的孩子的扎眼的行为
近 intruding, prominent, highlighted, striking
反 unobtrusive 不引人注目的

obdurate [ˈɑːbdərət]
【考法 1】 *adj.* 固执的：**resistant** to persuasion or softening **influences**
例 She is known for her obdurate determination. 她以坚定不移著称。
近 adamant, hard-nosed, headstrong, inflexible, intransigent, pertinacious, stubborn, unbending, uncompromising, unrelenting, unyielding, willful
反 acquiescent, agreeable, amenable, compliant, complying, flexible, pliable, pliant, relenting, yielding 温顺的
【考法 2】 *adj.* 冷酷无情的：having or showing a **lack of sympathy** or tender feelings
例 the obdurate refusal of the crotchety old man to let the neighborhood kids retrieve their ball from his backyard 那个怪老头冷酷无情地拒绝了孩子们进他后院找球的请求
近 affectless, callous, compassionless, hard-hearted, heartless, indurate, inhuman, insensate, ironhearted, merciless, remorseless, ruthless, unsparing
反 charitable, compassionate, humane, kindhearted, kindly, merciful, softhearted, sympathetic, tender, warmhearted 同情的，有爱的

obedient [əˈbiːdiənt]
【考法】 *adj.* 服从的，顺从的：**submissive** to the restraint or command of **authority**
例 the obedient girl 顺从的女孩 ‖ unquestioningly obedient to the law 对法律绝对服从
近 amenable, compliant, submissive, tractable

反 contumacious, imperial, balky, contrary, contumacious, defiant, disobedient, froward, incompliant, insubordinate, intractable, noncompliant, obstreperous, rebel, rebellious, recalcitrant, refractory, restive, unamenable, ungovernable, unruly, untoward, wayward, willful 顽固的，不服从的

obeisance [oʊˈbiːsns]
【考法】 *n.* 敬礼，尊重：a movement of the body made in token of **respect** or **submission**
例 make obeisance to her mentors 向她的导师们致敬
派 obeisant *adj.* 恭敬的
反 impertinent, impudent, imperious 不敬的，无礼的

obfuscate [ˈɑːbfʌskeɪt]
【考法】 *vt.* 使困惑，使模糊：to make so **confused** or **opaque** as to be difficult to perceive or understand
例 obfuscate the reader 让读者困惑
近 becloud, befog, blur, cloud, fog, muddy
反 demystify, elucidate, illuminate, clarify, explain clearly 澄清，阐明
派 obfuscated *adj.* 模糊的
反 lucid 清晰的

obligatory [əˈblɪɡətɔːri]
【考法】 *adj.* 强制性的：of the nature of an obligation; **compulsory**
例 obligatory military service 强制性的服军役
近 compulsory, imperative, involuntary, peremptory, required
反 discretionary, selective, elective, optional, voluntary 自由选择的，志愿的

Unit 2

◼ OBLIGING	◼ OBLIQUE	◼ OBLITERATE	◼ OBLIVIOUS	◼ OBLOQUY
◼ OBSCURE	◼ OBSEQUIOUS	◼ OBSESS	◼ OBSTINATE	◼ OBSTREPEROUS

obliging [əˈblaɪdʒɪŋ]
【考法】 *adj.* 乐于助人的：willing to **do favors**
例 an obliging and warmhearted man 一个乐于助人热心的人
近 accommodative, friendly, indulgent

oblique [əˈbliːk]
【考法】 *adj.* 斜的：**inclined or twisted** to one side
例 The old woman gave the eavesdropper an oblique glance. 老妇人给了偷听者一个白眼。
近 askew, cant, inclined, leaning, listing, slanted, sloping, tilted
反 direct, even, level, straight 笔直的

obliterate [əˈblɪtəreɪt]
【考法】 *vt.* 除去：to **remove** from existence
例 The March snowstorm obliterated our hopes for an early spring. 三月的暴风雪摧毁了我们对于早春的念想。
近 efface, eradicate, expunge, expurgate, exterminate, extirpate, wipe out

oblivious [əˈblɪviəs]
【考法】 *adj.* 不知道的，不知情的：**lacking** conscious **awareness**; **not informed** about or aware of something
例 be oblivious to sth. 对某事不知情
近 incognizant, insensible, unaware, unconscious, uninformed, unwitting
反 mindful, vigilant, acquainted, cognizant, conscious, conversant, grounded, informed, knowing, mindful, witting 留意的，机警的

obloquy [ˈɑːbləkwi]
【考法】 *n.* 谩骂，诽谤：**abusively** detractive **language** or utterance; calumny
例 she unleashed a torrent of obloquy on her opponent. 她滔滔不绝地辱骂了对手一顿。
近 billingsgate, fulmination, invective, scurrility, vitriol, vituperation
反 adulation 极度谄媚

obscure [əbˈskjʊr]
【考法 1】 *adj.* 含义模糊的：**not clearly** understood or expressed; having an often intentionally **veiled** or **uncertain meaning** *vt.* 使模糊：to make dark, dim, or **indistinct**
例 a fantasy writer who likes to put lots of obscure references in her tales of wizards and warlocks 一个喜欢在巫师故事中添加很多含义模糊的引文的魔幻小说作家

近 ambiguous, arcane, enigmatic, equivocal, fuliginous, inscrutable, opaque; blear, blur, darken, dim, overshadow, shroud

反 explicit, manifest, clear, certain, accessible, nonambiguous, obvious, plain, unambiguous, unequivocal 明晰的，没有歧义的；elucidate, brighten, illuminate, light up, lighten 阐明

【考法2】 *adj.* 平凡的，不知名的：not prominent or **famous**

例 an obscure poet 无名的诗人

近 noteless, uncelebrated, unfamous, unknown, unrecognized, unsung

反 legendary, celebrated, famed, famous, noted, notorious, prominent, renowned, well-known 有名的

派 obscurity *n.* 无名之辈

反 celebrity 名人

obsequious [əbˈsiːkwiəs]

【考法】 *adj.* 谄媚的，奴性的：marked by or exhibiting a **fawning attentiveness**

例 She's constantly followed by obsequious assistants who will do anything. 她总是有一群谄媚的跟班，愿意为她赴汤蹈火。

反 supercilious 目中无人的

obsess [əbˈses]

【考法】 *vt.* 迷住；使困扰：to **haunt** or excessively preoccupy the mind of

例 The war obsesses her—she talks about nothing else. 那场战争困扰着她，她张口闭口都谈。

反 intensively disgust 极度厌恶

obstinate [ˈɑːbstɪnət]

【考法】 *adj.* 固执的：perversely adhering to an opinion, purpose, or course **in spite of** reason, arguments, or **persuasion**

例 obstinate resistance to change 坚决抵制改变

近 adamant, headstrong, intransigent, stubborn, uncompromising, unyielding, willful

反 acquiescent, agreeable, amenable, compliant, complying, flexible, pliable, pliant, relenting, yielding 顺从的，服从的

obstreperous [əbˈstrepərəs]

【考法】 *adj.* 不听话的，任性的：stubbornly resistant to control; **unruly**; given to resisting authority or another's control

例 The club's president was at his wits' end with obstreperous members who refused to cooperate. 俱乐部主席拿那些不合作的会员一点办法都没有。

近 balky, defiant, incompliant, insubordinate, intractable, rebellious, recalcitrant, refractory

反 disciplined, amenable, biddable, compliant, conformable, docile, obedient, ruly, submissive, tractable 守纪律的，顺从的

Unit 3

■ OBSTRUCT	■ OBTUSE	■ OBVIATE	■ OCCULT	■ ODIUM
■ OFFBEAT	■ OFFHAND	■ OFFICIOUS	■ OFFISH	■ OFF-KEY

obstruct [əbˈstrʌkt]

【考法】 *vt.* 妨碍，给…制造困难：to **impede**, retard, or interfere with; hinder; to **create difficulty** for the work or activity of

例 He was charged with obstructing justice by lying to investigators. 他被指控向检察官说谎，妨碍司法。

近 encumber, fetter, handicap, hinder, impede, inhibit, stymie, interfere with

反 facilitate, abet, aid, assist 促进，帮助

obtuse [əbˈtuːs]

【考法】 *adj.* 愚钝的：not having or showing an ability to **absorb ideas readily**

例 Are you being deliberately obtuse? 你是故意装笨吗？

近 dumb, fatuous, mindless, oafish, opaque, senseless, unintelligent, vacuous

反 insightful, apt, brainy, bright, brilliant, clever, fast, intelligent, keen, nimble, quick, quick-witted, sharp, sharp-witted, smart 有洞察力的，智慧的

obviate [ˈɑːbvieɪt]

【考法】 *vt.* 排除，使不必要：to anticipate and prevent (as a situation) or make **unnecessary** (as an action)

例 The new treatment obviates the need for surgery. 新的疗法使手术不再是必须的。

近 avert, forestall, preclude, stave off, head off

occult [əˈkʌlt]

【考法】 *adj.* 难以理解的：**not easily apprehended** or understood: abstruse, **mysterious**

例 an occult reference in the text that has puzzled scholars 文章中一处晦涩的、难倒了学者们的引注

近 ambiguous, arcane, equivocal, inscrutable, opaque, impenetrable

反 bare, manifest, patent, readily fathomable 暴露的，可理解的

odium [ˈoʊdiəm]

【考法】 *n.* 憎恶，讨厌：**strong dislike**, contempt, or aversion

例 Time did nothing to diminish the odium in which the traitor lived out his days. 时间也没有减少大家对这个叛徒的唾弃。

近 ignominy, infamy, obloquy, opprobrium

反 esteem, honor, respect, hankering, infatuation 尊敬，渴望，着迷

offbeat [ˌɔːfˈbiːt]

【考法】 *adj.* 不平常的：noticeably **different from** what is **generally found** or experienced

例 This writer has an enjoyably offbeat sense of humor. 这个作者有一种奇特而有趣的幽默感。

近 extraordinary, peculiar, queer, unaccustomed, uncommon, uncustomary, out-of-the-way

反 conventional, bathetic, hackneyed, common, ordinary, plain, usual 传统陈腐的，平常普通的

offhand [ˌɔːfˈhænd]

【考法】 *adj.* 即兴的，没有准备的：**without premeditation** or preparation

例 couldn't give the figures offhand 无法立即给出数字

近 ad-lib, extemporary, impromptu, improvised, unplanned, unpremeditated, unrehearsed

反 considered, planned, premeditated, prepared, rehearsed 事先谋划的

officious [əˈfɪʃəs]

【考法】 *adj.* 多管闲事的：**thrusting oneself** where one is not welcome or invited

例 an officious little man who was always telling everyone else how to do their jobs 一个多管闲事的人，总喜欢对他人的事情指手画脚

近 interfering, intruding, meddlesome, obtrusive, presuming, prying, snoopy

反 unobtrusive 不引人注目的

offish [ˈɔːfɪʃ]

【考法】 *adj.* 冷淡的：inclined to be distant and reserved; **aloof**

例 consistently surly and offish with the would-be suitors who came calling 对于追求者总是阴沉并且冷淡

近 aloof, detached, distant, remote, unbending, unsociable

反 sociable, cordial, friendly, social, warm 热情的

off-key [ˌɔːfˈkiː]

【考法】 *adj.* 不寻常的，不合适的：being **out of accord with** what is considered normal or appropriate

例 a high-flown, off-key speech by a newcomer 来自新手的颇有野心、不寻常的一次演讲

Unit 4

■ OMINOUS　　　　　■ OMNISCIENT　　　　■ ONEROUS　　　　　■ OPAQUE　　　　　■ OPINE
■ OPPORTUNE　　　　■ OPPROBRIOUS　　　■ OUTRAGEOUS　　　■ ORIENT　　　　　■ ORIGINAL

ominous [ˈɑːmɪnəs]

【考法】 *adj.* 凶兆的：of or being an **omen**, especially an **evil** one

例 an ominous threat of war 战争来临的凶兆

近 baleful, foreboding, inauspicious, portentous, sinister, threatening, minatory

反 auspicious, unthreatening 吉兆的，不具有威胁的

omniscient [ɑːmˈnɪsiənt]

【考法】 *adj.* 无所不知的：possessed of universal or **complete knowledge**

例 an omniscient deity 无所不知的神

反 vacuous 无知的

onerous [ˈɑːnərəs]

【考法】 *adj.* 费时间花心思的：**requiring much time**, **effort**, or careful attention

例 Building the scale model of the frigate was an onerous task. 建造军舰的小模型非常花时间。

近 arduous, burdensome, challenging, exacting, grueling, taxing, toilsome

反 requiring little effort, light, nondemanding, unchallenging, undemanding 轻松的，不费劲的

opaque [oʊˈpeɪk]
【考法】 *adj.* 晦涩的：so **obscure** as to be unintelligible
例 opaque prose 晦涩的诗歌
近 ambiguous, arcane, enigmatic, equivocal, inscrutable, occult
反 clear, accessible, obvious, plain, unambiguous, unequivocal 清晰易懂的

opine [oʊˈpaɪn]
【考法】 *v.* 表达观点；想，认为：to **express opinions**; to sate as an opinion
例 You can opine about any subject you like . 你可以畅所欲言。
近 comment, editorialize, note, observe, reflect, weigh in

opportune [ˌɑːpərˈtuːn]
【考法】 *adj.* 合适的，适当的：suitable or **convenient** for a particular occurrence
例 an opportune moment 方便的时机
近 seasonable, well-timed
反 inconvenient, untimely, inappropriate, unseasonable 不合适的

opprobrious [əˈproʊbriəs]
【考法1】 *adj.* 辱骂的: expressing contemptuous **reproach**; scornful or abusive
例 opprobrious language 脏话
近 scurrilous, vitriolic, vituperative, contumelious
【考法2】 *adj.* 臭名昭著的，令人鄙视的：bringing disgrace; shameful or **infamous**
例 opprobrious conduct 令人鄙视的行为
近 discreditable, disgraceful, dishonorable, ignominious, infamous, notorious, shameful, unrespectable
反 irreproachable, honorable, reputable, respectable 无可指责的，受人尊敬的
派 opprobrium *n.* 恶名
反 good repute 好名声

outrageous [aʊtˈreɪdʒəs]
【考法1】 *adj.* 过分的，难以容忍的：**exceeding the limits** of what is normal or tolerable
例 Outrageous tuition fees threaten our fundamental right to education. 过高的教育费用威胁着我们受教育的基本权利。
近 baroque, exorbitant, extravagant, lavish, overdue, overweening, unconscionable
反 acceptable, bearable, endurable, tolerable 可接受的，可容忍的；moderate, modest, reasonable, temper-ate 适度的，合适的
【考法2】 *adj.* 极坏的，极可怕的：enormously or flagrantly **bad or horrible**
例 The public was shocked by the outrageous treatment of prisoners . 民众对战俘所遭受的残暴虐待感到震惊。
近 atrocious, devious, evil, heinous, monstrous, nefarious, vicious, villainous, wicked
反 benign, benignant, kindhearted, humane, sympathetic, tenderhearted 善良的，好的

orient [ˈɔːrient]
【考法】 *vt.* 使确定方向，使熟悉或适应：to set or arrange in any **determinate position** especially in relation to the points of the compass; to **make familiar** with or adjusted to facts, principles, or a situation
例 orient students toward a career in medicine 指导学生从事医学的职业道路
近 accustom, familiarize, initiate, introduce, orientate
反 confuse 使迷惑

original [əˈrɪdʒənl]
【考法1】 *adj.* 创新的：independent and **creative** in thought or action: **inventive**
例 The car has a highly original design . 这车的设计很新颖。
近 ingenious, innovative, inventive
反 commonplace, banal, trite, familiar, hackneyed, time-honored, tired, warmed-over 陈腐的
【考法2】 *adj.* 最初的，最早的：coming **before** all others in time or order
例 The original plan had to be discarded when the situation changed drastically. 当环境发生剧烈变化时，最初的计划就该被放弃。
近 earliest, foremost, headmost, inaugural, initial, leadoff, maiden, pioneer, premier, virgin
反 final, last, latter, terminal, ultimate 最终的

Unit 5

orthodox ['ɔːrθədɑːks]
【考法】 *adj.* 传统的：following or agreeing with **established form**, **custom**, **or rules**
例 He believes in the benefits of both orthodox medicine and alternative medicine. 他既相信传统药物又相信替代药物的效用。
近 ceremonial, conventional, regular, routine
反 casual, freewheeling, informal, irregular, unceremonious, unconventional, unorthodox 不常见的

oscillate ['ɑːsɪleɪt]
【考法】 *vt.* 犹豫，变化：**vary** between opposing beliefs, feelings, or theories

ossify ['ɑːsɪfaɪ]
【考法】 *v.* (使)硬化，(使)僵化：to (cause to) become **hardened** or **conventional** and **opposed to change**
例 a disease that ossifies the joints 一种会使关节僵化的疾病
反 make pliant, transcend conventions, amenable to change 使柔软，超越传统

ostentatious [,ɑːsten'teɪʃəs]
【考法】 *adj.* 炫耀卖弄的：marked by or fond of **conspicuous** or vainglorious and sometimes **pretentious** display
例 She wears an ostentatious diamond ring on her finger. 她手指上戴着一枚巨大的钻戒。
近 flamboyant, flaring, flashy, splashy
反 modest, artless, austere, unpretentious, conservative, quiet, understated, unflamboyant, unflashy 谦让的，朴素的，保守的

ostracize ['ɑːstrəsaɪz]
【考法】 *vt.* 驱逐：to **exclude** from a group
例 He was ostracized from the scientific community for many years because of his radical political beliefs. 他因激进的政治理想被驱逐出了科学界很多年。
近 banish, bounce, chase, dismiss, expel, extrude, oust, boot out, cast out, run off, drum out, kick out, throw out, turf out
反 take in, include, embrace, welcome 接纳

oust [aʊst]
【考法】 *vt.* 驱逐：to **drive** or force **out**
例 She was ousted from her job after it was proven she'd been pilfering company supplies. 她贪污公司财物这事被证实后，她被驱逐出工作。
近 banish, boot out, cast out, chase, dismiss, drum out, expel, extrude, kick out, throw out, turf out, turn out

overweening [,oʊvər'wiːnɪŋ]
【考法】 *adj.* 傲慢的，专横的：having a **feeling of superiority** that shows itself in an **overbearing** attitude
例 His modesty is just a masquerade for his overweening conceit. 他的谦虚只不过是掩盖其傲慢本质的面具。
近 assumptive, arrogant, bumptious, haughty, imperious, peremptory, pompous, presuming, presumptuous, pretentious, supercilious
反 humble, modest 谦逊的

outlandish [aʊt'lændɪʃ]
【考法】 *adj.* 古怪的，奇异的：strikingly **out of the ordinary**; **bizarre**
例 an outlandish costume 奇装异服
近 bizarre, cranky, eccentric, erratic, offbeat, peculiar, remarkable
反 conventional, familiar, nonexotic, nonglamorous, plain-Jane, unglamorous, unromantic 常规的，平凡的

outmaneuver [,aʊtmə'nuːvər]
【考法】 *vt.* 以策略取胜：to **overcome** (an opponent) by artful, clever maneuvering
例 He outmaneuvered his congressional opponent. 他以计谋战胜了国会的对手。
近 outfox, outslick, outsmart, outthink, outwit
反 yield 屈服

outset [ˈaʊtset]
【考法】 *n.* 开端，开始：**beginning**, start
例 I wish you'd mentioned this problem at the outset . 我希望你开门见山地提这个问题。
近 alpha, commencement, genesis, inception, incipience, nascence
反 termination, close, conclusion, end, ending, omega 终止

Unit 6

■ OUTWIT	■ OVERBEARING	■ OVERLAP	■ OVERT	■ OVERTURE
■ OXYMORON	■ PACIFY	■ PADDING	■ PAEAN	■ PAINSTAKING

outwit [ˌaʊtˈwɪt]
【考法】 *vt.* 瞒骗，以智取胜：to **surpass** in cleverness or **cunning**; outsmart
例 a plan to outwit their opponents at their own game 在擅长的领域智取对手的计划
近 outfox, outmaneuver, outslick, outsmart, outthink

overbearing [ˌoʊvərˈberɪŋ]
【考法】 *adj.* 专横傲慢的：domineering in manner; **arrogant**
例 Her husband's overbearing manner made her miserable. 她的丈夫专横傲慢的态度，让她痛不欲生。
近 authoritative, despotic, dictatorial, imperious, masterful, peremptory
反 meek, unassuming 谦逊的

overlap [ˌoʊvərˈlæp]
【考法】 *v.* (与…)部分重叠：to occupy the **same area** in part
例 Baseball season overlaps football season in September. 棒球赛季和橄榄球赛季在九月有重合时间。
近 lap, overlay, overlie, overspread

overt [oʊˈvɜːrt]
【考法】 *adj.* 明显的，公开的：**open** and observable; not hidden, concealed, or secret
例 overt hostility 公然的敌意
反 shadowy 模糊的

overture [ˈoʊvərtʃər]
【考法 1】 *n.* 前言：an **introductory** section or part, as of a poem; a **prelude**
近 preamble, preliminary, prologue, warm-up, curtain-raiser
【考法 2】 *n.* 序曲：an instrumental composition intended especially as an **introduction** to an extended work, such as an **opera** or oratorio
例 the overture for festivities 节日活动的序曲
反 coda 结尾

oxymoron [ˌɑːksɪˈmɔːrɑːn]
【考法】 *n.* 矛盾修饰法：a **combination** of **contradictory** or incongruous words
例 The phrase "cruel kindness" is an oxymoron. "残酷的仁慈"就是矛盾修饰法的一个例子。

pacify [ˈpæsɪfaɪ]
【考法】 *vt.* 使平静，安慰：to **ease the anger** or agitation of
例 pacify a crying child 安抚一个哭泣的孩子
近 appease, assuage, conciliate, mollify, placate, propitiate
反 incite, rankle, tantrum, vex, discompose, truculent 煽动，激起

padding [ˈpædɪŋ]
【考法】 *n.* 夸张，废话：the representation of something in terms that **go beyond the facts**
例 That feature writer is sometimes guilty of padding , but he keeps it from getting out of hand. 这位专栏作者有时候夸夸其谈，但是保持了适度。
近 caricature, coloring, elaboration, embellishment, embroidery, hyperbole, magnification, overstatement, stretching
反 meiosis, understatement 轻描淡写

paean [ˈpiːən]
【考法】 *n.* 欢乐颂，赞扬：a **joyous song** or hymn of **praise**, tribute, thanksgiving, or triumph
例 paeans for hardworking 对辛勤工作的赞扬
近 accolade, citation, dithyramb, eulogium, eulogy, hymn, panegyric, tribute

painstaking [ˈpeɪnzteɪkɪŋ]
【考法】 *adj.* 煞费苦心的：taking pains: expending, showing, or involving **diligent care** and effort
例 It took months of painstaking research to write the book. 这本书的写作耗费了几个月的苦心研究。
近 careful, conscientious, fussy, meticulous, scrupulous
反 slipshod, cursory, careless 漫不经心的，草率的

Unit 7

■ PALATABLE	■ PALATIAL	■ PALL	■ PALLIATE	■ PALLID
■ PALMY	■ PALPABLE	■ PALTER	■ PALTRY	■ PAN

palatable [ˈpælətəbl]
【考法】 *adj.* 感到愉悦满足的：giving **pleasure or contentment** to the mind or senses
例 I always associate the palatable aroma of roasting turkey with Thanksgiving. 我总是把香喷喷的烤火鸡的味道和感恩节联系起来。
近 agreeable, blessed, congenial, delectable, delightful, delightsome, dreamy, dulcet, enjoyable, felicitous, grateful, gratifying, heavenly, jolly, luscious, pleasurable, satisfying, savory
反 disagreeable, pleasureless, unpalatable, unpleasant, unwelcome 不愉悦的

palatial [pəˈleɪʃl]
【考法】 *adj.* 宫殿般奢华的：of the nature of a palace, as in spaciousness or **ornateness**
例 a palatial penthouse apartment 一套豪华的顶层公寓
近 deluxe, lavish, luxuriant, opulent, sumptuous
反 ascetic, austere, humble, no-frills, spartan 简朴的

pall [pɔːl]
【考法】 *vi.* 失去兴趣：to lose in **interest** or **attraction**
例 His humor began to pall on us. 他的幽默开始使我们生腻了。
反 interest, intrigue 激发兴趣

palliate [ˈpælieɪt]
【考法】 *vt.* 平息，减轻：to make **less severe** or **intense**; mitigate
例 palliate his lonliness 减轻他的孤独
近 allay, alleviate, assuage, mitigate, mollify, relieve, soothe
反 aggravate, exacerbate, worsen, increase intensity 加剧，恶化
派 palliative *adj.* 缓和的，减轻的
例 palliative drug 缓解剂

pallid [ˈpælɪd]
【考法】 *adj.* 无生气的，缺乏活力的：**lacking** in **radiance** or **vitality**; dull
adj. 苍白无血色的：having an abnormally **pale** or wan complexion
例 The movie is a pallid version of the classic novel. 这部电影是这个经典小说缺乏活力的改版。
a pallid girl who looked as though she'd never seen the sun 一个面色苍白的姑娘，仿佛从来没有晒过太阳
近 ashen, ashy, blanched, pasty, wan
反 piquant 兴奋的; rubicund, blooming, florid, flush, full-blooded, glowing, ruddy, sanguine 红润的

palmy [ˈpɑːmi]
【考法】 *adj.* 繁荣的：marked by **prosperity**
例 the palmy days of the British drama 英国戏剧的繁荣时期
近 flourishing, prosperous, thriving, booming, lush, roaring, halcyon
反 failed, depressed, unprosperous, unsuccessful 不成功的，不繁荣的

palpable [ˈpælpəbl]
【考法】 *adj.* 明显的，易觉察的：easily perceived; **obvious**
例 a palpable difference 易觉察的差别
近 apprehensible, detectable, discernible, distinguishable, sensible
反 imperceptible, inappreciable, indistinguishable, insensible, undetectable 隐晦的，细微的

palter [ˈpɔːltər]
【考法】 *vi.* 欺骗；讨价还价：to act **insincerely** or **deceitfully**; haggle, chaffer
例 unwilling to palter over the price of the house 拒绝对房子讨价还价
近 chaffer, deal, dicker, haggle, horse-trade, negotiate, equivocate
反 candor 坦率

paltry ['pɔːltri]
【考法】 *adj.* 无价值的；微不足道的：lacking in **importance** or worth
例 paltry amounts of money 微不足道的钱
近 inconsequential, inconsiderable, insignificant, niggling, piddling, piffling, trivial
反 significant, important, big, consequential, considerable, material 意义重大的

pan [pæn]
【考法】 *vt./n.* 严厉批评：a **harsh criticism**
例 Almost all the movie critics have panned this latest sequel in a tired series. 几乎所有的影评家都批评这部最新续集，认为是狗尾续貂。
近 blame, censure, condemn, denounce, dispraise, reprehend
反 eulogize, extol, rave, laud, praise 称赞

Unit 8

■ PANACHE	■ PANDEMIC	■ PANDEMONIUM	■ PANEGYRIC	■ PANORAMIC
■ PROVENANCE	■ PARADIGM	■ PARADISE	■ PARADOX	■ PARAGON

panache [pə'næʃ]
【考法】 *n.* 炫耀：dash or **flamboyance** in style and action
例 play with panache 引人注意的炫耀
反 humility, unremarkable behavior, dullness 谦逊，寻常举止，平庸乏味

pandemic [pæn'demɪk]
【考法】 *adj.* 大范围流行的：**widespread**; general
例 pandemic malaria 大规模的疟疾
反 limited 有限的

pandemonium [ˌpændə'moʊniəm]
【考法】 *n.* 喧嚣，骚动：wild uproar or **noise**
例 When the market opened up, there was plenty of pandemonium. 市场一开市，就一片喧嚣。
近 bluster, bustle, disturbance, furor, fuss, hubbub, moil, pother, ruckus, ruction, tumult, turmoil, uproar
反 serene 安静

panegyric [ˌpænə'dʒɪrɪk]
【考法】 *n.* 赞颂之词，颂文：an **eulogistic** oration or writing
例 a panegyric on sth. 关于某事的赞颂
近 accolade, citation, commendation, dithyramb, eulogium, eulogy, hymn, paean
反 anathema, denunciation, condemnation 诅咒，谴责

panoramic [ˌpænə'ræmɪk]
【考法】 *adj.* 全景的：of an unobstructed or **complete view** of an area in every direction
例 a panoramic view of Los Angeles 洛杉矶的全景
近 compendious, complete, comprehensive, cyclopedic, embracive, exhaustive, thorough, in-depth
反 narrow 狭窄的
派 panorama *n.* 全景；全貌，概述
例 a panorama of American history 美国历史总览

provenance ['prɑːvənəns]
【考法】 *n.* 来源，起源：**origin, source**
例 The provenance of the ancient manuscript has never been confirmed. 这份古代手稿的来源仍未被确认。
近 derivation, fountain, inception, origin, root, source, wellspring

paradigm ['pærədaɪm]
【考法】 *n.* 典范，模范：one that serves as a **pattern** or model
例 He was the paradigm of the successful man. 他是成功人士的典范。
近 archetype, example, exemplar, ideal, model, pattern, paragon

paradise ['pærədaɪs]
【考法】 *n.* 快乐，狂喜：a state of overwhelming usually **pleasurable emotion**
例 that early stage of a romance when lovers are in paradise 恋爱初期，恋人们都处于快乐兴奋的状态
近 elation, euphoria, exhilaration, intoxication, rapture, rhapsody, transport
反 dejection, depression, gloominess, melancholy 沮丧，哀伤

paradox [ˈpærədɑːks]

【考法】 *n.* 矛盾，悖论：a statement that is seemingly contradictory or **opposed to common sense** and yet is perhaps true

例 reconcile the paradox 调和矛盾

近 dichotomy, incongruity

paragon [ˈpærəgɑːn]

【考法1】 *n.* 优秀模范：a model of excellence or perfection of a kind; a peerless **example**

例 a paragon of good husband 模范好丈夫

近 archetype, example, exemplar, ideal, model, pattern, paradigm

【考法2】 *vt.* 把…比作；显示相似：to **compare** with; parallel

例 paragon retreat with treachery 把撤退比作是背叛

近 assimilate, compare, equate, liken, match, parallel

反 contrast 对比，对照以产生反差

Unit 9

■ PARAMOUNT	■ PARANOID	■ PARAPHRASE	■ PARCH	■ PARENTHESIS
■ PARIAH	■ PARITY	■ PARODY	■ PAROXYSM	■ PARROT

paramount [ˈpærəmaʊnt]

【考法】 *adj.* 最重要的：of **chief** concern or **importance**

例 The paramount goal is to restore the colonial-era house with complete historical accuracy. 最重要的任务就是十分精确地依照历史重建殖民时期的建筑。

近 cardinal, chief, key, leading, main, predominant, preeminent, primary, principal, supreme

反 ancillary, secondary 次要的；paltry, petty, trifling, trivial 不重要的

paranoid [ˈpærənɔɪd]

【考法】 *adj.* 多疑的，对他人极端恐惧和怀疑的：exhibiting or characterized by **extreme** and irrational **fear or distrust** of others

例 a paranoid suspicion that the phone might be bugged 疑神疑鬼地担心电话被窃听了

近 distrustful, nervous, suspicious, unbelieving, worried

反 credulous 轻信的

派 paranoia *n.* 偏执狂

paraphrase [ˈpærəfreɪz]

【考法】 *v.* 转述，意译，改写：to express something (as a text or statement) **in different words**

例 paraphrase the diagnosis 转述诊断

近 rephrase, restate, reword, translate

反 quote (不加以修改地)引用

parch [pɑːrtʃ]

【考法】 *v.* 炽，烤，烤干：to make extremely **dry**, especially by exposure to heat

例 The Sun parches the fields. 太阳烤干了田野。

近 dehydrate, desiccate, dry, scorch, sear

反 douse, drench, hydrate, steep, wash, water, wet 弄湿

parenthesis [pəˈrenθəsɪs]

【考法】 *n.* 间断：an **interruption** of continuity; an interval

例 a parenthesis in an otherwise solid marriage 在本该是完满婚姻中的一个插曲

近 discontinuity, interim, interlude, intermission, interregnum, interruption, interstice, interval

反 continuation, continuity 持续不断；resumption 继续

pariah [pəˈraɪə]

【考法】 *n.* 被排斥或鄙视的人：one that is **despised or rejected**, outcast

例 a pariah of the society 被社会排斥的人

近 castaway, castoff, leper, reject

反 respectable person 值得尊敬的人

parity [ˈpærəti]

【考法】 *n.* 相称，同等，平等：the quality or state of **being equal** or equivalent

例 achieve parity with our competitors 取得与我们的竞争对手同等的地位

近 coequality, coordinateness, equality, equivalency, par, sameness

反 disparity, imparity, inequality 不公平；incommensurateness 不相称

parody ['pærədi]

【考法】 *n.* （以嘲笑原作作者的）模仿作品，恶搞：a literary or musical work in which the style of an author or work is closely **imitated for** comic effect or in **ridicule**

v. 模仿（以嘲弄）：to **copy** or exaggerate（someone or something）in order **to make fun** of

例 The Back Dormitory Boys specialize in parody of Backstreet Boys . 后舍男生擅长恶搞后街男孩。‖ parody a public figure's mannerisms 模仿嘲弄一个公共人物的举止

近 burlesque, caricature, spoof, travesty; imitate, mock, mimic

paroxysm ['pærəksɪzəm]

【考法】 *n.* （政治、社会领域的）大动荡：a violent **disturbance**（as of the political or social order）

例 Darwin's introduction of the theory of evolution created paroxysms in both religion and science that are still being felt today. 达尔文提出的进化论给宗教界和科学界都带来了巨大的冲击，时至今日我们仍然能感觉到。

近 bouleversement, cataclysm, earthquake, hurricane, storm, tempest, tumult, upheaval, uproar

parrot ['pærət]

【考法】 *vt.* （机械地）模仿，复制：to repeat or **imitate**, especially **without understanding**

例 parrot others blindly 盲目地人云亦云

近 copy, ditto, duplicate, echo, quote

反 coin, create, devise, invent 创造

Unit 10

■ PARRY   ■ PARSIMONIOUS   ■ PARTIAL   ■ PARTICULARIZE   ■ PARTISAN
■ PASTICHE   ■ PARTITION   ■ PATENT   ■ PATHOLOGICAL   ■ PATINA

parry ['pæri]

【考法】 *vt.* 躲避（问题）：to **evade** especially by an adroit answer

例 He parried the embarrassing question with a clever reply. 他以巧妙的回答躲避了这个令人尴尬的问题。

近 avoid, dodge, elude, eschew, evade, finesse, scape, shirk, shun

反 confront, face, meet 面对；embrace 欣然接受

parsimonious [ˌpɑːrsə'moʊniəs]

【考法】 *adj.* 过度节俭的，吝啬的：frugal to the point of **stinginess**

例 be parsimonious in the budgets 对预算吝啬

近 closefisted, mean, mingy, miserly, niggardly, penurious, stinting, tight, tightfisted, uncharitable, ungenerous

反 generous, liberal, munificent 慷慨的；dissolute, extravagant, prodigal, wasteful 浪费的，挥霍的

partial ['pɑːrʃl]

【考法 1】 *adj.* 偏袒的，偏爱的：inclined to favor one party more than the other: **biased**

例 He is partial to pretty girls . 他偏爱漂亮女孩。

近 biased, one-sided, partisan, prejudiced

反 disinterested, equitable, evenhanded, fair, impartial, neutral, objective, unbiased, unprejudiced 公平的

【考法 2】 *adj.* 部分的，不完整的：**lacking** some necessary part

例 a partial answer to the problem 一部分的解答

近 deficient, fragmental, fragmentary, half, halfway

反 complete, entire, full, intact, integral, perfect, whole 完整的

派 partially *adv.* 部分地；partiality *n.* 偏袒，偏爱

particularize [pər'tɪkjələraɪz]

【考法】 *vt.* 详述：to go into or **give details** or particulars

例 particularize the rules you must observe 详述你需要遵守的规定

近 detail, specificate, specify

反 abbreviate, abridge, condense, shorten 删减（内容等）

partisan ['pɑːrtəzn]

【考法】 *n.* 有偏见的人 *adj.* 偏袒的：inclined to favor **one side** over another

例 a shamelessly partisan news report 一篇无耻的、有倾向性的新闻报道

近 biased, one-sided, partial, prejudiced

反 disinterested, equitable, evenhanded, fair, impartial, neutral, objective, unbiased, unprejudiced 公平的

pastiche [pæ'stiːʃ]

【考法 1】 *n.* (带嘲讽的)模仿：a literary, artistic, musical, or architectural work that **imitates** the style of previous work, often **with satirical intent**

例 a pastiche of expensive interior design 高档室内设计的模仿

近 burlesque, caricature, imitation, parody, spoof, travesty

反 original work 原作

【考法 2】 *n.* 大杂烩：a pasticcio of incongruous parts; a **hodgepodge**

例 a pastiche of dishes from many countries 来自众多国家的饮食杂烩

近 agglomerate, collage, hodgepodge, jumble, jungle, medley, montage, motley, salad, variety, welter

partition [paːr'tɪʃn]

【考法】 *n.* 分割，划分：the act or process of **dividing** something into parts

例 Korea was partitioned in 1945. 朝鲜在 1945 年被划分了。

近 bifurcation, breakup, cleavage, disunion, division, fractionalization, schism, scission, split, sundering

反 unification, union 联合

patent ['peɪtnt]

【考法 1】 *adj.* 显而易见的，明显的：**readily visible** or intelligible: obvious

例 Unfortunately, the patent flaw of the proposal did not deter the city council from putting it up for a vote. 不幸的是，尽管提案中有着显而易见的缺陷，市议会依然将它拿出来进行投票。

近 apparent, blatant, conspicuous, evident, flagrant, manifest, obvious, plain

反 concealed, hidden, invisible 隐藏的，不可见的

【考法 2】 *n.* 专利：A patent is **an official right** to be the **only** person or company **allowed to make or sell** a new product for a certain period of time.

例 P&G applied for a patent on its cookies. 宝洁公司为其饼干申请了专利。

pathological [ˌpæθə'lɑːdʒɪkl]

【考法】 *adj.* 不正常的，病态的：being such to a degree that is extreme, excessive, or **markedly abnormal**

例 She has a pathological fear of snakes. 她对蛇有一种病态的恐惧。

近 abnormal, aberrant, anomalous, morbid

反 normal 正常的；natural 自然的

patina [pə'tiːnə]

【考法 1】 *n.* 外表：a **superficial** covering or exterior

例 a superficial patina of knowledge 表面肤浅的知识

近 façade, hull, skin, veneer

反 essential quality 本质；core, kernel 核心

【考法 2】 *n.* (由内而外散发的)氛围，气场：an **appearance or aura** that is derived from association, habit, or established character

例 Although the winery is brand-new, it has been constructed and decorated to give it a patina of old-world quaintness. 尽管酿酒厂是全新建造的，但它的构造和装饰都刻意营造出一种古色古香的奇异氛围。

近 air, ambience, aroma, atmosphere, climate, flavor, halo, odor, smell, temper, vibration

"不要把背 GRE 单词当成一种负担，要把它当成记忆的游戏、扩展视角的平台。"
（宋歆怡，2008 年 10 月，Verbal 700，录取院校：Newcastle University 口译系）

Unit 1

■ PATRICIAN	■ PATRIOT	■ PATRONIZE	■ PAUCITY	■ PROVINCE
■ PECK	■ PEDAGOGUE	■ PEDANT	■ PREDESTINE	■ PEDESTRIAN

patrician ［pə'trɪʃn］
【考法】 *n.* 贵族，名门望族：a man or woman of **high birth** or social position
adj. 贵族的，地位高的：of **high birth**, rank, or station
例 the rank of a patrician 贵族等级 ‖ come from a patrician family 出身贵族世家
近 aristocrat, noble, blue blood; aristocratic, genteel, gentle, grand, great, highborn, highbred, upper-class, wellborn
反 plebeian 平民，庶民; baseborn, common, humble, ignoble, low, lower-class, mean 地位低下的

patriot ［'peɪtrɪət］
【考法】 *n.* 爱国者：one who **loves** his or her **country** and supports its authority and interests
例 a fanatical patriot 狂热的爱国者
近 loyalist, nationalist, partisan
反 apostate, recreant, renegade, traitor, turncoat 叛徒; insurgent, mutineer, rebel 叛乱者
派 patriotism *n.* 爱国主义

patronize ［'peɪtrənaɪz］
【考法 1】 *vt.* 赞助：to **provide aid** or support for
例 a company that loyally patronizes the arts 一个一直以来坚持赞助艺术界的公司
近 advocate, back, champion, endorse, support, uphold
反 baffle, foil, frustrate, sabotage 阻挠，从中破坏
【考法 2】 *vt.* 以高人一等的态度对待：to adopt an air of condescension toward: **treat haughtily** or coolly
例 a director with an unpleasant habit of patronizing even his most gifted actors 一个有着令人讨厌的习惯的导演，他即便是对手下最有才华的演员也总是摆出傲慢的姿态
近 condescend
派 patron *n.* 赞助人

paucity ［'pɔːsəti］
【考法】 *n.* 少量，缺乏：smallness of number; **dearth**
例 an extreme paucity of natural resources 极度缺乏自然资源
近 dearth, deficit, drought, inadequacy, insufficiency, lack, scantiness, scarcity, shortage, undersupply, want
反 abundance, adequacy, amplitude, opulence, plenitude, sufficiency, wealth 大量，丰富

province ［'prɑːvɪns］
【考法】 *n.* 职能范围：sphere or **field of activity or authority**, as of a person
例 Increasingly, nurse practitioners are lessening the heavy workload of physicians by performing medical tasks once thought to be the exclusive province of doctors. 越来越多的护士开始执行原属于医生专属职能范畴的任务，从而大大减轻了医生的工作负担。
近 business, duty, function, role

peck ［pek］
【考法 1】 *n.* 大量：a **considerable amount**
例 Now you're in a peck of trouble. 现在你有一堆麻烦了。
近 abundance, bunch, bundle, dozen, mass, mountain, much, multiplicity, myriad, pile, plenitude, profusion, ton, volume, wealth
反 bit, glimmer, handful, hint, little, mite, nip, ounce, peanuts, pittance, spot, sprinkle, trace 少量

【考法 2】 *v.* (不情愿地) 小口咬：to **eat** reluctantly and **in small bites**
例 Fashion models never really eat: they just peck at small meals in expensive restaurants. 时装模特们几乎不吃东西——他们只是随便咬一口昂贵餐厅里的食物。
近 bite, nibble, sip, tipple
反 devour, gobble, gorge, guzzle, quaff, swill 贪婪地吃喝，大口吃喝

pedagogue [ˈpedəgɑːg]
【考法】 *n.* 教育者，老师：a person whose occupation is to **give formal instruction** in a school
例 a boring pedagogue who is called "PPT reader" 一个被戏称为"幻灯片朗读机"的无聊老师
近 educator, instructor, preceptor, teacher
反 disciple, pupil, student 弟子，学生

pedant [ˈpednt]
【考法】 *n.* 书呆子，墨守成规之人：one who pays undue attention to book learning and **formal rules**
例 He is a perfect type of pedant. 他是个十足的书呆子。
近 doctrinaire, dogmatist

predestine [ˌpriːˈdestɪn]
【考法】 *vt.* 预先注定：to determine the fate of **in advance**
例 a predestined victory 预先注定的胜利
近 doom, fate, foredoom, foreordain, ordain, predestine, predetermine, preordain
派 predestination *n.* 命中注定

pedestrian [pəˈdestriən]
【考法】 *adj.* 平庸无奇的，令人厌倦的：**causing weariness**, restlessness, or lack of interest
例 a pedestrian style 令人厌倦的风格
近 arid, dreary, dull, flat, jading, jejune, monochromatic, monotonous, stale, stodgy, tedious, wearisome
反 absorbing, engaging, engrossing, gripping, interesting, intriguing, involving, riveting 吸引人的

Unit 2

■ PEEP	■ PEER	■ PEEVE	■ PEJORATIVE	■ PELLUCID
■ PLAINTIVE	■ POLYMATH	■ PENCHANT	■ PENITENT	■ PENSIVE

peep [piːp]
【考法】 *n.* 一瞥：a **brief** and sometimes furtive **look**
例 take a peep at the new neighbors 偷偷瞄了新邻居一眼
近 gander, glance, glimpse, peek

peer [pɪr]
【考法 1】 *n.* 同等地位的人，同辈：a person who has **equal** standing with others
例 stand out among peers 在同辈当中很出众
近 coequal, compeer, coordinate, counterpart, equivalent, fellow, match, parallel
反 inferior 地位更低的人；superior 地位更高的人
派 peerless *adj.* 无与伦比的，不可比拟的
【考法 2】 *vi.* 好奇地凝视：to **look** narrowly or curiously
例 peer at the variety of marine life in the aquarium's huge tank 好奇地注视着巨大水族箱中丰富多样的海洋生物
近 blink, gape, gawk, gaze, goggle, rubberneck, stare
反 glance, glimpse 投去一瞥

peeve [piːv]
【考法】 *vt.* 打扰，惹恼：to **disturb** the peace of mind of (someone) especially by repeated disagreeable acts
例 be peeved by flattery 被拍马屁惹恼
近 aggravate, annoy, bother, exasperate, frost, gall, irk, nettle, pique, rile, ruffle, vex
反 becalm, compose, lull, lullaby, quiet, salve, settle, soothe, still, tranquilize 使镇定
派 peevish *adj.* 易怒的，脾气不好的

pejorative [pɪˈdʒɔːrətɪv]

【考法】 *adj.* 轻蔑的，贬低的：disparaging; belittling

例 pejorative attacks 贬义攻击

近 belittling, contemptuous, degrading, deprecatory, depreciative, derogative, disdainful, disparaging, scornful

反 commendatory, complimentary, laudatory 赞美的

pellucid [pəˈluːsɪd]

【考法】 *adj.* 清晰明确的，易懂的：transparently clear in style or meaning

例 Her poetry has a pellucid simplicity that betrays none of the sweat that went into writing it. 她的诗歌风格十分清新简约，丝毫没有体现出她为此付出的汗水。

近 apparent, distinct, evident, lucid, manifest, obvious, palpable, patent, perspicuous, plain, straightforward

反 clouded, cryptic, enigmatic, indistinct, mysterious, obfuscated, obscure 模糊难懂的

plaintive [ˈpleɪntɪv]

【考法】 *adj.* 悲伤的 expressing suffering or sadness

例 They lay on the firm sands, listening to the plaintive cry of the seagulls. 他们躺在硬实的沙地上，听着海鸥的哀鸣。

近 aching, anguished, bemoaning, deploring, doleful, grieving, heartbroken, lugubrious, mournful, plangent, sorrowful, weeping, woeful

polymath [ˈpɑːlimæθ]

【考法】 *n.* 学识渊博的人，博学者：a person of encyclopedic learning

例 To call him a mere polymath would be a gross understatement. 仅仅称他为"博学者"是大大地低估了他。

近 pundit, sage, savant, scholar

反 illiterate 文盲

penchant [ˈpentʃənt]

【考法】 *n.* 嗜好，迷恋：a strong and continued inclination

例 a penchant for Champaign 非常喜爱香槟

近 affection, bias, disposition, leaning, partiality, predilection, predisposition, proclivity, propensity, tendency

反 aversion, disfavor, disinclination, dislike, distaste, loathing, repugnance, repulsion 反感

penitent [ˈpenɪtənt]

【考法】 *adj.* 悔过的：feeling or expressing humble or regretful pain or sorrow for sins or offenses

例 a penitent criminal 一个悔过的罪犯

近 apologetic, compunctious, regretful, remorseful, repentant, rueful, sorry

反 impenitent, remorseless, unapologetic, unrepentant 不知悔改的

pensive [ˈpensɪv]

【考法】 *adj.* 沉思的，（尤指）哀思的：given to or marked by long, quiet and often musingly sad thinking

例 Rainy days often put her in a pensive mood. 雨天总是让她陷入深深的思考之中。

近 broody, cogitative, meditative, melancholy, musing, reflective, ruminant, ruminative, thoughtful

反 mindless, thoughtless, unreflective 不加思考的

Unit 3

■ PENURY	■ PERAMBULATE	■ PERCEPTIBLE	■ PEREMPTORY	■ PAROCHIAL
■ PERFIDY	■ PERFORATE	■ PERFUNCTORY	■ PERIMETER	■ PERIODICAL

penury [ˈpenjəri]

【考法 1】 *n.* 贫穷：extreme dearth; barrenness or insufficiency

例 be trapped in penury 被困于贫穷之中

近 destitution, impecuniosity, impoverishment, indigence, neediness, poorness, poverty, want

反 affluence, opulence, richness, wealth 富裕

【考法 2】 *n.* 吝啬，节俭：extreme and often niggardly **frugality**

例 They bitterly complained about their father's penury. 他们哀怨地抱怨父亲的节俭。

近 closeness, miserliness, niggardliness, parsimony, penuriousness, stinginess, tightfistedness, tightness

反 generosity, largesse, munificence, openhandedness, philanthropy 慷慨的

派 penurious *adj.* 贫穷的；吝啬的

perambulate [pəˈræmbjuleɪt]

【考法】 *v.* 徒步穿越，走过：to **travel over** or through especially on foot for exercise or pleasure

例 perambulate the desert 徒步穿越沙漠

近 amble, cross, go, navigate, pass, peregrinate, proceed, ramble, transit, travel, traverse

perceptible [pərˈseptəbl]

【考法】 *adj.* 可察觉的：capable of **being perceived** especially by the senses

例 You should be able to note a perceptible temperature change when you add the second reagents. 当你加入第二种试剂的时候，你应该能够察觉到明显的温度变化。

近 appreciable, apprehensible, detectable, discernible, distinguishable, palpable, sensible

反 impalpable, imperceptible, inappreciable, indistinguishable, insensible, undetectable 不能感知的

peremptory [pəˈremptəri]

【考法 1】 *adj.* 不容反抗的：**not allowing contradiction** or refusal; imperative

例 a peremptory order from the general 将军下达的不容反抗的命令

近 compulsory, forced, imperative, incumbent, involuntary, obligatory, required

反 elective, optional, voluntary 可选择的

【考法 2】 *adj.* 傲慢的：having a **feeling of superiority** that shows itself in an overbearing attitude

例 She had such a peremptory approach to running the club that people started to avoid her. 她用一种如此傲慢自大的方式来管理俱乐部，令大家纷纷开始躲避她。

近 assumptive, bumptious, haughty, imperious, lofty, pompous, presumptuous, pretentious, supercilious

反 humble, lowly, modest 谦逊的

parochial [pəˈroʊkiəl]

【考法】 *adj.* 狭隘的：**not broad** or open in views or opinions

例 the parochial outlook of the people in that rural backwater 在那个贫困乡村中的人们的狭隘观点

近 insular, narrow-minded, provincial, sectarian

反 broad-minded, catholic, cosmopolitan, liberal, open-minded 心胸宽广的，见过世面的

perfidy [ˈpɜːrfədi]

【考法】 *n.* 不忠，背信弃义：an act or an instance of **disloyalty**

例 As loyalty unites lovers, so perfidy estranges friends. 忠诚是爱情的纽带，背信弃义使友朋疏远。

近 backstabbing, disloyalty, infidelity, sellout, treachery, unfaithfulness, double cross

反 allegiance, devotion, faithfulness, fidelity, loyalty, staunchness, steadfastness 忠诚

派 perfidious *adj.* 不忠诚的

perforate [ˈpɜːrfəreɪt]

【考法】 *v.* 打孔，穿透：to **make a hole** through

例 perforate with a pin 用针穿孔

近 bore, drill, hole, pierce, punch, puncture, riddle

perfunctory [pərˈfʌŋktəri]

【考法】 *adj.* 敷衍的，呵呵的：characterized by routine or **superficiality** and often done merely as a duty

例 a perfunctory glance 敷衍的一瞥

近 automatic, cursory, mechanical, superficial

perimeter [pəˈrɪmɪtər]

【考法】 *n.* 边界，界限：the line or relatively narrow space that marks the **outer limit** of something

例 soldiers guarding the perimeter of the camp 守卫着营地边界的士兵

近 borderline, bound, boundary, circumference, confines, edge, frame, fringe, margin, periphery, skirt, verge

反 center, core, heart, kernel 核心

periodical [ˌpɪriˈɑːdɪkl]

【考法】 *adj.* 周期性的，有固定间隔的：occurring or recurring at **regular intervals**

例 periodical announcements from airline personnel concerning the delay 航空公司工作人员关于延误所进行的一遍又一遍的广播

近 continual, periodic, recurrent, recurring

反 constant, continuous, incessant, unceasing 持续不断的

Unit 4

peripatetic [ˌperipəˈtetɪk]
【考法】 *adj.* 巡游的，四处游历的：walking about or from **place to place**
例 peripatetic preachers 四处游历的传教士
近 ambulant, errant, nomadic, perambulatory, peregrine, vagabond, wandering
反 sedentary, settled 定居的

peripheral [pəˈrɪfərəl]
【考法】 *adj.* 辅助性的：available to **supply** something extra when needed
例 The IT consultant suggested that we update the drivers for all of the computer's peripheral devices. IT 咨询师建议我们更新电脑所有外围辅助设备的驱动程序。
近 accessorial, accessory, appurtenant, supplemental, supplementary
反 chief, main, principal 主要的

perish [ˈperɪʃ]
【考法】 *vi.* 死亡，消亡：to become destroyed or ruined: **cease to exist**
例 Thrive in calamity and perish in soft living. 生于忧患，死于安乐。‖ adapt or perish 适应或是消亡
近 decease, demise, die, end, expire, succumb, pass away
反 breathe, live, survive 活着，存活

permanent [ˈpɜːrmənənt]
【考法】 *adj.* 永恒的：**continuing or enduring** without fundamental or marked change; lasting **forever**
例 A temporary compromise has been accepted until a more permanent solution can be agreed upon. 在更为持久的决案被通过之前，一个暂时性的妥协方案被接受了。
近 ceaseless, dateless, deathless, endless, eternal, immortal, perpetual, undying, unending
反 ephemeral, evanescent, transient, transitory 稍瞬即逝的；provisional, temporary 暂时性的
派 permanence *n.* 永恒

permeable [ˈpɜːrmiəbl]
【考法】 *adj.* 可渗透的：capable of being permeated or **penetrated**, especially by liquids or gases
例 a permeable fabric that allows your body heat to escape 一种能使身体热量耗散的透气纤维
近 passable, penetrable, pervious, porous
反 waterproof 防水的；impassable, impenetrable, impervious, impermeable 不能渗透的

pernicious [pərˈnɪʃəs]
【考法】 *adj.* 有害的：highly **injurious** or destructive
例 Business may be troublesome but idleness is pernicious. 工作烦人，懒散害人。
近 adverse, baleful, damaging, deleterious, detrimental, hurtful, injurious, mischievous, nocuous, noxious
反 anodyne, benign, harmless, innocent, innocuous, inoffensive, safe 温和的，无害的

patchwork [ˈpætʃwɜːrk]
【考法】 *n./adj.* 混合物(的)：an unorganized collection or **mixture of various things**
例 this complex republic, a patchwork of cultures, religions and nationalities 这个复杂的共和国，各种文化、宗教和民族的混合体
近 assortment, hodgepodge, medley, montage, motley, pastiche, salad, stew, welter

perpetual [pərˈpetʃuəl]
【考法】 *adj.* 永恒的，不断的：**continuing forever**: everlasting
例 perpetual motion machine 永动机
近 ceaseless, dateless, deathless, endless, eternal, immortal, undying, unending
反 ephemeral, evanescent, transient, transitory 稍纵即逝的；provisional, temporary 暂时性的
派 perpetuate *vt.* 使永恒

persecute [ˈpɜːrsɪkjuːt]
【考法】 *vt.* 迫害，折磨：to **cause** persistent **suffering** to
例 persecuted minorities 被迫害的少数群体
近 agonize, anguish, curse, excruciate, harrow, plague, rack, torment, torture
派 persecution *n.* 迫害

persevere [ˌpɜːrsəˈvɪr]

【考法】 *vi.* 坚持不懈，不屈不挠: to **persist** in or remain constant to a purpose, idea, or task in the face of obstacles or discouragement

例 Although he was frustrated by the lack of financial resources and support, he persevered in his scientific research . 尽管因为资金不足而受阻，但他仍坚持进行科学研究。

近 carry on, endure, persist

反 renounce, succumb, surrender, yield 放弃，屈服

派 perseverance *n.* 坚持不懈

Unit 5

■ PERSIFLAGE   ■ PERSISTENCE   ■ PERSONABLE   ■ PERSPICACIOUS   ■ PERSPICUITY
■ PERTAIN   ■ PERTINACIOUS   ■ PERTINENT   ■ PENANCE   ■ PERUSE

persiflage [ˈpɜːrsɪflɑːʒ]

【考法】 *n.* 开玩笑: good-natured **teasing** or exchanging of clever remarks

例 an inappropriate persiflage 不合适的玩笑

近 backchat, badinage, chaff, jesting, joshing, raillery, repartee

persistence [pərˈsɪstəns]

【考法】 *n.* 坚持，持续: uninterrupted or **lasting existence**

例 The persistence of the fever for a week caused me great worry. 持续一周的发烧让我很不安。

近 ceaselessness, continuance, continuity, durability, endurance, subsistence

反 cessation, close, end, expiration, finish, stoppage, surcease, termination 停止

派 persistent *adj.* 持续不断的

personable [ˈpɜːrsənəbl]

【考法】 *adj.* 风度翩翩的，吸引人的: pleasing in personality or appearance; **attractive**

例 apparently be attracted by a personable young man 明显被一位风度翩翩的少年迷住了

近 alluring, appealing, attractive, captivating, charismatic, charming, comely, enchanting, handsome, pretty

反 grotesque, hideous, ugly 丑陋的; homely 相貌平庸的

perspicacious [ˌpɜːrspɪˈkeɪʃəs]

【考法】 *adj.* 极敏锐的，有洞察力的: having or showing **penetrating mental discernment**; clear-sighted

例 an impartial and perspicacious judge 一个明镜高悬(公正而极具洞察力)的法官

近 astute, savvy, sharp, sharp-witted, shrewd, smart

反 ignorant, oblivious, unknowing 未察觉的，无知的

派 perspicacity *n.* 敏锐，洞察力

perspicuity [ˌpɜːrspɪˈkjuːəti]

【考法】 *n.* 清晰明了: the quality of being perspicuous; **clearness and lucidity**

例 The key of modern enterprise system is the perspicuity of property right . 现代企业制度的核心是产权的明晰。

近 clarity, clearness, explicitness, lucidity, lucidness, perspicuousness

反 obscureness, obscurity, unclarity 模糊不清; ambiguity 模棱两可

pertain [pərˈteɪn]

【考法】 *vi.* 有关联: to **have a relation** or connection; relate

例 new evidence that pertains to the accident 与事故相关的新证据

近 appertain, bear, concern, refer, relate

派 pertaining *adj.* 有关系的

pertinacious [ˌpɜːrtnˈeɪʃəs]

【考法】 *adj.* 顽固的，固执地坚持的: **sticking** to an opinion, purpose, or course of action in spite of reason, arguments, or persuasion

例 the pertinacious crying boy 一个顽固的哭泣男孩

近 adamant, headstrong, implacable, inflexible, intransigent, mulish, obdurate, perverse, stubborn, willful

反 compliant, flexible, pliable, pliant, yielding 容易受影响的，容易控制的

pertinent ['pɜːrtnənt]

【考法】 *adj.* 相关的，恰当的：having a clear decisive **relevance** to the matter in hand

例 He impressed the jury with his concise, pertinent answers to the attorney's questions. 他对律师提出的问题给予了简洁而恰当的回答，这给陪审团留下了深刻的印象。

近 applicable, apposite, apropos, germane, material, pointed, relative, relevant

反 extraneous, immaterial, impertinent, inapplicable, inapposite, irrelevant, pointless 无关的

派 pertinence *n.* 相关，恰当

penance ['penəns]

【考法】 *n.* 忏悔：something that you do in order to **show** that you are **sorry about doing something wrong**

例 penance for her sin 为她的罪行忏悔

peruse [pə'ruːz]

【考法】 *vt.* 细读：to read or **examine**, typically **with great care**

例 peruse the manuscript to check for grammatical errors 细读手稿以检查语法错误

近 examine, scrutinize

反 glance, glimpse, scan, skim 一瞥，迅速浏览

Unit 6

■ PERVADE	■ PESSIMISTIC	■ PETITION	■ PETRIFY	■ PETTY
■ PHENOMENAL	■ PHILANTHROPIC	■ PHILISTINE	■ PHLEGMATIC	■ PIDDLING

pervade [pər'veɪd]

【考法】 *vt.* 弥漫，充满：to be present **throughout**; permeate

例 The mixed smell of sawdust and glue pervaded the whole factory. 锯末与胶水的味道弥漫了整个工厂。the corruption that pervades every stratum of society 充斥在社会每个阶层中的腐败

近 interpenetrate, percolate, riddle, suffuse, transfuse

派 pervasive *adj.* 弥漫的

pessimistic [,pesɪ'mɪstɪk]

【考法】 *adj.* 悲观的：tending to stress the negative or unfavorable or to **take the gloomiest possible view**

例 With that pessimistic attitude, it's no wonder you're depressed. 你的人生观悲观，难怪你会感到压抑。

近 bearish, defeatist, despairing, downbeat, hopeless

反 optimistic 乐观的

派 pessimism *n.* 悲观主义

petition [pə'tɪʃn]

【考法】 *n.* 请愿，正式的申请；申请书：a solemn **supplication or request** to a superior authority; an entreaty

v. (尤指正式地) 请求：to **make a request**, especially a formal written one

例 a petition for divorce 离婚申请书 ‖ She is petitioning to regain custody of the child. 为了重新获得孩子的监护权，她提出了正式申请。

近 appeal, cry, entreaty, pleading, solicitation, supplication; adjure, beseech, conjure, entreat, impetrate, implore, importune, plead, solicit, supplicate

派 petitioner *n.* 申请人，请愿者

petrify ['petrɪfaɪ]

【考法】 *vt.* 使僵化，使失去活力：to cause to **become stiff** or stone-like; deaden

例 Pressure from family has petrified his innovative mind. 家庭的压力使他的头脑失去了创造力。

近 damp, dampen, deaden, devitalize, enervate, lobotomize, ossify

反 brace, energize, enliven, invigorate, quicken, stimulate, vitalize, vivify 使有活力

派 petrification *n.* 石化，僵化

petty ['peti]

【考法】 *adj.* 细微的，不重要的：of **small importance**; trivial

例 play petty tricks 耍小聪明

近 inconsequential, inconsiderable, insignificant, measly, minute, paltry, peanut, slight, trifling, trivial

反 consequential, considerable, important, material, momentous, significant 重大的，重要的

phenomenal [fə'nɑːmɪnl]

【考法】 *adj.* 不寻常的，非凡的：being **out of the ordinary**; extraordinary; outstanding

例 the phenomenal growth that the suburb has experienced over the last decade 过去十年间郊区所经历的令人称奇的快速发展

近 especial, exceptional, extraordinary, peculiar, preternatural, rare, singular, uncommon, unusual

反 common, normal, ordinary, typical 普通的，典型的

philanthropic [ˌfɪlən'θrɑːpɪk]

【考法】 *adj.* 博爱的，为他人着想的：having or showing a concern for the **welfare of others**

例 the philanthropic aims of the organization 这个机构的博爱、利他的目标

近 altruistic, beneficent, benevolent, eleemosynary, good, humanitarian

反 misanthropic 反人类的；selfish 自私的

派 philanthropist *n.* 博爱的人

philistine ['fɪlɪstiːn]

【考法】 *n.* 市侩（注重物质而鄙视智慧或艺术的人）：a person who is **guided by materialism** and is usually disdainful of intellectual or artistic values

例 the philistine's vulgarity 市侩之人的庸俗

近 lowbrow, materialist

反 highbrow 文化修养高的人

phlegmatic [fleg'mætɪk]

【考法】 *adj.* 冷静的，无感情的，淡漠的：having or suggesting a **calm**, **sluggish temperament**; unemotional

例 a strangely phlegmatic response to what should have been happy news 对本该是一个让人开心的新闻的冷漠回应

近 affectless, apathetic, cold-blooded, emotionless, impassible, numb, stoic, stolid

反 demonstrative, emotional, fervent, fervid, impassioned, passionate, vehement 感情丰富的，热情的

piddling ['pɪdlɪŋ]

【考法】 *adj.* 微不足道的：so **trifling or trivial** as to be beneath one's consideration

例 raise a piddling objection to the plan 对计划提出一个微不足道的反对

近 inconsequential, inconsiderable, insignificant, measly, minute, paltry, peanut, slight, trifling, trivial

反 consequential, considerable, important, material, momentous, significant 重大的，重要的

Unit 7

■ PIEBALD	■ PIGMENT	■ PILFER	■ PRECOCIOUS	■ PILLORY
■ PILOT	■ PINE	■ PINNACLE	■ PINPOINT	■ PIQUANT

piebald ['paɪbɔːld]

【考法】 *adj.* 混合的，杂糅而成的：consisting of many things of **different sorts**

例 his piebald ethnic background 他身为混血儿的背景

近 assorted, eclectic, heterogeneous, hybrid, magpie, mixed, motley, promiscuous, varied

反 homogeneous 由相同类型事物组成的

pigment ['pɪgmənt]

【考法】 *n.* 颜料：a substance that imparts black or white or a **color** to other materials

vt. 给…上颜色：to **color** with or as if with pigment

例 natural red pigment 天然红色染料 ‖ pigmented silk 染过色的丝绸

近 colorant, dye, stain; paint, stain, tincture, tinge, tint

反 blanch 漂白；decolorize 使脱色

pilfer ['pɪlfər]

【考法】 *vt.* 偷窃：to **steal** stealthily in small amounts

例 pilfer the commercial document 偷窃商业文件

近 appropriate, filch, hook, lift, pinch, purloin, steal, thieve

precocious [prɪ'koʊʃəs]

【考法】 *adj.* 早熟的：occurring **before the usual** or expected time

例 a precocious child 一个早熟的孩子

近 early, premature, unseasonable

pillory [ˈpɪləri]

【考法】 *vt.* 当众嘲弄：to expose to **public contempt**, ridicule, or scorn

例 The candidate mercilessly pilloried his opponent. 候选人在大众面前无情地羞辱他的对手。
He resigned after being pilloried by the press. 在遭到媒体嘲弄之后他愤然辞职。

近 abase, debase, degrade, denounce, humiliate, ridicule

反 carol, eulogize, exalt, extol, laud 赞美

pilot [ˈpaɪlət]

【考法1】 *adj.* 初步的，试验性的：serving as a **tentative model** for future experiment or development

例 They carried out a pilot study before the larger, more expensive project was started. 在更大规模、更为昂贵的项目开始之前，他们进行了初步研究。

近 developmental, experimental, model, test, trial

反 eventual, final, ultimate 最终的

【考法2】 *vt.* 带领通过：**lead** or conduct over a usually difficult course

例 The lobbyists piloted the bill through the Senate. 游说集团使法案得到参议院的批准。

近 conduct, direct, guide, lead, route, show, steer

反 follow 跟随

pine [paɪn]

【考法】 *vi.* 渴望，奢望：to **yearn** intensely and persistently especially for something unattainable

例 pine for a lost love 渴望那段逝去的爱情

近 ache, crave, dream, hunger, itch, long, lust, repine, thirst, yearn

反 abhor, detest, loathe 厌恶，反感

pinnacle [ˈpɪnəkl]

【考法】 *n.* 顶峰：the **highest point** of development or achievement

例 a singer who has reached the pinnacle of career 已到达事业巅峰的歌手

近 acme, apex, climax, culmination, meridian, peak, summit, top, zenith

反 bottom, nadir 最低点

pinpoint [ˈpɪnpɔɪnt]

【考法1】 *adj.* 非常精确的：located, fixed, or directed with **extreme precision**

例 The commander demanded the pinpoint location of artillery fire. 指挥官需要火炮攻击的精确位置。

近 accurate, close, delicate, exact, fine, hairline, mathematical, precise, refined, rigorous

反 coarse, cursory, rough 粗略的；imprecise, inaccurate, inexact 不准确的

【考法2】 *vt.* 精确定位或确认：to locate, fix, determine, or **identify with precision**

例 pinpoint the target by tracking calls from his cellphone 通过跟踪手机信号精确定位目标 ‖ pinpoint the cause of failure 准确找出失败的原因

近 determine, distinguish, locate, identify, recognize, spot

反 estimate 估计

piquant [ˈpiːkənt]

【考法】 *adj.* 令人振奋的：appealingly **provocative**

例 a piquant glance 充满挑逗的一瞥

近 exciting, pungent, racy, stimulating

反 flat, pallid 单调的，无聊的

Unit 8

■ PIQUE   ■ PIRATE   ■ PITHY   ■ PITILESS   ■ PITTANCE
■ PLACATE   ■ PLACEBO   ■ PLAGIARIZE   ■ PLANGENT   ■ PLASTIC

pique [piːk]

【考法】 *vt.* 激起，刺激：to **excite or arouse** especially by a provocation, challenge, or rebuff

例 radical remarks that pique their curiosity 引起他们兴趣的激进评论

近 arouse, encourage, excite, fire, impassion, incite, instigate, move, stimulate, stir

反 allay, alleviate, assuage, ease, mitigate, mollify, palliate, relieve, soothe 平息，缓和

pirate [ˈpaɪrət]

【考法】 *vt.* 盗版，盗用：to take or make use of under a guise of authority but **without actual right**

例 a pirated version of the software 盗版软件

近 arrogate, commandeer, convert, expropriate, preempt, press, seize, usurp

pithy	[ˈpɪθi]
【考法】	*adj.* 精练的，简洁的：precisely meaningful; forceful and **brief**
例	The professor gave a pithy introduction to this course. 教授就这门课程做了简短的介绍。
近	apothegmatic, brief, capsule, compact, compendious, concise, laconic, succinct, telegraphic, terse
反	circuitous, circumlocutory, diffuse, rambling, prolix, verbose, windy, wordy 冗长累赘的
派	pithiness *n.* 简洁，犀利

pitiless	[ˈpɪtiləs]
【考法】	*adj.* 没有同情心的：**devoid of** or unmoved by **pity**
例	a pitiless humiliation 毫不留情的羞辱
近	affectless, callous, coldhearted, cruel, harsh, indurate, merciless
反	charitable, clement, compassionate, humane, merciful, sympathetic, tender 有同情心的，仁慈的

pittance	[ˈpɪtns]
【考法】	*n.* 少量津贴：a **small portion**, amount, or allowance
例	The internship offers only a pittance for a salary, but it is a great opportunity to gain experience. 实习所能挣到的报酬是很少的，但是它提供了获得经验的绝佳机会。
近	bit, mite, modicum, peanuts, trace
反	cornucopia, opulence 富饶；boodle, bundle, fortune 大笔财富

placate	[ˈpleɪkeɪt]
【考法】	*vt.* (通过让步以)平息抚慰：to **lessen the anger** or agitation of
例	The colonists implemented a new policy to placate local opposition. 殖民者采取了一项新政策以缓和当地的反抗情绪。
近	appease, assuage, conciliate, mollify, pacify, propitiate, tranquilize
反	anger, enrage, foment, gall, incense, inflame, infuriate, peeve, rile 激怒，使气恼
派	placation *n.* 安抚

placebo	[pləˈsiːboʊ]
【考法】	*n.* 安慰性的事物：something of no intrinsic remedial value that is **used to appease or reassure** another
例	Candies are often adopted as the placebo for the dying patients. 糖果通常作为安慰剂给重症患者服用。

plagiarize	[ˈpleɪdʒəraɪz]
【考法】	*v.* 剽窃，抄袭：to **steal** and pass off (the **ideas** or words of another) as one's own
例	In scientific community, plagiarizing other's paper is a felony. 在学术界，剽窃他人的论文是一项重罪。
近	steal
派	plagiarism *n.* 剽窃

plangent	[ˈplændʒənt]
【考法】	*adj.* 凄凉的，哀伤的：having an expressive and especially **plaintive** quality
例	a plangent song about a long-ago love 一首关于往日爱情的凄凉歌曲
近	doleful, dolorous, funeral, grieving, lamentable, lugubrious, plaintive, rueful, sorrowful, woeful
反	agreeable, cheerful, delightful, enjoyable, jolly, pleasing 令人愉快的

plastic	[ˈplæstɪk]
【考法】	*adj.* 可塑的：susceptible of being **modified** in form or nature
例	the plastic quality of modeling clay 模型泥的可塑性质
近	adaptable, ductile, flexible, malleable, pliable, pliant, resilient, supple
反	inflexible, rigid, stiff 僵硬的
派	plasticity *n.* 可塑性

Unit 9

■ PLATEAU	■ PLATITUDE	■ PLAUSIBLE	■ PLAGUE	■ POIGNANT
■ PLETHORA	■ PLIABLE	■ PLIANT	■ PLIGHT	■ PLODDING

plateau	[plæˈtoʊ]
【考法 1】	*n.* 高原：a usually extensive level land area **raised** sharply **above** adjacent land on at least one side
例	Qinghai-Tibetan Plateau 青藏高原
近	highland, mesa, tableland, upland
反	lowland 低谷；basin 盆地

【考法2】 *n.* 稳定时期，平台期：a relatively **stable level**, period, or state

例 reach a plateau of development 达到发展的稳定期

近 equilibrium, stage, stasis

platitude ['plætɪtuːd]

【考法】 *n.* 陈词滥调：a trite or **banal** remark or **statement**, especially one expressed as if it were original or significant

例 the platitude of most political oratory 政治说辞里的陈词滥调

近 banality, bromide, cliché, commonplace, homily, shibboleth, truism

plausible ['plɔːzəbl]

【考法】 *adj.* 可信的：**superficially** fair, **reasonable**, or valuable but often specious

例 a plausible argument 可信的论点

近 believable, credible, likely, possible, presumable, probable

反 paradoxical 看似矛盾的；implausible, improbable, incredible, unbelievable, unlikely 不太可能的

派 plausibility *n.* 看似有理

plague [pleɪg]

【考法1】 *n.* 瘟疫：a **widespread disease** resulting in a high rate of death

例 Half of the population was wiped out by the plague . 一半的人口在瘟疫中丧生。

近 pestilence

【考法2】 *v.* 折磨，使…痛苦：to **cause persistent suffering** to

例 She was plagued by weakness, fatigue, and dizziness . 她被虚弱、疲劳和眩晕折磨。

近 agonize, anguish, excruciate, harrow, persecute, afflict, torment, torture

poignant ['pɔɪnjənt]

【考法】 *adj.* 令人感伤的：**causing** a strong feeling of **sadness**

例 a poignant story of a love affair that ends in tragedy 一个以悲剧终结的令人感伤的爱情故事

近 affecting, impactful, impressive, moving, touching

反 unaffecting, unemotional, unimpressive 无动于衷的

plethora ['pleθərə]

【考法】 *n.* 过量，过剩：**excess**, superfluity

例 a plethora of advice and a paucity of assistance 给出大量建议而鲜有实质性援助

近 abundance, cornucopia, feast, overabundance, overflow, plentitude, profusion, surfeit, surplus

反 dearth, inadequacy, insufficiency, paucity, scarcity, undersupply 缺乏

派 plethoric *adj.* 过量的

pliable ['plaɪəbl]

【考法1】 *adj.* 易弯曲的，柔软的：**supple** enough to bend freely or repeatedly without breaking

例 pliable optical fiber 柔软的光纤

近 adaptable, ductile, flexible, limber, plastic, supple

反 inflexible, rigid, stiff, unbending 不易弯曲的

【考法2】 *adj.* 易受影响的，温顺的：**easily influenced**, persuaded, or swayed

例 He took advantage of the pliable mind of youth . 他利用了年轻人容易受他人教唆的思想。

近 compliant, docile, obedient, pliant, tractable, subdued

反 contumacious, insubordinate, intractable, obstreperous, recalcitrant, refractory, unruly 难控制的

pliant ['plaɪənt]

【考法1】 *adj.* 易弯曲的：**easily bent** or flexed

例 a pliant young tree 易弯曲的小树

近 adaptable, ductile, flexible, limber, plastic, supple

反 inflexible, rigid, stiff 不易弯曲的；unbending 难弯曲的

【考法2】 *adj.* 顺从的：**yielding** readily to influence or domination

例 She's proud and stubborn, you know, under that pliant exterior . 你知道，她外表温顺，内心却骄傲而固执。

近 compliant, docile, obedient, pliant, tractable, subdued

反 contumacious, insubordinate, intractable, obstreperous, recalcitrant, refractory, unruly 难控制的

plight [plaɪt]

【考法】 *n.* 困境：a situation, especially a bad or **unfortunate** one

例 the plight of poor families 穷困家庭的困境

近 dilemma, jam, predicament, quandary

plodding	[ˈplɑːdɪŋ]
【考法】	*adj.* 无聊的，单调乏味的：characterized by **dullness and monotony**; lacking variety or excitement
例	How can you stick with this show through the first four plodding episodes？你是怎么坚持把前四季枯燥无味的节目看完的？
近	dreary, dull, humdrum, jejune, monotone, monotonous, pedestrian, stale, stodgy
反	absorbing, engaging, engrossing, gripping, interesting, intriguing, involving, riveting 令人感兴趣的

Unit 10

■ PLUCK	■ PLUMB	■ PLUMMET	■ PLUMP	■ PLUNGE
■ POLARIZE	■ POLEMIC	■ POLISHED	■ POLITIC	■ POMPOUS

pluck	[plʌk]
【考法】	*n.* 敢于面对困难的勇气：resourceful **courage** and daring in the face of difficulties
例	full of pluck 充满了勇气
近	backbone, courage, dauntlessness, grit, guts, resolution, spirit, spunk
反	cowardice, coward, spinelessness 胆小，怯懦
派	plucky *adj.* 勇敢的

plumb	[plʌm]
【考法1】	*adj.* 完全的，绝对的：having **no exceptions** or restrictions
派	Such a movie is plumb trash and further evidence of the deterioration of popular culture. 这样的电影就是彻头彻尾的垃圾，它进一步证明了大众文化的堕落和腐化。
近	absolute, categorical, complete, consummate, definite, pure, sheer, thorough, utter, very
反	doubtful, dubious, equivocal, questionable, uncertain 不确定的；qualified 有条件的
【考法2】	*vt.* 仔细深入地检查；探索，探究：to **examine** closely or **deeply**
例	plumb the book's complexities 审阅这本书的复杂度 ‖ questions that plumb the depths of stupidity 探究智商下限的问题
近	explore, delve, inquire, investigate, probe

plummet	[ˈplʌmɪt]
【考法】	*vi.* 突然下降：to **decline suddenly** and steeply
例	Overall GPA plummeted 0.5 points. 平均学分骤降 0.5。
近	crash, decline, descend, dip, dive, fall, plunge, sink, tumble
反	skyrocket, soar 飙升

plump	[plʌmp]
【考法1】	*adj.* 丰满的：**well-rounded** and full in form
例	In Tang Dynasty, being plump was a sign of ultimate beauty. 在唐代，身材丰满是最美丽的象征。
近	chubby, fleshy, fat, gross, obese, rotund, round
反	lean, slender, svelte, thin 纤瘦的，苗条的；angular 因消瘦而棱角分明的
【考法2】	*v.* 鼎力支持，赞不绝口：to **give full support** or praise
例	We will plump for candidate who supports stem cell research. 我们会鼎力支持那些拥护干细胞研究的候选人。
近	advocate, back, champion, endorse, patronize
反	baffle, foil, frustrate, sabotage 阻挠，从中破坏

plunge	[plʌndʒ]
【考法】	*vi.* 突然下降：to **descend** or dip **suddenly**
例	Stock's value plunged. 股票价值骤然下降。
近	crash, decline, descend, dip, dive, fall, plummet, sink, tumble
反	skyrocket, soar 飙升

polarize	[ˈpoʊləraɪz]
【考法】	*vt.* 使分开对立，使两极分化：to **break** up **into opposing** factions or groupings
例	The controversy has polarized voters into pro-abortion and anti-abortion groups. 这一争议使得选民分化成支持堕胎和反对堕胎两个群体。
近	bifurcate, diverge, divide
反	coalesce, unite 合并，联合
派	polarization *n.* 两极分化

polemic [pəˈlemɪk]
【考法】 *n.* 争执：a controversial **argument**
例 The polemic between science and religion has never ceased. 科学和宗教之间的争论从未停息。
近 contention, controversy, disagreement, disputation
反 agreement 一致，协议
派 polemical *adj.* 好争论的

polished [ˈpɑːlɪʃt]
【考法】 *adj.* 有教养的：showing a **high degree of refinement** and the assurance that comes from wide social experience
例 He maintained a very polished tone in his correspondences. 他在通信中保持着一种极有教养的口吻。
近 cultivated, cultured, genteel, refined, urbane
反 gauche, rustic, philistine 粗俗的；uncivilized, untutored 未开化的

politic [ˈpɑːlətɪk]
【考法】 *adj.* 合时宜的，明智的，高情商的：**suitable** for bringing about a desired result under the circumstances
例 a politic decision 一个明智的决定
近 advisable, desirable, prudent, tactical
反 imprudent, inadvisable, injudicious, unwise 不明智的，不合时宜的

pompous [ˈpɑːmpəs]
【考法1】 *adj.* 浮夸的：excessively elevated or **ornate**
例 The candidate was given to windy and pompous rhetorical speeches. 听众们听了一场冗长而浮夸的演讲。
近 affected, bombastic, flowery, grandiloquent, magniloquent, rhetorical
反 homely 朴素的
【考法2】 *adj.* 傲慢的：having or exhibiting **self-importance**
例 a pompous politician who insisted on boarding the plane first 一个坚持要求优先登机的傲慢政客
近 arrogant, egocentric, haughty, pontifical, presumptuous, supercilious
反 humble, modest, unpretentious 谦逊的

If you put out your hands, you are a laborer; if you put out your hands and mind, you are a craftsperson; if you put out your hands, mind, heart and soul, you are an artist.

如果你用双手工作,你是一个劳力;如果你用双手和头脑工作,你是一个工匠;
如果你用双手和头脑工作,并且全身心投入,你就是一个艺术家。

——美国电影 *American Heart and Soul*

List 19

"多看多背多做题，不烦不倦不放弃。"
（赵墨非，Verbal 790，Quantitative 800，录取学校：UCLA 经济学 PHD）

Unit 1

■ PONDERABLE	■ PONDEROUS	■ PONTIFICATE	■ PORE	■ POROUS
■ PORTENTOUS	■ POSEUR	■ POSIT	■ POSTULATE	■ POSTURE

ponderable ['pɑːndərəbl]
【考法】 *adj.* 有价值的，值得考虑的：**considerable** enough to be weighed or assessed
例 Climate change has exerted a ponderable influence on world politics. 气候变化对世界政局有着不容忽视的影响。
近 appreciable, perceptible, sensible
反 inappreciable 微不足道的

ponderous ['pɑːndərəs]
【考法】 *adj.* 沉重的：of very **great weight**
例 a ponderous machine 沉重的机器
近 cumbersome, heavy, hefty, massive, onerous, weighty
反 ethereal, gossamer, light, weightless 轻飘飘的

pontificate [pɑːn'tɪfɪkeɪt]
【考法】 *vi.* 傲慢地做或说：to **speak** or express opinions in a **pompous** or dogmatic way
例 pontificate to show a sense of superiority 傲慢地说以显示高人一等的优越感
反 condescend 屈尊，俯就
派 pontification *n.* 傲慢的言行；pontifical *adj.* 傲慢的

pore [pɔːr]
【考法】 *vi.* 仔细浏览，仔细研究：to **read or study attentively**（usually used with over）
例 The committee will probably pore over the results of the study for a long time before making their decision. 在正式做决定之前，委员会可能需要花很长的时间来仔细研究调查结果。
近 cogitate, consider, contemplate, deliberate, meditate, perpend, ruminate, study, weigh, chew over
反 flip, glance, leaf, riffle, skim 粗略地看，迅速浏览

porous ['pɔːrəs]
【考法】 *adj.* 多孔可渗透的：**admitting** the passage of gas or **liquid** through pores or interstices
例 Lava rock has a porous structure which makes the material lightweight and highly moisture-retentive. 火山岩的多孔结构使得它密度很小，同时有很高的吸湿性。
近 passable, penetrable, permeable, pervious
反 impassable, impenetrable, impermeable, impervious 无法穿透的
派 porosity *n.* 多孔性

portentous [pɔːr'tentəs]
【考法】 *adj.* 预兆性的，凶兆的：being or showing a **sign of evil** or calamity to come
例 an eerie and portentous stillness 阴森神秘、充满凶兆的寂静
近 baleful, direful, doomy, foreboding, inauspicious, menacing, minatory, ominous, sinister, ill-omened
反 auspicious, propitious 吉兆的

poseur [poʊ'zɜːr]
【考法】 *n.* 故作姿态、不真诚的人：an **affected** or **insincere** person
例 a pretending poseur 一个虚伪不真诚的人
近 grandstander, poser

posit ['pɑːzɪt]

【考法】 *vt.* 假定，断定：to assume or **affirm** the existence of

例 The committee posited that he was qualified for the election. 委员会假定他是够格参加选举的。

近 assume, postulate, presuppose, premise, presume

反 falsify 证明为假

postulate ['pɑːstʃəleɪt]

【考法】 *n.* 假定，假设：something taken as being true or factual and used as a **starting point** for a course of action or reasoning   *vt.* 假定为真：to **assume** or claim as **true**, existent, or necessary

例 postulate a causal relationship 假定存在因果关系

近 premise, presumption, presupposition, supposition; assume, conjecture, hypothesize, posit, presuppose, premise, presume, suppose

反 conclusion 结论；belie, disprove, falsify 证明为假

派 postulation *n.* 推测

posture ['pɑːstʃər]

【考法】 *vi.* 故作姿态，装模作样：to assume an artificial or **pretended attitude**

例 posture to impress 故作姿态以给别人留下印象

近 attitudinize, feign, grandstand, masquerade, pose, pretend

派 posturer *n.* 故作姿态之人

Unit 2

■ POTABLE	■ POTENTATE	■ POTENTIATE	■ POUT	■ PRACTITIONER
■ PREMIUM	■ PRATE	■ PREACH	■ PRECARIOUS	■ PRECEDENT

potable ['poʊtəbl]

【考法】 *n.* 饮品，尤指有酒精饮料：a **beverage**, especially an alcoholic beverage
adj. 适于饮用的：**suitable for drinking**

例 Potables are offered at bar counter for free. 饮料可以在吧台免费领取。 ‖ Price of the potable water has soared. 饮用水价格飙升。

近 beverage, drink, juice, liquor, spirits; drinkable, edible

反 non-intoxicant, soft drink 软饮料；undrinkable 不能饮用的

potentate ['poʊtnteɪt]

【考法】 *n.* 有权势的人：one who **has the power** and position to rule over others

例 a son of a potentate 官二代

近 authority, autocrat, monarch, ruler, sovereign

反 figurehead (有名无权的) 傀儡

potentiate [poʊ'tenʃɪeɪt]

【考法】 *vt.* 激活，加强：to make effective or active, or more effective or **more active**

例 additives to potentiate the drug 增强药效的添加剂

近 activate, energize, enhance, intensify, stir, wake, vitalize

反 deactivate 使无效；abate, attenuate, dwindle, lessen, moderate, reduce 减弱，削弱

pout [paʊt]

【考法】 *vi.* (尤指撅嘴或板着脸) 表示不悦：to **show displeasure**, especially by thrusting out the lips or wearing a sullen expression

例 She pouted and didn't say a word to anyone all morning. 她整个早上都闷闷不乐，没和别人说一句话。

近 grump, mope, sulk

反 grin 露齿而笑

practitioner [præk'tɪʃənər]

【考法】 *n.* 职业人士：one who practices a **profession**

例 medical practitioner 医护人员，行医者

近 expert, guru, professional, specialist, virtuoso

反 fledgling 无经验的人；quack 冒充内行的人

premium	[ˈpriːmiəm]

【考法】 *adj.* 高端的：of **superior quality or value**
例 premium gasoline 质优价高的汽油
近 expensive, extravagant, precious, costly, valuable

prate	[preɪt]

【考法】 *vi.* 闲聊，空谈：to **talk** long and **idly**
例 They have been prating on the phone for hours. 他们已经煲了几个小时的电话粥了。
近 babble, chat, chatter, converse, gabble, jabber, prattle, twitter
派 prater *n.* 闲聊的人

preach	[priːtʃ]

【考法】 *vi.* 传道，布道：to deliver a **sermon**
例 a minister who loves to preach 一个爱布道的牧师
近 discourse, sermonize
派 preacher *n.* 布道者；preachy *adj.* 说教的

precarious	[prɪˈkeriəs]

【考法1】 *adj.* 危险的，不稳定的：dangerously **lacking** in **security** or **stability**
例 a precarious livelihood 不稳定的生计
近 delicate, fragile, sensitive, touchy, unstable
反 firm, stable 稳定的；safe, secure 安全的
【考法2】 *adj.* 可疑的，不明确的：dependent on **uncertain** premises
例 His entire argument relies on a precarious assumption. 他的整篇论证都建立在一个可疑的假设之上。
近 ambiguous, doubtful, dubious, equivocal, uncertain, unfounded
反 indubitable, unambiguous, unequivocal, unquestionable 明确的，毋庸置疑的

precedent	[ˈpresɪdənt]

【考法1】 *n.* 先例，前例：an **earlier occurrence** of something similar
例 a landmark decision that set a legal precedent 在法律上首开先河的重大决议
近 example, instance, model, paradigm, pattern, standard
【考法2】 *adj.* 先前的：**prior** in time, order, arrangement, or significance
例 Her violent behaviors may be explained by some precedent events in her troubled life. 她的暴力行径或许可以由她之前苦难生活中遭遇到的一些事件来解释。
近 antecedent, anterior, former, preceding, previous, prior
反 ensuing 继而发生的
派 unprecedented *adj.* 前所未有的

Unit 3

■ PLOY	■ PRECIPITATE	■ PRECIPITATION	■ PRECIPITOUS	■ PRECLUDE
■ PRECURSOR	■ PREDECESSOR	■ PREDILECTION	■ PREEMINENT	■ PREEMPT

ploy	[ˈplɔɪ]

【考法】 *n.* 计策，手段：**a clever often underhanded means** to achieve an end
例 a successful marketing ploy 一个成功的营销策略
近 artifice, device, knack, trick, scheme, stratagem, wile

precipitate	[prɪˈsɪpɪteɪt]

【考法1】 *adj.* 匆忙的：acting or done with excessive or **careless speed**
例 the army's precipitate withdrawal from the field of battle 匆忙将军队从战场上撤下
近 cursory, flying, headlong, hurried, overhasty, precipitous, rash, rushed
反 deliberate 慎重考虑的；leisurely, unhurried, unrushed 从容不迫的，不慌不忙的
派 precipitation *n.* 急促；沉淀；降水
【考法2】 *vt.* 促使，导致：to **cause to happen**, especially suddenly or prematurely
例 precipitate an international crisis 产生国际危机
近 accelerate, escalate, expedite, hasten, impel, speed, trigger
反 check, encumber, enfetter, hamper, handicap, hinder, manacle, obstruct, retard, trammel 阻碍

precipitation [prɪˌsɪpɪˈteɪʃn]

【考法 1】 *n.* 沉积物，尤指降水：something precipitated as a **deposit** on the earth of hail, mist, **rain**, sleet, or **snow**

例 The storm brought several inches of precipitation . 风暴带来的降水量达数英寸。

近 deposit, sediment

【考法 2】 *n.* 仓促：excited and often showy or **disorderly speed**

例 I fear that I may have acted with some precipitation on this matter , so I would like to reconsider. 我害怕自己在这个事情上考虑得太仓促了，因此我想再想想。

近 haste, hastiness, hustle, precipitousness, rush

反 deliberation 深思熟虑

precipitous [prɪˈsɪpɪtəs]

【考法 1】 *adj.* 非常陡峭的：very **steep**, perpendicular, or overhanging in rise or fall

例 a precipitous gorge 险峻的峡谷

近 abrupt, arduous, sheer, steep

反 flat, level 平坦的

【考法 2】 *adj.* 匆忙的：acting or done with excessive or **careless speed**

例 They soon regretted their precipitous actions in international affairs. 他们很快就为他们在国际事务中的匆忙举动感到后悔。

近 cursory, flying, headlong, hurried, overhasty, precipitate, rash, rushed

反 deliberate 慎重考虑的；leisurely, unhurried, unrushed 从容不迫的，不慌不忙的

preclude [prɪˈkluːd]

【考法】 *vt.* 预先防止：to **make impossible**, as by action taken **in advance**

例 Age alone will not preclude him from standing as a candidate . 年龄并没有阻止他成为候选人。

近 avert, deter, forestall, obviate, prevent, stave off

precursor [priːˈkɜːrsər]

【考法】 *n.* 先驱者，先导：one that **precedes** and indicates the approach of another

例 18th-century lyric poets like Robert Burns were precursors of the Romantics . 十八世纪的抒情诗人（如罗伯特·彭斯）是浪漫主义的先驱。

近 foregoer, forerunner, harbinger, herald, outrider

反 sequela, successor 后继者；descendant 后代

派 precursory *adj.* 先驱性的，开创性的

predecessor [ˈpredəsesər]

【考法】 *n.* 前任，先辈：a person who has **previously occupied** a position or office to which another has succeeded

例 a political legacy left by his predecessor 他的前任留下来的政治遗产

近 ancestor, antecedent, foregoer, forerunner, precursor

反 successor 继任者；descendant 后代

predilection [ˌpredlˈekʃn]

【考法】 *n.* 爱好，偏袒：a partiality or **disposition** in **favor** of something

例 a predilection for travel 热爱旅行

近 affection, affinity, bias, disposition, inclination, leaning, penchant, predisposition, propensity, tendency

反 aversion, loathing, nausea, repugnance, repulsion, revulsion 反感

preeminent [priˈemɪnənt]

【考法】 *adj.* 优秀的，重要的：having **paramount** rank, dignity, or importance

例 the writer's preeminent style 作者出色的文风

近 distinguished, illustrious, incomparable, notable, outstanding, peerless, superb, supreme, unmatchable

反 negligible, trivial 不重要的

派 preeminence *n.* 杰出

preempt [priˈempt]

【考法】 *vt.* 预先占有：to appropriate, **seize**, or take for oneself **before others**

例 The naughty children had preempted front-row seats that were reserved for the guests of honor. 调皮的孩子们把前排留给贵宾的座位占了。

近 appropriate, arrogate, commandeer, convert, expropriate, seize, usurp

派 preemptive *adj.* 先发制人的；先买的

Unit 4

preen ［priːn］
【考法】 *vt.* 打扮修饰：to **dress** or groom (**oneself**) with **elaborate** care
例 She always preens herself in an elaborate suit before going to the opera. 她去听歌剧之前总要精心打扮一番，穿上最华丽的服装。
近 groom, plume, primp

preface ［ˈprefəs］
【考法】 *n.* 序言：a **preliminary statement** or essay introducing a book that explains its scope, intention, or background and is usually written by the author
例 An informal brunch served as a preface to the three-day conference. 一顿非正式的早午餐作为为期三天的会议的序曲。
近 exordium, foreword, introduction, overture, preamble, prelude, prologue
反 epilogue 尾声
派 prefatory *adj.* 序言的

pregnant ［ˈpregnənt］
【考法】 *adj.* 重要的，意味深长的：weighty or significant; **full of meaning**
例 the pregnant phrases of the Bible 《圣经》中充满哲理的话语
近 eloquent, meaningful, momentous, profound, revelatory, significant, suggestive
反 inane 空洞的

premeditate ［ˌpriːˈmedɪteɪt］
【考法】 *vi.* 预先考虑：to think, **consider**, or deliberate **beforehand**
例 carefully premeditate each step of his plan 细致谋略他计划的每一步
近 deliberate, prearrange, prepare, preplan
反 disregard, ignore, neglect, omit, overlook 忽视
派 premeditation *n.* 谋略，事先考虑

preoccupation ［priˌɑːkjuˈpeɪʃn］
【考法】 *n.* 非常关心，全神贯注：**extreme** or excessive **concern** with something
例 He kept sinking back into gloomy preoccupation. 他陷入了深深的忧虑之中。
近 absorption, engagement, engrossment, immersion
反 apathy, indifference, nonchalance, unconcern 漠不关心
派 preoccupied *adj.* 全神贯注的

preponderant ［prɪˈpɑːndərənt］
【考法】 *adj.* 占优势的，更重要的：having **superior** weight, force, **importance**, or influence
例 a preponderant misconception 一个影响甚广的错误概念
近 dominant, paramount, predominant, prevalent, overruling
反 secondary, subsidiary 次要的
派 preponderance *n.* 优势地位

prepossessing ［ˌpriːpəˈzesɪŋ］
【考法】 *adj.* 给人好感的，有魅力的：serving to **impress favorably**
例 He was fascinated by her prepossessing appearance at first sight. 他第一眼就被她迷人的外表吸引了。
近 alluring, attractive, appealing, captivating, charming, enchanting, pleasing, riveting
反 abhorrent, appalling, disgusting, hideous, loathsome, repellent, repulsive 令人反感的
派 unprepossessing *adj.* 其貌不扬的

preposterous ［prɪˈpɑːstərəs］
【考法】 *adj.* 荒谬的，不符合常理的：**contrary** to nature, reason, or **common sense**
例 a preposterous conclusion of quantum mechanics 量子力学里有悖于常理的结论
近 absurd, asinine, fallacious, fatuous, lunatic, ludicrous, insane, irrational, unreasonable
反 commonsensical 常识性的；reasonable, sensible 有道理的

presage	['presɪdʒ]

【考法】 *n.* 征兆: something believed to be a **sign or warning** of a future event

vt. 预示，预言: to foretell or **predict**

例 The sight of the first robin is always a welcome presage of spring. 第一只知更鸟的出现总是迎接春天到来的象征。‖ The incident may presage war. 这个事件可能是战争的征兆。

近 augury, auspice, boding, foreboding, foreshadowing, portent, prefiguring; adumbrate, augur, forecast, foretell, portend, predict, prognosticate, prophesy

prescience	['presɪəns]

【考法】 *n.* 预知，先见: **knowledge** of actions or events **before** they occur

例 God's prescience 上帝的预知

近 foresight, forethought, providence

反 improvidence, myopia, shortsightedness 目光短浅

Unit 5

■ PRESCRIPTION	■ PRIMITIVE	■ PRESTIGE	■ PRESUMPTUOUS	■ PRETENSE
■ PRETERNATURAL	■ PROGNOSIS	■ PREVALENT	■ PREVARICATE	■ PRIMORDIAL

prescription	[prɪˈskrɪpʃn]

【考法 1】 *n.* 处方: a **written message from a doctor** that officially tells someone to use a medicine, therapy

例 a prescription drug 处方药 ‖ prescription from the doctor 医生的处方

【考法 2】 *n.* 规定，传统的规矩: something prescribed as a **rule**; especially an inherited or established way of thinking, feeling, or doing

近 convention, custom, decree, law, regulation, rule

派 prescribe *v.* 开药方; 设立规定

primitive	['prɪmətɪv]

【考法】 *adj.* 原始的: belonging to or characteristic of an **early level** of skill or development

例 primitive wooden tools 原始的木质工具

近 rudimentary, elemental

反 advanced, developed, evolved 高级的

prestige	[preˈstiːʒ]

【考法】 *n.* 声望，威望: the level of **respect** at which one is regarded by others

例 The prestige of the university has been irrevocably impaired by the plagiarism scandal. 这所大学的声望已经因剽窃丑闻而受到了不可挽回的损失。

近 credit, fame, influence, reputation

反 infamy 坏名声

派 prestigious *adj.* 有名望的

presumptuous	[prɪˈzʌmptʃuəs]

【考法】 *adj.* 傲慢的: having a **feeling of superiority** that shows itself in an overbearing attitude

例 the presumptuous and impatient doctor 这位傲慢、没耐心的医生

近 assumptive, bumptious, cavalier, haughty, imperious, lofty, overweening, peremptory, supercilious

反 humble, modest 谦卑的

pretense	['priːtens]

【考法 1】 *n.* 虚假，伪装: the act of **pretending**; a false appearance or action intended to **deceive**

例 There is too much pretense in his piety. 他的虔诚大多都是伪装。

近 affectation, camouflage, deceit, disguise, imposture, mask, masquerade

反 sincerity 真诚

【考法 2】 *n.* 自大，优越感: an **exaggerated sense of one's importance** that shows itself in the making of excessive or unjustified claims

近 assumption, hauteur, imperiousness, loftiness, lordliness, pomposity, superciliousness, superiority

反 humility, modesty 谦逊

preternatural	[ˌpriːtərˈnætʃrəl]

【考法】 *adj.* 超乎寻常的: **surpassing** the normal or **usual**

例 They exhibited preternatural courage in face of danger. 他们在危险面前显示出了超乎寻常的勇气。

近 aberrant, abnormal, anomalous, extraordinary, phenomenal, magical, miraculous, unearthly

反 common, ordinary, prosaic 平凡的

prognosis [prɑːɡˈnoʊsiːz]

【考法】 *n.* 预兆：a declaration that **something will happen in the future**

例 a gloomy prognosis for economic recovery 经济复苏的黯淡预兆

近 augury, forecast, foretelling, predicting, presaging, prediction, prophecy

prevalent [ˈprevələnt]

【考法】 *adj.* 流行的，普遍的：widely or **commonly** occurring, existing, **accepted**, or practiced

例 The kinds of accidents are frequently seen in places where snowmobiles are prevalent . 这类事故在摩托雪橇盛行的地区很常见。

近 conventional, dominant, common, popular, predominant, preponderant, prevailing, rife

反 absent, rare 缺少的，稀少的；unusual 与众不同的

派 prevalence *n.* 流行，遍及

prevaricate [prɪˈværɪkeɪt]

【考法】 *vi.* 支吾其词，撒谎：to stray from or **evade the truth**

例 During the hearings the witness did his best to prevaricate . 听证会上证人在竭尽全力地支吾其词。

近 equivocate, fabricate, falsify, lie, palter

派 prevarication *n.* 支吾其词

primordial [praɪˈmɔːrdiəl]

【考法】 *adj.* 原始的，最初的：being or **happening first** in sequence of time

例 primordial forms of life 最原始的生命形态

近 ancient, early, primal, primeval, primitive

反 late, recent 最近的

Unit 6

■ PRIMP　　　　■ PEDDLE　　　　■ PRISTINE　　　　■ PRIVATION　　　　■ PROBE
■ PROBITY　　　■ PROCLIVITY　　■ PROCRASTINATE　■ PROCURE　　　　■ PROD

primp [prɪmp]

【考法】 *v.* 精心打扮：to dress, **adorn**, or arrange in a careful or **finicky** manner

例 She primps for hours before a date . 她出门约会前要花数小时打扮。

近 preen, dress up

peddle [ˈpedl]

【考法】 *v.* 叫卖，兜售：to **sell** from place to place usually in small quantities

例 peddle fruits and vegetables 沿街兜售果蔬

近 hawk

pristine [ˈprɪstiːn]

【考法】 *adj.* 纯净的，质朴的，未被文明腐蚀的：remaining in a **pure** state; uncorrupted by civilization; remaining **free from dirt or decay**; clean

例 a pristine forest 一片未被文明影响的森林

近 immaculate, spotless, stainless, unsoiled, unstained, unsullied

反 tainted, squalid, contaminated, besmirched, corrupted by civilization 污染的，被文明腐蚀的

privation [praɪˈveɪʃn]

【考法】 *n.* 缺乏，穷困：**lack** of what is needed for existence

例 The constant privation of sleep was starting to affect his work. 长期以来的睡眠不足开始影响他的工作。

近 deprivation, loss

反 repletion 充满

probe [proʊb]

【考法】 *v./n.* 深入调查：a **penetrating** or critical **investigation**

例 probe into his background 深入调查他的背景

近 delve, explore, inquire; delving, disquisition, exploration, inquisition

probity [ˈproʊbəti]

【考法】 *n.* 正直：faithfulness to high **moral standards**

例 A person of indisputable probity should head the disciplinary panel. 一个真正正直的人应该来领导纪律委员会。

近 honesty, integrity, rectitude, righteousness, uprightness

反 unscrupulousness, shiftiness, baseness, dishonor, lowness 肆无忌惮，欺骗

proclivity	[prəˈklɪvəti]
【考法】	*n.* 癖性，偏好：a natural propensity or **inclination**; predisposition
例	show artistic proclivities at an early age 在很小的时候就表现出了对艺术的喜好
近	aptitude, disposition, leaning, partiality, penchant, predilection, propensity
反	aversion, antipathy, disinclination 厌恶，反感

procrastinate	[proʊˈkræstɪneɪt]
【考法】	*vi.* (因为懒散)拖延：to **put off** doing something, especially out of habitual carelessness or **laziness**
例	She procrastinated and missed the submission deadline. 她一直拖拖拉拉，导致错过了截止日期。

procure	[prəˈkjʊr]
【考法】	*vt.* 获得，取得：to **get possession** of
例	procured the prisoner's release 得到了释放囚犯的许可
近	acquire, attain, garner, knock down, pull down, bring in
反	relinquish, forfeit, lose 放弃

prod	[prɑːd]
【考法】	*vt.* 促使…行动：to try to **persuade** (someone) through earnest appeals to follow a course of action
例	The strike may prod the government into action. 罢工也许会迫使政府采取行动。
近	encourage, exhort, goad, nudge, prompt, spur, egg on
反	rein 抑制

Unit 7

■ PRODIGAL	■ PRODIGIOUS	■ PROFANE	■ PROFFER	■ PROFICIENT
■ PROFLIGATE	■ PUSHOVER	■ PROFUSION	■ PROHIBITIVE	■ PROLIFERATE

prodigal	[ˈprɑːdɪɡl]
【考法】	*adj.* 挥霍的：recklessly **spendthrift** *n.* 败家子：someone who **spends** money **freely** or foolishly
例	prodigal outlays for her clothes 买衣服时挥金如土
近	extravagant, profligate, squandering, unthrifty, wasteful; fritterer, high roller, profligate, spender, spendthrift, squanderer, waster, wastrel
反	frugal, parsimonious, conserving, economical, economizing, penny-pinching, scrimping, skimping, thrifty 节省的，吝啬的; economizer, penny-pincher 吝啬的人
派	prodigality *n.* 浪费，挥霍
反	penury 贫困; husbandry 节约

prodigious	[prəˈdɪdʒəs]
【考法1】	*adj.* 巨大的：impressively **great in size**, force, or extent; **enormous**
例	a prodigious supply of canned food kept in the basement 地下室贮存着的大量罐头食品
近	colossal, elephantine, enormous, gigantic, titanic, tremendous
反	slight 微小的
派	prodigy *n.* 天才，神童
【考法2】	*adj.* 惊人的，了不起的：causing wonder or **astonishment**
例	stage magicians performing prodigious feats for rapt audiences 舞台魔术师在全神贯注的观众们面前表演惊人的技艺
近	amazing, astonishing, astounding, awesome, fabulous, miraculous, portentous, staggering, stunning, stupendous, sublime, surprising

profane	[prəˈfeɪn]
【考法】	*vt.* 亵渎：to **treat** (something sacred) with **abuse**, **irreverence**, or **contempt**
例	Invading troops profaned the altar by playing poker on it. 侵略军亵渎了祭坛，竟然在上面打扑克。
近	defile, violate
派	profaned *adj.* 被亵渎的
反	unviolated, inviolable 未被亵渎的，不可亵渎的

proffer	[ˈprɑːfər]
【考法】	*v./n.* 献出，提供：to **offer** for acceptance; tender
例	She proffered her assistance in helping the two sides reach a compromise. 她在斡旋双方达成妥协过程中尽了力。
近	extend, give, tender, trot out
反	retain, withhold 保留

proficient	[prəˈfɪʃnt]
【考法】	*adj.* 熟练的，精通的：having or marked by an **advanced** degree of **competence**, as in an art, vocation, profession, or branch of learning
例	proficient in translating foreign languages 精通外语翻译
近	accomplished, complete, expert, skilled, versed, virtuoso
反	inept, incompetent, amateur, inexperienced, inexpert, jackleg, unprofessional, unseasoned, unskilled 无能的，没有经验的

profligate	[ˈprɑːflɪgət]
【考法】	*adj./n.* 挥金如土的，挥霍的：recklessly **wasteful**; wildly extravagant
	n. 败家子：someone who **spends money freely** or foolishly
例	leading a profligate life 过着骄奢淫逸的生活
近	extravagant, high-rolling, spendthrift, squandering, thriftless, unthrifty, wasteful; fritterer, high roller, spender, spendthrift, squanderer, waster, wastrel
反	parsimonious, provident, thrift, economical, frugal, conserving 吝啬的，节俭的; economizer, penny-pincher 吝啬的人

pushover	[ˈpʊʃoʊvər]
【考法】	*n.* 容易做的工作；易如反掌的事：**something that is easy to do**
例	GRE is not a pushover to crack. GRE 不是一件容易攻克的事。
近	breeze, cake, picnic, snap
反	headache, labor, pain 费力的事

profusion	[prəˈfjuːʒn]
【考法】	*n.* 丰富，大量：the state of being profuse; **abundance**
例	snow falling in profusion 雪量很大
近	abundance, mass, plentitude, scads, volume, wealth
反	paucity 极小量
派	profuse *adj.* 丰富的
反	scanty 缺乏的

prohibitive	[prəˈhɪbətɪv]
【考法】	*adj.* (价格高得)抑制购买的：so high or burdensome as to discourage **purchase** or use
例	prohibitive prices 抑制购买的高价

proliferate	[prəˈlɪfəreɪt]
【考法】	*vi.* 快速繁殖；激增：to **grow or multiply by rapidly** producing new tissue, parts, cells, or **offspring**; to increase at a rapid rate
例	Rumors about the accident proliferated on the Internet. 关于事故的小道消息在网上迅速扩散。
近	balloon, boom, build up, escalate, expand, mushroom, snowball
反	decrease in amount, dwindle, contract, decrease, diminish, lessen, recede, wane 数量减少，缩小

Unit 8

■ PROLIX	■ PROLOGUE	■ PROLONG	■ PROMULGATE	■ PROOFREAD
■ PROPAGATE	■ PROPENSITY	■ PROPHETIC	■ PROPITIATE	■ PROPITIOUS

prolix	[ˈproʊlɪks]
【考法】	*adj.* 啰嗦的，冗长的：tending to speak or write at **excessive length**
例	prolix reality 冗长的现实
近	diffuse, garrulous, rambling, verbose, windy
反	pithy, taciturn, terse, succinct, concise, extremely brief 精炼的，寡言的

prologue	[ˈproʊlɔːg]
【考法】	*n.* 序言：the **preface** or introduction to a literary work
例	The burglary, which he committed while still a teen, was but a prologue to a wasted life of crime 他青少年时犯过的入室抢劫拉开了他偷盗生涯的序幕。
近	exordium, foreword, preamble, preface, prelude, proem, prolusion
反	epilogue 结尾

	prolong	[prə'lɔːŋ]

【考法】 *vt.* 延长，拖延: to **lengthen** in extent, scope, or range
例 Additives are used to prolong the shelf life of packaged food. 添加剂被用来延长包装食品的保存期限。
近 elongate, lengthen, outstretch, protract, stretch, drag (out), draw out
反 abbreviate, abridge, curtail, cut, cut back, shorten, truncate 截短

	promulgate	['prɑːmlgeɪt]

【考法】 *vt.* 正式宣布: to **make known** openly or publicly
例 The law was promulgated in June 1988. 法律在 1988 年 6 月出台。
近 annunciate, declare, enunciate, proclaim, publicize, herald
反 keep secret 保密

	proofread	['pruːfriːd]

【考法】 *vt.* 校对: to read (copy or proof) in order to **find errors and mark corrections**
例 She proofread the paper carefully. 她仔细把论文校对了。

	propagate	['prɑːpəgeɪt]

【考法】 *vt.* 传播，宣传: to cause to **spread out** and affect a greater number or greater area; extend
例 the various ways in which churches can propagate the faith 不同的宣传教义的方法
近 broadcast, circulate, disseminate
反 check 阻止
派 propaganda *n.* 宣传(活动)

	propensity	[prə'pensəti]

【考法】 *n.* 倾向，癖好: an often intense natural **inclination** or preference
例 a neighbor who has an unfortunate propensity for snooping 好管闲事的邻居
近 affinity, aptitude, bent, partiality, penchant, predilection, predisposition, proclivity
反 aversion 厌恶

	prophetic	[prə'fetɪk]

【考法】 *adj.* 预言的，预示的: **foretelling** events: predictive
例 Those lower-than-expected sales numbers were a prophetic indicator of the financial trouble the company would soon be in. 那些低于预期的销售数字就是公司即将陷入金融危机的先兆。
近 predictive

	propitiate	[prə'pɪʃieɪt]

【考法】 *vt.* 抚慰，劝解: to conciliate (an offended power); **appease**
例 propitiate sb. 安抚某人
近 appease, assuage, conciliate, disarm, mollify, placate
反 enrage, incense, inflame, infuriate, ire, madden, outrage, antagonize, arouse hostility 激怒

	propitious	[prə'pɪʃəs]

【考法】 *adj.* 吉祥的: **favorably** disposed: pointing toward a **happy outcome**
例 propitious sign 吉祥的征兆
近 auspicious, encouraging, fair, heartening, optimistic, promising, upbeat
反 dim, discouraging, disheartening, futureless, hopeless, inauspicious, unfavorable, unpromising, unpropitious 不吉利的

Unit 9

■ PROPONENT	■ PROPRIETY	■ PROSAIC	■ PROSCRIBE	■ PROSECUTION
■ PROSELYTIZE	■ PROSPECT	■ PROSPEROUS	■ PROSTRATE	■ PROTEAN

	proponent	[prə'poʊnənt]

【考法】 *n.* 建议者，支持者: one who argues in **support** of something; an advocate
例 a proponent of sth. 某事的支持者
近 advocate, apostle, champion, expounder, espouser, friend, promoter, supporter, protagonist
反 adversary, antagonist, opponent, detractor 诋毁者，反对者

	propriety	[prə'praɪəti]

【考法】 *n.* 适当，得体: the quality or state of being especially **suitable or fitting**
例 the propriety of doing sth. 做某事得体
近 appositeness, aptness, felicity, fitness, properness, rightness, seemliness, suitability
反 improperness, impropriety, inappositeness, inappropriateness, inaptness, infelicity, unfitness, unseemliness, unsuitability, wrongness 不得体

prosaic [prəˈzeɪɪk]

【考法】 *adj.* 单调的，常见的：being of the type that is encountered in the **normal course of events**

例 prosaic advice 老掉牙的建议

近 commonplace, everyday, routine, unexceptional, unremarkable, workaday

反 abnormal, exceptional, extraordinary, odd, out-of-the-way, strange, exciting, preternatural, ingenious, imaginary 不寻常的，有独创性的

proscribe [prouˈskraɪb]

【考法】 *vt.* 禁止，排斥：to prohibit; **forbid**

例 acts proscribed by law 被法律禁止的行为

近 ban, enjoin, interdict, outlaw, prohibit

反 sanction, permit, allow, let, suffer 允许

prosecution [ˌprɑːsɪˈkjuːʃn]

【考法】 *n.* 实行，执行：the **doing** of an action

例 oversee the prosecution of the president's foreign policy 监督总统对外政策的执行情况

近 accomplishment, achievement, discharge, enactment, execution, fulfillment, implementation, performance, perpetration, pursuance

反 nonfulfillment, nonperformance 不履行，不完成

proselytize [ˈprɑːsələtaɪz]

【考法】 *v.* (使)改变信仰：to persuade to **change** to one's **religious faith**

例 The efforts of early missionaries to proselytize the Native Americans of Minnesota were largely unproductive. 早期传教士对明尼苏达土著人进行的改变信仰的努力大多无功而返。

近 convert

prospect [ˈprɑːspekt]

【考法】 *v.* 探查，勘探：to **go into** or range over for purposes of **discovery**

例 People had arrived in the valley to prospect for gold. 人们来到山谷淘金。

近 hunt, probe, search, skirr

prosperous [ˈprɑːspərəs]

【考法】 *adj.* 成功的，繁盛的：marked by **vigorous growth** and **well-being** especially economically

例 thriving and prosperous 繁荣昌盛

近 booming, flourishing, halcyon, lush, palmy, roaring, thriving

反 depressed 萧条的；impecunious 贫穷的

prostrate [ˈprɑːstreɪt]

【考法 1】 *adj./vt.* 平躺(的)/使平躺：**lying flat** or at full length

例 He was lying prostrate on the bed. 他平躺在床上。

反 erect, upright 直立的

【考法 2】 *adj./v.* 衰弱的/使衰竭：to reduce to extreme **weakness** or incapacitation

例 illness that prostrated an entire family 将整个家庭拖垮的疾病

近 debilitated, effete, enervated, enfeebled, languid, sapped; debilitate, devitalize, enervate, enfeeble, etiolate, sap, tire

反 fortify, strengthen, beef up 加强

protean [ˈproʊtiən]

【考法】 *adj.* 善变的；多才多艺的：displaying great **diversity** or **variety; versatile**

例 He loved to show off his protean talent. 他喜欢炫耀自己多样的才华。

近 adaptable, universal, all-around

反 static 固定的

Unit 10

| ■ PROTOCOL | ■ PROTRACT | ■ PROTRUDE | ■ PROTUBERANT | ■ PROVIDENT |
| ■ PROVIDENTIAL | ■ PROVINCIAL | ■ PROVISIONAL | ■ PROVISORY | ■ PROVOKE |

protocol [ˈproʊtəkɔːl]

【考法】 *n.* 正确的礼仪规范：a code of **correct conduct**

例 a breach of protocol 对社交礼仪的破坏

protract [prəˈtrækt]

【考法】 *vt.* 延长，拖长：to draw out or **lengthen** in time; **prolong**
近 elongate, lengthen, prolong, stretch, drag out, draw out
反 curtail, abridge, abbreviate, shorten, cut back 缩减

protrude [proʊˈtruːd]

【考法】 *vi.* 突出：to jut out; **project**; bulge
例 a handkerchief protruding from his breast pocket 手帕从他的上衣口袋里伸出来
近 bulge, overhang, poke, project, stand out, stick out
反 concave 凹陷

protuberant [proʊˈtuːbərənt]

【考法】 *adj.* 隆起的，凸出的：**thrusting out** from a surrounding or adjacent surface often as a rounded mass
例 protuberant eyes 暴鱼眼
反 depressed 下陷的
派 protuberance *n.* 隆起
反 concavity 凹陷

provident [ˈprɑːvɪdənt]

【考法 1】 *adj.* 节俭的：**frugal**; **economical**
例 It is possible to be provident without being miserly. 人可以做到节俭但不吝啬。
近 economical, sparing, thrifty, farsighted, provident, scrimpy
反 profligate 挥霍的
【考法 2】 *adj.* 有远见的：having or showing **awareness** of and preparation **for the future**
例 Her provident measures kept us safe while we waited out the hurricane. 她之前有远见的准备措施让我们在等待飓风结束的期间安然无恙。
近 farseeing, farsighted, forehanded, foreseeing, forethoughtful, prescient, proactive, visionary
反 half-baked, half-cocked, improvident, myopic, shortsighted 目光短浅的

providential [ˌprɑːvɪˈdenʃl]

【考法】 *adj.* 天意的，幸运(的)：happening as if through **divine intervention**
例 a providential escape 幸运的逃脱
近 lucky, fluky, fortuitous
反 unfortunate, mishap, hapless, ill-fated, ill-starred, luckless, star-crossed 不幸的

provincial [prəˈvɪnʃl]

【考法】 *adj./n.* 狭隘(的)：**limited** in **perspective**; narrow and self-centered
例 an artist who has been criticized for being provincial 一个被批评非常狭隘的艺术家
近 illiberal, insular, parochial, sectarian, narrow-minded
反 ecumenical, broad-minded, catholic, cosmopolitan, liberal, open, open-minded, receptive, tolerant 世界范围的，开放的，包容的

provisional [prəˈvɪʒənl]

【考法】 *adj.* 临时的：provided or serving only for the time being; **temporary**
例 He was appointed provisional executor of the industrialist's vast estate. 在遗嘱中，他被指定为那位实业家的庞大资产的临时保管人。
近 impermanent, interim, provisionary, short-term
反 long-term, permanent 永久的

provisory [prəˈvaɪzəri]

【考法】 *adj.* 有附带条件的；临时的：depending on a proviso; **conditional**; serving in a position for the time being
例 a provisory permit to block off the street while movie scenes were being shot 一个同意在电影拍摄期间封锁道路的临时许可
近 interim, provisional, provisionary, provisory
反 unconditional, long-term, permanent 无条件的，永久的

provoke [prəˈvoʊk]

【考法 1】 *vt.* 激怒：to **incite** to **anger** or resentment
例 His teasing finally provoked her. 他的调戏最终把她激怒了。
近 arouse, excite, incite, instigate, pique, stimulate, stir, fire up
【考法 2】 *vt.* 驱使，激起：to **stir** to action or **feeling**
例 rankings that are sure to provoke an argument among film critics 必将引发影评家们争论的排名
近 abet, ferment, foment, instigate, stir up, whip up

List 20

"生如夏花，在追求结果绚烂的同时享受过程中的美好。"

（杨璐，2008 年 10 月，Verbal 800, Quantitative 800, AW 5.5,
录取学校：Massachusetts Inst. of Technology）

Unit 1

■ PROWESS	■ PROWL	■ PRUDE	■ PRUDENT	■ PRUDISH
■ PRUNE	■ PRY	■ PSEUDONYM	■ PUTATIVE	■ PECUNIARY

prowess ［'prauəs］
【考法】 *n.*英勇，勇敢：**superior** strength, **courage**, or daring, especially in battle
例 his prowess on the football field 他在球场上过人的勇气
近 bravery, courageousness, daring, gallantry, guts, intrepidity
反 timid, cowardice, cravenness, dastardliness, poltroonery 胆小，懦弱

prowl ［'praʊl］
【考法】 *v.* 巡游以猎取食物；徘徊：to **roam through** stealthily, as in **search of prey** or plunder
例 I prowled the shop looking for sales. 我在商店里转悠，寻找打折商品。

prude ［pruːd］
【考法】 *n.*过分正经的人：一个过分关心自己是否得体、谦逊或正确的人：a person who is **greatly concerned** with **seemly behavior and morality** especially regarding sexual matters
例 a hypocritical prude 一个虚伪的过分正经的人
近 bluenose, moralist, puritan
反 immoralist 不道德的人

prudent ［'pruːdnt］
【考法 1】 *adj.*明智的：marked by **wisdom** or **judiciousness**; **wise**
例 prudent advice 明智的建议
近 advisable, desirable, judicious, politic, tactical, intelligent
反 foolish 傻的
【考法 2】 *adj.*小心谨慎的，审慎的：marked by **circumspection**

prudish ［'pruːdɪʃ］
【考法】 *adj.*过分守礼的：marked by **prudery**
例 By the prudish standards of the 19th century, any depiction of the nude was scandalous. 根据 19 世纪的保守标准，任何对裸露的刻画描述都是下流无耻的。
近 nice-nelly, prim, puritanical

prune ［pruːn］
【考法】 *vt.*修剪；修整：to cut off or remove dead or living parts or branches of （a plant, for example）to improve shape or growth
例 The students were asked to prune their essays. 学生们被要求修改文章。
近 shave, shear, snip, trim

pry ［praɪ］
【考法】 *vi.*刺探，打听：to look or **inquire closely**, **curiously**, or impertinently
例 Don't go prying into other people's business. 别去打探别人的事。
近 interlope, intermeddle, intrude, nose, obtrude, snoop

pseudonym ［'suːdənɪm］
【考法】 *n.*假名，笔名：a **fictitious** name
例 the pseudonym of sb. 某人的笔名
近 alias, nom de guerre

putative [ˈpjuːtətɪv]

【考法】 *adj.* 推测的，假定的：generally **regarded as such**

例 putative customers in this market 市场中假定的客户群体

近 assumed, ostensible, presumed, reputed, seeming, supposed

pecuniary [pɪˈkjuːnieri]

【考法】 *adj.* 金钱上的：of or relating to **money**, banking, or investments

例 The insurance company will compensate you for your pecuniary loss in the snow disaster. 保险公司会赔偿你在雪灾中所蒙受的金钱损失。

近 fiscal, monetary, financial

反 nonfinancial 非财务的

Unit 2

■ PUCKISH	■ PUERILE	■ PUISSANCE	■ PULCHRITUDE	■ PULVERIZE
■ PERMEATE	■ PUNCTILIOUS	■ PUNDIT	■ PUNGENT	■ PUNY

puckish [ˈpʌkɪʃ]

【考法】 *adj.* 淘气的，顽皮的：**mischievous**; **impish**

例 She had a puckish smile on her face. 她脸上挂着顽皮的笑容。

近 devilish, impish, prankish, waggish

反 sober, grave, staid 严肃的

puerile [ˈpjʊrəl]

【考法】 *adj.* 幼稚的，不成熟的：**immature**; lacking in adult experience or maturity

例 puerile remarks 幼稚的评论

近 adolescent, green, immature, unfledged, unformed, unripened

反 adult, experienced, grown-up, mature, ripe, sagacious 睿智的，成熟的

puissance [ˈpwɪsəns]

【考法】 *n.* 权力：**power**; might

例 The president pledged to put the full puissance of the nation into the war effort. 总统下令全国进入战争状态。

近 force, might, potency, strength, vigor, sinew

反 powerlessness, impotence, weakness 无力

pulchritude [ˈpʌlkrɪtjuːd]

【考法】 *n.* 美丽：great physical **beauty** and appeal

反 ugliness, homeliness, hideousness 丑陋，平庸

pulverize [ˈpʌlvəraɪz]

【考法】 *vt.* 将…研磨成粉；将…彻底摧毁：to pound, crush or grind to powder or dust; to bring to a **complete end** the physical soundness, existence, or usefulness of

例 Bits of pulverized rock filled the air. 被碾碎的岩石碎片充斥在空气里。

反 solidify, build, construct, erect, put up, raise, rear, set up 硬化，构建

permeate [ˈpɜːrmieɪt]

【考法】 *v.* 弥漫，渗透：to **spread throughout**

例 The smell of roast beef permeated the air. 烤牛肉的气味弥漫在空气中。

近 interpenetrate, pervade, suffuse, transfuse

punctilious [pʌŋkˈtɪliəs]

【考法】 *adj.* 注意细节的，一丝不苟的：strictly **attentive** to minute **details** of form in action or conduct

近 decorous, proper, starchy, stilted

反 remiss, slipshod, casual, easygoing, informal, laid-back, unceremonious 粗心的

pundit [ˈpʌndɪt]

【考法】 *n.* 权威人士，专家：a person who gives **opinions** in an **authoritative** manner usually through the mass media

例 The new laptop has gotten a thumbs-up from industry pundits. 新出的笔记本电脑受到了业界专家的一致好评。

近 savant, scholar

pungent [ˈpʌndʒənt]

【考法】 *adj.* 辛辣的，讽刺的：marked by the **use of wit** that is intended to **cause hurt feelings**

例 pungent language 辛辣讽刺的语言

近 acerbic, acid, acrid, caustic, mordant, sardonic, scalding, scathing

puny ['pju:ni]

【考法】 *adj.* 微小的，弱小的：of **inferior size**, strength, or significance; **weak**

例 a puny youth/dog 一个弱小的年轻人/狗

近 diminutive, dwarfish, slight, subnormal

反 enormous, considerable, grand, husky, king-size, outsize, overscale, substantial, whacking, whopping 巨大的

Unit 3

■ PURPORT   ■ PURLIEU   ■ PURLOIN   ■ PURVEY   ■ PUSILLANIMOUS
■ QUACK   ■ QUAFF   ■ QUAIL   ■ QUALIFY   ■ QUANDARY

purport [pər'pɔːrt]

【考法】 *v.* 声称，打算：to state as a fact usually forcefully

例 a book that purports to tell the whole truth 一本声称讲出全部真相的书

近 claim, affirm, allege, assert, aver, avouch, avow, profess

反 deny, gainsay 否认，反对

purlieu ['pɜːrluː]

【考法1】 *n.* 常去的地方：a place for spending time or for **socializing**

例 The restaurant, the preferred purlieu of the theatergoing crowd, is always packed an hour or two before showtime. 观剧的人群经常去的那间餐厅总是在演出开始前一两个小时爆满。

近 haunt, rendezvous, resort, stamping ground, stomping ground

【考法2】 *n.* 临近的地区：an **adjoining region** or space

例 We stopped at one of the several pubs in the purlieus of the stadium. 我们在体育馆附近的一间酒吧前停下来。

近 backyard, neighborhood, vicinage, vicinity

purloin [pɜːr'lɔɪn]

【考法】 *vt.* 偷窃：to **steal**, often in a violation of trust

例 fearing that someone might attempt to purloin a copy of the script for the show's season finale 害怕该剧的完季那集剧本被盗

近 appropriate, filch, pilfer, snitch, thieve

purvey [pər'veɪ]

【考法】 *v.* （大量）供给，供应：to **supply** (food, for example); furnish

例 a little shop purveying handmade merchandise 出售手工商品的小店

pusillanimous [ˌpjuːsɪ'læniməs]

【考法】 *adj.* 懦弱的，胆小得令人鄙视的：lacking courage and resolution, marked by contemptible **timidity**

例 pusillanimous politicians who vote according to whichever way the political wind is blowing 胆小懦弱的政客，舆论风吹向谁就投票给谁

近 craven, dastardly, gutless, poltroon, recreant, spineless

反 brave, courageous, daring, dauntless, doughty, gallant, gutsy, intrepid, lionhearted, stalwart, stout, stout-hearted, valiant, valorous 勇敢的

quack [kwæk]

【考法】 *n.* 骗子医生，江湖郎中：a **pretender** to medical skill

例 Don't bother to see that guy, as I've heard he's a quack with no actual training. 别再找他看病了，我听说他就是个没有真才实学的江湖郎中。

近 charlatan, fake, fraud, hoaxer, mountebank, phony

反 honest practitioner 诚实从业者

quaff [kwæf]

【考法】 *vt.* 大口地喝：to **drink** (a beverage) **heartily**

例 He stopped at a bar and quaffed a few beers. 他在酒吧停下来，痛饮了几杯啤酒。

近 gulp, swig, swill

quail [kweɪl]

【考法】 *vi.* 胆怯，畏缩：to shrink back in **fear**; **cower**

例 She quailed at the thought of seeing him again. 她想到还要再见他就害怕。

近 blench, cringe, recoil, shrink, wince

反 become resolute, give bold 变得坚决、大胆

	qualify	[ˈkwɑːlɪfaɪ]

【考法 1】 *vt.* 限定：to **reduce** from a **general** to a particular or restricted form

派 qualified *adj.* 有限制的，不完全的

例 |qualified support| 有限的支持

反 unreserved, absolute, categorical 无保留的，不受限制的

【考法 2】 *vt.* 使有资格，使有能力：to **make competent**（as by training, skill, or ability）for a particular office or function

例 |a qualified advice columnist| 一个有能力的专栏作家

近 equip, fit, prepare, ready, season, train

	quandary	[ˈkwɑːndəri]

【考法】 *n.* 困惑，窘境：a state of **perplexity** or **doubt**

例 I've had two job offers, and I'm in |a real quandary about/over which one to accept|. 我有两个工作机会，但实在是进退两难，不知道应该选哪一个。

近 catch-22, double bind

反 state of complete certainty 胸有成竹

Unit 4

■ QUARANTINE	■ QUALM	■ QUASH	■ QUIRKY	■ QUELL
■ QUENCH	■ QUERULOUS	■ QUIBBLE	■ QUIESCENT	■ QUIXOTIC

	quarantine	[ˈkwɔːrəntiːn]

【考法】 *n.* 隔离：enforced **isolation** or restriction of free movement imposed to prevent the spread of contagious disease

例 The cows will be |kept in quarantine| for another two weeks. 牛群还需要被隔离观察两周。

	qualm	[kwɑːm]

【考法】 *n.* 担忧，不安：a sudden **uneasy feeling** about the rightness

例 |I have no qualms about recommending this approach.| 我会没有疑虑地推荐这一方法。

近 compunction, misgiving, scruple

	quash	[kwɔːʃ]

【考法】 *vt.* 镇压，阻止：to **put a stop to**（something）by the use of force

例 |quash a rebellion| 镇压一次叛变

近 repress, squelch, subdue, suppress, clamp down on, crack down on

反 engender, foment 引起，煽动

	quirky	[ˈkwɜːrki]

【考法】 *adj.* 古怪的，奇葩的：**different from the ordinary** in a way that causes curiosity or suspicion

例 |styles her hair in a quirky way| 用奇怪的方法设计发型

近 bizarre, eccentric, erratic, outlandish, peculiar, odd, strange, weird

	quell	[kwel]

【考法 1】 *vt.* 压制：to put down forcibly；**suppress**

例 |quell riot| 镇压骚乱

近 quash, repress, squash, squelch, subdue, suppress, clamp down on, crack down on

【考法 2】 *vt.* 使平静，使安静：to **pacify**；quiet

例 |quell fears| 减轻害怕

近 dumb, extinguish, hush, mute, settle

反 foment, instigate, rouse, incite 煽动

	quench	[kwentʃ]

【考法 1】 *vt.* 熄灭：to **put out**（a fire, for example）；extinguish

例 We |thoroughly quenched the campfire| before we headed to bed. 我们在睡前把营火完全熄灭了。

近 blanket, douse, put out, snuff out

反 fire, ignite, inflame, kindle, light 点燃

【考法 2】 *vt.* 使满足：to **put a complete end to**（a physical need or desire）

例 This lemonade really |quenches my thirst|. 这杯柠檬汁真是解渴。

近 assuage, sate, satiate, slake

querulous ['kwerələs]
【考法】 *adj.* 抱怨的，爱发牢骚的：habitually **complaining**
例 a querulous voice 抱怨的声音
近 crabby, cranky, grouchy, grumpy
反 forbearing, long-suffering, patient, stoic, tolerant, uncomplaining 容忍的

quibble ['kwɪbl]
【考法】 *vi.* 吹毛求疵：to find fault or **criticize** for petty reasons; **cavil**
例 She spent the entire evening quibbling about the historical inaccuracies in the television series on World War II. 她一整晚都在对那部关于二战的电视剧里的历史错误吹毛求疵。
近 carp, cavil, fuss, niggle, nitpick

quiescent [kwi'esnt]
【考法】 *adj.* 平静的，静止的：being **quiet**, still, or at rest; **inactive**
例 a group of quiescent loungers 一群平静懒散的流浪汉
近 dull, inert, lethargic, sluggish, torpid
反 rambunctious, tumultuous, active, restlessly active 骚乱的

quixotic [kwɪk'sɑːtɪk]
【考法】 *adj.* 不切实际的，空想的：having or marked by a tendency to be guided **more by ideals than by reality**
例 She had quixotic dreams about the future. 她对未来有着幻想。
近 impractical, ideal, romantic, starry, utopian, visionary
反 clear-eyed, clear-sighted 聪明的

Unit 5

■ QUOTA	■ QUOTIDIAN	■ RABBLE	■ RABID	■ RACY
■ RAFFISH	■ RECAPITULATE	■ RAGE	■ RAGGED	■ RAIL

quota ['kwoʊtə]
【考法】 *n.* 配额，限额：a **proportional** part or share
例 The department set new sales quotas in May. 部门设定了五月的销售定额。
近 allowance, portion, proportion
反 unlimited number 不限数量

quotidian [kwoʊ'tɪdiən]
【考法】 *adj.* 每日的；平凡的：everyday; **commonplace**
例 plagued by a quotidian coughing 每天被咳嗽困扰
近 commonplace, everyday, frequent, ordinary, routine, ubiquitous
反 remarkable, striking, extraordinary, unusual, rare, infrequent, seldom 不平常的

rabble ['ræbl]
【考法】 *n.* 混乱的人群；暴民；下层民众：a **disorganized** or disorderly **crowd of people**; the lowest class of people
例 The crown prince was reminded that even the rabble deserved his attention and compassion. 太子应该知道即使是草民，也值得他的关注和同情。
近 ragtag and bobtail, riffraff, scum, rag, trash, unwashed

rabid ['ræbɪd]
【考法】 *adj.* 狂热的，不冷静的：extremely zealous or enthusiastic; **fanatical**
例 soccer fans whose **rabid enthusiasm** makes them go berserk when their team wins 不冷静的粉丝们在球队获胜以后变得很狂暴
近 delirious, ferocious, feverish, fierce, frantic, frenetic, violent
反 logical, detached 合常理的，客观的

racy ['reɪsi]
【考法】 *adj.* 活泼生动的：**vigorous**; lively
例 vivid writing and a racy plot that keeps readers turning the pages 栩栩如生的手法和生动新鲜的情节让读者手不释卷
近 animate, brisk, frisky, jaunty, perky, spirited, vivacious
反 tame, dead, inactive, inanimate, lackadaisical, languid, languorous, leaden, lifeless, limp, listless, spiritless, vapid 乏味的，死气沉沉的

243

raffish	[ˈræfɪʃ]

【考法】 *adj.* 低俗的 : marked by or suggestive of flashy vulgarity or **crudeness**

例 The dowager cringed at the thought of raffish tourists tromping all over her Persian rugs. 孀居贵妇一想到低俗的游客践踏她的波斯地毯就痛苦不已。

近 crass, lowbred, uncouth, uncultivated, uncultured, unpolished, unrefined, vulgar

反 civilized, cultivated, cultured, genteel, polished, refined, ultrarefined, well-bred 有教养的

recapitulate	[ˌriːkəˈpɪtʃuleɪt]

【考法】 *v./n.* 概括，摘要 : to **make into a short statement** of the main points

例 recapitulate the essential points 概括要点

近 abstract, outline, summarize, synopsize

rage	[reɪdʒ]

【考法】 *n./v.* 暴怒 : **violent** and uncontrolled **anger**

例 Her rages rarely last more than a few minutes. 她的暴躁来得快去得也快。

近 agitation, deliriousness, delirium, distraction, furor, hysteria, rampage

ragged	[ˈrægɪd]

【考法】 *adj.* 凹凸不平的，不光滑的 : <u>not</u> having a level or **smooth** surface

例 She cut herself on the ragged edge of the tin can's lid. 她被罐头盖的锋利边缘割伤了。

近 broken, bumpy, coarse, irregular, jagged, lumpy, pebbly, rough, roughened, rugged, scraggy

反 even, flat, level, plane 平整的；smooth 光滑的

rail	[reɪl]

【考法】 *vi.* 怒骂，猛烈抨击 : to **revile or scold** in harsh, insolent, or abusive language

例 We could hear the cook in the kitchen railing against his assistant and wondered if we'd ever get our food. 我们可以听到厨师在厨房怒斥他的助手，由此我们怀疑我们点的菜还能不能做好。

近 baste, berate, castigate, chastise, hammer, lambaste, rebuke, reprimand, reproach, upbraid

反 accredit, applaud, commend, eulogize, extol, laud, praise 表扬，赞扬

派 raillery *n.* 善意的打闹

Unit 6

▉ RAKISH	▉ RAMBLE	▉ RAMBUNCTIOUS	▉ RAMSHACKLE	▉ RANCOR
▉ RANDOM	▉ RANKLE	▉ RANT	▉ RAPACIOUS	▉ RAPPORT

rakish	[ˈreɪkɪʃ]

【考法】 *adj.* 放荡的，行为不检点的 : having or showing **lowered moral character** or standards; dissolute

例 He wore his hat at a rakish angle. 他帽子戴得吊儿郎当的。

近 debased, debauched, demoralized, depraved, dissolute, libertine, perverse, perverted, reprobate

反 good, moral, pure, righteous, virtuous 有美好品德的；uncorrupted 不放荡的

派 rake *n.* 行为不检点的人，放荡的人

ramble	[ˈræmbl]

【考法】 *vi.* 漫谈；长篇大论(并经常离题)地说或写 : to talk at length **without** sticking to **a topic** or getting to a point

例 Sometimes she spoke sensibly; sometimes she rambled. 有时她说话很有道理；有时却漫无边际。

近 blather, chat, chatter, drivel, maunder, patter, prattle

rambunctious	[ræmˈbʌŋkʃəs]

【考法】 *adj.* 喧闹的，骚乱的 : being rough or **noisy** in a high-spirited way

例 a very rambunctious and energetic class 一个十分喧闹活跃的课堂

近 boisterous, clamorous, raucous, riotous, rowdy, tumultuous, turbulent

反 orderly 有秩序的；calm, noiseless, peaceful, placid, quiet, serene, silent, soundless, tranquil 安静的

ramshackle	[ˈræmʃækl]

【考法】 *adj.* 摇摇欲坠的 : appearing **ready to collapse**; rickety

例 a deserted and ramshackle village 一个废弃的、摇摇欲坠的小木屋

近 rickety, shaky, tottering

反 concrete, firm, solid, sturdy 坚固的；stable 稳定的

rancor	[ˈræŋkər]
【考法】	*n.* 敌意，深仇：a bitter deep-seated **ill will**
例	dispel the rancor 驱散敌意
近	animosity, animus, antagonism, antipathy, bitterness, gall, grudge, hostility, jaundice
反	amity, harmony, goodwill, rapport, rapprochement 和睦，友好；friendship 友谊

random	[ˈrændəm]
【考法】	*adj.* 随机的，随意的：**lacking** a definite plan, purpose, or **pattern**
例	We received several answers and picked one at random. 我们收到了若干答案，并随机抽取了一个。
例	aimless, arbitrary, desultory, erratic, haphazard, scattered, slapdash, stray
反	methodical, orderly, organized, regular, systematic, systematized 井然有序的，系统化的
派	randomly *adv.* 随机地；randomize *v.* 随机挑选、排列

rankle	[ˈræŋkl]
【考法】	*vt.* 激怒：to **cause anger**, irritation, or deep bitterness
例	Her comments rankled me. 她的评论激怒了我。
近	aggravate, enrage, exasperate, incense, inflame, infuriate, ire, madden, rile, roil
反	delight, gratify, please 使愉悦；appease, assuage, conciliate, mollify, placate, propitiate 安抚

rant	[rænt]
【考法】	*n.* (尤指长时间的)训斥，责骂：a long **angry** speech or **scolding**
例	After complaining about the hotel's lousy service, the woman went off on another rant about the condition of her room. 在抱怨完旅店差劲的服务之后，她继续对房间的条件开骂。
近	castigation, diatribe, harangue, lambasting, philippic, reprimand, reproach, vituperation
反	encomium, eulogy, panegyric, rhapsody, tribute 赞美之词

rapacious	[rəˈpeɪʃəs]
【考法】	*adj.* 过度贪婪的：excessively grasping or **covetous**
例	a rapacious exploitation policy 一项贪婪的剥削政策
近	acquisitive, avaricious, avid, coveting, covetous, grasping, mercenary, moneygrubbing
反	content, sated, satiated, satisfied 心满意足的
派	rapaciousness *n.* 贪婪

rapport	[ræˈpɔːr]
【考法】	*n.* 和睦，友好：a **friendly relationship** marked by ready communication and mutual understanding
例	build rapport and trust 建立友好和信任
近	amity, communion, concord, fellowship, harmony, rapprochement
反	animosity, antagonism, antipathy, bitterness, enmity, hostility, jaundice, rancor 敌意

Unit 7

■ RAPPROCHEMENT   ■ RAPSCALLION   ■ RAPT   ■ RAREFY   ■ RASH
■ RASPY   ■ RATIFY   ■ RATIOCINATION   ■ RATION   ■ RATIONAL

rapprochement	[ˌræprouʃˈmɑːn]
【考法】	*n.* 和睦，友好：establishment of or state of having **cordial relations**
例	a new era of rapprochement between China and Russia 中俄两国睦邻友好关系的新纪元
近	amity, communion, concord, fellowship, harmony, rapport
反	animosity, antagonism, antipathy, bitterness, enmity, hostility, jaundice, rancor 敌意

rapscallion	[ræpˈskæliən]
【考法】	*n.* 流氓，恶棍：a mean, **evil**, or unprincipled person
例	an unsafe place frequented by drunkards and rapscallions 一个酒鬼和流氓经常造访的不安全的地方
近	brute, devil, evildoer, fiend, knave, miscreant, rascal, reprobate, rogue, savage, scamp, varlet, wretch
反	saint 圣人；cavalier, chevalier (尤指对女士)彬彬有礼的绅士

rapt	[ræpt]
【考法】	*adj.* 狂喜的，狂热的：experiencing or marked by overwhelming usually **pleasurable emotion**
例	a rock band that still attracts rapt crowds 一个仍然拥有着狂热粉丝的摇滚乐队
近	elated, elevated, enraptured, entranced, euphoric, exhilarated, intoxicated, rapturous, rhapsodic
反	crestfallen, dejected, depressed 沮丧的；doleful, gloomy, melancholy, mournful, woeful 哀伤的

rarefy ['rerfaɪ]

【考法】 *vt.* 使稀薄：to **make rare**, thin, porous, or less dense: to expand without the addition of matter

例 rarefy the air 使空气变得稀薄

近 attenuate, dilute, thin

反 concentrate, condense 使稠密，浓缩

派 rarefaction *n.* 稀薄，稀疏

rash [ræʃ]

【考法】 *adj.* 草率的，仓促的：marked by or proceeding from undue haste or **lack** of deliberation or **caution**

例 a rash move 草率的一招

近 cursory, gadarene, headlong, hurried, overhasty, precipitate, precipitous, rushed

反 deliberate 慎重考虑的；leisurely, unhurried, unrushed 从容不迫的，不慌不忙的

派 rashly *adv.* 草率地，仓促地

raspy ['ræspi]

【考法】 *adj.* 声音刺耳的：**harsh** and dry in sound

例 The dying man was speaking in a raspy and barely discernible voice . 将死的人在用一种沙哑刺耳且难以听清的语调说话。

近 cacophonous, coarse, croaky, harsh, grating, gravelly, gruff, husky, rasping, rusty, scratchy, throaty

反 mellifluous, sweet 声音甜美的；gentle, soft, tender 声音轻柔的

ratify ['rætɪfaɪ]

【考法】 *vt.*（官方地）认可，批准：to give **official acceptance** of as satisfactory

例 Lincoln's home state of Illinois was the first to ratify the 13th Amendment to the U.S. Constitution , which pro-vided for the abolition of slavery. 林肯的老家——伊利诺伊是美国第一个通过《宪法第十三修正案》的州，该决案提供了废除奴隶制的法律基础。

近 accredit, approbate, authorize, certify, endorse, finalize, formalize, pass, sanction, validate, warrant

反 decline, deny, disallow, disapprove, negative, reject, veto 否决

派 ratification *n.* 正式批准

ratiocination [ˌreɪʃiousɪ'neɪʃn]

【考法】 *n.* 推理：the **thought processes** that have been established as leading to valid solutions to problems

例 As an expert in ratiocination , the detective Sherlock Holmes has few rivals. 作为推理专家，大侦探福尔摩斯可谓无人能及。

近 deduction, intellection, reason, reasoning, sense

ration ['ræʃn]

【考法】 *vt.* 按比例分配：to give as a **share or portion**

例 The region has had to ration water during times of drought. 干旱时该地区不得不按比例分配水资源。

近 allocate, allot, allow, apportion, assign, distribute, lot

反 keep, retain, withhold 扣留，拒绝给予

rational ['ræʃnəl]

【考法】 *adj.* 理性的：**based on** sound **reasoning** or information

例 Betting all of your savings on the lottery is not a rational move . 把你所有的存款赌在彩票上可不是一个理智的决定。

近 commonsensical, firm, informed, just, justified, levelheaded, sober, solid

反 groundless, unfounded, unjustified 无理由的，无根据的

派 rationalize *vt.* 使合理化；找借口

Unit 8

■ RAVE	■ RAVEL	■ RAVISH	■ RAZE	■ ROW
■ REACTIONARY	■ REAM	■ RAMIFICATION	■ REASSURE	■ REBUFF

rave [reɪv]

【考法 1】 *vi.* 狂热赞扬：to make an **exaggerated display of affection** or enthusiasm

例 Critics raved about the new play. 新剧得到了评论家们的热烈赞扬。

近 drool, effuse, enthuse, fuss, rhapsodize, slobber

反 blame, censure, condemn, criticize, denounce, pan, reprehend 批评，指责

【考法2】 *vi.* （发疯般地）怒吼： to **talk** irrationally and wildly in or **as if in delirium**
例 a man standing outside the city hall, raving like a lunatic about his tax bill 站在市政大厅外、像疯子一样叫嚷着自己税单的人
近 bluster, fulminate, huff, rant, roar, spout
反 grumble, murmur, mutter 小声抱怨

ravel ［ˈrævl］
【考法1】 *vt.* 解开，松开： to **separate** the various **strands** of
例 Since the sweater is too small, you could ravel the yarnout and make something else with it. 既然这个毛衣太小，你可以把它拆了然后织些新的东西。
近 disentangle, extricate, unbraid, unsnarl, untwine, unweave
反 braid, knit, plait, weave 编织
【考法2】 *vt.* 阐明： to **clarify by separating** the aspects of
例 The difficulty will soon ravel out. 困难很快就会得到解决。
近 clarify, clear, elucidate, untangle, unravel
反 complex, complicate, entangle, perplex, sophisticate, snarl, tangle 使复杂化
【考法3】 *vt.* 使纠缠，使复杂化： to **tangle** or complicate
例 a ravelled story 一个复杂的故事
近 complex, complicate, entangle, perplex, sophisticate, snarl, tangle
反 clarify, clear, elucidate, untangle, unravel 阐明

ravish ［ˈrævɪʃ］
【考法】 *vt.* 使陶醉，使沉迷： to **overcome with emotion** (as wonder or delight)
例 I was completely ravished by those marvelous pictures taken by HST. 用哈勃太空望远镜拍摄的那些壮观图片让我彻底地陶醉了。
近 captivate, enchant, enrapture, enthrall, rapture, transport
反 disenchant, sober 使清醒
派 ravishing *adj.* 极美丽的

raze ［reɪz］
【考法】 *vt.* 摧毁，粉碎： to **destroy completely** by or as if by knocking down or breaking to pieces
例 Excavators were began to raze old school building. 挖土机开始夷平学校的老建筑。
An entire city block was razed by a terrible fire. 大火摧毁了整个街区。
近 annihilate, decimate, demolish, devastate, level, nuke, pulverize, ruin, smash, vaporize, wreck, tear down
反 build, construct, erect, raise, rear, set up 建造
派 razor *n.* 剃须刀

row ［roʊ］
【考法】 *n.* 争吵，争执： an often noisy or angry **expression of differing opinions**
例 The incipient row regarding taxes could affect trade between the two countries much more than the festering dispute over banana imports, which has been going on for years. Unfortunately, the trade regulators seem to be ignoring both disagreements. 关于税收的初期争端会比持续多年的香蕉进口纠纷对两国贸易影响更大，但不幸的是这两起争执都被贸易监督机构忽略了。
近 altercation, controversy, disagreement, dispute, dissension, fight, imbroglio, quarrel, squabble, wrangle
反 accord, assent, agreement, consensus, harmony, unanimity, unison 一致同意

reactionary ［riˈækʃəneri］
【考法】 *adj.* 反对变革的，极保守的： characterized by reaction, especially **opposition to progress** or liberalism; extremely conservative
例 reactionary rulers 保守的统治者
近 brassbound, conservative, die-hard, hidebound, traditionalistic, ultraconservative
反 liberal 允许变革的；progressive 进步的；radical, aggressive 激进的

ream ［riːm］
【考法】 *vt.* 怒斥，训斥： to **criticize** (someone) severely or angrily especially for personal failings
例 You are so going to get reamed out when the boss learns that you wrecked the company car. 要是老板知道你把公司的车弄坏了，你肯定会挨骂的。
近 baste, berate, castigate, chastise, hammer, lambaste, rail, rebuke, reprimand, reproach, upbraid
反 accredit, applaud, commend, eulogize, extol, laud, praise 表扬，赞扬

ramification ［ˌræmɪfɪˈkeɪʃn］
【考法】 *n.* 影响，结果： something that is the **result** of an action, decision
例 the ramifications of a court decision 法庭判决的结果
近 consequence, outgrowth, effect, result

reassure	[ˌriːə'ʃʊr]

【考法】 *vt.* 使安心，打消疑虑：to **restore to confidence**

例　reassure her worry 使她安心

近　assure, cheer, console, solace, soothe

反　distress, torment, torture, trouble 使忧虑，折磨

派　reassurance *n.* 消除疑虑

rebuff	[rɪ'bʌf]

【考法】 *vt.* 严词拒绝：to **reject** or criticize sharply

例　She rebuffed an invitation from her colleagues. 她回绝了同事们的邀请。
She rebuffed him when he asked her for a date. 她拒绝了他的约会邀请。

近　decline, deny, refuse, reject, repudiate, repulse, snub, spurn

反　accept 接受；approve 赞同；welcome 欢迎

Unit 9

■ RECALCITRANT　　■ RECANT　　■ RECESSIVE　　■ RECIDIVATE　　■ RECIPROCATE
■ RECKLESS　　■ RECLUSE　　■ RECOIL　　■ RECONCILE　　■ RECONDITE

recalcitrant	[rɪ'kælsɪtrənt]

【考法】 *adj.* 顽抗的，不顺从的：marked by stubborn **resistance** to and **defiance** of authority or guidance

例　a recalcitrant teenager 执拗的少年 ‖ The manager worried that the recalcitrant employee would try to undermine his authority. 经理担心那些不服管理的员工会削弱他的权威。

近　balky, contumacious, defiant, incompliant, insubordinate, intractable, obstreperous, rebellious, refractory, unruly

反　amenable, compliant, conformable, docile, governable, obedient, ruly, submissive, tractable 服从的，顺从的

派　recalcitrance *n.* 固执，不服从命令

recant	[rɪ'kænt]

【考法】 *vt.* 撤回，放弃，改变：to **withdraw** or repudiate (**a statement** or belief) formally and publicly

例　The man has refused after torture to recant his heresy. 这个人在受折磨后依旧拒绝放弃他的异教信仰。

近　abjure, abnegate, forswear, renege, renounce, repeal, repudiate, retract, withdraw

反　adhere, insist, maintain, stick 坚持

派　recantation *n.* 改变论调

recessive	[rɪ'sesɪv]

【考法】 *adj.* 内向的，内敛的：**not comfortable around people**

例　For such a recessive genius, the most comfortable thing is working alone in his lab. 对于这样一个内向的天才而言，最舒服的事情就是一个人在实验室里干活。

近　backward, bashful, coy, demure, diffident, introverted, modest, retiring, self-effacing, sheepish, withdrawn

反　extroverted, immodest, outgoing 外向的；gregarious, sociable 好交际的

派　recession *n.* 后退，衰退

recidivate	[riː'sɪdəveɪt]

【考法】 *vi.* 回到原先的习惯，尤指重新犯罪：to return to a previous pattern of behavior, especially to **return to criminal habits**

例　The suspect has recidivated for several times. 这个嫌犯是个惯犯了。

近　regress, relapse, retrogress, revert

反　habilitate, reclaim, redeem, regenerate, rehabilitate 洗心革面，使改正

派　recidivism *n.* 再犯，重犯；recidivist *n.* 再次犯罪的人

reciprocate	[rɪ'sɪprəkeɪt]

【考法】 *vt.* 报答，回报：to **return** in kind or degree

例　They reciprocated the favor by driving their neighbor to the airport. 他们开车送邻居去机场以还人情。

近　recompense, repay, requite, retaliate, return

反　owe 欠（钱、人情等）

派　reciprocal *adj.* 相互之间的，互惠的

reckless	['rekləs]

【考法】 *adj.* 不考虑后果的，大胆鲁莽的：**careless** of consequences; foolishly adventurous or bold

例　His reckless driving accounted for the accident. 他鲁莽的开车行为导致了这场事故。

近　audacious, bold, brash, brassy, brazen, careless, daredevil, rash, madcap, temerarious

反　careful, cautious, circumspect, guarded, heedful, prudent, wary 慎重的，小心的

recluse [ˈrekluːs]

【考法】 *n.* 隐士：a person who **lives away** from others

adj. 隐居的，不爱社交的：marked by **withdrawal from society**

例 He was sick of cities and crowds, so he decided to go live by himself in the woods as a recluse. 他厌倦了城市和拥挤的人群，因此他决定像隐士一样遁隐山林。‖ a recluse poet who left a large amount of literature legacies 一个留下了大量文学遗产的隐居诗人 ‖ My neighbor is so recluse that I only see him about once a year. 我的邻居太神秘了，一般我一年只能见他一面。

近 anchorite, eremite, hermit, isolate, solitary; cloistered, hermetic, secluded, secluse, seclusive, sequestered

反 gregarious, social 好交际的

派 reclusive *adj.* 隐居的

recoil [ˈriːkɔɪl]

【考法】 *vi.* 退却，畏缩：to **shrink back**, as under pressure or in fear or repugnance

例 recoil from the snake 因为害怕蛇而畏缩不前 ‖ She recoiled from his touch. 她因害怕与他接触而退缩。

近 blench, cringe, flinch, quail, shrink, squinch, wince

反 confront, meet 面对

reconcile [ˈrekənsaɪl]

【考法】 *vt.* 使和解，协调：to restore to friendship or **harmony**

例 All efforts to reconcile her with her husband were in vain. 使她与她丈夫和解的一切努力都白费了。

近 accommodate, attune, conciliate, conform, coordinate, harmonize, key

反 disharmonize 使不和谐；estrange 离间

派 reconciliation *n.* 协调

recondite [ˈrekəndaɪt]

【考法】 *adj.* 深奥的，难解的：**difficult** or impossible for one of ordinary understanding or knowledge **to comprehend**

例 I think Quantum Mechanics and Random Process are the two most recondite courses in our curriculum this semester. 我觉得量子力学和随机过程是这学期课表中最难的两门课程。

近 abstruse, arcane, deep, enigmatic, esoteric, hermetic, occult, profound

反 facile, shallow, superficial 肤浅的；easy, simple 简单的

Unit 10

■ RECONNOITER	■ RECONSTITUTE	■ REPENTANT	■ RECTITUDE	■ RECUMBENT
■ RECUPERATE	■ REDOLENT	■ REDOUBTABLE	■ REDUNDANT	■ REEL

reconnoiter [ˌriːkəˈnɔɪtər]

【考法】 *vt.* 侦察，勘查：to **make a preliminary inspection** of, especially in order to gather military information

例 The wide utilization of unmanned aerial vehicles makes it much less risky to reconnoiter a certain area. 无人飞行器的广泛运用大大减少了军事侦察的风险。

近 probe, scout, survey

派 reconnaissance *n.* 侦察

reconstitute [ˌriːˈkɑːnstətuːt]

【考法】 *vt.* 重建，(尤其是通过加水)使复原：to constitute again or anew; to **restore** to a former condition, especially **by adding water**

例 reconstitute Jewish community after war 战后重建犹太人社区

近 reconstruct, reorder, reorganize, reshuffle, retool

反 annihilate, decimate, demolish, devastate, level, nuke, pulverize, ruin, smash, vaporize, wreck 摧毁

派 reconstitution *n.* (加水)复原

repentant [rɪˈpentənt]

【考法】 *adj.* 悔过的：**feeling sorrow** for a wrong that one has done

例 Certainly the image of a repentant playboy helps sell books. 毫无疑问，一个花花公子浪子回头的形象能帮助书的销售。

近 apologetic, compunctious, contrite, penitent, regretful, remorseful, rueful, sorry

反 impenitent, remorseless, unapologetic, unrepentant 不知悔改的

rectitude	[ˈrektɪtuːd]
【考法】	*n.* 正直: the quality or state of being straight; **moral integrity**
例	The principal encouraged the graduates to go on to live lives of rectitude . 校长鼓励毕业生们在今后的生活中做一个正直的人。
近	honesty, integrity, probity, righteousness, scrupulousness, uprightness, virtue, virtuousness
反	badness, evil, immorality, iniquity, sin, villainy, wickedness 邪恶，罪恶

recumbent	[rɪˈkʌmbənt]
【考法】	*adj.* 躺着的: **lying down**, especially in a position of comfort or rest
例	lying recumbent on the floor 躺在地板上
近	decumbent, procumbent, prone, prostrate, reclining, supine
反	erect, upright 直立的

recuperate	[rɪˈkuːpəreɪt]
【考法】	*v.* 恢复(健康或力量)，康复: to **recover health** or strength
例	He is gradually recuperating from a serious back injury . 他正渐渐地从严重的背部损伤中恢复过来。
近	convalesce, heal, rally, recoup, recover, rehabilitate
反	deteriorate, flag, wane, weaken 衰退，变得衰弱；die, expire, perish, pass away 死亡
派	recuperative *adj.* 有助于康复的

redolent	[ˈredələnt]
【考法】	*adj.* 芳香的: having or emitting **fragrance**
例	be redolent with the aroma of baking bread 充满了烤面包的香味
近	ambrosial, aromatic, fragrant, perfumed, savory, scented, sweet
反	unscented 没有香味的; fetid, foul, malodorous, noisome, rancid, reeky, stinky 恶臭的，腐臭的
派	redolence *n.* 芳香，香味

redoubtable	[rɪˈdaʊtəbl]
【考法 1】	*adj.* 杰出的，值得尊敬的: **worthy of respect** or honor
例	a surprising discovery by one of the most redoubtable figures in Egyptian archaeology 埃及考古学领域最值得敬重的人物之一所做出的一个惊人发现
近	bright, distinguished, illustrious, luminous, notable, noteworthy, outstanding, preeminent, prestigious
反	average, inferior, mediocre 平庸的，中等偏下的
【考法 2】	*adj.* 可怕的: **arousing fear** or awe
例	His next opponent would be by far the most redoubtable adversary the young boxer had ever faced. 年轻的拳击手的下一个对手将会是迄今为止他见过的最可怕的敌人。
近	direful, dreadful, fearsome, formidable, frightening, ghastly, horrifying, intimidating, scary, terrifying
反	calming, comforting, consoling, lulling, pacifying, quieting, reassuring, relaxing, soothing 令人放松的

redundant	[rɪˈdʌndənt]
【考法】	*adj.* 多余的，冗余的: **exceeding** what is **necessary** or normal
例	a redundant word/person 一个多余的字/人
近	excess, extra, supererogatory, superfluous, supernumerary, surplus
反	deficient, inadequate, insufficient, meager, niggardly, scant, scarce, short, sparse 缺乏，稀疏
派	redundancy *n.* 过剩，过多

reel	[riːl]
【考法】	*vi.* 感到眩晕: to be in a confused state as if **from being twirled around**
例	His mind reeled at the question . 他的脑子被这个问题搅混了。
近	spin, swirl, turn, whirl
反	calm 保持镇定

List 21

Unit 1

■ REFEREE	■ REFINE	■ REFLECT	■ REFRACTORY	■ REFULGENT
■ REFUTE	■ REGENERATE	■ REGIMEN	■ REGRESS	■ REHABILITATE

referee [ˌrefəˈriː]
【考法】 *n.* 仲裁者；裁判员：a person who **impartially** decides or **resolves a dispute** or controversy
vt.（就纠纷或争议）给出意见：to **give an opinion** about（something at issue or in dispute）
例 serve as the unofficial referee in disputes over the family business 作为一个非官方协调员，解决家庭事务中的纠纷 ‖ Their father usually ends up refereeing any disputes concerning use of the big TV. 最后往往是他们的父亲决定该看什么电视频道，从而解决了相关争执。
近 adjudicator, arbiter, arbitrator, judge, umpire; adjudge, adjudicate, arbitrate, decide, determine, settle
反 consult 咨询

refine [rɪˈfaɪn]
【考法】 *vt.* 改善，改进：to **improve or perfect** by pruning or polishing
例 You'd better refine your backhand before the big tennis match if you want to throne. 如果你想获得冠军的话，你最好在网球大赛开赛前再提升一下反手的技术。
近 ameliorate, amend, better, enhance, enrich, help, meliorate, perfect, polish, upgrade
反 deteriorate, worsen 恶化，降低
派 refined *adj.*（物）精雕细琢的，（人）彬彬有礼的；refinery *n.* 炼油厂

reflect [rɪˈflekt]
【考法 1】 *vt.* 反映，显露：to **make manifest** or apparent: show
例 Her book clearly reflects her religious beliefs. 她的书明确地反映了她的宗教信仰。
近 bespeak, betray, demonstrate, evince, manifest, reveal, show
反 conceal, cover, hide, mask, obscure, occlude, veil 隐藏
【考法 2】 *vi.* 思考：to **think seriously**
例 I reflected on my path as an undergraduate and my future as a PhD candidate. 我思考了我作为一名本科生的成长足迹以及我进修博士的未来。
近 consider, cogitate, contemplate, deliberate, meditate, muse, ponder, ruminate, think
派 reflective *adj.* 思考的，深思熟虑的

refractory [rɪˈfræktəri]
【考法】 *adj.* 倔强的，不顺从的：**resisting control** or authority
例 Refractory players will be ejected from the game. 不服从的球员将会被驱逐出场。
近 balky, contumacious, defiant, incompliant, insubordinate, intractable, obstreperous, rebellious, unruly
反 amenable, compliant, conformable, docile, governable, obedient, ruly, submissive, tractable 服从的，顺从的

refulgent [rɪˈfʌldʒənt]
【考法】 *adj.* 辉煌的，灿烂的：**shining radiantly**; resplendent
例 Refulgent sunlight broke through the clouds, creating huge swaths of light in the valley below us. 耀眼的阳光穿透了云层，在我们脚下的峡谷中投下了一块巨大的光斑。
近 beaming, brilliant, dazzling, incandescent, lucid, luminous, lustrous, radiant, resplendent, splendid
反 dim, dull, lackluster 黯淡无光的
派 refulgence *n.* 灿烂，光芒四射

refute [rɪˈfjuːt]
【考法】 *vt.* 否认：to **declare not to be true**
例 While the spokeswoman was publicly refuting rumors of a merger, behind the scenes the CEO was

working to effect that very outcome. 尽管女发言人一再公开否认合并的谣言，首席执行官却正在幕后为这一目标而努力。

近 contradict, disaffirm, disavow, disclaim, disconfirm, deny, gainsay, negate, negative, reject, repudiate

反 acknowledge, admit, avow, concede, confirm 承认

regenerate [rɪˈdʒenəreɪt]

【考法】 vt. 使重获新生, 使焕然一新: to **bring back to life**, practice, activity or a former condition of vigor

例 The lizard is able to regenerate its tail . 蜥蜴能够重新长出断尾。‖ The whole community was regenerated thanks to a government grant for repairing all the old buildings. 多亏了政府用于维修老楼的专项拨款，整个社区焕然一新。

近 recharge, refresh, rejuvenate, rekindle, renew, restore, resurrect, resuscitate, revitalize, revivify

反 degenerate, deteriorate, worsen 衰退, 恶化

派 regeneration n. 复兴

regimen [ˈredʒɪmən]

【考法】 n. (政治上的)统治: **lawful control** over the affairs of a political unit (as a nation)

例 A new party will have regimen over the nation and, hopefully, bring some much-needed change. 一个新的政党将要上台，希望他们能带来一些迫切需要的改革。

近 administration, authority, governance, jurisdiction, regime

regress [rɪˈgres]

【考法】 vi. 退化, 恶化: to become **worse** or of less value

例 regress to babyish behavior 退步到幼稚的行为

近 atrophy, crumble, decay, decline, degenerate, descend, deteriorate, ebb, retrograde, rot, sink, worsen

反 ameliorate, improve, meliorate 改善

派 regressive adj. 后退的, 退化的; regression n. 后退, 退化

rehabilitate [ˌriːəˈbɪlɪteɪt]

【考法】 vt. 使复原, 使康复: to **restore to** a former state （as of efficiency, good management, or solvency）or a **healthy condition**

例 new policies in hopes of rehabilitating the national economy 被指望能振兴国家经济的新政策 ‖ She decided to undergo physical therapy to help rehabilitate her broken elbow . 她决定采取理疗来治疗受伤的手肘。

近 cure, fix, mend, rejuvenate, resuscitate, revitalize, revive, set up

反 debilitate, enervate, enfeeble, weaken 使虚弱; relapse 旧病复发

派 rehabilitation n. 康复, 复原

Unit 2

| ■ REHEARSAL | ■ REIGN | ■ REIN | ■ REITERATE | ■ REJOICE |
| ■ RELAPSE | ■ REHASH | ■ RELENTLESS | ■ RELEVANT | ■ REMINISCENT |

rehearsal [rɪˈhɜːrsl]

【考法】 n. 排练, 彩排: the act of **practicing in preparation** for a public performance

例 We made a few mistakes in rehearsal , but we were pretty sure that we'd be OK on opening night. 彩排过程中我们犯了几个错误，但正式开幕式当晚我们有信心做得很好。

近 practice, trial, dry run

反 extemporization, impromptu, improvisation (无准备的)即兴表演

reign [reɪn]

【考法】 n. 统治权: the **right** or means **to command** or control others vi. 占统治地位或盛行: to **be predominant** or prevalent

例 A healthy nation should be governed by the reign of law and not by the will of its chief executive. 一个健康的国家应该是法制的，而非由最高领导人的意志统领。‖ They accused him of carrying out a reign of terror . 他们指责他搞独裁暴政。‖ Chaos reigned in the classroom. 整个教室一片混乱。‖ Panic reigned as the fire spread. 随着大火的扩散，恐慌也迅速蔓延。

近 arm, authority, clutch, command, control, dominion, grip, hold, mastery, sway; dominate, domineer, prevail, predominate, rule

反 impotence, impotency, powerlessness 无权, 无能

rein [reɪn]

【考法】 n. 抑制, 限制: the act or practice of **keeping** something (as an activity) **within certain boundaries**
vi. 抑制, 控制: to **keep from exceeding** a desirable degree or level (as of expression)

例 The oversight committee called on the corporation to keep a much tighter rein on the activities of its contractors. 监督委员会要求这个公司对其承包商的行为采取更为严格的管控。 || A good man knows how to rein in his temper. 君子知道如何按捺住火气。

近 circumscription, confinement, limitation, stint; bridle, check, constrain, contain, curb, govern, hold, inhibit, keep, measure, manacle, regulate, restrain, rule, tame

反 liberate, loose, loosen, unleash 释放，不再加以管束

reiterate [riˈɪtəreɪt]
【考法】 v. 重申: to say or **state again**
例 Let me reiterate our stance. 让我来重述我们的立场。 || I want to reiterate that under no circumstances are you to leave the house. 我想再次重申: 无论如何你都不能离开这间房子。
近 chime, din, iterate, recapitulate, rehearse, repeat

rejoice [rɪˈdʒɔɪs]
【考法】 vi. 欣喜，喜悦: to **feel joy** or great delight
例 We rejoiced over our unexpected victory on the soccer field. 我们为预料之外的足球胜利而感到欢喜。
近 crow, delight, exuberate, glory, jubilate, joy, kvell, triumph
反 bemoan, bewail, deplore, grieve, lament, moan, mourn, regret, weep 感到伤感、痛苦或遗憾
派 rejoiced adj. 高兴的

relapse [rɪˈlæps]
【考法】 vi. 重蹈覆辙，再犯: to slip or **fall back** into a former worse state
例 The patient wondered whether his illness would relapse. 病人想知道他的病会不会复发。
近 recidivate, regress, retrogress, revert
反 habilitate, reclaim, redeem, regenerate 变好，洗心革面; convalesce, rehabilitate 康复

rehash [ˈriːhæʃ]
【考法】 v. 重复，老调重弹: to **present** (something) **again** in a slightly different form
例 rehash details of decades past 老调重弹过去几十年的细节

relentless [rɪˈlentləs]
【考法1】 adj. 残酷的，无情的: showing or promising **no abatement of severity**, intensity, strength, or pace
例 relentless pressure 无情的压力
近 grim, inexorable, ironfisted, merciless, mortal, ruthless, unrelenting
反 charitable, clement, merciful, lenient 仁慈的
【考法2】 adj. 固执的，不肯妥协的: showing no signs of slackening or **yielding in one's purpose**
例 The team's offense was relentless in trying to score. 进攻球员毫不妥协地努力得分。
近 adamant, dogged, headstrong, mulish, obdurate, pertinacious, rigid, uncompromising, unyielding
反 acquiescent, amenable, compliant, complying, flexible, pliable, pliant, relenting, yielding 易屈服的

relevant [ˈreləvənt]
【考法】 adj. 有关系的，重要的: **having** a bearing on or **connection** with the matter at hand
例 Make sure your answers during the interview are short and relevant. 确保你在面试时的回答简短而恰当。
You need to bring all the relevant certificates with you. 你需要携带所有的相关证明。
近 applicable, apposite, apropos, germane, material, pertinent, pointed, relative
反 extraneous, immaterial, impertinent, inapplicable, inapposite, irrelevant, pointless 无关的
派 relevance n. 关联

reminiscent [ˌremɪˈnɪsnt]
【考法】 adj. 怀旧的，引发回忆的: **provoking a memory** or mental association
例 reminiscent of life in the United States 回想起来在美国的生活
近 evocative, suggestive

Unit 3

■ RELINQUISH ■ RELISH ■ RELUCTANT ■ REMISS ■ RESENT
■ REMONSTRANCE ■ REMORSE ■ REMUNERATE ■ REND ■ RENEGADE

relinquish [rɪˈlɪŋkwɪʃ]
【考法】 vt. 放弃(职位、权力等): to **give up** (as a position of authority) formally
例 relinquish power 放弃权力
近 abnegate, cede, renounce, resign, surrender
反 inaugurate 就职; usurp 篡位

relish ['relɪʃ]

【考法 1】 *n.* 喜好，偏好：an appetite for something; a strong **appreciation or liking**

vt. 享受，喜欢：to **take** keen or zestful **pleasure** in

例 She has great relish for early morning walks , which she takes nearly every day. 她对早晨散步有格外的喜好——几乎每天早上她都会坚持出去。|| I relish the challenge of doing jobs that others turn down. 我喜欢挑战别人拒绝做的工作。

近 appetite, fancy, favor, fondness, like, love, partiality, preference, taste; adore, enjoy, like, love, rejoice, revel, savor

反 aversion, disfavor, disgust, dislike, distaste, hatred, loathing 反感，厌恶感; abhor, abominate, detest, dislike, hate, loathe 厌恶，讨厌

reluctant [rɪ'lʌktənt]

【考法】 *adj.* 不情愿的，不要嘛：feeling or **showing** aversion, hesitation, or **unwillingness**

例 be reluctant to ask for help 不愿意寻求帮助

近 averse, disinclined, indisposed, loath, unwilling

反 willing 乐意的; disposed, inclined 倾向于做某事的; eager 渴望的

派 reluctance *n.* 不愿意，不情愿

remiss [rɪ'mɪs]

【考法】 *adj.* 疏忽的，不留心的：exhibiting **carelessness** or slackness

例 I would be remiss if I did not do something about it . 如果我对此不做点什么就是懈怠。

近 careless, derelict, disregardful, heedless, lax, lazy, neglectful, neglecting, slack

反 attentive, careful, conscientious, meticulous, painstaking, scrupulous 细致的，仔细的

resent [rɪ'zent]

【考法】 *v.* 怨恨，憎恨 to be **angry or upset** about (someone or something that you think is unfair)

例 resent us for our methods 怨恨我们所采用的方式

近 begrudge, envy

remonstrance [rɪ'mɑːnstrəns]

【考法】 *n.* 抗议，抱怨：an **expression of protest**, **complaint**, or reproof, especially a formal statement of grievances

例 She seems deaf to her son's remonstrances . 她似乎对儿子的抗议充耳不闻。|| Aggravated by the noisy metro construction, many residents wrote letters of remonstrance to city officials . 许多被地铁建设的噪音激怒的居民向市政府投去了抗议信。

近 challenge, complaint, demur, difficulty, fuss, objection, protest, question, remonstration, stink

反 acceptance, acquiescence, agreement, approval, assent, sanction 同意，接受

remorse [rɪ'mɔːrs]

【考法】 *n.* 懊悔，悔恨：moral anguish arising from repentance for past misdeeds; **bitter regret**

例 be full of remorse 充满悔恨

近 contriteness, contrition, penitence, regret, remorsefulness, repentance, rue, self-reproach, shame

反 impenitence, remorselessness 不知悔改

派 remorseful *adj.* 懊悔的，悔恨的

remunerate [rɪ'mjuːnəreɪt]

【考法】 *vt.* 支付报酬，补偿：to **pay** an equivalent to for a service, loss, or expense

例 He promptly remunerated the repair company for fixing the satellite TV. 他迅速地支付了维修公司修理卫星电视酬劳。

近 compensate, indemnify, recompense, recoup, redress, remedy, repay, requite

派 remunerative *adj.* 有报酬的

rend [rend]

【考法】 *vt.* 撕裂，猛拉：to **tear or split apart** or into pieces violently

例 Wolves rend a game to pieces . 狼群会把猎物撕成碎片。|| pain that rends the heart 撕心裂肺般的痛

近 cleave, lacerate, ribbon, rip, rive, rupture, shred, split, tatter, tear

反 associate, coalesce, combine, conjoin, conjugate, connect, fuse, interfuse, join, link, unify 联合

renegade ['renɪɡeɪd]

【考法】 *n.* 背教者，叛徒：one who **rejects** a religion, cause, **allegiance**, or group for another; a deserter

例 a renegade without respect for the rule of law 毫不尊重法规的叛逆者

近 apostate, betrayer, defector, deserter, recreant, traitor, turncoat

反 adherent, loyalist, partisan 忠诚者

Unit 4

renounce [rɪˈnaʊns]
- 【考法】 *vt.* (正式地)放弃: to **give up**, refuse, or resign usually by formal declaration
- 例 renounce his nationality 退出国籍
- 近 abnegate, cede, relinquish, resign, surrender
- 反 inaugurate 就职; usurp 篡位
- 派 renunciation *n.* 放弃

renovate [ˈrenəveɪt]
- 【考法】 *vt.* 修复，维修: to **restore** to a former better state (as by cleaning, repairing, or rebuilding)
- 例 We will have to renovate the house extensively before we can move in. 在入住之前我们必须大规模翻修一下这栋房子。
- 近 doctor, fix, patch, recondition, repair, revamp
- 反 blemish, break, damage, deface, disfigure, harm, hurt, impair, injure, mar, ruin, vandalize, wreck 破坏

repartee [ˌrepɑːrˈtiː]
- 【考法】 *n.* 打趣，善意的玩笑: **good-natured teasing** or exchanging of clever remarks
- 例 some witty repartee 妙语如珠
- 近 backchat, badinage, chaff, jesting, joshing, persiflage, raillery

repatriate [ˌriːˈpeɪtrieɪt]
- 【考法】 *vt.* 遣返: to restore or **return to the country** of origin, allegiance, or citizenship
- 例 As soon as the war ends, the government will start to repatriate war refugees. 只要战争一结束，政府就会开始遣返战争难民。
- 反 banish, deport, expatriate 放逐，驱逐

repeal [rɪˈpiːl]
- 【考法】 *vt.* 撤销，废除(法律等): to **rescind or annul** by authoritative act
- 例 The company called the furniture store to repeal the order for six new desks. 公司要求家具店撤销六张新桌子的订单。|| In 1933, Congress passed the 21st Amendment which repealed the Prohibition Amendment of 1919, thus making the sale, distribution, and use of alcohol legal once again. 1933 年，国会通过了《第二十一修正案》，该法案废除了于 1919 年制订的《禁酒法》，从而使得酒的买卖、配送和使用再次合法化。
- 近 abort, abrogate, annul, cancel, disannul, invalidate, negate, null, nullify, rescind, revoke, vacate, void
- 反 continue, keep 继续; enact, establish, legislate 立法，制订

repel [rɪˈpel]
- 【考法】 *vt.* 使厌恶: to **cause aversion** in: disgust
- 例 Evil odors always repel me. 臭味总是让我恶心。
- 近 disgust, nauseate, repulse, revolt, sicken
- 反 allure, attract, bewitch, captivate, charm, enchant, entice, fascinate, lure, seduce, tempt 吸引，诱惑
- 派 repelling *adj.* 令人厌恶的

repertoire [ˈrepərtwɑːr]
- 【考法】 *n.* (技术、设备或原料等的)详单: the **complete list** or supply of skills, devices, or ingredients used in a particular field, occupation, or practice
- 例 The chef's repertoire of specialties seems to be limited, with several of the dishes appearing over and over again in slightly varied guises. 这个厨师的所有拿手好戏看来是很有限的，因为上来的几盘菜看起来只是稍微换了一下装饰而已。
- 近 budget, fund, inventory, pool, reservoir, stock

repine [rɪˈpaɪn]
- 【考法 1】 *vi.* 抱怨，表达不满: to feel or **express discontent** or dejection
- 例 repine the fate 抱怨命运
- 近 carp, complain, fuss, gripe, grouch, grouse, growl, grumble, inveigh, moan, murmur, mutter, wail, whine
- 反 crow, delight, rejoice 高兴
- 【考法 2】 *vi.* 渴望: to **long for** something
- 例 During the deep cold of winter, I repine for warm tropical beaches. 在寒冬，我渴望温暖的热带海滩。
- 近 ache, covet, crave, desiderate, hunger, itch, long, lust, pine, salivate, thirst, want, wish, yearn
- 反 abhor, abominate, detest, dislike, hate, loathe 厌恶，讨厌

| **replete** | [rɪˈpliːt] |

【考法】 *adj.* 充满…的，富于…的：**possessing** or covered with **great numbers** or amounts of something specified

例 Financial history is replete with bubbles and crashes 金融的历史充满危机和泡沫

近 abounding, abundant, awash, flush, fraught, lousy, swarming, teeming, thick, thronging

反 depleted, drained, exhausted 耗竭的；deficient, incomplete, insufficient, short 缺乏的

派 repletion *n.* 装满

| **repose** | [rɪˈpoʊz] |

【考法1】 *n.* (劳作后的)休息：a **state of resting** after exertion or strain *vi.* 休息：to **take a rest**

例 The doctor ordered a period of repose for the patient suffering from insomnia. 医生要求正在饱受失眠折磨的病人好好休息一阵。‖ They have to repose on couches because all beds have been occupied. 因为所有的床都有人占了，他们不得不在沙发上休息。

近 ease, leisure, relaxation; idle, loll, lounge, relax, rest

反 exertion, labor, toil, work 劳动，工作; drudge, hustle, moil, strive, struggle, sweat, travail 努力工作

【考法2】 *n.* 平静，宁静：a state of **freedom from storm** or disturbance

例 We enjoyed the repose of a summer evening on a remote island. 我们在遥远的小岛上共享了夏日傍晚的片刻安宁。

近 calmness, hush, peace, placidity, quietness, restfulness, serenity, still, tranquility

反 commotion, pandemonium, tumult, turmoil, unrest, uproar 骚乱，动乱

Unit 5

| ■ REPREHEND | ■ REPRESS | ■ REPRIEVE | ■ REPROACH | ■ REPROBATE |
| ■ REPROOF | ■ REPROVE | ■ REPUDIATE | ■ REPUGNANT | ■ REPULSE |

| **reprehend** | [reprɪˈhend] |

【考法】 *vt.* 谴责，责难，批评：to **express** one's **unfavorable opinion** of the worth or quality of

例 Our conscience reprehends us. 我们的良心谴责我们。

近 berate, blame, castigate, censure, condemn, denounce, dispraise, fault, knock, lambaste, pan, upbraid

反 extol, laud, praise 表扬

派 reprehensible *adj.* 应受谴责的

| **repress** | [rɪˈpres] |

【考法1】 *vt.* 镇压：to **put down by force**, usually before total control has been lost; quell

例 Military quickly repressed the rebellion in the city and restored order. 军方迅速平息了市内的暴乱，恢复了秩序。

近 crush, quash, quell, silence, squash, squelch, subdue, suppress

反 foment, incite, instigate, provoke, stir 煽动，激起

【考法2】 *vt.* 阻止（正常的表达、活动或发展等）：to **prevent** the natural or normal **expression**, activity, or development of

例 You can't repress your feelings forever, so tell her that you love her. 你不可能永远压抑自己的感受，所以大胆地向她表白吧。

近 bridle, check, curb, muffle, smother, stifle, strangle, swallow

反 express, loose, release, take out, unleash, vent (情感等)表达，宣泄

派 repression *n.* 阻止，镇压

| **reprieve** | [rɪˈpriːv] |

【考法】 *vt.* 对…暂缓处刑，免罪：to **postpone or cancel** the **punishment** of

例 reprieve the criminal 给予罪犯缓刑

近 absolve, acquit, amnesty, condone, excuse, forgive, pardon, remit, respite, spare

反 penalize, punish 惩罚

| **reproach** | [rɪˈproʊtʃ] |

【考法】 *vt.* 批评，责备：to **express** disapproval, **criticism**, or disappointment in（someone）

例 reproached by their mother for untidiness 因为邋遢而被他们的母亲批评

近 admonish, berate, castigate, chide, condemn, denounce, lambaste, rebuke, reprimand, reprove, upbraid

反 commend, eulogize, extol, laud, praise 表扬

派 irreproachable *adj.* 无可指责的

reprobate ['reprəbeɪt]

【考法】 *n.* 堕落者，道德败坏的人：a morally **unprincipled person** *adj.* 堕落的，放荡的：**morally corrupt**

例 The program rehabilitates reprobates and turns them into hard-working, law-abiding citizens. 这个项目让那些堕落的人改过自新，并将他们变成勤劳守法的好公民。‖ He is a reprobate judge who could be bribed, and often with astonishing ease. 他是一个堕落的法官，极其容易就被贿赂了。

近 brute, devil, fiend, miscreant, rapscallion, rascal, villain; debased, debauched, degraded, depraved, dissipated, dissolute, libertine, perverse, perverted, rakish

反 saint 圣人; good, moral, righteous, virtuous 有道德的; pure, uncorrupted 纯净的，未受污染的

reproof [rɪ'pruːf]

【考法】 *n.* 批评，反对：**criticism** for a fault, rebuke

例 The head teacher speaks in tones of gentle reproof. 校长的话语中带有轻微的批评。

近 commination, condemnation, denunciation, excoriation, rebuke, reprimand, reproach, stricture

反 commendation, eulogy, praise 赞扬; endorsement 同意

reprove [rɪ'pruːv]

【考法】 *vt.* 温和地责备，警告：to **scold** or correct usually **gently** or with kindly intent

例 My piano teacher often reproves me for slouching while playing, observing that good posture helps one play better. 我的钢琴老师常常会因为懒散的坐姿而批评我，他认为良好的坐姿能让我弹得更好。

近 admonish, blame, chide, criticize, reprimand, reproach

反 lambaste 严厉地责备; commend, eulogize, extol, laud, praise 表扬

repudiate [rɪ'pjuːdieɪt]

【考法】 *vt.* 否认：to **declare not to be true**

例 She repudiated the charge that she had lied on her résumé. 她否认了她在简历中作假的指控。

近 contradict, disaffirm, disavow, disclaim, disconfirm, disown, gainsay, negate, negative, refute, reject

反 acknowledge, admit, allow, avow, concede, confirm 承认

repugnant [rɪ'pʌɡnənt]

【考法】 *adj.* 令人厌恶的：**arousing** disgust or **aversion**

例 be repugnant to sb. 让某人感到厌恶

近 abhorrent, abominable, awful, disgusting, distasteful, hideous, loathsome, noisome, obnoxious, repulsive

反 innocuous, inoffensive 无害的; agreeable, delightful, enjoyable, gratifying, pleasing 令人愉悦的

repulse [rɪ'pʌls]

【考法】 *vt.* 使厌恶，排斥：to rebuff or **reject with** rudeness, coldness, or **denial**

例 The scenes of violence in the film may repulse some viewers. 电影中某些暴力场景可能会使观众反感。

近 disgust, nauseate, repel, revolt, sicken

反 allure, attract, bewitch, captivate, charm, enchant, entice, fascinate, lure, seduce, tempt 吸引，诱惑

派 repulsion *n.* 排斥

Unit 6

■ REPUTE	■ REQUITE	■ REQUISITE	■ RESCIND	■ RESERVED
■ RESIDUE	■ RESIGN	■ RESILIENCE	■ RESOLUTE	■ RESONANT

repute [rɪ'pjuːt]

【考法】 *n.* （尤指好的）名声，名誉：a **good reputation**

例 Before his national bestseller, he was a writer of little repute. 在他的全国畅销书面市之前他是个没什么名声的作家。

近 celebrity, fame, name, renown, reputation

反 infamy, notoriety 坏名声

派 reputable *adj.* 有好名声的

requite [rɪ'kwaɪt]

【考法1】 *vt.* 酬谢，报答：to **make repayment** or return for

例 requite her love with hatred 恩将仇报

近 indemnify, reciprocate, recompense, recoup, reimburse, remunerate, repay

【考法2】 *vt.* 报仇：to **punish in kind** the wrongdoer responsible for

例 The future writer would later requite the abuse he suffered at the hands of his classmates by creating scathing portraits of them in his novels. 未来的作家会把在同学那里受了委屈的账算清的——他会在小说中把他们描绘成恶人。

近 avenge, redress, retaliate, revenge

反 absolve, condone, forgive, pardon 饶恕，宽恕

requisite [ˈrekwɪzɪt]

【考法】 *n.* 必需品: **something necessary**, indispensable, or unavoidable

adj. 必不可少的，必备的: essential, **necessary**

例 A is a requisite for B A 是 B 的必需品 ‖ Oxygen is requisite for human to survive. 氧气是维持人类生存的必要条件。

近 condition, demand, necessity, need, requirement; critical, compulsory, imperative, indispensable, mandatory, necessary, obligatory, required, vital

反 needless, unnecessary 不必要的; dispensable, optional 可替换的，可选择的

rescind [rɪˈsɪnd]

【考法】 *vt.* 废除，取消: to **make void**

例 The government refused to rescind the order of curfew. 政府拒绝撤销宵禁的决定。

近 abolish, abrogate, annul, cancel, invalidate, negate, null, nullify, recall, repeal, revoke, void

反 establish, enact 建立; continue, keep 维持，保持

reserved [rɪˈzɜːrvd]

【考法】 *adj.* 内向的，缄默的: **restrained** in words and actions

例 He was unemotional, quiet and reserved. 他不动感情、安静并且内向。

近 closemouthed, constrained, laconic, reticent, restrained, silent, taciturn

反 communicative, expansive, talkative 健谈的; garrulous, loquacious 话多的

派 unreserved *adj.* 无保留的，外向的

residue [ˈrezɪduː]

【考法】 *n.* 剩余物: something that **remains** after a part is taken, separated, or designated

例 residue incoal 煤的残渣

近 debris, remainder, remnant

派 residual *adj.* 剩余的

resign [rɪˈzaɪn]

【考法】 *vt.* 辞职，放弃(职位): to **give up** one's job or **office**

例 She resigned her position at the university. 她自动放弃她在大学的职位。

近 abnegate, cede, relinquish, renounce, surrender, step down

反 assume, inaugurate 就职，承担(责任); usurp 篡位

派 resigned *adj.* 辞职的，放弃的

resilience [rɪˈzɪliəns]

【考法】 *n.* 恢复能力: the **ability to recover quickly** from illness, change, or misfortune

例 Her mental resilience helped her promptly walk out of the shadow of her father's death. 她的精神恢复能力让她很快地走出了父亲去世的阴影。

近 adaptability

派 resilient *adj.* 有弹性的; 能迅速恢复的

resolute [ˈrezəluːt]

【考法】 *adj.* 坚定的: marked by **firm determination**

例 We are glad to have such a resolute ally. 我们很高兴能拥有这样一个坚定的盟友。

近 bound, decided, faithful, resolved, unwavering

反 faltering, hesitant, indecisive, irresolute, jittery, vacillating, wavering 犹豫的，踌躇的

派 resolution *n.* 坚定的决心

resonant [ˈrezənənt]

【考法】 *adj.* (声音)洪亮的，共鸣的: **strong** and deep **in tone**

例 A deep resonant voice rang out. 传来了洪亮的声音。

近 consonant, orotund, plangent, resounding, reverberant, sonorous, vibrant

反 faint, low, muffled, muted, smothered, soft, weak 声音模糊的，低声的

派 resonance *n.* 洪亮

Unit 7

■ RESOURCEFUL	■ RESPITE	■ RETROACTIVE	■ RESPLENDENT	■ RESPONSIVE
■ RESTIVE	■ RESTLESS	■ REVELATION	■ RESURGENCE	■ RESUSCITATE

resourceful [rɪˈsɔːrsfl]

【考法】 *adj.* 有创造力的，机智的: able to **act** effectively or **imaginatively**, especially in difficult situations

例 an inventive and resourceful man 一个有创造力又足智多谋的人

近 able, adroit, competent, talented

派 resourcefulness *n.* 足智多谋

respite ['respɪt]

【考法】 *n.* 间歇，休息：an interval of **rest** or relief

例 toil without respite 埋头苦干 || In the middle of each semester there came a short respite . 在每个学期的期中，会有一个短暂的休假。

近 break, lull, intermission, recess, pause, rest

反 resumption 继续进行；exertion, labor, toil, work 劳动，工作

retroactive [ˌretroʊˈæktɪv]

【考法】 *adj.* 有追溯效力的：**extending in** scope or **effect to a prior time** or to conditions that existed or originated in the past

例 retroactive law 具有追溯效力的法律

resplendent [rɪˈsplendənt]

【考法】 *adj.* 华丽辉煌的：shining **brilliantly**

例 look resplendent in a fine suit 穿西装看起来光彩照人

近 brilliant, glorious, gorgeous, grand, magnificent, splendid, sublime, superb

反 dim, dull, lackluster 黯淡无光的

派 resplendence *n.* 辉煌

responsive [rɪˈspɑːnsɪv]

【考法】 *adj.* 反应的；敏感的：**quick to respond** or react appropriately or sympathetically

例 Children are often the most responsive members of the audience. 儿童通常是观众中最为敏感的群体。

近 prompt, sensible, sensitive, susceptible

反 dispassionate 无动于衷的；detached, indifferent 冷漠的

派 responsiveness *n.* 有反应；热诚

restive ['restɪv]

【考法】 *adj.* 急躁的，忧虑的：marked by **impatience** or **uneasiness**

例 I spent a restive night worrying about the next day's exam . 我度过了忧虑的一晚，担心明天的考试。

近 restless, nervy, uneasy, uptight

反 imperturbable 沉着的；phlegmatic 冷静的

restless ['restləs]

【考法】 *adj.* 不平静的：marked by or causing a **lack of quiet**, repose, or rest

例 The patient felt restless from pain . 病人因疼痛而无法平静。

近 agitating, anxious, distressful, disturbing, fraught, restive, perturbed, uneasy, unquiet, unsettled

反 halcyon, peaceful, serene, tranquil 平静的，安宁的

revelation [ˌrevəˈleɪʃn]

【考法】 *n.* 爆料，揭示：the act of **making known** something previously unknown or concealed

例 the revelation of the movie star's secret marriage by the tabloids 小报爆料了电影明星的秘密婚姻

近 disclosure, divulgence, exposure

resurgence [rɪˈsɜːrdʒəns]

【考法】 *n.* 复兴：a **restoration** to use, acceptance, activity, or vigor

例 Let's witness the resurgence of classical school . 让我们见证古典乐派的复兴。

近 reanimation, rebirth, regeneration, rejuvenation, renewal, resurrection, resuscitation, revitalization

反 decay, degradation, deterioration, downfall, ebb, fall 衰落

派 resurgent *adj.* 正在复兴的

resuscitate [rɪˈsʌsɪteɪt]

【考法】 *vt.* 使复活，使苏醒：to **restore consciousness**, vigor, or life to

例 resuscitated by the kiss of the prince 因王子的吻而苏醒

近 reanimate, recharge, refresh, rejuvenate, rekindle, renew, resurrect, revitalize, revive, revivify

反 faint 昏迷

派 resuscitation *n.* 复活，复兴；resuscitated *adj.* 复活的

Unit 8

retainer [rɪ'teɪnər]

【考法】 *n.* 家仆: a person attached or owing **service** to a household

例 Knights are dressed for battle by their retainers. 骑士们在上战场之前是由他们的家仆帮助着装打扮的。

近 menial, servant

反 lord, master 主人

retaliate [rɪ'tælieɪt]

【考法】 *v.* 报复，反击: to **pay back** (as an injury) in kind

例 We swear to retaliate for our losses. 我们发誓要以牙还牙。

近 avenge, redress, requite, revenge

反 absolve, condone, forgive, pardon 饶恕，宽恕

派 retaliation *n.* 报复

retard [rɪ'tɑːrd]

【考法】 *vt.* 减速，延迟: to **cause** to move or proceed **slowly**; delay or impede

例 Language barriers retarded their negotiating progress. 语言障碍让谈判进程受阻。

近 bog, brake, decelerate, delay, detain, hamper, impede, mire, slacken

反 accelerate, catalyze, expedite, hasten, precipitate 加速，促进

repetitious [ˌrepə'tɪʃəs]

【考法】 *adj.* 重复的，反复的: **repeated many times** and therefore boring

例 a painfully repetitious task 一项痛苦、不断重复的任务

近 duplicative, reiterative, repetitive

reticent ['retɪsnt]

【考法】 *adj.* 沉默不语的: **inclined to be silent** or uncommunicative in speech

例 reticent about achievements 对成就保持缄默

近 closemouthed, constrained, laconic, reserved, restrained, silent, taciturn

反 communicative, expansive, talkative 健谈的; garrulous, loquacious 话多的

retort [rɪ'tɔːrt]

【考法】 *n.* （尤指机智的）回应，回答: something spoken or written in reaction especially to a question, especially a **quick**, **witty**, or cutting **reply**

例 She responded to the heckler with a scathing but hilarious retort that instantly won over the audience. 面对故意起哄捣乱的人，她那严厉但不失幽默的回答立刻得到了观众的肯定。

近 comeback, rejoinder, repartee, reply, response, return, riposte

反 inquiry, query, question 问题，问询

retouch [ˌriː'tʌtʃ]

【考法】 *v.* 润饰，改进: to **improve** or change (a photographic negative or print)

例 She was retouching her painting before the deadline. 在截止日期到来之前，她一直在润色她的画作。

近 ameliorate, enhance, furbish, meliorate, perfect, polish, refine, upgrade

反 deteriorate, downgrade, worsen 恶化，降低

retract [rɪ'trækt]

【考法】 *vt.* 收回，否认: to **take back**

例 The newspaper had to retract its allegations against the mayor. 报纸不得不收回针对市长的谣言。

近 abjure, abnegate, disavow, forswear, recall, recant, renounce, repeal, repudiate, withdraw

反 tender 提出（建议，想法）; adhere, stick 坚持

派 retractable *adj.* 可收回的

retrench [rɪ'trentʃ]

【考法】 *vi.* 削减开支: to **curtail expenses**

例 Declining business forced the company to retrench. 衰减的业务迫使公司削减开支。

近 economize, reduce, cut down

反 enlarge, expand 扩大，扩张

派 retrenchment *n.* 削减开销

retribution [ˌretrɪˈbjuːʃn]

【考法】 *n.* 报偿，报应：the dispensing or receiving of **reward or punishment** especially in the hereafter

例 retribution karma in Buddhism 佛教的因果报应

近 avengement, payback, recompense, reparation, repayment, requital, retaliation, revenge, vengeance

派 retributive *n.* 报应的

Unit 9

■ RETROGRADE	■ RETROSPECTIVE	■ REVEL	■ REVENGE	■ REVERE
■ RESONATE	■ REVIVE	■ REVOKE	■ REVOLT	■ RIBALD

retrograde [ˈretrəɡreɪd]

【考法】 *adj.* 倒退的：**moving** or tending **backward** *vi.* 退步，退化：to **decline** to a worse condition

例 This is a retrograde step and you will regret it. 这是后退的一步，你以后肯定会后悔的。‖ The Dark Ages is the period following the fall of the Roman Empire when Western civilization seriously retro-graded. "黑暗时代"指的是罗马帝国崩溃之后，西方文明严重退步的一个历史时期。

近 backward, receding, regressive, reversed, withdrawing; atrophy, crumble, decay, decline, degenerate, descend, deteriorate, ebb, regress, rot, sink, worsen

反 progressive 前进的; ameliorate, improve, meliorate 改善

retrospective [ˌretrəˈspektɪv]

【考法】 *adj.* 回顾的：**looking back** on, contemplating, or directed to the past

例 a retrospective glance at my youth 朝我少年时代投去的回顾性一瞥

近 backward

反 anticipatory, prospective 预期的，未来的

revel [ˈrevl]

【考法】 *v.* 享乐，陶醉：to **take intense pleasure** or satisfaction

例 reveled in her unaccustomed leisure 喜爱她尚未习惯的休闲

近 binge, carouse, roister

revenge [rɪˈvendʒ]

【考法】 *n.* 报复，复仇：an act or instance of **retaliating** in order to get even

vt. 为…复仇：to avenge (as oneself) usually by **retaliating in kind** or degree

例 Both sides were determined to get revenge for losses and showed little interest in ending the feud. 双方都下定决心要为失去的东西报仇，对于结束他们之间的世仇毫无兴趣。‖ The bombing was in revenge for the assassination of their leader. 此次轰炸是对暗杀他们领袖的报复行动。‖ He finally revenged the death of his brother. 他终于为兄弟的死报了仇。

近 avengement, payback, reprisal, requital, retaliation, retribution, vengeance; avenge, redress, requite, retaliate

反 forgiveness, pardon 饶恕，原谅; absolve, condone, forgive, pardon 原谅，宽恕

revere [rɪˈvɪr]

【考法】 *vt.* (尤指对神的)尊崇，尊敬：to offer honor or **respect** to (someone) as a divine power

例 He is revered for his valor. 他因为英勇而受到尊敬。‖ In some cultures people revere their ancestors, even leaving food offerings for them. 在一些文化中，人们非常敬重先人，甚至将一些食物留下来供他们享用。

近 adore, deify, glorify, esteem, regard, respect, venerate, worship

反 blaspheme, desecrate, profane, violate 亵渎

派 reverence *n.* 尊重; reverent *adj.* 恭敬的，虔诚的

resonate [ˈrezəneɪt]

【考法】 *v.* 有重要性：**beneficial to the health** of body or mind

近 the issues resonating with voters 投票者特别关心的问题

反 ring true

revive [rɪˈvaɪv]

【考法】 *vi.* 再获新生：to become **active** or flourishing **again**

例 Around midnight, I usually need to revive myself with a cup of strong coffee. 在午夜时分，我需要一杯浓咖啡来提神。‖ The success of the movie has revived her career. 这部电影的成功让她的事业焕发第二春。

近 reanimate, recharge, refresh, rejuvenate, rekindle, renew, resurrect, resuscitate, revitalize, revivify

反 degenerate, deteriorate, worsen 衰退，恶化

派 revival *n.* 复苏

	revoke	[rɪˈvoʊk]
【考法】	*vt.* 撤回，宣告无效: to **annul** by recalling or taking back
例	revoke a will 废除遗嘱
近	abolish, abrogate, annul, cancel, invalidate, negate, null, nullify, recall, repeal, void
反	establish, enact 建立; continue, keep 维持，保持
派	revocation *n.* 撤销，废除

	revolt	[rɪˈvoʊt]
【考法】	*vt.* 使厌恶，使反感: to **fill with disgust** or abhorrence
例	The smell of seafood revolts him. 他对海鲜的腥味十分反感。
近	disgust, nauseate, repel, repulse, sicken
反	allure, attract, bewitch, captivate, charm, enchant, entice, fascinate, lure, seduce, tempt 吸引，诱惑

	ribald	[ˈraɪbɔːld]
【考法】	*adj.* (举止、言语) 下流粗俗的: characterized by or indulging in **vulgar**, lewd humor
例	entertain the guests with ribald jokes 用荤段子来取悦客人
近	bawdy, blue, coarse, crude, dirty, filthy, gross, indecent, nasty, obscene, pornographic, profane, vulgar
反	decent, proper, seemly 恰当的，得体的

Unit 10

■ RICKETY	■ RESTORATIVE	■ RIDICULE	■ RIFE	■ RIFT
■ RILE	■ RIPEN	■ RIOT	■ RITE	■ RIVE

	rickety	[ˈrɪkəti]
【考法】	*adj.* 不稳的: **lacking stability** or firmness
例	The rickety coalition may break at any moment. 脆弱的联盟随时都可能破裂。
近	insecure, precarious, shaky, unsound, unsteady, weak
反	firm, sound, stable, sturdy 稳定的，稳固的

	restorative	[rɪˈstɔːrətɪv]
【考法】	*adj.* 有益健康的: **beneficial to the health** of body or mind
例	the restorative power of sleep 睡眠有助于健康的能力
反	tonic, curing, healing, remedial, sanative, wholesome

	ridicule	[ˈrɪdɪkjuːl]
【考法】	*vt.* 嘲笑: to **make fun** of
例	They always ridiculed everything she said. 他们总是嘲笑她说的话。 ‖ The term "big bang theory" was originally coined to ridicule the belief that the universe was created by a giant explosion. "大爆炸理论"起初是为了嘲笑一种观点而创造的，这种观点认为宇宙源自一场巨大的爆炸。
近	deride, gibe, jape, jeer, lout, mock, taunt
反	commend, praise 表扬
派	ridiculous *adj.* 荒谬的

	rife	[raɪf]
【考法】	*adj.* 丰富的，普遍的: possessing or covered with **great numbers** or amounts of something specified
例	a video game rife with violence and abuse 充满暴力与虐待的电子游戏
近	abounding, abundant, awash, flush, fraught, lousy, replete, swarming, teeming, thick, thronging
反	deficient, incomplete, insufficient, short 缺乏的

	rift	[rɪft]
【考法】	*n.* 分裂，不和: a **break** in **friendly** relations *vt.* 使开裂: to cause to split open or **break**
例	a rift between two once allied nations 两个往昔盟国的决裂 ‖ Hills were rifted by the earthquake. 地震使得山崩地裂。
近	crack, fissure, fracture, schism; cleave, divide, rip, split, sunder, tear
反	reconciliation, rapprochement 调和; associate, coalesce, combine, conjugate, join, link 接合

	rile	[raɪl]
【考法】	*vt.* 刺激，惹怒: to **make agitated** and angry
例	The new work schedules riled the employees. 新的工作时间表激怒了员工。
近	aggravate, annoy, enrage, exasperate, grate, inflame, infuriate, irritate, nettle, peeve, pique, provoke, roil
反	allay, alleviate, assuage, ease, mitigate, mollify, palliate, relieve, soothe 平息，缓和

	ripen	['raɪpən]
【考法】		*v.* 使成熟，变成熟: to **make** or become **ripe** or riper
例		Age ripens a good wine . 时间酿出好酒。
近		age, develop, grow, mature
反		fade, flag, shrivel, wane, wilt, wither 使枯萎
派		ripened *adj.* (酒、果实等)成熟的

	riot	['raɪət]
【考法】		*n.* 喧闹，暴乱: **public violence**, tumult, or disorder
例		Special police units equipped with riot shields quickly arrived at the airport. 装备有防暴盾牌的特警们迅速抵达了飞机场。
近		clamor, commotion, disorder, ferment, tumult, turmoil, upheaval, uproar
反		serenity, tranquility 宁静; order 秩序

	rite	[raɪt]
【考法】		*n.* 惯例，仪式: a **prescribed form** or manner governing the words or actions for a ceremony
例		the marriage rites 婚礼仪式的章程
近		ceremony, form, observance, protocol, ritual, solemnity
派		ritual *n.* 仪式

	rive	[raɪv]
【考法】		*v.* 撕开: to wrench open or **tear apart** or to pieces
例		Lightning rived the tree . 闪电把树劈裂了。
近		cleave, lacerate, rend, ribbon, rip, rupture, shred, split, tatter, tear
反		associate, coalesce, combine, conjoin, conjugate, connect, fuse, interfuse, join, link, unify 联合
派		riven *adj.* 被撕开的

Jovons saw the kettle boil and cried out with the delighted voice of a child;
Marshal too had seen the kettle boil and sat down silently to build an engine.
杰文斯看见壶开了,高兴得像孩子似地叫了起来;马歇尔也看见壶开了,却悄悄地坐下来造了一部蒸气机。
——英国经济学家 凯恩斯(John Maynard Keynes, British economist)

List 22

Unit 1

■ RIVETING	■ RENAISSANCE	■ ROBUST	■ ROIL	■ ROSY
■ ROOKIE	■ ROTE	■ RATIONALE	■ ROUSE	■ ROYALTY

riveting [ˈrɪvɪtɪŋ]
【考法】 *adj.* 吸引人的，极迷人的: wholly **absorbing** or **engrossing** one's attention
例 the riveting story 吸引人的故事
近 absorbing, arresting, engaging, engrossing, enthralling, fascinating, immersing, intriguing, involving
反 insipid, vapid 索然无味的；boring, dull, monotonous, tedious 单调的

renaissance [ˈrenəsɑːns]
【考法】 *n.* 复兴: **becomes popular again** after a time when people were not interested in it
例 an educational renaissance 一场教育的复兴
近 regeneration, rejuvenation, revival, resurgence, resurrection, resuscitation, revitalization, renewal

robust [roʊˈbʌst]
【考法】 *adj.* 精力充沛的；强壮，健康的: **full of** health and **strength**
例 a robust older man who still bicycles 10 miles a day 一个每天骑行 10 英里的充满活力的老人
近 bouncing, dynamic, energetic, gingerly, hale, potent, strong, sound, vigorous, vital, wholesome
反 delicate, frail, weak 弱不禁风的；ailing, diseased, ill, sick, unfit, unhealthy, unsound 不健康的
派 robustness *n.* 健壮，活力四射

roil [rɔɪl]
【考法】 *vt.* 激怒: to **displease** or disturb
例 Some of his roommate's habits began to roil him. 他室友的某些习惯开始让他恼火。
近 aggravate, enrage, exasperate, incense, inflame, infuriate, irritate, provoke, rile, vex
反 delight, gratify, please 使愉快

rosy [ˈroʊzi]
【考法】 *adj.* 乐观的: having qualities which **inspire hope**
例 a rosy view of the economic situation 对于经济形势的乐观看法
近 auspicious, encouraging, heartening, optimistic, promising, propitious
反 bleak, depressing, discouraging, gloomy, inauspicious, pessimistic, unpromising, unpropitious 暗淡的，没有前途的

rookie [ˈrʊki]
【考法】 *n.* 新兵；新手；菜鸟: **recruit**; novice
例 The rookie replaced the injured regular at first base. 这个新手代替了受伤的一垒手。
近 apprentice, fledgling, freshman, greenhorn, neophyte, novice, recruit, tyro
反 veteran 老兵

rote [roʊt]
【考法】 *n.* 死记硬背: a memorizing process **using routine or repetition**, often without full attention or comprehension
例 learn by rote 死记硬背地学习
近 drill, groove, pattern, routine, treadmill

rationale [ˌræʃəˈnæl]
【考法】 *n.* 基本原理，解释: a statement given to **explain** a belief or act
例 the rationale for the actions you should take 你应该采取行动的基本原理
近 account, accounting, argument, case, explanation, reason

rouse [raʊz]

【考法 1】 *vt.* 激起，煽动：to **stir up**

例 He was roused to fury. 他大为光火。

近 agitate, excite, motivate, provoke, stimulate

反 allay, alleviate, assuage, ease, mitigate, mollify, palliate, relieve, soothe 平息，缓和

【考法 2】 *vt.* 唤醒：to cause to **stop sleeping**

例 The piercing siren roused her from a deep sleep. 刺耳的警笛声将她从沉睡中唤醒。

近 arouse, awake, awaken, waken

反 lull 使睡着

royalty ['rɔɪəlti]

【考法 1】 *n.* 皇家身份：**regal character** or bearing

近 aristocracy, nobility

【考法 2】 *n.* 版税；专利权税：a **payment** to an author or composer for each copy of a work sold or to an inventor for each item sold under a patent

例 charge KTV owners royalty fee 向 KTV 索取版权费

Unit 2

■ RUBICUND　　■ RUDIMENTARY　　■ RUE　　　　■ RUFFLE　　　■ RUMINATE
■ RUMPLE　　　■ REVISION　　　■ RUNIC　　　■ RUPTURE　　■ RUSE

rubicund ['ruːbɪkənd]

【考法】 *adj.* 红润的，健康的：inclined to a **healthy rosiness**

例 A rubicund complexion indicates good health. 红润的气色意味着身体健康。

近 blooming, florid, flush, rosy, ruddy, sanguine

反 ashen, pale, pallid, wan 苍白的，虚弱的

rudimentary [ˌruːdɪ'mentri]

【考法 1】 *adj.* 初始的，未发展的：being in the **earliest** stages of **development**

例 The equipment of these past empire-builders was rudimentary. 过去这些帝国的建造者们使用的都是极其原始的工具。

近 incipient, nascent, primitive, primordial

反 developed, full-blown, mature, ripe 成熟的，发展完全的

【考法 2】 *adj.* 最根本的，基础的：consisting in **first principles**：fundamental

例 The dropout had only a rudimentary knowledge of science. 这个辍学的孩子对科学知识只有最基本的一些了解。

近 basic, elemental, essential, fundamental, rudimental, underlying

反 advanced, higher 进阶的，高级的

rue [ruː]

【考法】 *n.* 后悔，遗憾：the **feeling of regret**, remorse, or sorrow for

例 With rue my heart is laden. 我的内心充满了遗憾。

近 contriteness, contrition, penitence, regret, remorse, remorsefulness, repentance

反 impenitence, remorselessness 不知悔改

派 rueful *adj.* 后悔的

ruffle ['rʌfl]

【考法 1】 *vt.* 使粗糙：to **destroy** the **smoothness** or evenness of

例 The acid ruffled the surface of the catalyst. 酸使得催化剂的表面变得粗糙。

近 abrade, chafe, erode, roughen, rub, wear

反 glaze, smooth 使平滑

【考法 2】 *vt.* 扰乱，打扰：to **disturb** the peace of mind of（someone）especially by repeated disagreeable acts

例 The stream of minor complaints finally ruffled him into snapping, "If you don't like the way I'm doing it, do it yourself!" 一系列斤斤计较的抱怨终于让他爆发："如果你不喜欢我做事的方法，你就自己去做！"

近 annoy, bother, chafe, frost, gall, grate, itch, nettle, peeve, persecute, pique, rasp, rile, vex

反 allay, alleviate, assuage, ease, mitigate, mollify, palliate, relieve, soothe 平息，缓和

ruminate	['ruːmɪneɪt]
【考法】	*v.* 反复思考：to **go over in the mind** repeatedly and often casually or slowly
例	ruminate the reason of past failures 沉思以往失败的原因
近	cogitate, contemplate, deliberate, meditate, perpend, ponder, weigh
反	ignore, neglect, overlook 忽视
派	ruminative *adj.* 沉思的

rumple	['rʌmpl]
【考法】	*vt.* 打乱，使不整齐：to **undo the proper order** or arrangement of
例	The aunt would invariably rumple the little boy's hair whenever she came to visit. 不论小男孩的姨妈何时来拜访，她总是要弄乱他的头发。
近	disarray, disorder, disorganize, disrupt, disturb, mess, muddle, upset
反	arrange, array, order, organize, regulate 整理，使有序
派	rumpled *adj.* 褶皱的

revision	[rɪ'vɪʒn]
【考法】	*n.* 修订：he act, process, or result of **making different**
例	The phase of writing that is actually most important is revision. 写作中真正最重要的阶段是修改。
近	alteration, modification, remodeling, revise, change, variation
反	fixation, stabilization 固定不变

runic	['ruːnik]
【考法】	*adj.* 神秘的：having some secret or **mysterious** meaning
例	painstaking efforts to decipher the runic inscriptions 为破解神秘的碑文付出的辛勤劳动
近	arcane, enigmatic, impenetrable, inscrutable, mysterious, mystic, occult, uncanny
反	comprehensible, fathomable 可理解的

rupture	['rʌptʃər]
【考法】	*v.* 打破；打碎，破裂：to **part** by violence
例	Jealousy ruptured our friendly relationship. 嫉妒破坏了我们之间的友谊。
近	breach, burst, disjoin, dissect, fracture, separate, split, sunder, tear
反	associate, coalesce, combine, conjoin, conjugate, connect, fuse, interfuse, join, link, unify 联合

ruse	[ruːz]
【考法】	*n.* 诡计：a wily **subterfuge**
例	This is a ruse to divide them. 这是一招反间计。
近	artifice, maneuver, stratagem, trick, wile

Unit 3

■ RUSTIC	■ RUSTLE	■ SABOTAGE	■ SACCHARINE	■ SACRILEGE
■ SADDLE	■ SAFEGUARD	■ SAGE	■ SALIENT	■ SALUBRIOUS

rustic	['rʌstɪk]
【考法 1】	*n.* 乡下人，头脑简单的人：an **awkward or simple person** especially from a small town or the country *adj.* 乡村的：of, relating to, associated with, or typical of **open areas with few buildings** or people
例	a rustic who was awed by the prices that city dwellers had to pay 一个被大城市房价所吓到的乡下人 ‖ We went to a rustic area that is devoid of skyscrapers and shopping malls. 我们去了一个没有摩天大楼和购物中心的乡村原野。
近	bumpkin, churl, countryman, provincial, rube, yokel; bucolic, country, pastoral
反	cosmopolitan, cosmopolite, sophisticate 见多识广的人; urban 都市的
【考法 2】	*adj.* 粗俗的：**lacking** in social graces or **polish**
近	clumsy, discourteous, gauche, impertinent, impolite, inelegant, rude, stiff
反	graceful, polished, urbane 文雅的
派	rustically *adv.* 粗俗地

rustle	['rʌsl]
【考法】	*vi.* 快速地行动：to **move or act** energetically or **with speed**; to proceed or move quickly
例	The little boy rustled around enthusiastically on the first morning of the trip. 旅行的第一个早晨，小男孩充满热情地跑来跑去。
近	bolt, breeze, careen, career, hasten, hustle, jump, run, rush, scurry
反	crawl, creep 匍匐前行; poke 缓慢行动

sabotage [ˈsæbətɑːʒ]

【考法】 *n.* 妨害，破坏：treacherous action to defeat or **hinder a cause** or an endeavor; deliberate subversion
vt. 从事破坏活动：to **practice sabotage** on

例 sabotage of the project by government officials 被政府官员阻止的项目 ‖ He sabotaged his opponent's campaign with rumors. 他用谣言来破坏对手的竞选活动。 ‖ My ex-wife deliberately sabotages my access to the children. 我的前妻故意阻止我和我的孩子们见面。

近 damage, impairment, subversion, undermining; disrupt, foil, frustrate, obstruct, undermine

反 assistance 支援; assist, support 支持; advance, cultivate, forward, foster, further, nurture, promote 促进

saccharine [ˈsækərɪn]

【考法 1】 *adj.* 像糖一样的，有甜味的：of, relating to, or resembling that of **sugar**

例 a powdery substance with a saccharine taste 有甜味的粉状物质

近 cloying, sugary

反 bitter 苦涩的

【考法 2】 *adj.* 做作的，矫情的：**appealing to the emotions** in an obvious and tiresome way

例 The movie was funny, but it had a saccharine ending in which everyone lives happily ever after. 电影还是很有意思的，但是结局太做作了——所有人从此都幸福地生活在了一起。

近 fruity, maudlin, mawkish, mushy, sentimental, sugarcoated

反 unsentimental 不动感情的

sacrilege [ˈsækrəlɪdʒ]

【考法】 *n.* 亵渎圣物：desecration, **profanation**, misuse, or theft of something **sacred**

例 It is a sacrilege to offend democracy. 这是一种对民主的亵渎。

近 blasphemy, defilement, desecration, irreverence, impiety, profanation, violation

反 adoration, glorification, respect, reverence 爱慕，尊敬

派 sacrilegious *adj.* 不敬的，亵渎神明的

saddle [ˈsædl]

【考法】 *vt.* 使某人负担：to **load** or burden

例 saddle sb. with sth. 某事成了某人的负担

近 burden, encumber, freight, lade, lumber, impose, inflict, tax, weight

反 disburden, discharge, disencumber, unburden, unlade, unload 卸下

safeguard [ˈseɪfɡɑːrd]

【考法】 *n.* 保护措施：a technical contrivance to **prevent accident** *vt.* 保护：to **make safe**; protect

例 legal safeguards against fraud 防止欺诈的法律措施 ‖ Sheepdogs safeguard the flock from attacks by wolves. 保护羊群免受狼群攻击的牧羊犬。

近 aegis, caution, defense, fail-safe, guard, palladium, precaution, preventive, security; bulwark, cover, defend, fence, fend, guard, keep, protect, screen, secure, shield, ward

反 assail, assault, attack 攻击

sage [seɪdʒ]

【考法】 *n.* 智者：one (as a profound philosopher) distinguished for **wisdom**

例 The young prince made a pilgrimage to the sage, hoping to learn the meaning of life. 年轻的王子走上了向智者取经的道路，希望能领悟到生命的真谛。

近 expert, illuminati, master, mentor, savant, scholar

反 dolt, fool, idiot, simpleton 傻子

派 sagacious *adj.* 睿智的; sagacity *n.* 聪慧

salient [ˈseɪliənt]

【考法】 *adj.* 显著的，最突出的：standing out **conspicuously**

例 read the salient facts 阅读最突出的事实

近 conspicuous, noticeable, outstanding, prominent, remarkable, striking

反 inconspicuous, unnoticeable 不明显的

派 salience *n.* 突出; 特点

salubrious [səˈluːbriəs]

【考法】 *adj.* 有益健康的：favorable to or **promoting health** or well-being

例 Every year I go to Kunming to enjoy its cool and salubrious climate. 每年我都会去昆明享受它那凉爽宜人的气候。

近 good, healthy, restorative, salutary, tonic, wholesome

反 debilitating, deleterious, noxious, virulent 有害的，有毒的

Unit 4

salutary ['sæljəteri]

【考法 1】 *adj.* 有益健康的：beneficial, **promoting health**

例 salutary exercise 有益健康的锻炼

近 good, healthy, restorative, salubrious, tonic, wholesome

反 debilitating, deleterious, noxious, virulent 有害的，有毒的

【考法 2】 *adj.* 有利的，利好的：**promoting** or contributing to personal or social **well-being**

例 The low interest rates should have a salutary effect on business. 低利率对于商业而言应该是有利的。
a salutary warning 善意的警告

近 advantageous, benefic, beneficent, benignant, favorable, friendly, helpful, kindly, profitable

反 bad, disadvantageous, unfavorable, unfriendly, unhelpful, unprofitable 不利的

salutation [ˌsælju'teɪʃn]

【考法】 *n.* 赞扬：a formal expression of **praise**

例 The speaker introduced the evening's honored guest with a lavish salutation. 主持人用大量赞扬的话介绍了今晚的嘉宾。

近 accolade, citation, commendation, eulogium, eulogy, homage, hymn, paean, panegyric, tribute

salvage ['sælvɪdʒ]

【考法】 *vt.* (从灾难中)抢救：to **save from loss** or destruction

例 salvage the torpedoed vessel 拯救被鱼雷击中的舰艇

近 rescue, retrieve, save

反 abandon, desert, forsake 放弃，抛弃

派 salvageable *adj.* 可以挽回的

salve [sælv]

【考法】 *v.* 减轻，缓解：quiet, **assuage**

例 The company give him a raise in salary to salve his feelings. 公司决定给他加薪以安抚他的情绪。

近 allay, balm, becalm, compose, lull, lullaby, quiet, settle, soothe, still, tranquilize

反 agitate, discompose, disquiet, disturb, perturb, upset, vex 打扰，扰乱

sanctify ['sæŋktɪfaɪ]

【考法】 *vt.* 使神圣，将…敬为神：to **make holy**

例 The Constitution sanctified the rights of the people. 宪法认为人权是至高无上的。

近 consecrate, hallow

反 desecrate, profane 亵渎

派 sanctification *n.* 敬为神明

sanctimonious [ˌsæŋktɪ'moʊniəs]

【考法】 *adj.* 假装虔诚的：**hypocritically pious** or devout

例 a sickening sanctimonious smile 令人厌恶的伪善的笑容

近 canting, deceiving, hypocritical

反 devout, religious, pious 虔诚的

sanction ['sæŋkʃn]

【考法】 *vt.* 批准，同意，认可：to **make valid** or binding usually by a formal procedure (as ratification)

例 The President sanctioned covert operations. 总统批准了秘密行动。‖ The administration will sanction almost any field trip with educational value. 基本上任何有教育意义的实地考察都可以得到批准。

近 accredit, approbate, authorize, certify, confirm, finalize, formalize, license, ratify, warrant

反 interdict, prohibit, proscribe 禁止；decline, deny, disallow, disapprove, negative, reject, veto 否决

sanctuary ['sæŋktʃueri]

【考法】 *n.* 避难所：a place of refuge and **protection**

例 In earlier times a criminal could use a church as a sanctuary. 在以前，犯罪分子可以将教堂当作避难所。

近 asylum, cover, harbor, haven, port, refuge, shelter

showcase	[ˈʃoʊkeɪs]

【考法】 *vt.* 展示（优点）: to **exhibit** especially **in an attractive** or favorable **aspect**

例 Restored films are being showcased this month at a festival in Paris. 本月的巴黎电影节将展映一些修复版的电影。

近 brandish, disport, exhibit, expose, flash, flaunt, parade, show off, trot out

反 conceal, hide, secrete 隐藏

sanguine	[ˈsæŋgwɪn]

【考法】 *adj.* 乐观的，确信的: having or showing a mind **free from doubt**

例 I'm reasonably sanguine about the adoption of the latest proposal. 我非常看好最新的那项提议获得通过。

近 assured, confident, doubtless, implicit, positive

反 doubtful, dubious, uncertain, unsure 怀疑的，不确信的

Unit 5

■ SANITARY	■ SAP	■ SAPIENT	■ SARCASM	■ SARTORIAL
■ SATE	■ SATIATE	■ SCANDALOUS	■ SATIRIZE	■ SATURATE

sanitary	[ˈsænəteri]

【考法】 *adj.* 健康的，清洁的: of or relating to **health**

例 sanitary measures 清洁措施

近 aseptic, germfree, hygienic, sterile

反 noxious 有毒的

sap	[sæp]

【考法 1】 *vt.* 削弱: to **weaken** or exhaust the **energy** or **vitality** of

例 Weeks of hard work had sapped him and left him exhausted. 连续几周辛苦工作让他削弱筋疲力尽。

近 debilitate, devitalize, enervate, enfeeble, etiolate, prostrate

反 bolster, fortify, invigorate, beef up 增强，使有活力

【考法 2】 *n.* 健康，活力: **active strength** of body or mind

例 a child full of sap and vivacity 活力满满的孩子

近 dynamism, energy, esprit, get-up-and-go, gusto, verve, vim, vitality

反 lethargy, listlessness, sluggishness, torpidity 无精打采

sapient	[ˈseɪpiənt]

【考法】 *adj.* 聪明的，有洞察力的: having or showing **deep understanding** and **intelligent** application of knowledge

例 a man who is always good for valuable insights and some sapient advice 一个以见解深刻、建议明智著称的男人

近 discerning, insightful, perceptive, prudent, sagacious, sage

反 foolish, unperceptive, unwise 愚蠢的，不明智的

sarcasm	[ˈsɑːrkæzəm]

【考法】 *n.* 讽刺，轻蔑: a sharp and often satirical or **ironic** utterance designed to cut or give pain

例 a voice full of sarcasm 充满轻蔑的言论

近 affront, barb, indignity, offense, slap, slight, slur

反 praise 表扬

sartorial	[sɑːrˈtɔːriəl]

【考法】 *adj.* 裁缝匠的，裁缝的: of or relating to a tailor or tailored **clothes**

例 poor sartorial taste 很烂的穿衣品位

sate	[seɪt]

【考法】 *vt.* 使饱足，充分满足: to glut; to **satisfy** (an appetite) **fully**

例 The information sated her curiosity. 这个消息充分满足了她的好奇心。

近 cram, glut, stuff, surfeit, satiate

反 starve 饿

satiate	[ˈseɪʃieɪt]
【考法】	vt./adj. (使)饱足(的), 过分满足(的): to **satisfy fully** or to excess
例	A long drink of water satiated my thirst. 一顿痛饮之后我的口渴得到了缓解。
近	replete, sate, stuff, surfeit
反	tantalize 挑逗, 不去满足

scandalous	[ˈskændələs]
【考法】	adj. 引起反感的, 丢脸的: causing intense displeasure, **disgust**, or resentment
例	criminal and scandalous behavior 犯罪和令人反感的行为
近	abhorrent, abominable, hideous, horrible, noisome, odious, repellent repugnant, shocking
反	innocuous, inoffensive 不会引起反感的

satirize	[ˈsætəraɪz]
【考法】	vt. 讽刺: to **ridicule** or attack by means of satire
例	The movie satirizes contemporary life. 这部电影讽刺当下生活。
派	satire n. 讽刺诗, 讽刺文学: a literary work holding up human vices and follies to ridicule or scorn
例	a satire about the music industry in which a handsome but untalented youth is turned into a rock star 一部关于一个长得帅却没才华的年轻人如何被打造成一个摇滚巨星的讽刺文学作品
近	lampoon, pasquinade

saturate	[ˈsætʃəreɪt]
【考法】	vt./adj. 使饱和, 浸透: to **wet thoroughly** with liquid
例	Saturate the sponge with water. 将海绵浸透。
近	bathe, douse, drench, soak, souse, bedraggle
反	wring out 拧出(水)来

Unit 6

■ SATURNINE	■ SAUNTER	■ SAVANT	■ SAVORY	■ SAVVY
■ SCADS	■ SCANT	■ SCATHING	■ SCHISM	■ SCINTILLATE

saturnine	[ˈsætərnaɪn]
【考法】	adj. 忧郁的, 阴沉的: causing or marked by an atmosphere **lacking in cheer**
例	The men awaiting interrogation by the police shared a saturnine silence. 等待警察审问的人们脸色阴沉, 沉默不语。
近	bleak, depressive, dismal, dreary, miserable, solemn
反	jovial, bright, cheerful, comforting, cordial, festive, heartwarming, sunshiny 欢乐的

saunter	[ˈsɔːntər]
【考法】	vi. 闲逛, 漫步: to travel **by foot** for exercise or pleasure
例	saunter slowly down the street 在街上闲逛
近	amble, ramble, range, stroll, wander, perambulate

savant	[sæˈvɑːnt]
【考法】	n. 博学之士, 学者: a person of **learning**
例	a savant in the field of medical ethics 医学伦理方面的专家
近	pundit, scholar
反	unlearned person 没有学问的人

savory	[ˈseɪvəri]
【考法】	adj. 令人愉悦的: giving **pleasure or contentment** to the mind or senses
例	can't find savory things to occupy their time 找不到愉悦的事打发时间
近	agreeable, blessed, congenial, delectable, delicious, delightful, dulcet, enjoyable, felicitous, grateful, gratifying, heavenly, jolly, luscious, palatable, pleasurable, satisfying, tasty, welcome
反	disagreeable, pleasureless, unpalatable, unpleasant, unwelcome 讨厌的, 不受欢迎的

savvy	[ˈsævi]
【考法 1】	n. 老练, 机智: **knowledge** gained by **actually doing** or living through something
例	political savvy 政治上的老练精明
近	chops, expertise, proficiency, know-how
反	simplicity, tactlessness, inexperience 单纯, 缺乏经验

【考法2】 *adj.* 有见识的，精明能干的：having or showing a **practical cleverness or judgment**

例 A particularly savvy investor, he was among the first to see the potential in tech stocks. 他是一个有卓识远见的投资者，是第一批看到科技类股票升值潜力的人。

近 astute, canny, clear-eyed, clear-sighted, hard-boiled, hardheaded, heady, sharp, sharp-witted, smart

反 unknowing 无知的

scads [skædz]

【考法】 *n.* 许多，大量：a **large number** or quantity

例 scads of people showed up for the party 参加派对的人们蜂拥而至

近 abundance, plenitude, profusion, slew, spate, wealth

反 paucity 极小量

scant [skænt]

【考法】 *adj.* 不足的，缺乏的：barely or **scarcely** sufficient

例 Jobs for teenagers were scant that summer. 那年暑假适合青少年们做的工作很少。

近 exiguous, niggardly, scarce, sparse, stingy

反 considerable, copious, voluminous, profuse, myriad 大量的，相当多的

scathing [ˈskeɪðɪŋ]

【考法】 *adj.* 尖酸刻薄的：marked by the use of wit that is intended to **cause hurt feelings**

例 a scathing review of the book 尖刻的书评

近 acerbic, acid, acrid, pungent, scalding, snarky, tart

反 polite, calm compliment 礼貌的，平静的称赞

schism [ˈskɪzəm]

【考法】 *n.* 不一致：a **lack of agreement** or harmony

例 a schism between political parties 党派间的冲突

近 conflict, discordance, disharmony, dissidence, dissonance, disunion, friction, strife

反 accord, agreement, concord, harmony, peace 一致

scintillate [ˈsɪntɪleɪt]

【考法】 *vi.* 闪耀：to emit **sparks**

例 diamond ring scintillated in the sunlight 钻戒在阳光下闪闪发光

近 gleam, glimmer, glisten, glister, luster, sparkle, winkle

派 scintillating *adj.* 才华横溢的：brilliantly lively, stimulating, or witty

例 a scintillating conversation 智慧火花四溅的交谈

反 dull, foolly 迟钝的

Unit 7

■ SEDITIOUS　　■ SCISSION　　■ SCOFF　　■ SCORCH　　■ SCORN
■ SCOTCH　　■ SCOUR　　■ SCOWL　　■ SCRAPPY　　■ SCRAP

seditious [sɪˈdɪʃəs]

【考法】 *adj.* 煽动性的，意在制造混乱的：tending to **excite political disorder** or insurrection

例 Several activists were jailed for leading protests that the government branded as seditious. 众多激进分子因为带头参与被政府认定为煽动性的示威集会而锒铛入狱。

近 agitational, incendiary, instigative, provocative

反 conciliatory, consoling, pacific 安抚性的

scission [ˈsɪʒən]

【考法】 *n.* 切断，分离，分裂：a **division** or split in a group or union: schism

例 The scission of the labor union will compromise the workers' bargaining power. 工会内部的分裂会削弱工人讨价的力量。

近 bifurcation, cleavage, dissolution, division, partition, schism, sundering

反 unification, union 统一

scoff [skɔːf]

【考法】 *v.* 嘲笑：to treat or address with **derision**: **mock**

例 scoff at the idea 对这个提议不屑一顾

scorch [skɔːrtʃ]
【考法】 *v.* 炙烤，烘干: to **burn** on the surface; to **make dry**
例 scorching sun 火辣辣的太阳
近 dehydrate, desiccate, parch, sear, singe
反 dampen, hydrate, wash, water, wet 使潮湿

scorn [skɔːrn]
【考法】 *vt.* 轻蔑，鄙视，不屑: **reject** or dismiss as **contemptible** or unworthy
例 They were scorned as fanatics. 他们被指责为狂热分子。
近 despise, disregard, flout, contemn, disdain, slight, look down (on *or* upon)
反 adulate 谄媚；venerate, honor, respect, revere 尊敬

scotch [skɑːtʃ]
【考法】 *vt.* 停止: to **put an** abrupt **end to**
例 The prime minister scotched the rumors of her illness. 首相出面澄清了关于她生病的谣言。
近 hinder, thwart

scour [ˈskauər]
【考法】 *vt.* 搜查: to look through (as a place) carefully or thoroughly in an effort **to find or discover** some-thing
例 The police scoured the city for the criminal. 警方全城搜索罪犯。
近 comb, dig through, dredge, hunt through, rake, ransack, rifle, rummage, sort through, troll

scowl [skaul]
【考法】 *vi.* 皱眉(表现出不高兴): to contract the brow in an **expression** of **displeasure**
例 scowl down at the misbehaving child 对淘气的孩子皱起眉
近 frown, pout, glare, gloom, glower, lower
反 beam, grin, smile 微笑(表示高兴)

scrappy [ˈskræpi]
【考法】 *adj.* 好斗的，好吵架的: having an **aggressive** and determined spirit, quarrelsome
例 She was a scrappy girl despite—or, perhaps, because of—her small size. 这个妹子好打斗，但是身材娇小，不过这很可能是原因。
近 aggressive, assaultive, combative, militant, pugnacious, truculent
反 nonaggressive, nonbelligerent, pacific, peaceful, unbelligerent, uncombative, timorous 胆小的，爱好和平的

scrap [skræp]
【考法】 *vt.* 抛弃: to **get rid of** as useless or unwanted
例 We've decided to scrap the first car. 我们决定丢弃第一辆车。
近 ditch, dump, jettison, junk, toss, throw away
反 retrieve 找回

Unit 8

| ■ SCRAWL | ■ SCRIBBLE | ■ SCRUPULOUS | ■ SCRUTABLE | ■ SCRUTINIZE |
| ■ SCUFF | ■ SCURRILOUS | ■ SCURVY | ■ SEAMY | ■ SECLUDED |

scrawl [skrɔːl]
【考法】 *vt.* 乱涂，潦草地写: to **write** or draw awkwardly, hastily, or **carelessly**
例 He scrawled a quick note, stuck it in their mailbox, and hurried off. 他草草写了张便条，塞进他们的信箱然后匆匆跑了。
近 scratch, squiggle, scribble
反 write carefully 仔细地写

scribble [ˈskrɪbl]
【考法】 *v.* 潦草地书写，乱写: to cover with scribbles, doodles, or **meaningless** marks
例 Students scribbled furiously as the teacher lectured. 老师一边讲，学生们一边狂抄笔记。
近 scratch, scrawl, squiggle

scrupulous [ˈskruːpjələs]
【考法 1】 *adj.* 正直的: guided by or in accordance with one's sense of right and wrong; **principled**
例 Less scrupulous companies find ways to evade the law. 道德程度略低的公司钻法律的空子。
近 conscionable, ethical, honest, honorable, moral, principled
反 cutthroat, dishonest, dishonorable, immoral, unconscionable, unethical, unjust, unprincipled 不道德的

【考法 2】 *adj.* 一丝不苟的：taking, showing, or involving **great care and effort**

例 The task requires scrupulous attention to detail . 这项任务需要对细节一丝不苟。

近 careful, conscientious, fussy, meticulous

---

scrutable ［ˈskruːtəbl］

【考法】 *adj.* 可以理解的：capable of being **understood** through study and observation; **comprehensible**

例 a lot of srutable information 很多可以理解的信息

近 accessible, apprehensible, comprehensible, fathomable, legible

反 mysterious, incoherent, incomprehensible, inscrutable, insensible 神秘而不可知的

---

scrutinize ［ˈskruːtənaɪz］

【考法】 *vt.* 仔细检查：to examine or **observe** with **great care**

例 I closely scrutinized my opponent's every move . 我仔细注意着对手的每一个举动。

近 examine, review, scan, survey, plumb, check（out）

反 casually glance, gloss over 随意一瞥，敷衍处理

---

scuff ［skʌf］

【考法】 *v.*（使）磨损：to become scratched, chipped, or **roughened by wear**

例 a countertop that won't scuff 一块不易磨损的厨房台面

近 abrade, graze, scratch

---

scurrilous ［ˈskɜːrələs］

【考法】 *adj.* 说粗话的：given to the use of **vulgar**, coarse, or abusive language

例 scurrilous and untrue stories 粗俗不实的故事

近 contumelious, invective, opprobrious, truculent, vitriolic, vituperative

---

scurvy ［ˈskɜːrvi］

【考法】 *adj.* 下流的，让人鄙视的：mean; **contemptible**

例 She was beset by a whole scurvy swarm of con artists . 她被一群下流的骗子艺术家蜂拥围攻。

近 deplorable, despicable, grubby, lousy, scummy, wretched

反 admirable, commendable, creditable, laudable, meritorious, praiseworthy 让人称赞的

---

seamy ［ˈsiːmi］

【考法】 *adj.* 肮脏的，堕落的：**sordid**; **base**

例 the seamy side of urban life 城市生活的肮脏面

近 sordid, base

反 decent and respectable 适当而值得尊敬的

---

secluded ［sɪˈkluːdɪd］

【考法】 *adj.* 僻静的，隐蔽的：screened or **hidden** from view

例 secluded monks 隐居的僧人

近 cloistered, covert, isolated, remote, retired, sheltered

Unit 9

■ SECRETE	■ SEDATE	■ SEDENTARY	■ SEDUCE	■ SEDULOUS
■ SEEMLY	■ SEGMENT	■ SELF-ABASEMENT	■ SELF-ABSORBED	■ SEMINAL

---

secrete ［sɪˈkriːt］

【考法 1】 *vt.* 隐藏：to **conceal** in a hiding place: cache

例 The police found the weapon secreted under the driver's seat of the getaway car. 警方在逃逸车辆驾驶座下发现了隐藏的武器。

近 bury, cache, conceal, ensconce

反 divulge, display, exhibit 泄密，展示

【考法 2】 *vt.* 分泌：to **generate** and separate（a substance）from cells or bodily fluids

反 absorb 吸收

---

sedate ［sɪˈdeɪt］

【考法】 *adj.* 淡定的，安静的：**free from** emotional or mental **agitation**

例 She remained sedate under pressure . 她在压力下仍保持镇静。

近 collected, composed, self-possessed, serene, tranquil, undisturbed, unperturbed, unruffled

反 agitated, discomposed, disturbed, flustered, perturbed, upset 不淡定的，狂乱的

sedentary ['sednteri]

【考法】 *adj.* 固定不动的: **not migratory**: settled

例 a sedentary lifestyle 很宅的生活方式

反 migratory, peripatetic 流动的, 巡游的

seduce [sɪˈduːs]

【考法】 *vt.* 劝说(使不忠, 使不服从), 诱…误入歧途: to attract or **persuade** to disobedience or disloyalty

例 The other firm seduced him with a better offer. 另一家公司用更高的待遇想挖他墙脚。

近 allure, decoy, entice, solicit, tempt, lead on

反 repulse, ward off 厌恶, 不被吸引

sedulous ['sedʒələs]

【考法】 *adj.* 勤奋认真的: involving or accomplished with **careful perseverance**

例 a sedulous student 一个勤奋的学生

近 assiduous, diligent, industrious, laborious, occupied, tied-up

反 idle, inactive, unbusy, unemployed, unoccupied 懒惰的

seemly ['siːmli]

【考法】 *adv.* 得体的, 遵守礼节的: **following the established traditions** of refined society and good taste

例 a young lady of seemly appearance, robust health, and keen intelligence 一个打扮得体、身体健康、头脑敏锐的姑娘

近 befitting, decent, decorous, genteel, respectable

反 uncouth, ribald, indecorous, improper, inappropriate, indecent, indelicate, unbecoming, ungenteel, unseemly 粗俗的, 不礼貌的

segment ['segmənt]

【考法】 *vt./n.* 分割; 部分: to **separate** into segments

例 I think I lost one segment of this model kit. 这套模型的一个零件我找不到了。

近 member, partition, portion, section

self-abasement [ˌselfə'beɪsmənt]

【考法】 *n.* 自卑, 自谦: degradation or **humiliation** of oneself

反 self-asserting 自信

self-absorbed [ˌselfəb'sɔːrbd]

【考法】 *adj.* 自恋的, 自私的: **absorbed in one's own** thoughts, activities, or interests

例 the self-absorbed perspective of satisfying one's greed 满足某人贪欲的自私角度

近 narcissistic, self-centered, self-infatuated, self-obsessed, self-oriented, self-preoccupied

反 self-forgetting, selfless, unselfish 无私的

seminal ['semɪnl]

【考法】 *adj.* 创新的: of, relating to, or having the power to originate; **creative**

例 a seminal novel 新颖的小说

反 derivative 派生的

Unit 10

■ SENSATION	■ SIFT	■ SHOWMANSHIP	■ SEPULCHRAL	■ SEPTIC
■ SEQUELA	■ SEQUESTER	■ SERE	■ SERENDIPITY	■ SERENE

sensation [sen'seɪʃn]

【考法】 *n.* 轰动事件: a state of **intense** public **interest** and excitement

例 the rookie hitting sensation of the American League 这个菜鸟的表现轰动了整个全美大联盟

近 flash, marvel, miracle, phenomenon, portent, prodigy, splendor

反 unnoticed event 不知名的小事

sift ['sɪft]

【考法】 *v.* 审查: to **examine** and sort carefully

例 sift the evidence 审查证据

近 audit, examine, oversee, review, survey

showmanship [ˈʃoʊmənʃɪp]

【考法】 *n.* 擅于表演、展示的技巧: the skill or ability of an individual who has a sense or knack for **dramatically effective presentation**

例 Even among the staid, unemotional denominations of the 1830s and 1840s, the renewal of religious fervor and the necessity of competing with more charismatic clerics inevitably led to a greater cultivation of ministerial showmanship. 即便在 19 世纪 30、40 年代那些缺乏感情色彩的、严肃古板的教派中，宗教热情的复兴以及与更有魅力的牧师竞争的必要性也不可避免地加强了对牧师表演技巧的培养。

近 grandstanding

sepulchral [səˈpʌlkrəl]

【考法】 *adj.* 阴沉的; 丧葬的: causing or marked by an atmosphere **lacking in cheer**; funereal

例 The decrepit mansion had a sepulchral tone that gave everybody a chill. 破旧的公馆有着一种坟墓的气息，让人皆为之一颤。

近 depressing, desolate, dismal, dreary, morose, sullen, tenebrous

反 merry, bright, cheery, comforting, cordial, festive, heartwarming, sunshiny 欢快的

septic [ˈseptɪk]

【考法】 *adj.* 腐败的，感染的: of, relating to, or causing **putrefaction**

反 free of infection 未被感染的

sequela [siˈkwiːlə]

【考法】 *n.* 结果: a **secondary** consequence or **result**

反 precursor 先兆

sequester [sɪˈkwestər]

【考法】 *vt.* 使隔绝，分离: to set apart: **segregate**

例 sequester a jury 让陪审团分开讨论

近 insulate, seclude, segregate, separate, cut off

反 permit to mingle, desegregate, integrate, reintegrate 混合，综合

sere [sɪə]

【考法】 *adj.* 干枯的，凋萎的: being **dried** and **withered**

例 a sere region that can't support agriculture 一片贫瘠不能发展农业的地区

近 arid, droughty, thirsty, waterless

反 lush, damp, dank, humid, moist, wet 葱绿的，湿润的

serendipity [ˌserənˈdɪpəti]

【考法】 *n.* 意外发现珍奇 (或称心) 事物的本领: the faculty of making fortunate discoveries **by accident**

例 They found each other by pure serendipity. 他俩的相识属于缘分天注定。

serene [səˈriːn]

【考法】 *adj.* 安静的: **free from** disturbing noise or **uproar**

例 a serene vacation spot 一处宁谧的度假胜地

近 arcadian, calm, hushed, peaceful, placid, restful, still, tranquil

反 boisterous, clamorous, clattery, deafening, raucous, roistering, romping, rowdy, tumultuous, unquiet, uproarious 喧闹的

List 23

"行百里者半九十，不要等到发现 GRE 成为自己申请的短板时才追悔不已。"

(蔺琳, Verbal 700, Quantitative 800, AW 5.0)

Unit 1

■ SERMON	■ SERPENTINE	■ SELF-DEFEATING	■ SERRIED	■ SERVILE
■ SHIFTY	■ SHACKLE	■ SHADOW	■ STALE	■ SHAM

sermon ['sɜːrmən]
【考法】 *n.* 布道，说教：**public speech** usually by a member of the clergy for the purpose of giving **moral guidance or uplift**
例 preach a sermon 布道
近 homily

serpentine ['sɜːrpəntiːn]
【考法】 *adj.* 弯曲的：**winding** or turning one way and another
例 The country inn lies at the end of a rather serpentine road . 乡村小酒吧坐落在一条非常蜿蜒的道路的尽头。
近 curved, curvy, devious, sinuous, tortuous, twisted, winding
反 direct, straight, straightaway 直的

self-defeating [ˌselfdɪ'fiːtɪŋ]
【考法】 *adj.* 适得其反的，自我拆台的：**causing more problems** than it solves
例 a self-defeating strategy 一个自我拆台的政策

serried ['serid]
【考法】 *adj.* 密集的：having **little space** between items or parts
例 Flowers came up every spring in their serried ranks . 大量的鲜花在春季盛开(密集地开放)。
近 compact, dense
反 widely separated, airy, loose, open, uncrowded 稀疏的

servile ['sɜːrvl]
【考法】 *adj.* 低下的，卑屈的：meanly or cravenly **submissive**: **abject**
例 He had always maintained a servile attitude around people with money. 他对有钱人总是卑躬屈膝。
近 base, humble, menial, slavish

shifty ['ʃɪfti]
【考法】 *adj.* (显得)狡诈的，(显得)欺诈的：having, displaying, or suggestive of **deceitful character**
例 shifty practices such as turning back the odometers on used cars 一些欺骗性的花招，比如把旧车的里程表调零 ‖ He had a shifty face so I won't trust him. 他看起来贼眉鼠眼的，我不会相信他。
近 crooked, deceitful, deceptive, duplicitous, fraudulent, guileful, rogue, shady, sharp, underhanded
反 aboveboard, honest, straight 正派的，光明正大的

shackle ['ʃækl]
【考法 1】 *vt.* 束缚：to deprive of freedom especially of action by means of **restrictions** or handicaps
例 unwilling to shackle the dogs to the wall of the house 不愿意把狗拴在墙边
近 chain, enchain, enfetter, fetter, gyve, handcuff, manacle, pinion, trammel
反 loose, emancipate, unbind, unfetter, unshackle 解放
【考法 2】 *vt.* 限制，阻碍：to **create difficulty** for the work or activity of
例 shackled by poverty and ignorance 被贫穷和无知所阻碍
近 clog, cramp, encumber, fetter, hinder, impede, inhibit, interfere with, manacle, obstruct, short-circuit, stymie, tie up, trammel
反 aid, assist, facilitate, help 促进，帮助

shadow ['ʃædoʊ]
【考法 1】 *vt.* 偷偷尾随：to follow especially **secretly**: **trail**
例 shadow the suspect to see what he was up to 尾随嫌犯行踪
近 chase, course, pursue, trace, track, trail

【考法2】 *v.* 遮蔽，（使）变暗：to (cause to) become **gloomy** or dark
派 shadowy *adj.* 模糊的：faintly perceptible: indistinct
例 He had only a shadowy idea of what they wanted him to do. 他对要做的事只有一个模糊的想法。

stale [steɪl]
【考法】 *adj.* 陈旧乏味的：used or heard **so often as to be dull**
例 The Government were sticking to stale ideas. 政府仍在抱残守缺。
近 banal, cliché, commonplace, hackneyed, moth-eaten, musty, shopworn, stereotyped, threadbare, timeworn, trite
反 fresh, new, novel, original, unhackneyed 新的

sham [ʃæm]
【考法1】 *v.* 掩饰，假装：to **present a false appearance** of
例 sham a most unconvincing limp just to get sympathy 非常拙劣地假装自己腿脚不便，以博得同情
近 act, affect, bluff, counterfeit, cloak, dissemble, fake, simulate, pretend, profess, put on, pass for
【考法2】 *adj.* 虚假的：not genuine; **fake**
例 street vendors selling sham designer handbags to gullible tourists 街头小贩向易上当的游客兜售山寨的设计师手包
近 bogus, forged, phony, spurious, unauthentic
反 genuine, authentic, bona fide, real, unfaked 真正的

Unit 2

| ■ SHIFTLESS | ■ SHIPSHAPE | ■ SHIRK | ■ SHOAL | ■ SHOPWORN |
| ■ SHRED | ■ SHREWD | ■ SHRINK | ■ SHROUD | ■ SHRUG |

shiftless [ˈʃɪftləs]
【考法】 *adj.* 胸无大志的，懒惰的：**lacking** in **ambition** or incentive: lazy
例 shiftless spongers who never thought to do anything for themselves 无志气的弃民们，从来没有想过改变自己
近 idle, indolent, slothful
反 industrious 勤奋的

shipshape [ˈʃɪpʃeɪp]
【考法】 *adj.* 井然有序的：marked by meticulous **order** and neatness
例 I like to keep my car shipshape. 我喜欢打理我的车。
近 antiseptic, kempt, orderly, prim, uncluttered, well-groomed
反 disheveled, disordered, disorderly, messy, sloven, unkempt, untidy 混乱的，不整洁的

shirk [ʃɜːrk]
【考法】 *v.* 逃避，规避：to get or **keep away from**（as a responsibility）through cleverness or trickery
例 shirk one's duty 逃避责任
近 avoid, dodge, elude, eschew, evade, shun, weasel out of

shoal [ʃoʊl]
【考法】 *adj.* 浅的：having **little depth**: shallow
例 shoal waters of the bay 海湾附近的浅水区
反 deep 深的

shopworn [ˈʃɑːpwɔːrn]
【考法】 *adj.* 陈旧的：**worn-out**, as from overuse: trite
例 the shopworn suggestion to job applicants to "just be yourself" 老掉牙的让应征者"做你自己"的提议
近 banal, cliché, commonplace, hackneyed, trite, well-worn
反 new, fresh, novel, original, unclichéd, unhackneyed 新的

shred [ʃred]
【考法】 *n.* 少量：a **small amount**; a particle
例 He struggled to retain a shred of his dignity. 他勉强挽救了一点尊严。
近 crumb, driblet, mite, scintilla, spark, speck, sprinkling, tad

shrewd [ʃruːd]
【考法】 *adj.* 精明的，机敏的：having or showing a practical **cleverness or judgment**
例 He's shrewd about his investments. 他对投资很精明。
近 crafty, cunning, devious, sly, subtle, wily, astute, savvy, sharp
反 foolish, naïve, unknowing 愚蠢的，幼稚的

shrink [ʃrɪŋk]

【考法】 *vi.* (在数量或价值方面)降低，减小: to become **reduced** in amount or value: dwindle

例 His savings quickly shrank . 他的存款急剧减少。

近 compress, condense, constrict

反 balloon, expand, snowball, swell 增大，膨胀

shroud [ʃraʊd]

【考法】 *vt.* 将…从视线中隔离，遮蔽: to **shut off from sight**; screen

例 She shrouded the fact that the child had been adopted. 她将孩子是领养的这个事实隐藏起来。

近 belie, blanket, cloak, conceal, cover, curtain, disguise, mask, occult, screen, veil, blot out, paper over

反 bare, disclose, display, divulge, expose, reveal, show 展示，暴露

shrug [ʃrʌg]

【考法】 *vt.* 轻视，忽略: to **dismiss** as of little importance

例 The administration was willing to shrug off the problem . 当局有意忽略这个问题。

近 bypass, disregard, gloss, ignore, neglect, minimize, overlook, overpass, slight, slur

反 attend, heed, mind 留心，注意

Unit 3

- ■ SHUN
- ■ SIDESTEP
- ■ SIGNAL
- ■ SIMPLETON
- ■ SIMULATE
- ■ SELF-PERPETUATING
- ■ SENSUALITY
- ■ SINECURE
- ■ SINEW
- ■ SINGE

shun [ʃʌn]

【考法】 *vt.* 避开，避免: to avoid deliberately; **keep away** from

例 After his divorce he found himself being shunned by many of his former friends . 自从他离婚以来，他发现许多曾经的朋友都刻意躲着他。

近 avoid, dodge, duck, elude, eschew, evade, finesse, scape, shirk

反 accept, embrace, welcome 接受，欢迎; pursue, seek 追寻

sidestep [ˈsaɪdstep]

【考法】 *vt.* (通过逃避而)不遵守: to **avoid having to comply with** (something) especially through cleverness

例 The eager enlistee sidestepped the regulations by lying about his age. 急切的应募者通过谎报自己的年龄躲过了规定的限制。

近 beat, bypass, dodge, shortcut, skirt

反 comply, follow, keep, obey, observe 遵守

signal [ˈsɪgnəl]

【考法1】 *adj.* (在重要性、成就方面)非同寻常的: **standing above** others in rank, importance, or achievement

例 The Louisiana Purchase is cited by many historians as one of the most signal events in American history. 从法国手中购买路易斯安那被许多历史学家认为是美国历史上最重要的事件之一。‖ a signal feat 一项非同寻常的伟业

近 distinguished, illustrious, luminous, notable, noteworthy, outstanding, preeminent, prestigious, redoubtable

反 average, inferior, mediocre 一般的，低下的; insignificant, minor, unimportant 不重要的

【考法2】 *v.* 给出信号: to **direct or notify** by a movement or gesture

例 They signaled at me to come over . 他们向我打招呼要我到他们去。‖ A lock on the suit-case might signal that there's something of value inside . 手提箱上的锁可能意味着里面有贵重物品。

近 beckon, flag, gesture, wave

simpleton [ˈsɪmpltən]

【考法】 *n.* (缺乏常识的)笨蛋: a person **lacking in common sense**; a stupid person

例 His silly antics at office parties have earned him a reputation as a simpleton . 他在办公室聚会上愚蠢古怪的行为让他被人认为是个蠢货。

近 airhead, dolt, donkey, dullard, fool, idiot, moron

反 intellectual, sage, wit 智者; genius, prodigy 天才

simulate [ˈsɪmjuleɪt]

【考法】 *vt.* 假装，模仿: to have or **take on the appearance**, form, or sound of: imitate

例 cosmetics that simulate a suntan 用来模仿晒黑效果的化妆品

近 act, affect, assume, counterfeit, dissemble, fake, imitate, pretend, profess, sham

self-perpetuating	[ˌselfpərˈpetʃueɪtɪŋ]

【考法】 *adj.* 自续的，能使自身永久存在的：**continuing** or prevailing **without any external intervention**

例 self-perpetuating economic declines 持续存在的经济衰退

sensuality	[ˌsenʃuˈæləti]

【考法】 *n.* 感官享乐：excessive **pursuit of fleshly pleasures**

例 the true sensuality of sushi 食用寿司的真正感官享受

近 carnality, debauchery, hedonism, voluptuousness

反 abstinence, asceticism, sobriety, temperance 克制

sinecure	[ˈsaɪnɪkjʊr]

【考法】 *n.* 拿钱不干事的职务；闲差事：an office or position that **requires little or no work** and that usually provides an income

例 capture a sinecure 获得了一个美差

反 drudge, drudgery, moil, sweat, toil, travail 艰苦的工作，苦活

sinew	[ˈsɪnjuː]

【考法】 *n.* 活力，力量：**vigorous strength**; muscular power

例 Money is the sinew of love as well as war. 爱情和战争都要用金钱来保证。

近 energy, firepower, force, horsepower, might, muscle, potency, power, puissance, strength, vigor

反 impotence, impotency, powerlessness, weakness 无力，虚弱

singe	[sɪndʒ]

【考法】 *vt.* 轻微烧焦：to **burn superficially** or lightly

例 The iron is too hot, and you'll singe the nightdress. 熨斗太烫了，你会把睡衣烫坏的。

近 char, scorch, sear

反 incinerate 烧成灰烬

Unit 4

■ SINUOUS	■ SNAG	■ SACROSANCT	■ SCOURGE	■ SKIMP
■ SCRUPLE	■ SKIRT	■ SLACK	■ SLAKE	■ SLANT

sinuous	[ˈsɪnjuəs]

【考法】 *adj.* 蜿蜒的，迂回的：marked by a long series of **irregular curves**; not direct

例 The river flowed in a sinuous path through the lush valley. 蜿蜒曲折的河流流过茂密的山谷。‖ Thirty-year-old men are novel, rich in content and sinuous in plots. 三十岁的男人是小说，内容丰富，情节曲折。

近 bending, curling, curved, curving, devious, serpentine, tortuous, twisted, winding, windy

反 straight, straightaway 直的，直接的

snag	[snæg]

【考法】 *n.* 障碍：a danger or **difficulty** that is hidden or not easily recognized

例 hit a snag 碰到一个小困难

反 hitch, catch-22, gotcha, pitfall

sacrosanct	[ˈsækroʊsæŋkt]

【考法】 *adj.* 极为神圣的，不可侵犯的：**most sacred** or holy

例 Freedom of the press is sacrosanct. 出版自由是神圣的。

近 hallowed, holy, inviolable, sacred, unassailable, untouchable

反 blasphemous, irreverent, profane, sacrilegious 亵渎的

scourge	[skɜːrdʒ]

【考法】 *n.* 祸害：a **source of harm** or misfortune

例 The sheer ubiquity of food seems to be the scourge of humanity, as evidenced by the obesity epidemic. 无所不在的食品似乎要成为人类的祸害了，这一点可以从肥胖病的泛滥得以佐证。

近 affliction, bane, curse, nemesis

反 benefit, blessing, boon, felicity, godsend, manna, windfall 恩赐，福音

skimp	[skɪmp]

【考法 1】 *adj.* 缺乏的，不足的：**less plentiful** than what is normal, necessary, or desirable

例 The dieter complained about skimp meals that were served at the fat farm. 这个节食者抱怨说减肥疗养地的伙食少得可怜。

近 exiguous, meager, niggardly, poor, scant, scanty, scarce, skimpy, slender, slim, sparing, sparse, stingy

反 abundant, ample, bountiful, copious, generous, liberal, plenteous, plentiful 大量的，丰富的

【考法2】 *vi.* 节省花费，吝啬: to **give insufficient** or barely sufficient attention or effort to or **funds** for

例 skimp on security 不注意安全

近 pinch, save, scrimp, spare, stint

反 dissipate, lavish, prodigalize, squander, waste 浪费，挥霍

scruple ['skruːpl]

【考法】 *n.* (良心上的)不安: an **uneasy feeling about the rightness** of what one is doing or going to do

例 The survey showed that many students had few scruples about cheating on papers or exams. 调查显示，很多学生对于在论文中或考试时作弊没有丝毫的愧疚。

近 compunction, misgiving

反 assurance, certainty, certitude, confidence, conviction, sureness 确信

skirt [skɜːrt]

【考法】 *vt.* 绕行，避开: to **go around** or keep away from in order to avoid danger or discovery

例 skirt the construction zone 绕开建筑工地 || The new bill would make it harder for companies to skirt environmental regulations. 新的规定会增加公司逃脱环境监管的难度。

近 bypass, circumvent, detour, shortcut, sidestep

反 pursue, seek 追寻

slack [slæk]

【考法1】 *adj.* 松弛的: **not tightly fastened**, tied, or stretched

例 slack rope 松弛的绳子

近 insecure, lax, loosened, relaxed, slackened, unsecured

反 taut, tense, tight 拉紧的

【考法2】 *adj.* 疏忽的，大意的: **failing to give proper care** and attention

例 This building contractor is known mainly for his firm's slack workmanship and slipshod construction. 这个建筑承包商因其公司不负责任的粗糙做工和马虎建造的建筑物而臭名远扬。

近 careless, derelict, disregardful, lax, lazy, neglectful, neglecting, negligent, remiss

反 attentive, careful, conscientious 专心的; alert, heedful, mindful, observant, regardful, vigilant, wary, watchful 警惕的

slake [sleɪk]

【考法】 *vt.* 使满足: to **satisfy** (a craving); quench

例 Mountain climbing has largely slaked my desire for adventure. 登山很大程度上满足了我对探险的渴望。

近 assuage, quench, sate, satiate, satisfy

反 tantalize, tease 诱惑，挑逗; arouse, excite, pique, stimulate 激起，唤起

slant [slænt]

【考法1】 *n.* (看待问题、思考的)角度，看法: a **way of looking** at or thinking about something

例 an interesting slant on the problem of underage drinking 在青少年饮酒这个问题上一个有趣的视角

近 angle, outlook, perspective, standpoint, viewpoint

【考法2】 *adj.* 倾斜的: running in a **slanting direction**

例 The computer keyboard has a slightly slant surface so that typing is more comfortable for the wrists. 电脑键盘有一个微小的倾斜角，因此打字不会使手腕感到不适。

近 canted, graded, inclined, leaning, listing, oblique, pitched, raked, slanted, sloping, tilting

反 perpendicular, plumb, vertical 垂直的; horizontal, level 水平的

Unit 5

| ■ SLATE | ■ SLEW | ■ SLIGHT | ■ SLING | ■ SLIPPERY |
| ■ SLIPSHOD | ■ SLOPPY | ■ SLOTH | ■ SLOUCH | ■ SLOVENLY |

slate [sleɪt]

【考法】 *vt.* 列入名单，计划，安排: to **put** (someone or something) **on a list**

例 You've been slated for a three o'clock interview. 你的面试被安排在三点。

近 catalog, enroll, enter, index, inscribe, record, register, schedule

反 delete, erase 删除，除名

slew [sluː]

【考法】 *n.* 大量，许多：a **large amount** or number

例 donate a slew of books to the university library 向大学图书馆捐赠了大量的书籍

近 abundance, bundle, dozen, multiplicity, myriad, plentitude, profusion, scad, shipload, volume, wealth

反 ace, bit, driblet, glimmer, handful, hint, mite, mouthful, nip, ounce, pittance, sprinkle, trace 少量

slight [slaɪt]

【考法 1】 *adj.* 不重要的：**deficient in weight**, importance

例 a slight comedy that did nothing to further her career 一个对她事业发展没有任何帮助的小喜剧

近 fiddling, frivolous, inconsequential, inconsiderable, insignificant, little, minor, minute, nugatory, trifling, trivial

反 consequential, eventful, important, meaningful, momentous, significant, substantial, weighty 重要的

【考法 2】 *vt.* 轻蔑，看不起：to **treat with disdain** or indifference

例 Those snobbish music critics slight any style of music. 那帮自命不凡的音乐评论家看不起所有音乐。

近 contemn, disdain, disrespect, snub, look down

反 esteem, honor, respect, revere, venerate 尊敬

【考法 3】 *vt.* 忽略，疏忽：to **fail to give proper attention** to

例 She slighted several major authors in her survey of 20th-century fiction. 她在调查 20 世纪小说时忽略了几个重要的作家。

近 bypass, disregard, ignore, neglect, overlook, overpass, shrug, slur

反 attend, heed, mind 留心，注意

sling [slɪŋ]

【考法】 *vt.* 投掷：to **send through the air** especially with a quick forward motion of the arm

例 sling stones at the checkpoint 朝着检查站扔石头

近 cast, chuck, dash, fire, fling, heave, hurl, hurtle, launch, lob, loft, pelt, pitch, toss

反 catch 接住

slippery ['slɪpəri]

【考法 1】 *adj.* 光滑的：causing or tending to cause something to **slide** or fall

例 slippery road after rain 雨后湿滑的道路

近 greased, greasy, lubricated, oiled, slicked, slithery

反 coarse, rough 粗糙的

【考法 2】 *adj.* 意义不明确的：**not precise** or fixed **in meaning**, elusive or tricky

例 a slippery concept that we had trouble understanding 一个我们难以理解的模糊概念

近 ambiguous, elusive, equivocal, evasive, fugitive, obscure, unintelligible, vague

反 apparent, clear, distinct, evident, manifest, obvious, palpable, patent, plain, unambiguous, unequivocal 明确的

slipshod ['slɪpʃɑːd]

【考法】 *adj.* 粗心的，随意的：marked by carelessness or **indifference to exactness**, **precision**, **and accuracy**

例 a slipshod piece of research 一项随意的研究 || The hotel had always been run in a slipshod way. 酒店总是在以一种随意的状态运营。

近 botchy, careless, messy, slapdash, sloppy, slovenly, untidy

反 fastidious, meticulous 极仔细的；accurate, exact, precise 准确的

sloppy ['slɑːpi]

【考法 1】 *adj.* 邋遢的，不整洁的：**lacking neatness** in dress or person

例 a sloppy child who always seems to have spilled something on his clothes 一个外表邋遢的小孩子，他的衣服似乎总被沾上了什么东西

近 blowsy, dowdy, frowsy, slovenly, unkempt, untidy

反 dapper, dashing, sharp, smart, spruce 外表整洁的

【考法 2】 *adj.* 混乱的：**lacking in order**, neatness, and often cleanliness

例 dump the papers in a sloppy pile on the desk 把纸张随意地叠放在书桌上

近 chaotic, disarranged, disarrayed, disheveled, disorderly, jumbled, littered, rumpled, tousled, tumbled

反 bandbox, crisp, kempt, neat, orderly, organized, shipshape, snug, tidy, trim 整洁有序的

sloth [sloʊθ]

【考法】 *n.* 怠惰，懒惰：**disinclination to action** or labor: indolence

例 Sloth is the mother of poverty. 懒惰是贫穷的原因。

近 idleness, indolence, inertia, languor, laziness, lethargy, shiftlessness, sluggishness, torpor

反 assiduity, diligence, industry 勤奋

派 slothful *adj.* 懒惰的

slouch [slaʊtʃ]

【考法】 *vi.* 缓慢行走：to go or **move slowly** or reluctantly

例 He slouched towards the church as if going to his own funeral. 他缓缓地向教堂走去，仿佛是要去参加自己的葬礼一般。

近 creep, drag, inch, limp, nose, ooze, plod, poke, snail

反 fly, race, speed, whiz, zip 快走

slovenly [ˈslʌvnli]

【考法】 *adj.* 邋遢的，不整洁的：**lacking neatness** in dress or person

例 For the sake of their image, the band members transformed themselves from clean-cut lads to slovenly rockers. 为了他们自身的形象，乐队成员从健康向上的青年变成了邋遢的摇滚乐手。

近 blowsy, dowdy, frowsy, sloppy, unkempt, untidy

反 dapper, dashing, neat, sharp, smart, spruce, trim 外表整洁的

Unit 6

■ SLUGGARD	■ SLUGGISH	■ SLUMBER	■ SLUR	■ SLY
■ SMARMY	■ SKULLDUGGERY	■ SMATTERING	■ SMIRK	■ SMOTHER

sluggard [ˈslʌɡərd]

【考法】 *n.* 懒人：an habitually **lazy person**

例 The teacher tried to wake up the sluggards who were still sleeping at that late hour. 老师尝试去叫醒那些还在睡觉的懒鬼们。

近 deadbeat, drone, idler, loafer, slouch, slug

反 doer, hummer, hustler, rustler 活跃的人，精力充沛的人

sluggish [ˈslʌɡɪʃ]

【考法】 *adj.* 缓慢的，迟缓的：markedly **slow in movement**, flow, or growth

例 The sluggish pace of the project is worrisome. 项目的缓慢进展让人担忧。

近 crawling, creeping, dallying, dilatory, dragging, lagging, languid, leisurely, snaillike, tardy, unhurried

反 bolting, brisk, fast, fleet, hasty, lightning, meteoric, quick, racing, rapid, rocketing, speedy, swift 快速的

slumber [ˈslʌmbər]

【考法】 *vi.* 睡着：to be in a state of **sleep**

例 She slumbered for hours while the train rolled on. 她在火车行进过程中睡了几个小时。

近 catnap, doze, nap, rest, sleep, snooze

反 arouse, awake, waken 醒来

slur [slɜːr]

【考法 1】 *n.* 耻辱：a **mark of guilt** or disgrace

例 Your drunken behavior at the wedding has cast a slur on this family. 你在婚礼上醉酒后的行为给整个家族都带来了耻辱。

近 blot, brand, onus, smirch, smudge, spot, stigma, taint

反 award, credit, glory, honor 荣誉，荣耀

【考法 2】 *vt.* 疏忽，忽略：to slide or slip over **without due** mention, **consideration**, or emphasis

例 This documentary slurs over certain important facts as it offers a very biased case for a conspiracy theory. 这部纪录片忽略了许多重要的客观事实，而只给出了带有偏见的阴谋论解释。

近 bypass, disregard, forget, ignore, overlook, overpass, slight

反 attend, heed, mind 留心，注意

sly [slaɪ]

【考法】 *adj.* 狡猾的：**clever or cunning**, especially in the practice of deceit

例 The movie pairs a sly, dissembling ex-con with an upstanding, straight-arrow cop. 电影把一个狡猾、善于骗人的出狱犯和正直、坦率的警察搭配在了一起。

近 beguiling, cagey, crafty, cunning, designing, devious, foxy, guileful, scheming, shrewd, subtle, tricky, wily

反 artless, guileless, ingenuous, innocent, undesigning 天真纯朴的，无伪装的

smarmy	[ˈsmɑːrmi]

【考法】 *adj.* 虚情假意的，过分恭维的：**hypocritically**, complacently, or effusively **earnest**

例 smarmy commendation 恭维和表扬

近 fulsome, oily, slick, soapy, unctuous

反 artless, earnest, genuine, heartfelt, sincere, unaffected 真诚的，真挚的

skullduggery	[skʌlˈdʌgəri]

【考法】 *n.* 欺诈，诡计：the **use of clever underhanded actions** to achieve an end

例 intrigue and political skullduggery 密谋和政治欺诈

近 artifice, chicanery, trickery, subterfuge, wile

smattering	[ˈsmætərɪŋ]

【考法】 *n.* 少量：a **small** scattered number or **amount**

例 Only a smattering of spectators presented. 只有少数几个观看者出席了。

近 ace, bit, driblet, glimmer, handful, hint, mite, mouthful, nip, ounce, pittance, sprinkle, trace

反 abundance, bundle, dozen, multiplicity, myriad, plentitude, profusion, scad, shipload, slew, volume, wealth 大量

smirk	[smɜːrk]

【考法】 *vi.* (自鸣得意地)笑：to smile in an affected, often **offensively self-satisfied** manner

例 She tried not to smirk when they announced the winner. 当他们宣布她获得了胜利时，她尽可能地保持不露出笑容。

近 grin, simper

反 cry, weep 哭泣；groan, moan, sigh 叹息

smother	[ˈsmʌðər]

【考法】 *vt.* 抑制(表达、说出)，压制：to **refrain** from openly showing or uttering

例 He quickly smothered his inappropriate laughter at the funeral ceremony. 他很快就控制住了自己在葬礼上不适当的笑声。‖ Management smothered the true facts of the case. 管理层隐瞒了案件的真相。

近 bridle, check, choke, control, curb, muffle, quash, quell, repress, squelch, suppress

反 unleash, vent (感情)爆发，宣泄；express 表达

Unit 7

■ SMUG	■ SMUGGLING	■ SNARE	■ SNARL	■ SNEER
■ SNOBBISH	■ SNUB	■ SOAK	■ SOBER	■ SODDEN

smug	[smʌg]

【考法】 *adj.* 自大的，自鸣得意的：having too high an **opinion of oneself**

例 smug belief/smile/attitude 自大的想法/微笑/态度

近 complacent, egoistic, overweening, pompous, proud, self-satisfied, vain

反 egoless, humble, modest 谦逊的

smuggling	[ˈsmʌglɪŋ]

【考法】 *n.* 走私，私运：secret **importation or exportation contrary to the law** and especially without paying duties imposed by law

例 He was arrested for smuggling drugs into the country. 他因为向境内走私毒品而被逮捕。

近 bootlegging, contraband

snare	[sner]

【考法1】 *n.* 无法逃脱的困境：something that **catches and holds**

例 Someday you'll find that your lies are a snare from which you can't escape. 总有一天你会发现，你所说过的谎话都会变成你无法逃脱的困境。‖ caught in the snare of drug addiction 处于吸毒上瘾的困境之中

近 entanglement, mesh, morass, net, noose, quagmire, quicksand, toil, trap

【考法2】 *vt.* 捕捉：to **capture by** or as if by use of a snare

例 They snared a rabbit earlier in the day. 今天的早些时候他们捕获了一只兔子。‖ The car salesman successfully snared three potential customers. 汽车销售员成功地让三个潜在客户上钩了。

近 catch, enmesh, ensnare, ensnarl, entrap, tangle

反 disentangle 解开；free, liberate 释放

snarl [snɑːrl]

【考法】 *v.* 纠缠，纠结: to **twist** together into a usually confused mass

例 You'll be awfully sorry if you snarl your fishing line . 要是你把渔网给缠在一起，你肯定会非常后悔的。
The new regulation has succeeded in nothing but snarling up rush-hour traffic throughout the city. 新的政策将全城高峰时期的交通变得更为复杂难解。

近 entangle, ensnarl, interlace, intertwine, intertwist, interweave, knot, ravel, tangle
反 disentangle, extricate, unravel, unsnarl, untwine, untwist 解开

sneer [snɪr]

【考法】 *vt.* (轻蔑地)嘲笑: to speak in a **scornful**, contemptuous, or derisive manner

例 sneer a contempt 嗤之以鼻
近 deride, gibe, laugh, jeer, jibe, mock, ridicule
反 esteem, honor, respect, revere, venerate 尊敬

snobbish [ˈsnɑːbɪʃ]

【考法】 *adj.* 谄上傲下的，自大的: being or characteristic of a person who has an **offensive air of superiority** and tends to ignore or disdain anyone regarded as inferior

例 snobbish belief/smile/attitude 自大的想法/微笑/态度
近 aristocratic, bumptious, elitist, haughty, imperious, persnickety, pompous, presumptuous, supercilious
反 egoless, humble, modest 谦逊的，不自大的

snub [snʌb]

【考法】 *vt.* 轻视，不理睬: to treat with **contempt or neglect**

例 snub her in public 在公共场合轻视她
近 contemn, disdain, disrespect, slight, look down
反 esteem, honor, respect, revere, venerate 尊敬

soak [souk]

【考法】 *vt.* 使…湿透: to **make thoroughly wet** or saturated by or as if by placing in liquid

例 That downpour soaked my hair , and now I look like a sight. 那场大雨把我的头发淋湿了，所以我现在看起来格外滑稽。 ‖ We ran for home as soon as the rain started, but our clothes still ended up soaked . 我们一发觉下雨就开始往家里跑，但我们的衣服还是湿透了。

近 douse, drench, drown, impregnate, macerate, saturate, sodden, sop, souse, steep
反 dehydrate, dry, desiccate 脱水；parch, sear, scorch 烤干，烧焦；wring 拧干

sober [ˈsoubər]

【考法 1】 *adj.* 严肃的: marked by **seriousness**, gravity, or solemnity of conduct or character

例 She made a sober reply to what was only a teasing comment. 她很严肃地回复了那个恶搞的评论。
Illness is a sober reminder of our mortality . 疾病是死亡给我们发出的严肃警告。

近 earnest, grave, humorless, sedate, severe, sober, solemn, staid, weighty
反 facetious, flip, flippant, humorous, jesting, jocular, joking, playful 轻佻的，幽默有趣的

【考法 2】 *adj.* 节制的: given to or marked by **restraint** in the satisfaction of one's appetites

例 The millionaire decided to live a sober life after bankruptcy. 那个百万富翁破产以后决定过有节制的生活。
近 abstentious, abstinent, continent, self-denying, temperate
反 hedonistic, licentious, self-indulgent, sensual, sybaritic, voluptuary 纵欲的，享乐主义的

sodden [ˈsɑːdn]

【考法】 *adj.* 湿透的: containing, covered with, or thoroughly **penetrated by water**
vt. 使…湿透: to **wet thoroughly** with liquid

例 We stripped off our sodden clothes and wrung them dry. 我们脱下湿透了的衣服并将它拧干。
Soldiers' boots were soddened by endless hours in muddy trenches. 长时间身处泥泞的战壕使得士兵的靴子湿透了。

近 awash, bathed, doused, drenched, logged, saturated, soaked, watered, waterlogged; douse, drench, drown, impregnate, macerate, saturate, soak, sop, souse, steep
反 arid, dry 干燥的；dehydrate, dry, desiccate 脱水；parch, sear, scorch 烤干，烧焦；wring 拧干

Unit 8

■ SOLACE	■ SOLDER	■ SOLEMNITY	■ SOLICITOUS	■ SOLID
■ SOLILOQUY	■ SOLITUDE	■ SOLVENT	■ SOMATIC	■ SOMBER

solace [ˈsɑːləs]

【考法】 *n.* 安慰：**comfort in sorrow**, misfortune, or distress

vt. 安慰，安抚：to comfort, cheer, or **console**, as in trouble or sorrow

例 The kind words brought a little solace to the grieving widow . 这些同情的话语给痛苦的寡妇带来了些许安慰。‖ I did my best to solace those bereaved children . 我尽力去安抚那些失去双亲的孩子们。

近 consolation, relief; cheer, comfort, console, soothe

反 agonize, distress, harrow, torment, torture, trouble 使痛苦，折磨

solder [ˈsɑːdər]

【考法】 *v.* 连接，联合：to join or **unite**

例 Wires are soldered onto the circuit board . 电线被焊接在电路板上。‖ The agreement soldered the factions into an alliance . 两个派系因这份协议而结成同盟。

近 associate, coalesce, combine, conjoin, conjugate, connect, couple, fuse, interfuse, join, link, marry, unify

反 disassociate, disconnect, disjoin, divide, sever, split, sunder 分开

solemnity [səˈlemnəti]

【考法】 *n.* 庄严，严肃：the quality or condition of being **solemn**

例 The coronation ceremony requires absolute solemnity . 加冕典礼需要绝对的庄严肃穆。

近 earnest, graveness, gravity, intentness, seriousness, sobriety, solemnness, staidness

反 facetiousness, flightiness, flippancy, frivolity, frivolousness, levity, lightheartedness, play 轻佻，欢快

solicitous [səˈlɪsɪtəs]

【考法】 *adj.* 为他人操心的，体谅他人的：given to or made with heedful anticipation of the needs and **happiness of others**

例 The solicitous husband had already cleaned the house and cooked dinner by the time his wife returned home from work. 这个十分体谅妻子的好丈夫在他妻子回家之前就把家里清理干净，还把晚餐都做好了。

近 attentive, considerate, kind

反 heedless, inconsiderate, thoughtless, unthinking 不关心的

派 solicitude *n.* 关切，挂念

solid [ˈsɑːlɪd]

【考法】 *adj.* 有理有据的：based on **sound reasoning** or information

例 the only solid conclusion that the jury could have reached 陪审团唯一可能做出的合理结论

近 firm, informed, justified, levelheaded, logical, rational, reasonable, sensible, sober, valid, well-founded

反 groundless, illogical, invalid, unfounded, uninformed, unjustified, unreasonable, unsound 没有道理的

soliloquy [səˈlɪləkwi]

【考法】 *n.* (尤指自言自语的)独白：a dramatic or literary form of discourse in which a character talks to himself or herself or reveals his or her thoughts **without addressing a listener**

例 a monotonous soliloquy 一段无聊的独白

近 monologue

反 chorus, ensemble 合唱

solitude [ˈsɑːlətuːd]

【考法】 *n.* 孤独，避世：the quality or state of **being alone** or remote from society

例 He sought the kind of solitude where his thoughts would be his only companions. 他在寻找一种孤独感，只有他的思想陪伴着他。‖ She wished to work on her novel in solitude. 她想一个人安静地完成小说。

近 aloneness, insulation, privacy, seclusion, segregation, separateness, sequestration, solitariness

反 camaraderie, companionship, company, comradeship, fellowship, society 陪伴

solvent [ˈsɑːlvənt]

【考法 1】 *adj.* 有偿付能力的：**able to pay** all legal **debts**

例 They're going to have to prove that the company is now solvent . 接下来他们必须要证明公司有偿贷能力。

反 bankrupt 破产的

【考法 2】 *n.* 溶剂: a substance in which **another substance is dissolved**, forming a solution

例 Some organic solvents, such as benzene, pyridine, furan, are poisonous to human's reproductive system. 一些有机溶剂(比如苯、吡啶、呋喃)对人体的生殖系统有毒性。

反 solute 溶质

somatic [səˈmætɪk]

【考法】 *adj.* 肉体的: **of the body**, especially as distinguished from a body part, the mind, or the environment

例 a somatic disorder that was once thought to be "all in the patient's head" 曾被认为"全是病人头脑中的问题"的生理机能紊乱

近 animal, bodily, carnal, corporal, corporeal, fleshly, material, physical

反 mental, spiritual 精神上的; nonmaterial, nonphysical 非肉体的

somber [ˈsɑːmbər]

【考法】 *adj.* 悲伤的, 不愉快的: causing or marked by an atmosphere **lacking in cheer**

例 Her death put us in a somber mood. 她的死让我们陷入了悲伤沮丧的情绪之中。

近 depressing, dire, dismal, funereal, lugubrious, melancholy, miserable, morbid, morose, saturnine, sullen

反 cheerful, delighted, festive, gay, jocund, jovial 快乐的

Unit 9

■ SOMNOLENCE	■ SLAPDASH	■ SOOTHE	■ SOP	■ SOPHISM
■ SOPHISTICATED	■ SOPORIFIC	■ SORDID	■ SOUND	■ SPARSE

somnolence [ˈsɑːmnələns]

【考法】 *n.* 瞌睡, 嗜睡: the quality or state of desiring or **needing sleep**

例 the readers' somnolence spells their indifference 读者的嗜睡说明他们不感兴趣

近 doziness, drowsiness

反 insomnia, sleeplessness, wakefulness 失眠

slapdash [ˈslæpdæʃ]

【考法】 *adj.* 马虎的: to do things **carelessly** without much thinking or planning

例 a slapdash worker 粗心的工作者

近 aimless, arbitrary, desultory, erratic, haphazard, stray

反 methodical, nonrandom, orderly, organized, regular, systematic

soothe [suːð]

【考法】 *vt.* 带来慰藉, 安慰: to **bring comfort**, solace, or reassurance to

例 There seemed to be no words sufficient to soothe the widow. 任何话语好像都不足以安慰这个寡妇。

近 cheer, comfort, console, solace

反 agonize, distress, harrow, torment, torture, trouble 使痛苦, 折磨

sop [sɑːp]

【考法 1】 *n.* 安慰物: something yielded to **placate or soothe**

例 provide with the salary raise as a sop 提高工资作为安慰

近 balm, emollient, placebo, salve, unguent

反 irritant, stimulant 刺激物

【考法 2】 *vt.* 浸湿, 湿透: to **wet thoroughly**

例 a thoroughly sopped book 一本完本浸湿的书

近 douse, drench, drown, impregnate, macerate, saturate, soak, sodden, souse, steep

反 dehydrate, dry, desiccate 脱水; parch, sear, scorch 烤干, 烧焦; wring 拧干

sophism [ˈsɑːfɪzəm]

【考法】 *n.* 假推理, 诡辩: **deceptive** or fallacious **argumentation**

例 Political selection is more dependent on sophism and less on economic literacy. 政治选举更多的是依靠诡辩, 而非精练的文笔。

近 sophistry

sophisticated [səˈfɪstɪkeɪtɪd]

【考法 1】 *adj.* 精明的, 老于世故的: having acquired **worldly knowledge or refinement**; lacking natural simplicity or naiveté

例 On the train I met a surprisingly sophisticated and widely traveled child. 在火车上我见到了一个老练得让人惊讶的、见多识广的孩子。

近 cosmopolitan, debonair, knowing, smart, suave, urbane, worldly

反 guileless, ingenuous, innocent, naïve 天真的

【考法2】 *adj.* 复杂的：very **complex** or complicated

例 a very sophisticated machine that is a marvel of modern design 一个十分复杂的机器，是现代设计的最高成就

近 baroque, byzantine, complicated, convoluted, elaborate, intricate, involved, knotty, labyrinthine, tangled

反 plain, simple 简单的

派 sophistication *n.* 精明；复杂

---

soporific [ˌsɑːpəˈrɪfɪk]

【考法】 *n.* 催眠的药剂，安眠药：a drug or other substance that **induces sleep**

adj. 催眠的：causing or tending to **cause sleep**

例 Alcohol is a poor soporific because it disturbs sleep patterns, and so can worsen sleep disorders. 酒精是一种欠佳的安眠药，因为它会干扰睡眠的固定模式，从而恶化睡眠紊乱的情况。

近 hypnotic; narcotic, opiate, slumberous, somniferous, somnolent

反 stimulant 兴奋剂；arousing, waking, invigorating, stimulating 刺激性的

---

sordid [ˈsɔːrdɪd]

【考法1】 *adj.* 肮脏的，不干净的：not clean

例 I will not let my children grow up in such a sordid environment. 我绝不会让我的孩子在这样一个肮脏的环境之中成长。

近 besmirched, dirty, dusty, filthy, foul, grubby, muddy, nasty, smudged, soiled, stained, sullied, unclean

反 clean, immaculate, spotless, stainless, unsoiled, unstained, unsullied 干净的

【考法2】 *adj.* 卑鄙的：marked by **baseness** or grossness

近 Behind his generous donation were sordid motives. 在他慷慨捐资的背后有着卑鄙的动机。

近 base, contemptible, despicable, detestable, dishonorable, execrable, ignominious, mean, vile, wretched

反 honorable, lofty, noble, straight, upright, venerable, virtuous 高尚的，值得尊敬的

---

sound [saʊnd]

【考法1】 *adj.* 牢固的，不可动摇的：marked by the ability to **withstand stress without structural damage** or distortion

例 The bridge is structurally sound. 这座大桥在结构上是稳固的。

近 bombproof, fast, firm, stalwart, strong, sturdy

反 ramshackle 摇摇欲坠的；rickety, unstable, unsteady 不稳定的

【考法2】 *adj.* 健康的，强壮的：**free from injury** or disease; exhibiting normal health

例 an old but sound horse 老当益壮的马

近 bouncing, fit, hale, healthy, hearty, robust, well, well-conditioned, wholesome

反 ailing, diseased, ill, sick 生病的；decrepit, enfeebled, feeble, infirm 虚弱的

【考法3】 *adj.* (逻辑上)严谨的：based on **valid reasoning**

例 Sound reasoning alone should tell you that the result is invalid. 从纯粹严谨的逻辑演绎出发，这个结论是不正确的。

近 analytic, coherent, consequent, rational, reasonable, sensible, valid, well-founded, well-grounded

反 illegitimate, illogical, incoherent, inconsequent, invalid, irrational, unreasonable, unsound, weak (逻辑上)站不住脚的

派 soundness *n.* (逻辑上的)无瑕疵

---

sparse [spɑːrs]

【考法】 *adj.* 稀疏的，稀少的：**less plentiful** than what is normal, necessary, or desirable

例 Many slopes are rock fields with sparse vegetation. 许多山坡都是不长植物的石坡。

近 exiguous, meager, niggardly, poor, scant, scanty, scarce, skimpy, slender, slim, sparing, stingy

反 abundant, ample, bountiful, copious, generous, liberal, plenteous, plentiful 大量的，丰富的

Unit 10

■ SPARTAN	■ SPAT	■ SPATE	■ SLEEK	■ SPECIOUS
■ SPECK	■ SPECTATOR	■ SPECTRUM	■ SPECULATE	■ SPENDTHRIFT

---

spartan [ˈspɑːrtn]

【考法】 *adj.* 简朴的，节约的：marked by **simplicity**, frugality, or avoidance of luxury and comfort

例 spartan decoration 简朴的装饰

近 austere, plain, simple, stark

反 deluxe, luxurious, plush 奢华的

spat [spæt]

【考法】 *n.* (小的)争吵: a brief petty **quarrel** or angry outburst

例 Like any other couple, they have their spats . 像其他夫妻一样，他们也会有争执。‖ They were typical sisters, spatting one minute, playing together the next . 她们是典型的姐妹：上一分钟还在吵架，下一分钟就又玩在一起了。

近 altercation, controversy, disagreement, dispute, imbroglio, quarrel, squabble, tiff, wrangle

反 amity, concord, harmony, rapport, rapprochement 和睦，友好

spate [speɪt]

【考法】 *n.* 大量: a **large number** or amount

例 a spate of books about GRE 很多关于 GRE 的书

近 abundance, bundle, dozen, multiplicity, myriad, plentitude, profusion, scad, shipload, slew, volume, wealth

反 ace, bit, driblet, glimmer, handful, hint, mite, mouthful, nip, ounce, pittance, sprinkle, trace 少量

sleek [sliːk]

【考法】 *adj.* 时髦的，优美的: stylish and **attractive**

例 sleek modern furniture 造型优美的现代家具

近 chic, fashionable, trendy, voguish

specious [ˈspiːʃəs]

【考法】 *adj.* 似是而非的，欺骗性的: having a **false look of truth** or genuineness

例 a specious argument that really does not stand up under close examination 经不起仔细推敲的欺骗性论证

近 beguiling, deceitful, deceiving, deluding, delusive, delusory, fallacious, false, misleading

反 aboveboard, forthright, straightforward 明确的

speck [spek]

【考法】 *n.* 小点，少量: a very **small amount**: bit

例 She writes without even a speck of humor . 她字里行间一点幽默感也没有。

近 ace, bit, driblet, glimmer, handful, hint, mite, mouthful, nip, ounce, pittance, sprinkle, trace

反 abundance, bundle, dozen, multiplicity, myriad, plentitude, profusion, scad, shipload, slew, volume, wealth 大量

spectator [ˈspekteɪtər]

【考法】 *n.* 观众，目击者，旁观者: one who looks on or **watches**

例 join the organization as a temporary spectator 作为短期观察员加入该组织 ‖ The accident attracted a large crowd of spectators . 事故引来了大量的围观群众。

近 bystander, observer, onlooker, viewer, watcher

反 actor, performer, player 表演者

spectrum [ˈspektrəm]

【考法】 *n.* 光谱；范围，系列: a broad **sequence or range** of related qualities, ideas, or activities

例 the whole spectrum of 20th-century thought 20 世纪所有不同的思潮 ‖ A political spectrum is a way of modeling different political positions by placing them upon one or more geometric axes symbolizing independent political dimensions. 所谓的政治光谱是一种将不同的政治立场可视化的模型，它通过一条或者多条几何坐标轴来定位不同的政治态度。

近 diapason, gamut, scale, spread, stretch

speculate [ˈspekjuleɪt]

【考法】 *v.* 推测，揣测: to **take to be true** on the basis of insufficient evidence

例 speculate on their motives 猜测他们的动机

近 assume, conjecture, daresay, imagine, presume, speculate, suppose, surmise, suspect

反 prove, substantiate, validate 证明

spendthrift [ˈspendθrɪft]

【考法 1】 *n.* 挥霍者，败家子: a person who **spends improvidently** or wastefully

adj. 挥霍的，不节俭的: given to **spending money freely** or foolishly

例 Spendthrift consumers amassed a mountain of debt on their credit cards. 那些爱挥霍财富的消费者们在他们的信用卡上累积了一大笔债务。

近 fritterer, profligate, spender, squanderer, waster, wastrel; extravagant, improvident, squandering, thriftless, unthrifty, wasteful

反 economizer, penny-pincher 节约的人；hoarder, miser, niggard 吝啬鬼；conserving, economical, frugal, penny-pinching, provident, scrimping, skimping, thrifty 节俭的

List 24

Unit 1

■ SPENT	■ SLUMP	■ SPINY	■ SPLEEN	■ SPLICE
■ SPONTANEOUS	■ SPOOF	■ SPORADIC	■ SPRAWL	■ SPRIGHTLY

spent ［spent］
【考法 1】 *adj.* 精疲力竭的：**drained of energy** or effectiveness
例 spent runner after the marathon 马拉松后疲惫的选手
近 beaten, bleary, done, drained, enervate, exhausted, fatigued, jaded, prostrate, tired, wearied, worn-out
反 active, energetic, invigorated, peppy, strengthened, strong, tireless, vitalized, weariless 充满活力的
【考法 2】 *adj.* 用废的：used up and **no longer useful**
例 Radioactive waste is simply spent fuel . 放射性废物就是用后的燃料。
近 consumed, depleted

slump ［'slʌmp］
【考法】 *n./v.* 暴跌，急剧下降：to **decline suddenly** as in activity, prices, or business
例 a stock market slump 股市暴跌
近 recession, depression
反 boom 繁荣

spiny ［'spaɪni］
【考法】 *adj.* 棘手的，麻烦的：**requiring exceptional skill** or caution in performance or handling
例 This promises to be a spiny problem to negotiate . 这有可能成为谈判过程中棘手的问题。
近 catchy, delicate, difficult, knotty, problematic, sensitive, sticky, ticklish, thorny, tough, troublesome
反 easy, effortless, manageable, painless, simple, straightforward, uncomplicated, undemanding 简单的

spleen ［spliːn］
【考法】 *n.* 怒气，怨恨：feelings of **anger or ill will** often suppressed
例 She vented her spleen on her boyfriend and felt much better for having done so. 在她把怒气一股脑地倾泻到她男朋友身上之后，她感觉好多了。
近 angriness, choler, furor, fury, indignation, ire, madness, outrage, rage, wrath
反 delight, pleasure 高兴，愉悦

splice ［splaɪs］
【考法】 *vt.* 接合，叠接：to **unite** (as two ropes) by interweaving the strands, or to join (as two pieces of film) at the ends
例 He taught me to edit and splice film . 他教我如何剪辑和叠接胶卷。
近 associate, coalesce, combine, conjoin, conjugate, connect, couple, fuse, interfuse, join, link, marry, unify
反 disassociate, disconnect, disjoin, divide, sever, split, sunder 分开

spontaneous ［spɑːn'teɪniəs］
【考法】 *adj.* 自发的，不经思索的：acting or activated **without apparent thought** or deliberation
例 Hugging a crying child is simply a spontaneous reaction . 拥抱一个哭泣的小孩是很自然而然的反应。
近 automatic, impulsive, instinctive, involuntary, mechanical, natural
反 calculated, deliberate, intentional, planned, predetermined, premeditated, studied 有计划的，故意的

spoof ［spuːf］
【考法】 *n.* 轻松幽默的模仿，小恶搞：a work that imitates and **exaggerates** another work **for comic effect**
例 Many viewers thought that the spoof of a television newscast was the real thing. 许多观众认为这则新闻报道被恶搞之后的作品才是真实的东西。
近 burlesque, caricature, mimicking, parody, travesty

sporadic [spəˈrædɪk]

【考法】 *adj.* 断断续续的：**not often occurring** or repeated

例 On the whole, situation has significantly improved with only sporadic disturbances . 总体而言，局势得到了明显的改善，现在只有偶尔发生的骚乱。

近 few, infrequent, occasional, odd, rare, scarce, seldom, uncommon

反 frequent, habitual, repeated 时常发生的

sprawl [sprɔːl]

【考法】 *v.* 杂乱无序地发展；蔓生，蔓延：to grow, develop, or spread **irregularly** and without apparent design or plan

例 The city sprawls down the whole coast . 城市顺着整条海岸线蔓延。

近 ramble, scramble, straddle

派 sprawling *adj.* 蔓延的，不规则伸展的

sprightly [ˈspraɪtli]

【考法】 *adj.* 活泼的，充满活力的：**full of** spirit and **vitality**

例 the sprightly 85-year-old president 那位充满活力的 85 岁总统

近 active, airy, animated, brisk, energetic, frisky, gay, jaunty, kinetic, mettlesome, racy, spirited, vital, vivacious

反 dead, inactive, inanimate, lackadaisical, languid, languishing, leaden, lifeless, listless, spiritless, vapid 没精神的

Unit 2

■ SPUR	■ SPURIOUS	■ SPURN	■ SANITY	■ SQUALID
■ SQUALL	■ SQUANDER	■ SQUAT	■ SOFT–PEDAL	■ SQUELCH

spur [spɜːr]

【考法】 *n.* 刺激物：something that **arouses action** or activity *vt.* 刺激，激励：to **incite** or stimulate

例 Appreciation spurred his ambition . 赞扬激起了他的雄心壮志。

近 boost, catalyst, impetus, incentive, incitement, instigation, momentum, motivation, provocation, stimulus; arouse, excite, exhort, goad, instigate, prod, stir, urge

反 deterrent, disincentive 阻碍物；bridle, check, constrain, curb, deter, fetter, hamper, inhibit, manacle, shackle 制止，阻碍，束缚

spurious [ˈspjʊriəs]

【考法】 *adj.* 假的，伪造的：**lacking authenticity** or validity in essence or origin; not genuine

例 spurious coins 伪币

近 apocryphal, bogus, counterfeit, fake, forged, phony, sham

反 authentic, bona fide, genuine, real 真实的

派 spuriously *adv.* 伪造地，虚假地

spurn [spɜːrn]

【考法】 *vt.* 摈弃，拒绝：to **reject with disdain** or contempt

例 They spurned his recommendation . 他们拒绝了他的推荐。‖ Fiercely independent, the elderly couple spurned all offers of financial help . 这对老夫妻极其独立，回绝了所有经济援助。

近 decline, disapprove, negative, refuse, reject, reprobate, repudiate

反 accede, accept, agree, approve, assent, consent, embrace 同意，接受

派 spurned *adj.* 被摈弃的，被拒绝的

sanity [ˈsænəti]

【考法】 *n.* 心智健全，神志正常：the normal or **healthy condition** of the mental abilities

例 preserve one's sanity 保持神志正常

近 reason, saneness, mind

反 dementia, insanity, madness, mania 疯狂

squalid [ˈskwɑːlɪd]

【考法】 *adj.* 污秽的，肮脏的：**dirty** and wretched

例 The migrants have been living in squalid conditions . 移民们一直生存在肮脏的条件下。

近 black, dirty, filthy, foul, impure, nasty, slipshod, slovenly, unclean

反 clean, immaculate, spotless, unsoiled, unsullied 干净的

squall	[skwɔːl]

【考法】 *v.* 尖叫：to **scream** or cry loudly and harshly
例 The baby squalled in pain . 婴儿因为疼痛而大叫。
近 cry, howl, screech, shout, shriek, shrill, squeal, thunder, yelp, yell
反 murmur, mutter, whisper 低声细语

squander	[ˈskwɑːndər]

【考法】 *vt.* 浪费：to **spend wastefully** or extravagantly
例 He squandered his inheritance on women and gambling . 他把他继承的遗产浪费在女人和赌博上。
近 blow, dissipate, fritter, lavish, misspend, waste
反 conserve, husband 节约，节俭
派 squandering *adj.* 浪费的

squat	[skwɑːt]

【考法】 *adj.* 又矮又胖的：being compact and **broad in build** and often **short in stature**
例 a squat but adroit craftsman 一个又胖又矮，但是手艺灵巧的工匠
近 chunky, dumpy, heavyset, squatty, stocky, stout, stubby, stumpy, thickset
反 gangling, lanky 瘦高的

soft-pedal	[sɔːft ˈpedl]

【考法】 *v.* 降低…的力度：to **reduce** in apparent importance
例 soft-pedal an investigation into the scandal 降低对该丑闻的调查力度
近 de-emphasize, downplay, play down

squelch	[skweltʃ]

【考法】 *vt.* 压制，镇压（运动）：to put a **stop** to (something) **by** the use of **force**
例 The authority tried to squelch the workers' protest . 政府试图镇压工人的抗议游行。
近 crush, muffle, quell, repress, squash, subdue, suppress, crack down
反 abet, aid, assist, back, help, support, prop up 支持，帮助
派 squelcher *n.* 镇压者

Unit 3

■ SECEDE	■ STALWART	■ STAMINA	■ STAMMER	■ STARTLE
■ STATIC	■ STATURE	■ STEADFAST	■ STEALTH	■ STEEP

secede	[sɪˈsiːd]

【考法】 *vi.* 脱离，退出（组织、团体、联盟等）：to **withdraw from an organization** (as a religious communion or political party or federation)
例 They threatened to secede from the coalition . 他们以退出联盟相要挟。
近 demit, disaffiliate, quit, withdraw
反 enlist, enroll, join, sign up 加入

stalwart	[ˈstɔːlwərt]

【考法】 *adj.* 坚定的：**firm** and **resolute**
例 a stalwart supporter of the UN 联合国的坚定支持者
近 adament, obstinate, unbending, willful

stamina	[ˈstæmɪnə]

【考法】 *n.* 耐力：physical or **moral strength** to resist or withstand illness, fatigue, or hardship
例 A marathon challenges a runner's stamina . 马拉松挑战参赛者的耐力。
近 endurance, tolerance
反 frailty 脆弱

stammer	[ˈstæmər]

【考法】 *vi.* 口吃，结巴：to **speak with** involuntary **pauses** or repetitions
例 He decided to master his stammer . 他决心纠正他的口吃。
近 falter, stutter
反 articulate 清楚地说

startle	['stɑːrtl]
【考法】	*vt.* 使吓一跳，使大吃一惊: to **frighten or surprise** suddenly and usually not seriously
例	They were startled at the prohibitive price. 他们被高得离谱的价格吓到了。
近	amaze, astonish, astound, dumbfound, rock, scare, shock, stun, stupefy
反	reassure 消除（恐惧或疑虑）
派	startling *adj.* 惊人的

static	['stætɪk]
【考法】	*adj.* 静态的；停滞的: characterized by a **lack of movement**, animation, or progression
例	Both your pictures are of static subjects. 你的两张照片都是静物。 ‖ a static economy 停滞不前的经济
近	inactive, fixed, immobile, immotile, immovable, inert, stable, stagnant, stationary, still
反	active, dynamic, lively, vibrant 充满活力的；mobile, movable 可移动的

stature	['stætʃər]
【考法1】	*n.* 高度，身高: natural **height**（as of a person）in an upright position
例	a man of surprisingly great stature 拥有惊人身高的人
近	altitude, elevation, inch
【考法2】	*n.* 才干，水平: **quality** or **status** gained by growth, development, or achievement
例	This club has grown in stature over the last 20 years. 过去二十年间里这家俱乐部的水平得到了提升。
近	merit, quality, value, virtue, worth

steadfast	['stedfæst]
【考法】	*adj.* 坚定的，忠诚的: **firm in belief**, determination, or adherence
例	Her comrades remained steadfast despite brutal tortures. 尽管经受了残酷的折磨，她的同志们都依然坚定忠诚。
近	constant, dedicated, devoted, devout, loyal, pious, staunch, steady, true-blue
反	disloyal, perfidious, recreant, traitorous, treacherous, unfaithful 不忠的

stealth	[stelθ]
【考法】	*adj.* 秘密的: intended **not to attract attention**
例	The SWAT team carried out a stealth raid on the house, which was believed to be harboring a terrorist cell. 特警们对这间被认为是恐怖分子老巢的房屋进行了秘密的突袭。
近	backstairs, clandestine, covert, furtive, private, sneak, stealthy, surreptitious, undercover, underground
反	open, overt, public 公开的，光明正大的
派	stealthy *adj.* 秘密的，隐秘的

steep	[stiːp]
【考法1】	*adj.* 陡峭的: having an incline **approaching** the **perpendicular**
例	a very steep rock face that is nearly impossible to climb 一面非常陡峭、不可能攀爬的岩石
近	abrupt, precipitate, sheer
反	gradual 逐渐变化的；flat 平坦的
【考法2】	*adj.* 过分的，过高的: going **beyond** a normal or acceptable **limit** in degree or amount
例	extremely steep demands 过高的要求
近	exorbitant, extravagant, extreme, immoderate, inordinate, insane, lavish, overdue, overweening, plethoric, stiff
反	moderate, modest, reasonable, temperate 适度的

Unit 4

■ STENCH	■ STENTORIAN	■ STERILE	■ STICKLER	■ STIFF
■ STIFLE	■ STIGMA	■ STINT	■ STINGY	■ SEQUEL

stench	[stentʃ]
【考法】	*n.* 臭气，恶臭: a strong, **foul odor**
例	We finally discovered the dead rat that was causing the stench in the living room. 我们终于发现是死老鼠带来了卧室里的恶臭。
近	fetor, funk, malodor, reek, stink
反	aroma, fragrance, perfume, scent 香气

stentorian [sten'tɔːriən]

【考法】 *adj.* 声音洪亮的：extremely **loud**

例 an tenor with a stentorian voice 拥有洪亮声音的男高音 ‖ The professor's stentorian voice was enough to keep even the drowsiest student awake. 教授洪亮的声音足以使最困的学生保持清醒。

近 blaring, blasting, clamorous, deafening, earsplitting, plangent, resounding, roaring, sonorous, thunderous

反 gentle, low, soft 声音轻柔的

sterile ['sterəl]

【考法 1】 *adj.* 贫瘠的：**not productive** or effective

例 a sterile land which used to be a forest 曾经是森林的一块贫瘠土地

近 barren, effete, fruitless, impotent, infertile

反 verdant（因长满植物而）青翠的；fat, fertile, fruitful 肥沃的

【考法 2】 *adj.* 无菌的：**free from** live **bacteria** or other microorganisms

例 The hospitals in the war-torn city often lack necessary drugs and sterile surgical supplies. 在这个被战争所蹂躏的城市中，医院里通常缺乏必需的药物和无菌手术用品。

近 aseptic, germfree, hygienic

反 insanitary, unhygienic 不卫生的；contaminated, polluted 受污染的

派 sterilize *v.* 消毒，杀菌

stickler ['stɪklər]

【考法】 *n.* 坚持细节的人，一丝不苟的人：one who **insists on exactness** or completeness in the observance of something

例 a stickler for perfection 完美主义者 ‖ a stickler for neatness 有洁癖的人

近 disciplinarian, pedant, purist, martinet

stiff [stɪf]

【考法 1】 *adj.* 僵硬的，无法弯曲的：**lacking** in **suppleness** or flexibility

例 a stiff cardboard packing box 不易弯折的硬纸板盒 ‖ When I got out of bed this morning my back was stiff as a board. 今早起床时我的背和木板一样僵硬。

近 immalleable, impliable, inflexible, petrified, rigid, unbending, unyielding

反 flexible, floppy, pliable, pliant, supple, yielding 柔软的

【考法 2】 *adj.* 艰苦的，费力的：**requiring** considerable physical or mental **effort**

例 We'll have a stiff climb to actually reach the summit. 我们还有一段艰苦的征途才能登顶。

近 arduous, challenging, difficult, formidable, grueling, laborious, strenuous, sweaty, testing, toilsome, tough

反 easy, effortless, facile, light, mindless, simple, soft, undemanding 容易的

stifle ['staɪfl]

【考法】 *vt.* 抑制（声音、呼吸等）；阻止，扼杀：to cut off (as the voice or breath); to keep in or **hold back**

例 stifle free expression 限制言论自由

近 choke, muffle, mute, repress, smother, strangle, suffocate, suppress

反 foment, incite, instigate, provoke, stir 激发，激起

派 stifling *adj.* 抑制的

stigma ['stɪɡmə]

【考法】 *n.* 耻辱，污名：a **mark of shame** or discredit

例 the stigma of cowardice 懦弱的污名 ‖ There's a social stigma attached to receiving welfare. 接受福利有一种社会耻辱感。

近 blemish, brand, onus, slur, smirch, smudge, spot, stain, taint

反 award, credit, honor 荣誉；fame, glory, renown, repute 好名声

stint [stɪnt]

【考法】 *vi.* 吝惜，节省：to **be** sparing or **frugal**

例 They never stint with their praise. 他们从不吝啬他们的赞美之词。

近 scrimp, skimp

反 blow, dissipate, fritter, lavish, misspend, squander, waste 浪费

stingy ['stɪndʒi]

【考法】 *adj.* 小气的，吝啬的：being **unwilling** or showing unwillingness **to share** with others

例 too stingy to tip the waiter 小气到不肯给小费

近 closefisted, mean, mingy, miserly, niggardly, parsimonious, penurious, sparing, stinting, tightfisted

反 bountiful, charitable, freehanded, generous, liberal, munificent, openhanded 慷慨的

派 stinginess *n.* 小气

sequel [ˈsiːkwəl]

【考法】 *n.* 结果：a **result** or consequence

例 Higher prices are a logical sequel to higher costs for manufacturers. 从逻辑上来说，更高的价格是生产商付出更高的生产成本的结果。

近 aftermath, conclusion, consequence, fate, fruit, outcome, product, result, sequence

反 antecedent, causation, cause, occasion, reason 起因，原因

Unit 5

■ STIPULATE	■ STITCH	■ STOCK	■ SECTARIAN	■ STODGY
■ STOKE	■ STOIC	■ STOLID	■ STOMACH	■ STONEWALL

stipulate [ˈstɪpjuleɪt]

【考法】 *v.* 规定，特定要求：to **specify** or arrange in an **agreement**

例 Total disarmament was stipulated in the peace treaty. 和平条约中要求彻底解除武装。

近 claim, designate, detail, particularize, qualify

反 relinquish, surrender, yield, waive 放弃（权利等）

派 stipulation *n.* 规范，要求

stitch [stɪtʃ]

【考法】 *n.* 突然剧痛：a **sharp unpleasant sensation** usually felt in some specific part of the body

例 an unexpected stitch 意想不到的阵痛

近 ache, pang, prick, shoot, smart, sting, throe, tingle, twinge

反 comfort, ease, easiness 舒适的感觉

stock [stɑːk]

【考法】 *adj.* 普通的，常备的：**commonly used** or brought forward

例 the stock answers to sensitive questions 对于敏感问题的常备回答

近 common, conventional, general, ordinary, prosaic, routine, standard, universal

反 unique 独特的

sectarian [sekˈteriən]

【考法】 *adj.* 狭隘的：**not broad** or open in views or opinions

例 sectarian positions 狭隘的观点

近 illiberal, insular, narrow-minded, parochial, provincial, narrow

反 broad-minded, catholic, cosmopolitan, liberal, open-minded

stodgy [ˈstɑːdʒi]

【考法】 *adj.* 平庸的，乏味的：**dull**, unimaginative, and commonplace

例 a stodgy plot 乏味的情节

近 arid, dreary, dull, flat, jading, jejune, monochromatic, monotonous, pedestrian, stale, tedious, wearisome

反 absorbing, engaging, engrossing, gripping, interesting, intriguing, involving, riveting 吸引人的

派 stodginess *n.* 乏味，无趣

stoke [stoʊk]

【考法】 *vt.* 增大，促进：to **make greater** in size, amount, or number

例 stoke workers' commitment to the company by raising their salaries 通过加薪来提升员工对公司的忠诚度

近 aggrandize, amplify, augment, boost, enlarge, escalate, expand, extend, multiply, raise

反 abate, decrease, diminish, downsize, dwindle, lessen, lower, minify, reduce, subtract 减少

stoic [ˈstoʊɪk]

【考法】 *adj.* 隐忍的，冷静的：seemingly indifferent to or **unaffected by pleasure or pain**

例 stoic resignation in the face of hunger 默默忍受着饥饿

近 aloof, apathetic, detached, forbearing, indifferent, impassive, phlegmatic, stolid, tolerant, unemotional

反 demonstrative, emotional, fervent, fervid, impassioned, passionate, vehement 充满热情的

stolid [ˈstɑːlɪd]

【考法】 *adj.* 无动于衷的，感情麻木的：having or revealing **little emotion** or sensibility

例 Her face showed nothing but stolid indifference. 她的脸上只露出了麻木和冷漠。

近 apathetic, catatonic, deadpan, emotionless, impassive, indifferent, numb, phlegmatic, stoic

反 demonstrative, emotional, fervent, fervid, impassioned, passionate, vehement 充满热情的

派 stolidity *n.* 麻木，无动于衷

stomach	[ˈstʌmək]
【考法】	*vt.* 容忍：to **bear** without overt reaction or resentment
例	I can't stomach his bragging . 我受不了他自吹自擂了。
近	abide, brook, countenance, endure, handle, stand, tolerate
反	decline, refuse, reject, repudiate, spurn 拒绝

stonewall	[ˌstoʊn ˈwɔːl]
【考法】	*v.* 拒绝(合作)，阻挠：to be **uncooperative**, **obstructive**, or evasive
例	lobbying efforts to stonewall passage of the legislation 意在阻止法律通过的游说行动
近	blockade, filibuster, hinder, impede, obstruct
反	collaborate, cooperate 合作

Unit 6

■ STOUTHEARTED	■ STRATAGEM	■ SONOROUS	■ STRAND	■ STRATIFY
■ STRAY	■ STRENUOUS	■ STRIATE	■ STRICTURE	■ SOOTHSAYER

stouthearted	[ˌstaʊt ˈhɑːrtɪd]
【考法】	*adj.* 勇敢的：having a **stout** heart or **spirit**
例	a stouthearted army officer who risked his life to save his men 为了拯救部下宁愿牺牲自己的勇敢军官
近	bold, brave, courageous, dauntless, fearless, gallant, intrepid, stalwart, stout, valiant, valorous
反	cowardly, craven, fearful, gutless, nerveless, pusillanimous, spineless, spiritless, timorous 怯懦的

stratagem	[ˈstrætədʒəm]
【考法】	*n.* 谋略，策略：an artifice or trick in war for **deceiving** and outwitting the enemy
例	deceitful stratagem 有欺骗性的策略
近	artifice, device, gambit, gimmick, intrigue, maneuver, ruse, scheme, trick, wile

sonorous	[ˈsɑːnərəs]
【考法】	*adj.* 声音洪亮的：marked by **conspicuously full and rich** sounds or tones
例	sonorous voice 洪亮的嗓音
近	plangent, resounding, reverberant, resonant, vibrant

strand	[strænd]
【考法】	*vt.* 遗弃，使置于困境：to **leave in a** strange or an **unfavorable place** especially without funds or means to depart
例	The convoy was stranded in the desert . 车队被困在了沙漠之中。
近	abandon, desert, forsake, maroon, quit
反	evacuate, reclaim, rescue 救出

stratify	[ˈstrætɪfaɪ]
【考法】	*vt.* 将…分成各种等级：to **divide into classes**, castes, or social strata
例	Income distribution often stratifies a society . 收入分配往往将社会分层。
近	assort, categorize, classify, differentiate, distinguish, separate
反	homogenize 使均匀；commingle, mingle 混合
派	stratification *n.* 分层化

stray	[streɪ]
【考法】	*adj.* 漫无目的的：**lacking** a definite plan, **purpose**, or pattern
例	a stray dog 一只走失的狗
近	aimless, arbitrary, desultory, erratic, haphazard, scattered, slapdash
反	methodical, orderly, organized, regular 有条理的，有组织的；systematic, systematized 系统性的

strenuous	[ˈstrenjuəs]
【考法1】	*adj.* 有活力的：**vigorously active**
例	strenuous workers 干劲十足的工作人员
近	aggressive, dynamic, energetic, forceful, vigorous
【考法2】	*adj.* 艰巨的，费力的：**requiring considerable** physical or mental **effort**
例	a strenuous task 一项艰巨的任务
近	arduous, challenging, demanding, exacting, formidable, grueling, laborious, severe, toilsome, tough
反	easy, effortless, facile, undemanding 轻松的

striate	['straɪɪt]

【考法】 *vt.* 加条纹：to **mark with striations** or striae

例 The inner surface of the bark is smooth, of a pale, yellowish brown and very finely striated . 树皮的内部十分光滑，显着偏暗偏黄的棕色，并且有着十分精细的条纹。

近 furrow, streak, stripe

派 striated *adj.* 有条纹的

stricture	['strɪktʃər]

【考法】 *n.* 责难，批评：an adverse **criticism**

例 The reviewer made several strictures upon the author's style. 评论家就作者的文风发出了不少责难。

近 censure, condemnation, denunciation, excoriation, obloquy, rebuke, reprimand, reproach, reproof

反 commendation, eulogy 表扬，赞扬

soothsayer	['suːθseɪər]

【考法】 *n.* 预言家：one who **predicts future** events or developments

例 Warren Buffett, billionaire investor and economic soothsayer 沃伦巴菲特，身家亿万的投资者、经济预言家

近 augur, diviner, forecaster, foreteller, prognosticator, prophet, visionary

Unit 7

■ STRIDENT	■ STRIKE	■ STRINGENT	■ STRIP	■ STRUT
■ SPIKE	■ STULTIFY	■ STUPOR	■ STUNT	■ STURDY

strident	['straɪdnt]

【考法】 *adj.* 刺耳的：characterized by **harsh**, insistent, and discordant **sound**

例 plagued by the strident noise 被刺耳的噪声所折磨

近 grating, harsh, hoarse, jarring, rasping, raucous, squawky

反 mellifluous（声音）甜美的；harmonious 和谐的

派 stridence *n.* 喧闹，刺耳

strike	[straɪk]

【考法1】 *n.* 攻击：the act or action of setting upon with **force or violence**

vt. 击打：to aim and usually **deliver a blow**, stroke, or thrust（as with the hand, a weapon, or a tool）

vt. 袭击，攻击：to take sudden, **violent action** against

例 The drunkard angrily struck the security guard . 酒鬼愤怒地殴打保安。|| A rattlesnake strikes its prey with lightning speed. 响尾蛇以惊人的速度攻击了它的猎物。

近 aggression, assault, charge, offense, onset, onslaught, raid, rush; bat, beat, hammer, hit, knock, nail, punch, swat; assail, beset, storm, set on

【考法2】 *vt.* 撞击：to come into usually **forceful contact** with something

例 One bullet-train struck the other one which had been forced to stop on a viaduct due to lightning strike, resulting in huge casualties. 一辆动车撞向了另一辆因雷击而停在高架桥上的动车，造成了巨大的人员伤亡。

近 bang, bash, bump, collide, crash, impact, impinge, ram, slam, smash, swipe, thud

派 striking *adj.* 引人注目的

stringent	['strɪndʒənt]

【考法】 *adj.* 严格的：**marked by rigor**, strictness, or severity especially with regard to rule or standard

例 stringent drug-testing procedures 严格的药检程序

近 draconian, exacting, ironhanded, rigorous, severe, strict, uncompromising

反 lenient 宽大的，仁慈的

strip	[strɪp]

【考法】 *vt.* 脱衣，剥去：to **remove clothing**, covering, or surface matter from

例 Guards stripped and started to search the prisoners . 守卫剥光了犯人，开始搜身。

近 denude, disrobe, doff, unclothe, undress

反 dress, gown, robe 穿衣；bedeck 穿衣打扮

strut	[strʌt]

【考法】 *vi.* 趾高气扬地走：to **walk** with a **pompous** and affected air

例 A pompous general strutted off the parade ground . 盛气凌人的将军从阅兵场上趾高气扬地走过。

近 parade, prance, stalk, swagger

spike	[ˈspaɪk]	

spike [ˈspaɪk]
【考法】 *v.* 激励 : to give life, **vigor**, or spirit to
例 a clumsy attempt to spike rumors of a cabinet split 一个促进内阁分裂的流言的笨拙尝试
近 brace, energize, enliven, invigorate, liven, animate, stimulate, vitalize, vivify
反 damp, dampen, deaden 抑制，减弱

stultify [ˈstʌltɪfaɪ]
【考法】 *vt.* 使无效，抑制 : to deprive of vitality and **render futile** especially by enfeebling or repressive influences
例 The accident stultified his previous efforts . 这场意外使他过去的努力都白费了。
近 constipate, stagnate, stifle, trammel
反 encourage, foster, nourish 鼓励，培养
派 stultifying *adj.* 抑制的

stupor [ˈstuːpər]
【考法】 *n.* 迟钝，麻痹，无知觉 : a condition of greatly dulled or completely **suspended sense** or sensibility
例 The heartbreaking man lapsed into an alcoholic stupor . 那个伤心的男人陷入了无知觉的酒醉状态。
近 coma, dullness, languor, lethargy, lassitude, listlessness, torpidity, torpor
反 alertness, vigilance 警惕，警戒；vigor, vim, vitality, vivacity 活力，精力

stunt [stʌnt]
【考法】 *vt.* 阻碍(成长) : to **hinder** the normal **growth**, development, or progress of
例 The inhospitable climate had stunted all vegetation . 不佳的气候条件抑制了所有植物的生长。
近 check, curb, dwarf, suppress
反 advance, boost, foster, nourish, nurture, promote 培养，促进

sturdy [ˈstɜːrdi]
【考法】 *adj.* 强健的，结实的 : marked by or reflecting physical **strength** or vigor; substantially made or built
例 sturdy young athletes 年轻有力的运动员 ‖ Remember to wear sturdy boots because we will be going over sharp rocks and uneven terrain. 别忘了穿一双靠谱的靴子，因为我们要在锋利的岩石和崎岖的地面上行走。
近 durable, firm, robust, rugged, stalwart, stout, strong, sound, tough, vigorous
反 delicate, feeble, frail, weak, wimpy 脆弱的；rickety, unsound, unstable, unsteady 不稳固的
派 sturdiness *n.* 强健

Unit 8

■ STYGIAN	■ STYMIE	■ SUBDUE	■ SUBJECT	■ SUBJUGATE
■ SUBLIME	■ SUBLIMINAL	■ SUBMERGE	■ SUBMISSIVE	■ SUBORDINATE

stygian [ˈstɪdʒiən]
【考法】 *adj.* 极阴暗的 : **extremely dark**, gloomy, or forbidding
例 the stygian blackness of the cave 山洞里令人恐惧的黑暗
近 black, caliginous, dark, dim, gloomy, pitch-black
反 bright, brilliant, illuminated, illumined, light, lightsome, lucent, lucid, luminous 明亮的

stymie [ˈstaɪmi]
【考法】 *vt.* 阻碍 : to **present an obstacle** to
例 stymied by red tape 被冗长的政策条款所阻碍
近 encumber, fetter, handcuff, handicap, hinder, impede, inhibit, manacle, obstruct, shackle, trammel
反 aid, assist, facilitate, help 帮助，促进
派 stymieing *adj.* 阻碍的

subdue [səbˈduː]
【考法】 *vt.* 使顺从；征服 : to **conquer** and bring into subjection; to bring under one's control by force of arms
例 They subdued the native tribes after years of fighting. 他们经过多年征战终于征服了当地的部落。
近 conquer, defeat, squelch, subjugate, vanquish
反 capitulate, surrender 投降；lose 失败
派 subdued *adj.* 臣服的；柔和的

subject [ˈsʌbdʒekt]
【考法】 *adj.* 取决于(其他因素)的，受制于 : contingent on or **under the influence** of some later action
例 The price of seafood is subject to weather conditions . 海鲜的价格受天气影响。
近 affected, conditional, contingent, dependent, reliant, subordinate
反 independent, unconditional 独立的，无条件的

subjugate	[ˈsʌbdʒugeɪt]
【考法】	*vt.* 征服，镇压：to **bring under control** and governance as a subject
例	subjugate an unruly boy 制服顽童
近	conquer, dominate, overpower, pacify, quash, squelch, subdue, vanquish
反	capitulate, surrender 投降；lose 失败
派	subjugation *n.* 征服

sublime	[səˈblaɪm]
【考法】	*adj.* 崇高的，庄严的：of **high** spiritual, **moral**, or intellectual worth
例	the sublime virtue of having given all one's worldly goods to the poor 将所有财产都捐给穷人的崇高美德
近	chivalrous, elevated, gallant, greathearted, lofty, magnanimous, noble
反	base, debased, degenerate, degraded, ignoble, low 可鄙的

subliminal	[ˌsʌbˈlɪmɪnl]
【考法】	*adj.* 下意识的，潜在意识的：**below** the threshold of conscious **perception**
例	subliminal advertising in movies 电影中的潜意识广告
近	concealed, hidden, subconscious
反	apparent, clear, evident, manifest, obvious, patent 明显的

submerge	[səbˈmɜːrdʒ]
【考法】	*vt.* 使淹没：to put **under water**
例	The river bursted its banks, submerging an entire village. 河水冲上了堤岸，淹没了整个村庄。
近	dip, douse, drench, drown, immerse, inundate, sop, submerse
反	emerge 显现
派	submerged *adj.* 被淹没的

submissive	[səbˈmɪsɪv]
【考法】	*adj.* 服从的，顺从的，恭顺的：**submitting** to others
例	submissive employees 顺服的员工 ‖ It's not in her nature to be submissive. 服从不是她的本性。
近	amenable, biddable, compliant, conformable, docile, obeisant, obsequious, servile, subservient, tractable
反	contumacious, defiant, intractable, obstreperous, rebellious, recalcitrant, refractory, unruly 不顺从的
派	submission *n.* 服从，顺从

subordinate	
【考法 1】	[səˈbɔːrdɪnət] *adj.* 下级的；次要的：belonging to a **lower** or inferior class or **rank**
例	His contention is that environment plays a subordinate role to heredity in determining what we become. 他的观点就是：在决定我们成长的因素——环境和遗传之中，前者处于更次要的地位。
近	inferior, junior, lower, minor, secondary, subject, tributary
反	greater, higher, major, primary, prime, senior, superior 更优等的，更高等的
【考法 2】	[səˈbɔːrdɪneɪt] *vt.* 征服：to bring **under one's control** by force of arms
例	It is one of the lessons of history that more powerful civilizations often subordinate weaker ones. 强大的文明往往征服弱势的文明，这是历史的教训之一。
近	conquer, dominate, overpower, pacify, subdue, subject, subjugate, vanquish
反	capitulate, surrender 投降；lose 失败

Unit 9

■ SUBSERVIENT	■ SUBSIDE	■ SUBSIDIARY	■ SUBSIDY	■ SUBSTANTIAL
■ SUBSTANTIATE	■ SUBSTANTIVE	■ SUBTERFUGE	■ SUBTLE	■ SUBVERT

subservient	[səbˈsɜːrviənt]
【考法】	*adj.* 奉承的，屈从的：**obsequiously** submissive
近	amenable, biddable, compliant, conformable, docile, obeisant, obsequious, servile, submissive, tractable
反	contumacious, defiant, intractable, obstreperous, rebellious, recalcitrant, refractory, unruly 不顺从的
派	subservience *n.* 服从

subside	[səbˈsaɪd]
【考法】	*vi.* 下陷，下沉，减弱：to tend **downward**
例	Local officials say the flood waters have subsided. 当地官员表示洪水已经退去。 ‖ As the noise of the siren subsided, I was able to fall back to sleep. 随着警笛声的减弱，我可以再次睡着了。 ‖ The pain will subside in a couple of hours. 几个小时之内疼痛感就会退去。
近	abate, decline, decrease, diminish, drop, dwindle, ebb, fall, lessen, moderate, recede, wane
反	balloon, burgeon, escalate, expand, grow, increase, intensify, rise, snowball, soar, wax 上升，增大
派	subsidence *n.* 下沉

subsidiary	[səbˈsɪdieri]
【考法】	*adj.* 次要的：of **secondary importance**
例	The river has several subsidiary streams . 这条河拥有数条支流。
近	minor, secondary, subordinate, tributary
反	capital, cardinal, central, chief, key, leading, main, paramount, predominant, primary, principal, supreme 主要的，重要的

subsidy	[ˈsʌbsədi]
【考法】	*n.* 补助金，津贴：**monetary** assistance granted by a government to a person or group in **support** of an enterprise regarded as being in the public interest
例	a timely subsidy 及时的补助金
近	allotment, allowance, appropriation, grant, subvention
派	subsidize *vt.* 提供补助

substantial	[səbˈstænʃl]
【考法】	*adj.* 有重大意义的：**considerable in importance**, value, degree, amount, or extent
例	made a substantial progress 取得了实质性的进展
近	consequential, considerable, earthshaking, important, meaningful, momentous, significant, weighty
反	inconsequential, inconsiderable, insignificant, little, minor, negligible, slight, trifling, trivial 微不足道的

substantiate	[səbˈstænʃieɪt]
【考法】	*vt.* 证实：to **support with proof** or evidence
例	There is little scientific evidence to substantiate the claims . 现在还缺乏足够的科学证据来证实这种言论。
近	attest, authenticate, confirm, corroborate, justify, validate, verify
反	controvert, disprove, rebut, refute 反驳
派	substantiated *adj.* 经证实的

substantive	[səbˈstæntɪv]
【考法】	*adj.* 本质的，关键的：of or **relating to the essence** or substance
例	The substantive information is their political stance. 关键信息是他们的政治立场。
近	constitutional, elemental, essential, fundamental, substantial, vital
反	inconsequential, inconsiderable, insignificant, insubstantial, negligible, nominal 不重要的

subterfuge	[ˈsʌbtərfjuːdʒ]
【考法】	*n.* 诡计：**deception** by artifice or stratagem in order **to conceal**, escape, or evade
例	The spy obtained the documents by subterfuge . 间谍通过狡猾的计谋获得了文件。
近	artifice, cheat, chicanery, deception, fraud, trickery, wile

subtle	[ˈsʌtl]
【考法】	*adj.* 微妙的，难以感知的：(so slight as to be)**difficult** to understand or **perceive**
例	subtle differences in meaning between the words 单词词义之间的细微差别
近	delicate, elusive, evasive, faint, fine, impalpable, intangible, nice, slight
反	blatant, conspicuous, obvious, patent, plain 明显的；open, public 公开的
派	subtlety *n.* 微妙；微妙的想法

subvert	[səbˈvɜːrt]
【考法】	*vt.* 颠覆：to **overturn** or overthrow from the foundation
例	an alleged plot to subvert the state 一个旨在推翻政权的谣传中的阴谋
近	overthrow, overturn, topple
反	reinforce 加强
派	subversion *n.* 颠覆

Unit 10

■ SUCCINCT	■ SUCCOR	■ SUFFOCATE	■ SUFFUSE	■ SULK
■ SULLEN	■ SECULAR	■ SUMMIT	■ SUMMON	■ SUMPTUOUS

succinct	[səkˈsɪŋkt]
【考法】	*adj.* 简明的，简洁的：characterized by **clear**, **precise** expression in few words
例	succinct and perspicacious speech 简洁而一针见血的发言
近	apothegmatic, brief, compact, compendious, concise, laconic, pithy, summary, telegraphic, terse

| 反 | circuitous, circumlocutory, diffuse, long, prolix, rambling, verbose, windy, wordy 冗长的 |
| 派 | succinctness *n.* 简洁，扼要 |

succor [ˈsʌkər]

【考法】 *vt.* 救援，援助：to go to the **aid** of

例 We see it as our duty to succor anyone in need. 我们视帮助他人为自己的职责。

近 aid, assist, help, relieve, support

suffocate [ˈsʌfəkeɪt]

【考法】 *vt.* 使窒息：to **deprive of oxygen**

例 She was suffocated with tension. 她紧张到窒息。

近 asphyxiate, choke, smother, stifle, strangle

派 suffocating *adj.* 令人窒息的，压抑的

suffuse [səˈfjuːz]

【考法】 *vt.* (色彩等)弥漫，染遍，充满：to **spread through** or over, as with liquid, color, or light

例 a room suffused with warm sunlight 一个充满温暖阳光的房间

近 flush, fill, imbue, infuse, interpenetrate, percolate, pervade, transfuse

派 suffusing *adj.* 弥漫的

sulk [sʌlk]

【考法】 *vi.* 生气，愠怒：to be sullenly aloof or withdrawn, as in silent **resentment** or protest

例 He would sulk for hours whenever he didn't get what he wanted. 每当他的愿望没被满足时，他都会生几个小时的闷气。

近 frown, grump, mope, pout

反 crow, delight, exuberate, jubilate, rejoice, triumph 感到高兴，雀跃

派 sulky *adj.* 生气的，不悦的

sullen [ˈsʌlən]

【考法】 *adj.* 闷闷不乐的：causing or marked by an atmosphere **lacking in cheer**

例 She remained sullen amid festivities alone. 她独自一人在喜庆的气氛中闷闷不乐。‖ sullen skies that matched our mood on the day of the funeral 葬礼当天与我们很搭调的沉闷天气

近 bleak, cheerless, dark, depressing, dire, gloomy, glum, gray, lugubrious, morose, saturnine, sulky, surly

反 bright, cheerful, cheering, cordial, festive, gay, lighthearted 欢快的，高兴的

secular [ˈsekjələr]

【考法】 *adj.* 世俗的，尘世的：of or relating to the **worldly or temporal**

例 secular state/perspective 世俗国家/角度

近 carnal, earthborn, earthbound, fleshly, material, mundane, sublunary, temporal, terrene, terrestrial, worldly

反 heavenly, unearthly, unworldly 非尘世间的；spiritual 精神上的；religious 宗教的；clerical 牧师的

summit [ˈsʌmɪt]

【考法】 *n.* 顶点：the **highest point**

例 the summit of his ambition 他雄心壮志的顶点

近 acme, apex, climax, crescendo, crest, crown, culmination, meridian, peak, pinnacle, top, zenith

反 bottom, nadir 最低点

summon [ˈsʌmən]

【考法】 *vt.* 召集，召唤：to **call together**

例 The general summoned all his troops before the operation. 行动之前，将军把所有的部队召集到了一起。

近 assemble, convene, convoke, muster, rally

反 dismiss 解散

sumptuous [ˈsʌmptʃuəs]

【考法】 *adj.* 豪华的，奢侈的：**extremely** costly, rich, **luxurious**, or magnificent

例 The hotel claims to offer sumptuous furnishings and exquisitely prepared cuisine. 酒店宣称有奢华的装潢和精心准备的食物。

近 deluxe, lavish, lush, luxurious, opulent, palatial, resplendent, splendid, superb

反 ascetic, austere, humble, spartan 简朴的

List 25

"面对辞藻堆砌的高峰，我们不应因身处词汇匮乏的谷底而绝望，征服都是从脚下开始的。"
（姚佳雄，Verbal 700，Quantitative 800，AW4.5，
录取院校：Johns Hopkins University）

Unit 1

■ SUNDER	■ SUPERCILIOUS	■ SUPERFICIAL	■ SUPERFLUOUS	■ STAGNANT
■ SUPINE	■ SUPPLE	■ SUPPLANT	■ SUPPLEMENT	■ SUPPLICATE

sunder [ˈsʌndər]
【考法】 *vt.* 分裂，分离：to **break apart** or in two
例 a city sundered by racial conflict 一个因种族冲突而分裂的城市
近 disassociate, disconnect, disjoin, disunite, divide, part, rend, rive, separate, sever, unyoke
反 bond, connect, join, link, unify, unite, yoke 连接，结合
派 asunder *adv.* 开开地，分裂地

supercilious [ˌsuːpərˈsɪliəs]
【考法】 *adj.* 高傲的，傲慢的：feeling or showing **haughty** disdain
例 a supercilious lady 傲慢的女人
近 arrogant, assumptive, bumptious, haughty, imperious, pompous, presumptuous, overbearing, superior
反 humble, moderate, modest 谦逊的

superficial [ˌsuːpərˈfɪʃl]
【考法】 *adj.* 表面的，肤浅的：**lacking** in **depth**, solidity, and comprehensiveness
例 The official's superficial report on the situation provoked wide blame on the Internet. 官员对于情况的敷衍陈述激起了网络上的广泛谴责。
近 cursory, facile, perfunctory, shallow, sketchy, skin-deep
反 profound 深刻的；comprehensive, exhaustive 全面的
派 superficiality *n.* 表面现象

superfluous [suːˈpɜːrfluəs]
【考法】 *adj.* 多余的，过剩的：**exceeding** what is **sufficient** or necessary
例 a complicated algorithm that could filter all superfluous information 一个能滤除所有多余信息的复杂算法
近 excessive, extra, redundant, surplus
反 deficient, inadequate, insufficient, scanty, scarce, short, skimpy, sparse 不足的
派 superfluity *n.* 多余，过剩

stagnant [ˈstægnənt]
【考法】 *adj.* 停滞不前的：**not advancing** or developing
例 a stagnant economy 停滞不前的经济

supine [ˈsuːpaɪn]
【考法】 *adj.* 懒散的，倦怠的，消极的，漠不关心的：showing **lethargy**, passivity, or blameworthy **indifference**
例 a supine legislature that is afraid to take action 害怕采取行动的不作为的立法机关
近 inert, passive, dormant, torpid
反 vigilant 警惕的

supple [ˈsʌpl]
【考法】 *adj.* 易弯曲的，柔软的：readily **bent**; **pliant**
例 supple limbs 柔软的四肢 ‖ a supple mind 灵活的头脑
近 bendy, flexible, limber, lissome, lithe, pliable, pliant, lithesome
反 inflexible, stiff, rigid 坚硬的
派 suppleness *n.* 柔软

supplant [səˈplænt]

【考法】 *vt.* 排挤，篡夺…的位置: to **usurp the place of**, especially through intrigue or underhanded tactics

例 Old traditions were fading away and being supplanted by modern ways . 老传统逐渐式微，被现代方式所取代。

近 displace, displant, substitute, supersede, cut out

supplement [ˈsʌplɪmənt]

【考法】 *n./v.* 增补，补充: something that serves to **complete** or make up **for a deficiency** in something else

例 The handout is a supplement to the official manual. 这本分发的印刷品是官方手册的补充。

近 addendum, addition, expansion, increment, proliferation, step-up

supplicate [ˈsʌplɪkeɪt]

【考法】 *v.* 恳求，乞求: to **make a request** to (someone) in an **earnest or urgent** manner

例 She supplicated the judge for protection . 她恳请法官保护。

近 beseech, conjure, entreat, impetrate, implore, solicit, plead to, appeal to

反 demand 强求

Unit 2

■ SUPPOSITION　　　■ SUPPRESS　　　■ SURCHARGE　　　■ SURFEIT　　　■ SURRENDER
■ SURREPTITIOUS　　■ SUSCEPTIBLE　　■ SUSPEND　　　■ SUTURE　　　■ SVELTE

supposition [ˌsʌpəˈzɪʃn]

【考法】 *n.* 猜想，推测: an opinion or judgment based on **little or no evidence**

例 It's pure supposition on your part that there's something illegal going on next door. 你说隔壁在进行非法勾当纯属猜测。

近 hypothesis, proposition, surmise, premise, presumption

反 certainty 确定

suppress [səˈpres]

【考法 1】 *vt.* 用暴力终止，镇压: to **put a stop to** (something) by the use of **force**

例 Nothing could suppress the rising tide of protest . 任何事物都无法控制越来越激烈的游行示威活动。

近 clamp down on, crack down on, put down, quash, repress, silence, slap down, snuff out, squash, squelch, subdue

【考法 2】 *v.* 封锁，删除: to deliberately **exclude** (unacceptable desires or thoughts) from the mind

例 suppress the information 封锁消息

近 censor, clean, expurgate

surcharge [ˈsɜːrtʃɑːrdʒ]

【考法】 *v./n.* 过高收费: to **charge** (someone) too **much** for goods or services

例 The airline has added a $30 fuel surcharge on all international flights. 该航空公司对所有国际航线上涨了 30 美元的燃油税。

近 gouge, soak, sting

surfeit [ˈsɜːrfɪt]

【考法】 *v./n.* (使)过量，(使)饮食过度: to feed or **supply** to **excess**

例 He surfeited himself with chocolate 他巧克力吃多了。

近 overabundance, overage, overflow, plethora, redundancy, superfluity, surplus

反 deficiency, deprivation, insufficient supply, famish, starve 短缺，匮乏

surrender [səˈrendər]

【考法】 *vt.* 交出，放弃，投降: to **give** (something) **over to** the control or possession of another usually under duress

例 surrender a contractual right 放弃契约上规定的一项权利

近 abnegate, cede, relinquish, renounce, resign

反 appropriate 挪用，占为己有

surreptitious [ˌsɜːrəpˈtɪʃəs]

【考法】 *adj.* 偷偷摸摸的，保密的: undertaken or done so as to **escape being observed** or known by others

例 He took a surreptitious glance at her knees. 他偷偷瞟了一下她的膝盖。

近 backstairs, clandestine, covert, furtive, privy, underground, underhanded, behind-the-scenes

反 barefaced, aboveboard, open, overt, public 光明正大的

susceptible	[səˈseptəbl]

【考法】 *adj.* 容易受伤害的: being in a situation where one is **likely to meet with harm**

例 Some people are more susceptible to depression during the winter . 一些人更容易在冬天受到沮丧情绪的影响。

近 endangered, exposed, sensitive, subject, vulnerable

反 insusceptible, invulnerable, unexposed, unsusceptible 不受影响的

suspend	[səˈspend]

【考法】 *vi.* 暂停，中止: to **bring to a formal close** for a period of time

例 suspend the trial 暂停审判

近 prorogue, recess

反 invoke 实行

suture	[ˈsuːtʃər]

【考法】 *n./v.* 缝合: the process of **joining** two surfaces or edges together along a line by or as if by sewing

例 The doctor sutured the wound . 医生将伤口缝合。

反 incision, avulse 切开，撕脱

svelte	[svelt]

【考法】 *adj.* (女人)体态苗条的，优雅的: slender or graceful in figure or outline; **slim**

例 The svelte dancer seemed to float across the stage. 苗条的舞者看起来就像轻盈地漂浮在舞台上。

近 bony, lean, skinny, slender, slim

反 plump, corpulent, paunchy and awkward 丰满的，大腹便便而笨拙的

Unit 3

■ SWAGGER	■ SWEAR	■ SWELTERING	■ SWERVE	■ STERLING
■ SWINDLE	■ SYBARITE	■ SYCOPHANT	■ SYLLABUS	■ SYLLOGISM

swagger	[ˈswæɡər]

【考法】 *vi.* 自夸，吹嘘: to **boast**, brag

例 I would swagger if I'd won first place in the bowling tournament. 如果我赢得保龄球锦标赛的冠军，我肯定会自夸。

近 brag, vapor, vaunt, gasconade

swear	[swer]

【考法 1】 *vi.* 咒骂: to use profane or obscene language: **curse**

例 No one is allowed to swear in this house . 这个房间里禁止说脏话。

近 blaspheme, curse, cuss

反 accolade 赞美

【考法 2】 *v.* 宣誓: to promise or pledge with a solemn **oath**; vow

例 He swore his oath of allegiance to the queen. 他宣誓效忠女王。

近 attest, depose, covenant, pledge, vow

sweltering	[ˈsweltərɪŋ]

【考法】 *adj.* 酷热的: oppressively **hot**

例 a sweltering summer 酷热夏季

近 boiling, scorching, searing, sultry, torrid, fiery

反 algid, arctic, bone-chilling, freezing, frigid, frozen, glacial, ice-cold, iced, icy 严寒的

swerve	[swɜːrv]

【考法】 *vi.* 突然改变方向: to **turn aside abruptly** from a straight line or course

例 The car swerved sharply to avoid the squirrel in the road. 为了避开路上的松鼠，汽车猛地转向。

近 detour, deviate, diverge, sheer, swing, veer

反 maintain direction, straighten 保持方向，直行

sterling	[ˈstɜːrlɪŋ]

【考法】 *adj.* 优秀的: of the very **best kind**

例 Those are sterling qualities to be admired in anyone. 那些优秀品质在任何人身上都值得称道。

近 awesome, fabulous, fantastic, first-class, noble, splendid, excellent, superb, superlative, wonderful

反 atrocious, awful, execrable, poor, terrible, vile, wretched 极差的

swindle	['swɪndl]
【考法】	*vt.* 欺骗，骗取：to **cheat** or defraud of money or property
例	Hundreds of people were swindled out of their savings . 几百人都被骗去了存款。
近	bilk, con, hustle, fiddle, gyp, bunco, flimflam
sybarite	['sɪbəraɪt]
【考法】	*n.* 沉溺于奢侈逸乐者，酒色之徒：a person **devoted** to pleasure and **luxury**; a voluptuary
例	The prince was remembered as a self-indulgent sybarite . 王子酒色之徒的名声远扬。
近	debauchee, decadent, hedonist, sensualist
反	spartan, ascetic 禁欲者
sycophant	['sɪkəfænt]
【考法】	*n.* 马屁精：a servile self-seeking **flatterer**
例	When her career was riding high, the self-deluded actress often mistook sycophants for true friends . 当这位演员的事业如日中天之时，她常常把一些马屁精误以为真朋友。
近	fawner, flunky, lickspittle, toady, apple-polisher, bootlicker, brownnoser
syllabus	['sɪləbəs]
【考法】	*n.* 提纲，摘要；课文、演讲或研究课题的概要或提纲：an outline or a **summary** of the main points of a text, lecture, or course of study
例	Have you got next year's syllabus ? 你拿到明年的教学大纲了吗？
syllogism	['sɪlədʒɪzəm]
【考法】	*n.* 由一般到个别的推理，演绎：**reasoning** from the general to the specific; **deduction**
例	form a syllogism 形成演绎
派	syllogize *v.* 用三段论论证

Unit 4

■ SYMBIOSIS	■ SYMMETRY	■ SYNCHRONOUS	■ SYNERGIC	■ SYNONYMOUS
■ SYNOPSIS	■ SYNTHESIS	■ TACIT	■ TACITURN	■ TACKLE

symbiosis	[ˌsɪmbaɪ'oʊsɪs]
【考法】	*n.* 共生关系：the **living together** in more or less intimate association or close union of two dissimilar
例	The bird lives in symbiosis with the hippopotamus . 这种鸟和河马是共生关系。
反	unrelated growth 无关联的生长
symmetry	['sɪmətri]
【考法】	*n.* 对称：**balanced proportions**
例	The building has perfect symmetry . 这栋房子是完美的对称构造。
近	balance, coherence, consonance, proportion
反	disproportion, asymmetry, discordance, disproportion, disunity, imbalance, incoherence, violence 不均衡，混乱
synchronous	['sɪŋkrənəs]
【考法】	*adj.* 同时期的，同步的：having **identical period** and **phase**
例	synchronous discharger 同步放电器
近	coetaneous, coeval, coexistent, concurrent, contemporaneous, simultaneous
反	occurring at different times, noncontemporaneous, out-of-phase 发生在不同时代的
synergic	[sɪ'nɜːrdʒɪk]
【考法】	*adj.* 合作的，1+1>2 的：working together：**cooperating**
例	synergic muscles 协同肌肉
反	antagonistic 敌对的
synonymous	[sɪ'nɑːnɪməs]
【考法】	*adj.* 同义的：having the **same** or a **similar meaning**
例	Paris has always been synonymous with elegance , luxury and style. 巴黎在人们心中就是优雅、奢侈和时尚的同义词。

synopsis	[sɪ'nɑːpsɪs]
【考法】	*n.* 摘要，概要：a brief **outline** or general view; an **abstract** or a **summary**
例	Just give me a synopsis of the movie. 把电影的大致情节给我说说就行。
近	abstract, brief, digest, recapitulation, roundup, summarization, epitome

synthesis	['sɪnθəsɪs]
【考法】	*n.* 合成，综合：the **combination** of parts or elements so as to form a whole
例	a philosophy that is a kind of synthesis of several schools of Western and Eastern thought 哲学是东西方很多思想流派的综合
近	admixture, alloy, amalgamation, compound, conflation, fusion, meld
反	analysis, taking apart 分解

tacit	['tæsɪt]
【考法】	*adj.* 暗示的：**implied** or indicated (as by an act or by silence) but **not actually expressed**
例	tacit consent 默许
近	implied, unexpressed, unspoken, unvoiced, wordless
反	explicit, express, expressed, spoken, stated, voiced 明确表达的，直率的

taciturn	['tæsɪtɜːrn]
【考法】	*adj.* 沉默寡言的，话少的：temperamentally **disinclined to talk**
例	A taciturn man never initiates a conversation. 一个寡言的人从不主动和人说话。
近	laconic, reserved, reticent, tight-lipped, uncommunicative
反	garrulous, loquacious, glib, expansive, prolix, voluble 多话的

tackle	['tækl]
【考法】	*vt.* 着手处理：to **start work** on energetically
例	Once I clean the kitchen, I think I'll tackle the bathroom. 等我把厨房打扫干净了，就去收拾浴室。
近	dive into, wade in

Unit 5

■ TACT	■ TACTILE	■ TACTLESS	■ TILT	■ TAINT
■ TAMPER	■ TANGENT	■ TANGIBLE	■ TANGY	■ TANTALIZE

tact	[tækt]
【考法】	*n.* 机敏，精明，不冒犯：a **keen sense** of what to do or say in order to **maintain good relations** with others or avoid offense
例	She talked to her neighbor with supreme tact. 她和邻居说话十分圆滑。
近	diplomacy
反	clumsiness, insensitivity, tactlessness 笨拙

tactile	['tæktl]
【考法】	*adj.* 有触觉的，能触知的：perceptible by **touch**: **tangible**
例	The thick brushstrokes give the painting a tactile quality. 粘稠的笔触给了这幅画一种厚实的感觉。

tactless	['tæktləs]
【考法】	*adj.* 不机智的，笨拙的：bluntly **inconsiderate** or **indiscreet**
例	a tactless remark/manner 不明智的言论/行为
近	graceless, ill-advised, imprudent, indelicate, injudicious, undiplomatic
反	advisable, discreet, judicious, prudent, tactful, wise 小心谨慎的，明智的

tilt	[tɪlt]
【考法 1】	*v.* 倾斜：to set or cause to be **at an angle**
例	The mirrors are controlled by an electrical signal that causes it to tilt either toward or away from the laser source. 电信号控制着这组镜片，使其转向或者远离激光光源。
近	angle, cant, heel, list, incline, pitch, slant, slope, tip
反	erect 竖立
【考法 2】	*n.* 倾斜：the act of positioning or an instance of **being positioned at an angle**
例	She expressed her approval with a slight tilt of her head. 她斜着头，表达她的认可。
近	bend, grade, gradient, inclination, lean, leaning

taint	[teɪnt]
【考法】	*vt.* 使(品质)污损: to affect slightly with something **morally bad** or undesirable
例	taint sb.'s reputation 玷污某人名誉
近	blemish, darken, mar, spoil, tarnish, vitiate
派	tainted *adj.* 污损的
反	pristine, unspoiled, wholesome, unadulterated 纯洁的，健全的

tamper	[ˈtæmpər]
【考法】	*v.* 恶意窜改，损害: to handle thoughtlessly, ignorantly, or **mischievously**
例	tamper with tradition 坏了规矩
近	diddle with, fiddle with, fool with, mess with

tangent	[ˈtændʒənt]
【考法】	*n./adj.* 离题(的)，不相关(的): diverging from an original purpose of course: **irrelevant**
例	tangent remarks 不相关的评论
近	excursive, digressive
反	essential 重要的

tangible	[ˈtændʒəbl]
【考法】	*adj.* 可感知的: **capable** of being **perceived**
例	tangible property/material benefits/art 有形的财产/物质利益/艺术
近	palpable, touchable
反	impalpable, intangible, unable to perceive 无法感知的

tangy	[ˈtæŋi]
【考法】	*adj.* 刺激的: having a **powerfully stimulating** odor or flavor
例	a tangy sauce with a strong aftertaste 味道刺激的酱料，回味无穷
近	pungent, strong
反	bland, mild, smooth 不刺激的

tantalize	[ˈtæntəlaɪz]
【考法】	*vt.* 激起，挑逗，引诱: to **excite** (another) by exposing something desirable while keeping it out of reach
例	tantalize sb. 挑逗某人
反	comfort, console, solace, alleviate, assuage, relieve, satiate 安慰，缓和

Unit 6

■ TANTAMOUNT	■ TANTRUM	■ TAPER	■ TARDY	■ TARNISH
■ TASTY	■ TATTY	■ TAUNT	■ TAUT	■ TAWDRY

tantamount	[ˈtæntəmaʊnt]
【考法】	*adj.* 等价的，与…相等的: **equivalent** in value, significance, or effect
例	a relationship tantamount to marriage 到了谈婚论嫁地步的关系
反	incommensurate 不相称的

tantrum	[ˈtæntrəm]
【考法】	*n.* 勃然大怒，发脾气: a fit of **bad temper**
例	have a tantrum 大发脾气
近	blowup, explosion, fit
反	pacification 平静

taper	[ˈteɪpər]
【考法】	*v.* 逐渐减少，减弱: to **diminish** or lessen **gradually**
例	The storm finally tapered off. 风暴逐渐平静下来。
近	subside, die down, phase down, fall away, let up

tardy	[ˈtɑːrdi]
【考法】	*adj.* 缓慢的，迟缓的: moving **slowly**: sluggish
例	He was tardy to work. 他做事拖拖拉拉。
近	crawling, creeping, dallying, dawdling, dilatory, dragging, lagging, languid, sluggish
反	bolting, brisk, fleet, flying, meteoric, rocketing, scooting, scudding, scurrying, swift, whirling 迅速的

tarnish ['tɑːrnɪʃ]

【考法】 *vt.* 玷污: to affect slightly with something **morally bad** or undesirable

例 An arrest for shoplifting tarnished her reputation . 因在商店行窃被捕玷污了她的名誉。

近 blemish, mar, stain, vitiate

tasty ['teɪsti]

【考法】 *adj.* 美味的；令人愉悦的: giving **pleasure or contentment** to the mind or senses

例 the tasty prospect of getting his revenge 他报仇成功的诱人前景

近 agreeable, delectable, delightful, satisfying, savory

反 uninteresting, disagreeable, unpalatable, unpleasant, unwelcome 无趣的，令人失望的

tatty ['tæti]

【考法】 *adj.* 破旧的，褴褛的: somewhat worn, **shabby**, or dilapidated

例 a tatty shirt 破旧的衬衣

近 dilapidated, scruffy, seedy, sleazy, tatterdemalion, threadbare

反 smart 整洁漂亮的

taunt [tɔːnt]

【考法】 *vt.* 嘲弄性质疑，挑衅: to reproach or **challenge** in a mocking or insulting manner: **jeer at**

例 The boys continually taunted each other . 男孩子们不断互相挑衅。

近 bait, hassle, haze, heckle, needle, ride

taut [tɔːt]

【考法】 *adj.* 紧绷的: **not loose** or flabby

例 taut muscles 紧实的肌肉

反 lax, loose, slack 松弛的

tawdry ['tɔːdri]

【考法】 *adj.* 俗丽的，花哨而庸俗的: cheap and **gaudy** in appearance or quality; ignoble

例 a tawdry attempt to smear his opponent 企图污蔑对手的下三滥的手段

近 meretricious, gaudy, flashy, garish

反 exquisite 高雅的

Unit 7

| ■ TAXING | ■ TEDIOUS | ■ TEETER | ■ TEETOTALISM | ■ TELLING |
| ■ TEMERITY | ■ TEMPORIZE | ■ TEMPERATE | ■ TEMPESTUOUS | ■ TENABLE |

taxing ['tæksɪŋ]

【考法】 *adj.* 繁重的，费力的: **requiring much time**, **effort**, or careful attention

例 a taxing journey/plan/task 艰辛的旅途/计划/任务

近 arduous, burdensome, exacting, grueling, laborious, onerous, toilsome

反 light, easy 轻快的

tedious ['tiːdiəs]

【考法】 *adj.* 冗长乏味的: **tiresome** because of length or **dullness**: **boring**

例 a tedious public ceremony 冗长无聊的公开仪式

近 drab, dreary, jading, monotonous, stale, stodgy, stuffy, weary, drudging

反 entertaining, absorbing, stimulating, engaging, engrossing, gripping, interesting, intriguing, involving, riveting 令人愉快的，吸引人的

teeter ['tiːtər]

【考法 1】 *vi.* 蹒跚，不稳定地行走: to move **unsteadily**: wobble

例 She teetered down the street in her high heels. 她穿着高跟鞋，摇摇晃晃地沿街走着。

近 careen, dodder, lurch, reel

反 stabilize 使…稳固

【考法 2】 *vi.* 犹豫不决: to show **uncertainty** about the right course of action

例 He was teetering on the brink of making a decision about college. 他正在为选择哪所大学而犹豫不决。

近 balance, dither, falter, hang back, scruple, shilly-shally, stagger, vacillate, waver, wobble

反 dive in, plunge in 积极做

teetotalism	[ˌtiːˈtoʊtlɪzəm]
【考法】	*n.* 禁酒：the principle or practice of complete **abstinence** from **alcoholic** drinks
反	intemperance 饮酒过度

telling	[ˈtelɪŋ]
【考法】	*adj.* 有效的，显著的：**effective**, expressive
例	the most telling evidence 最有力的证据
近	compelling, conclusive, convincing, forceful, persuasive, satisfying
反	inconclusive, indecisive, ineffective, uncompelling, unconvincing, unpersuasive 无效的

temerity	[təˈmerəti]
【考法】	*n.* 鲁莽，冒失：**foolhardy** disregard of danger; **recklessness**
例	She was punished for her temerity. 她因冒失吃到了苦头。
近	audacity, brashness, presumption, presumptuousness
反	circumspection, cautious approach, pusillanimity 谨慎

temporize	[ˈtempəraɪz]
【考法】	*vi.* 行动躲躲闪闪以争取时间、躲避争论等，打哈哈：to **act evasively** in order to gain time, avoid argument, or postpone a decision
例	temporize between two parties 两党间的妥协

temperate	[ˈtempərət]
【考法】	*adj.* (言行举止) 有分寸的：**avoiding extremes** in behavior or expression
	adj. 有节制的：given to or marked by **restraint** in the satisfaction of one's appetites
例	He is rather temperate in his appraisal of the movie, calling it good but not great. 他对这部电影的赞赏很适度，说其"还好"而不是"很棒"。 ‖ temperate manner/criticism/language 有分寸的行为/批评/语言
近	abstentious, abstinent, continent, self-abnegating, self-denying, sober
反	immoderate, extreme, frivolous 极端的；self-indulgent 放纵的

tempestuous	[temˈpestʃuəs]
【考法】	*adj.* 突然的，剧烈的：marked by **sudden or violent** disturbance
例	In terms of social change, the 1960s are generally considered the most tempestuous decade in recent American history. 就社会变革来说，20世纪60年代是近现代美国历史上最动荡的十年。
近	cataclysmal, tumultuous, turbulent
反	serene 平静的

tenable	[ˈtenəbl]
【考法】	*adj.* 有据可依的，无懈可击的：**capable** of being held or **defended**; **reasonable**
例	a tenable theory 一个站得住脚的理论 ‖ a tenable outpost 一个守得住的前哨
近	defendable, justifiable, maintainable, supportable, sustainable
反	unjustified, unsound, specious, indefensible, fallacious 不合理的

Unit 8

■ TENACIOUS	■ TENDENTIOUS	■ TENDER	■ TENUOUS	■ TEPID
■ TERMINOLOGY	■ TERMINUS	■ TRAUMATIC	■ TERSE	■ TESTIMONY

tenacious	[təˈneɪʃəs]
【考法】	*adj.* 顽固的，不屈不挠的：**persistent** in maintaining something valued or habitual
例	a tenacious advocate of civil rights 公民权利的坚定捍卫者
近	dogged, insistent, persevering, pertinacious
反	negotiable, vacillated 可商量的，踌躇的

tendentious	[tenˈdenʃəs]
【考法】	*adj.* 有偏见的：marked by a tendency in favor of a particular point of view: **biased**
例	He made some extremely tendentious remarks. 他的一些评论颇具偏向性。
近	partial, distorting, subjective, biased
反	unbiased, unprejudiced 公平的

tender	[ˈtendər]
【考法1】	*vt.* 正式提出：to **offer** formally
例	tender a letter of resignation 正式提交辞职信
近	extend, proffer, trot out
反	withdraw 撤回

【考法 2】 *adj.* 考虑周到的，关心同情的: having or marked by **sympathy** and **consideration** for others

例 an especially tender teacher who loves having kids with special educational needs in her class 特别无微不至的老师，爱着那些需要特别教育的孩子们

近 beneficent, benevolent, benignant, compassionate, softhearted

反 atrocious, barbarous, bestial, brutal, callous, cruel, fiendish, inhuman, insensate, sadistic, savage, truculent, uncompassionate, vicious 尖酸刻薄的

tenuous [ˈtenjuəs]

【考法】 *adj.* 没有实际内容的，空洞的: having **little substance**; flimsy

例 a tenuous argument 站不住脚的论点

反 substantial 实质的

tepid [ˈtepɪd]

【考法】 *adj.* 不太热心的: showing **little or no interest** or enthusiasm

例 a tepid response 冷漠的回应 ‖ the tepid conservatism of the fifties 五十年代那种温和的保守主义

近 lukewarm, halfhearted, uneager, unenthusiastic

反 ardent, ebullient, feverish, keen, passionate, wholehearted 热心的

terminology [ˌtɜːrməˈnɑːlədʒi]

【考法】 *n.* 专业术语: the **special terms or expressions** of a particular group or field

例 the terminology favored by sportscasters 体育节目转播员喜欢用的那些术语 ‖ medical terminology that can be hard for the patient to understand 那些病人们难以理解的医学术语

近 argot, cant, dialect, jargon, jive, lingo, patois, patter, slang

terminus [ˈtɜːrmɪnəs]

【考法】 *n.* 终点，终点站: the final point; the **end**

例 Stockholm is the terminus for the southbound train. 斯德哥尔摩是向南去的列车的终点站。

反 outset, sustain 开始，持续

traumatic [trɑʊˈmætɪk]

【考法】 *adj.* 造成创伤的，痛苦的: something shocking and upsetting, and may **cause psychological damage**

例 a traumatic experience 一次痛苦的经历

terse [tɜːrs]

【考法】 *adj.* 简洁的，简明的: **brief** and to the point; effectively concise

例 terse statement/style/manner 简洁的声明/风格/行为

近 compact, compendious, laconic, pithy, succinct

反 circuitous, circumlocutory, diffuse, long-winded, prolix, rambling, verbose, windy, wordy 冗长啰嗦的

testimony [ˈtestɪmoʊni]

【考法】 *n.* 证词，声明: firsthand **authentication** of a fact

例 The jury heard 10 days of testimony. 陪审团进行了 10 天的听证。

近 attestation, confirmation, documentation, substantiation, testament, validation

反 disproof 反驳

Unit 9

■ TESTY	■ TETHER	■ THEATRICAL	■ THERAPEUTIC	■ THORNY
■ THREADBARE	■ THRONG	■ THWART	■ TICKLISH	■ TIFF

testy [ˈtesti]

【考法】 *adj.* 易怒的，暴躁的: **easily annoyed**: irritable

例 testy taxi driver/teacher 暴躁的出租车司机/老师

近 choleric, irascible, peevish, perverse, pettish, petulant

反 affable, good humor, unable to irritate, imperturbable, patient 和蔼可亲的，冷静的，有耐心的

tether [ˈteðər]

【考法】 *vt.* (用绳、铁链)拴系，束缚: to **fasten** or **restrain** by or as if by a tether

例 They tethered the horses in the shade. 他们把马拴在棚子里。

反 detach, tear loose 分开，撕裂

theatrical [θiˈætrɪkl]

【考法】 *adj.* 做作的，夸张的，矫揉造作的: marked by **exaggerated** self-display and **unnatural** behavior

例 assume a theatrical pose 摆出夸张的姿势

近 dramatic, histrionic, melodramatic, stagy

反 natural, understated, reserved, restraint 自然的，保留的

therapeutic [ˌθerəˈpjuːtɪk]

【考法】 *adj.* 治疗的，有疗效的: of or relating to the **treatment** of **disease** or disorders by remedial agents or methods

例 Gentle exercise can be therapeutic for hospital patients . 适量的运动对病人恢复有好处。

近 curative, healing, officinal, remedial, restorative

thorny [ˈθɔːrni]

【考法】 *adj.* 棘手的: full of **difficulties** or controversial points: ticklish

例 a thorny problem 棘手的问题

近 catchy, delicate, knotty, prickly, ticklish

threadbare [ˈθredber]

【考法】 *adj.* 陈腐的: overused to the point of being worn out; **hackneyed**

例 a novel filled with nothing but threadbare clichés 一部满是陈词滥调的小说

近 banal, cliché, commonplace, hackney, shopworn, trite

throng [θrɔːŋ]

【考法】 *v./n.* 大量聚集: to **crowd** together **in great numbers**

例 a throng of questions 大量问题

近 flock, mob, swarm

thwart [θwɔːrt]

【考法】 *vt.* 阻挠: to **oppose** successfully

例 She did all she could to thwart his plans . 她竭尽所能阻挠他的计划。

近 baffle, balk, checkmate, discomfit

反 advance, cultivate, encourage, forward, foster, further, nurture, promote, support, aid, bolster, abet, foment, facilitate 促进，支持

ticklish [ˈtɪklɪʃ]

【考法1】 *adj.* 易怒的: **easily offended** or upset; touchy

例 ticklish cabdriver/teacher/bess 易怒的出租车司机/教师/老板

近 huffy, tetchy, thin-skinned

反 imperturbable 镇静的

【考法2】 *adj.* 棘手的，对技巧要求高的: requiring **exceptional skill or caution** in performance or handling

例 Trying to tell him that his zipper is down without embarrassing him will be a ticklish task . 如何体面得体地提醒他拉链没关好是一个技巧活儿。

近 catchy, delicate, difficult, dodgy, knotty, prickly, problematic, sensitive, spiny, sticky, thorny, touchy, tough, tricksy

tiff [tɪf]

【考法】 *n./v.* 小争吵: a **petty quarrel**

例 The couple got into a little tiff about what color sheets to buy for their bed. 夫妇俩对于买什么颜色的床单争吵起来。

近 altercate, bicker, brabble, hassle, quarrel, quibble, row, scrap, spat, squabble

Unit 10

■ TIGHTFISTED	■ TIMEWORN	■ TIMID	■ TIMOROUS	■ TINGE
■ TINKER	■ TRUISM	■ TIRADE	■ TOADY	■ TONIC

tightfisted [ˈtaɪtˌfɪstɪd]

【考法】 *adj.* 吝啬的: close-fisted; **stingy**

例 tightfisted employer/boss 吝啬的雇主/老板

近 mean, miserly, parsimonious, penurious, sparing, stinting

反 bounteous, bountiful, charitable, freehanded, generous, liberal, munificent, openhanded, unsparing, unstinting 慷慨大方的

timeworn ['taɪmˌwɔːrn]

【考法】 *adj.* 陈腐的：**hackneyed**, stale

例 timeworn jokes 老掉牙的笑话

近 banal, cliché, commonplace, hackneyed, stereotyped, threadbare, trite

反 fresh, new, novel, original, unclichéd, unhackneyed 新奇的

timid ['tɪmɪd]

【考法】 *adj.* 胆小的，不自信的：**lacking** in **courage** or **self-confidence**

例 He gave her a timid smile. 他给了她一个羞赧的微笑。

近 fainthearted, fearsome, scary, timorous, tremulous

反 stalwart, adventurous, audacious, bold, daring, dashing, gutsy, venturous 坚定勇敢的

timorous ['tɪmərəs]

【考法】 *adj.* 胆小的：of a timid disposition: **fearful**

例 timorous voice/rabbit 胆小的声音/兔子

近 timid, undaring, quailing, recoiling, scary, skittish

反 stalwart, intrepid, adventurous, audacious, bold, daring, dashing, gutsy, venturous 大胆的

tinge [tɪndʒ]

【考法】 *vt.* 给…着上少量的色彩：to **color** with a slight shade or stain: **tint**

例 Just slightly tinge the frosting with yellow food coloring to give it a lemony look. 略微在霜糖表面加一点黄色色素，有一点柠檬的感觉就可以了。

近 dye, pigment, stain, tincture, tint, suffuse

反 decolorize 使脱色

tinker ['tɪŋkər]

【考法】 *v.* 乱修，乱调整：to handle **thoughtlessly**, ignorantly, or mischievously

例 tinker with the engine 胡乱调整发动机

近 diddle with, fiddle with, fool with, mess with, toy with, twiddle with

反 adjust, repair 调整，修理

truism ['truːɪzəm]

【考法】 *n.* 陈词滥调：an idea or expression that has been **used by many people**

例 the truism that nothing succeeds like success "一事成功百事顺"的陈词滥调

近 banality, bromide, cliché, platitude, commonplace, trope

tirade ['taɪreɪd]

【考法】 *n.* 长篇抨击性演讲：a long **angry** or violent speech, usually of a **censorious or denunciatory** nature; a diatribe

例 a tirade of angry protest 一个表达愤怒的抗议的长篇抨击性演讲

近 harangue, diatribe, jeremiad, philippic, rant

反 eulogy, encomium, panegyric, tribute 颂词

toady ['toʊdi]

【考法】 *n./v.* 马屁精；拍马屁：one who **flatters** in the hope of **gaining favors**

例 He criticized that I was a toady. 他批评说我是一个马屁精。

近 sycophant, groveler, flatterer

tonic ['tɑːnɪk]

【考法】 *adj.* 滋补的，有益健康的：producing or **stimulating** physical, mental, or emotional **vigor**; **beneficial** to the health of body or mind

例 tonic medicine 补药

近 medicinal, restorative, salubrious, salutary, salutiferous, sanative, wholesome

反 insalubrious, noxious, unhealthful, unhealthy, unwholesome 不健康的

List 26

"若干年前，有人跟我说，没有GRE的人生是不完整的。现在我跟别人说，没有GRE的人生确实不是完整的。"

（李丹，录取院校：Princeton University, Civil and Environmental Engineering）

Unit 1

■ TOPSY-TURVY	■ TORPID	■ TORPOR	■ TORRENTIAL	■ TORRID
■ TORTUOUS	■ TOUT	■ TOY	■ TRACTABLE	■ TRANQUILITY

topsy-turvy [ˌtɑːpsɪ ˈtɜːrvi]
【考法】 *adj.* 混乱的：**lacking in order**, neatness, and often cleanliness
例 a topsy-turvy room 混乱的房间
近 disordered, chaotic, messy, anarchic, jumbled
反 kempt, neat, orderly, organized, shipshape, tidy, trim, uncluttered, well-ordered 有序的

torpid [ˈtɔːrpɪd]
【考法】 *adj.* 麻木的，没有知觉的：lacking in **sensation** or feeling
例 torpid state/tongue 麻木的状态/舌头
近 asleep, benumbed, dead, insensitive, numbed, unfeeling
反 feeling, sensible, sensitive 有同情心的，敏感的

torpor [ˈtɔːrpər]
【考法1】 *n.* 缺乏兴趣：**lack of interest** or concern
例 After a lifetime of setbacks, defeats, and failures, he could only greet the latest bad news with a resigned fatalism and dull torpor. 一生都充满了挫折、失败，他只能用宿命论和麻木不仁来迎接又一次的坏消息。
近 apathy, casualness, complacence, disinterestedness, disregard, incuriosity, insouciance, nonchalance
反 concern, interest, regard 有兴趣
【考法2】 *n.* (肉体或精神上的)迟钝，懒散：physical or mental **inertness**
例 Following Thanksgiving dinner, we spent the rest of the day lounging about in a contented torpor. 吃完感恩节晚餐后，我们慵懒地靠在沙发上度过剩下的时间。
近 languor, lassitude, listlessness, stupor
反 vigor, vim, vitality, vivacity 活力

torrential [təˈrenʃl]
【考法】 *adj.* 急流的：caused by or resulting from action of **rapidstreams**
例 a torrential rain 倾盆大雨
反 trickling 涓涓细流的

torrid [ˈtɔːrɪd]
【考法1】 *adj.* 酷热的：**intensely hot**
例 the dry, torrid summers in southern Arizona 南亚利桑那州干燥、炎热的夏天
近 hot, scalding, scorching, sweltering
反 arctic, bone-chilling, freezing, frigid, frozen, glacial, icy 寒冷的
【考法2】 *adj.* 热情的，情感深厚的：having or expressing **great depth of feeling**
例 torrid love affair 炙热的爱
近 ardent, burning, fervid, flaming, glowing, impassioned, incandescent, intense, passionate, vehement
反 dispassionate, emotionless, impassive, unemotional 冷漠的

tortuous [ˈtɔːrtʃuəs]
【考法】 *adj.* 转弯抹角的：marked by devious or **indirect** tactics: crooked, tricky
例 a tortuous path 一条蜿蜒的道路
近 bending, curling, curvy, devious, serpentine, sinuous, twisted, windy
反 direct, straightforward 直接的

tout	[taʊt]

【考法】 *vt.* 极力赞扬：to promote or **praise** energetically; publicize

例 tout victory in the war 鼓吹战果

近 acclaim, laud, praise, ballyhoo

反 asperse, censure, denounce, berate, rate, revile, vituperate 指责

toy	[tɔɪ]

【考法】 *vi.* 草率或不认真地对待：to **handle thoughtlessly**, ignorantly, or mischievously

例 toy with great issues 把大问题当儿戏

近 diddle with, fiddle with, fool with, mess with, monkey with, tinker with, twiddle with

tractable	[ˈtræktəbl]

【考法】 *adj.* 易驾驭的，温顺的：readily **giving in** to the command or authority of another

例 a tractable horse 一匹温顺的马

近 obedient, amenable, docile, flexible, manageable, compliant, submissive, tame

反 balky, contumacious, defiant, disobedient, incompliant, insubordinate, obstreperous, rebellious, recalcitrant, refractory, restive, unamenable, ungovernable, unruly, untoward, wayward, willful 任性的，难以驯服的

tranquility	[træŋˈkwɪləti]

【考法】 *n.* 宁静，淡定：a state of **freedom from storm** or disturbance

例 enjoyed the tranquillity of the snow-covered field at dusk 享受傍晚时分被雪覆盖的田野的静谧

近 calm, quiet, silence, serenity

反 bustle, commotion, hubbub, pandemonium, tumult, turmoil, unquietness, unrest, uproar 喧闹，骚乱

Unit 2

■ TRANSCEND	■ TRANSFIGURE	■ TRANSGRESS	■ TRANSIENT	■ TRANSITORY
■ TRANSLUCENT	■ TRANSPARENT	■ TRAVAIL	■ TRAVERSE	■ TRAVESTY

transcend	[trænˈsend]

【考法】 *vt.* 超越，超过极限：to rise above or go **beyond the limits** of

例 a person who believes that any true understanding of God transcends human intelligence 认为对上帝的真正理解是超越人类智商极限的人

近 break, outreach, outrun, overpass, overreach, overrun, overshoot, overstep, surpass

transfigure	[trænsˈfɪgjər]

【考法】 *vt.* 使改变外观：to **alter** the outward **appearance** of; **transform**

例 transfigure the AutoCAD drawings with elegant symbols 用优美的符号使 AutoCAD 图变得美观

近 alchemize, metamorphose, transform, transmute, transpose, transubstantiate, make over

transgress	[trænzˈgres]

【考法】 *vt.* 违背；犯错：to **fail to keep**; to **commit an offense**

例 Don't even think about transgressing the drug laws of that Asian country, for punishments are severe and there's nothing that our government can do to intervene. 别指望违背那个亚洲国家的药品相关法，因为惩罚非常严厉，我们政府完全无法干涉。

近 breach, break, contravene, fracture, infringe, offend, traduce

反 follow, mind, obey, observe, comply with, conform to 遵守

transient	[ˈtrænʃnt]

【考法】 *adj.* 短暂的，瞬时的：passing with time; **transitory**

例 transient pleasure 短暂的快乐

近 transitory, ephemeral, evanescent, fleeting, temporary

反 ceaseless, dateless, deathless, endless, enduring, eternal, everlasting, immortal, lasting, long-lived, permanent, perpetual, timeless, undying, unending 永恒持久的

transitory	[ˈtrænsətɔːri]

【考法】 *adj.* 短暂的：existing or **lasting only a short time**; short-lived or temporary

例 transitory period/moment 短暂的阶段/时光

近 transient, ephemeral, evanescent, fleeting, temporary

反 ceaseless, dateless, deathless, endless, enduring, eternal, everlasting, immortal, lasting, long-lived, permanent, perpetual, timeless, undying, unending 永恒持久的

translucent [trænsˈluːsnt]

【考法】 *adj.* 透明的: **permitting** the **passage** of **light**; clear, **transparent**

例 translucent dewdrop 透明的露珠

近 transparent, limpid, pellucid, lucent, lucid, transpicuous

反 opaque 不透明的

transparent [trænsˈpærənt]

【考法】 *adj.* 没有歧义的, 清晰易懂的: **not subject to misinterpretation** or more than one interpretation

例 transparent lie 明显的谎言

近 obvious, clear, apparent, patent, understandable, apprehensible, comprehensible, fathomable

反 ambiguous, clouded, cryptic, enigmatic, equivocal, indistinct, mysterious, obfuscated, obscure, unapparent, unclarified, unclear, unclouded 难以理解的

travail [ˈtræveɪl]

【考法】 *n./v.* 辛苦劳动: work, especially when **arduous** or involving painful effort

例 writer's literary travail 作家辛勤的文学创作 ‖ Labor Day is the day on which we recognize those men and women who daily travail with little appreciation or compensation . 劳动节是我们向那些平日辛勤劳作但是很少受到大家关注并得到应有补偿的工人致敬的日子。

近 drudgery, fatigue, grind

traverse [trəˈvɜːrs]

【考法】 *vt.* 横穿: to travel or **pass across**, over, or through

例 The spider traversed the wall from end to end . 蜘蛛侠攀岩走壁。

近 course, cover, cross, cut across, navigate, pass over, perambulate, peregrinate, proceed along, transit, travel

travesty [ˈtrævəsti]

【考法】 *n./v.* 拙劣的、嘲弄性模仿: an **exaggerated** or grotesque **imitation**, such as a parody of a literary work

例 a travesty of his classmate's manner 滑稽的模仿其他同学的举止

近 caricature, burlesque, parody, spoof, mock

反 paragon 完美的模范

Unit 3

■ TREACHEROUS	■ TRENCHANT	■ TREPIDATION	■ TRESPASS	■ TRIBUTE
■ TRICKLE	■ TRITE	■ TRIVIAL	■ TRUANT	■ TRUCE

treacherous [ˈtretʃərəs]

【考法】 *adj.* 背叛的: marked by **betrayal** of fidelity, confidence, or trust

例 a treacherous ally 不忠的盟友

近 faithless, disloyal, perfidious, recreant, traitorous, unfaithful, unloyal, betraying

反 constant, dedicated, devoted, staunch, down-the-line, faithful, fast, loyal, steadfast, steady, true 忠诚的

trenchant [ˈtrentʃənt]

【考法】 *adj.* (言辞) 一针见血的: vigorously effective and **articulate**

例 trenchant criticisms 一针见血的批评

近 incisive

反 vague 含糊的

trepidation [ˌtrepɪˈdeɪʃn]

【考法】 *n.* 恐惧, 战栗: the emotion experienced in the presence or threat of danger; **apprehension**

例 trepidation about starting a new career 对开创一项新事业感到恐惧

近 fear, fright, horror, apprehension

反 boldness, bravery, dauntlessness, intrepidity 大胆

trespass [ˈtrespəs]

【考法】 *vi.* 非法侵入; 违反, 冒犯: to **enter unlawfully** upon the land of another; to commit an **offense**

例 I consider him to be trespassing against all of us when he trespasses against any one of us. 当他冒犯我们当中一个人的时候, 他就冒犯了我们全部。

近 transgress, invade, intrude

反 withdraw, retreat 撤退

tribute	[ˈtrɪbjuːt]
【考法】	*n.* 称颂，颂词：a gift, payment, **declaration**, or other acknowledgment of **gratitude**, respect, or admiration
例	pay a high tribute to 赞颂
近	accolade, eulogy, encomium, panegyric, tribute 颂词
反	denunciation, condemnation, criticism, censure, reproof, reprobation 批评，指责

trickle	[ˈtrɪkl]
【考法】	*vi.* 一滴一滴地流，缓缓地流：to issue or **fall in drops**
例	Tears trickled down her cheeks. 眼泪从她的脸上一滴一滴地流下。
反	pour, roll, stream, gush 喷涌

trite	[traɪt]
【考法】	*adj.* 陈腐的，陈词滥调的：**hackneyed** or boring from much use, not fresh or original
例	"You win some, you lose some" is a trite expression. "有得必有失"是老生常谈了。
近	bathetic, cliché, hackneyed, threadbare, timeworn, banal
反	fresh, new, novel, original, unclichéd, unhackneyed 新鲜的

trivial	[ˈtrɪviəl]
【考法】	*adj.* 无足轻重的，不重要的：of little worth or **importance**
例	Why spend so much time on trivial decisions, like whether the cola should be regular or diet? 为什么花这么多时间在这种琐碎的决定上，比如可乐要喝一般的还是健怡的?
近	inconsiderable, insignificant, minor, petty, inconsequential, paltry, trifling
反	consequential, material, momentous, weighty, indispensable, substantive, grandiose, massive 重要的

truant	[ˈtruːənt]
【考法】	*adj./ n./ vi.* 逃避责任(的)；逃避责任者：**shirking responsibility**; one who **shirks duty**
例	play truant 逃学
近	shirk, malinger, goldbrick, avoid, escape, evade, parry, sidestep, circumvent, fence, hedge, avert, elude, shun, skirt, dodge, bilk, eschew
反	dutiful 尽职尽责的

truce	[truːs]
【考法】	*n.* 休战，休战协定：a **suspension** of **fighting** especially of considerable duration by agreement of opposing forces
例	truce agreement 休战协议
近	armistice, cease-fire, peace

Unit 4

■ TRUCULENT	■ TRUDGE	■ TRUMPET	■ TRUNCATE	■ TREMENDOUS
■ TUMULT	■ TURBID	■ TURBULENT	■ TURGID	■ TURMOIL

truculent	[ˈtrʌkjələnt]
【考法】	*adj.* 好战的，好斗的：feeling or displaying **eagerness to fight**
例	in an aggressively truculent manner 以好斗的、进攻性的方式
近	belligerent, bellicose, combative, militant, aggressive, feisty
反	nonaggressive, nonbelligerent, pacific, peaceable, peaceful, uncombative, uncontentious 好和平的

trudge	[trʌdʒ]
【考法】	*vi.* 吃力而笨拙地走：to move **heavily or clumsily**
例	trudge over hill 翻山越岭
近	plod, lug, slog, flounder
反	breeze, glide, slide, waltz, whisk, flit 快速通过

trumpet	[ˈtrʌmpɪt]
【考法】	*v.* 大声说出或宣告：to **make known** openly or publicly
例	The losing party lost no time in trumpeting allegations of election fraud. 落败的政党马不停蹄地开始公开宣称选举存在作假。
近	advertise, annunciate, blare, broadcast, declare, proclaim, promulgate, release, give out

truncate	['trʌŋkeɪt]
【考法】	vt. 截短；缩短（时间、篇幅等）：to **shorten** by or as if by cutting off
例	a truncated version of the 11 o'clock newscast following the awards show, which ran over its time slot 颁奖典礼之后缩短版的 11 点新闻节目，已经超出了预定时长
近	abbreviate, abridge, curtail, retrench
反	elongate, extend, lengthen, prolong, protract 延长

tremendous	[trə'mendəs]
【考法】	adj. 极大的：unusually **large**
例	a tremendous amount of information 海量的信息
近	astronomical, colossal, elephantine, enormous, gargantuan, gigantic, immense, mammoth, massive, monumental, titanic, vast
反	diminutive, infinitesimal, minuscule, minute, pocket, tiny 极小的

tumult	['tuːmʌlt]
【考法】	n. 骚动，暴动：a **disorderly** commotion or **disturbance**, a riot
例	His mind was in a tumult. 他心烦意乱。
近	disorder, disturbance, commotion, convulsion, ferment, turmoil, pandemonium, uproar
反	quietude, quiescence, serenity, tranquility 安静

turbid	['tɜːrbɪd]
【考法】	adj. 混浊的：**deficient in clarity** or purity
例	a turbid stream 一条混浊的河
近	muddy, murky, obscure
反	clear, limpid, lucid, pellucid, crystalline 清澈的

turbulent	['tɜːrbjələnt]
【考法】	adj. 动荡的：marked by sudden or violent **disturbance**
例	a turbulent period in history 历史上的动荡时期
近	cataclysmal, stormy, tempestuous, tumultuous

turgid	['tɜːrdʒɪd]
【考法】	adj. 浮夸的，过分装饰的：excessively **embellished** in style or language
例	turgid prose 浮华的散文
近	flatulent, bombastic, pompous
反	simple, austere, unadorned, undecorated, unembellished 简朴的

turmoil	['tɜːrmɔɪl]
【考法】	n. 骚动，混乱：a state or condition of extreme confusion, **agitation**, or **commotion**
例	My mind is in a turmoil. 我心里很乱。
近	commotion, agitation, tumult, turbulence, disorder, ferment, clamor
反	calm, ease, peace, peacefulness, quiet, tranquility, silence, serenity 安静

Unit 5

■ TURNCOAT	■ TURPITUDE	■ TROPE	■ TYPO	■ TYRO
■ UBIQUITOUS	■ UNASSAILABLE	■ UNCANNY	■ UNCOUTH	■ UNCTUOUS

turncoat	['tɜːrnkoʊt]
【考法】	n. 叛徒：one who **switches** to an opposing side or party; specifically: **traitor**
例	He was labeled as a turncoat. 他是一个叛徒。
近	renegade, traitor, apostate, recreant, betrayer, quisling
反	loyalist, partisan, adherent, supporter 支持者，追随者

turpitude	['tɜːrpətuːd]
【考法】	n. 卑鄙：inherent **baseness**: depravity
例	moral turpitude 道德上的卑鄙
近	abjection, corruptness, debasement, debauchery, decadency, degeneration, degradation, demoralization, depravity, dissipatedness, dissoluteness, libertinism, perversion, rakishness
反	probity 正直

	trope	[troʊp]

【考法 1】 *n.* 比喻：a word or expression used in a **figurative** sense

例 in-one-ear-and-out-the-other, which was my mother's trope for a failure to connect 一个耳朵进，一个耳朵出，我妈妈总是用这句比喻来形容连接失败

近 metaphor, simile

【考法 2】 *n.* 陈词滥调：an idea or expression that has been **used by many people**

例 The scheme became a common trope in detective fiction. 这种作案手法成了侦探小说中的常见套路。

近 banality, bromide, cliché, platitude, commonplace, truism

	typo	[ˈtaɪpoʊ]

【考法】 *n.* 打字错误：an **error** in typed or typeset material

例 make one typo on the memo 在样张上打错一个字

近 misprint, bug

	tyro	[ˈtaɪroʊ]

【考法】 *n.* 新手，业余爱好者：a **beginner** in learning: **novice**

例 a tyro in the art of piano 钢琴界的新手

近 novice, apprentice, neophyte, rookie, amateur, dabbler, dilettante, fledgling, recruit

反 old hand, old-timer, vet, expert, professional, veteran 专家

	ubiquitous	[juːˈbɪkwɪtəs]

【考法】 *adj.* 无所不在的，普通的：being **everywhere** at the same time; **often observed** or encountered

例 ubiquitous mosquito 无所不在的蚊子

近 omnipresent, universal, general, common

反 extraordinary, infrequent, rare, seldom, uncommon, unfamiliar, unusual, unique, particular 独特的，不常见的

	unassailable	[ˌʌnəˈseɪləbl]

【考法】 *adj.* 无可争辩的，无法否认的，不可亵渎的：**not to be violated**, criticized, or tampered with

例 an unassailable article 无可争辩的文章

近 undeniable, inviolable, sacrosanct, irrefutable, indisputable, unexceptionable, unimpeachable

反 controversial 有争议的

	uncanny	[ʌnˈkæni]

【考法】 *adj.* 离奇的，奇异的：being so **extraordinary or abnormal** as to suggest powers which violate the laws of nature

例 an uncanny ability to forsee the future 预见未来的能力

近 magical, miraculous, phenomenal, preternatural, superhuman, supernormal, transcendent, transcendental, unearthly

反 ordinary, commonplace, normal 平凡的

	uncouth	[ʌnˈkuːθ]

【考法】 *adj.* 粗俗的，没有品位的：**lacking in refinement** or good taste

例 The movie's uncouth humor seemed to be purposely offensive. 电影里一些恶俗的幽默貌似是故意的。

近 crass, rude, discourteous, disgracious, ungraceful, crude, ill-bred, ill-mannered, uncivil, unrefined

反 genteel, cultivated, cultured, polished, urbane, seemly 得体的，有教养的

	unctuous	[ˈʌŋktʃuəs]

【考法】 *adj.* 油嘴滑舌的，谄媚的：overly or insincerely **flattering**

例 an unctuous appraisal of the musical talent shown by the boss's daughter 拍老板马屁，说他女儿在音乐方面有着非常卓越的天赋

近 adulatory, gushing, hagiographic, oily, oleaginous, soapy

Unit 6

■ UPBEAT	■ UNDERGIRD	■ USHER	■ UNDERSCORE	■ UNDERSTATE
■ UNDUE	■ UNEXCEPTIONABLE	■ UNFLAPPABLE	■ UNGAINLY	■ UNIMPEACHABLE

	upbeat	[ˈʌpbiːt]

【考法 1】 *adj.* 心情好的：having or showing **a good mood** or disposition

例 The line was incredibly long, but people were patient and upbeat. 队伍长得不可思议，但好在人们很有耐心，心情也不错。

近 blithe, buoyant, chipper, eupeptic, gay, lightsome, winsome

反 dour, gloomy, glum, morose, saturnine, sulky, sullen 忧郁的，心情沉重的

【考法 2】 *adj.* 给人希望的，象征好运的：having qualities which **inspire hope**
例 Several upbeat signs imply that the economy is recovering. 一些迹象给人们以希望，表明经济正在复苏。
近 auspicious, bright, encouraging, fair, heartening, optimistic, promising, propitious
反 bleak, dark, depressing, desperate, dismal 压抑的，令人绝望的

undergird [ˌʌndərˈgɜːrd]
【考法】 *vt.* 加强，巩固…的底部：to support or **strengthen** from beneath
例 Facts and statistics undergird his commentary. 事实和数据支持了他的评论。
近 strengthen, support, fortify, reinforce, bear, bolster, brace, buttress, carry, stay, sustain, underpin, uphold, prop up, shore up
反 undermine, weaken, debilitate, enfeeble, enervate 削弱

usher [ˈʌʃər]
【考法】 *v.* 开启：to mark or observe the **beginning** of
例 usher in a new era of stability in Europe 开启欧洲稳定新纪元
近 begin, embark, launch, start, commence
反 conclude, end, finish, terminate 终结

underscore [ˌʌndərˈskɔːr]
【考法】 *vt.* 强调：**to emphasize**; stress
例 underscore the value of education 强调教育的重要性
近 accentuate, italicize, stress, underline, bring out
反 deemphasize, downplay 轻描淡写

understate [ˌʌndərˈsteɪt]
【考法】 *vt.* 保守陈述：to state or present with **restraint** especially for effect
例 understate a problem 低调处理问题
近 downplay
反 vaunt, exaggerate, overstate 夸大
派 understated *adj.* 不夸张的；朴素的：avoiding obvious emphasis or embellishment
近 conservative, low-key, muted, repressed, restrained, sober, subdued, unflashy, unpretentious
反 flamboyant, flaring, flashy, garish, gaudy, glitzy, ostentatious, splashy 夸张的；华丽的

undue [ˌʌnˈdjuː]
【考法】 *adj.* 过度的，过多的：**going beyond a normal** or acceptable limit in degree or amount
例 put undue pressure on ourselves 对自己施加过度压力
近 baroque, exorbitant, extravagant, extreme, immoderate, steep, excessive
反 middling, moderate, modest, temperate 适度的

unexceptionable [ˌʌnɪkˈsepʃənəbl]
【考法】 *adj.* 无懈可击的：not open to objection or criticism，**beyond reproach**
例 unexceptionable movie/book/argument 无懈可击的电影/书/论点
近 unassailable, undeniable, irrefutable, indisputable, unimpeachable
反 assailable, controversial 有争议的

unflappable [ˌʌnˈflæpəbl]
【考法】 *adj.* 镇定的，从容不迫的：**not easily upset** or excited
例 a unflappable general 一个镇定的将军
近 collected, composed, disimpassioned, imperturbable
反 perturbable, shakable, disturbed, nervous 紧张的

ungainly [ʌnˈgeɪnli]
【考法】 *adj.* 笨拙的，不雅的：having or showing an **inability** to move **in a graceful manner**
例 ungainly movements 笨拙的动作
近 clumsy, awkward, blundering, maladroit
反 coordinated, graceful, adroit, dexterous, lissome 协调的，灵巧的

unimpeachable [ˌʌnɪmˈpiːtʃəbl]
【考法】 *adj.* 无可置疑的：beyond doubt; **unquestionable**
例 an unimpeachable evidence 无可置疑的证据
近 unassailable, undeniable, irrefutable, indisputable, unexceptionable
反 assailable, controversial, open to question 可争辩的

Unit 7

unkempt [ˌʌnˈkempt]

【考法】 *adj.* 凌乱的，无序的：**lacking in order**, neatness, and often cleanliness

例 unkempt hotel rooms 凌乱的酒店房间

近 slovenly, slipshod, sloppy, unneat, untidy, topsy-turvy, jumbled

反 bandbox, neat, orderly, organized, shipshape, tidy, trim, uncluttered, well-ordered 有序的，井井有条的

---

unlettered [ˌʌnˈletərd]

【考法】 *adj.* 未受教育的，文盲的：not adept at reading and writing; **deficient in the knowledge** that can be acquired from books; **illiterate**

例 unlettered sector of society 未受教育的地区

近 ignorant, illiterate, uneducated, untutored

反 educated, knowledgeable, erudite, literate, schooled, well-informed, well-read 博学的，受过教育的

---

unpretentious [ˌʌnprɪˈtenʃəs]

【考法 1】 *adj.* 低调的，谦逊的：lacking pretension or affectation; **modest**

例 an unpretentious virtuoso 一位谦虚的大师

近 demure, down-to-earth, lowly, meek, unassuming, humble, modest, unostentatious

反 arrogant, bumptious, conceited, egotistic, fastuous, haughty, imperious, lordly, overweening, peremptory, pompous, presuming, presumptuous, self-asserting, supercilious, superior, toplofty, uppish, flamboyant, ostentatious 傲慢的，自负的

【考法 2】 *adj.* 坦诚的，自然的：**free from** any intent to **deceive** or impress others

例 a simple and unpretentious account about growing up in the rural South 一段简单坦率的关于在南部乡村成长经历的叙述

近 artless, genuine, honest, ingenuous, innocent, naive, simple, sincere, true, unpretending

反 affected, artful, artificial, assuming, dissembling, dissimulating, fake, guileful, insincere, phony 做作的，虚伪的

---

unflagging [ˌʌnˈflæɡɪŋ]

【考法】 *adj.* 不懈的，不知疲倦的：**not declining in strength** or vigor

例 I'm greatly indebted to my editor, without whose unflagging efforts this book cannot be published on time. 我非常感谢我的编辑，没有他/她的不懈努力这本书不可能如期上市。

近 indefatigable, inexhaustible, tireless, unrelenting, weariless

反 dull, lackadaisical, languid, lethargic, listless, sluggish, torpid 无精打采的

派 unflaggingly *adv.* 不懈地

---

unsung [ˌʌnˈsʌŋ]

【考法】 *adj.* 被埋没的；不知名的 **not celebrated** or praised（as in song or verse）

例 They are among the unsung heroes of our time. 他们是我们这个时代的无名英雄。‖ Although little known and unsung, it is one of the grandest little towns you could ever wish to see. 它虽然名不见经传，但却是不可错过的最具恢宏气势的小镇之一。

近 noteless, obscure, uncelebrated, unfamous, unknown, unrecognized

反 celebrated, famed, famous, noted, prominent, renowned, well-known 出名的

---

unruly [ʌnˈruːli]

【考法】 *adj.* 难驾驭的，不守规矩的：**difficult** or impossible **to discipline**, control, or rule

例 an unruly monkey/pet 一个不听话的猴子/宠物

近 indocile, indomitable, intractable, recalcitrant, uncontrollable, undisciplined, ungovernable, unmanageable, insubordinate

反 amenable, biddable, compliant, conformable, docile, obedient, submissive, tractable, subdued, mild, manageable, disciplined 顺从的，守纪律的

untenable	[ʌnˈtenəbl]
【考法】	*adj.* 防守不住的，站不住脚的：not able to be **defended**
例	an untenable remark/evidence 一个站不住脚的评论/证据
近	assailable, controversial, open to question 可质疑的
反	unassailable, undeniable, irrefutable, indisputable, unexceptionable, unimpeachable 无可指责的，无懈可击的

untold	[ʌnˈtoʊld]
【考法】	*adj.* 数不清的，无数的：too great or **numerous** to count
例	untold issues/weakness 无数的问题/弱点
近	incalculable, innumerable, countless, innumerous, uncountable, uncounted
反	countable, enumerable, numberable, quantifiable, calculable 可以计算的

untoward	[ʌnˈtɔːrd]
【考法1】	*adj.* 倒霉的，不吉利的：**not favorable**, **unpropitious**
例	an untoward experience 不幸的经历
近	unpropitious, unlucky, misfortunate, unfortunate
反	auspicious, propitious, favorable, fortunate 吉利的，幸运的
【考法2】	*adj.* 难以驯服的，难以驾驭的：given to **resisting control or discipline** by others
例	a program for untoward teenagers that is designed to give them the kind of discipline that their parents were unable or unwilling to administer 一个以任性、桀骜不驯青少年为对象的项目，旨在弥补家长管教不周之处
近	froward, headstrong, intractable, recalcitrant, refractory, unruly, wayward, willful
反	controllable, governable, manageable, tractable 易管教的，顺从的

unwitting	[ʌnˈwɪtɪŋ]
【考法】	*adj.* 不知道的，未觉察的：not knowing, **unaware**
例	Please forgive my unwitting interruption of your conversation. 请原谅我无意间打断了你们的谈话。
近	unaware, ignorant
反	acquainted, aware, cognizant, conscious, conversant, grounded, informed, knowing, mindful 有意识的

Unit 8

■ UNWONTED	■ UPBRAID	■ UPHOLD	■ URBANE	■ USURP
■ UNIVOCAL	■ VACCINATE	■ VACILLATE	■ VACUOUS	■ VAGARY

unwonted	[ʌnˈwoʊntɪd]
【考法】	*adj.* 不习惯的，不寻常的：**not habitual** or **ordinary**; **unusual**
例	He's honored for the unwonted courage he showed in battle. 他因在战争中表现出的过人的勇气而受到嘉奖。
近	uncommon, unordinary, unusual
反	wonted, usual, routine, habitual, accustomed, customary 平常的

upbraid	[ʌpˈbreɪd]
【考法】	*vt.* (严厉地)谴责，责骂：to **reproach severely**
例	upbraid sb with his ingratitude 责备某人忘恩负义
近	baste, scold, revile, berate, vituperate
反	laud, extol, glorify, hymn, magnify, panegyrize, flatter, fawn, cringe, adulterate 赞扬

uphold	[ʌpˈhoʊld]
【考法】	*vt.* 支持，赞成：to give **support** to
例	He determined to uphold her views in the face of all challenges. 他下定决心支持她的观点，尽管全世界都反对她。
近	support, bolster, advocate, champion, endorse, espouse

urbane	[ɜːrˈbeɪn]
【考法】	*adj.* 彬彬有礼的，文雅的：notably **polite** or finished in manner
例	a gentlemanly and urbane host 有绅士风度、彬彬有礼的主持人
近	debonair, civilized, genteel, cultivated, cultured, polished, refined, well-bred, courteous, gracious
反	boorish, churlish, classless, clownish, loutish, uncouth 粗鲁的

usurp [juːˈzɜːrp]

【考法】 *vt.* 篡夺，篡位：to **seize** and hold （the **power** or rights of another, for example）by force and **without legal authority**

例 usurp the throne 篡夺王位

近 arrogate, commandeer, convert, expropriate, pirate, preempt, press, seize, take over

反 abdicate 退位；crown 授予职位

univocal [ˌjuːˈnɪvoʊkl]

【考法】 *adj.* 含义明确的：so **clearly expressed** as to leave no doubt about the meaning

例 a univocal message of support 明确表示支持

近 clear-cut, definitive, unambiguous, unequivocal, explicit

反 ambiguous, equivocal, indefinite, inexplicit, unspecific, vague 模糊的

vaccinate [ˈvæksɪneɪt]

【考法】 *v.* 预防接种疫苗：to inoculate with a vaccine in order to **produce immunity** to an infectious disease, such as diphtheria or typhus

例 vaccinate sb for smallpox 为某人接种牛痘疫苗以防天花

近 immunize

vacillate [ˈvæsəleɪt]

【考法1】 *vi.* 犹豫不决：to waver in mind, will, or feeling; **hesitate** in choice of opinions or courses

例 Parents vacillate between saying no and yes, but actually neither response seems satisfactory to their children. 父母总是犹豫不定，不知道是该同意还是该反对，但是事实上哪种答案对他们的孩子都不理想。

近 hesitate, dither, waver, teeter, falter

反 resolute, decide, dive in, plunge in 决定

【考法2】 *vi.* 摇动，摇摆：to sway from one side to the other; **oscillate**

近 oscillate, fluctuate

反 equipoise 平衡；静止

vacuous [ˈvækjuəs]

【考法】 *adj.* 茫然的，愚蠢的：marked by **lack of** ideas or **intelligence**

例 a movie that was derided for its vacuous dialogue 一部因为对白十分愚蠢而被嘲讽的电影

近 airhead, brainless, dull, dumb, fatuous, foolish, inane, moronic, obtuse, simple, stupid, witless

反 apt, bright, brilliant, clever, intelligent, keen, sharp, smart 聪明的

派 vacuity *n.* 愚蠢；空虚，空白

vagary [ˈveɪɡəri]

【考法】 *n.* 不可预测的思想或行为：an **erratic**, **unpredictable**, or extravagant manifestation, action, or notion

例 Recently he had been prone to strange vagaries. 最近他逐渐变得行为古怪起来。

近 caprice, fancy, freak, humor, vagrancy, whimsy

Unit 9

■ VAGUE	■ VALEDICTION	■ VALIANT	■ VERSED	■ VANQUISH
■ VAPID	■ VAPORIZE	■ VARIANCE	■ VARIEGATED	■ VARNISH

vague [veɪɡ]

【考法】 *adj.* 表达不清的：**not clearly expressed**

adj. 轮廓不清晰的：**lacking definite shape**, form, or character

例 the vague outline of a building through the dense fog 浓雾中建筑物模糊的轮廓

近 ambiguous, enigmatic, equivocal, indefinite, inexplicit, unclear; dim, faint, foggy, hazy, indistinct, indistinguishable, misty, murky, nebulous, obscure, opaque

反 clear, definite, express, explicit, specific 清楚明确的; pellucid 清澈透明的

valediction [ˌvælɪˈdɪkʃn]

【考法】 *n.* 告别词：an **address** or statement of **farewell** or leave-taking

例 a touching valediction 动人的告别词

派 valedictory *adj.* 告别的

valiant [ˈvæliənt]

【考法】 *adj.* 勇敢的，英勇的：possessing or acting with **bravery** or boldness

例 a valiant and moral knight 一个勇敢和有道德感的骑士 ‖ Despite their valiant efforts, they lost the game. 尽管他们英勇奋战，但还是输掉了比赛。

近 audacious, bold, brave, courageous, dauntless, fearless, gallant, intrepid, stalwart, stout, valorous

反 cowardly, craven, gutless, nerveless, pusillanimous, spineless, timorous 胆怯的

派 valiance *n.* 英勇

versed [vɜːrst]

【考法 1】 *adj.* 熟知的：**having information** especially as a result of study or experience

例 versed in the latest developments in aeronautics 熟知航空业的最新发展情况

近 abreast, acquainted, conversant, informed, knowledgeable, well-informed

反 ignorant, unacquainted, unfamiliar, uninformed, unknowledgeable 无知的

【考法 2】 *adj.* 精通的：having or showing **exceptional knowledge**, experience, or skill in a field of endeavor

例 well versed in the techniques of laser surgery 精通激光手术方面的技术

近 accomplished, adept, complete, consummate, experienced, expert, master, practiced, professed, skilled, veteran, virtuoso

反 amateur, inexperienced, inexpert, jackleg, unprofessional, unseasoned, unskilled 业余的，不精通的

vanquish [ˈvæŋkwɪʃ]

【考法】 *vt.* 打败，征服：to **defeat** in a conflict or contest

例 He vanquished his inner fear. 他战胜了内心的恐惧。

近 conquer, dominate, overpower, pacify, subdue, subject, subjugate, subordinate

反 capitulate, surrender, yield 投降，屈服

vapid [ˈvæpɪd]

【考法】 *adj.* 无趣的，乏味的：**lacking** liveliness, animation, or **interest**

例 a song with vapid lyrics 一首歌词乏味的歌曲

近 driveling, dull, flat, inane, insipid, jejune, sapless, tasteless

反 absorbing, arresting, engaging, engrossing, enthralling, fascinating, immersing, intriguing, riveting 吸引人的

vaporize [ˈveɪpəraɪz]

【考法】 *vt.* 彻底消灭：to **destroy** by or as if by converting into vapor

例 vaporize an army 消灭一支军队

近 annihilate, decimate, demolish, devastate, extinguish, nuke, pulverize, raze, ruin, smash, wreck

反 build, construct, erect, establish, raise, rear 建造

派 vaporous *adj.* 模糊的，空洞的

variance [ˈveriəns]

【考法】 *n.* 不一致，不和谐：a **lack** of agreement or **harmony**

例 Persistent variance within the band eventually caused it to break up. 乐团中持续不断的分歧最终导致了它的解散。

近 conflict, disaccord, discordance, disharmony, dissent, division, friction, schism, variation, war

反 accord, agreement, concord, concordance, harmony, peace 和谐，一致

派 variant *adj.* 有差异的，不同的

variegated [ˈveriɡeɪtɪd]

【考法】 *adj.* 杂色的，斑驳的：having discrete markings of **different colors**

例 variegated costumes of the dancers in the nightclub 夜总会舞者身上色彩斑驳的服装

近 chromatic, kaleidoscopic, iridescent, motley, rainbow

反 monochromatic 单色的；colorless 无色的

派 variegation *n.* 杂色

varnish [ˈvɑːrnɪʃ]

【考法】 *vt.* 粉饰（令人不悦的东西）：to cover or **conceal** （as something **unpleasant**）with something that gives an attractive appearance

例 She tried to varnish her mistakes. 她试图掩盖她的失误。

近 blanch, extenuate, gloss, palliate, sugarcoat, veneer

反 bare, disclose, discover, divulge, expose, reveal, uncloak, uncover, unmask, unveil 揭露

Unit 10

■ VALORIZE ■ VAUNT ■ VEER ■ VEHEMENT ■ VENAL
■ VENDOR ■ VENEER ■ VENERATE ■ VENIAL ■ VENOM

valorize ['væləraɪz]
【考法】 *v.* 提升，赞美： to **enhance** or try to enhance the price, value, or status
例 using subsidies to valorize coffee 用补贴去提升咖啡
近 exalt

vaunt [vɔːnt]
【考法】 *vi.* 吹嘘： to speak **boastfully**
例 He always vaunted his country's military might . 他总是吹嘘他的国家的军事实力。
近 boast, brag, brandish, swagger
反 belittle, deprecate, diminish, minimize, underrate, undervalue 轻视，瞧不起
派 vaunting *adj.* 吹嘘的

veer [vɪr]
【考法】 *v.* (使)转向，(使)改变航线： to **change direction** or course
例 He veered the car abruptly to the right to avoid a collision. 他向右猛打方向盘以避免撞击。
近 avert, deviate, deflect, divert, redirect, swerve, swing, wheel
反 straighten (使)直行

vehement ['viːəmənt]
【考法】 *adj.* (情感)强烈的，热情的： having or expressing **great depth of feeling**
例 vehement criticism/storm/defender 强烈的批评/暴风雨/维权者
近 ardent, demonstrative, emotional, fervid, impassioned, intense, passionate, perfervid, torrid
反 cold, cool, dispassionate, emotionless, impassive, unemotional 冷淡的
派 vehemence *n.* 强烈

venal ['viːnl]
【考法】 *adj.* 贪污受贿的： **open to corrupt** influence and especially bribery
例 a venal officer/administration/authority 一个贪污受贿的官员/政府/当局
近 bribable, corruptible, dirty, purchasable
反 incorruptible 不受贿赂的；scrupulous 正直的

vendor ['vendər]
【考法】 *n.* 小贩，商贩： one that **sells** or vends
例 We're thinking of making a deal with that other software vendor . 我们在考虑和那个软件供应商做交易。
近 broker, dealer, merchandiser, retailer, seller, trader
反 buyer, consumer, purchaser 消费者

veneer [və'nɪr]
【考法】 *vt.* 粉饰(不好的东西)： to cover over with a veneer; especially to **conceal** (as a **defect** of character) under a superficial and deceptive attractiveness
近 blanch, extenuate, gloss, palliate, sugarcoat, varnish
反 bare, disclose, discover, divulge, expose, reveal, uncloak, uncover, unmask, unveil 揭露

venerate ['venəreɪt]
【考法】 *vt.* 尊敬： to **regard with** reverential **respect** or with admiring deference
例 She is venerated by the public as a saint . 她被当作圣人，受万众景仰。
近 adore, deify, esteem, regard, respect, revere
反 despise, disdain, disregard, flout, scorn 轻视，蔑视
派 veneration *n.* 尊敬

venial ['viːniəl]
【考法】 *adj.* 可宽恕的： **easily excused** or forgiven
例 Taking the restaurant's menu as a souvenir seems like a venial offense . 把餐厅的菜单当成纪念品带走似乎是一个可以宽恕的罪行。
近 condonable, excusable, forgivable, pardonable, remissible, remittable
反 heinous, indefensible, inexcusable, mortal, unforgivable, unpardonable 罪大恶极的，不可饶恕的

venom ['venəm]
【考法】 *n.* 恶意，恶毒的用心： the **desire to cause pain** for the satisfaction of doing harm
例 She spoke of him with venom in her voice. 她对他的评论怀揣着恶意。
近 despite, malevolence, maliciousness, malignance, malignity, meanness, nastiness, spite, viciousness
反 comity, friendship, goodwill 友善

List 27

"信仰、勇敢的心和自我控制是最强者的本能。"

（刘栩志，录取院校：Harvard Kennedy School）

Unit 1

■ VERACIOUS	■ VERBATIM	■ VERBOSE	■ VERDANT	■ VERIFY
■ VERISIMILAR	■ VILE	■ VERNACULAR	■ VERSATILE	■ VERSE

veracious [vəˈreɪʃəs]
【考法】 *adj.* 诚实的，说实话的: being in the habit of **telling the truth**
例 a veracious witness 诚实的证人 ‖ He has a reputation for being veracious, so people generally take his word for things. 他诚实的名声让其他人通常都相信他说的话。
近 honest, truthful
反 dishonest, lying, mendacious, prevaricating, untruthful 说谎的，不诚实的
派 veracity *n.* 诚实

verbatim [vɜːrˈbeɪtɪm]
【考法】 *adv.* 逐字地，一字不差地: in the **exact words**
例 You can't just copy the encyclopedia article verbatim for your report—that's plagiarism. 你不能一字不差地抄百科全书上的内容——这是剽窃。
近 ad verbum, directly, exactly, word for word
反 inaccurately, inexactly 不准确地
派 verbalism *n.* 言辞，措词

verbose [vɜːrˈboʊs]
【考法】 *adj.* 冗长的，啰嗦的: containing **more** words **than necessary**
例 a verbose orator 啰嗦的演讲者 ‖ She has a verbose writing style. 她的文风很啰嗦。
近 circuitous, circumlocutory, diffuse, garrulous, long-winded, prolix, rambling, verbose, windy
反 brief, compact, concise, pithy, succinct, terse 简洁的
派 verbosity *n.* 冗长，啰嗦

verdant [ˈvɜːrdnt]
【考法】 *adj.* (因长满植物而)翠绿的，郁郁葱葱的: **green with vegetation**; covered with green growth
例 verdant fields 翠绿的田野
近 green, grown, leafy, luxuriant, overgrown
反 barren, impoverished, infertile, leafless, sterile 贫瘠的

verify [ˈverɪfaɪ]
【考法】 *vt.* 校验，证实: to **determine** or test the truth or **accuracy** of, as by comparison, investigation, or reference
例 We need to verify your passport. 我们需要校验阁下的护照。
近 attest, authenticate, certify, corroborate, substantiate, support, validate, vindicate
反 disprove, rebut, refute 反驳，驳斥
派 verified *adj.* 经证实的；verification *n.* 证实
派 veritable *adj.* 真正的，确实的: being in fact the thing named and not false, unreal, or imaginary
例 a veritable manuscript 一份原稿
近 authentic, credible, genuine, real, true, unquestionable, bona fide
反 bogus, counterfeit, fake, false, mock, phony, pseudo, sham, spurious 伪造的，虚假的

verisimilar [ˌverɪˈsɪmɪlər]
【考法】 *adj.* 似乎真实的: **appearing to be true** or real
例 a verisimilar tale 一个似乎为真的传奇
近 likely, plausible, probable
反 implausible, incredible, unbelievable 难以置信的

vile	[vaɪl]
【考法 1】	*adj.* 丑陋的：**unpleasant to look at**
例	a truly vile combination of colors 着实丑陋的混搭色调
近	grotesque, hideous, homely, monstrous
反	aesthetic, attractive, beautiful, comely, cute, fair, gorgeous, handsome, ravishing, seemly 漂亮迷人的
【考法 2】	*adj.* (道德上)可鄙的，卑鄙的：**morally despicable** or abhorrent
例	Nothing is so vile as intellectual dishonesty. 没什么比智力上的欺骗更为可鄙的了。
近	base, contemptible, despicable, detestable, dishonorable, execrable, ignominious, mean, nasty, paltry, sordid, wretched
反	honorable, lofty, noble, straight, upright, venerable, virtuous 有道德的，高尚的

vernacular	[vərˈnækjələr]
【考法 1】	*n.* 方言：a **nonstandard language** or dialect of a place, region, or country
例	phrases that occur in the common vernacular 常见方言中的词组
近	argot, cant, dialect, jargon, lingo, slang
【考法 2】	*adj.* 非正式的，口头的：used in or **suitable for speech** and not formal writing
例	write essays in a very easy-to-read, vernacular style 用一种易懂的口头化风格写作
近	conversational, informal, nonliterary, vulgar
反	bookish, formal, learned, literary 书面的，正式的

versatile	[ˈvɜːrsətl]
【考法】	*adj.* 多才多艺的，全能的：able to do many **different** kinds of **things**
例	We have found a versatile baseball player who can play any position. 我们发现了一个能打任何位置的全能型球员。
近	adaptable, all-around, ambidextrous, protean, universal
反	limited 受限制的，有限的

verse	[vɜːrs]
【考法 1】	*vt.* 使精通，使熟悉：to **familiarize** by close association, study, or experience
例	well versed in the theater 精通剧院
近	acquaint, familiarize, inform
反	misinform, mislead 误导
【考法 2】	*n.* 诗歌：a composition using **rhythm** and often rhyme to create a **lyrical effect**
例	compose a short verse for his father's birthday 为他父亲的生日创作了一首小诗
近	ballad, lyric, poetry, song
反	prose 散文

Unit 2

■ VERTIGO	■ VERVE	■ VENUE	■ VESTIGE	■ VOCATION
■ VETERAN	■ VETO	■ VEX	■ VIABLE	■ VICARIOUS

vertigo	[ˈvɜːrtɪgoʊ]
【考法】	*n.* 眩晕：a **dizzy** confused state of mind
例	He had a dreadful attack of vertigo at the top of the tower. 他站在塔顶，感到一阵令人窒息的眩晕。
近	dizziness, giddiness
反	sobriety 清醒

verve	[vɜːrv]
【考法】	*n.* 活力，热情：**vitality**, liveliness
例	The instrumentalists played with skill and verve. 器乐表演者们有着高超的技巧与饱满的热情。
近	animation, dynamism, energy, exuberance, liveliness, robustness, vibrancy, vigorousness, vim, vitality
反	lethargy, listlessness, sluggishness, torpidity 精神不振

venue	[ˈvenjuː]
【考法】	*n.* 场地：the **area or space** occupied by or intended for something
例	the historic library is a perfect venue for the poetry readings 历史图书馆是读诗的最佳场所
近	locale location, locus, position, site, spot, place

vestige [ˈvestɪdʒ]

【考法】 *n.* 微小的遗迹，小痕迹：the **smallest** quantity or **trace**

例 A few strange words carved on a stone were the only vestige of the lost civilization. 石碑上刻着的几个奇怪的字符是这个失落文明的唯一遗迹。|| the fossilized vestige of a dinosaur that traversed that muddy landscape millions of years ago 数百万年横跨那块泥泞土壤的恐龙的化石碎片

近 echo, ghost, relic, remain, remnant, residual, shadow, trace

派 vestigial *adj.* 退化的，发育不全的：(of certain organs or parts of organisms) having attained a simple structure and reduced size and function during the evolution of the species

例 snake that has vestigial limbs 拥有退化四肢的蛇

近 incomplete, rudimentary, undeveloped

反 adult, full-blown, full-fledged, matured, ripe, ripened 成熟的，发育完全的

vocation [voʊˈkeɪʃn]

【考法】 *n.* 职业：the work in which a person is regularly **employed**

例 His vocation coincides with his avocation. 他的职业同他的爱好完全一致。

近 calling, employment, occupation, profession, trade, work

反 hobby 爱好

派 vocational *adj.* 职业的，为职业做准备的

veteran [ˈvetərən]

【考法】 *n.* 老兵；有丰富经验的人：an old soldier; one having **knowledge** or ability gained **through long experience** *adj.* 经验丰富的，资深的：having or showing exceptional **knowledge**, **experience**, or skill in a field of endeavor

例 As a veteran of overseas travel, she offered us solid advice about planning our trip. 作为一名资深的海外旅行家，她给我们提供了许多关于旅行规划的中肯建议。|| She is a veteran teacher who can mentor new teachers. 她是一位资深教师，可以教新教师。

近 doyen, expert, master, maven, warhorse; accomplished, adept, consummate, experienced, masterful, professed, skilled, versed, virtuoso

反 beginner, colt, fledgling, freshman, greenhorn, neophyte, novice, recruit, rookie, tenderfoot, tyro 新手；amateur, inexperienced, inexpert, unprofessional, unseasoned, unskilled, unskillful 业余的，经验不足的

veto [ˈviːtoʊ]

【考法】 *n./vt.* 否决，禁止：to **forbid** or **prohibit** authoritatively

例 The President vetoed the bill. 总统否决了提案。|| We wanted to do a cross-country trip, but our parents vetoed it. 我们想来一次跨国旅行，但是父母不肯批准。

近 blackball, decline, disallow, disapprove, kill, negative, refuse, reject

反 accredit, approbate, authorize, clear, confirm, finalize, formalize, ratify, sanction, warrant 批准

vex [veks]

【考法】 *vt.* 使烦恼，使恼怒：to **bring** trouble, distress, or **agitation** to

例 She was vexed by her son's failure to clean his room. 她因为儿子不清理房间而恼怒。

近 aggravate, annoy, bother, exasperate, gall, grate, irk, nettle, peeve, rile

反 appease, assuage, conciliate, mollify, placate, propitiate 平息

派 vexation *n.* 烦恼

viable [ˈvaɪəbl]

【考法】 *adj.* 可行的：capable of **being done** or carried out

例 a viable solution to the problem 解决问题的一个可行方案

近 achievable, attainable, doable, feasible, practicable, realizable, workable

反 hopeless, impossible, impracticable, infeasible, unattainable, unviable, unworkable 不可行的

派 viability *n.* 可行性

vicarious [vaɪˈkeriəs]

【考法】 *adj.* 代理的，取代的：performed or suffered by one person as a **substitute for another** or to the benefit or advantage of another

例 use Internet as a vicarious form of social life 把互联网当作一种虚拟的社交生活

近 indirect, substitute, surrogate

反 firsthand 直接的

Unit 3

- VICIOUS　　　- VICISSITUDE　　　- VICTIMIZE　　　- VIGILANT　　　- VIGNETTE
- VIGOROUS　　　- VILIFY　　　- VIM　　　- VINDICATE　　　- VINDICTIVE

vicious　[ˈvɪʃəs]
【考法】 *adj.* 凶恶的，恶毒的：having or showing the **desire to inflict** severe pain and suffering on others
例　vicious slander 恶意诽谤
近　atrocious, barbaric, barbarous, brutal, butcherly, fiendish, heartless, inhumane, sadistic, savage, truculent
反　benign, benignant, compassionate, humane, kind, kindhearted, merciful, sympathetic 仁慈的
派　viciousness *n.* 邪恶

vicissitude　[vɪˈsɪsɪtuːd]
【考法】 *n.* 自然变化，变迁兴衰：**natural change** or mutation visible in nature or in human affairs
例　vicissitude of daily life 日常生活的跌宕起伏
近　fluctuation, mutation, shift, variation
反　uniformity 一致性，无差异
派　vicissitudinous *adj.* 有变化的

victimize　[ˈvɪktɪmaɪz]
【考法】 *vt.* 使受骗：to **subject to deception** or fraud
例　victimized by a confidence man with a slick story 被一个骗子用圆滑的故事欺骗
近　cheat, cozen, deceive, defraud, dupe, fool, hoax, swindle
反　disabuse, disenchant, disillusion, undeceive 使醒悟

vigilant　[ˈvɪdʒɪlənt]
【考法】 *adj.* 警醒的，警惕的：**alertly watchful** especially to avoid danger
例　Police warned the public to be vigilant and report anything suspicious. 警方要求公众保持警惕，并上报任何有嫌疑的人或事。‖ When traveling through the city, tourists should be extra vigilant. 在这个城市旅行的游客应该保持格外的警惕。
近　alert, attentive, awake, cautious, observant, sharp, watchful
反　careless, heedless, inattentive, unmindful, unthinking, unwary 不谨慎的
派　vigilance *n.* 警惕

vignette　[vɪnˈjet]
【考法】 *n.* 简介，短文：a **vivid representation** in words of someone or something
例　The general's memoirs are filled with revealing vignettes of some of the war's most compelling personalities. 将军的回忆录里充满了短小的文章，它们揭露了战争中最引人注意的人物。
近　definition, delineation, depiction, picture, portrait, portraiture, portrayal, rendering, sketch

vigorous　[ˈvɪɡərəs]
【考法】 *adj.* 精力旺盛的：having **active strength** of body or mind
例　a strong and vigorous politician 一位身体强壮、精力旺盛的政治家
近　brisk, dynamic, energetic, lively, robust, spirited, vital
反　dull, lethargic, listless, sluggish, torpid 没有精神的

vilify　[ˈvɪlɪfaɪ]
【考法】 *vt.* 诽谤，辱骂：to **utter slanderous** and abusive **statements** against
例　be vilified by the press because of her radical views 因为她激进的观点而被媒体抨击
近　asperse, blacken, calumniate, defame, libel, malign, smear, traduce
反　acclaim, applaud, commend, praise 表扬
派　vilification *n.* 辱骂

vim　[vɪm]
【考法】 *n.* 活力，精力：robust **energy** and enthusiasm
例　A little rest should give me back some of my vim. 稍事休息我应该就能回复些许精力。
近　animation, bounce, dynamism, energy, liveliness, robustness, verve, vibrancy, vigorousness, vitality
反　lethargy, listlessness, sluggishness, torpidity 精神不振

vindicate　[ˈvɪndɪkeɪt]
【考法 1】 *vt.* 为…平反，为…辩护，使无罪：to **free from** allegation or **blame**
例　The evidence would completely vindicate him. 这个证据将彻底证明他的清白。
近　absolve, acquit, exculpate, exonerate
反　incriminate 使有罪

【考法 2】 *vt.* 证明，证实：to **give evidence** or testimony to the truth or factualness of

例 Recent discoveries have generally vindicated the physicist's theories. 近期的发现整体上证明了物理学家的理论。

近 attest, authenticate, certify, corroborate, substantiate, support, validate, verify

反 disprove, rebut, refute 反驳，驳斥

vindictive [vɪnˈdɪktɪv]

【考法】 *adj.* 复仇的，有寻仇倾向的：disposed to **seek revenge**

例 vindictive hatred for his brother 对他兄弟的仇恨

近 avenging, resentful, retaliatory, revengeful, vengeful

反 forgiving, merciful, relenting 仁慈的

Unit 4

■ VIRTUOSO	■ VIRTUOUS	■ VIRULENT	■ VISCID	■ VISCOUS
■ VISIONARY	■ VITALITY	■ VITIATE	■ VITRIOLIC	■ VITUPERATE

virtuoso [ˌvɜːrtʃuˈoʊsoʊ]

【考法 1】 *n.* 艺术鉴赏家，专家：a person with **masterly skill** or technique in the arts

例 a violin virtuoso 资深小提琴艺术家

近 adept, connoisseur, maestro, master, maven, proficient, wizard

反 amateur, inexpert 业余爱好者，非专业玩家

【考法 2】 *adj.* 经验丰富的，技艺精湛的：having or showing **exceptional knowledge**, experience, or skill in a field of endeavor

例 The American virtuoso cellist Lynn Harrell joins the orchestra as soloist in Shostakovich's technically challenging *Cello Concerto No 2.* 来自美国的技艺精湛的大提琴家林恩·哈勒尔作为独奏者加入了乐队，共同演绎肖斯塔科维奇充满挑战的《第二大提琴协奏曲》。

近 accomplished, adept, consummate, experienced, masterful, professed, skilled, versed, veteran

反 amateur, inexperienced, inexpert, unprofessional, unseasoned, unskilled, unskillful 业余的，经验不足的

派 virtuosity *n.* 精湛技艺

virtuous [ˈvɜːrtʃuəs]

【考法】 *adj.* 品德高尚的，正直的：having or **showing** virtue, especially **moral excellence**

例 Virtuous behavior is its own reward. 美德本身就是一种回报。 || She felt that she had made a virtuous decision by donating the money to charity. 她觉得把钱捐赠给慈善基金是一个高尚的决定。

近 decent, ethical, honest, honorable, moral, noble, righteous, straight, upright

反 bad, evil, immoral, indecent, sinful, unethical, unrighteous, wicked, wrong 邪恶的

virulent [ˈvɪrələnt]

【考法】 *adj.* 有毒的：extremely **poisonous** or venomous

例 virulent bacteria 有毒的细菌

近 poisonous, toxic, venomous

反 innocuous 无害的；healthy, salubrious, wholesome 有益健康的

viscid [ˈvɪsɪd]

【考法】 *adj.* 有粘性的：having a **glutinous** consistency

例 viscid tree resin 粘性的树脂

近 adherent, adhesive, clingy, gluey, glutinous, tenacious, viscous

反 slick 光滑的

viscous [ˈvɪskəs]

【考法】 *adj.* 粘稠的，粘的：**viscid**; sticky

例 viscous syrup that takes forever to pour from a narrow-neck bottle 不知要花多久才能从窄口瓶中倒出来的粘稠糖浆

近 glutinous, syrup, viscid

反 fluid, watery 流体的，易流动的

visionary [ˈvɪʒəneri]

【考法 1】 *adj.* 空想的，不切实际的：having or marked by a tendency to be **guided** more **by ideals** than by reality

例 a visionary plan for a manned flight to Mars 一个构想中的载人火星计划

近 idealistic, imaginary, impractical, quixotic, romantic, utopian

反 pragmatic 实事求是的，务实的

【考法2】 *adj.* 有远见的: having or marked by **foresight** and imagination
例 a visionary and legendary leader 一个有远见的传奇领袖
近 farseeing, farsighted, forehanded, foreseeing, forethoughtful, prescient, proactive, provident
反 improvident, myopic, shortsighted 目光短浅的

vitality [vaɪˈtæləti]
【考法】 *n.* 活力，生命力: physical or mental **vigor** especially when highly developed
例 lose intellectual vitality 失去思维活力
近 animation, bounce, dynamism, energy, liveliness, robustness, verve, vibrancy, vigorousness, vim
反 lethargy, listlessness, sluggishness, torpidity 精神不振
派 vitalize *vt.* 激发，使有活力

vitiate [ˈvɪʃieɪt]
【考法】 *v.* 削弱，损害: to **reduce the value** or impair the quality of
例 Too many grammatical errors can vitiate the soundness of your writing , so double-check is recommended before submission. 太多的语法错误会削弱你论证的力度，所以建议交稿前检查几遍。
近 blemish, cripple, deface, degrade, deteriorate, flaw, harm, impair, mar, undermine
反 doctor, fix, mend, patch, rebuild, recondition, reconstruct, renovate, repair, revamp 修复，再生

vitriolic [ˌvɪtriˈɑːlɪk]
【考法】 *adj.* (言辞)刻薄的: bitterly **scathing**
例 vitriolic criticism 刻薄的批评
近 acerbic, acid, acrid, bitter, biting, caustic, corrosive, harsh, mordant, scalding, scathing, sharp, tart
反 balmy, benign, bland, delicate, light, mellow, mild, nonabrasive, soft, soothing, tender 柔和的
派 vitriol *n.* 刻薄的话语

vituperate [vaɪˈtuːpəreɪt]
【考法】 *vt.* 谩骂，责骂: to **abuse or censure** severely or abusively
例 He was vituperated for betraying his friends . 他因为背叛朋友而被责骂。
近 abuse, assail, belabor, berate, castigate, excoriate, lambaste, reprimand, scold, rail, revile, upbraid
反 admire, commend, laud, praise 赞赏
派 vituperative *adj.* 辱骂的

Unit 5

- ■ VIVACIOUS
- ■ VOCIFEROUS
- ■ VOLATILE
- ■ VOLITION
- ■ VOLUBLE
- ■ VOLUMINOUS
- ■ VOLUPTUOUS
- ■ VORACIOUS
- ■ VOTARY
- ■ VOUCH

vivacious [vɪˈveɪʃəs]
【考法】 *adj.* 活泼的，快活的: **lively** in temper, conduct, or spirit
例 a vivacious girl who became a successful sales rep 一个成为成功销售代表的活泼女孩
近 active, animated, bouncing, brisk, energetic, frisky, kinetic, mettlesome, spirited, sprightly, vital, zippy
反 dead, inactive, inanimate, languid, languorous, leaden, lifeless, listless, spiritless, vapid 无活力的
派 vivacity *n.* 活力，活泼

vociferous [voʊˈsɪfərəs]
【考法】 *adj.* 喧哗的，大叫大嚷的: making, given to, or marked by noisy and **vehement outcry**
例 vociferous applause 喧闹的欢呼
近 blatant, boisterous, clamant, clamorous, obstreperous, strident, yowling
反 reticent, taciturn 沉默的；serene, tranquil 宁静的

volatile [ˈvɑːlətl]
【考法】 *adj.* 多变的: characterized by or subject to **rapid** or unexpected **change**
例 a boss of volatile moods 一个性情多变的老板 ‖ The stock market can be very volatile. 股市瞬息万变。
近 capricious, changeable, fluid, inconstant, mercurial, skittish, temperamental, variable, versatile
反 certain, changeless, constant, immutable, invariable, settled, stable, stationary, steady, unchangeable, unvarying 固定的，不变的
派 volatility *n.* 易变性，易挥发性

volition [vəˈlɪʃn]
【考法】 *n.* 意志，自愿选择的行为：the act or power of **making one's own choices** or decisions
例 beyond his volition or control 超出了他的意志和控制范围
近 choice, decision, discretion, will
反 coercion, compulsion, constraint, duress, force, pressure 强迫，迫使

voluble [ˈvɑːljəbl]
【考法】 *adj.* 健谈的，话多的：characterized by **ready** or rapid **speech**
例 The voluble gadfly ruined the party. 聚会被那个话又多又让人讨厌的人破坏了。
近 chatty, eloquent, garrulous, glib, loquacious, talkative, vocative
反 reticent, taciturn 沉默的；laconic, reserved, succinct 惜字如金的
派 volubility *n.* 口若悬河

voluminous [vəˈluːmɪnəs]
【考法】 *adj.* 卷数多的，大量的，庞大的：having **great** volume, fullness, size, or **number**
例 try to keep a track of voluminous academic database 尝试追踪数目庞大的学术数据库
近 colossal, considerable, elephantine, enormous, gargantuan, gigantic, mammoth, numerous, oversize
反 scanty, scarce 缺乏的；dwarf, little, small, undersized 数量少的

voluptuous [vəˈlʌptʃuəs]
【考法】 *adj.* 奢侈逸乐的，沉溺酒色的：given to or spent in **enjoyments** of **luxury**, pleasure, or sensual gratifications
例 They spent a long and voluptuous holiday in Venice. 他们在威尼斯度过了一个漫长而奢华的假期。
近 carnal, epicurean, luscious, lush, luxurious, indulgent, sensual, sensuous
反 ascetic, spartan, self-denying 克己的，自制的
派 voluptuary *n.* 酒色之徒

voracious [vəˈreɪʃəs]
【考法1】 *adj.* 有很大食量的，贪吃的：having a **huge appetite**
例 He has a voracious appetite. 他的食量惊人。
近 edacious, esurient, gluttonous, swinish
反 abstemious, abstentious 有节制的
【考法2】 *adj.* 贪婪的，如饥似渴的：having or marked by an **insatiable** appetite for an activity or pursuit
例 a voracious reader who locked himself up in the study 一个把自己锁在书房里如饥似渴读书的人
近 acquisitive, avid, covetous, grasping, greedy, hungry, rapacious, ravenous, thirsty
反 apathetic, indifferent, uneager, unenthusiastic 无所谓的
派 voracity *n.* 食欲，贪婪

votary [ˈvoʊtəri]
【考法】 *n.* 崇拜者，信徒：a person who is **fervently devoted**, as to a leader or ideal; a faithful follower
例 votaries of the religious leader 宗教领袖的追随者们
近 acolyte, adherent, devotee, disciple, fan, fanatic, partisan, pupil, zealot
反 bellwether, leader 领导；apostate, defector, renegade, traitor, turncoat 叛徒

vouch [vaʊtʃ]
【考法】 *v.* 担保，声称为真：to declare (something) to be true or genuine; to **give a guarantee**
例 willing to vouch for her integrity 愿意担保她的人格
近 attest, avouch, guarantee, testify, warrant

Unit 6

■ VULGAR	■ VULNERABLE	■ WADDLE	■ WAFFLE	■ WAFT
■ WAG	■ WAN	■ WARBLE	■ WANE	■ WANTING

vulgar [ˈvʌlgər]
【考法】 *adj.* 粗俗的，无教养的：morally **crude**, undeveloped, or unregenerate
例 He is a vulgar man but his music is quite divine. 虽然他是一个粗俗的人，但他的音乐却十分神奇。
近 bawdy, coarse, crass, crude, dirty, filthy, gross, lowbred, indecent, nasty, obscene, ribald, rude, uncouth
反 civilized, cultivated, cultured, genteel, polished, refined, urbane, well-bred 有教养的

	vulnerable	[ˈvʌlnərəbl]
【考法】	*adj.* 易受攻击的，脆弱的: **open to attack** or damage
例	the vulnerable group of people 弱势群体
近	assailable, endangered, exposed, subject, susceptible
反	guarded, protected, shielded 有保护的；invincible, invulnerable 无敌的
派	vulnerability *n.* 弱点，易受伤害

waddle	[ˈwɑːdl]
【考法】	*vi.* 摇摇摆摆地走: to walk with short steps that **tilt the body from side to side**
例	The duck waddled back into the water. 鸭子一摇一摆地回到了水中。
近	careen, dodder, reel, teeter, totter
派	waddling *adj.* 摇摇摆摆的

waffle	[ˈwɑːfl]
【考法】	*vi.* 胡扯: to **talk** or write **foolishly**
例	This lecturer will waffle on for hours. 这个老师会胡说八道地扯几个小时。
近	babble, blather, drivel, gabble, prattle
反	articulate 清楚地说

waft	[wɑːft]
【考法】	*v.* 飘荡，漂浮: to **float** easily and gently, as on the air
例	Heavenly aromas wafted from the kitchen. 令人欣悦的香气从厨房飘出。‖ A feather wafted past us and settled on the grass. 一片羽毛飘过我们身边，落在草地上。
近	buoy, drift, glide, hang, hover, raft
反	flounder, sink 沉没；submerge 下沉

wag	[wæg]
【考法】	*v.* 摆动: to **move to and fro or up and down** especially with quick jerky motions
例	The dog wagged its tail. 狗摆动着它的尾巴。
近	swish, switch, waggle

wan	[wæn]
【考法】	*adj.* 苍白的，病态的: suggestive of **poor health**
例	She looks a little wan after all that tiring work. 在完成那些繁重的工作之后她看起来有些虚弱。
近	ashen, ashy, blanched, livid, lurid, sickly, pale, pallid
反	blooming, florid, flush, full-blooded, glowing, red, rosy, rubicund, ruddy, sanguine 红润的，健康的

warble	[ˈwɔːrbl]
【考法】	*v.* 柔和地唱歌: to **sing with** trills, runs, or other **melodic embellishments**
例	warble me now for joy of lilac. 为我歌唱丁香花季节的喜悦吧。
近	quaver, trill, croon

wane	[weɪn]
【考法】	*vi.* 减少，衰退，降低: to **decrease** in size, extent, or degree
例	In the evening the storm finally waned. 傍晚时分风暴终于减弱了。‖ The moon waxes and then wanes. 月有阴晴圆缺。
近	abate, decline, diminish, dwindle, ease, ebb, fall, lessen, lower, moderate, recede, shrink, subside, taper
反	accumulate, balloon, burgeon, enlarge, escalate, expand, grow, increase, intensify, mushroom, rise, snowball, soar, wax 增加，扩大，上升
派	waning *adj.* 衰退的，减少的

wanting	[ˈwɑːntɪŋ]
【考法 1】	*adj.* 未出现的，缺少的: **not present** or in evidence
例	find young workers wanting in skill 认为许多年轻员工缺乏技术
近	absent, lacking, missing, nonexistent
反	existent, present 存在的，出现的
【考法 2】	*adj.* 未达到要求的: **not being up to standards** or expectations
例	He examined her work and found it wanting. 他检查了她的工作，发现不合要求。‖ We tried her cooking and found it to be very wanting. 我们试了试她的厨艺，结果发现很不尽人意。
近	deficient, dissatisfactory, ill, inferior, lousy, paltry, poor, unacceptable, unsatisfactory, wretched
反	acceptable, adequate, passable, tolerable 可接受的；satisfactory 令人满意的

Unit 7

warmonger ['wɔːrmʌŋgər]
【考法】 *n.* 好战者：one who **urges** or attempts to stir up **war**
- 例 Fortunately, the warmongers met with overwhelming opposition . 幸运的是，好战者们碰到了巨大的阻力。
- 近 belligerent, hawk, jingoist, war hawk
- 反 dove, pacifist 和平主义者

warp [wɔːrp]
【考法】 *vt.* 曲解：to change so much as to create a wrong impression or **alter the meaning** of
- 例 The faulty English translation really warps the meaning of the original Chinese text. 错误的英语翻译曲解了中文的原意。
- 近 distort, falsify, misinterpret, misrepresent, twist
- 反 clarify, clear, explain, illuminate, illustrate 澄清

warrant ['wɔːrənt]
【考法】 *vt.* 批准，认可：to give **official acceptance** of as satisfactory
- 例 The law warrants these measures . 法律允许这些措施。
- 近 approbate, authorize, clear, confirm, finalize, formalize, ratify, sanction
- 反 decline, deny, disallow, disapprove, negative, reject, veto 禁止，否决
- 派 warranted *adj.* 担保的；warranty *n.* 保证，承诺

wary ['weri]
【考法】 *adj.* 小心的，机警的，谨慎的：marked by keen **caution**, cunning, and watchfulness
- 例 be wary of strangers 提防陌生人
- 近 alert, cautious, chary, circumspect, conservative, guarded, heedful, vigilant, watchful
- 反 careless, heedless, incautious, unguarded, unmindful, unwary 不谨慎的
- 派 wariness *n.* 谨慎，小心

wastrel ['weɪstrəl]
【考法】 *n.* 肆意挥霍的人，败家子：one who **expends** resources foolishly and **self-indulgently**
- 例 He ended up being a wastrel and a drunkard . 他最后成了一个花天酒地的败家子，还是一个酒鬼。
- 近 fritterer, profligate, spender, spendthrift, squanderer, waster
- 反 economizer, penny-pincher 节约的人；hoarder, miser, niggard 吝啬鬼

watershed ['wɔːtərʃed]
【考法】 *n.* 重要关头，分水岭：a crucial dividing point: **turning point**
- 例 a watershed moment in her life 她命运的分水岭
- 近 climax, corner, event, landmark, milestone

wax [wæks]
【考法】 *vi.* 增大，增强：to **increase** in size, numbers, strength, prosperity, or intensity
- 例 The vast empire is waxing. 那个巨大的帝国在强大。
- 近 accelerate, accumulate, appreciate, balloon, boom, burgeon, enlarge, escalate, expand, proliferate, rise
- 反 contract, decrease, diminish, dwindle, lessen, recede 减少，减弱
- 派 waxing *adj.* 增加的

waylay [weɪ'leɪ]
【考法】 *vt.* 埋伏，伏击：to lie in wait for or **attack** from ambush
- 例 Unsuspecting tourists are often waylaid by gangs . 不警惕的旅客们常常被犯罪团伙偷袭。‖ We were way-laid by a group of protestors with rocks. 我们被一群示威者用石头偷袭了。
- 近 ambush, assault, lurk

welter ['weltər]
【考法】 *n.* 混乱，动乱：a state of wild **disorder**
- 例 There was a welter of pushing and shoving . 到处是推搡和拥挤的混乱局面。‖ The troop withdrawal would plunge the country into a welter of anarchy and endless civil war. 撤军会使得这个国家陷入无政府的动乱状态和无尽的内战中。
- 近 disturbance, furor, hurricane, pandemonium, turmoil, uproar, whirl
- 反 calm, peace, tranquility 平静，宁静；order 秩序

wheedle	['wiːdl]
【考法】	v. (用花言巧语)诱惑，哄骗: to persuade or attempt to **persuade by flattery** or guile
例	wheedle him into working for them 哄骗他为他们工作 ‖ She pleaded and wheedled, but I wouldn't be swayed. 她软磨硬泡地求我，但我仍不动摇。
近	adulate, blandish, cajole, coax
反	coerce, compel, demand, force, oblige, require 迫使，强求

Unit 8

■ WHET	■ WINNOW	■ WHIMSICAL	■ WHOLESOME	■ WICKED
■ WINCE	■ WINDBAG	■ WINDY	■ WINSOME	■ WIT

whet	[wet]
【考法】	vt. 刺激，激起: to make keen or **more acute**
例	Media moguls intend to whet a public zeal for the low-fat burger. 传媒巨头们希望能够掀起一场低脂肪汉堡的狂潮。
近	arouse, bestir, elicit, excite, evoke, ignite, kindle, rally, stimulate, waken
反	assuage, allay, mitigate, mollify, pacify, soothe 平息，缓和

winnow	['wɪnoʊ]
【考法】	v. 筛选: to **examine closely** in order to separate the good from the bad
例	winnowed the list of candidates to three. 将候选人名单筛减到三人。
近	sift, pick, select, separate

whimsical	['wɪmzɪkl]
【考法】	adj. 反复无常的: prone to **sudden illogical changes** of mind, ideas, or actions
例	a whimsical personality 变化无常的个性 ‖ his whimsical art 他反复无常的艺术作品
近	capricious, fickle, freakish, mercurial, volatile
反	resolute, unwavering 坚决的
派	whimsicality n. 反复无常

wholesome	['hoʊlsəm]
【考法】	adj. 有益身心健康的: **promoting** mental, moral, or social **health**
例	try to eat a more wholesome diet 尽可能有更健康的饮食习惯
近	healthy, restorative, salubrious, recuperative, tonic
反	insalubrious, noxious, unhealthy, unwholesome 不健康的，有害的
派	wholesomeness n. 健康

wicked	['wɪkɪd]
【考法】	adj. 邪恶的: **morally** very **bad**
例	a wicked attack 邪恶的攻击
近	dark, evil, immoral, iniquitous, nefarious, sinful, vicious, villainous
反	decent, ethical, good, honest, honorable, moral, righteous, sublime, upright, virtuous 高尚的
派	wickedness n. 邪恶

wince	[wɪns]
【考法】	vi. 畏缩: to **shrink back** involuntarily as **from pain**
例	wince at the horrible corpses 在令人恐惧的尸体面前畏缩
近	blench, cringe, quail, quiver, recoil, shrink, tremble
反	confront, face, meet 直面; challenge 挑战

windbag	['wɪndbæg]
【考法】	n. 健谈的人: an exhaustively **talkative** person
例	a talktive windbag 一个话多健谈的人
近	babbler, conversationalist, gabbler, gasbag, prattler

windy	['wɪndi]
【考法】	adj. 冗长的: characterized by wearisome **verbosity**
例	a windy saleswoman who told us a lot more than we wanted to know about vacuum cleaners 一个啰嗦的女销售员，一个劲地说着我们不想知道的关于吸尘器的细节
近	circuitous, circumlocutory, diffuse, garrulous, prolix, rambling, verbose
反	compact, concise, crisp, pithy, succinct, terse 简洁的

winsome ['wɪnsəm]

【考法】 *adj.* 迷人的，漂亮的：generally **pleasing and engaging** often because of a childlike charm and innocence

例 fascinated by her winsome smile 为她动人一笑所倾倒

近 adorable, charming, disarming, enchanting, endearing, sweet, winning

反 abhorrent, abominable, detestable, hateful, loathsome, odious 令人厌恶的

派 winsomeness *n.* 迷人

wit [wɪt]

【考法】 *n.* 机智，智慧：the natural **ability to** perceive and **understand**

n. 智者，有智慧的人：a person of exceptional **intelligence**

例 lack the wit to judge 缺乏判断的智慧 ‖ a man who fancied himself as a great wit 一个把自己想象成智慧的化身的男子

近 astuteness, brilliance, foxiness, intelligence, keenness, perspicacity, sagacity, sharpness, shrewdness; illuminati, pundit, sage, savant, scholar

反 brainlessness, dullness, fatuity, lunacy, silliness 愚蠢；dolt, fool, idiot, simpleton 傻子

派 witty *adj.* 有智慧的

Unit 9

■ WITHDRAW　　■ WITHER　　■ WITHHOLD　　■ WIZEN　　■ WOBBLE
■ WORLDLY　　■ WINDFALL　　■ WRANGLE　　■ WRETCHED　　■ WRY

withdraw [wɪð'drɔː]

【考法】 *v.* 撤退：to **take back** or away

例 The army was forced to withdraw from the frontline. 部队被迫从前线撤回。

近 recede, retreat, fall back

反 advance 前进；place, position, put 放置，安置

派 withdrawal *n.* 撤退；withdrawn *adj.* 性格内向的，离群的

wither ['wɪðər]

【考法】 *vi.* 枯萎，凋谢：to **become** dry and **sapless**

例 The crops will wither. 庄稼会枯萎。

近 dry, fade, shrivel, wane, wilt, wizen

反 revive 复活；bloom, flourish, prosper, thrive 繁茂

派 withering *adj.* 凋谢的，凋亡的

withhold [wɪð'hould]

【考法】 *vt.* 抑制；扣压，不给予：to hold back from action; to **refrain from** granting, **giving**, or allowing

例 withhold sensitive information 限制敏感信息的传播

近 decline, disallow, disapprove, detain, refuse, reject, reprobate, restrain, retain

反 allow, concede, grant, permit 授予

wizen ['waɪzn]

【考法】 *v.* (使)凋谢，(使)枯萎：to **become** dry, shrunken, and **wrinkled** often as a result of aging or of failing vitality *adj.* 凋谢的，枯萎的：shriveled or **dried up**

近 dry, mummify, shrivel, wither; faded, withered

反 revive 复活；bloom, flourish, prosper, thrive 繁茂；blooming 盛开的

wobble ['wɑːbl]

【考法1】 *vi.* 摇晃，颤抖：to **move or proceed** with an irregular rocking or staggering motion or **unsteadily** and clumsily from side to side

例 The drunk stood up, wobbled for a moment, and fell forward. 醉汉站了起来，晃动了一阵，然后向前倒了下去。

近 rock, totter

反 stabilize 使稳定

【考法2】 *vi.* 犹豫不决：to **show uncertainty** about the right course of action

例 We cannot tolerate the government wobbling at this critical time. 我们不能容忍政府在这种关键时刻犹豫不决。

近 falter, stagger, teeter, vacillate, waver

worldly ['wɜːrldli]

【考法 1】 *adj.* 世间的，世俗的：of this world **rather than spiritual** or religion affairs

例 preoccupied with worldly concerns 纠缠于世俗的忧虑 ‖ It is time you woke up and focused your thoughts on more worldly matters. 现在你应该停止做梦，然后把自己的精力集中在更现实的问题上了。

近 carnal, corporeal, material, mundane

反 mental, spiritual 精神的；heavenly 天国的

【考法 2】 *adj.* 老练的：**experienced** in human affairs

例 My little sister was worldly and sophisticated, quite unlike me. 与我截然不同的是，我的妹妹在为人处世方面非常老练。

近 cosmopolitan, sophisticated

反 ingenuous, innocent, naïve, unsophisticated 天真的

windfall ['wɪndfɔːl]

【考法】 *n.* 好运，幸事 an **unexpected**, unearned, or sudden **gain or advantage**

例 Hitting the jackpot was an unbelievable windfall for the recently laid-off worker. 对这个刚失业的人来说中彩票头奖是令人难以置信的天赐好运。

近 benediction, blessing, boon, felicity, godsend, manna

反 apocalypse, calamity, cataclysm, catastrophe, debacle, disaster 大灾难；bane, scourge 祸害

wrangle ['ræŋɡl]

【考法】 *n.* 纷争，争端：an often noisy or angry expression of **differing opinions**

vi. 争吵：to **quarrel** noisily or angrily

例 There was a bit of a wrangle over how much money to give the high school for its sports programs. 这个高中应该获得多少体育项目的拨款引起了一阵纷争。 ‖ Local residents wrangled for hours about property taxes. 当地居民就房产税的问题争吵不休。

近 altercation, controversy, disagreement, dispute, fight, imbroglio, quarrel, squabble; altercate, argue, bicker, controvert, hassle, quibble, spat, tiff

反 harmony 和谐

派 wrangler *n.* 争吵的人

wretched ['retʃɪd]

【考法 1】 *adj.* 极差的：very **poor in quality** or ability

例 the wretched conditions of the refugee camp 难民营极恶劣的条件

近 bad, coarse, inferior, low-grade, mediocre, miserable, poor, rubbishy, terrible, trashy

反 excellent, fine, first-class, first-rate, good, high-grade, superior 优质的

【考法 2】 *adj.* 沮丧的：deeply afflicted, **dejected**, or distressed in body or mind

例 in a wretched mood 心情沮丧

近 blue, crestfallen, dejected, doleful, dolorous, gloomy, melancholy, mournful, rueful, sorrowful, woeful

反 blissful, buoyant, cheerful, delighted, glad, happy, joyful, jubilant 欢乐的

派 wretchedness *n.* 沮丧

wry [raɪ]

【考法】 *adj.* 坚持错误的：**stubborn** in adherence **to wrong** opinion or principles

近 headstrong, obstinate, pertinacious, perverse, stubborn, wrongheaded

反 amenable, compliant, complying, flexible, pliable, pliant, relenting, yielding 容易改变立场的

Unit 10

■ XENOPHOBE   ■ YOKE   ■ YOKEL   ■ ZEAL   ■ ZEALOT
■ ZENITH   ■ ZESTY

xenophobe ['zenəfəʊb]

【考法】 *n.* 仇视（或畏惧）外国人（或外国事物）者：one unduly **fearful of what is foreign** and especially of people of foreign origin

例 an extreme xenophobe 一个极端仇视外国者

反 xenomania 崇洋媚外的人

派 xenophobia *n.* 仇外情绪

yoke [joʊk]

【考法】 *v.* 连接: to **become joined** or linked

例 yoke several ideas together to propose a novel theory 将几个想法结合起来提出一个全新的理论

近 chain, conjugate, hook, interconnect, join, link, unite

反 disconnect, disjoin, dissever, disunite, separate, sunder, unchain, unlink, unyoke 分开

yokel ['joʊkl]

【考法】 *n.* 乡下人，天真纯朴的人: a naive or gullible **inhabitant of a rural area** or small town

例 a lame comedy about the misadventures of yokels in the big city 讲述乡下人在大都市中不幸遭遇的蹩脚喜剧

近 bucolic, bumpkin, churl, provincial, rustic

反 cosmopolitan 云游四海的人

zeal [ziːl]

【考法】 *n.* 热心，热诚: **enthusiastic devotion** to a cause, ideal, or goal and tireless diligence in its furtherance

例 preaches with fanatical zeal 带着狂热进行传教

近 ardor, devotion, enthusiasm, fervidness, fervor, passion

反 apathy, indifference, nonchalance, torpor, unconcern 麻木，冷漠

派 zealous *adj.* 狂热的

zealot ['zelət]

【考法】 *n.* 狂热者，极端主义者: someone whose views and actions are very **extreme**, especially in **following a** particular **political or religious belief**

例 religious zealots 宗教狂热者

近 enthusiast, extremist, fanatic, fiend, freak, partisan, maniac, nut

反 moderate 温和派

派 zeal *n.* 狂热

zenith ['zenɪθ]

【考法】 *n.* 最高点，巅峰: **culminating** point

例 at the zenith of his power 他到达了权力巅峰

近 acme, apex, apogee, climax, crescendo, crest, peak, pinnacle, summit, top

反 bottom, nadir 最低点

zesty [zesti]

【考法】 *adj.* 刺激的，开胃的: appealingly **piquant** or lively

例 a zesty sauce 味道刺激的酱汁

近 peppery, piquant, pungent, salty, savory, spicy, zingy

反 bland, insipid, vapid, zestless 乏味的

List 28

Unit 1

■ ABREAST ■ APPURTENANCE ■ ACCLAIM ■ APOSTLE ■ ACCORD
■ ACCUSTOM ■ ACQUIRE ■ ACQUISITIVE ■ ADJUDICATE ■ ADVERSITY

abreast [əˈbrest]
【考法】 *adj.* 熟知的：up to a particular standard or level especially of **knowledge of recent developments**
例 She tried to keep abreast of the latest fashion trends . 她总是尽可能地跟上时尚的潮流。
近 acquainted, conversant, informed, knowledgeable, versed, well-informed
反 ignorant, unacquainted, unfamiliar, uninformed, unknowledgeable 无知的，不熟悉的

appurtenance [əˈpɜːrtɪnəns]
【考法】 *n.* 附属物：a **subordinate** part or adjunct
例 It is rather difficult, if not impossible, to determine how large the management consulting industry is mainly because there is so little agreement on its appurtenance . 由于对其附属产业的看法不统一，大家很难确定管理咨询产业的规模究竟有多大。
近 accessory, adjunct, affiliate, appendage, appendix, attachment

acclaim [əˈkleɪm]
【考法】 *n.* 称赞：**public acknowledgment or admiration** for an achievement
vt. 赞扬，赞颂：to declare enthusiastic **approval** of
例 Many people were involved in the search, but the person who actually found the missing girl got all the acclaim . 许许多多的人都参与了搜救行动，但是只有真正找到那个迷失的小女孩的人才受到了称赞。
He was acclaimed as the country's greatest modern painter. 他被盛赞为国内最优秀的现代画家。
近 accolade, applause, credit, distinction, homage, honor, kudos, laud, laurels; accredit, applaud, cheer, commend, endorse, exalt, hail, praise, salute, tout
反 castigate, excoriate, lambaste, pan, slam 猛烈抨击

apostle [əˈpɑːsl]
【考法】 *n.* （政策或思想等的）信奉者，支持者：a person who **actively supports** or favors a cause
例 Her mother was a dedicated apostle of healthy eating . 她母亲是健康饮食矢志不渝的倡导者。
近 advocate, champion, crusader, expounder, espouser, exponent, partisan, promoter, proponent, protagonist, supporter, zealot
反 adversary, antagonist, opponent 反对者

accord [əˈkɔːrd]
【考法1】 *n.* 一致：a state of **consistency** *vi.* 相符合，相一致：to be consistent or **in harmony**
例 These results accord with our predictions . 这些结果和我们的预测一致。
近 accordance, agreement, conformity, congruence, congruity, consensus, consonance, harmony, tune; agree, chord, cohere, coincide, conform, correspond, fit, harmonize, jibe, sort, square, tally
反 conflict, disagreement, incongruence, incongruity, incongruousness 不一致；differ, disagree 不相同，不一致
派 accordance *n.* 一致，和谐
【考法2】 *vt.* 授予，给予：to **grant or give** especially as appropriate, due, or earned
例 accord women the right to vote 给予妇女投票权 ‖ accord a tumultuous welcome 给予热烈欢迎
近 accord, award, grant, vest, vouchsafe
反 withhold 保留，不给予；recant, retract, withdraw 撤回，收回

accustom [əˈkʌstəm]
【考法】 *vt.* 使习惯：to **make familiar with** something through use or experience
例 As a kid from Southern California, the first challenge in his PhD life is to accustom himself to the harsh winter climate in Boston. 身为来自南加州的小孩，他博士生涯的第一道挑战就是习惯波士顿寒冷的冬天。
近 familiarize, habituate, inure, orient, wont
反 alienate, estrange, wean 使疏远

337

acquire [əˈkwaɪər]
【考法】 *vt.* 获取，获得: to **get as one's own**
例 bacteria that acquire tolerance to antibiotics 产生了抗药性的细菌 ‖ I have never acquired a taste for wine. 我从来就不具备对葡萄酒的品味能力。
近 attain, capture, draw, gain, garner, get, make, obtain, procure, realize, reap, secure, win, bring in
反 forfeit, lose 丧失
派 acquired *adj.* 后天的

acquisitive [əˈkwɪzətɪv]
【考法】 *adj.* 贪婪的: strongly **desirous** of acquiring and possessing
例 Acquisitive developers are trying to tear down the ancient temple and build a shopping mall instead. 贪婪的开发商打算铲平这座古老的神庙，取而代之建造一座购物中心。
近 avaricious, avid, coveting, covetous, grabby, grasping, mercenary, moneygrubbing, rapacious
反 benevolent, generous, liberal, philanthropic, munificent 慷慨的

adjudicate [əˈdʒuːdɪkeɪt]
【考法】 *v.* 裁决，判定: to hear and **settle** (a case, dispute or conflict)
例 When my wife and I asked the salesclerk to adjudicate our disagreement, she agreed with me that the white shoes looked better. 我和我妻子要求售货员来裁决我们之间的争论，她同意我的观点，认为白色的鞋子看起来更漂亮。
近 adjudge, arbitrate, decide, determine, judge, referee, settle, umpire

adversity [ədˈvɜːrsəti]
【考法】 *n.* 厄运，逆境: a state, condition, or instance of serious or continued **difficulty** or adverse fortune
例 The fire is the test of gold, adversity of strong man.(Martha Graham) 烈火试真金, 逆境炼勇士。——玛莎·葛兰姆 ‖ They finally overcame all the adversities of the Great Depression and rebuilt their fortunes. 他们终于度过了大萧条的困境，开始重新创造他们的财富。
近 ill, hardship, misadventure, mischance, mishap, tragedy
反 fortune, fluke, luck, serendipity 好运气

Unit 2

■ AFFECTATION   ■ AFFIRM   ■ AFFIX   ■ AFFLICTION   ■ AGAPE
■ AGILITY   ■ AGONIZE   ■ AGREEABLE   ■ ALIENATE   ■ ALLOY

affectation [ˌæfekˈteɪʃn]
【考法】 *n.* 虚伪，做作: the act of taking on or displaying an attitude or mode of behavior **not natural** to oneself or **not genuinely felt**
例 His little affectations irritated her. 他做作的小动作激怒了她。
近 façade, guise, mannerism, pose, pretense, show
反 artlessness, genuineness, innocence, naivety 天真，淳朴

affirm [əˈfɜːrm]
【考法】 *vt.* 声称…为真，肯定…属实: to assert (as a judgment or decree) as **valid or confirmed**
例 affirm the commitment to the ceasefire 申明答应停火
近 allege, assert, aver, avouch, avow, contend, declare, insist, maintain, profess, protest, purport, warrant
反 deny, gainsay, disclaim, recant 否定，反对
派 affirmation *n.* 肯定，确认

affix [əˈfɪks]
【考法】 *vt.* 粘合: to **attach physically**
例 affix a stamp to a letter 把邮票贴在信封上
近 attach, bend, fix
反 detach, undo, unfasten, unhook 松开，分开

affliction [əˈflɪkʃn]
【考法】 *n.* 痛苦，悲伤，折磨: a state of **great suffering** of body or mind
例 She listened with deep affliction as her daughter told her about the latest trouble she was in. 听着女儿诉说自己目前艰难的处境，她感到深深的心痛。
近 agony, anguish, dolor, excruciation, grief, hurt, misery, pain, rack, torment, torture, travail, tribulation, woe
反 bliss, cheer, delight, ecstasy, elation, euphoria, exhilaration, exuberance, exultation, felicity, joy, jubilation, pleasure, rapture 喜悦，高兴

agape [əˈgeɪp]

【考法】 *adj.* 急切盼望的: having or showing signs of **eagerly awaiting** something

例 She stood looking at Carmen with her mouth agape. 她站着，张大嘴看着卡门。

近 agog, anticipant, anticipatory

反 apathetic, indifferent, unconcerned, uninterested 不感兴趣的，不为所动的

agility [əˈdʒɪləti]

【考法】 *n.* (身手)敏捷: **quickness, ease and grace** in physical activity

例 His agility on the parallel bars has won him several medals. 他在双杠上的矫捷身姿助他赢得了数枚奖牌。

近 deftness, dexterity, nimbleness, sleight, spryness

反 awkwardness, clumsiness, gaucheness, gawkiness, gracelessness, ungainliness (行动)笨拙

agonize [ˈæɡənaɪz]

【考法】 *vt.* 折磨，使痛苦: to cause to suffer **agony**

例 agonize over the moral issues 被道德问题折磨

近 bedevil, beset, besiege, curse, excruciate, harrow, persecute, plague, rack, torment, torture

反 comfort, console, solace, soothe 安抚，安慰

派 agony *n.* 痛苦; agonizing *adj.* 痛苦的

agreeable [əˈɡriːəbl]

【考法 1】 *adj.* 令人愉悦的: **pleasing to the mind or senses** especially as according well with one's tastes or needs

例 Would you mind putting on some agreeable music for dinner? 你介意晚饭时放一些令人愉快的音乐吗？
the agreeable melancholy resulting from a sense of the transitoriness of natural beauty 因为感慨自然之美稍纵即逝而产生的令人愉悦的忧伤

近 congenial, delectable, delicious, delightful, dulcet, enjoyable, felicitous, gratifying, heavenly, palatable, pleasing, satisfying, savory

反 abhorrent, abominable, disagreeable, disgusting, loathsome, nauseating, repellent, repugnant, repulsive, revolting 令人厌恶的

【考法 2】 *adj.* 相一致的: being **in harmony**

例 A be agreeable with B A 与 B 相一致

近 amicable, compatible, congenial, consistent, consonant, frictionless, kindred, unanimous, united

反 disagreeable, discordant, disunited, incompatible, inharmonious 不一致的

alienate [ˈeɪliəneɪt]

【考法】 *vt.* 使…疏远: to make **unfriendly, hostile,** or **indifferent** especially where attachment formerly existed

例 alienate many followers 疏远许多支持者

近 alien, disaffect, disgruntle, sour

反 reconcile 使…重归于好

alloy

【考法 1】 [ˈælɔɪ] *n.* 合金; 混合物: a distinct entity formed by the **combining of two or more different things**

例 Television news has always been an alloy of journalism and show business. 电视新闻一直以来都是新闻界和演艺圈的混合体。

近 admixture, amalgam, cocktail, composite, compound, fusion, intermixture, mix, mixture, synthesis

反 element (构成整体的)单个元素

【考法 2】 [əˈlɔɪ] *vt.* 掺杂，降低…的纯度: to **debase by the addition** of an inferior element

例 idealism that was alloyed with political skill 因为掺入了政治技巧而被削弱的理想主义

近 adulterate, contaminate, dilute, extend, lace, pollute, sophisticate, thin

反 purify 纯化

派 unalloyed *adj.* 纯粹的，未掺杂的

Unit 3

■ AMBIVALENT   ■ ANACHRONISM   ■ ANALOGOUS   ■ ANNEX   ■ ANNOTATE
■ ANTEDATE   ■ ANTIPATHY   ■ ANTIQUATED   ■ ANTITHETICAL   ■ APPARITION

ambivalent [æmˈbɪvələnt]

【考法】 *adj.* (尤指感情、态度)矛盾的: having a mixture of **opposing feelings**

例 He maintained an ambivalent attitude to religion throughout his life. 他一生都对宗教抱有矛盾的心理。

近 conflicting, contradictory, mixed

反 certain, decided, definite, positive, resolute, sure, unquestioning 明确的，毫无疑问的

派 ambivalence *n.* 矛盾心理

anachronism [əˈnækrənɪzəm]

【考法 1】 *n.* 不合时代的人或事物；过时现象：something or someone that is not in its correct historical or chronological time, especially **a thing or person that belongs to an earlier time**

例 The bow and arrow is an anachronism in modern warfare. 弓箭在现代战争中早已过时。

反 fad, fashion, vogue 潮流，时尚

【考法 2】 *n.* 时代错误，年代误植(指所叙人、事与时代不符的错误)：**an error in chronology** in which a person, object, event, etc., is assigned a date or period other than the correct one

例 The last paragraph contains an anachronism: the Holy Office no longer existed at that time. 最后一段有一个时代错误：异端裁判所那时已经不存在了。

analogous [əˈnæləɡəs]

【考法】 *adj.* 相似的，可比较的：having qualities in **common**

例 A is analogous to B A 和 B 相似

近 akin, cognate, comparable, connate, corresponding, matching, parallel, resembling, similar, suchlike

反 different, disparate, dissimilar, diverse, unlike 不同的，不相似的

annex [əˈneks]

【考法】 *vt.* 添加，合并：to **join** (something) to a mass, quantity, or number so as to bring about an overall increase

例 plan to annex the supply room so as to make the classroom bigger 计划将工具房并入教室，从而扩充其容量

近 adjoin, affix, append, attach, subjoin, tack

反 abate, deduct, remove, subtract 削减

annotate [ˈænəteɪt]

【考法】 *vt.* 给…作注解：to furnish (a literary work) with critical **commentary or explanatory notes**

例 annotate the diary selections 给日记选篇做注

近 commentate, footnote, gloss

派 annotation *n.* 注解，注释

antedate [ˌæntiˈdeɪt]

【考法】 *vt.* 比…早，早于：to be of an **earlier date** than

例 The church antedates the village itself. 这座教堂甚至在村庄之前就存在了。

近 antecede, forego, predate, preexist

反 follow, postdate, succeed 晚于

antipathy [ænˈtɪpəθi]

【考法】 *n.* 厌恶，反感：settled **aversion** or **dislike**

例 I feel no antipathy towards any of my opponents in the tournament. 我对锦标赛中碰到的任何对手都不存在反感。

近 animosity, animus, antagonism, bitterness, enmity, gall, grudge, hostility, jaundice, rancor

反 amity 友好，和睦；liking, partiality, predilection, prepossession 偏爱，喜爱

antiquated [ˈæntɪkweɪtɪd]

【考法】 *adj.* 古老的，过时的：outmoded or discredited by reason of age: being **out of style** or fashion

例 antiquated methods of farming 过时的耕种技术

近 antique, archaic, dated, fossilized, moribund, moth-eaten, obsolete, outdated, outmoded, outworn, prehistoric, rusty

反 contemporary, current, modern, recent 当前的，现代的

antithetical [ˌæntiˈθetɪkl]

【考法】 *adj.* 完全对立的，相反的：being in **direct and unequivocal opposition**

例 A is antithetical to B A 与 B 相对立

近 antipodal, antipodean, contradictory, contrary, diametric, opposite, polar

反 equivalent, identical, same 完全一致的，相等的

派 antithesis *n.* 对立，相反

apparition [ˌæpəˈrɪʃn]

【考法】 *n.* 鬼魂，幽灵：**a ghostly figure**

例 An eccentric claimed to have photographed an apparition in her very own house. 一个行为怪异的人声称在她的住所里拍了一张幽灵的照片。

近 ghost, phantasm, phantom, shade, shadow, specter, spirit, spook, sprite, vision, visitant, wraith

反 entity, substance 实体

Unit 4

applicable [ˈæplɪkəbl]

【考法 1】 *adj.* 可用的，可行的：capable of being **put to use** or account
例 The new approach is a applicable to different problems . 新方法适用于不同的问题。
近 actionable, applicative, applied, functional, practicable, serviceable, useful, workable
反 impractical, inapplicable, unusable, unworkable, useless 不可用的，不可行的

【考法 2】 *adj.* 相关的，有关的：**having to do with** the matter at hand
例 He rarely makes comment that is applicable to our discussion . 他的评论很少和我们讨论的题目搭边。
近 apposite, apropos, germane, material, pointed, relative, relevant
反 extraneous, immaterial, impertinent, inapposite, irrelevant, pointless 无关的

apprehensive [ˌæprɪˈhensɪv]

【考法 1】 *adj.* 知晓的，理解的：having specified facts or feelings actively **impressed on the mind**
例 I am fully apprehensive of the opinions , I assure you. 我向你保证这些观点我都理解了。
近 alive, aware, cognizant, mindful, sensible, sentient, ware, witting
反 ignorant, insensible, oblivious, unaware, unconscious, unmindful, unwitting 不知晓的，无知觉的

【考法 2】 *adj.* 恐惧的，害怕的：**anxious** or **fearful** about the future
例 People apparently haven't recovered from the devastating terrorist attack and are still terribly apprehensive about the future . 人们显然没有从那场严重的恐怖袭击中恢复过来，对于未来仍然充满了恐惧。
近 afraid, aghast, fearful, frightened, horrified, hysterical, scared, shocked, terrified
反 dauntless, fearless, intrepid, unafraid 无所畏惧的；confident 充满自信的
派 apprehension *n.* 理解；忧虑，恐惧

arable [ˈærəbl]

【考法】 *adj.* 适合耕种的：fit for or used for the **growing of crops**
例 explore the west for arable land 向西探索适合耕种的土地
近 cultivable, tillable
反 barren, sterile, infertile, unfruitful, unproductive 贫瘠的

arbitrary [ˈɑːrbətreri]

【考法 1】 *adj.* 专横的，独断专行的：having or showing a tendency to **force one's will on others** without any regard to fairness or necessity
例 an arbitrary piano teacher who makes all her students do the same exercises over and over again 一个让学生反复练习相同曲子的专横的老师
近 dictatorial, imperious, peremptory, willful

【考法 2】 *adj.* 缺乏计划的，随意的：**lacking a definite plan**, purpose, or pattern
例 an unpredictable arbitrary decision 一个难以预料、随意的决定
近 aimless, desultory, erratic, haphazard, scattered, slapdash, stray, willy-nilly
反 methodical, orderly, organized, regular, systematic, systematized 有序的，有组织的

arcane [ɑːrˈkeɪn]

【考法】 *adj.* 深奥的，难以理解的：**difficult** for one of ordinary knowledge or intelligence **to understand**
例 arcane grammatical rules 深奥的语法规则
近 abstruse, cryptic, deep, enigmatic, esoteric, hermetic, impenetrable, inscrutable, recondite, uncanny
反 easy, facile, shallow, simple, superficial 浅显易懂的

argument [ˈɑːrgjumənt]

【考法 1】 *n.* 争吵，争论：an often noisy or angry **expression of differing opinions**
例 The couple's arguments were often loud enough to be heard all over the neighborhood. 这对夫妻吵架的声音往往大到能被所有邻居听见。
近 altercation, controversy, disagreement, dispute, hassle, imbroglio, quarrel, squabble, tiff, wrangle

【考法 2】 *n.* (逻辑上的)论证：a coherent series of statements leading **from a premise to a conclusion**
例 the author's argument 作者的论证
近 account, accounting, argumentation, case, explanation, rationale, reasoning

arid [ˈærɪd]

【考法 1】 *adj.* 干燥的：marked by **little or no precipitation** or humidity
例 arid wastelands unfit for human habitation 不适合人类居住的干燥荒原
近 droughty, dry, sere, thirsty, waterless
反 damp, dank, humid, moist, wet 湿润的，潮湿的

【考法 2】 *adj.* 无趣的，无聊的：causing weariness, restlessness, or **lack of interest**
例 a technically perfect but arid musical performance 技术纯熟但音乐毫无感染力的表演
近 dreary, dull, flat, humdrum, jading, jejune, monochromatic, monotonous, pedestrian, stale, stodgy, tedious, wearisome
反 absorbing, engaging, engrossing, gripping, interesting, intriguing, involving, riveting 有趣的，吸引人的

array [əˈreɪ]

【考法】 *n.* 排列，阵列：a regular and imposing grouping or **arrangement**
vt. 排列，摆放：to **arrange or display** in or as if in an array
例 a marching band's carefully choreographed array 前进中的乐队所摆出的经过精心编排的队列阵形 ‖ data arrayed in descending order 按照降序排列的数据 ‖ He arrayed his baseball cards in order of their rarity and consequent monetary value. 他把他的棒球卡按照稀有程度以及随之附有的价值排列。
近 arrangement, disposal, disposition, distribution, ordering, sequence, setup; arrange, classify, codify, dispose, marshal, organize, range, systematize, draw up, lay out
反 disorder, disorganization 混乱，无序；derange, disarrange, disarray, disorder, mess, rumple, upset 弄乱，打乱

assail [əˈseɪl]

【考法】 *vt.* 抨击，严厉批评：to **criticize harshly** and usually publicly
例 The union organizers assailed the chemical company for failing to provide a safe working environment. 工会主席严厉批评这家化工企业不能为员工提供安全的生产环境。
近 abuse, bash, belabor, blast, castigate, excoriate, lambaste, savage, scathe, slam, trash, vituperate
反 acclaim, commend, compliment, hail, laud, praise 表扬，称赞

atrophy [ˈætrəfi]

【考法】 *vi.* 萎缩，衰退：to **waste away**; wither or deteriorate
例 Memory can atrophy through lack of use. 记忆力不常使用就会衰退。
近 crumble, decay, decline, degenerate, descend, devolve, ebb, regress, retrograde, rot, sink, worsen
反 ameliorate, improve, meliorate 改善，提升

Unit 5

■ ATTEST	■ ATTUNE	■ AUGUST	■ AUSPICIOUS	■ AUSTERE
■ AUTOMATIC	■ AVOWAL	■ BACKFIRE	■ BACKSLIDE	■ BAFFLE

attest [əˈtest]

【考法】 *vt.* 证实，为…作证：to **give evidence** or testimony to the truth or factualness of
例 Her fine work attests her ability. 她的优秀作品能够证明她的能力。
近 argue, authenticate, certify, corroborate, substantiate, support, testify, validate, verify, vindicate
反 contradict, disprove, gainsay, rebut, refute 反驳，否定

attune [əˈtuːn]

【考法】 *vt.* 使协调，使和谐：to bring **into harmony**
例 After years spent in academia, he found it difficult to attune himself to the corporate culture. 在学术圈摸爬滚打多年之后，他发现自己很难融入企业文化之中。
近 accommodate, conciliate, conform, coordinate, key, reconcile
反 disharmonize 使不和谐；disarray, disorder, disorganize, disrupt 弄乱，打乱
派 attunement *n.* 调音；协调

august [ɔːˈɡʌst]

【考法】 *adj.* 威严的，庄重的：having or showing a **formal and serious or reserved manner**
例 Unsurprisingly, the head of the bank is an august white-haired gentleman. 不出所料，银行的总裁是一名白发苍苍的、令人顿生敬意的绅士。
近 distinguished, imposing, portly, solemn, staid, stately
反 flighty, frivolous, giddy, goofy, silly, undignified 轻浮的，不庄重的

auspicious [ɔːˈspɪʃəs]

【考法】 *adj.* 好兆头的：pointing **toward a happy outcome**

例 an auspicious start 开门红

近 bright, encouraging, golden, heartening, hopeful, promising, propitious

反 baleful, dark, direful, doomy, foreboding, gloomy, menacing, minatory, ominous, portentous, sinister, threatening 不祥的，凶兆的

austere [ɔːˈstɪr]

【考法】 *adj.* 朴素的，朴实无华的：markedly **simple** or unadorned

例 an austere bedroom 朴素的卧室 ‖ the monk's austere way of look 僧侣的朴素生活方式

近 plain, spartan, stark, unadorned

反 deluxe, lavish, luxurious, plush, sumptuous 奢华的；elaborate, fancy 花哨的

派 austerity *n.* 节俭，朴素

automatic [ˌɔːtəˈmætɪk]

【考法】 *adj.* 自发的，情不自禁的：acting or done **spontaneously or unconsciously**

例 Breathing is an automatic function of the body. 呼吸是自发的功能。‖ My reaction was automatic. 我的反应是情不自禁的。

近 impulsive, instinctive, involuntary, mechanic, mechanical, natural, spontaneous

反 calculated, deliberate, intentional, planned, predetermined, premeditated, studied 有计划的，蓄意的

派 automatically *adv.* 自动地

avowal [əˈvaʊəl]

【考法】 *n.* 承认，公开宣布：a solemn and often public **declaration** of the truth or existence of something

例 With jingoism rampant, the peace candidate felt compelled to make an avowal of his patriotism. 在沙文主义肆虐的情况下，这位爱好和平的候选人被迫公开承认自己是个爱国主义者。

近 affirmation, assertion, asseveration, avouchment, claim, declaration, insistence, profession

反 disavowal 否认，否定

backfire [ˌbækˈfaɪr]

【考法】 *vi.* 产生相反的结果，事与愿违：to have the **reverse** of the desired or expected effect

例 Unfortunately, the plan backfired. 不幸的是，计划产生了相反的效果。

近 boomerang

反 succeed 成功

backslide [ˈbækslaɪd]

【考法】 *vi.* (情况等)倒退，变坏：to **revert to a worse condition**

例 Keep these things in mind to help prevent you from backsliding. 牢记这些东西，它们能防止你旧病复发。

近 degenerate, lapse, recidivate, relapse, retrograde, retrogress

反 advance, progress 进步，前进

baffle [ˈbæfl]

【考法】 *vt.* 使疑惑：to throw into a state of **mental uncertainty**

例 His behavior baffles me. 他的行为使我难以琢磨。

近 befog, befuddle, bewilder, confound, discombobulate, disorient, maze, mystify, perplex, puzzle, vex

反 clarify, elucidate 澄清，阐明

派 baffling *adj.* 令人困惑的，难以理解的：making great mental demands; hard to comprehend or solve

例 I was constantly ill, with a baffling array of symptoms. 我常常生病，伴随着一系列令人困惑的症状。

近 befuddling, bewildering, confounding, confusing, enigmatic, puzzling, perplexing

反 apparent, distinct, evident, lucid, manifest, obvious, patent, pellucid, perspicuous, plain, transparent 明确的，明显的

Unit 6

| ■ BOHEMIAN | ■ BASH | ■ BEHOLDEN | ■ BEHOOVE | ■ BEIGE |
| ■ BUREAUCRATIC | ■ BELLIGERENT | ■ BESET | ■ BEWITCHING | ■ BLACKMAIL |

bohemian [boʊˈhiːmiən]

【考法】 *n.* 特立独行之人：a person（as an artist）who has an unconventional life-style that often reflects **protest against or indifference to convention**

例 Due to the lifestyle of modern-dance pioneer Isadora Duncan was considered a bohemian , since it was marked by unconventional behavior and attitudes. 现代舞先驱伊莎多拉·邓肯的生活方式叛逆不羁，充满了反传统的举止和态度，因此她被认为是特立独行之人。
近 deviant, heretic, iconoclast, maverick, nonconformist
反 conformer, conformist 循规蹈矩的人

bash [bæʃ]
【考法】 *vt.* 抨击，严厉批评：to **criticize harshly** and usually publicly
例 In all of talk radio no other host seems to enjoy bashing liberals as much as he does. 在所有电台节目中再没有像他一样热衷于抨击自由主义者的主持人了。
近 abuse, assail, belabor, blast, castigate, excoriate, lambaste, savage, scathe, slam, trash, vituperate
反 acclaim, commend, compliment, hail, laud, praise 表扬，称赞

beholden [bɪˈhoʊldən]
【考法】 *adj.* 欠他人人情的：**owing** something, such as **gratitude**, to another
例 Not wanting to be beholden to anyone, he insisted on paying his own way. 因为不想欠别人的人情，所以他坚持出自己的那一份钱。
近 indebted, obligated, obliged

behoove [bɪˈhuːv]
【考法】 *vt.* 对…有利：to be **necessary**, **proper** or **advantageous** for
例 It behooves you at least to try . 你至少也应该尝试一下。
近 befit, beseem, fit, serve, suite

beige [beɪʒ]
【考法】 *adj.* 缺乏特征的：**lacking distinction**
例 Some food critics have dismissed that chef's version of French cuisine as beige and boring . 一些美食评论家认为那名厨师所做的法国菜平凡无奇，令人厌倦。
近 characterless, faceless, featureless, indistinctive, neutral, noncommittal, vanilla
反 diagnostic, discriminating, distinct, distinctive, distinguishing, identifying, peculiar, typical 有特征的

bureaucratic [ˌbjʊərəˈkrætɪk]
【考法】 *adj.* 官僚主义的：involving **complicated rules** and procedures which can cause **long delays**
例 The department has become a bureaucratic nightmare . 该部门的官僚作风非常严重。
近 governmental, complicated

belligerent [bəˈlɪdʒərənt]
【考法】 *adj.* 好斗的，好战的：inclined to or exhibiting **assertiveness**, **hostility**, or **combativeness**
例 a belligerent attitude 寻衅的态度
近 aggressive, agonistic, assaultive, bellicose, combative, contentious, disputatious, feisty, gladiatorial, militant, pugnacious, quarrelsome, truculent, warlike
反 dove, pacific, peaceful 爱好和平的
派 belligerence *n.* 好斗，好战：an aggressive or truculent attitude, atmosphere, or disposition
例 Among the Native American tribes of the colonial period, the Iroquois were known for their belligerence . 在殖民时期的美洲土著部落中，易洛魁人因为他们的好战而著名。
近 aggressiveness, assaultiveness, bellicosity, combativeness, contentiousness, disputatiousness, feistiness, militance, pugnacity, quarrelsomeness, scrappiness, truculence
反 pacifism 爱好和平

beset [bɪˈset]
【考法 1】 *vt.* 使苦恼，骚扰：to **cause persistent suffering** to
例 He has been beset by a lack of self-confidence virtually his entire life. 事实上他的一生都被缺乏自信所困扰。
近 agonize, anguish, bedevil, besiege, curse, excruciate, harrow, persecute, plague, rack, torment, torture
反 comfort, console, solace, soothe 安抚，安慰
【考法 2】 *vt.* 攻击，袭击：to **set upon**
例 The settlers were beset by savages . 这些移民遭到了野蛮人的袭击。‖ The unsuspecting tourists were suddenly beset by robbers . 丝毫没有准备的游客遭到了歹徒的突然袭击。
近 assail, assault, attack, charge, raid, rush, storm, strike, set on
反 defend, guard, protect, shield 防御，守卫

bewitching [bɪˈwɪtʃɪŋ]
【考法】 *adj.* 迷人的，令人着迷的：having an often mysterious or magical power to **attract**
例 a bewitching woman who has never lacked for suitors 一个从不缺乏追求者的迷人女子
近 alluring, appealing, attractive, captivating, charismatic, enchanting, engaging, entrancing, glamorous, luring, magnetic, seductive
反 repellent, repelling, repugnant, repulsive, revolting 令人反感的

| **blackmail** | [ˈblækmeɪl] |

【考法】 *n./vt.* 敲诈，勒索：**extortion of money** or something else of value from a person by the threat of exposing a criminal act or discreditable information

例 emotional/moral blackmail 情感上/道德上的胁迫

近 extortion

Unit 7

| ■ BLUFF | ■ BOGUS | ■ BORE | ■ BRANDISH | ■ BRIM |
| ■ BUMBLE | ■ BUSTLE | ■ CALAMITY | ■ CALCULATED | ■ CANNY |

| **bluff** | [blʌf] |

【考法 1】 *adj.* 直率的，（说话）直截了当的：being or characterized by **direct**, **brief**, and **potentially rude** speech or manner

例 Frankly speaking, he is a bluff but good-hearted teacher. 老实说，这个老师说话很直接，但是心地善良。

近 abrupt, brusque, crusty, curt, downright, forthright, snippy, straightforward, unceremonious

反 circuitous, mealy-mouthed（说话）拐弯抹角的

【考法 2】 *vt.* 欺骗：to cause to believe what is untrue; **deceive**

例 I successfully bluffed the interviewer into believing that I could really speak French and thus would be the perfect person to serve in the newspaper's Paris bureau. 我成功地欺骗了面试官，让他相信我会法语，从而成为报社在巴黎办事处的不二人选。

近 bamboozle, beguile, cozen, deceive, delude, dupe, fool, hoax, misguide, misinform, mislead, trick

反 disabuse, disenchant, disillusion 使清醒

| **bogus** | [ˈboʊɡəs] |

【考法】 *adj.* 伪造的，假冒的：**being such in appearance only** and made or manufactured with the intention of committing fraud

例 bogus evidence 伪造的证据

近 counterfeit, fake, false, forged, inauthentic, phony, queer, sham, snide, spurious, unauthentic

反 authentic, genuine, real, unfaked, bona fide 真实的

| **bore** | [bɔːr] |

【考法】 *n.* 令人厌烦的人或事物：one that **causes boredom**

vt. 使厌倦，使厌烦：to **make weary** by being dull, repetitive, or tedious

例 For once, the graduation speaker wasn't a real bore. 就这一次，毕业演讲者不是那么令人厌倦。
The professor's lifeless and unimaginative teaching style bored the students to death. 教授毫无生气和想象力的教学方式让学生厌倦至极。

近 drip, droner, snoozer, yawner; jade, pall, tire, weary

反 absorb, engage, engross, enthrall, fascinate, grip, interest, intrigue 使充满兴趣，使全神贯注

派 boring *adj.* 令人厌烦的；boredom *n.* 厌烦，乏味

| **brandish** | [ˈbrændɪʃ] |

【考法】 *vt.*（带有威胁性地）挥舞：to **shake** or wave（as a weapon）**menacingly**

例 I could see that the suspect was brandishing a knife and was in no way inclined to surrender. 我可以看到嫌犯在挥舞着一把刀，完全没有要投降的倾向。

近 shake, swing, wave

反 drop 放下（武器等）

| **brim** | [brɪm] |

【考法 1】 *n.* 边缘，边界：an upper or **outer margin**

例 The brim of the teacup was banded with gold. 茶杯的边缘被镀上了金。

近 borderline, bound, boundary, circumference, confines, edge, frame, fringe, margin, perimeter, periphery, skirt, verge

反 center, core, heart, kernel 核心

【考法 2】 *vi.* 充满：to be or become **full often to overflowing**

例 a secondhand bookstore that was brimming with bargains 一个到处都是减价品的二手书店
eyes brimming with tears 饱含热泪的双眼

近 bristle, bulge, burst, bustle, buzz, crawl, hum, overflow, pullulate, swarm, teem

反 lack, need, want 缺少，缺乏

bumble	[ˈbʌmbl]

【考法】 *vi.* 含糊不清地说，杂乱无章地说：to speak **rapidly**, **inarticulately**, and usually unintelligibly

例　Overcome with stage fright, I could only bumble through the speech . 由于怯场，我结结巴巴地说完了演讲稿。

近　babble, drivel, drool, gabble, gibber, jabber, prattle, sputter

反　articulate, enunciate, pronounce 清楚地说

bustle	[ˈbʌsl]

【考法1】 *n.* 忙乱，喧闹：**noisy**, **energetic**, and often obtrusive activity

例　the hustle and bustle of the big city 熙熙攘攘的大都市

近　bluster, coil, disturbance, furor, hurricane, pandemonium, stir, storm, tumult, turmoil, uproar, welter, whirl

反　calm, hush, peace, quiet, rest, stillness, tranquillity 宁静，祥和；order 秩序

【考法2】 *vi.* (快速地)行走，奔忙：to **move briskly** and often ostentatiously

例　The hostess bustled about, taking care of last-minute preparations for the party. 女主人四处走着，为聚会做最后的准备。

近　blast, bolt, careen, career, dash, fly, hustle, rush, rustle, speed, whirl

反　crawl, creep, lag, poke 缓慢行进

calamity	[kəˈlæməti]

【考法】 *n.* 大灾难：a **disastrous event** marked by great loss and lasting distress and suffering

例　an economic calamity 金融风暴

近　apocalypse, cataclysm, catastrophe, debacle, disaster, tragedy

反　benediction, boon, felicity, godsend, manna, windfall 天赐好运，幸事

calculated	[ˈkælkjuleɪtɪd]

【考法】 *adj.* 经过计算(成败得失)的，经过深思熟虑的：engaged in, undertaken, or displayed after **reckoning or estimating** the statistical probability of success or failure

例　He took a calculated risk and got in on the ground floor of the new enterprise. 他深思熟虑一番之后决定冒这个险，踏出了迈向新计划的第一步。

近　advised, considered, deliberate, knowing, measured, reasoned, studied, thoughtful, weighed

反　automatic, casual, instinctive, spontaneous, unstudied 随意的，不假思索的

canny	[ˈkæni]

【考法】 *adj.* 精明的，聪明的：**careful and shrewd**, especially where one's own interests are concerned

例　He is a canny card player who is good at psyching out his opponents. 他是一个善于琢磨对手心思的精明的扑克玩家。

近　astute, clever, hardheaded, heady, knowing, savvy, sharp, shrewd, smart

反　ignorant, unknowing 无知的；foolish, idiotic, imbecile, moronic, silly, thoughtless, witless 愚笨的

Unit 8

■ CANONIZE	■ CAPTIOUS	■ CAREEN	■ CAREFREE	■ CASCADE
■ CELLULAR	■ CEREMONIOUS	■ CERTITUDE	■ CHANNEL	■ CHAPERONE

canonize	[ˈkænənaɪz]

【考法】 *vt.* 使崇高，使神圣：to assign a **high status or value** to

例　Some movie buffs canonized David Fincher as today's most preeminent director . 一些影迷把戴维·芬彻视作当今世界上最为出色的导演。

近　aggrandize, deify, dignify, elevate, ennoble, enshrine, ensky, enthrone, glorify, magnify

反　abase, degrade, demean, humble, humiliate 贬低，瞧不起

captious	[ˈkæpʃəs]

【考法】 *adj.* 吹毛求疵的，爱挑毛病的：marked by an often ill-natured inclination to **stress faults and raise objections**

例　a captious and cranky eater who has never met a vegetable he didn't hate 一个古怪又挑剔的食客，从来就没有他不讨厌的蔬菜

近　carping, caviling, critical, faultfinding, hypercritical, judgmental, overcritical

反　appreciative 表示欣赏的

careen	[kəˈriːn]

【考法】 *vi.* 蹒跚而行，不稳地行走：to **lurch or swerve** while in motion

例　He careened unsteadily to the couch after hitting his head. 在撞到头以后，他摇摇摆摆地走向沙发。

近　dodder, lurch, reel, sway, teeter, totter, waddle, wobble

carefree ['kerfriː]

【考法】 *adj.* 无忧无虑的：free from care as having **no worries or troubles**

例 passengers on a luxury cruise ship enjoying a carefree vacation 在豪华游轮上享受着无忧旅途的乘客
carefree college students on spring break 春假期间无忧无虑的大学生

近 blithe, debonair, gay, insouciant, lighthearted, lightsome, slaphappy, unconcerned

反 careworn 焦虑的

cascade [kæ'skeɪd]

【考法】 *n.* 一连串，大量：something falling or **rushing forth in quantity**

例 The women have lustrous cascades of black hair. 那些女子拥有瀑布般乌黑亮泽的秀发。

近 deluge, avalanche

cellular ['seljələr]

【考法】 *adj.* 多孔的：containing cavities; having a **porous** texture

例 the cellular construction of a beehive 蜂巢的多孔结构

近 porous

ceremonious [ˌserə'moʊniəs]

【考法】 *adj.* 讲究礼节的，庄重的：marked by or showing **careful attention to set forms** and details

例 a ceremonious reception 隆重的接待仪式

近 correct, decorous, formal, nice, proper, punctilious, starchy, stiff, stilted

反 casual, easygoing, informal, unceremonious 随意的，不正式的

certitude ['sɜːrtɪtuːd]

【考法】 *n.* 确信无疑：the state of being or feeling **certain**

例 definite certitude 确信

近 assurance, assuredness, certainty, confidence, conviction, doubtlessness, positiveness, sureness, surety

反 doubt, dubiety, incertitude, uncertainty 不确定

channel ['tʃænl]

【考法】 *vt.* 将···导向，投入：to cause to **move to a central point** or along a restricted pathway

例 a youth who channeled all of his energy into sports 一个将所有精力都投入体育之中的少年

近 canalize, channelize, conduct, direct, funnel, pipe, siphon

chaperone ['ʃæpəroʊn]

【考法】 *vt.* 同行，护送：to **go along with** in order to provide assistance, protection, or companionship

例 chaperone the young girl 护送那个年轻女孩

近 accompany, attend, companion, company, convoy, escort, squire

反 abandon, desert, ditch, dump, forsake 抛弃，不顾

Unit 9

| ■ CHARISMA | ■ CHERISHED | ■ CHIVALROUS | ■ CHORALE | ■ CLAMOR |
| ■ CLAN | ■ CLEAVE | ■ CLING | ■ COARSE | ■ COHESIVE |

charisma [kə'rɪzmə]

【考法】 *n.* 魅力，吸引力：a special magnetic **charm** or appeal

例 a movie star with unique charisma 有着独特魅力的电影明星 ‖ The candidate was lacking in charisma. 这位候选人就是缺乏了点个人魅力。

近 allure, appeal, attractiveness, captivation, enchantment, fascination, glamor, seductiveness, witchery

反 repulsion, repulsiveness 反感，厌恶

派 charismatic *adj.* 有魅力的，吸引人的

cherished ['tʃerɪʃt]

【考法】 *adj.* 受喜爱的，珍爱的：**granted special treatment** or attention

例 a cherished heirloom that has been in the family for generations 在这个家族里流传了几代的备受珍爱的传家宝 ‖ He described the picture with his wife as his most cherished possession. 他把这张与妻子的合影看作自己最为珍爱的财富。

近 beloved, dear, favored, favorite, fond, loved, pet, precious, special, sweet

反 abhorred, abominated, despised, detested, disdained, disliked, execrated, hated, loathed 被厌恶的

chivalrous [ˈʃɪvlrəs]

【考法】 *adj.* 有骑士风度的，（尤指对女性）彬彬有礼的：marked by **gracious courtesy and high-minded consideration**（especially to women）

例 The elderly gentleman still engages in chivalrous behavior, such as opening doors for people. 这位年迈的绅士仍然坚持着有风度的行为，比如帮别人开门。

近 big, elevated, gallant, great, greathearted, high, high-minded, lofty, lordly, magnanimous, natural, sublime

反 base, debased, degenerate, degraded, ignoble, ignominious, low 品行低劣的，可鄙的

派 chivalry *n.* 骑士风度

chorale [kəˈrɑːl]

【考法1】 *n.* 赞美诗：a **hymn or psalm** sung to a traditional or composed melody **in church**

例 practice a chorale to perform in church 练习吟唱要在教堂表演的赞美诗

近 anthem, canticle, carol, hymn, paean, psalm, spiritual

【考法2】 *n.* 合唱班，合唱团：an organized **group of singers**

例 a chorale that is regarded as being among the best in the state 一个被认为是国内一流的合唱班

近 choir, chorus, consort, ensemble

clamor [ˈklæmər]

【考法】 *n.* 喧闹，喧哗，噪声：**loud**, confused, and usually **inharmonious** sound

例 the clamor of the market 市场上鼎沸的人声

近 blare, bluster, cacophony, clangor, discordance, howl, racket, rattle, roar, tumult, uproar, vociferation

反 quiet, silence, still, stillness 寂静；calm, lull, serenity, tranquility 宁静，祥和

派 clamorous *adj.* 喧闹的

clan [klæn]

【考法】 *n.* (有共同爱好的)团体，帮派：a group **united by a common interest** or common characteristics

例 That clan of football fans has parties every weekend on which the New England Patriots play. 只要是新英格兰爱国者队有比赛的周末，那帮球迷就会举行聚会。

近 body, bunch, circle, clique, community, coterie, coven, crowd, fold, network, pack, ring, set

反 clannish *adj.* 派系的；团结的

cleave [kliːv]

【考法1】 *vi.* 紧贴，坚持：to **adhere** firmly and closely or loyally and unwaveringly

例 You should resolutely cleave to the facts in your report. 你应该在报道中坚持客观的原则。

近 adhere, cling, hew, stick

反 defect 叛变

【考法2】 *vt.* 分隔，割裂，劈开：to **divide** by or as if by a cutting blow

例 His spade cleaved the firm sand with a harsh crunch. 他的锹凿开了坚实的砂土，发出尖锐刺耳的嘎扎声。

近 cut, decouple, disconnect, disjoin, dissever, dissociate, divide, part, ramify, sever, slice, split, sunder

反 join, link, unify, unite 连接，接合

cling [klɪŋ]

【考法】 *vi.* 紧贴；支持：to **adhere** as if glued firmly

例 a dozen magnets clinging to the refrigerator 贴靠在冰箱门上的一打磁石 ‖ The couple continued to cling to the old ideas of child rearing long after they had gone out of fashion. 这对夫妇仍然坚持关于抚养孩子的老观念，尽管它们已经过时。

近 adhere, cleave, hew, stick

反 defect 叛变

coarse [kɔːrs]

【考法1】 *adj.* 粗糙的，表面不平整的：**not** having a level or **smooth** surface

例 the coarse surface of the sandpaper 砂纸的粗糙表面

近 broken, bumpy, irregular, jagged, lumpy, pebbly, ragged, rough, roughened, rugged, scraggy

反 even, flat, level, plane 表面平整的；smooth 表面光滑的

【考法2】 *adj.* 粗俗的：**lacking** in delicacy or **refinement**

例 coarse manners/laughter 粗俗的举止/笑声

近 crass, crude, gross, incult, lowbred, raffish, rude, uncouth, uncultivated, unpolished, unrefined, vulgar

反 civilized, cultivated, cultured, genteel, polished, refined, smooth, tasteful 有教养的，举止得体的

cohesive [kouˈhiːsɪv]

【考法】 *adj.* 有粘性的；有凝聚力的：exhibiting or producing **cohesion or coherence**

例 a cohesive social unit 有凝聚力的社会个体 ‖ cohesive soils 有粘性的土壤

近 adherent, adhesive, clingy, gluey, glutinous, gummy, tacky, tenacious, viscid

反 non-adhesive, non-viscous 无粘性的

派 cohesion *n.* 粘结；凝聚力

Unit 10

■ COMMISERATE   ■ COMPATIBLE   ■ COMPELLING   ■ COMPLACENT   ■ COMPLEMENTARY
■ COMPLICATE   ■ COMPREHEND   ■ CONCRETE   ■ CONDEMN   ■ CONDITIONAL

commiserate [kəˈmɪzəreɪt]

【考法】 *vi.* 表示怜悯，同情：to feel or express **sympathy**

例 He commiserated over their failure. 他对他们的失败表示同情。‖ We commiserated with him but there was little we could do to make the situation better. 我们很同情他的遭遇，但是也只能表示无能为力。

近 ache, bleed, compassionate, condole, sympathize, yearn

compatible [kəmˈpætəbl]

【考法】 *adj.* 一致的，能共存的：capable of existing together **in harmony**

例 A is compatible with B   A 与 B 能共存

近 accordant, coherent, concordant, conformable, congruent, congruous, consonant, harmonious

反 conflicting, incompatible, incongruous, inconsistent, inharmonious 有冲突的，矛盾的

compelling [kəmˈpelɪŋ]

【考法】 *adj.* 极具说服力的：having the power to **persuade**

例 make a compelling argument against military intervention 就反对军事干预提出了很有说服力的论证

If you can't present any compelling evidence to prove your innocence, you will be found guilty. 如果你找不出任何能证明你清白的有力证据，你就会被定罪。

近 conclusive, convincing, decisive, effective, forceful, persuasive, satisfying, strong, telling

反 feeble, weak 说服力不足的

complacent [kəmˈpleɪsnt]

【考法】 *adj.* 自满的，自鸣得意的：feeling or showing an often **excessive or unjustified satisfaction** and pleasure in one's status, possessions, or attainments

例 be complacent over success 对成功自满

近 assured, consequential, egoistic, overweening, pompous, prideful, proud, smug, vain, vainglorious

反 egoless, humble, modest, uncomplacent 谦逊的，谦卑的

派 complacency *n.* 自满

complementary [ˌkɑːmplɪˈmentri]

【考法】 *adj.* 互补的：mutually **supplying each other's** lack

例 two complementary strategies 两个互补的策略

近 correlative, interdependent, reciprocal, supplemental, supplementary

反 contradictory, incompatible 矛盾的

complicate [ˈkɑːmplɪkeɪt]

【考法】 *vt.* 使复杂化：to make **complex or difficult**

例 Don't complicate matters by getting the parents involved. 不要把父母牵扯进来，这会让问题更复杂。

近 complex, embarrass, entangle, ravel, perplex, sophisticate, tangle

反 simplify, streamline 简化

派 complicated *adj.* 复杂的，麻烦的

comprehend [ˌkɑːmprɪˈhend]

【考法 1】 *vt.* 理解，了解：to **grasp** the nature, significance, or meaning of

例 the age at which children can comprehend the difference between right and wrong 一个小孩可以开始分辨是非的年龄

近 appreciate, apprehend, assimilate, behold, catch, cognize, conceive, discern, grasp, perceive, recognize, savvy, see, seize, sense, understand

反 misapprehend, misconceive, misinterpret, misperceive, misunderstand 误解

【考法 2】 *vt.* 包括，包含：to **contain or hold within** a total scope, significance, or amount

例 comprehend more explanations 包含更多解释

近 carry, contain, embrace, encompass, entail, involve, number, subsume, take in

反 exclude, leave, omit, preclude 排除，忽略

派 comprehensive *adj.* 全面的，综合的；comprehension *n.* 理解；comprehensible *adj.* 可理解的

concrete	[ˈkɑːŋkriːt]
【考法】	*adj.* 事实性的，明确的：existing **in fact** and not merely as a possibility
例	Concrete evidence , and not just a theory, must be presented at a trial. 在法庭上需要出示确凿的证据，而非臆测。
近	effective, existent, factual, genuine, real, true, very, de facto
反	conjectural, hypothetical, ideal, platonic, suppositional, theoretical 猜测的，理论上的

condemn	[kənˈdem]
【考法】	*vt.* 谴责（…为不道德的、邪恶的）：to **declare to be reprehensible**, **wrong**, **or evil** usually after weighing evidence and without reservation
例	a policy widely condemned as racist 一个被广泛谴责为种族歧视的政策 ‖ It is a sign of human progress that slavery, which was once common, is now universally condemned . 曾经很平常的奴隶制如今却沦落到人人谴责的境地，这不能不说是人类文明的进步。
近	anathematize, censure, damn, decry, denounce, execrate, reprimand, reprehend, reproach, reprobate
反	commend, endorse, extol, laud, praise 赞扬，赞颂

conditional	[kənˈdɪʃənl]
【考法】	*adj.* 有条件的，受制约的：subject to, implying, or **dependent** upon a condition
例	a conditional offer 有条件限制的录取
近	contingent, dependent, subject, tentative
反	absolute, categorical, unconditional 不受制约的；independent 独立的

We often hear of people breaking down from overwork, but in nine cases out of ten they are really suffering from worry or anxiety.

我们常常听人说，人们因工作过度而垮下来，但是实际上十有八九是因为饱受担忧或焦虑的折磨。

—— 英国银行家 卢伯克. J.（John Lubbock, British banker）

List 29

"人最大的悲剧是眼睁睁地让梦想一点点蜕变成空想。与其纠结每个小节的意义，不如放手一搏，不求无憾，但求无悔。"

（翟冰，录取院校：Texas A&M University，生物学系）

Unit 1

■ CONFLAGRATION	■ CONFLATE	■ CONFORM	■ CONJURE	■ CONSENT
■ CONSIGN	■ CONSTERNATION	■ CONTEMPLATE	■ CONTEMPT	■ CONTEND

conflagration [ˌkɑːnfləˈɡreɪʃn]

【考法】 *n.* 武装冲突，战争：a state of **armed violent struggle** between states, nations, or groups

例 What began as a skirmish over disputed territory erupted into a conflagration that swept the continent. 这场席卷整个大陆的战争是由之前关于有纠纷的领土的小冲突引发的。

近 conflict, war, warfare

反 peace 和平；truce 休战

conflate [kənˈfleɪt]

【考法】 *vt.* 混合：to **turn into a single mass** or entity that is more or less the same throughout

例 conflate past and present 把过去与现在结合在一起

近 amalgamate, combine, composite, fuse, homogenize, immingle, incorporate, integrate, interfuse, meld, merge, mingle, mix

反 disunite, divide, part, separate, sunder 使分离

派 conflation *n.* 合并

conform [kənˈfɔːrm]

【考法1】 *vt.* 使协调：to **bring into harmony** or accord

例 conform to new safety regulations 符合新的安全标准

近 accommodate, attune, conciliate, coordinate, key, reconcile

反 disharmonize 使不和谐

【考法2】 *vi.* 遵照，遵从：to be **obedient** or **compliant**

例 an independent-minded person who refuses to conform to another's wishes 一个思想独立、拒绝遵照他人的意愿行动的人

近 adhere, comply, follow, goose-step, mind, observe

反 defy, disobey, rebel 不服从，反抗

派 conformist *n.* 墨守成规的人；conformism *n.* 守旧

conjure [ˈkʌndʒər]

【考法1】 *vt.* 请求，恳求：to charge or **entreat earnestly** or solemnly

例 I conjure you to hear my plea for mercy. 请您发发慈悲吧。

近 appeal, beseech, besiege, entreat, impetrate, implore, importune, petition, plead, pray, solicit, supplicate

【考法2】 *vt.* 在脑海中浮现，想起：to **form a mental picture** of

例 With certain flowers I instantly conjure up memories of our Caribbean honeymoon. 这些鲜花让我立即回想起我们加勒比海的蜜月之旅。

近 conceive, dream, envisage, envision, fancy, fantasize, feature, ideate, image, picture, vision, visualize

consent [kənˈsent]

【考法】 *n.* 同意，赞同：the **approval** by someone in authority for the doing of something

vi. 同意：to give assent or **approval**

例 We had to get our neighbor's consent in order to trim the tree from his side. 想要从邻居家那边修剪树木，我们得先得到他的同意。|| consent to being tested in her neurobiology experiment 同意在她神经生物学的实验中作测试对象 || refuse to consent to the marriage 拒绝这桩婚事

近 allowance, approval, authorization, clearance, concurrence, granting, license, sanction, warrant; acquiesce, agree, approve, assent, subscribe

反 interdiction, prohibition, proscription 禁止；dissent 反对；deny, veto 否决

consign [kənˈsaɪn]

【考法】 *vt.* 转交，转移（给他人）: to give, transfer, or deliver into the hands or **control of another**

例 The record shows that the deliveryman had consigned our package to a next-door neighbor . 记录显示邮递员把我们的包裹转投给隔壁邻居了。‖ a writer consigned to oblivion 湮没无闻的作家

近 commend, commit, confide, delegate, deliver, entrust, hand, recommend, repose, transfer, transmit, vest

反 hold, keep, retain 保留

consternation [ˌkɑːnstərˈneɪʃn]

【考法】 *n.* 惊愕，恐慌，恐惧: a state of **paralyzing dismay**

例 The two girls stared at each other in consternation without any idea about what to do. 两个小女孩惊恐地望着对方，显得不知所措。

近 alarm, apprehension, dread, fear, fright, horror, terror, trepidation

反 bravery, courage, dauntlessness, fearlessness, fortitude, intrepidity, stoutness, valor 勇气，无畏

contemplate [ˈkɑːntəmpleɪt]

【考法】 *v.* 沉思，仔细思索: to view or **consider** with continued attention

例 contemplate the vastness of the universe 沉思着宇宙的广袤无垠 ‖ She contemplated the problem for several hours before reaching a decision. 关于这个问题，她苦苦思索了几个小时后才做出决定。

近 cogitate, consider, deliberate, meditate, mull, perpend, pore, revolve, ruminate, study, weigh, wrestle

反 disregard, ignore, overlook, slight 忽视

派 contemplation *n.* 沉思，思索

contempt [kənˈtempt]

【考法】 *n.* 蔑视，鄙视: open dislike for someone or something considered **unworthy of one's concern or respect**

例 my undying contempt for people who abuse animals 我对于虐待动物者的无尽鄙视 ‖ Her contempt for illiterate was obvious. 你可以很明显地看出她对文盲的鄙夷。

近 contemptuousness, despisement, despite, despitefulness, disdain, misprision, scorn

反 admiration, esteem, estimation, regard, respect, reverence, veneration 尊敬，敬仰

派 contemptible *adj.* 可鄙的；contemptuous *adj.* 蔑视的

contend [kənˈtend]

【考法1】 *vi.* 竞争，争夺: to **strive or vie in contest** or rivalry or against difficulties

例 two traditional rivals contending for the championship 两个争夺冠军头衔的老对手

近 battle, fight, race, rival, vie

反 capitulate, quit, succumb, surrender, give in 投降

【考法2】 *vt.* 声明，声称: to **state as a fact** usually forcefully

例 I would contend that the minister's thinking is flawed on this point. 我声明部长的想法在这一点上有漏洞。

近 affirm, allege, assert, aver, avouch, avow, declare, insist, maintain, profess, protest, purport, warrant

反 deny, gainsay 否认

Unit 2

| ■ CONTRADICT | ■ CONTRIVED | ■ CONVENE | ■ CORRELATE | ■ COUNTERPART |
| ■ COUNTERPRODUCTIVE | ■ COURTEOUS | ■ COY | ■ CREDIT | ■ CROW |

contradict [ˌkɑːntrəˈdɪkt]

【考法】 *vt.* 否认，反驳；与…相矛盾: to assert the **contrary** of; to imply the opposite or a denial of

例 contradict a rumor 反驳谣言 ‖ Your actions contradict your words . 你的行为和你说的话相互矛盾。

近 deny, disaffirm, disavow, disclaim, disconfirm, disown, gainsay, negate, negative, refute, reject, repudiate

反 acknowledge, admit, avow, concede, confirm 承认

派 contradictory *adj.* 矛盾的，相反的

contrived [kənˈtraɪvd]

【考法】 *adj.* 不自然的，刻意的: **lacking** in natural or **spontaneous quality**

例 We are bored with the contrived applause of a TV studio audience that has been told when to clap. 摄影棚中的观众会被告知什么时候鼓掌，这种经过刻意安排的掌声让我们倍感厌倦。

近 affected, assumed, bogus, factitious, feigned, plastic, pretended, pseudo, simulated, unnatural

反 artless, natural, spontaneous, unaffected, uncontrived, unfeigned, unforced 真诚的，不虚伪的

convene [kənˈviːn]

【考法】 *vt.* 召开，召集: to **bring together in assembly** by or as if by command

例 convene the members of the council for an emergency session 召集委员会的成员进入紧急议程

近 assemble, call, muster, summon

反 disband, dispel, disperse, dissipate, dissolve, squander 驱散，驱逐

correlate [ˈkɔːrəleɪt]

【考法】 *vt.* 使…相关联: to establish a **mutual or reciprocal relation** between

例 a demanding father who always correlated success with hard work 一个总将成功和辛勤工作挂钩的严格父亲 ‖ In this work, we correlate the simulation in the lab and the observation in the field to examine the validity of our theory. 本文中，我们将实验室的模拟结果和实际观测数据联系起来以验证理论的真实性。

近 connect, identify, link, relate

反 separate 分离

派 correlation *n.* 关联，关系

counterpart [ˈkaʊntərpɑːrt]

【考法】 *n.* (地位、功能)对等的人或物: one having the **same function or characteristics** as another

例 U.S. presidents and his British counterpart 美国总统和英国首相

近 coequal, compeer, coordinate, equivalent, fellow, like, match, parallel, peer, rival

counterproductive [ˌkaʊntərprəˈdʌktɪv]

【考法】 *adj.* 反效果的，阻碍预期目标的: **not producing** or tending to hinder the attainment of a **desired goal**

例 Violence as a means to achieve an end is counterproductive. （W. E. Brock）用暴力来达到目标往往是事与愿违的。——W. E. 布洛克

近 feckless, hamstrung, ineffective, ineffectual, inefficacious, inefficient, inexpedient

反 effective, effectual, efficacious, efficient, expedient, operant 行之有效的

courteous [ˈkɜːrtiəs]

【考法】 *adj.* 礼貌的，谦恭有礼的: marked by **polished manners**, gallantry, or ceremonial usage of a court

例 Their customer service department always gives courteous responses, even to rude people. 哪怕是对粗鲁的消费者，他们的客服部总是用一种非常有礼貌的态度回复。

近 civil, civilized, couth, genteel, gracious, mannerly, suave, urbane, well-bred

反 discourteous, ill-bred, ill-mannered, impertinent, impolite, impudent, insolent, rude 粗鲁的，不礼貌的

派 courtesy *n.* 礼貌，谦恭

coy [kɔɪ]

【考法】 *adj.* 不愿与人交往的，内向的: **tending to avoid people** and social situations

例 She was modest without being coy. 她很低调，但又不至于内向。

近 backward, bashful, diffident, introverted, modest, recessive, retiring, sheepish, shy, withdrawn

反 extroverted, immodest, outgoing 外向的

credit [ˈkredɪt]

【考法 1】 *n.* 信任，信赖: **mental conviction of the truth** of some statement or the reality of some being or phenomenon

例 I give full credit to this report on the prevalence of cheating among college students today. 我非常相信这则有关大学中作弊成风的报道。

近 belief, credence, faith, trust

反 disbelief, doubt, dubiety, incertitude 不信任，不确定

【考法 2】 *n.* 表扬，赞扬: public **acknowledgment or admiration** for an achievement

例 She deserves all the credit, since she did all the work. 是她完成了所有的工作，因此荣誉都应该属于她。

近 acclaim, accolade, applause, commendation, distinction, endorsement, homage, honor, kudos, laud

反 denunciation, excoriation, rebuke, reprimand, reproach, reproof, stricture 谴责，责难

crow [kroʊ]

【考法】 *vi.* 感到高兴: to feel or express **joy or triumph**

例 He won't stop crowing about his victory. 他滔滔不绝地夸耀自己的胜利。

近 delight, exuberate, glory, jubilate, joy, rejoice, triumph

反 bemoan, bewail, grieve, lament, weep 感到悲伤，叹息

Unit 3

damn ［dæm］
【考法】 *vt.* (在道德上)谴责: to declare to be **morally wrong or evil**
例 a cleric who damned gambling and strong drink 一位严厉谴责赌博和酗酒的牧师
近 anathematize, censure, decry, denounce, execrate, reprehend, reprobate
反 bless, eulogize, exalt, extol, glorify, laud, praise 赞颂

dampen ［'dæmpən］
【考法】 *vt.* 抑制，压抑(感情、精力等)，泼冷水: to check or **diminish the feeling, activity or vigor** of
例 Nothing could dampen their enthusiasm. 没有什么能扼杀他们的激情。
近 benumb, blunt, castrate, deaden, devitalize, enervate, geld, lobotomize, petrify
反 brace, energize, enliven, invigorate, quicken, stimulate, vitalize, vivify 使充满活力

dashing ［'dæʃɪŋ］
【考法】 *adj.* 爱好冒险的，大胆的: inclined or willing to **take risks**
例 the dashing heroes in stories about the American West 美国西部故事中那些勇敢无畏的英雄
近 adventurous, audacious, daring, emboldened, enterprising, gutsy, nerved, nervy, venturous
反 cowardly, craven, pusillanimous, timid, timorous 胆小的

dated ［'deɪtɪd］
【考法】 *adj.* 过时的: having **passed its time of use** or usefulness; out-of-date
例 His jokes are awfully dated, referring to things that happened years ago. 他的笑话全是些关于几年前的事情的过时货。
近 antiquated, archaic, fossilized, medieval, moribund, moth-eaten, obsolete, outdated, outmoded, outworn, prehistoric, rusty
反 contemporary, current, modern, recent 当前的，现代的

deadlock ［'dedlɑːk］
【考法1】 *n.* 僵局: **a state of inaction or neutralization** resulting from the opposition of equally powerful uncompromising persons or factions
例 The deadlock was broken with a key compromise. 一个关键性的妥协打破了僵局。
近 gridlock, halt, impasse, logjam, stalemate, standoff, standstill
【考法2】 *vt.* 使陷入僵局，使停顿: to bring or come **to a deadlock**
反 expedite 加速进程

debonair ［ˌdebə'ner］
【考法1】 *adj.* 无忧无虑的，不在乎的: having or showing **freedom from worries or troubles**
例 His debonair dismissal of my inquiry concerning his financial situation led me to believe that nothing was wrong. 对于我提出的有关他个人财务状况的问题，他表现得毫不担忧，这使我相信(他的财务)确实没有出现问题。
近 blithe, carefree, gay, insouciant, lighthearted, lightsome, slaphappy, unconcerned
反 careworn 焦虑的
【考法2】 *adj.* 风度翩翩的: having or showing very **polished and worldly manners**
例 The debonair gentleman charmed all of the ladies in the room. 风度翩翩的绅士吸引了房间里的所有女士。
近 civilized, graceful, polished, refined, smooth, sophisticated, suave, svelte, urbane
反 boorish, churlish, loutish, uncouth 粗鲁的，粗野的; clumsy, gauche, graceless 笨拙的

decadent ［'dekədənt］
【考法】 *adj.* 堕落的，腐败的: having or showing **lowered moral character** or standards
n. 道德上堕落的人: a person in a condition or process of mental or **moral decay**
例 Opponents of gambling casinos claim that gambling is a decadent form of entertainment. 赌场的反对者们宣称赌博是一种堕落腐化的娱乐形式。
近 debased, debauched, degenerate, depraved, dissolute, perverse, perverted, reprobate, warped; deviate
反 pure, uncorrupted 纯净的，未腐化的; saint 圣人

decry ［dɪ'kraɪ］
【考法】 *vt.* 强烈反对，否定: to express **strong disapproval** of
例 Scientists were quick to decry the claims of the psychic. 通灵者的说法很快就遭到了科学家的反对。
decry the excessive emphasis on sex 谴责对于性的过分重视

近 belittle, denigrate, denounce, deprecate, depreciate, derogate, disapprove, dismiss, disparage, minimize
反 acclaim, applaud, exalt, extol, glorify, laud, magnify, praise 表扬，称颂

deflect [dɪˈflekt]
【考法】 *vt.* 使偏斜，使转向：to **turn aside** especially **from a straight course** or fixed direction
例 They are trying to deflect the public attention from the troubled economy. 他们试图将公众的注意力从经济的困境中转移开。
近 divert, redirect, swing, veer, wheel, whip
派 deflection *n.* 偏转，偏离

defray [dɪˈfreɪ]
【考法】 *vt.* 支付：to **undertake the payment** of
例 The government has committed billions toward defraying the costs of the war. 政府为战争付出了数十亿元的代价。‖ I don't have sufficient fund to defray the expense. 我身上的现金不够买单。
近 disburse, expend, pay
反 acquire, earn, gain, garner, procure, realize, secure, win 获得，获取；charge 收取

Unit 4

■ DEIGN	■ DELEGATE	■ DELINEATE	■ DEMOTE	■ DEPENDABLE
■ DEPLORABLE	■ DICHOTOMY	■ DICTATE	■ DISCREET	■ DISENCHANT

deign [deɪn]
【考法】 *vi.* （不情愿地）屈尊，俯就：to **condescend reluctantly** and with a strong sense of the affront to one's superiority that is involved
例 I would never deign to answer that absurd accusation. 我根本不屑于去解释那样一个荒谬的指责。
近 condescend, stoop

delegate [ˈdelɪɡət]
【考法1】 *n.* 代理人，代表：a person authorized to act as **representative for another**
例 The real estate developer sent a delegate to the town meeting to represent his interests. 房地产开发商派了一名能代表自己利益的代理前往镇上开会。‖ the U.N. delegates from African countries 非洲国家的驻联合国代表
近 agent, assignee, commissary, deputy, emissary, envoy, legate, minister, proxy, representative
派 delegation *n.* 代表团
【考法2】 *vt.* 移交（权力、任务等）：to put（something）into the **possession or safekeeping of another**
例 The manager is reluctant to delegate authority to subordinates while abroad. 经理不愿意在国外期间将自己的权力转交给下级。
近 commit, confide, consign, deliver, entrust, repose, transfer, transmit, vest, give over, hand over, turn over
反 hold, keep, retain 保持，持有

delineate [dɪˈlɪnieɪt]
【考法】 *vt.* 描写，描绘：to **describe, portray**, or set forth with accuracy or in detail
例 delineate the steps to be taken by the government 具体描述了政府所应该采取的措施 ‖ The film does a remarkable job of delineating the emotions that immigrants feel upon their arrival in a strange country. 这部电影成功地描绘了移民者踏上陌生国土时的心情。
近 depict, display, draw, image, limn, paint, picture, portray, render
反 color, distort, falsify, garble, misrepresent, misstate, pervert, twist, warp 曲解，篡改本意
派 delineation *n.* 描绘

demote [ˌdiːˈmoʊt]
【考法】 *vt.* 降职，降级：to reduce to **a lower grade** or rank
例 The court-martial's decision was to demote the officer responsible for the failed mission. 军事法庭决定对为此次任务失败负责的军官进行降职处理。
近 break, bust, degrade, disrate, downgrade, reduce
反 advance, elevate, promote, raise 提升，晋升
派 demotion *n.* 降职

dependable [dɪˈpendəbl]
【考法】 *adj.* 可靠的，值得信赖的：capable of being **depended on**
例 a dependable source of income 可靠的收入来源 ‖ He was a good friend and a dependable companion. 他是一个好朋友，一个值得信赖的好伙伴。
近 calculable, reliable, responsible, safe, secure, solid, trustable, trustworthy
反 undependable, unreliable, unsafe, untrustworthy 不值得信赖的

deplorable [dɪˈplɔːrəbl]

【考法】 *adj.* 可鄙的，可耻的：worthy of severe **condemnation or reproach**

例 We will not tolerate such deplorable behavior in a house of worship. 我们绝不能容许这样一种可鄙的行为出现在礼拜堂中。

近 despicable, dirty, grubby, lousy, mean, nasty, paltry, scurvy, wretched

反 admirable, commendable, creditable, laudable, meritorious, praiseworthy 值得表扬的

dichotomy [daɪˈkɑːtəmi]

【考法】 *n.* 对立：a **division into two** especially mutually exclusive or contradictory groups or entities

例 a dichotomy between A and B A 与 B 的对立

近 bifurcation, breakup, cleavage, division, fractionalization, partition, schism, scission, split, sundering

反 unification, union 统一

dictate [ˈdɪkteɪt]

【考法】 *vt.* (仗着地位、权力) 下令：to **request** the doing of by virtue of one's authority

例 They are in no position to dictate terms 他们没有资格发号施令

近 call, decree, direct, impose, mandate, ordain, order, prescribe

反 cancel, countermand, rescind 撤销命令

派 dictator *n.* 独裁者

discreet [dɪˈskriːt]

【考法】 *adj.* (言行) 谨慎的：having or showing **good judgment and restraint** especially in conduct or speech

例 make a few discreet enquiries 审慎地询问清楚

近 intelligent, judicious, prudent

反 imprudent, indiscreet, injudicious 不谨慎的

disenchant [ˌdɪsɪnˈtʃænt]

【考法】 *vt.* 使清醒：to **free from illusion**

例 disenchant voters 使选民清醒

近 disabuse, undeceive

反 beguile, cozen, delude, dupe, fool, gull, hoax, hoodwink, misguide, misinform, mislead 诱骗

Unit 5

■ DISHEARTEN	■ DISJUNCTIVE	■ DISPROVE	■ DISTINCTIVE	■ DOCTRINAIRE
■ DOMINEER	■ DRAB	■ DRAMATIC	■ DREAD	■ DUPLICATE

dishearten [dɪsˈhɑːrtn]

【考法】 *vt.* 使沮丧，使失去信心：to cause to **lose spirit or morale**

例 We were greatly disheartened by the news that our grandmother was seriously ill. 听到祖母病重的消息，我们都很沮丧。

近 chill, daunt, demoralize, discourage, dismay, dispirit, frustrate, unnerve

反 embolden, encourage, hearten, nerve, steel 使大胆，鼓励

disjunctive [dɪsˈdʒʌŋktɪv]

【考法】 *adj.* 分离的：marked by **breaks or disunity**

例 a disjunctive narrative sequence 散乱的叙述顺序

反 conjunctive, connective 连接的

派 disjunction *n.* 分离

disprove [ˌdɪsˈpruːv]

【考法】 *vt.* 反驳，证明为假：to **prove to be false** or wrong

例 Magellan's circumnavigation of the globe disproved any lingering notions that the earth is flat. 麦哲伦的环球旅行彻底反驳了任何残存的"地球是平的"的观念。

近 belie, confound, confute, debunk, disconfirm, discredit, falsify, rebut, refute, shoot down

反 confirm, establish, prove, validate, verify 证实，证明为真

distinctive [dɪˈstɪŋktɪv]

【考法 1】 *adj.* 完全不同的：being **not of the same kind**

例 She seems to alternate between two distinctive hairstyles. 她的发型似乎在两种截然不同的样式中变换。

近 disparate, dissimilar, distant, distinct, distinguishable, diverse, unalike, unlike

反 identical, indistinguishable, same 相同的；alike, analogous, kindred, like, parallel, similar 相似的

派 distinction *n.* 区别，差别

【考法 2】 *adj.* 特征性的，典型的: **serving to identify** as belonging to an individual or group
例 Jerusalem has a distinctive Middle East flavor . 耶路撒冷有着典型的中东风情。
近 characteristic, classic, diagnostic, discriminating, distinguishing, identifying, peculiar, symptomatic, typical
反 atypical, uncharacteristic, untypical 非典型的

doctrinaire [ˌdɑːktrə'ner]
【考法】 *adj.* 教条主义的，照本宣科的: given to or marked by the forceful expression of **strongly held opinions**
例 A doctrinaire conservative , the columnist takes special delight in baiting liberals. 这个专栏作家是个谨遵教条的顽固保守主义者，他很享受挑衅那些自由主义者的感觉。
近 dogmatic
反 latitudinarian (宗教方面) 能容纳不同意见的

domineer [ˌdɑːmə'nɪr]
【考法】 *vt.* 专制统治: to exercise arbitrary or **overbearing control**
例 He tried to domineer over everyone . 他试图统治任何人 。
近 tyrannize
派 domineering *adj.* 专横的，盛气凌人的

drab [dræb]
【考法】 *adj.* 单调的，无聊的: characterized by **dullness and monotony**
例 The new city hall turned out to be another drab pile of masonry for the town. 新的市政大厅结果又是城镇里一座单调无趣的砖瓦堆积物。
近 arid, dreary, drudging, humdrum, jading, jejune, monochromatic, monotonous, pedestrian, ponderous, stale, stodgy, tedious, tiresome, wearisome
反 absorbing, engaging, engrossing, gripping, interesting, intriguing, involving, riveting 令人感兴趣的

dramatic [drə'mætɪk]
【考法】 *adj.* 显著的，惹人注意的: **striking** in appearance or effect
例 a dramatic drop in the temperature overnight 夜晚气温的显著下降
近 arresting, bold, brilliant, catchy, conspicuous, flamboyant, prominent, remarkable, splashy, striking
反 discreet, inconspicuous, invisible, subtle, unnoticeable, unobtrusive 不易引起注意的
派 dramatically *adv.* 显著地

dread [dred]
【考法】 *n.* 恐惧: great **fear** especially in the face of impending evil
例 We were filled with dread when we saw the rapids we would be rafting down. 当我们看到竹筏驶向激流时，我们的内心被恐惧所占据。
近 alarm, apprehension, consternation, fear, fright, horror, terror, trepidation
反 bravery, courage, dauntlessness, fearlessness, fortitude, intrepidity, stoutness, valor 勇气，无畏
派 dreadful *adj.* 令人恐惧的

duplicate
【考法】 ['duːplɪkət] *n.* 复制品: either of two things **exactly alike** and usually produced at the same time or by the same process ['duːplɪkeɪt] *vt.* 复制: to **make a copy** of
例 a duplicate of a house key 房间钥匙的复制品 ‖ Art students are trying to duplicate paintings in the museum's collection as part of their training. 艺术生们正在努力临摹博物馆中的作品，作为他们训练的一部分。
近 copy, dupe, duplication, facsimile, imitation, mock, reduplication, replica, replication, reproduction; clone, copycat, imitate, reduplicate, render, replicate, reproduce
反 archetype, original, prototype 原型; originate 原创
派 duplicable *adj.* 可模仿的

Unit 6

■ ECLECTIC	■ EFFICACIOUS	■ ELUDE	■ ENAMORED	■ ENDEAVOR
■ ENTHRALL	■ EQUILIBRIUM	■ ESCORT	■ ETHOS	■ EXORCISE

eclectic [ɪ'klektɪk]
【考法】 *adj.* 混合的，多元化的: composed of elements drawn **from various sources**
例 The museum's eclectic collection has everything from a giraffe skeleton to medieval musical instruments. 博物馆里的展品丰富多样，从长颈鹿的骨架到中世纪的乐器都有。
近 assorted, diverse, heterogeneous, indiscriminate, magpie, mixed, motley, piebald, ragtag, varied
反 homogeneous, uniform 同一性的

efficacious [ˌefɪˈkeɪʃəs]
- 【考法】 *adj.* 有效的：having the power to **produce a desired effect**
- 例 efficacious new drug 有效的新药
- 近 effective, effectual, efficient, fruitful, operative, potent, productive
- 反 bootless, fruitless, ineffective, ineffectual, inefficient, inoperative, unproductive, useless 无效的

elude [iˈluːd]
- 【考法 1】 *vt.* 躲闪，躲避：to **avoid adroitly**
- 例 manage to elude capture 成功躲过追捕
- 近 avoid, dodge, duck, eschew, evade, finesse, scape, shirk, shun, sidestep, weasel
- 反 confront 直面，面对
- 【考法 2】 *vt.* 使无法理解，使困惑：to **escape the perception**, understanding, or grasp of
- 例 a metaphor that eluded them 一个让他们无法理解的比喻
- 近 baffle, befog, befuddle, bewilder, confound, discombobulate, disorient, maze, mystify, perplex, puzzle, vex
- 反 clarify, elucidate, explicate, expound, illuminate, illustrate 解释，阐明
- 派 elusive *adj.* 隐秘的；难懂的

enamored [ɪˈnæmərd]
- 【考法】 *adj.* 迷恋的，热爱的：filled with an **intense or excessive love** for
- 例 Many teenage girls became enamored of the movie idol for her boyish good looks. 很多年轻的女孩子因为该影星男性化的帅气面庞而对她深深迷恋。
- 近 besotted, bewitched, captivated, crazy, dotty, enraptured, fascinated, infatuated, mad, nuts, obsessed
- 反 apathetic, detached, indifferent, insouciant, nonchalant 无所谓的，冷漠的

endeavor [ɪnˈdevər]
- 【考法】 *n.* 努力，奋斗：a **conscientious or concerted effort** toward an end
- *vt.* 努力做，拼搏：to **devote serious and sustained effort**
- 例 endeavor to improve the quality of life in the inner city 努力改善市内的生活质量 ‖ They endeavored to create a government that truly serves its people. 他们在努力地创立一个一心为人民服务的政府。
- 近 attempt, essay, striving, struggle, trial, undertaking; assay, drudge, hustle, moil, plod, slave, strain, strive, sweat, seek, toil, travail, tug
- 反 drop, quit 放弃

enthrall [ɪnˈθrɔːl]
- 【考法】 *vt.* (像用魔咒般)吸引：to **hold the attention** of as if by a spell
- 例 Enthralled by the flickering aurora in the sky, we lost all track of time. 我们被夜空里变化莫测的极光深深地吸引，以至于忘却了时间。
- 近 absorb, arrest, bedazzle, enchant, engross, fascinate, grip, hypnotize, immerse, mesmerize, spellbind
- 反 bore, jade, pall, tire, weary 使厌恶，使厌倦
- 派 enthralling *adj.* 吸引人的

equilibrium [ˌiːkwɪˈlɪbriəm]
- 【考法】 *n.* 均势，平衡：a condition in which **opposing forces are equal** to one another
- 例 find an equilibrium between A and B 在 A 和 B 之间找到一个平衡点
- 近 counterpoise, equilibration, equipoise, poise, stasis
- 反 disequilibration, disequilibrium, imbalance, nonequilibrium, unbalance 不平衡

escort [ɪˈskɔːrt]
- 【考法】 *vt.* 同行，护送：to **go along with** in order to provide assistance, protection, or companionship
- 例 a VIP escorted by an army of bodyguards and journalists 被一群保镖和记者包围的重要人物
- 近 accompany, attend, chaperone, companion, company, convoy, squire
- 反 abandon, desert, ditch, dump, forsake 抛弃，不顾

ethos [ˈiːθɑːs]
- 【考法】 *n.* 道德准则：the **code of good conduct** for an individual or group
- 例 Rigorous self-discipline was central to the ethos of the ancient Spartans. 严格的自律是古代斯巴达人所尊崇的核心道德准则。
- 近 ethics, morality, morals, norms, principles, standards

exorcise [ˈeksɔːrsaɪz]
- 【考法】 *vt.* 除去：to **get rid of** (something troublesome, menacing, or oppressive)
- 例 exorcise the unhappy memories from her mind 把不愉快的记忆从她的脑海中除去
- 近 cashier, cast, ditch, dump, fling, jettison, lose, pitch, reject, scrap, shed, slough, throw, toss, unload
- 反 adopt, employ, use, utilize 采用，使用
- 派 exorcism *n.* 除魔，驱鬼

Unit 7

explicate ['eksplɪkeɪt]

【考法】 *vt.* 解释，说明：to give a **detailed explanation** of

例 The physicist did his best to explicate the wave theory of light for the audience of laymen. 物理学家尽其所能向一群非专业的听众解释了光的波动性理论。

近 clarify, clear, construe, demonstrate, demystify, elucidate, explain, expound, illuminate, illustrate, interpret, simplify, unriddle

反 obscure 使晦涩

派 explication *n.* 解释

exterminate [ɪk'stɜːrmɪneɪt]

【考法】 *vt.* 根除，消灭：to get rid of completely usually by **killing off**

例 We hope that the fumigant exterminates the whole colony of cockroaches, for any survivors may be resistant to any poison. 我们希望所有的蟑螂都能被这种杀虫熏剂根除，因为任何幸存者都可能产生抗药性。

近 annihilate, decimate, efface, eradicate, expunge, extirpate, liquidate, obliterate, raze, sweep, wipe out

反 conserve, preserve, protect 保护；rescue, save 拯救

派 extermination *n.* 消灭

extrapolate [ɪk'stræpəleɪt]

【考法】 *vt.*（通过逻辑）推断：to **form an opinion** or reach a conclusion **through reasoning** and information

例 We can extrapolate from past economic recessions the probable course of the current one. 通过以往经济衰退我们可以推断出本次危机的可能发展趋势。

近 conclude, decide, deduce, derive, gather, judge, reason, understand

反 conjecture, guess, speculate, surmise（无根据地）猜测，揣测

派 extrapolation *n.* 推论

fabulous ['fæbjələs]

【考法1】 *adj.* 幻想中的，不真实的：not real and existing only **in the imagination**

例 a story of a fabulous land where the people know nothing of war and live together in perfect harmony 一个有关世外桃源的故事，当地的居民不知道战争为何物，和谐融洽地生活在一起

近 chimerical, dreamy, illusory, phantom, unreal, visionary

反 actual, existent, existing, real 真实存在的

【考法2】 *adj.* 极好的：**extremely pleasing** or successful

例 We had a fabulous time on our vacation. 我们的假期赞极了。

近 awesome, divine, fantastic, heavenly, marvelous, noble, prime, splendid, superb, superior, terrific

反 atrocious, awful, execrable, lousy, pathetic, poor, rotten, terrible, wretched 极差劲的

fad [fæd]

【考法】 *n.*（短暂的）流行，时尚：a practice or interest that is very **popular for a short time**

例 a passing fad 昙花一现 ‖ the latest/current fad 最新/当前的时尚

近 buzz, craze, enthusiasm, fashion, trend, vogue

反 classic 经典；standard 标准

fallible ['fæləbl]

【考法】 *adj.* 可能出错的：tending or likely to be **erroneous** or capable of making an error

例 They are only human and all too fallible. 他们都是人类，因此难免犯错。‖ a hasty, fallible generalization 有可能出错的仓促结论

近 errant

反 fail-safe, foolproof, infallible, unfailing 万无一失的，不可能出错的

派 fallibility *n.* 易错

fanciful ['fænsɪfl]

【考法】 *adj.* 不切实际的，荒谬的：conceived or made **without regard for reason** or reality

例 a fanciful dream 一个不切实际的梦想

近 absurd, bizarre, crazy, foolish, insane, nonsensical, preposterous, unreal, wild

反 realistic, reasonable 现实的，有理的

favoritism ['feɪvərɪtɪzəm]

【考法】 *n.* 偏爱，偏袒：the showing of **special favor**

例 The students accused the teacher of favoritism. 学生指责老师偏心。

| 近 | favor, one-sidedness, partiality, prejudice, tendentiousness |
| 反 | impartiality, neutrality, objectivity, open-mindedness, unbiasedness 公平，公正 |

featureless [ˈfiːtʃərləs]
【考法】 *adj.* 缺乏特征的：**lacking distinguishing characteristics** or features
例 the featureless landscape of the steppe 大草原上缺乏特色的地貌
近 beige, characterless, faceless, indistinctive, neutral, noncommittal, vanilla
反 diagnostic, discriminating, distinct, distinctive, distinguishing, identifying, peculiar, typical 特征的

feisty [ˈfaɪsti]
【考法】 *adj.* 好斗的，好争论的：having or showing a lively **aggressiveness**
例 a feisty child 一个好斗的孩子
近 aggressive, agonistic, assaultive, bellicose, belligerent, combative, contentious, disputatious, gladiatorial, militant, quarrelsome, truculent
反 pacific, peaceful, peace-loving 热爱和平的

Unit 8

| ■ FELONY | ■ FEROCIOUS | ■ FERVENT | ■ FIGMENT | ■ FITFUL |
| ■ FLEETING | ■ FORAGE | ■ FOREBODE | ■ FOREGROUND | ■ FORFEIT |

felony [ˈfeləni]
【考法】 *n.* 重罪：one of several **grave crimes**, such as murder, rape, or burglary, punishable by a more stringent sentence than that given for a misdemeanor
例 a felony punishable by life imprisonment 可被判处无期徒刑的重罪
近 crime
反 misdemeanor, peccadillo 轻罪

ferocious [fəˈroʊʃəs]
【考法 1】 *adj.* 激烈的，爆发性的：marked by **bursts of destructive force** or intense activity
例 a ferocious battle 激烈的战争
近 cyclonic, explosive, furious, paroxysmal, rabid, stormy, tempestuous, tumultuous, turbulent, volcanic
反 nonviolent, peaceable, peaceful 平静的，平和的
【考法 2】 *adj.* 凶猛的，残暴的：violently **unfriendly or aggressive** in disposition
例 captured and slaughtered by the ferocious tribesmen 被残暴的部落居民所抓获并惨遭屠杀
近 feral, grim, savage, vicious
反 gentle, mild, unaggressive 温和的，不具攻击性的
派 ferocity *n.* 凶猛，残暴

fervent [ˈfɜːrvənt]
【考法】 *adj.* 充满感情的，热情洋溢的：exhibiting or marked by **great intensity of feeling**
例 fervent ethical arguments 充满感情的伦理道德争辩
近 ardent, demonstrative, fervid, flaming, glowing, impassioned, incandescent, passionate, perfervid, torrid, vehement, zealous
反 cold, cool, dispassionate, emotionless, impassive, unemotional 冷漠的

figment [ˈfɪɡmənt]
【考法】 *n.* 虚构的事物，幻觉：something **made up** or contrived
例 Unable to find any tracks in the snow the next morning, I was forced to conclude that the shadowy figure had been a figment of my imagination. 第二天一早，我没有在雪地上发现任何足迹，由此我不得不相信昨晚幽灵一样的物体只是我的空想。‖ Thus far, the invisible human being has been nothing more than a figment of fantasy writers. 到目前为止，隐形人还仅仅是玄幻小说作家笔下的构想。
近 chimera, conceit, daydream, delusion, dream, fancy, fantasy, hallucination, illusion, phantasm, vision
反 fact, materiality, reality 客观存在的事物

fitful [ˈfɪtfl]
【考法】 *adj.* 断断续续的：having an **erratic or intermittent** character
例 slow and fitful progress in the negotiations 谈判中取得的缓慢、断断续续的进展
近 aperiodic, casual, discontinuous, episodic, erratic, intermittent, irregular, occasional, sporadic, unsteady
反 constant, continuous, incessant 持续不断的；periodic, regular, repeated 定期的

fleeting [ˈfliːtɪŋ]

【考法】 *adj.* 稍纵即逝的，短暂的: lasting only **for a short time**; passing swiftly

例 They have been waiting for more than 4 hours but caught only a fleeting glimpse of the movie star. 他们苦等了四个多小时，却最终只匆匆地瞟到了了电影明星一眼。

近 brief, ephemeral, evanescent, flash, fugitive, impermanent, passing, temporary, transient, transitory

反 ceaseless, deathless, eternal, everlasting, immortal, lasting, permanent, perpetual, timeless 永恒的

forage [ˈfɔːrɪdʒ]

【考法】 *vi.* 寻找: to make a **search**

例 go foraging for change for the parking meter 寻找付停车费的零钱

近 chase, hunt, pursue, quest, rummage, search

反 ignore, neglect 忽视，忽略; conceal, hide 隐藏

派 forager *n.* 为动物寻找饲料的人

forebode [fɔːrˈboʊd]

【考法】 *v.* 预示，预兆: to **show signs** of coming ill or misfortune

例 Black clouds forebode a storm. 乌云预示有暴风雨。

近 augur, predict, promise

派 foreboding *n.* 预感，预兆

foreground [ˈfɔːrɡraʊnd]

【考法】 *vt.* 强调，重视: to **indicate the importance** of by centering attention on

例 He repeatedly foregrounded his experience in international affairs in the course of his campaign for the presidency. 在竞选总统的过程中，他一再强调自己在处理国际事务方面的经验。

近 accent, accentuate, emphasize, feature, highlight, illuminate, press, punctuate, stress

反 de-emphasize, understate, play down 轻描淡写

forfeit [ˈfɔːrfət]

【考法】 *n.* 罚金: a sum of money to be paid as a **punishment**

例 pay forfeit 付罚金

近 damages, fine, forfeiture, mulct, penalty

反 bonus, premium, prize 奖金

Unit 9

■ FORSAKE　　　■ FROSTY　　　■ GAWKY　　　■ GERMINATE　　　■ GLACIAL
■ GLIDE　　　　■ GLOWER　　　■ GRAFT　　　■ GRIT　　　　　　■ GROGGY

forsake [fərˈseɪk]

【考法】 *vt.* 彻底放弃，抛弃: to **renounce** or turn away from entirely

例 forsake ideals 抛弃理想

近 abandon, desert, maroon, quit, renounce, strand

反 reclaim 重新获得; hold, keep, retain, withhold 保留

派 forsaken *adj.* 被抛弃的

frosty [ˈfrɔːsti]

【考法 1】 *adj.* 寒冷的: having a **low** or subnormal **temperature**

例 a frosty autumn that was a sign of the brutal winter that followed 一个极为寒冷的秋天，它预示着随之而来的、可能更加冷酷的冬季

近 algid, arctic, bitter, chilling, coldish, cool, freezing, frigid, gelid, glacial, icy, nippy, numbing, polar, snappy

反 ardent, blazing, burning, fervent, fervid, molten, roasting, scalding, scorching, searing, sultry, sweltering, torrid 炎热的

【考法 2】 *adj.* 无强烈感情的，冷淡的: **lacking in friendliness or warmth** of feeling

例 a frosty reception 冷遇

近 antiseptic, apathetic, brittle, chilly, cold-blooded, frozen, indifferent, unfriendly, unsympathetic, wintry

反 cordial, friendly, genial, hearty, sympathetic, warm, warm-blooded, warmhearted 友善的，热心的

gawky [ˈɡɔːki]

【考法】 *adj.* (举止)笨拙的: having or showing an **inability to move in a graceful manner**

例 The pathetic gawky woman was once a lithe ballerina but got severely injured in a car accident. 这个可怜的步态笨拙的妇女本来是一名轻巧优雅的芭蕾舞女演员，但是在一次车祸中受了重伤。

近 awkward, clumsy, gawkish, graceless, uncoordinated, ungainly

反 agile, graceful, lithe, nimble 灵巧的，敏捷的; elegant 优雅的

派 gawkiness *n.* 笨拙

germinate [ˈdʒɜːrmɪneɪt]

【考法 1】 *vi.* 发芽: to **begin to grow**
- 例 Some seed varieties germinate very quickly. 有一些种子的变异体能够迅速发芽。
- 近 burgeon, shoot, sprout
- 反 fade, flag, wilt, wither 枯萎
- 派 germination *n.* 萌芽

【考法 2】 *vi.* 出现: to **come into being**
- 例 An idea for a novel began to germinate in her mind. 一部小说的构思已经在她的头脑中发芽。
- 近 develop, evolve, grow
- 反 disappear, vanish 消逝, 消失

glacial [ˈɡleɪʃəl]

【考法 1】 *adj.* 极冷的: **extremely cold**
- 例 The air from the sea felt glacial. 海上的空气冷极了。
- 近 algid, arctic, bitter, chilling, coldish, cool, freezing, frigid, frosty, gelid, icy, nippy, numbing, polar, snappy
- 反 ardent, blazing, burning, fervent, fervid, molten, roasting, scalding, scorching, searing, sultry, sweltering, torrid 炎热的

【考法 2】 *adj.* 冷漠的, 无感情的: **devoid of warmth** and cordiality
- 例 The Duchess gave him a glacial look and moved on. 公爵夫人冷冷地看了他一眼, 然后就继续上路了。
- 近 antiseptic, apathetic, brittle, chilly, cold-blooded, frozen, indifferent, unfriendly, unsympathetic, wintry
- 反 cordial, friendly, genial, hearty, sympathetic, warm, warm-blooded, warmhearted 友善的, 热心的

glide [ɡlaɪd]

【考法】 *v.* 轻松地行动, 轻松地通过: to move or proceed **smoothly**, **continuously**, and **effortlessly**
- 例 swans gliding over the lake 在湖面悠然划水的天鹅
- 近 bowl, breeze, brush, coast, cruise, drift, roll, sail, skim, slide, slip, stream, sweep, whisk
- 反 flounder, struggle 挣扎

glower [ˈɡlaʊər]

【考法】 *vi.* 怒目而视: to look or **stare with** sullen annoyance or **anger**
- 例 Baseball fans glowered at their TVs as they watched their favorite team lose. 看着他们支持的球队输球, 棒球迷们恶狠狠地盯着电视屏幕。
- 近 glare, gloom, lower, scowl
- 反 beam, grin, smile 笑

graft [ɡræft]

【考法】 *vt.* 移植, 移接: to **implant** (living tissue) **surgically** or as if surgically
- 例 graft old traditions onto the new ones 把老传统移植到新的习俗中
- 近 implant, transplant

grit [ɡrɪt]

【考法】 *n.* (面对困难时所表现出来的) 毅力: the strength of mind that enables a person to **endure pain or hardship**
- 例 She was an athlete with true grit, continuing her training despite bad weather and an injury. 她是一个有着惊人毅力的真正的运动员, 即便是在受了伤外加天气恶劣的情况下仍然坚持训练。
- 近 backbone, constancy, fiber, grittiness, guts, intestinal fortitude, pluck, spunk
- 反 cowardliness, cravenness, gutlessness, pusillanimity, spinelessness 懦弱

groggy [ˈɡrɑːɡi]

【考法】 *adj.* 虚弱的, (走路) 不稳的: **weak and unsteady** on the feet or in action
- 例 She was feeling a bit groggy when I saw her. 当我看到她的时候她显得有些走路不稳。
- 近 rickety, rocky, shaky, unbalanced, unsound, unstable, unsteady, wobbly
- 反 balanced, stable, steady, sound 平衡的, 稳定的

Unit 10

| ■ GRUDGE | ■ GRUMBLE | ■ HALFHEARTED | ■ HECKLE | ■ HIERARCHICAL |
| ■ HOBBLE | ■ HUMDRUM | ■ HUMILIATE | ■ HYPOTHETICAL | ■ IDIOSYNCRASY |

grudge [ɡrʌdʒ]

【考法】 *n.* 怨恨, 仇恨: a feeling of deep-seated resentment or **ill will**
- 例 There has been a grudge between the two families for years. 两家之间积怨已深。 ‖ He has had a deep grudge against her ever since she snubbed him at the dance. 自从她在舞会上对他不理不睬之后, 他就对她怀有深深的怨念。

近	animosity, animus, antagonism, antipathy, bitterness, gall, hostility, jaundice, malice, rancor, resentment
反	amity 和睦，友好
派	grudging *adj.* 勉强的，不情愿的

grumble ['grʌmbl]

【考法】 *vi.* (尤指低声地)抱怨，埋怨：to **complain** in a surly manner; mutter discontentedly

例 The governed will always find something to grumble about. (Crane Brinton) 被统治者总能找到发牢骚的理由。——克莱恩·布林顿

近 carp, croak, fuss, gripe, grouch, grouse, grump, moan, murmur, mutter, repine
反 crow, delight, rejoice 感到高兴

halfhearted [ˌhɑːf'hɑːrtɪd]

【考法】 *adj.* 不感兴趣的，不热情的：**lacking heart**, spirit, or interest

例 a halfhearted apology 一个不热情的道歉
近 lukewarm, tepid, uneager, unenthusiastic
反 eager, enthusiastic, keen, passionate, warm 充满热情的；hearty, wholehearted 全心投入的

heckle ['hekl]

【考法】 *vt.* 起哄，使难堪：to **harass** and try to disconcert with questions, challenges, or gibes

例 a controversial singer who was constantly heckled by the fans 一个时常被粉丝起哄的有争议的歌手
Several protesters were heckling the speaker at the rally. 不少示威者在集会上起哄让发言者难堪。
近 badger, bait, hassle, haze, hector, needle, ride, taunt

hierarchical [ˌhaɪə'rɑːrkɪkl]

【考法】 *adj.* 分等级的，等级制的：**classified** according to various criteria into successive levels or layers

例 the traditional hierarchical system of military organization 军队中传统的等级制度
近 graded, graduated, ranked
派 hierarchy *n.* 等级制度

hobble ['hɑːbl]

【考法】 *vt.* 阻碍，妨碍：to **hamper the action** or progress of

例 hobble the economy 阻碍经济发展
近 encumber, fetter, handicap, hamper, hinder, impede, inhibit, manacle, obstruct, shackle, stymie, trammel
反 aid, assist, facilitate 帮助

humdrum ['hʌmdrʌm]

【考法】 *adj.* 无聊的，乏味的：**lacking** variety or **excitement**

例 trapped in a humdrum but well-paid job 陷于无聊但是收入可观的工作之中
近 arid, drab, dreary, drudging, jading, jejune, monochromatic, monotonous, pedestrian, ponderous, stale, stodgy, tedious, tiresome, wearisome
反 absorbing, engaging, engrossing, gripping, interesting, intriguing, involving, riveting, thrilling 令人感兴趣的

humiliate [hjuː'mɪlieɪt]

【考法】 *vt.* 羞辱，使丧失尊严：to reduce **to a lower position** in one's own eyes or others' eyes

例 He humiliated me in front of my parents and I swear to retaliate. 他在我的父母面前让我难堪，我发誓要报复他。
近 abase, chasten, cheapen, debase, degrade, demean, discredit, disgrace, dishonor, shame, sink, smirch
反 aggrandize, canonize, deify, elevate, exalt 使崇高
派 humiliation *n.* 羞辱，蒙羞

hypothetical [ˌhaɪpə'θetɪkl]

【考法】 *n.* 假设，前提条件：something taken as being true or factual and used as a **starting point** for a course of action or reasoning　*adj.* 假定的：existing only as an **assumption** or **speculation**

例 He believes that predictions of the extinction of certain species as the result of global warming are based upon too many hypotheticals. 他认为所谓全球变暖会导致某些物种灭绝的说法基于过多的假设。
We talked about what we would do in various hypothetical emergencies. 我们讨论了在各种假定的紧急情况下的对策。
近 assumption, given, postulate, premise, presumption, presupposition, supposition; conjectural, speculative, supposed, suppositional
反 conclusion, consequence, deduction, induction, inference 结论；actual, factual, real 事实的

idiosyncrasy [ˌɪdiə'sɪŋkrəsi]

【考法】 *n.* 独特而奇怪的习惯：an **odd or peculiar habit**

例 an idiosyncrasy of this particular custom 这个特殊习俗的独特习惯
近 crotchet, eccentricity, individualism, mannerism, oddity, peculiarity, quirk, singularity, trick, twist
反 conformity, sameness 合乎(礼节等)，千篇一律

List 30

Unit 1

■ IDLE	■ ILL-BRED	■ ILLUSTRIOUS	■ IMPERISHABLE	■ IMPLICIT
■ IMPUNITY	■ INCENTIVE	■ INCUMBENT	■ INDECOROUS	■ INFRACTION

idle [ˈaɪdl]

【考法 1】 *adj.* 闲置的，未使用的：**not turned to** normal or appropriate **use**

例 The car was idle for two weeks while they went on vacation. 因为他们出去旅行了，他们的车闲置了两周。

近 dead, dormant, fallow, free, inert, inoperative, latent, unused, vacant

反 active, alive, employed, functioning, operative, running, working 使用中的

【考法 2】 *adj.* 懒散的：shiftless, **lazy** *v.* 懒散度日，无所事事：to pass (time) **without working** or while avoiding work

例 idle the afternoon away 打发下午的时光 || an idle employee who always seems to be either on break or at lunch 一个懒散的员工似乎不是在休息就是在吃饭

近 indolent, lazy, shiftless, slothful; dally, dillydally, drone, laze, loaf, loll, lounge

反 diligent, industrious 勤奋的；drudge, grind, hustle, labor, moil, plod, slave, sweat, toil, travail, work （辛苦地）干活，工作

派 idlly *adv.* 懒散地

ill-bred [ˈɪlˈbred]

【考法】 *adj.* 没有教养的，没有礼貌的：badly brought up or showing bad upbringing: **impolite**

例 Only an ill-bred, conceited person would demand that everyone cater to his whims. 只有一个没有教养、狂妄自大的人才会要求所有人都去迎合他的想法。

近 discourteous, disrespectful, impertinent, impolite, inconsiderate, rude, uncivil, ungracious, unmannerly

反 civil, considerate, courteous, genteel, gracious, mannerly, polite, urbane, well-bred 有礼貌的，得体的

illustrious [ɪˈlʌstriəs]

【考法】 *adj.* 著名的，杰出的：well known and very **distinguished**

例 the most illustrious scientists of the century 本世纪最为杰出的科学家

近 distinguished, luminous, noble, notable, noteworthy, outstanding, preeminent, prestigious, redoubtable, signal

反 average, inferior, mediocre 平凡的，较差的

imperishable [ɪmˈperɪʃəbl]

【考法】 *adj.* 不朽的，永恒的：enduring or **occurring forever**

例 imperishable masterpiece/memory 永恒的杰作/回忆

近 ageless, continuing, eternal, everlasting, immortal, lasting, perennial, perpetual, timeless, undying

反 ephemeral, evanescent, fleeting, transient, transitory 稍纵即逝的

implicit [ɪmˈplɪsɪt]

【考法】 *adj.* 不言而喻的，心照不宣的：capable of being **understood** from something else **though unexpressed**

例 The implicit agreement among members of the outing club is that everyone pays his or her own way on all trips. 野外俱乐部成员之间一条心照不宣的约定就是：沿途所有开销都 AA。

近 implied, unexpressed, unspoken, unvoiced, wordless

反 explicit, expressed, spoken, stated, voiced 明确声明的

impunity [ɪmˈpjuːnəti]

【考法】 *n.* 免责，免受处罚：exemption or **freedom from punishment**, harm, or loss

例 She mistakenly believed that she could insult people with impunity. 她错误地认为她可以肆无忌惮地羞辱他人，不受处罚。

近	exemption, immunity
反	liability 责任

incentive [ɪnˈsentɪv]

【考法】 *n.* 刺激，诱因：something that **incites** or has a tendency to incite to determination or action

例 A little bonus will give employees an incentive to work harder. 一点点奖金就可以刺激雇员更加努力地工作。

近 boost, goad, impetus, incitement, instigation, momentum, motivation, motive, provocation, spur, stimulant, stimulus, yeast

反 deterrent, disincentive 抑制剂，阻碍物

incumbent [ɪnˈkʌmbənt]

【考法】 *adj.* 义不容辞的，必须的：imposed as an **obligation** or **duty**

例 It is incumbent upon sb. to do sth. 做……事是……应尽的义务

近 compulsory, forced, imperative, involuntary, necessary, obligatory, peremptory, required

反 elective, optional, voluntary 可选择的

indecorous [ɪnˈdekərəs]

【考法】 *adj.* 不合乎礼节的，不得体的：**conflicting with accepted standards** of good conduct or good taste

例 How can you make such an indecorous joke for a solemn moment in the marriage ceremony? 你怎么能在庄严肃穆的结婚典礼上开那样一个不得体的玩笑呢？

近 amiss, graceless, improper, inapposite, infelicitous, malapropos, perverse, unbecoming, unfit, unseemly, unsuitable, wrong

反 appropriate, becoming, befitting, decorous, felicitous, fit, genteel, meet, proper, seemly, suitable 得体的，合乎礼节的

infraction [ɪnˈfrækʃn]

【考法】 *n.* 违背，违犯：a **failure to uphold the requirements** of law, duty, or obligation

例 Speeding is only a minor infraction, but vehicular homicide is a serious felony. 超速只是小的违章，但是用机动车故意杀人就是重罪了。

近 breach, contravention, infringement, transgression, trespass, violation

反 observance 遵守

Unit 2

■ JUSTIFY	■ LAG	■ LANCE	■ LAX	■ LICENSE
■ LIONIZE	■ LUDICROUS	■ LUMINOUS	■ LURID	■ MACHINATION

justify [ˈdʒʌstɪfaɪ]

【考法】 *vt.* 证明…的合理性，为…辩解：to **prove** or show **to be just**, **right**, or reasonable

例 fail to justify the need for a new expressway at this time 没能证明当前修建新的高速公路的合理性

近 excuse, rationalize, warrant

派 justification *n.* (正当的)理由

lag [læg]

【考法1】 *vi.* 缓慢行走：to proceed or develop with comparative **slowness**

例 The tired puppy was lagging behind the rest of the pack. 疲倦的小狗在队伍的后面缓缓地走着。

近 crawl, creep, dally, dawdle, dillydally, linger, loiter, poke, tarry

反 blast, bolt, bustle, careen, career, dash, fly, hustle, rush, rustle, speed, whirl 疾行，快速行走

派 lagging *n.* 延迟

【考法2】 *vi.* 萎靡，失去活力：to **lose bodily strength** or vigor

例 During the fourth quarter the whole team seemed to lag. 到了第四节整支队伍似乎都已经精疲力竭了。

近 decay, droop, emaciate, fade, fail, languish, sink, waste, wilt, wither, mope

反 convalesce, rally, rebound, recover, recuperate 康复，复原

lance [læns]

【考法】 *vt.* 刺穿，刺破：to **penetrate** or hold (something) with a pointed object

例 Doctors used to lance infected sores, so that they could drain clean. 以前医生会刺破受感染的疮，从而使脓液流出。

近 gore, harpoon, jab, pierce, puncture, spike, stab, stick

lax [læks]

【考法1】 *adj.* 松弛的，不紧的，不严格的：**not tense**, **firm**, **or rigid**

例 exercises to improve lax muscles 改善松弛的肌肉的锻炼

近 flabby, flaccid, insecure, loose, loosened, relaxed, slackened, unsecured
反 taut, tense, tight 紧固的，牢固的；hard, harsh, rigid, rigorous, severe, stern, strict 严格的
【考法2】 adj. 懈怠的，漫不经心的：failing to give proper care and attention
例 The university has been lax about enforcing these rules. 学校对于这些规定的施行显得漫不经心。
近 careless, derelict, disregardful, heedless, lazy, neglectful, neglecting, negligent, remiss, slack
反 attentive, careful, cautious, conscientious, heedful, mindful, vigilant, wary 注意的，留心的

license [ˈlaɪsns]
【考法1】 n. 许可，认可：the approval by someone in authority for the doing of something
例 The company is seeking license to operate several more power plants in the state. 公司正在寻求在国内多建造几个电厂的许可。|| A restaurant owner has to get a license to serve food and drink. 餐厅营业者必须获得食物和饮品的销售许可。
近 allowance, authorization, clearance, concurrence, consent, empowerment, granting, sanction, warrant
反 interdiction, prohibition, proscription 禁止
【考法2】 n. 自由：the right to act or move freely
例 Military commanders on the ground must be granted considerable license, as wars cannot be micromanaged by people back in Washington. 战地指挥官应该被赋予相当大的自由，因为一场战争只靠华盛顿的人是不可能打赢的，他们无法进行具体指挥。
近 freedom, latitude, liberty
反 confinement, custody, imprisonment 拘留，囚禁

lionize [ˈlaɪənaɪz]
【考法】 vt. 追捧，把…捧为名人：to look on or treat (a person) as a celebrity
例 The press began to lionize him enthusiastically. 媒体开始狂热吹捧他。
近 aggrandize, canonize, deify, dignify, elevate, ennoble, enshrine, ensky, enthrone, glorify, magnify
反 abase, degrade, demean, humble, humiliate 贬低，瞧不起

ludicrous [ˈluːdɪkrəs]
【考法】 adj. 荒唐的，可笑的：meriting derisive laughter or scorn as absurdly inept, false, or foolish
例 the ludicrous idea 可笑的想法
近 absurd, comical, derisive, derisory, farcical, laughable, ridiculous, pathetic, preposterous, risible, silly
反 logical, rational, reasonable, sensible 有道理的

luminous [ˈluːmɪnəs]
【考法】 adj. 杰出的，重要的：standing above others in rank, importance, or achievement
例 some of the most luminous writers in the nation's history 该国历史上最杰出的一批作家
近 astral, brilliant, distinguished, illustrious, notable, noteworthy, preeminent, prestigious, redoubtable, signal
反 average, inferior, mediocre 一般的，中庸的

lurid [ˈlʊrɪd]
【考法】 adj. 恐怖的，令人反感的：causing horror or revulsion
例 We quickly drove past the lurid scene of the crash. 我们迅速驶过了可怕的车祸现场。
近 appalling, atrocious, dreadful, frightful, ghastly, gruesome, hideous, horrid, horrific, macabre, monstrous, nightmarish
反 agreeable, appealing, delicious, delightful, enjoyable, enticing, inviting, pleasant, satisfying 令人愉悦的

machination [ˌmæʃɪˈneɪʃn]
【考法】 n. 诡计：a scheming or crafty action or artful design intended to accomplish some usually evil end
例 The incredibly complicated machination to assassinate the president inevitably failed. 刺杀总统的诡计极其复杂，最终不可避免地失败了。
近 conspiracy, design, intrigue, plot, scheme

Unit 3

| ■ MADCAP | ■ MAGNITUDE | ■ MALEVOLENT | ■ MALIGNANT | ■ MANEUVER |
| ■ MARGINAL | ■ MEDITATE | ■ MENIAL | ■ MERETRICIOUS | ■ MILIEU |

madcap [ˈmædkæp]
【考法】 n. 热爱冒险的人：a person who seeks out very dangerous or foolhardy adventures with no apparent fear
adj. 大胆的，鲁莽的：behaving or acting impulsively or rashly; foolishly adventurous or bold

例 an incorrigible madcap who loves drag racing and white-water rafting 一个热爱飙车和激流竹筏的无药可救的冒险狂

近 daredevil, madman; audacious, bold, brash, daredevil, overbold, overconfident, reckless, temerarious

反 careful, cautious, circumspect, guarded, heedful, prudent, wary 谨慎的，小心的

magnitude [ˈmæɡnɪtuːd]

【考法】 *n.* 重要，重大: **greatness in significance** or influence

例 The magnitude of the issue is severely underestimated. 这个事件的重要性被严重低估了。

近 account, consequence, importance, moment, momentousness, significance, weight, weightiness

反 insignificance, littleness, puniness, slightness, smallness, triviality 不重要

malevolent [məˈlevələnt]

【考法】 *adj.* 恶意的，恶毒的: having, showing, or arising from intense often **vicious ill will**, **spite**, or **hatred**

例 The novel grossly oversimplified the conflict as a struggle between relentlessly malevolent villains on one side and faultless saints on the other. 小说把这场冲突彻底简化成凶残恶毒的坏人和完美无瑕的圣人间的斗争。

近 cruel, despiteful, evil, malicious, malign, malignant, mean, nasty, spiteful, vicious, virulent

反 benevolent, benign, benignant 善意的，和善的

派 malevolence *n.* 恶意，恶毒

malignant [məˈlɪɡnənt]

【考法】 *adj.* 恶毒的，邪恶的: having or showing a **desire to cause someone pain** or suffering for the sheer enjoyment of it; disposed to do evil

例 a malignant breast tumor 一个恶性乳腺瘤

近 atrocious, brutal, cruel, despiteful, malevolent, malicious, malign, mean, nasty, spiteful, vicious, virulent

反 benevolent, benign, benignant 慈善的，和蔼的; merciful 仁慈的

maneuver [məˈnuːvər]

【考法】 *vt.* 巧妙地操纵: to **guide with adroitness and design** or to bring about or secure as a result of skillful management

例 They maneuvered him into signing the contract. 他们巧妙地诱使他签下合同。|| The host maneuvered the conversation so as to avoid the touchy subject of her divorce. 主人巧妙地控制着对话的内容，以避免触及有关她离婚的敏感话题。

近 contrive, finagle, finesse, frame, machinate, manipulate, mastermind, negotiate, wangle

反 botch, bungle, fumble, mishandle, muff, scamp, mess up 弄砸

marginal [ˈmɑːrdʒɪnl]

【考法】 *adj.* 不重要的: **not of central importance**

例 regard violence as a marginal rather than a central problem 并不把暴力问题当作重要的核心问题来看

近 inconsequential, inconsiderable, insignificant, minor, minute, negligible, nugatory, slight, trifling, trivial

反 consequential, eventful, important, meaningful, momentous, significant, substantial, weighty 重要的

meditate [ˈmedɪteɪt]

【考法】 *vt.* 思索，沉思: to **focus** one's thoughts on

例 meditate a visit to her professor 思索着去拜访她的导师 || I have been meditating a career change for months. 我这几个月一直在考虑换一个工作。

近 cogitate, consider, contemplate, deliberate, mull, perpend, ponder, ruminate, study, weigh, wrestle

反 disregard, ignore, overlook, slight 忽视

派 meditation *n.* 沉思

menial [ˈmiːniəl]

【考法】 *adj.* 卑贱的，低下的: showing, expressing, or offered in a **spirit of humility or unseemly submissiveness**

例 low-paid menial jobs such as cleaning the street 一些低收入的卑贱工作，比如扫大街

近 base, humble, lowly, servile, slavish, subservient

反 arrogant, haughty, imperious, lordly, supercilious, superior 自大的，狂妄的

meretricious [ˌmerəˈtrɪʃəs]

【考法】 *adj.* 艳俗的，俗气的: attracting attention in a **vulgar manner**

例 vulgar, meretricious and shabby souvenirs 各种俗气花哨和劣质的纪念品

近 flamboyant, flaring, flashy, garish, gaudy, glaring, loud, ostentatious, tawdry

反 conservative, quiet, understated, unflamboyant 低调的，不张扬的

milieu [miːˈljɜː]

【考法】 *n.* 环境，氛围: the **physical or social setting** in which something occurs or develops

例 Young, innovative artists thrive in the freewheeling milieu that a big city offers. 在大都市所提供的自由氛围

中，年轻而富有创造力的艺术家们在事业上蓬勃发展。‖ |a historical milieu conducive to democracy| 有助于民主制度的历史背景

近 ambient, atmosphere, climate, context, environment, environs, medium, setting, surroundings, terrain

Unit 4

■ MISAPPREHENSION　■ MONARCH　　　■ MONOPOLIZE　　■ NIRVANA　　　■ NOSTALGIA
■ NOTORIETY　　　　■ NOURISH　　　　■ NOVICE　　　　　■ NULLIFICATION　■ NUMB

misapprehension [ˌmɪsæprɪˈhenʃn]
【考法】 *n.* 错误的理解、判断：a **failure to understand** correctly; a **wrong judgement**
例 tried to |eliminate all misapprehensions| about the planned riverfront development 尽可能消除所有关于河流沿岸发展计划的误解 ‖ |a common misapprehension about how our language functions| 有关我们的语言如何运作的常见误判
近 incomprehension, misconstruction, misconstruing, misimpression, misinterpretation, misknowledge, misreading, misunderstanding, miscalculation, misjudging, misjudgment, misstep, slip, slipup

monarch [ˈmɑːnərk]
【考法】 *n.* 君主，帝王：one who **rules** over a people with a sole, supreme, and usually hereditary authority
例 |The ruling monarch| of Britain at that time was Queen Elizabeth I. 伊丽莎白一世是当时英国的君主。
近 autocrat, lord, potentate, ruler, sovereign

monopolize [məˈnɑːpəlaɪz]
【考法】 *vt.* 垄断，主宰：to have **complete control** over
例 They are virtually |monopolizing the market|. 他们实际上已经垄断了整个市场。‖ To their surprise it was the vice president who |monopolized the conversation|. 令他们惊讶的是，主导整个谈话的居然是副总裁。
近 control, dominate, govern, reign, rule, sew up
派 monopoly *n.* 垄断，垄断权

nirvana [nɪrˈvɑːnə]
【考法】 *n.* 天堂，极乐世界：an often imaginary place or state of **utter perfection and happiness**
例 They believe in a continuous cycle of births and deaths until the soul is perfected and |achieves nirvana|. 他们相信生命会不断轮回，直到灵魂变得完美并升入天堂。
近 empyrean, fantasyland, heaven, lotusland, utopia
反 hell, inferno 地狱

nostalgia [nəˈstældʒə]
【考法】 *n.* 怀旧，怀念：a wistful or excessively **sentimental yearning for return** to or of some past period or irrecoverable condition
例 |He felt a wave of nostalgia for the life he had left behind him|. 他开始怀念往昔的时光。
近 reminiscence
反 oblivion 遗忘
派 nostalgic *adj.* 怀旧的

notoriety [ˌnoʊtəˈraɪəti]
【考法】 *n.* 坏名声：the quality or condition of being notorious; **ill fame**
例 |the notoriety of Somali piracy| 索马里海盗的坏名声
近 infamy, obloquy, odium, opprobrium
反 anonymity, oblivion, obscurity 不知名，默默无闻；celebrity, fame, renown, repute 好名声

nourish [ˈnɜːrɪʃ]
【考法】 *vt.* 培养，促进：to **help the growth** or development of
例 |a friendship nourished by trust| 在信任的基础之上开出的友谊之花
近 advance, cultivate, encourage, forward, further, incubate, promote
反 discourage, frustrate, hinder, inhibit 阻碍，妨碍

novice [ˈnɑːvɪs]
【考法】 *n.* 新手，初学者：a person **new** to a field or activity
例 |a novice chess player| 象棋初学者
近 apprentice, colt, fledgling, freshman, greenhorn, neophyte, newcomer, recruit, rook, tenderfoot, tyro, virgin
反 doyen, maven, veteran 有经验的人

nullification [ˌnʌlɪfɪˈkeɪʃn]

【考法】 *n.* (尤指法律条文等正式的)废除，废弃: the **doing away** with something by formal action

例 the nullification of a treaty 废除条约

近 abolishment, abrogation, annulment, cancellation, invalidation, negation, repeal, rescindment, voiding

反 enactment, legislation 立法; establishment, founding, institution 建立

numb [nʌm]

【考法】 *adj.* 麻木的，无感情的: **devoid of emotion**

例 Apparently in shock, he answered the police officer's questions with a numb expression on his face . 他显然是受到了惊吓，在回答警官的问题时一脸茫然。 ‖ Years of physical and emotional abuse had rendered the woman numb and withdrawn . 长年累月的肉体和精神上的折磨已让她麻木而寡言。

近 affectless, apathetic, catatonic, deadpan, emotionless, impassible, passionless, phlegmatic, stoic, stolid

反 demonstrative, emotional, fervent, fervid, impassioned, passionate, vehement 充满感情的

Unit 5

■ OAF　　■ OBSERVANT　　■ OBSOLETE　　■ ONSET　　■ ORDEAL
■ OSTENSIBLE　　■ OUTGROWTH　　■ OUTMODED　　■ OVERRIDE　　■ OVERSHADOW

oaf [oʊf]

【考法】 *n.* 愚蠢的人: a **stupid person**

例 Anyone who took him for an oaf and tried to cheat him would be in for a nasty surprise. 任何把他当成傻子然后想借机欺骗他的人就等着大吃一惊吧。

近 airhead, dolt, dope, dullard, dumbhead, fool, idiot, imbecile, moron, simpleton

反 brain, intellectual, sage, wit 智者; genius, prodigy 天才

observant [əbˈzɜːrvənt]

【考法1】 *adj.* 警惕的，警觉的: **paying close attention** usually for the purpose of anticipating approaching danger or opportunity

例 Good reporters are keenly observant of everything around them . 优秀的记者应该对身边所有的事情都保持高度的警惕。

近 alert, attentive, awake, cautious, sharp, vigilant, watchful

反 careless, heedless, inattentive, unmindful, unthinking, unwary 不谨慎的

【考法2】 *adj.* 严格遵守(规章、制度或原则)的: diligent in **observing** a law, custom, duty, or principle

例 observant of the speed limit 严格遵守速度限制 ‖ pious and religiously observant families 虔诚而严守教规的家庭

近 law-abiding

派 observance *n.* 遵守(规定)

obsolete [ˌɑːbsəˈliːʃ]

【考法】 *adj.* 过时的，被淘汰的: no longer in use or **no longer useful**

例 I was told my old printer was obsolete and I couldn't get replacement parts. 我被告知我的打印机已经被淘汰了，因此无法更换配件。 ‖ an obsolete word 一个已经废弃不用的单词

近 antiquated, archaic, dated, fossilized, medieval, moribund, moth-eaten, outdated, outmoded, outworn, prehistoric, rusty

反 contemporary, current, modern, recent 当前的，现代的

onset [ˈɑːnset]

【考法】 *n.* 起始，开始: the point at which something **begins**

例 If you take enough vitamin C at the onset of a cold , you'll probably recover faster. 如果你感冒刚一开始就服用足量的维生素 C，你可能会康复得更快。

近 alpha, baseline, commencement, dawn, genesis, inception, kickoff, launch, nascence, outset, threshold

反 close, conclusion, end, ending, omega, termination 结束

ordeal [ɔːrˈdiːl]

【考法】 *n.* 严峻的考验: a **severe trial** or experience

例 The hikers were finally rescued after a three-day ordeal in the wilderness . 在野外度过了三天的严峻考验之后，登山者们终于获救了。

近 calvary, crucible, fire, gauntlet

反 delight, enjoyment, pleasure 令人愉快的事物

ostensible [ɑːˈstensəbl]

【考法】 *adj.* 表面上的，佯装的：**appearing to be true** on the basis of evidence that may or may not be confirmed

例 ostensible independent organizations 名义上的独立组织

近 apparent, assumed, evident, ostensive, presumed, putative, reputed, seeming, supposed, prima facie

反 actual, real 真实的

派 ostensibly *adv.* 表面上

outgrowth [ˈaʊtɡroʊθ]

【考法】 *n.* 结果，后果：a condition or occurrence **traceable to a cause**

例 Crime is often an outgrowth of poverty. 犯罪往往可以归因于贫穷。‖ A predictable outgrowth of the suburb's ever growing population will be the need for more schools. 郊区人口攀升所导致的一个可以预见的后果就是需要更多的学校。

近 aftereffect, aftermath, consequence, fate, fruit, outcome, precipitate, product, result, sequel, sequence

反 antecedent, cause, occasion, reason 原因；origin, root, source 源头

outmoded [ˌaʊtˈmoʊdɪd]

【考法】 *adj.* 过时的，废弃的：**no longer** acceptable, current, or **usable**

例 outmoded computers that can be recycled 可回收的废旧电脑

近 antiquated, archaic, demoded, fossilized, moribund, moth-eaten, obsolete, outworn, prehistoric, rusty

反 contemporary, current, modern 现代的，当代的

override [ˌoʊvərˈraɪd]

【考法】 *vt.* 推翻：to **set aside**

例 The Congress overrode the President's veto and passed the law. 国会推翻总统的否决，强行通过了那项法令。‖ He overrode all opposition to his plans. 他对所有的反对意见不予理睬。

近 disregard, ignore, neglect, overlook, overpass, pass over

反 comply, observe 遵守

overshadow [ˌoʊvərˈʃædoʊ]

【考法】 *vt.* (在重要性上)超越，超过：to **exceed in importance**

例 The forward's outstanding performance should not overshadow the achievements of the rest of the team. 其他队员的贡献不应该因前锋的精彩表现而被忽略。

近 eclipse, outrank, outshine, outstrip, overbalance, overweigh

反 fall behind 落后

Unit 6

| ■ OVERWHELM | ■ OVERWROUGHT | ■ PALAVER | ■ PALPITATION | ■ PANACEA |
| ■ PECULIARITY | ■ PEDAGOGICAL | ■ PEEL | ■ PERCEPTIVE | ■ PERILOUS |

overwhelm [ˌoʊvərˈwelm]

【考法】 *vt.* 淹没：to **cover** with or as if with a flood

例 That spring the massive runoff from melting snows overwhelmed the valley. 那个春天，整个山谷被融雪形成的洪流吞没了。

近 deluge, drown, engulf, inundate, overflow, submerge, submerse, swamp

反 drain 抽干

overwrought [ˌoʊvərˈrɔːt]

【考法 1】 *adj.* 十分激动的，非常不安的：being in a state of increased activity or **agitation**

例 be emotionally overwrought 情绪过分激动

近 agitated, excited, frenzied, heated, hectic, hyperactive, overactive

反 calm, collected, composed, placid, serene, tranquil 冷静的，沉着的

【考法 2】 *adj.* (装饰、文风等)过分华丽的：elaborately and often **excessively decorated**

例 The report is a little overwrought. 这篇报道有些过于华丽。

近 baroque, bedizened, flamboyant, florid, fussy, gingerbreaded, ornate, overdecorated

反 austere, plain, severe, stark, unadorned 朴素的

palaver [pəˈlævər]

【考法】 *n.* 对话，交流：an **exchange of views** for the purpose of exploring a subject or deciding an issue

vi. 闲聊：to talk **profusely or idly**

| 例 | seemingly endless palaver between the negotiating parties 谈判双方之间看似没有尽头的对话 ‖ Mothers were palavering and drinking coffee while watching their children play. 母亲们一边看着她们的孩子玩耍，一边喝着咖啡闲谈。 |
| 近 | argument, colloquy, conference, consult, council, counsel, debate, dialogue, parley; babble, chatter, converse, gabble, jabber, prate, prattle, rattle, twitter |

palpitation [ˌpælpɪˈteɪʃn]

【考法】	n. (有节奏的)舒张收缩: a rhythmic **expanding and contracting**
例	a palpitation of the blood vessels 血管有节奏的舒张收缩
近	beat, beating, pulse, throb

panacea [ˌpænəˈsiːə]

【考法】	n. 万能药，万灵药: a **remedy for all ills** or difficulties
例	Bicycles are not a panacea for the traffic problem. 自行车并不是解决交通问题的万能药。
近	catholicon, cure-all, elixir, nostrum

peculiarity [pɪˌkjuːliˈærəti]

【考法】	n. 特征，特点: a **distinguishing characteristic**
例	a strange peculiarity of the U.S. system 美国制度的一个奇怪的特性
近	attribute, character, criterion, diagnostic, differentia, feature, fingerprint, hallmark, mark, note, particularity, quality, specific, trait

pedagogical [ˌpedəˈɡɑːdʒɪkl]

【考法】	adj. 教学的；教师的: of, relating to, or befitting a **teacher or education**
例	improve teachers' pedagogical methods 提高老师的教学法
近	preceptorial
反	pupillary 学生的

peel [piːl]

【考法】	vi. 脱去(衣服等): to **take off** one's **clothes**
例	peel off the wet clothes 脱去湿衣服
近	doff, douse, put off, shrug off, take off
反	don, put on 穿上

perceptive [pərˈseptɪv]

【考法】	adj. 敏锐的: able to **sense slight** impressions or **differences**
例	perceptive U.S. political commentator 有洞察力的政治评论员
近	delicate, fine, keen, quick, sensitive, sharp
反	dead, imperceptive, insensible, insensitive, numb 反应慢的，麻木的

perilous [ˈperələs]

【考法】	adj. 危险的: involving **potential loss or injury**
例	perilous journey through hostile territory 穿过敌方领土的危险行程
近	dangerous, grave, grievous, hazardous, jeopardizing, menacing, risky, serious, threatening, venturesome
反	harmless, innocent, innocuous, safe, unthreatening 安全的，无害的

Unit 7

■ PERQUISITE　　　■ PETULANT　　　■ PIONEER　　　■ PIOUS　　　■ PITFALL
■ PIVOTAL　　　■ PLACID　　　■ PLAYFUL　　　■ PLEBEIAN　　　■ PLUSH

perquisite [ˈpɜːrkwɪzɪt]

【考法】	n. 额外的好处: something **given in addition** to what is ordinarily expected or owed
例	The use of a company car is one perquisite of the job . 能使用公司的汽车是这份工作的附加好处之一。
近	cumshaw, dividend, donative, extra, gratuity, gravy, lagniappe, perk, tip

petulant [ˈpetʃələnt]

【考法】	adj. 易怒的，爱发脾气的: **easily irritated** or annoyed
例	He is a petulant and fussy man who is always blaming everyone else for his problems. 他是一个对细节非常在意而又容易生气的人，还总是把自己的问题怪罪到别人的头上。
近	choleric, grouchy, grumpy, irascible, irritable, peevish, perverse, pettish, prickly, raspy, ratty, stuffy, testy

反 forbearing, obliging, patient, stoic, tolerant 容忍的，忍让的
派 petulance *n.* 易怒，坏脾气

pioneer [ˌpaɪəˈnɪr]
【考法 1】 *n.* 拓荒者，先驱者：one of the **first to settle** in a territory
例 the leading pioneer in journalism 新闻界的先驱
近 colonist, colonizer, homesteader, settler
反 follower 跟随者
【考法 2】 *vt.* 开创，创造：to **open up** (an area) or prepare (a way)
例 He single-handedly pioneered the university's institute for medical research. 他单枪匹马创建了这所大学的医学研究所。‖ rockets that pioneered outer space 开创了外太空纪元的火箭
近 begin, constitute, establish, inaugurate, initiate, innovate, institute, introduce, launch, plant, set up
反 close, end, shut, terminate, phase out 终止，淘汰
派 pioneering *adj.* 先驱性的，先导性的

pious [ˈpaɪəs]
【考法】 *adj.* (信仰上)虔诚的：marked by or showing reverence for deity and **devotion to divine worship**
例 a pious woman who decided to become a nun 一个决心成为修女的虔诚女子
近 devout, godly, religious, sainted, saintly
反 antireligious, faithless, godless, impious, irreligious, ungodly, unholy 不虔诚的，无宗教信仰的

pitfall [ˈpɪtfɔːl]
【考法】 *n.* 陷阱：a pit flimsily covered or camouflaged and used to **capture and hold animals** or men
例 caught in a pitfall 掉下了陷阱
近 catch, gimmick, gotcha, hitch, joker, snag, snare, trap

pivotal [ˈpɪvətl]
【考法】 *adj.* 最关键的，最为重要的：of the **greatest possible importance**
例 The report was missing a pivotal piece of information. 报告遗漏了最为重要的信息。
近 critical, crucial, decisive, key, vital
反 inconsequential, inconsiderable, insignificant, marginal, minor, minute, negligible, nugatory, slight, trifling, trivial 不重要的

placid [ˈplæsɪd]
【考法】 *adj.* 冷静的，淡定的：**free from** emotional or mental **agitation**
例 I know an exceptionally placid mother who was rarely upset by her six children. 我认识一个异常淡定的母亲，她几乎从未因为自己的六个孩子而烦恼过。
近 collected, composed, coolheaded, level, limpid, possessed, recollected, sedate, undisturbed, unperturbed
反 agitated, discomposed, disturbed, flustered, perturbed, upset 不安的，焦虑的
派 placidity *n.* 宁静，安宁

playful [ˈpleɪfl]
【考法】 *adj.* 爱开玩笑的，好打闹的：given to good-natured **joking or teasing**
例 The little girl was lighthearted and playful. 小女孩无忧无虑的，喜欢和别人打闹。
近 antic, coltish, elfish, fay, frisky, frolicsome, larky, rollicking, sportive
反 earnest, grave, serious, sober, solemn, somber 严肃的

plebeian [pləˈbiːən]
【考法】 *adj.* 平民的，社会下层的：belonging to the class of people of **low social or economic rank**
例 a man who rose to greatness but never forgot his plebeian past 一个仕途通达、但从未忘却自己平民出身的人
近 baseborn, common, humble, inferior, lowborn, lumpen, mean, prole, proletarian, unwashed, vulgar
反 aristocratic, genteel, gentle, highborn, highbred, lofty, noble, patrician, wellborn 上流社会的

plush [plʌʃ]
【考法】 *adj.* 奢华的，豪华的：**notably luxurious**
例 a plush castle filled with priceless art and antiques 一座充满了无价艺术品和古董的奢华城堡
近 deluxe, lavish, luxuriant, luxurious, opulent, palatial, silken, sumptuous
反 ascetic, austere, humble, spartan 朴素的，平凡的

Unit 8

poach ［poʊtʃ］
【考法】 *vt.* 水煮：to **cook in a liquid** heated to the point that it gives off steam
例 He poached an egg for breakfast. 他煮了一个荷包蛋做早饭。
近 coddle, parboil, simmer, stew

pointer ［ˈpɔɪntər］
【考法】 *n.* 忠告，建议：a useful **suggestion or hint** usually from an expert
例 Here are a few pointers to help you make a choice. 这里有一些能帮助你作抉择的建议。
近 advice, hint, lead, recommendation, tip

pragmatic ［præɡˈmætɪk］
【考法】 *adj.* 实用主义的，务实的：a **practical approach** to problems and affairs
例 Pragmatic men of power have had no time or inclination to deal with social morality.(K. B. Clark) 务实的当权者不会有时间或者意向去处理社会道德的问题。——K. B. 克拉克 ‖ a pragmatic man, not given to grand, visionary schemes 一个不迷恋花哨空想的计划，而更注重实际的人
近 down-to-earth, earthy, hardheaded, matter-of-fact, practical
反 fanciful, idealistic, impractical, unrealistic, utopian, visionary 幻想的，不务实的
派 pragmatism *n.* 实用主义，务实主义

premeditate ［priˈmedɪteɪt］
【考法】 *vt.* 预谋：to **think about** and revolve in the mind **beforehand**
例 He's carefully premeditating each step of his plan of campaign. 他正在仔细地计划竞选计划中的每一个步骤。
近 forethink, precogitate, predetermine
反 disregard, ignore, overlook, slight 忽略
派 premeditated *adj.* 有预谋的

prerequisite ［ˌpriːˈrekwəzɪt］
【考法】 *n.* 先决条件，前提：something that is **necessary to an end** or to the carrying out of a function
例 Competence is prerequisite to promotion. 能力是提升的必要条件。
近 condition, essential, must, necessity, precondition, requirement, requisite, sine qua non

prerogative ［prɪˈrɑːɡətɪv］
【考法】 *n.* 特权，权力：an exclusive or special **right**, **power**, or **privilege**
例 It is your prerogative to refuse to attend religious services. 你有权力不参加宗教活动。
近 appanage, birthright, entitlement, privilege, right

proclaim ［prəˈkleɪm］
【考法】 *vt.* 宣告，使…公之于众：to **declare publicly**, typically insistently, proudly, or defiantly and in either speech or writing
例 He launched a coup and proclaimed himself President. 他发动了一场政变，然后宣称自己已成为总统。
近 advertise, announce, blare, blazon, broadcast, declare, enunciate, herald, promulgate, publicize, publish, release, trumpet
反 conceal, hide 隐藏；silence, suppress 压制(观点的发表)

project ［prəˈdʒekt］
【考法】 *vt.* 预测，预计：to calculate, estimate, or predict (something in the future), **based on present data or trends**
例 project next year's expenses 预测明年的开销
近 augur, estimate, extrapolate, forecast, predict, predetermine, presage
派 projected *adj.* 计划的；projection *n.* 凸起物；投影

proprietary ［prəˈpraɪəteri］
【考法】 *adj.* 私营的：**privately owned** and managed and run as a profit-making organization
例 a proprietary hospital 私人医院
近 private
反 public 政府提供的；state-owned 国有的

prototype ['proʊtətaɪp]
- 【考法】 *n.* 原型: an **original model** on which something is patterned
- 例 The manufacturer exhaustively tested the prototype of the vehicle before approving production. 生产商在将该车型投入生产之前对样机进行了详细的测试。
- 近 archetype
- 反 copy, imitation, replica, reproduction 复制品

Unit 9

■ RAMPANT	■ RAVENOUS	■ REDEEM	■ REFRESHING	■ REMNANT
■ RENEGE	■ REPLENISH	■ REPLICATE	■ RESIDUAL	■ RESTITUTION

rampant ['ræmpənt]
- 【考法 1】 *adj.* (植物)生长茂盛的: **growing thickly** and vigorously
- 例 a rampant growth of weeds in the neglected yard 废弃的院子里杂草疯长
- 近 lush, luxuriant, prosperous, weedy
- 反 sparse 稀疏的
- 【考法 2】 *adj.* 猖獗的，不受限制的: **occurring without restraint** and frequently, widely, or menacingly
- 例 Mayor promised to put a stop to the rampant crime that plagued the city. 市长承诺要采取措施，终止那些扰乱城市治安的猖獗的犯罪活动。‖ rampant corruption in city government 市政府中猖獗的腐败
- 近 abandoned, intemperate, runaway, unbounded, unbridled, unchecked, uncontrolled, unhampered, unhindered, unrestrained
- 反 bridled, checked, constrained, controlled, curbed, governed, hampered, hindered, restrained, temperate 受制约的

ravenous ['rævənəs]
- 【考法】 *adj.* 食量大的，贪食的；贪婪的: having a **huge appetite**; greedy for gratification
- 例 He had moderated his ravenous appetite. 他控制了自己的食欲。‖ ravenous for power 渴望权力
- 近 edacious, esurient, gluttonous, greedy, rapacious, voracious
- 反 content, sated, satiated, satisfied 心满意足的

redeem [rɪ'diːm]
- 【考法】 *vt.* 改过自新: to **make better** in behavior or character
- 例 redeem one's sin 弥补某人的罪恶
- 近 habilitate, reclaim, regenerate, rehabilitate
- 派 redeemable *adj.* 可赎回的，可挽救的

refreshing [rɪ'freʃɪŋ]
- 【考法】 *adj.* 令人身心振奋的，提神的: having a **renewing effect** on the state of the body or mind
- 例 refreshing news/music 让人振奋的消息/音乐
- 近 bracing, cordial, invigorating, rejuvenating, restorative, reviving, stimulating, stimulative, vitalizing
- 反 deadening, debilitating, draining, enervating, enfeebling, exhausting, sapping, wearying 令人虚弱的

remnant ['remnənt]
- 【考法】 *n.* 残余，剩余物: something **left over**
- 例 a remnant of his past glory 他辉煌过去的一丝残余 ‖ The shop is selling remnants of cloth at half price. 商店在半价抛售剩余的衣物。
- 近 debris, remainder, remains, residue, vestige

renege [rɪ'niːg]
- 【考法】 *vt.* 放弃，摒弃: to solemnly or **formally reject** or go back on (as something formerly adhered to)
- 例 She refused to renege the principles by which she had always lived her life, even if it resulted in losing her business. 尽管有可能使她失去她的事业，但她仍然拒绝放弃生命中所坚持的那些原则。
- 近 abnegate, forswear, recant, renounce, repeal, repudiate, retract, withdraw
- 反 adhere 坚持
- 派 renegade *n.* 叛徒

replenish [rɪ'plenɪʃ]
- 【考法】 *vt.* 补充: to **fill** or make complete **again**; add a new stock or supply to
- 例 replenish stocks 补充仓库
- 近 refill, reload
- 反 consume, drain, empty, exhaust 清空，耗尽

replicate [ˈreplɪkeɪt]

【考法】 *vt.* 复制，复刻：to **make an exact likeness** of

例 We replicated the famous painting in our art class. 我们在艺术课上临摹一幅名画。

近 clone, copy, copycat, duplicate, imitate, reduplicate, render, reproduce

反 originate 原创

residual [rɪˈzɪdʒuəl]

【考法】 *adj.* 剩余的，残存的：of, relating to, or characteristic of a **residue**

例 residue pesticide 残存的杀虫剂

近 leftover, remaining, vestigial

反 comprehensive, entire, full, integral, total, whole 全部的，完整的

restitution [ˌrestɪˈtuːʃn]

【考法】 *n.* 补偿，赔偿：a making good of or giving an equivalent **for some injury**

例 The victims are demanding full restitution. 受害者要求全额补偿。

近 damages, indemnity, quittance, recompense, recoupment, redress, remuneration, reparation, reprisal, requital

Unit 10

■ RESURRECT　　　■ RETENTIVE　　　■ RETRIEVE　　　■ REVERBERATE　　　■ RHETORICAL
■ RIGMAROLE　　　■ RUTHLESS　　　■ SCREEN　　　■ SCRIMP　　　■ SECTARIANISM
---

resurrect [ˌrezəˈrekt]

【考法】 *vt.* 使重生，使复苏：to **bring back to life**, practice, or activity

例 People believed that his body would be resurrected. 人们相信他的身体将会复活。

近 reanimate, recharge, regenerate, rejuvenate, rekindle, renew, resuscitate, revitalize, revive, revivify

反 kill 杀死

派 resurrection *n.* 重生，复苏

retentive [rɪˈtentɪv]

【考法】 *adj.* 记性好的：having the ability or capacity to **retain knowledge or information** with ease

例 Her retentive memory helped her sail through the history test. 她的好记性帮助她顺利通过了历史考试。

反 absentminded, forgetful, oblivious 健忘的

派 retentiveness *n.* 好记性

retrieve [rɪˈtriːv]

【考法】 *vt.* 寻回，找回：to **get back again**

例 I need to retrieve the book from my friend so I could return it to the library. 我需要先把书从朋友那里拿回来才能还给图书馆。

近 reacquire, recapture, reclaim, re-collect, recoup, recover, regain, repossess, retake

反 lose, mislay, misplace 丢失

reverberate [rɪˈvɜːrbəreɪt]

【考法】 *vi.* 回荡，回响：to **continue or be repeated** in a series of reflected **sound waves**

例 The sound of thunder reverberated from one end of the mountain to the other. 打雷的声音在山间不断回荡。

近 echo, reecho, resonate, resound

派 reverberation *n.* 回响，回音

rhetorical [rɪˈtɔːrɪkl]

【考法】 *adj.* 言辞华丽（却往往无内涵）的：full of fine words and **fancy** expressions **but** mostly **meaningless** words and phrases

例 You can skip over the rhetorical passages and still get the gist of the essay. 你可以跳过那些词藻华丽的段落，直接获取文本的主旨。‖ The new governor delivered a long rhetorical speech about our state's bright future but laid out no specific programs for ensuring it. 新的执政官发表了词藻华丽的长篇演说，畅谈国家的美好未来，但却没有提出实现这一目标的具体措施。

近 bombastic, flatulent, florid, fustian, gaseous, gassy, grandiloquent, oratorical, orotund, purple, windy

反 prosaic 平凡无奇的；plain, simple 简单的

rigmarole [ˈrɪgmərəʊl]

【考法】 *n.* 混乱而无意义的话：language marked by abstractions, jargon, euphemisms, and circumlocutions; **confused or meaningless talk**

例 The security guard gave me some kind of rigmarole about passes and authorizations. 保安不知所云地跟我说了一些关于通关和授权的话。

近 abracadabra, babble, drivel, gabble, gibber, jabber, nonsense, prattle

ruthless	['ruːθləs]

【考法】 *adj.* 没有怜悯心的，残忍的: having **no pity**

例 an office supervisor with a ruthless disregard for others' feelings 一个从不顾及他人感情的无情领导

近 cruel, heartless, inhumane, ironfisted, iron-hearted, pitiless, merciless, mortal, relentless, remorseless

反 charitable, compassionate, humane, kindhearted, merciful, sympathetic, tender 有同情心的，善良的

screen	[skriːn]

【考法1】 *n.* 掩护物，屏障: something that **shelters**, **protects**, **or hides**

例 The target will be difficult to reach as it is behind a screen of anti-aircraft batteries . 目标在防空炮火的掩护之下难以靠近。‖ Please keep away from the screen door . 请不要倚靠屏蔽门。

近 aegis, ammunition, armor, cover, guard, protection, safeguard, security, shield, wall, ward

【考法2】 *vt.* 掩护，遮蔽: to keep secret or **shut off from view**

例 screen sth from sth 把某物与某物隔绝起来

近 belie, cloak, conceal, curtain, disguise, enshroud, mask, obscure, occult, shroud, veil

反 disclose, expose, reveal, uncloak, uncover, unmask, unveil 揭露

scrimp	[skrɪmp]

【考法】 *vi.* 节俭: to **avoid** unnecessary **waste** or expense

例 They had to scrimp and save for years in order to be able to afford a house. 他们不得不节俭度日才能攒够钱买房。

近 conserve, economize, husband, pinch, save, skimp, spare

反 dissipate, lavish, squander, waste 浪费

sectarianism	[sek'terɪənɪzəm]

【考法】 *n.* 宗派主义，顽固: stubborn or intolerant **adherence to** one's opinions or **prejudices**

例 An ideological sectarianism prevented the political party from ever being anything more than a fringe group. 意识形态上的顽固和保守使得这个政党只能成为一个边缘团体。

近 dogmatism, illiberalism, intolerance, narrow-mindedness, partisanship, small-mindedness

反 broad-mindedness, liberalism, open-mindedness, tolerance 开明

The man who has made up his mind to win will never say "impossible".

凡是决心取得胜利的人是从来不说"不可能的"。

——法国皇帝 拿破仑 (Bonaparte Napoleon, French emperor)

List 31

Unit 1

■ SECULAR	■ SIMILE	■ SKITTISH	■ SPARING	■ SPLUTTER
■ SQUEAMISH	■ STAUNCH	■ STEREOTYPE	■ STIGMATIZE	■ SUBSTITUTE

secular ［ˈsekjələr］
【考法】 *adj.* 世俗的，尘世的：of or relating to the **worldly or temporal**
例 That's an issue for the secular authorities, not the church. 这个问题和宗教无关，是一件世俗事务。
近 carnal, earthborn, earthbound, fleshly, material, mundane, sublunary, temporal, terrene, terrestrial, worldly
反 heavenly, unearthly, unworldly 非尘世间的；spiritual 精神上的；religious 宗教的；clerical 牧师的

simile ［ˈsɪməli］
【考法】 *n.* 明喻：a figure of speech **comparing two unlike things** that is often introduced by like or as
例 Even though both similes and metaphors are forms of comparison, similes indirectly compare the two ideas and allow them to remain distinct in spite of their similarities, whereas metaphors compare two things directly. For instance, a simile that compares a person with a bullet would go as follows: "Chris was a record-setting runner as fast as a speeding bullet." A metaphor might read something like, "When Chris ran, he was a speeding bullet racing along the track." 尽管明喻和暗喻都是比喻的手法，明喻会间接地对两个对象进行比较，同时允许差异的存在，而暗喻则直接对两者进行比较。比如说，用明喻来把一个人比作子弹会这样说："克里斯是一个不断打破纪录的选手，他跑得就和高速子弹一样快。"而暗喻可能会说："当克里斯奔跑的时候，他就是一颗在赛场上高速飞行的子弹。"
反 metaphor 暗喻

skittish ［ˈskɪtɪʃ］
【考法1】 *adj.* 容易受到惊吓的，胆小的：**easily frightened**
例 skittish horses/kitty 易受惊吓的马匹/小猫
近 fainthearted, fearful, fearsome, mousy, scary, timid, timorous, tremulous
反 adventuresome, adventurous, audacious, bold, daring, dashing, gutsy, venturesome, venturous 大胆的
【考法2】 *adj.* 善变的，多变的：**likely to change** frequently, suddenly, or unexpectedly
例 The skittish housing market had both buyers and sellers on edge. 变幻莫测的房市让买家和卖家都坐立不安。
近 capricious, changeful, flickery, fluctuating, fluid, inconstant, mercurial, mutable, temperamental, uncertain, unstable, unsteady, volatile
反 changeless, constant, immutable, invariable, settled, stable, stationary, steady, unvarying 不变的

sparing ［ˈsperɪŋ］
【考法】 *adj.* 节俭的，节约的：marked by or practicing **careful restraint**（as in the use of resources）
例 be sparing with money 用钱很节约
近 economical, economizing, provident, scrimping, thrifty
反 prodigal, profligate, spendthrift, squandering, wasteful 浪费的

splutter ［ˈsplʌtər］
【考法】 *vi.* 急切而不清楚地说：to speak **hastily and incoherently**, as when confused or angry
例 They begin to splutter and move restlessly about if they feel time is slipping away without some return. 当他们感到时间在悄悄流逝却一无所得时，他们便开始激动地说话，不安地走动。
近 babble, drivel, gabble, gibber, jabber, sputter, stammer, stutter
反 articulate, enunciate, pronounce 清楚地说

squeamish ['skwiːmɪʃ]

【考法】 *adj.* 恶心的，晕船的：affected with **nausea**

例 The rolling of the ship made the young sailor squeamish. 摇晃的船只让年轻的水手感到恶心。

近 ill, nauseated, qualmish, queasy, queer, queerish, sick, sickish

反 healthy, well 状态良好的

staunch [stɔːntʃ]

【考法】 *adj.* 忠诚的，坚定的：**steadfast in loyalty** or principle

例 a staunch believer in the democratic system 民主制度的坚定拥护者 ‖ No matter what happens I will be your staunchest supporters. 不论发生什么，我都会是你最忠诚的支持者。

近 constant, dedicated, devoted, devout, faithful, fast, loyal, pious, steadfast, steady, true, true-blue

反 disloyal, inconstant, perfidious, recreant, traitorous, treacherous 不忠诚的；fickle 善变的

stereotype ['steriətaɪp]

【考法】 *n.* 成见，老套的理念：a **conventional**, **formulaic**, **and oversimplified** conception, **opinion**, or image

例 a stereotype about sth. 对于某事的成见

近 concept, conception, generality, notion

stigmatize ['stɪgmətaɪz]

【考法】 *vt.* 使蒙上污名：to characterize or brand as **disgraceful or ignominious**

例 stigmatize overweight teenagers 贬低超重青年

近 abase, debase, degrade, demean, discredit, disgrace, dishonor, foul, humiliate, shame, sink, smirch

反 aggrandize, canonize, deify, elevate, exalt 提升（名誉、声望等）

substitute ['sʌbstɪtuːt]

【考法】 *n.* 取代者，替代品：a person or thing that **takes the place** or function **of another**

vt. 取代，替代：to **take the place of**

例 substitute moral power for physical force 用道德的力量取代暴力 ‖ BFR molecules have some atoms substituted by bromide atoms, which makes it fire-resistant. 在溴化阻燃剂的分子中，一部分原子被溴原子取代，从而使它不易燃烧。

近 backup, cover, fill-in, relief, replacement, reserve, stand-in, surrogate; displace, relieve, replace, supersede, supplant, cut out

派 substitution *n.* 取代

Unit 2

| ■ SUCCUMB | ■ SUPERSEDE | ■ SURLY | ■ SURMISE | ■ SURMOUNT |
| ■ SURPASS | ■ SURROGATE | ■ SURVEILLANCE | ■ TAME | ■ TANGLE |

succumb [sə'kʌm]

【考法 1】 *vi.* 屈服：to **yield to superior strength** or force or overpowering appeal or desire

例 She refused to succumb to her fears and defiantly walked through the dark cemetery. 她拒绝向自己的恐惧屈服，而是倔强地走过了幽暗的墓地。

近 bow, capitulate, concede, submit, surrender, give in

反 resist 抵抗

【考法 2】 *vi.* 死亡：to be brought to an end (as **death**) by the effect of destructive or disruptive forces

例 The patient lay so still and pale that everyone thought he had succumbed, and then he opened his eyes. 面色惨白的病人静静地躺在床上，正当所有人都以为他已经过世时，他突然睁开了眼睛。 ‖ The doctor worked tirelessly until finally he, too, succumbed to the plague. 医生不知劳累地工作，直至最后，他也死于瘟疫。

近 decease, demise, expire, perish, pass away

反 endure, stand 忍受住；breathe, live, survive 存活

supersede [ˌsuːpər'siːd]

「考法」 *vt.* 取代，替代：to **displace** in favor of another

例 That edition of the dictionary that you have has been superseded by a more recent one. 你买的那版字典已经被最近新出的版本取代了。

近 displace, relieve, replace, substitute, supplant, cut out

surly [ˈsɜːrli]
【考法】 *adj.* 脾气不好的: irritably sullen and **churlish in mood** or manner
例 a surly and rude person 一个粗暴无礼的人
近 acid, bearish, bilious, cantankerous, disagreeable, dyspeptic, ill-humored, ill-natured, ornery, splenetic
反 amiable, good-humored, good-natured, good-tempered 性格好的

surmise [ˈsɜːrmaɪz]
【考法】 [ˈsɜːrmaɪz] *n.* (根据不足的)推测，揣测: a thought or idea **based on scanty evidence**
[sərˈmaɪz] *vt.* 推测: to form a notion of **from scanty evidence**
例 My surmise is that the couple's "good news" is the announcement that they are going to have a baby. 我猜那对夫妻说的"好消息"就是他们要有小孩了。‖ From his tone I surmised that he was unhappy. 从他的语气中我猜测他并不高兴。
近 guess, hypothesis, shot, supposition, theory; assume, conjecture, daresay, imagine, infer, presume, speculate, suppose, suspect
反 fact 事实; demonstrate, prove, substantiate, validate 证明

surmount [sərˈmaʊnt]
【考法】 *vt.* 战胜，获得胜利: to **achieve a victory** over
例 an Olympic swimmer who surmounted endless obstacles to achieve her goals 一个克服重重困难最终实现目标的奥运游泳运动员
近 conquer, defeat, overbear, overcome, overmatch, prevail, subdue, triumph, win
反 lose 失败

surpass [sərˈpæs]
【考法】 *vt.* 超越，强于: to **become better**, greater, or stronger than
例 She always tried to surpass her older brother at anything he did, which results in his diffidence. 她在任何一个方面都要比她哥哥优秀，由此导致了他自信心的缺乏。
近 beat, better, eclipse, exceed, excel, outclass, outmatch, outshine, outstrip, overtop, transcend
反 fall behind 落后

surrogate [ˈsɜːrəgət]
【考法】 *n.* 替代品: one that **takes the place** of another
例 a surrogate mom 代孕母亲
近 backup, cover, fill-in, relief, replacement, reserve, stand-in, substitute

surveillance [sɜːrˈveɪləns]
【考法】 *n.* 监视，监控: **close observation** of a person or group, especially one under suspicion
例 government surveillance of suspected terrorists 政府对于恐怖分子嫌疑人的监控
近 oversight, supervision, watch

tame [teɪm]
【考法 1】 *adj.* 被驯化的: **reduced from a state of native wildness** especially so as to be tractable and useful to humans
例 Every evening, a wild Canada goose is at the food trough with our tame geese. 每天傍晚的食槽边总会出现一只野生加拿大鹅和我们饲养的家鹅一起进食。
近 domestic, domesticated, tamed
反 feral, savage, undomesticated, untamed, wild 野生的
【考法 2】 *vt.* 控制，抑制: to **keep from exceeding** a desirable degree or level (as of expression)
例 Try to tame your language when you are in front of the kids. 在孩子面前注意一下你的措辞。
近 bridle, check, constrain, contain, curb, govern, hold, inhibit, keep, measure, regulate, rein, restrain, rule
反 unleash 宣泄(感情等)

tangle [ˈtæŋgl]
【考法】 *vt.* 纠缠，使…纠结: to seize and hold in or as if **in a snare**
例 He was at last tangled in the web of lies that he had told to everyone. 他最终被自己所编织的谎言缠住了。
近 enmesh, ensnare, ensnarl, entrap, mesh, net, snare, trap
反 disentangle 解开

Unit 3

teeming ['tiːmɪŋ]
【考法】 *adj.* 大量的: possessing or covered with **great numbers** or amounts of something specified
例 oceans teeming with life 孕育着无穷生命的海洋
近 abundant, ample, awash, cornucopian, flush, fraught, lousy, replete, swarming, thick, thronging
反 bare, barren, blank, devoid, empty, stark, vacant, void 贫瘠的, 空无一物的

temporal ['tempərəl]
【考法】 *adj.* 世俗的, 尘世的: of or relating to **earthly life**
例 spiritual and temporal leader of the people 人们的精神和俗世领袖
近 carnal, earthborn, earthbound, fleshly, material, mundane, secular, sublunary, terrene, terrestrial, worldly
反 heavenly, unearthly, unworldly 非尘间的; spiritual 精神上的; religious 宗教的

tentative ['tentətɪv]
【考法】 *adj.* 暂时性的, 尝试的: **not fully** worked out or **developed**
例 Our plans are only tentative at this point and will depend on whether you can come. 我们的计划只是暂时性的, 具体还要看你能否前来。
近 ad interim, impermanent, interim, provisional, provisionary, provisory, short-term, temporary, trial
反 final 最终的; ceaseless, endless, eternal, immortal, permanent, perpetual, undying 永久性的

thick-skinned [ˌθɪk 'skɪnd]
【考法】 *adj.* 冷漠无情的, 不顾及他人感受的: largely **unaffected** by the needs and feelings of other people
例 a cold and thick-skinned person 一个冷漠无情的人
近 affectless, callous, cold-blooded, heartless, indurate, inhumane, insensitive, merciless, obdurate, ruthless
反 charitable, compassionate, humane, kindhearted, merciful, sympathetic, tender, warmhearted 慈善的

thrill [θrɪl]
【考法】 *n.* 强烈的兴奋感, 快感: a **pleasurably intense stimulation** of the feelings
vt. 使兴奋, 使激动: to cause to experience a sudden sharp feeling of **excitement**
例 the thrill of another joy 又是一阵喜悦激动 ‖ I was thrilled to hear that you got the promotion that you'd been so desperately wanting. 听到你终于获得了梦寐已久的升职, 我感到非常激动。
近 bang, boot, exhilaration, frisson, jollies, kick, rush, titillation, wallop; arouse, charge, electrify, excite, exhilarate, galvanize, intoxicate, provoke, stimulate, titillate, pump up
反 bore, jade, pall, tire, weary 使厌倦
派 thrilling *adj.* 刺激的; thriller *n.* 恐怖电影

timely ['taɪmli]
【考法】 *adj.* 恰到好处的, 合乎时宜的: **appropriate** or adapted to the times or the occasion
例 Timely invitation to lunch came just as I was starting to feel hungry. 正当我开始感到饥饿的时候, 就有人适时地邀请我吃午饭了。
近 opportune, seasonable, well-timed
反 inopportune, unseasonable, untimely 不合时宜的

trifling ['traɪflɪŋ]
【考法】 *adj.* 细微的, 不重要的: **lacking in significance** or solid worth
例 Deciding what you want to do for a living is no trifling matter. 决定维持生计的行当可不是一件小事。
trifling differences between the theatrical and DVD versions of the movie 这部电影影院版和 DVD 版的细微区别
近 frivolous, inconsequential, inconsiderable, insignificant, minor, minute, negligible, nugatory, slight, trivial
反 consequential, eventful, important, meaningful, momentous, significant, substantial, weighty 重要的

[taɪˈkuːn]
n. 大亨, 巨头: a **person of rank**, **power**, or **influence** in a particular field
an oil tycoon who's widely considered the most powerful man in the county 被认为是郡上最有势力的一个石油大亨 ‖ The automobile tycoon is on the verge of bankruptcy. 汽车巨头濒临破产的边缘。
baron, captain, king, lion, lord, magnate, mogul, monarch, prince
nobody, nothing, zero 不起眼的人物

tyrant [ˈtaɪrənt]
- 【考法】 n. 暴君 : a ruler who exercises absolute power **oppressively or brutally**
- 例 The people universally feared the tyrant , who was notorious for his frequent use of torture. 人们都非常恐惧这个暴君，因为他有着经常折磨人的臭名。
- 近 dictator, oppressor, pharaoh, strongman
- 派 tyranny n. 暴政，苛政

umbrage [ˈʌmbrɪdʒ]
- 【考法】 n. 不悦，生气 : the **feeling of being offended or resentful** after a slight or indignity
- 例 He would take umbrage at the slightest suggestion of disrespect. 哪怕是一点点的不敬也会让他不悦。
- 近 dudgeon, huff, miff, offense, peeve, resentment
- 反 contentment, delight, gratification, happiness, pleasure 满意，高兴

Unit 4

■ UNANIMOUS	■ UNAVAILING	■ UNREMITTING	■ VOUCHSAFE	■ WAYWARD
■ WEATHER	■ WILLFUL	■ WILLY-NILLY	■ WILT	■ WILY

unanimous [juˈnænɪməs]
- 【考法】 adj. 一致同意的 : having the agreement and **consent of all**
- 例 a unanimous vote to upgrade the school's computer facilities 一致同意对学校的计算机设备进行升级
- 近 consentaneous, uncontested
- 派 unanimity n. 一致同意

unavailing [ˌʌnəˈveɪlɪŋ]
- 【考法】 adj. 徒劳的，无果的 : **producing no results**
- 例 an unavailing effort to avert a war 试图避免战争的徒劳尝试
- 近 abortive, barren, bootless, fruitless, ineffectual, unproductive, unprofitable, unsuccessful, useless, vain
- 反 effective, effectual, efficacious, fruitful, potent, productive 有效的；successful 成功的

unremitting [ˌʌnrɪˈmɪtɪŋ]
- 【考法】 adj. 连续不断的 : going on and on **without any interruptions**
- 例 Unremitting rain lasted for six days . 连续下了六天的雨。
- 近 ceaseless, continual, continuing, incessant, nonstop, perpetual, unbroken, uninterrupted
- 反 discontinuous, intermittent 不连续的，有间断的

vouchsafe [ˌvaʊtʃˈseɪf]
- 【考法】 vt. 允诺，给予 : to **grant** or furnish often **in a gracious or condescending manner**
- 例 refuse to vouchsafe an explanation 拒绝给出任何解释
- 近 accord, award, grant, vest
- 反 withhold 保留，不给予；recant, retract, withdraw 撤回，收回

wayward [ˈweɪwərd]
- 【考法】 adj. 刚愎自用的，不服管束的 : **following one's own** capricious, wanton, or depraved **inclinations**
- 例 wayward children with a history of behavioral problems 过去行为上有些问题的调皮小孩
- 近 balky, contrary, contumacious, defiant, intractable, obstreperous, rebellious, recalcitrant, refractory, unruly
- 反 amenable, biddable, compliant, conformable, docile, obedient, ruly, submissive, tractable 顺从的

weather [ˈweðər]
- 【考法】 vt. 安全度过（危机等），经受住 : to **come through** (something) safely
- 例 We have weathered worse crises , and so we'll survive this one. 我们闯过了更为严重的危机，这个也不会有问题的。‖ They weathered a terrible storm while at sea. 他们在海上平安渡过了一场巨大的风暴。
- 近 survive
- 反 decease, die, expire, perish, succumb, pass away 死亡，消亡

willful [ˈwɪlfl]
- 【考法】 adj. 固执的，倔强的 : obstinately and often perversely **self-willed**
- 例 Finally the parents sought professional counseling for the willful child . 最终家长不得不为倔强的小孩寻求专业咨询。
- 近 adamant, headstrong, immovable, implacable, inconvincible, inflexible, intransigent, mulish, obdur pertinacious, perverse, stubborn, unyielding, wrongheaded
- 反 acquiescent, agreeable, amenable, compliant, flexible, pliable, pliant, relenting, yielding 易受影响f

willy-nilly [ˌwɪli ˈnɪli]
【考法】 *adj.* 无秩序的，随意的：**without order** or plan
例 willy-nilly taxing laws 杂乱无序的税收法
近 aimless, arbitrary, desultory, erratic, haphazard, scattered, slapdash, stray
反 methodical, orderly, organized, regular, systematic 有序的，有组织的

wilt [wɪlt]
【考法】 *vi.* 精神萎靡，憔悴：to feel or exhibit the effects of **fatigue or exhaustion**
例 His brain wilted from hitherto unprecedented weariness. 在前所未有的疲劳面前，他开始变得脑力衰弱。
近 decay, droop, emaciate, fade, fail, lag, languish, sink, waste, wither
反 convalesce, rally, rebound, recover, recuperate 康复，复原

wily [ˈwaɪli]
【考法】 *adj.* 狡诈的，狡猾的：clever at attaining one's ends by indirect and often **deceptive means**
例 He is an experienced and wily old statesman. 他是一个经验丰富而狡诈的老政治家。
近 beguiling, cagey, crafty, cunning, devious, foxy, guileful, scheming, shrewd, slick, sly, subtle, tricky
反 artless, guileless, ingenuous, innocent, undesigning 天真的，单纯的

Unit 5

■ WIRETAP　　■ WISTFUL　　■ WREST　　■ WRONGHEADED

wiretap [ˈwaɪərtæp]
【考法】 *n./vt.* 偷听，窃听：to tap a telephone or telegraph wire in order to **get information**
例 wiretap the hotel room 窃听酒店房间
近 eavesdrop, overhear, tap

wistful [ˈwɪstfl]
【考法】 *adj.* (带着忧伤而)渴望的，怀念的：full of **yearning or desire** tinged **with melancholy**
例 There was a wistful look in his eyes when he spoke of his childhood. 当他谈起他的童年时，眼眶中不禁流露出一种带有忧伤的怀念之情。
近 longing, nostalgic, reminiscent, yearning
反 apathetic, indifferent, insouciant, nonchalant, perfunctory, unconcerned 无所谓的，不感兴趣的

wrest [rest]
【考法】 *vt.* 辛苦地获得：to **gain with difficulty** by or as if by force, violence, or determined labor
例 farmers who were used to wresting a living from the barren land 一度依靠贫瘠的土地辛苦度日的农民
近 scrape, scrounge, squeeze

wrongheaded [ˌrɔːŋˈhedɪd]
【考法】 *adj.* 固执己见的，坚持(错误观点)的：**stubborn in adherence** to wrong opinion or principles
例 In spite of other's objections, he is always wrongheaded in his opinions. 他总是不管他人的反对而固执地坚持自己哪怕是错误的观点。
近 adamant, headstrong, immovable, implacable, inconvincible, inflexible, intransigent, mulish, obdurate, pertinacious, perverse, stubborn, unyielding, willful
反 acquiescent, agreeable, amenable, compliant, flexible, pliable, pliant, relenting, yielding 易受影响的

索 引

belligerent / 344
bellwether / 28
beneficent / 28
benign / 28
berate / 28
beseech / 28
beset / 344
besmirch / 28
bewitching / 344
bifurcate / 29
bigot / 29
blackmail / 345
bland / 29
blandishment / 29
blase / 29
blast / 29
blatant / 29
blazon / 29
blemish / 30
blight / 30
bliss / 30
blithe / 30
blueprint / 30
bluff / 345
blunder / 30
blunt / 30
blur / 31
blurt / 31
bluster / 31
boggle / 31
bogus / 345
bohemian / 343
boisterous / 31
bolster / 31
bombast / 31
bonhomie / 32
boo / 32
boon / 32
boorish / 32
bootless / 32
bore / 345
bound / 32
boycott / 32
bracing / 32
brake / 33
brandish / 345
brash / 33
brassy / 33
bravado / 33
bravura / 33
brazen / 33
breach / 33
brevity / 33
bribe / 33
bridle / 34
brim / 345
brisk / 34
bristle / 34

brittle / 34
broach / 34
bromide / 34
brook / 34
browbeat / 34
bruit / 34
buck / 34
budge / 35
bulge / 35
bully / 35
bumble / 346
bumptious / 35
bungle / 35
buoy / 35
buoyant / 35
bureaucratic / 344
burgeon / 35
burlesque / 35
burnish / 36
bustle / 346
buttress / 36
byzantine / 36
cache / 36
cachet / 36
cacophony / 36
cagey / 60
cajole / 36
calamity / 346
calcify / 37
calculated / 346
calibrate / 37
calligraphy / 37
callous / 37
callow / 37
calumniate / 37
camaraderie / 37
camouflage / 37
canard / 38
candor / 38
canny / 346
canon / 38
canonize / 346
cantankerous / 53
canvass / 39
capitulate / 39
caprice / 39
captious / 346
captivate / 39
cardinal / 39
careen / 346
carefree / 347
careworn / 39
caricature / 39
carnal / 40
carouse / 40
carp / 40
cascade / 347
cast / 40

castigate / 40
cataclysmal / 41
catalyze / 40
catastrophe / 40
categorical / 41
caterwaul / 64
catharsis / 37
catholic / 41
caustic / 41
cavalier / 36
caveat / 41
cavil / 41
cede / 41
cellular / 347
cement / 41
censor / 41
censure / 42
ceremonious / 347
certitude / 347
cessation / 42
chaff / 42
chagrin / 42
chameleon / 42
champion / 42
channel / 347
chaperone / 347
charisma / 347
charlatan / 43
chary / 43
chase / 43
chasm / 43
chauvinistic / 43
check / 43
cherished / 347
cherubic / 43
chic / 42
chicanery / 43
chide / 44
chimera / 43
chivalrous / 348
chokehold / 45
choleric / 44
chorale / 348
chord / 44
chromatic / 44
chronic / 44
churlish / 44
cipher / 44
circuitous / 44
circumlocution / 44
circumscribe / 45
circumspect / 45
circumvent / 45
civility / 45
clamor / 348
clan / 348
clandestine / 45
clarion / 45

clarity / 45
clasp / 45
cleave / 348
clement / 45
cliche / 46
cling / 348
cliquish / 40
cloak / 59
clog / 46
clot / 46
clout / 46
clownish / 50
cloying / 46
clumsy / 46
cluster / 48
coagulate / 46
coalesce / 47
coarse / 348
coax / 47
coda / 47
coerce / 47
coeval / 47
cogent / 47
cognizant / 47
cohesive / 348
collapse / 47
collude / 48
colossal / 48
coltish / 48
coma / 48
combustible / 48
comity / 48
commencement / 48
commend / 49
commensurate / 49
commingle / 49
commiserate / 349
commitment / 49
committed / 49
commodious / 49
commonplace / 53
commonsensical / 49
commotion / 49
compatible / 349
compelling / 349
compendium / 50
complacency / 50
complacent / 349
complaisance / 50
complementary / 349
compliant / 50
complicate / 349
compliment / 50
compose / 50
compound / 51
comprehend / 349
compress / 51
compromise / 51

compulsive / 42
compunction / 51
concatenate / 52
conceal / 52
concede / 52
concentrate / 52
concerted / 52
conciliate / 52
concoct / 52
concomitant / 42
concord / 53
concrete / 350
concur / 53
condemn / 350
condescending / 53
condign / 53
conditional / 350
condole / 53
condone / 53
conducive / 53
confine / 54
conflagration / 351
conflate / 351
confluence / 54
conform / 351
confound / 54
confront / 54
congeal / 54
congenial / 54
congruent / 54
conjecture / 55
conjure / 351
connive / 55
connoisseur / 55
conscientious / 55
consensus / 55
consent / 351
consequence / 55
conservative / 55
conservatory / 56
considerable / 56
consign / 352
consilience / 56
console / 56
consolidate / 56
consonant / 56
consort / 60
conspicuous / 56
conspire / 57
consternation / 352
constitute / 57
constrain / 57
constringe / 57
construct / 57
consummate / 57
contagious / 57
contaminate / 58
contemplate / 352